Securing the Fruits of Labor

Published with the assistance of the Cardozier Fund

Securing the Fruits of Labor

The American Concept of Wealth Distribution

1765–1900

JAMES L. HUSTON

Louisiana State University Press   *Baton Rouge*

Designer: Michele Myatt Quinn
Typeface: AGaramond
Typesetter: Wilsted & Taylor Publishing Services
Printer and binder: Thomson-Shore, Inc.

Portions of Chapters, 1, 2, and 3 first appeared in the article "The American Revolutionaries, the Political Economy of Aristocracy, and the American Concept of the Distribution of Wealth, 1765–1900," *American Historical Review,* XCVIII (1993), 1079–1105, and are reprinted with permission. Portions of Chapters 5 and 7 were first published as part of the article "Virtue Besieged: Virtue, Equality, and the General Welfare in the Tariff Debates of the 1820s," *Journal of the Early Republic,* XIV (1994), 523–47, and are reprinted with permission. Portions of the March 6, 1860, speech of Abraham Lincoln are taken from *The Collected Works of Abraham Lincoln,* ed. Roy P. Basler, copyright © 1953 by the Abraham Lincoln Association. Reprinted by permission of Rutgers University Press. Portions of J. Hector St. John de Crèvecoeur, *Letters from an American Farmer* (1782; rpr. New York, 1912), are reprinted by permission of Everyman's Library, David Campbell Publishers Ltd. Portions of John Locke, *Two Treatises of Government,* ed. Peter Laslett (Cambridge, Eng., 1988), are reprinted by permission of Cambridge University Press.

Library of Congress Cataloging-in-Publication Data
Huston, James L., 1947–
     Securing the fruits of labor : the American concept of wealth distribution,
1765–1900 / James L. Huston.
          p.   cm.
     Incudes bibliographical references and index.
     ISBN 0-8071-2206-8 (cloth : alk. paper)
          1. Income distribution—United States—History.   2. Distributive justice—
United States—History.   3. Wealth—Moral and ethical aspects—United States—
History.   I. Title.
HC110.I5H87   1998
339.2'0973—dc21   97-44939
                                                                                    CIP

To my wife, Kathy Jane Simmons Huston

Contents

TABLES

PREFACE

My interest in the topic of the American concept of the distribution of wealth began nearly two decades ago as a by-product of my dissertation. I had chosen to explore the political ramifications of the Panic of 1857 for the sectional controversy, and as I outlined my plan of attack I determined to look at the explanations of economic phenomena by mid-nineteenth-century political economists. That choice led me to the protectionist writings of Henry Charles Carey, Erasmus Peshine Smith, Francis Bowen, Calvin Colton, Horace Greeley, Stephen Colwell, and others. Embedded in verbose and at times quirky tomes on political economy were comments on the distribution of wealth that were highly intriguing, for these high-tariff advocates argued for an equal or equitable distribution of wealth, a position I had not at all expected to find.

Protectionist writings were so tantalizing in their implications about American developments that I decided to pursue the matter more thoroughly as my next project. Part of the study would include the protectionist analysis of a society's distribution of wealth. As I delved into the research, it became obvious that virtually no literature on American distributive concepts existed. Economists have published extensively on the actual distribution of wealth, but little has been done concerning American attitudes toward proper wealth distribution. Comments about the distribution of wealth abound in the secondary literature, but they are often little more than one or two lines or perhaps a paragraph. The labor literature has perhaps the most sustained investigation of popular attitudes to wealth distribution, but even here the amount of material is thin.[1] The allure of the subject increased as historians in the revolutionary and early national periods flooded the profession with monographs and articles about the political philosophy of republicanism. For these scholars, the American revolutionaries and their immediate successors held a set of ideas, derived from political theorists in ancient and modern Europe, that described the essential institutions and behaviors required for a republic to endure—and the American experiment was preeminently an experiment in republicanism. A central tenet in republicanism was the necessity of securing and then maintaining a nearly equal distribution of wealth among the voting citizenry.[2] Thus my natural inclination to investigate American theories about the distribution of wealth obtained a broader validation because an equitable, if not exactly equal, distribution of wealth was seen by the Founders as a crucial condition of the success of self-government in the United States. Over time, the subsidiary topic of wealth distribution became more and more the focal point of my efforts. Some years ago, I thought the research might yield either a very lengthy article or even a very short book; my powers of prognostication have not proven to be very formidable.

Yet the research became wondrously frustrating and enticing at the same time. Declarations by all types of Americans from the Revolution to the Civil War indicated a fervent belief that the United States required—and indeed had obtained—an egalitarian distribution of wealth, but the declarations were marked by an absence of a delineation of the principles of wealth distribution. Those Americans who addressed the issue usually simply mentioned the necessity of equitability and then failed to provide an explanation of how the condition was to be obtained. Indeed, before the 1880s, few tracts on the distribution of wealth were even published. Rather, an understanding of the American concept of the distribution of wealth has to be mined out of inter-

1. The best existing works are Peter D. McClelland, *The American Search for Economic Justice* (Cambridge, Eng., 1990); J. R. Pole, *The Pursuit of Equality in American History* (Berkeley, 1978). Among economists, see Martin Bronfenbrenner, *Income Distribution Theory* (Chicago, 1971); Lee Soltow, *Men and Wealth in the United States, 1850–1870* (New Haven, 1975); and Jeffrey G. Williamson and Peter H. Lindert, *American Inequality: A Macroeconomic History* (New York, 1980).

2. The subject of republicanism will be treated more fully in Chapter 2. The key books concerning republicanism are Gordon S. Wood, *The Creation of the American Republic, 1776–1787* (Chapel Hill, 1969); J. G. A. Pocock, *The Machiavellian Moment: Florentine Political Thought and the Atlantic Republican Tradition* (Princeton, 1975); and Paul A. Rahe, *Republics Ancient and Modern: Classical Republicanism and the American Revolution* (Chapel Hill, 1992).

minable debates over tariffs, banking legislation, internal improvements, and other political controversies. Even then, the mountains of words produce only a few nuggets of explicit references to wealth distribution.[3]

An understanding of antebellum ideas concerning wealth distribution eluded me for some years. How equality in material condition was to be wrung out of concerns about special privilege, aristocratic tendencies, monopolistic practices, and laissez-faire principles simply did not make any sense to me (nor has it for most historians). Such terms might be useful in describing how Americans feared unequal advantages, but they seemed wholly inadequate as principles to follow in order to obtain an equal distribution of wealth. At last I came to realize that the basic problem was my frame of reference—my intellectual heritage that economic results are determined by an economic system. The appropriate frame of reference for Americans in the late eighteenth century and throughout the nineteenth was that economic results were determined by the political system. I had discovered the necessity of grappling with context in a most forceful manner.

Four broad perspectives frame this study while a host of smaller observations dwell within the framework. First, the discussion of the distribution of wealth was transatlantic in terminology, mode of analysis, and reference to experiences. It quickly becomes obvious that it is not possible to understand how Americans handled this subject without bringing in the European context. Second, derivative of the first, is the vital role of aristocracy in the debate. Political discourse in the United States continuously evoked a special dichotomy to explain distributionist principles: the republicanism (or democracy) of the United States could be understood only in reference to the European tradition of aristocracy—or at least to what Americans thought the European experience had been. European aristocracy and American republicanism marched together as foils for each other's antagonisms and self-definitions for over a century. It was only after 1900 or thereabouts that the threat of aristocracy faded in the face of a new potential enemy, industrial consolidation—a circumstance that forced a reevaluation of both the enemy of the republic and the political meaning of the republic itself.

3. One can find some discussion of the subject in the literature on Jacksonian America, for example, Lawrence Frederick Kohl, *The Politics of Individualism: Parties and the American Character in the Jacksonian Era* (New York, 1989); Edward Pessen, *Riches, Class, and Power Before the Civil War* (Lexington, Mass., 1973); Harry L. Watson, *Liberty and Power: The Politics of Jacksonian America* (New York, 1990); John Ashworth, *"Agrarians" and "Aristocrats": Party Political Ideology in the United States, 1837–1846* (Cambridge, Eng., 1983).

Third, this book is about the development of American economic thought, academic and public, on a single topic through time and especially as it surfaced in the political realm. As such, it is a history of a particular kind of thought and not about political philosophy, religious values, or other intellectual concerns. The fourth and final broad perspective is the element of time. The concept of the distribution of wealth that emerged during the Revolution became a firmament in American economic thinking for nearly one and one-quarter centuries. Even those who questioned the fairness of wealth and income distribution in the United States had difficulty breaking out of its conceptual power. Behind this attention to time and the duration of the revolutionaries' ideas is my assertion that the economic and political processes of the country were evolving in a predictable and reinforcing fashion. Rather than describing American society as being buffeted by change in the nineteenth century, I argue for a continuity of processes and the ideas that coincided with those processes.

The heart of the specific interpretation is that during the Revolution public leaders had created four axioms that then became the American understanding of the distribution of wealth. The first was an ethical component to be able to tell whether wealth was properly distributed; that was the labor theory of property and value. Justice in distribution was achieved when each man—not yet woman—received the just fruits of his labors. The equality that American citizens hoped for arose from the agrarian nature of the society. In a nation of farmers where each farmer obtained only the rewards he worked for, the effect would be a general equality of material condition. Injustice occurred because of the political system of aristocracy, the second axiom of the revolutionaries' thinking. By looking at the system as it operated in Europe, revolutionaries affirmed that the few rich and the many poor were created when aristocrats used their monopoly over political power to steal the fruits of labor from producers. During the years of struggle with England, various leaders found those aristocratic policies to be high taxes, manipulation of currency, establishment of a bureaucracy, legislative creation of monopolies, and the maintenance of a state-sponsored church. Closely connected to the second axiom was the third. Aristocrats also created improper wealth distributions by controlling the land by inheritance laws, in particular the laws of primogeniture and entail. These laws were considered by most Americans before 1900 as a separate category of aristocratic malfeasance, and so I have kept them apart from the other elements in the American concept of wealth distribution. The final axiom was population growth. At first only dimly perceived by the revolutionaries, it became, until 1900, an enormously pervasive argument for explaining inequality. Explication of the details of these axioms is presented in Chapters 1 and 2.

By the time the Constitution was implemented, then, the American concept of the distribution of wealth was complete and in place. It carried several implications. Those implications obviously involved the institution of slavery, which by 1790 already was seen as violating the first and second axioms. But as well, these economic musings by the leadership set the stage for the free labor ideology that would emerge in the 1840s and 1850s. Likewise, the direction of the analysis was tilting public policy in the direction of laissez-faire capitalism, as was witnessed in the complementary explanations of economic activity offered by Adam Smith and the revolutionary leaders. The theory of wealth distribution also had its ambiguities and failures. These are the topics discussed in Chapter 3.

In Part II, I trace the evolution of the revolutionaries' understanding of the distribution of wealth throughout the nineteenth century. Few ventured far from the rules the revolutionary generation laid down. Chapter 4 begins the discussion of the nineteenth century by exploring the nation's economic and political institutions. The argument I offer is that the longevity of distributionist ideas among various Americans stemmed from a similarity in economic processes throughout the nineteenth century, which originated in the mid-eighteenth century. I propose that the essential era in American history is the Age of the Revolution, 1765 to 1880. The entire time span was characterized by the working out of the premises of the Revolution; the Revolution established the themes, and in the decades following, the variations and possibilities within those themes were investigated. The economic process that provided this political stability was a commercial agrarian economy in which commerce was always extending but not impoverishing the population. Ultimately, the reason why commercialization did not force the United States into a wrenching transformation was the existence of western lands; subsistence farmers in the East could become commercial farmers in the West. Moreover, the economic expansion that did occur was horizontal, an expansion of units of production rather than their consolidation. American political republicanism was the product of the proprietorship, the partnership, the small shop. When that economic base disappeared, so did revolutionary republicanism. In this analysis, comparisons with European states and British finances reveal the unique quality of American republicanism in the European context. As a by-product of this analysis, it is propounded that early-nineteenth-century industrialization has been badly overemphasized.

Chapter 5 returns to the verbal evolution of the revolutionaries' ideas by delving into the works of British classical economists and their American counterparts. British authors after Adam Smith saddled capitalist theory with a depressing outlook for the bulk of humankind in the doctrines of rent and population, giving rise to a justification for a massively skewed distribution of wealth. In their analysis was as well a major break, for the British writers saw economics as an inquiry independent from any political system. They created the field of economics from what had been political economy. American economic thinkers tended on the whole to stay within the confines of the revolutionary concept of the forces operating on the distribution of wealth and continued to insist that the political form of government played a major role in distributive justice. An important division emerged, however. American free traders, who lavished praise upon the British classicals, found their salvation from rent and population laws in the American frontier. Land made the United States the European exception. Protectionists, however, devised an alternative distribution scheme based on productivity, human skills, and scientific knowledge. They offered a particular analysis to understand the miseries of England's working class. At center stage in the debate between Americans and Europeans was the content of wage labor and whether it inevitably meant subsistence wages.

Throughout much of the nineteenth century, literate Americans indulged in celebrations about the egalitarian nature of the American distribution of wealth. They were not alone. The distribution of wealth in the United States was part of a transatlantic dialogue weighing the burdens and benefits of aristocratic systems versus republican ones. Within this discourse, commentators testified that, first, American property was unusually broadly distributed; second, the distribution was a result of lack of aristocratic controls; and, third, American egalitarianism and its republican foundations depended on the western frontier. Indeed, the idea of the frontier as the guarantor of equal property distribution incited a spirit of imperialism to seize more land to preserve a horizontal form of American-European civilization. This spirit was termed Manifest Destiny. Part of the reason why so many writers gushed rhapsodic about American wealth distribution, however, was that they openly excluded certain groups in their reckonings. Those left out, such as recent immigrants and slaves, totaled a hefty percentage of the population. These matters are discussed in Chapter 6.

How the revolutionaries' ideas on wealth distribution influenced national politics is the subject of Chapter 7, and the focus there is on party systems and the controversies over banking and tariffs. The parties tended to divide on economic policy in the fashion of the economists, free traders versus protectionists, Jeffersonian adherents versus Hamiltonian followers. In both instances, however, politicians relentlessly paraded their allegiance to the labor theory of property/value and a fear of aristocratic control of the economy—the political economy of aristocracy. The interesting entanglement was the rise of a protectionist argument that as a republic depended on equality for its existence, the state had to ensure that wages (or remuneration generally) would be high enough to allow social mobility. This could not be accomplished when virtuous republican nations traded with aristocratic ones because aristocratic nations purposely depressed wages so as to win foreign markets. To avoid an inegalitarian fate and the demise of free government, republics had to avoid trading with lands that suppressed wage rates.

Not everyone agreed with the politicians and economists about the glories of the American distribution of wealth. Dissenters are covered in Chapter 8. Foremost among the dissenters were working-class orators who decried the nation's actual distribution of wealth, provided some numbers for the first time, and insisted that workers were not receiving the fruits of their labor. This was true of other dissenters as well, such as anarchists, women's rights advocates, and utopian socialists. Yet even dissent seemed imprisoned in the revolutionaries' concept of the distribution of wealth, for the alleged solution to wealth imbalances usually turned out to be less government, the laissez-faire policy. Workers indicated the limitations of the political analysis by forming unions and attacking their employers, thereby behaviorally indicating that they found the true source of inequality to be a wage relationship or a hierarchical economic entity. But their verbal solutions were usually political laissez-faire, especially among their leaders. Only the utopians really broke free of the revolutionary heritage.

Distribution themes ran through the controversy over slavery, the subject of Chapter 9. On the one hand, the abolitionists excessively applied the labor theory of property/value to the institution to prove how slavery injured the welfare of the slave, a point stressed particularly by black abolitionists. The distributionist theme of the abolitionists dealt in part with the superiority of wage labor to slave labor. In their analysis, the abolitionists showed no hesitation in stating that, under conditions of equal bargaining power and noncoercion, wage labor was superior to slave labor and would restore an equitable distribution of income by ensuring that the laborer received the just fruits of his or her labor. Political antislavery, on the other hand, fastened on the political economy of aristocracy and used it to reveal the slaveholders as aristocrats who endangered the survival of the republic—the slave power conspiracy. In its fight against slaveholders, however, the Republican party in particular stumbled into the odd position of questioning the rights of property and in fact created the justification for each generation to decide for itself what it was and was not willing to consider property—a feat the Democrats utterly failed to perform. This chapter concludes with a look at the reward of the vote to the freedmen as a substitute for southern property redistribution. Although a feeble attempt at distributive justice, by the lights of the American concept of the distribution of wealth the right to vote was crucial in maintaining an equitable distribution of wealth because producers used the vote to protect themselves from the incursions of aristocrats. Without political control and coercion, aristocrats could not usurp the fruits of the labors of others.

Part III concludes the story of the revolutionaries' ideas about the forces that shaped wealth distribution. It details the death of the revolutionaries' ideas and, in a more fundamental sense, the demise of the Revolution's influence on American life. The end of Reconstruction did not herald the end of political and popular allegiance to the American concept of wealth distribution as established by the revolutionaries. Indeed, that set of ideas continued strong into the 1880s. What unraveled its power was the creation of the large-scale business organization, the commercial and industrial corporation. In a wave of pools, trusts, and then mergers, large business enterprise took over the core production of the American economy. That change induced a panic mentality among commentators who feared that now the distribution of wealth was becoming permanently warped and unsuitable for republican institutions. For the first time, numerical investigations into the distribution of wealth were conducted—with shocking results. And then the pillars of the American concept of the distribution of wealth began to crumble. The labor theory of property/value was replaced by marginal productivity theory. Only the new robber barons relied on the laws of entail and primogeniture to ensure "equitable" wealth distribution. The frontier closed, and the specter of overpopulation, the European social condition, began to absorb thinking on wealth distribution. And the old enemy of republicanism, aristocracy, seemed frail and impotent. The new challenger was corporate industry. In the economy born in the last decade or so of the nineteenth century came a new understanding of the distribution of wealth—a product of the economy that could be rectified only by political intervention in the economy so as to ensure a distribution suitable to popular government.

A brief afterword is provided to put the story in twentieth-century perspective and gives what I believe was the key failure of the revolutionary generation. They should have provided a mechanism for intelligent redistribution of property. That failure has injured welfare in the United States for well over two centuries. A final note is given in two appendixes which try to offer a different formulation of distribution theory that does not rely so heavily on individualism and which give my justification of redistribution based on the view that the principles of civilization outweigh the principles of economic theory.

The nature of this study requires some caveats and additional explanations to avoid confusion over terms and interpretations. In economic terminology, wealth is a stock and income is a flow. Wealth has always been more poorly distributed than has income, and they are treated analytically as separate topics. That separation seems to have come in the early twentieth century in the pioneering work of Willford Isbell King, *Wealth and Income of the People of the United States* (1915), who so far as I can tell first elaborated the difference. Wealth and income were almost interchangeable in eighteenth- and nineteenth-century discourse, which makes a certain amount of sense for a society that was primarily agrarian. For most of this book and unless otherwise directly specified, wealth in pre-twentieth-century parlance was almost always a surrogate for income.

Perhaps a more important warning needs to be issued about my use of the word *republican.* For three decades now the American historical profession has been deluged by works on republicanism, which have extended its explanatory domain close to the beginning of the twentieth century. Much of the work on republicanism involves the ideas of the participatory citizen, the fear of government, the premium on individual liberty, the belief that local community is best, the dangers of commerce and finance, the horror of bureaucracy, and the fear of political parties and patronage. And this list only begins to compile some of the attributes that historians have found in neoclassical republicanism and its American variant. But the essence of the historical interest in republicanism is lodged in the word *virtue,* which means a willingness to forgo self-interest in order to pursue the general welfare. The search that so many historians have engaged in is to find when self-interest triumphed over virtue, when liberal capitalism overran neoclassical republicanism.[4]

This book is primarily about economic thought and economic values—in a sense, about political economy. It is not possible in this age to write on such a topic in the early history of the republic and not become entangled in the debates raging over republicanism. I believe that republicanism has been overdone and its significance exaggerated in certain directions. The core of republicanism, its essential contribution, is the idea of popular sovereignty in the form of representative government. That idea has persisted and informed Americans about their politics from the beginning until (we hope, with some trepidations) this day. That contribution of republicanism is really not debatable, for it is fundamental. Corruption, virtue, and the other appendages of republicanism were neither vital nor fundamental. They were the social garb that clothed the essential doctrine. When times called for sacrifice (the Revolution, the Mexican War, the Civil War), virtue was in style. When people wanted the nation to adhere to agrarian roots or maintain the institution of slavery or preserve planter hegemony, they used country opposition ideology and the rhetoric of agrarian simplicity. When people expected to profit from laissez-faire, they naturally found it the most equitable of all systems. The garb that republicanism could wear—not to mention ideas about political parties and patronage—changed and varied over time as new experiences were assessed, new philosophies developed, new economic phenomena encountered. But popular sovereignty and representative government persevered in an almost pristine form. Unless otherwise indicated, when I use the words *republican* or *republic,* I am referring to what I think most nineteenth-century citizens were most proud of: a nation politically organized by popular sovereignty and representative government without aristocratic or monarchical influences.

I have found that American economic ideas, most of them expressed in the revolutionaries' understanding of the distribution of wealth, were far more stable and resilient than the garb that clothed republicanism. Economic ideas did not change greatly, although policy by public officials did. And the implication of that finding probably should be emphasized. The ideas springing

---

4. On this debate, see the discussion in James L. Huston, "Virtue Besieged: Virtue, Equality, and the General Welfare in the Tariff Debates of the 1820s," *Journal of the Early Republic,* XIV (1994), 523–26.

up in the economic arena were those of individualism, a modified Lockean view of property (via creation by labor and not simply by possession), and a willingness to accept market mechanisms. Specific socioeconomic groups clashed over these values at times, and debate did erupt on certain specific doctrines such as population, rent, productivity, and racial characteristics. On the whole, however, the essence of individualism suited a land of agrarian small enterprise.[5]

Overall, I postulate as well something of a consensus on the American idea of the distribution of wealth. That consensus requires understanding. The consensus existed over the notion that an equitable and natural distribution of wealth was created when each laborer received the fruits of his or her labor, and the equitability was disturbed when aristocrats manipulated political power to deprive individuals of their just fruits. That consensus existed in a transatlantic context; this was part of the way that Americans trumpeted their difference from Europeans. But the consensus quickly broke down in the United States when terms had to be defined. What precisely were the laborer's just fruits and how to calculate them became a major bone of contention that split advocates along socioeconomic lines. Moreover, what policies constituted aristocratic interference in the economy produced heated political exchanges and in some ways were responsible for the divisions between political parties. Conflict was never far beneath the surface of any consensus on any generality in the early republic.

My attitudes toward wealth distribution and redistribution have probably influenced the writing of this book, and, although I believe an attentive reader can probably surmise them from reading the volume, I shall make them explicit. My political orientation is New Deal liberal with certain modifications that experience and the passage of time have dictated; I am a firm believer that any civilization worthy of the name and that expects to endure will enact measures to effect a redistribution of some magnitude from the wealthy to the impoverished. The amount of redistribution will be limited by the necessity of permitting talented individuals to exercise their talents and reap

5. This book actually belongs to the genre of the history of economic thought, as in the examples of Joseph Dorfman, *The Economic Mind in American Civilization* (5 vols.; 1946; rpr. New York, 1966), and Paul K. Conkin, *Prophets of Prosperity: America's First Political Economists* (Bloomington, 1980). Anyone reading this book will notice its striking similarities, however, especially in its emphasis on labor and antiaristocracy, with the recent work of Gordon S. Wood, *The Radicalism of the American Revolution: How a Revolution Transformed a Monarchical Society into a Democratic One Unlike Any That Had Ever Existed* (New York, 1992).

commensurate rewards. My rationale for these brief statements is a perspective based on the ideal of civilization. The purpose of civilization is that the members of a society have the capacity to live a civilized life. Capacity for enjoying a civilized life would at the least include competent standards of justice, sufficient material rewards, and participation in the work and political decisions of the community. Because civilization creates the possibilities of rewards for the very talented, the civilization has a right to claim some—not all—of the rewards any individual may earn and redistribute those rewards to other members of the community to ensure that all enjoy a civil life. The economists' desire for maximum economic efficiency is not an appropriate goal for civilization—and economic efficiency is the reason why most microeconomists oppose plans for income redistribution. Economic efficiency dictates that those individuals who do not possess the correct skills should die; death of the inefficient, after all, is one of the ways to maximize overall efficiency. How anyone could call this civilized behavior is beyond me. To create civilization, a community must acquire from its members civilized behavior. Thus civilized behavior deserves a reward—regardless of any economic activity or economic theory, including the labor theory of value. To expect civilized behavior from individuals who obtain only hardship from their participation in the society appears moronic. In Appendix B, I offer a brief explication of these ideas. It must be said, however, that my orientation has induced a certain amount of skepticism about the American call for an equitable distribution of wealth and income when balanced against the nation's failure ever to institute measures to obtain it.

I also wish to take a moment to apologize for omissions of scholarship. The process of publishing a book takes many months. During those months, other authors are not idle, and the relentless appearance of new historical works, not to mention ventures into interdisciplinary research, is overwhelming. It is barely possible to keep the notes current within one or two years of date of publication. In any event, I wish to make my amends to authors whom I do not cite and state that my reasons for not doing so have nothing to do with the merits of their works but much to do with my need for sleep.

The sources used for this study are, and have been so called now for nearly twenty-five years, elite sources—the written and spoken words of important politicians, reformers, political economists, essayists, editors, and intellectuals. I have generally relied on the printed word—published books, journals, tracts, congressional accounts, and some newspapers. For this project, manuscripts were not especially informative. Newspapers probably contained more valuable information, but to conduct an intelligent search over the nation's newspapers for a span of 130 years was a bit more labor than I wished to invest. One potential source of information was also eliminated because of its voluminous size: religious sermons. The attitude of the clergy to the distribution of wealth could well be a book of its own. Thus the interpretations I offer do not rest on the broadest evidentiary base. But I am sufficiently convinced of the validity of my interpretations to claim for them more pervasiveness in the population than a strict accounting of the sources I searched would legitimately allow.

I will make one final observation in this preface. This study can be justified in endless ways. The subject lends itself to discovering the values and expectations Americans had of their economic system and what constituted their sense of economic justice; it as well delineates quite clearly the struggle between community and individuality that has marked much of the American experience. American understanding of wages is gloriously detailed in debates over wealth distribution and thereby aids in examination of the free labor ideology. The topic discloses the extent of cognitive dissonance a society (or groups within the society) can accommodate when objective measures reveal how far reality has deviated from the commonly espoused ideal. Other justifications for this study could be presented, such as how this monograph fills various gaps in historical knowledge and the profession's understanding of the forces shaping the American people. But they are not the motivation behind it. I did not choose this topic because I sat down and rationally figured out what bits of knowledge the historical profession needed for a fuller comprehension of the American past. I chose the topic because I liked it. Watching people in the past figure out the mechanisms of the distribution of wealth and argue their way to an understanding of the world in which they lived was utterly exhilarating. I readily confess that in nearly every aspect I have thoroughly enjoyed this adventure.

Over the course of more years than I suspected it would take, the completion of this book has indebted me to a number of patient and wonderful friends and colleagues. A lengthy draft of this work was read and thoroughly criticized by Charles Cheape, H. James Henderson, Morton Keller, and George F. Jewsbury. They alerted me to omissions in scholarship, faulty or questionable generalizations, and excessive documentation; most important, however, they mixed these suggestions with much needed encouragement. As well, a draft was read by Larkin B. Warner, who admonished me, quite correctly, to spell out my purposes and conclusions at the beginning of the book. As always, I was challenged and supported in my endeavors by my mentor, Robert W. Johannsen. A synopsis of some of this work was published as an article in the _American Historical Review_ in 1993, and I would like to thank Joyce O. Appleby, James A. Henretta, and three anonymous critiquers for their comments, which also aided me in composing this manuscript. A sincere gesture of gratitude must be accorded two reviewers for Louisiana State University Press, who took a draft that had already gone through numerous revisions and applied such massive amounts of erudition and analytical testing to it that they induced a considerable rethinking of certain themes and an extensive reorganization of several chapters. The final version of this study, and whatever concision it exhibits, was the product of the excellent staff at Louisiana State University Press, including Freelance Coordinator Catherine Landry and Executive Editor John Easterly. The writing was vastly improved by my copy editor, Trudie Calvert. To them I am especially indebted.

Financial support for my efforts was provided by a grant from the Oklahoma Foundation for the Humanities in the summer of 1992, by the administration of Oklahoma State University for approving a sabbatical leave in the spring of 1992, and by my department chairs and the dean of the College of Arts and Sciences for supporting summer grants and travel funds. I would indeed be remiss if I did not mention the greatest support of all: my wife. To produce scholarly works, certain sacrifices have to be made, and she has accepted this fate with grace and good humor.

Over the years, librarians have come to my aid and directed me to vital material. To the staffs at the libraries of the University of Illinois, the Library of Congress Manuscript Division, Cornell University, Duke University, the University of North Carolina, and Oklahoma State University I offer the highest praise. As well, the staffs at historical societies were marvelous in their attention and knowledge: the Massachusetts Historical Society, Connecticut Historical Society, Ohio Historical Society, and the Historical Society of Pennsylvania. The services of interlibrary loan have been indispensable.

PART I

FOUNDATION, 1765–1790

In truth, the abuses of monarchy had so much filled the space of political contemplation, that we imagined everything republican which was not monarchy. We had not yet penetrated to the mother principle that "governments are republican only in proportion as they embody the will of their people, and execute it."
—Thomas Jefferson to Samuel Kercheval, July 12, 1816

I

Justice and the Fruits of Labor

It will be highly politic," proclaimed Connecticut Congregational minister Benjamin Trumbull in 1773 on the subject of a republican government in North America, "in every free state, to keep property as equally divided among the inhabitants as possible, and not to suffer a few persons to amass all the riches and wealth of a country." An anonymous writer asserted to a London newspaper that all Americans were united in defense of republican liberty because "every man thinks and acts for himself in a country where there is an equal distribution of property." Jacob Green, a New Jersey minister, argued that in a republic "there should, as much as possible, be . . . something like an equality of estate and property." Noah Webster, the linguist-politician of Massachusetts, writing in favor of adoption of the Constitution in 1787, flatly stated that "*a general and tolerably equal distribution of landed property is the whole basis of national freedom,*" and a widespread distribution of property was "the very *soul of a republic.*" An Antifederalist in Maryland, however, worried about the effect of a stronger central government and warned that an "unequal division of property silently and gradually undermines this foundation [of equality of citizens], almost as soon as society is formed."[1]

1. Benjamin Trumbull, *Discourse, Delivered at the Anniversary Meeting of the Freemen of the Town of New-Haven, April 12, 1773* (New-Haven, 1773), 30; Letter of a Gentleman in America to a British Member of Parliament, December 26, 1774, rpr. in Margaret Wheeler Willard, ed., *Letters on the American Revolution, 1774–1776* (1925; rpr. Port Washington, N.Y., 1968), 42; Jacob Green, quoted in Ruth Bogin, *Abraham Clark and the Quest for Equality in the Revolutionary Era, 1774–1794* (East Brunswick, N.J., 1982), 35–36; Noah Webster, *An Examination into the Leading Principles of the Federal Constitution, Proposed by the Late Convention Held at Philadelphia* (Philadelphia, 1787), 47; The Federal Farmer [Richard Henry Lee], "Letters of the

Numerous Americans testified that not only was an equitable distribution of wealth necessary for a republic but the colonies and then the new nation had achieved such a status. David Ramsay of South Carolina wrote a history of the Revolution in which he stressed the lack of ranks in American society and the widespread diffusion of property. The French visitor Marquis de Chastellux admitted that Americans enjoyed an enviable distribution of property, but he questioned Sam Adams about the continuation of that state of affairs. Adams assured him that American equality would continue. Congregational minister Ezra Stiles determined that the American distribution of wealth was unusually praiseworthy in the 1780s. Speaking at the conclusion of the war, he exalted the outcome as the victory of equality and liberty over hierarchy and despotism—and he included property in his vision of equality. He later wrote to Thomas Jefferson, then in France, that he did not fear degeneration in the United States because property continued to be widely distributed: it would be "impossible" for a powerful upper house in the Continental Congress to appear and "acquire a Power dangerous to LIBERTY so long as Property in the United States is so minutely partitioned and transfused among the Inhabitants."[2]

At the Constitutional Convention, South Carolina delegate Charles Pinckney denied the necessity for establishing an upper house for a national legislature because such a body was always meant to represent an aristocracy or the wealthy of an imbalanced society. The Americans had no such class divisions: "Among them there are fewer distinctions of fortune & less of rank, than among the inhabitants of any other nation." There were, however, those at the Constitutional Convention who opposed the ideas expressed by Pinckney.

Federal Farmer," in Herbert J. Storing, ed., *The Complete Anti-Federalist* (Chicago, 1981), II, 251–52; "Essays by a Farmer," *ibid.*, V, 55; Centinel [Samuel Bryan?], "Letters of Centinel," *ibid.*, I, 139.

2. David Ramsay, *The History of the American Revolution* (Philadelphia, 1789), I, 31; Marquis de Chastellux, *Travels in North America in the Years 1780, 1781 and 1782*, rev. trans. by Howard C. Rice, Jr. (Chapel Hill, 1963), I, 161, II, 398; Nathaniel Chipman, *Sketches of the Principles of Government* (Rutland, Vt., 1793), 172–76. A good discussion about the impressions of visitors on American wealth distribution is contained in Lee Soltow, *Distribution of Wealth and Income in the United States in 1798* (Pittsburgh, 1989), 9–13. See also Ezra Stiles, *The United States Elevated to Glory and Honor. A Sermon, Preached Before His Excellency Jonathan Trumbull, Esq L.L.D. . . . at the Anniversary Election May 8th, 1783* (New Haven, 1783), 6–9; Ezra Stiles to Thomas Jefferson, September 14, 1786, in Julian P. Boyd *et al.*, eds., *The Papers of Thomas Jefferson* (Princeton, 1950–), X, 386; Edmund S. Morgan, *The Gentle Puritan: A Life of Ezra Stiles, 1727–1795* (New Haven, 1962), 213, 343–44.

James Madison and Alexander Hamilton, both distressed by Shays's Rebellion and by the actions of the states during the 1780s, believed that a different government had to be installed to contain the social divisiveness growing out of embryonic antagonisms between rich and poor. Madison's fears were for the future, but Hamilton's pessimism was for the here and now: "It was certainly true: that nothing like an equality of property existed: that an inequality would exist as long as liberty existed, and that it would unavoidably result from that very liberty itself."[3]

Such pronouncements about the distribution of wealth in speeches, tracts, and broadsides were widespread during the years of the founding of the American republic, 1763 to 1800, and had a distinct cadence. During the revolutionary years, American commentators affirmed the equality of possessions in the states of North America. The 1780s were more turbulent economically and produced social conflicts, most dramatically Shays's Rebellion in Massachusetts. For some political leaders, the belief in an enduring and equal distribution of wealth evaporated in an acknowledgment of inequality. Optimism rebounded, however, when better economic times returned during the first years of the Washington administration.

These years constitute a rare period in American history when the topic of the distribution of wealth was widely deliberated. Questions about the distribution of wealth, of course, did not consume public debate or monopolize the concerns of the revolutionary leaders. The challenge of building a functioning republican political order—the detailing of constitutions, suffrage requirements, legislative powers, executive powers, and the like, not to mention the task of actually winning a war against Europe's most powerful nation—consumed most of the infant nation's verbal and physical energy. But the topic of the distribution of wealth played an important role in public discourse because the goal of the American revolutionaries was to found a republic that preserved the equality of citizens and individual liberty. The goal demanded that the society possess a nearly equal distribution of wealth.

---

3. Pinckney speech in James Madison, *Notes of Debates in the Federal Convention of 1787 Reported by James Madison* (Athens, Ohio, 1966), 181–86, quote on 181. The same speech can be found in Jonathan Elliot, ed., *Elliot's Debates [on the Ratification of the Constitution]* (2nd ed.; 1836–45; rpr. Philadelphia, 1937), V, 233–77; and Max Farrand, ed., *The Records of the Federal Convention of 1787* (New Haven, 1911), I, 410–12; Hamilton's speech, Madison's speech, in Madison, *Notes of Debates,* 196, 194. See Federalist No. 10, in William T. Hutchinson *et al.,* eds., *The Papers of James Madison* (Chicago, 1962–), X, 264–69; Drew R. McCoy, *The Elusive Republic: Political Economy in Jeffersonian America* (Chapel Hill, 1980), 128–29.

The intimate connection between the distribution of wealth and self-government was detailed in the political theory of republicanism. Republicanism filled a vast literature, consumed voraciously by the revolutionaries, that explained the operation, principles, and fate of republics in the past—Athens, Rome, Sparta, Florence, and Venice. The revolutionaries heeded the analyses provided by ancient, medieval, and modern philosophers of republics, but especially those by Niccolò Machiavelli, James Harrington, Baron de Montesquieu, and a host of English radical Whigs and Tories in the early eighteenth century. The republicanism that American leaders came to advocate held sacred the ideals of individual liberty, the equality of citizens before the law, distrust of governmental power and of political demagogues, simplicity and frugality in the behaviors of the people, and public exhibition of virtue—the willingness of citizens to sacrifice their individual self-interest to obtain the common good. An important economic corollary of republicanism established primarily by Englishman James Harrington (1611–77) during the Puritan Commonwealth was widely acknowledged by American revolutionaries: to endure, a republic had to possess an equal or nearly equal distribution of landed wealth among its citizens.[4]

Political theorists generally held that the form of a society dictated its form of government. Societies with an equitable distribution of property deserved a republican form of government, whereas societies with a few wealthy families naturally gravitated toward aristocratic government. In creating guidelines for the appropriate economic policy of their country, however, American political leaders pushed beyond that static analysis. The power of government over economic affairs could alter society and the government itself. Thus republics needed to know the policies that preserved republican character; likewise, they required understanding of the policies that ultimately led to various forms of despotism.

In particular, the revolutionaries had to unearth the principles governing wealth distribution. Here a paradox intrudes. On the one hand, orators and writers commonly attested to a republic's need for an egalitarian wealth distribution, but on the other hand these statements were seldom more than one or two sentences long. They were tucked away in speeches and treatises about governments, congresses, branches of government, attributes of a republican people, principles of justice, and the failings of European society. No pam-

4. Republicanism will be further refined and dealt with in Chapter 2. For the basic principles of republicanism, consult Wood, *Creation of the American Republic*, chap. 2; Joyce O. Appleby, *Capitalism and a New Social Order: The Republican Vision of the 1790s* (New York, 1984), 9–22; and Pocock, *Machiavellian Moment*, 334–504.

phlets or speeches were devoted solely to an examination of the distribution of wealth. The topic was always an appendage to some other subject.

Lacking was an analysis of what forces created an equitable or equal distribution of wealth and what forces distorted it. The revolutionaries irritatingly failed to provide explicitly and compactly the principles—economic as much as political—by which such a distribution could be established and then maintained over the ages. At first glance, except in a few instances such as some of the debates in the Constitutional Convention, exclamations favoring an equitable distribution of wealth were not followed by a delineation of such principles appropriate for a republic.

The revolutionaries did possess an almost complete analysis of how an equitable distribution of wealth was created and what institutions and policies would sustain the condition. But the analysis was almost entirely implicit and lodged in numerous policy debates over specific issues. When those debates are aggregated and the various distributionist strands pulled together, a full and logical explanation of the forces acting on a society's wealth distribution emerges.

Four principles constituted the revolutionaries' understanding of the forces controlling the distribution of wealth. First, equitability was achieved in wealth distribution when all citizens adhered to the labor theory of property/value. Second, distortions in the distribution of wealth arose primarily from politics—specifically, in the policies that aristocrats devised to transfer the fruits of others' labors to themselves. This was the political economy of aristocracy. Third, an additional skewing of wealth distribution was produced when laws governing the transmission of estates to future generations were implemented, the laws of primogeniture and entail. Fourth, economic inequality was an unavoidable result of the natural process of population growth. When population overtook the capacity of the nation to maintain small, independent freeholds, then riches became concentrated among the few and poverty became the fate of the many.

These four axioms and the logic behind them were the legacy of the revolutionary leaders to their nineteenth-century successors in regard to the distribution of wealth. The legacy was well understood by those who came afterward. These four axioms would have a ferociously tenacious grip on the American economic imagination and would pass nearly unaltered through American history for the next one and one-quarter centuries.

The essential axiom upon which the revolutionaries' understanding of the distribution of wealth rested was a labor theory of property/value. This theory provided the ethical standard—verbally, not mathematically—to enable observers to determine whether wealth distribution accorded with justice—whether individual economic actors obtained the income and reward they merited. The other three axioms (the political economy of aristocracy, the laws of primogeniture and entail, and population growth) were descriptions of policies, institutions, and processes that could upset an equitable distribution of wealth; they will be treated fully in the next chapter. But the basis, the bedrock, upon which the whole of the revolutionaries' understanding of their economic world rested was a labor theory of property/value.

The central idea behind the labor theory of property/value was simple enough. When a person bestowed his labor upon an object, the value thus created and added to the object morally belonged only to that person and to no other because of the act of individual labor.[5] The laborer had a nearly absolute right to the values or property that his labor produced and could dispose of those values or property as he thought proper. The labor theory of property/value became the standard by which to judge the righteousness of property distribution. When the laborer obtained full remuneration for the values he created, the resulting distribution of wealth (or income) was natural and just. Unjust wealth distributions occurred when by one means or another the fruits of labor were transferred from the laborer to a nonlaborer. In colonial eighteenth-century parlance, the key phrase indicating the operation of the principle of the labor theory of property/value was "the fruits of labor."[6]

By the time of the American Revolution, the public atmosphere in North America was saturated with the phrase *the fruits of labor* and with explicit allusions to the labor theory of property/value, but its presence was not an American contribution to either political science or economic thought. Several disparate strands of thought combined to designate the act of individual labor as the major criterion in determining the appropriateness of reward and as a standard by which individuals could evaluate the fairness of a country's distribution of wealth.

First, the Protestant ethic reinforced the idea that the individual deserved,

5. Until the middle of the nineteenth century the discussion of wealth distribution was always conducted in masculine terms. It would be historically inaccurate to demasculinize the discourse and so its bias will not be corrected here.

6. See Alfred Young, "Afterword: How Radical Was the American Revolution?" in *Beyond the American Revolution: Explorations in the History of American Radicalism,* ed. Alfred F. Young (De Kalb, Ill., 1993), 319–21.

and deserved only, the fruits of his labor. Revolting against dissipation and idleness, the early radical English Protestants insisted on an industrious life of labor. Though radical Protestants hedged the labor theory of property/value with Christian notions of hierarchy and communitarian sharing, the concept nonetheless arose that labor brought with it material rewards that belonged largely (but not entirely) to the individual. The importance of labor in the thinking of the earliest colonists was unmistakable. John Winthrop, first governor of the Massachusetts Puritans, wrote, "What soever wee stand in need of is treasured in the earth, by the Creator & is to be fetched thence by the sweat of or Browes."[7]

Republican theorists also stressed the importance of labor and industry and the avoidance of luxury and dissipation. James Harrington indicated that property was an accumulation of labor, and therefore private property was sanctified by the laws of nature. An important source of republican sentiment on the labor theory of property/value was the work of John Trenchard and William Gordon, two London republicans who between 1719 and 1721 wrote editorials ("Cato" was their pseudonym) castigating the British government for its laxity in adhering to true republican principles. In 1721, "Cato" wrote:

> By Liberty, I understand the Power which every Man has over his own Actions, and his Right to enjoy the Fruit of his Labour, Art, and Industry, as far as by it he hurts not the Society, or any Members of it, by taking from any Member, or by hindering him from enjoying what he himself enjoys. The Fruits of a Man's honest Industry are the just Rewards of it, ascertained to him by natural and eternal Equity, as is his Title to use them in the Manner which he thinks fit: And thus, with the above Limitations, every Man is sole Lord and Arbiter of his own private Actions and Property.—A Character of which no Man living can divest him but by Usurpation, or his own Consent.[8]

7. Winthrop, quoted in E. A. J. Johnson, *American Economic Thought in the Seventeenth Century* (1932; rpr. New York, 1961), 101, 66–67, 71, 104–107; consult Edmund S. Morgan, *The Challenge of the American Revolution* (New York, 1976), 91–92, 102–103. J. E. Crowley has delineated the limitations Puritans placed on individualism in *This Sheba, Self: The Conceptualization of Economic Life in Eighteenth-Century America* (Baltimore, 1974), 50–72.

8. *Cato's Letters,* January 20, 1721, no. 62, in David L. Jacobson, ed., *The English Libertarian Heritage: From the Writings of John Trenchard and Thomas Gordon in "The Independent Whig" and "Cato's Letters"* (Indianapolis, 1965), 128; Richard Schlatter, *Private Property: The History of an Idea* (New Brunswick, N.J., 1951), 16, 72–73. Paul A. Rahe concludes that ancient

The third influence establishing the sanctity of the labor theory of property/value for the American revolutionaries was John Locke. In justifying the Glorious Revolution and a limitation to royal powers, Locke in 1690 framed the labor theory of property in its most famous and telling form:

> 27. Though the Earth, and all inferior Creatures be common to all Men, yet every Man has a *Property* in his own *Person*. This no Body has any Right to but himself. The *Labour* of his Body, and the *Work* of his Hands, we may say, are properly his. Whatsoever then he removes out of the State that Nature hath provided, and left it in, he hath mixed his *Labour* with, and joyned to it something that is his own, and thereby makes it his *Property*. It being by him removed from the common state Nature placed it in, it hath by this *labour* something annexed to it, that excludes the common right of other Men. For this *Labour* being the unquestionable Property of the Labourer, no Man but he can have a right to what that is once joyned to, at least where there is enough, as good left in common for others.[9]

Locke's purpose in developing a labor theory of property was to place private property beyond the capacity of the king or the government to appropriate arbitrarily; this doctrine enabled him to justify the overthrow of a sovereign who violated natural rights. Locke evidently believed that he had found the true explanation of the inviolability of private property, and from his discovery of the origins of private property he went on to sanctify property transmissions via inheritance laws and the lopsided distribution of private property that existed in his own day. What the Americans seized on in particular, however, was neither the sanctity of private property nor Locke's legitimation of inheritance laws (which, incidentally, the American revolutionaries explicitly repudiated) but the basic concept that labor and labor alone created property and economic values.[10]

---

republicans had a different idea about labor (*Republics Ancient and Modern,* 71). On Trenchard and Gordon, see Bernard Bailyn, *The Ideological Origins of the American Revolution* (Cambridge, Mass., 1967), 85–93, 130–38.

9. John Locke, *Two Treatises of Government* [1690], ed. Peter Laslett (Cambridge, Eng., 1988), Second Treatise, 287–88.

10. On Locke in general, see Peter Laslett, Introduction to Locke, *Two Treatises of Government,* ed. Laslett, 70–72, 101–104; Schlatter, *Private Property,* 151–59; Alan Ryan, *Property and Political Theory* (Oxford, 1984), 18–25. For an example of the marginalization of Locke, see Pocock, *Machiavellian Moment,* 424–25, 436, 457–58. For those who stress the centrality of Locke for the Revolution, consult Rahe, *Republics Ancient and Modern,* 510–18; Isaac Kram-

The developing study of economics, most commonly denoted political economy until the beginning of the twentieth century, also promoted the concept of the labor theory of property and was thus the fourth influence leading the Americans to adopt the labor theory of property/value. In the hands of seventeenth- and eighteenth-century political economists, however, the idea that labor created property was refined more precisely to the notion that labor created value; that is, the act of labor added a desirable quality to an object (or to land) which made it valuable to the laborer and possibly to other people. It was the creation of value by labor that explained the rise of trade and commerce, in which values produced by the labor of one individual were traded (under rules of fairness) for the values produced by the labor of someone else.

Political economists developed (and argued about) the labor theory of value for nearly two centuries (approximately 1650 to 1850), and the theory took several different branches. William Petty, a mid-seventeenth-century writer on economic topics, clearly established the idea that only labor created value. Petty was sufficiently influential to have had an impact on Philadelphian and paper money advocate Benjamin Franklin. The earliest forms of systematic economic thought in western Europe, mercantilism and physiocracy, incorporated a notion of the labor theory of value, although mercantilists generally espoused low wages and maintained that most people were averse to labor and would work only under some form of compulsion.[11]

Importantly for the Americans, the philosophers of the Scottish Enlightenment and the "common-sense" school of philosophy promoted and celebrated the positive aspects of the labor theory of value. These philosophers found work far more pleasing and worthwhile when laborers were permitted

nick, *Republicanism and Bourgeois Radicalism: Political Ideology in Late Eighteenth-Century England and America* (Ithaca, N.Y., 1990), 1–2, 7–10; Morton White, *The Philosophy of the American Revolution* (New York, 1978), 41–42, 53–58, 97–99.

11. E. A. J. Johnson, *Predecessors of Adam Smith: The Growth of British Economic Thought* (New York, 1937), 95–98, 102, 240; Paul W. Conner, *Poor Richard's Politicks: Benjamin Franklin and His New American Order* (New York, 1965), 41; Benjamin Franklin, *A Modest Inquiry into the Nature and Necessity of a Paper-Currency* (1729), in Leonard W. Labaree and William B. Willcox, eds., *The Papers of Benjamin Franklin* (New Haven, 1959–90), I, 140–41, 149, 150; Joseph J. Spengler, "Mercantilist and Physiocratic Growth Theory," in Bert F. Hoselitz et al., *Theories of Economic Growth* (Glencoe, Ill., 1960), 22–23, 30–31, 55–56, 64. For an example of one who believed in the coercion of labor, see A Citizen of Massachusetts [James Sullivan], *The Path to Riches. An Inquiry into the Origin and Use of Money; and into the Principles of Stocks and Banks* (Boston, 1792), 43.

to retain the fruits of their labors. The aversion to work, most often posited by mercantilists and others, occurred when someone other than the laborer received the fruits of labor. William Hutcheson, Lord Kames, and David Hume adopted a labor theory of value. The apex of the development of the labor theory of value in the Scottish Enlightenment came with Adam Smith's exposition in *An Inquiry into the Nature and Causes of the Wealth of Nations.*[12]

Fundamental ambiguities always vexed a precise understanding of the labor theory of value. For in the seventeenth and eighteenth centuries, the labor theory of value was not *the* labor theory of value but only *a* labor theory of value. The troublesome question for those individuals was what constituted value and how it was to be measured. A simple answer appeared in the phrase *labor in general,* but the political economists also recognized that other factors contributed: skill, management, organization, government, capital. Most contemporaries indicated that labor was perhaps the essential creator of value, but there were other creators as well. Moreover, the word *labor* itself had for most people a broad definition—any person who engaged in economic activities was a laborer, and so store owners, bookkeepers, managers, lawyers (although lawyers were a point of controversy), scientists, and others could be included as laborers. It would require the acuity of nineteenth-century economist David Ricardo to posit a labor theory of value that excluded all other variables from contributing to value except labor and a definition of labor that pointed exactly to manual labor. A few decades later, Karl Marx would refine the labor theory of value even further and draw out the explicit moral implications of the doctrine for laborers and capitalists.[13]

The sudden emergence and widespread acceptance of some version of the

12. Helen Hill Miller, *George Mason, Gentleman Revolutionary* (Chapel Hill, 1975), 152–53; Garry Wills, *Inventing America: Jefferson's Declaration of Independence* (Garden City, N.Y., 1978), 217, 231–32; John B. Stewart, *The Moral and Political Philosophy of David Hume* (New York, 1963), 179, 188; Eugene Rotwein, Introduction to *David Hume: Writings on Economics* (Madison, 1955), xliii; Samuel Hollander, *The Economics of Adam Smith* (Toronto, 1973), 114–17; Herbert Hovencamp, *Enterprise and American Law, 1836–1937* (Cambridge, Mass., 1991), chap. 7, esp. 68, 71–72. On the Scottish Enlightenment generally, see James T. Kloppenberg, "The Virtues of Liberalism: Christianity, Republicanism, and Ethics in Early American Political Discourse," *Journal of American History,* LXXIV (1987), 17–19; John Patrick Diggins, *The Lost Soul of American Politics: Virtue, Self-Interest, and the Foundations of Liberalism* (New York, 1984), 10–12.

13. Joan Robinson, *An Essay on Marxian Economics* (2nd ed.; London, 1969), chap. 3; Ian Shapiro, "Resources, Capacities, and Ownership," *Political Theory,* XIX (1991), 47–72. The fullest elaboration on the history of the labor theory of value is Ronald L. Meek, *Studies in the*

labor theory of property/value was no fluke of history. The scholar Richard Schlatter tied the labor theory of property of John Locke to the birth of extensive commerce in England. Colonial economic growth, the demand for African slaves in the plantations of North and South America, and the emergence of Great Britain as a naval power saw a mushrooming oceanic commerce in the late seventeenth century that soon grew to enormous proportions in the eighteenth century. Schlatter wrote that Locke's theory of property was a "theory which grew out of the everyday experience of the middle class. In the ancient and medieval worlds where labour was done by slaves, serfs, and peasants, and its products were the property of masters and feudal magnates, Locke's ideas about property would have been irrelevant." But in a commercial world in which hundreds and thousands of newcomers could by enterprise amass fortunes, Locke's notion that labor was the source of property seemed "self-evident."[14] Once enunciated, however, the labor theory of property/value could not be confined solely to the realm of commerce. In its internal logic, the theory could make as much sense to a small farmer based in a semicommercial community or a skilled artisan in one of the manufacturing trades as to a merchant prince. The idea was soon outstripping the social limitations of the material circumstances responsible for its birth.[15]

American colonists by the 1760s absorbed wholly the labor theory of property/value and indicated its presence by the use of the phrase *the fruits of labor*. Historians of the American revolutionary period have focused attention on such words and phrases as *taxation without representation, sovereignty, virtue, independence, corruption, luxury, constitutions, virtual representation* and *direct representation*. As important—and more so for the development of American political economy—was the revolutionaries' ceaseless reiteration of the phrase *the fruits of labor.*[16]

Labour Theory of Value (New York, 1956), chaps. 1–5. See the criticisms of the theory in John E. Roemer, *Analytical Foundations of Marxian Economic Theory* (Cambridge, Eng., 1981), 12–13, 52–53; Jon Elster, *Making Sense of Marx* (Cambridge, Eng., 1985), 119–23, 131, 137.

14. Schlatter, *Private Property*, 155–56.

15. The phrase *labor theory of property/value* will be used in this study to indicate its broad Lockean origins and meaning and to avoid confusion with the labor theory of value, which without qualifications can possess contradictory political implications.

16. One of the few scholars to have recognized the importance of the phrase is William B. Scott, *In Pursuit of Happiness: American Conceptions of Property from the Seventeenth to the Twentieth Century* (Bloomington, 1977), 31 and *passim*. See also Stanley N. Katz, "Thomas Jefferson and the Right to Property in Revolutionary America," *Journal of Law and Economics*, XIX (1976), 480; Max Savelle, *Seeds of Liberty: The Genesis of the American Mind* (New York,

Samuel Adams, writing for the House of Representatives of Massachusetts, stated, "It is acknowledged to be an unalterable law in nature, that a
man should have the free use and sole disposal of the fruit of his honest industry, subject to no controul." Joseph Warren in 1775 gave a speech at Boston,
and in the first paragraph of substance he declared that "personal freedom is
the natural right of every man; and that property or an exclusive right to dispose of what he has honestly acquired by his own labor, necessarily arises
therefrom, are truths which common sense has placed beyond the reach of
contradiction." The colonial legislature of North Carolina addressed the
British Empire with the words, "To enjoy the fruits of our own honest industry; to call that our own which we earn with the labor of our hands, and the
sweat of our brows . . . these are the mighty boons we ask." John Rutledge addressed the Continental Congress in 1776 with the statement, "To the most
illiterate it must appear, that no power on earth can, of right, deprive them of
the hardly [*sic*] earned fruits of their honest industry, toil and labor." In the
early 1790s, northern agrarian radical George Logan argued, "Our rights over
the other species of property arise from the labor we have bestowed in acquiring them, or from the bounty of others."[17]

Out of the revolutionary period came a conviction that to labor was to
celebrate life and to participate in community affairs—so long as the fruits
of labor belonged to the laborer. Indeed, some believed the real value of the
Revolution was the establishment of the principle that the laborer deserved
the fruits of his labor. Upon announcement of peace with Great Britain, Ezra
Stiles provided the Connecticut legislature with a sermon extolling American
institutions. The United States was to be an experiment different from all
past republican experiments: "The enjoyment of this [civil and religious lib-

---

1948), 219–20; Richard L. Bushman, "Massachusetts Farmers and the Revolution," in *Society,
Freedom, and Conscience: The American Revolution in Virginia, Massachusetts, and New York,*
ed. Richard M. Jellison (New York, 1976), 89.

17. Samuel Adams, "The House of Representatives of Massachusetts to Henry Seymour
Conway," in Harry Alonzo Cushing, ed., *The Writings of Samuel Adams* (1904; rpr. New York,
1968), I, 190; Dr. Joseph Warren, *An Oration Delivered March Sixth, 1775, at the Request of the
Inhabitants of the Town of Boston, to Commemorate the Bloody Tragedy of the Fifth of March, 1770*
(Boston, 1775), 6; Address of the Provincial Congress of North Carolina to the British Empire,
September 3, 1775, in Hezekiah Niles, ed., *Principles and Acts of the Revolution in America,* rev.
by Samuel V. Niles (1822; rpr. New York, 1876), 316; speech of John Rutledge, President, to the
General Assembly, April 11, 1776, *ibid.,* 326; An American Farmer [George Logan], *Letters Ad-
dressed to the Yeomanry of the United States, Containing Some Observations on Funding and Bank
Systems* (Philadelphia, 1791), 27.

erty], with property, has filled the english settlers in america with a most amazing spirit, which has operated, and still will operate with great energy. *Never before has the experiment been so effectually tried, of every man's reaping the fruits of his labor, and feeling his share in the aggregate system of power.*" In the 1780s, Ben Franklin summed up the economic content of the American experiment when he lectured Europeans that titles counted for nothing in the United States; everyone had to labor to survive—"In short, America is the land of labour."[18] During the Revolution, American leaders fleshed out the economic content of their political republicanism, and it was little more than a condensation of the labor theory of property/value: the laborer deserved the full fruits of his or her labor.

In the struggle with England over appropriate imperial policy for North America, the labor theory of property/value of colonial politicians stood out in two particular arguments. The first, and most famous, was the colonial claim that Parliament could not tax the colonies because to do so violated the English dictum of no taxation without representation. Buttressing colonial claims was the idea that the people who have earned property by their labor should be consulted in measures of taxation. Because the colonists had no representation in London, parliamentary taxation meant that taxation laws were being devised by legislators who had no connection to the people who created property by their labor. Without this control, legislators had no respect for the effort entailed in creating property and so would not constrain their desire for public revenue to only the essentials needed by the polity.[19]

But the second argument was in a sense more interesting though less noticed. Colonists claimed the right of self-government because by their labor they had created civilization in North America. They denied England's right to legislate for North America because England had not "labored" in the settlement and maturation of the colonies. Their view was neither accurate nor

18. Stiles, *United States Elevated to Glory and Honor,* 35, emphasis added; Franklin, 1783, quoted in Carl Van Doren, *Benjamin Franklin* (New York, 1938), 704–705.

19. For example, see Charles Thomson to Benjamin Franklin, November 26, 1769, in Labaree and Willcox, eds., *Papers of Franklin,* XVI, 238; James Otis, *Rights of the British Colonies Asserted and Proved* (1764), in Bernard Bailyn, ed., *Pamphlets of the American Revolution, 1750–1776* (Cambridge, Mass., 1965), 423–24, 427, 434–35, 447–54, 474; Thomas Fitch et al., *Reasons Why the British Colonies, in America, Should Not Be Charged with Internal Taxes* (1764), *ibid.,* 386–88; John Dickinson, *Letters of a Farmer* (1768), in Paul Leicester Ford, ed., *The Political Writings of John Dickinson, 1764–1774* (1895; rpr. New York, 1970), 354–57. On the question of taxation, see Morgan, *Challenge of the American Revolution,* 55–56; Bailyn, *Ideological Origins of the American Revolution,* 99.

charitable, for it ignored the protection offered by the British fleet, the access to Britain's advanced economy, and the military efforts Britain made in colonial wars, especially the Seven Years' War. But then many revolutionary leaders did not feel like being reasonable or charitable. Sam Adams, only two years after the Seven Years' War, could write that all of American growth was at "their [the colonists'] own Expence" and "Britain reaps all this Advantage without any Expence of her own & solely at theirs."[20]

When Britain commenced its new colonial program under George Grenville, American politicians and orators responded with a barrage of statements insisting that only Americans deserved to legislate for America because they, not England, had built the civilization there. Richard Henry Lee wrote in 1764, "Can it be supposed that those brave adventurous Britons, who originally conquered and settled these countries, through great dangers to themselves and benefit to the mother country" would consent to be deprived of natural liberties? The Stamp Act Congress formulated a petition to the king asking for the preservation of rights and privileges to the Englishmen in North America because their ancestors had built the colonies by "Successful perseverance in the Midst of Inumerable Dangers and Difficulties together with a profusion of their Blood, and Treasure." In several places among the natural rights and constitutional arguments he propounded, Massachusetts lawyer James Otis claimed that Americans deserved control of America by their labor: "They [colonial charters] were given to their ancestors in consideration of their sufferings and merit in discovering and settling America. Our forefathers were soon worn away in the toils of hard labor on their little plantations and in war with the savages. They thought they were earning a sure inheritance for their posterity."[21]

No opponents of parliamentary taxation and regulation were more prominent in their sense of history than the New Englanders, evidently always mindful of the perfectionist vision of their Puritan progenitors. Spoke Joseph Warren in 1772, "Certainly it never entered the hearts of our ancestors, that after so many dangers in this then desolate wilderness, their hard-earned property should be at the disposal of the British Parliament." In 1775 he made

20. Samuel Adams to John Smith, December 19, 1765, in Cushing, ed., *Writings of Samuel Adams,* I, 40–41.

21. R. H. Lee to [?], May 31, 1764, in James Curtis Ballagh, ed., *The Letters of Richard Henry Lee* (1911–14; rpr. New York, 1970), I, 5; Stamp Act Congress petition in C. A. Weslager, *The Stamp Act Congress* (Newark, Del., 1976), 204–205; Otis, *Rights of the British Colonies Asserted,* in Bailyn, ed., *Pamphlets of the American Revolution,* 444.

the connection between the ancestors of New England and the labor theory of property/value explicit: "But (as has been before observed) every man has a right to personal freedom, consequently a right to enjoy what is acquired by his own labor. And it is evident that the property in this country has been acquired by our own labor." The Suffolk Resolves were also forthright in their use of the labor theory of property/value: "And whereas, this then savage and uncultivated desert was purchased by the toil and treasure, or acquired by the valor and blood, of those our venerable progenitors," the inheritors—the present generation—must fend off all would-be oppressors.[22]

The most famous employment of this theme of self-government earned by the dint of American toil unassisted by England came from Thomas Jefferson in his *Summary View of the Rights of British America* (1774). At the start of the tract Jefferson argued: "America was conquered, and her settlements made, and firmly established, at the expence of individuals, and not of the British public. Their own blood was spilt in acquiring land for their settlement, their own fortunes expended in making that settlement effectual; for themselves they fought, for themselves they conquered, and for themselves alone they have right to hold."[23] In so many ways the American Revolution was virtually built on the labor theory of property/value.[24]

The resounding cry from the colonials about the fruits of their labor may aid in clearing up some conundrums about the nature of the American resis-

22. Dr. Joseph Warren, *An Oration Delivered March 5th, 1772, at the Request of the Inhabitants of the Town of Boston; To Commemorate the Bloody Tragedy of the Fifth of March, 1770* (Boston, 1772), 11; Warren, *An Oration Delivered March Sixth, 1775*, 6–7, 12; Suffolk Resolves in Richard Frothingham, *Life and Times of Joseph Warren* (1865; rpr. New York, 1971), 529–30. British supporters of the American cause also used this theme; see speech of Isaac Barré quoted in Merrill Jensen, *The Founding of a Nation: A History of the American Revolution, 1763–1776* (New York, 1968), 63–64; Richard Price, "Observations on the Nature of Civil Liberty" (2nd ed., 1776), in Bernard Peach, ed., *Richard Price and the Ethical Foundations of the American Revolution* (Durham, N.C., 1970), 85.

23. Thomas Jefferson, *A Summary View of the Rights of British America* (1774), in Merrill D. Peterson, ed., *Thomas Jefferson: Writings* (New York, 1984), 106. For interpretations of this pamphlet, see Gilbert Chinard, *Thomas Jefferson: The Apostle of Americanism* (Boston, 1939), 48–55; William D. Grampp, "A Re-Examination of Jeffersonian Economics," *Southern Economic Journal,* XII (1946), 266; Richard K. Matthews, *The Radical Politics of Thomas Jefferson: A Revisionist View* (Lawrence, Kans., 1984), 24–25; Wills, *Inventing America,* 82–84; John Phillip Reid, *The Concept of Liberty in the Age of the American Revolution* (Chicago, 1988), 24; Katz, "Thomas Jefferson and the Right to Property," 476.

24. This is one of the strong themes of Wood, *Radicalism of the American Revolution,* 277–86; see also Savelle, *Seeds of Liberty,* 219.

tance to British regulation after 1763. One does not turn many pages of the literature generated by the colonists to find property rights elevated to nearly a sacrosanct position, that it was an "essential, natural right," in Sam Adams' words, "that a man shall quietly enjoy, and have the sole disposal of his own property." The emphasis revolutionaries placed on property rights has produced real consternation among historians. "On the surface the Americans' preoccupation with their property—more particularly their determination to resist the levy of taxes on it," Robert Middlekauf has written, "seems petty, demeaning, poor stuff with which to make a revolution."[25] Historians have exercised their imaginations to the utmost to find every possible meaning of the word *property* in an effort to raise the Americans above the level of incomprehensibly avaricious antitaxers.

Added to the puzzle of explaining the unbreakable bond that cemented the revolutionaries to the rights of property is the problem of understanding how different classes of colonials came together in such organizations as the Sons of Liberty to protest British policies and "pull down" the houses of their enemies. The rallying cry was "Liberty and Property!" While it is not unremarkable that the highly propertied of the cities might utter such a sentiment, such rallies were mostly populated by men and women of little or no property. For the unpropertied classes to adopt "liberty" for a revolutionary slogan poses no theoretical problems in interpretation, but for the unpropertied to cry "Liberty and Property" does. For the unpropertied to rally in revolutionary fervor to protect the property of their economic superiors defies almost every modern notion of self-interest or class interest, and its existence has evoked a sense of bewilderment.[26]

25. [Samuel Adams], "The House of Representatives of Massachusetts to Dennys De Berdt," in Cushing, ed., *Writings of Samuel Adams*, I, 135. See Morgan, *Challenge of the American Revolution*, 54–55; Reid, *Concept of Liberty*, 5, 71; Robert Middlekauff, *The Glorious Cause: The American Revolution, 1763–1789* (New York, 1982), 118. For assertions of the centrality of property rights in the Revolution, see James W. Ely, Jr., *The Guardian of Every Other Right: A Constitutional History of Property Rights* (New York, 1992), 28–30.

26. The cry "Liberty and Property" may be found in Herbert M. Morais, "The Sons of Liberty in New York," in *The Era of the American Revolution: Studies Inscribed to Evarts Boutell Greene*, ed. Richard B. Morris (New York, 1939), 284; Pauline Maier, *The Old Revolutionaries: Political Lives in the Age of Samuel Adams* (New York, 1980), 66–68. On classes, see Bogin, *Abraham Clark and the Quest for Equality*, 32–34; Gary B. Nash, *The Urban Crucible: Social Change, Political Consciousness, and the Origins of the American Revolution* (Cambridge, Mass., 1979), 342–43; Dirk Hoerder, *Crowd Action in Revolutionary Massachusetts, 1765–1780* (New York, 1977), 22–23, 76–80, 138–39, 372.

If one uses the labor theory of property/value that Locke espoused—which the colonists mostly used—and eliminates the Lockean emphasis on the sanctity of material property that he later postulated, however, the American revolutionary cry of "Liberty and Property" can be translated into "Liberty and the Fruits of Labor."[27] For the Americans, property was equivalent to the fruits of labor and was often used as a synonym for it. Once the substitution of *fruits of labor* for *property* is achieved, the possibilities of interclass alliances against British programs are revealed: the upper class to protect material property already obtained one way or another, the middling farming and artisan classes to protect the small amounts of material property acquired and the future property they intended to receive as the fruits of their future labor; and the unpropertied as a security that the fruits of their labor would at least not be subjected to onerous and pauperizing imperial taxation. Of course, internal conflicts over property could not be so easily covered by reference to the labor theory of value, but the cry that the "fruits of labor" were being endangered by an outside power had the possibility of rallying the different classes to an anti-British standard.[28]

The labor theory of property/value was a prominent theme in the American Revolution because it established a notion of a just distribution, revealing how much property any single individual could fairly claim. The theory had such a profound impact because it matched so many conditions in the American economy. As well, the theory had the capacity of being primarily egalitarian while at the same time permitting inegalitarian results. Not the least of its attractiveness, it had the capacity of being reconciled, given certain explicit assumptions and analyses about previous societies, with commercial activity. The labor theory of value would serve numerous people very well for a very long time.

By the third quarter of the eighteenth century, the American colonies were economically a land of semisubsistence household farmers. Most lived off the products they raised, with a small surplus to obtain goods not available in local markets. Commerce had made inroads along navigable rivers and

27. Note Jefferson's activity as described in Willi Paul Adams, *The First American Constitutions: Republican Ideology and the Making of the State Constitutions in the Revolutionary Era* (1973), trans. Rita Kimber and Robert Kimber (Chapel Hill, 1980), 193.

28. See Ronald Schultz, *The Republic of Labor: Philadelphia Artisans and the Politics of Class, 1720–1830* (New York, 1993), 5–6, 11–25, 106; James Oakes, *Slavery and Freedom: An Interpretation of the Old South* (New York, 1990), 115.

throughout the South, where farmers raised crops primarily for exchange. Yet as important as commercial development was, the bulk of the population lived subsistence lives because of the lack of transportation facilities.[29]

In this semicommercial agricultural economy, the operation of the labor theory of property/value potentially offered an egalitarian vista. The only wealth a semicommercial agrarian society could produce was from the land. If the land was divided roughly equally, and the farmer (or, more realistically, the household) was assured of retaining the bulk of the fruits of his (the household's) labor, then the system would maintain its egalitarian material structure until overwhelmed by demographic problems arising from over-population. By excessive work, exceptional foresight, and good fortune, some farmers might obtain more land and income than others over time, but a limit was quickly reached. The earth could yield only so much harvest under the best of circumstances, and so the economic distance between the average person and the best person had to be tightly circumscribed—that is, so long as all observed the principle that each laborer obtained only the fruits of his individual labor.

Americans thus had sound reasons for believing they had the capacity for achieving the egalitarianism that neoclassical republicanism demanded. For neoclassical republicanism—the republicanism of Machiavelli, Harrington, Montesquieu, Trenchard, Gordon, and others—called for an equality in *landed* possessions. European states had run out of land and run into grow-ing populations. Demography and geography seemingly precluded their be-ing republican societies. But the infant United States had a small population and vast stretches of uninhabited land—and potentially a continent of unin-habited land, when the Native Americans were disregarded, which Euro-American leaders regularly did. All that was left to be ensured was a system of inheritance so that a few individuals could not monopolize the soil (these two themes of population and inheritance are elaborated in Chapter 2). American

---

29. Jackson Turner Main, *The Social Structure of Revolutionary America* (Princeton, 1965), chaps. 1–4, and pp. 270–71, 277–80; David P. Szatmary, *Shays' Rebellion: The Making of an Agrarian Insurrection* (Amherst, Mass., 1980), xiv, 1–18; Nash, *Urban Crucible*, 161–76; Allan Kulikoff, *The Agrarian Origins of American Capitalism* (Charlottesville, 1992), 34–35; Jeanne Boydston, *Home and Work: Housework, Wages, and the Ideology of Labor in the Early Republic* (New York, 1990), 2–18. Scholars debate the extent of commercialization of agriculture; the contours of the argument can be found in John J. McCusker and Russell R. Menard, *The Econ-omy of British America, 1607–1789: Needs and Opportunities for Study* (Chapel Hill, 1985), 295–305.

leaders easily conceived that within their grasp was a nation in which each household reaped only the rewards of its labors, thereby producing a society of equals in material holdings. And this was a prescription for a republican form of government.

It was such an analysis that at the start of the Revolutionary War made John Adams so optimistic about a republic in the United States. Adams was a keen student of past civilizations, and he particularly favored the ideas of the seventeenth-century political writer James Harrington. Harrington had argued that a widespread distribution of property diluted power; when economic power became concentrated in a few hands, then political power flowed to those possessors and away from the citizens, ultimately resulting in an oligarchy or tyranny. In a letter of 1776, Adams acknowledged the truth of Harrington's hypothesis:

> The balance of power in a society, accompanies the balance of property in land. The only possible way, then, of preserving the balance of power on the side of equal liberty and public virtue, is to make the acquisition of land easy to every member of society; to make a division of the land into small quantities, so that the multitude may be possessed of landed estates. If the multitude is possessed of the balance of real estate, the multitude will have the balance of power, and in that case the multitude will take care of the liberty, virtue, and interest of the multitude, in all acts of government.[30]

The emphasis Harrington and other republican theorists placed on equality in landed possessions did not arise from a sentimental fondness for leveling. Rather, they believed the structure of a republic—free and equal citizens formulating their own laws and maintaining their liberties—necessitated more equality in possessions than did monarchy or aristocracy. To pass laws for the general welfare, citizens in a republic had to be free from the influences of self-interest or wealthy patrons. By owning their own land, farmers obtained their subsistence without being obliged to any individual or faction. Such individuals possessed independence. When individuals relied on others to obtain subsistence, they were dependent for the means of living on someone else and thus could be manipulated to support laws that

---

30. John Adams to James Sullivan, May 26, 1776, in Charles Francis Adams, ed., *The Works of John Adams, Second President of the United States* (Boston, 1856), IX, 376–77. John Adams has been most quotable on the distribution of wealth; see John R. Howe, Jr., *The Changing Political Thought of John Adams* (Princeton, 1966), 87, 136–37; Soltow, *Distribution of Wealth and Income,* 10–11, 17–22.

inured to the benefit of a few or a faction instead of the whole community, the "general welfare." Hence republics required independent citizens, and independent citizens could be most easily found wherever people owned their own freehold farms. The early United States seemed to fit this description.[31]

Of course, virtually all individuals who commented on the distribution of wealth qualified their claims of egalitarianism by insisting that some inequalities would always and rightfully exist. In most of the leaders' discourses, equal really meant equitability, and the revolutionaries hoped to achieve an equitable distribution of wealth rather than an equal one. Sam Adams emphatically rejected absolute equality of fortune: "The utopian schemes of levelling, and a community of goods, are as visionary and impracticable, as those which vest all property in the Crown, are arbitrary, despotic, and in our government unconstitutional." The role of the labor theory of property/value in promoting this inequality was explicit: because individual talents differed, amounts of individual property varied. A Charleston pamphleteer argued that monopolizers must be halted but emphasized that this would only lessen and not end inequality because variations in wealth-holding occur "from the difference of acquisition by different talents and industry." John Adams, for one, became skeptical of his earlier belief in equal distribution in his later years, primarily because he appreciated how inequalities in talents produced major differences in accumulations of wealth.[32]

Yet the inequality arising from different talents did not necessarily invalidate the requirement of widespread property ownership to sustain a republican form of government. The talented of society—the "natural aristocracy" of Thomas Jefferson and John Adams or the pecuniarily gifted of Alexander

---

31. On the idea of dependence and independence, see Lance Banning, *The Jeffersonian Persuasion: Evolution of a Party Ideology* (Ithaca, N.Y., 1978), 31–39, 67, 203–204; Wood, *Radicalism of the American Revolution*, 234; Wood, *Creation of the American Republic*, 71.

32. [Samuel Adams], "The House of Representatives of Massachusetts to Dennys De Berdt," in Cushing, ed., *Writings of Samuel Adams,* I, 137; Anonymous, "Rudiments of Law and Government Deduced from Nature" (Charleston, 1783), in Charles S. Hyneman and Donald S. Lutz, eds., *American Political Writing During the Founding Era, 1760–1805* (Indianapolis, 1983), I, 577–79; John Adams to Thomas Brand-Hollis, June 11, 1790, in Adams, ed., *Works of John Adams,* IX, 570; Reid, *Concept of Liberty,* 5; Wood, *Creation of the American Republic,* 72.

Hamilton—lived under the constraint of a simple agricultural society.[33] No matter how talented they were, individuals in a semicommercial agrarian society could use their talents only so far to increase their rewards by personal labor. A yeoman, agrarian society did not offer many opportunities for unusually large returns to individual labor so long as the labor theory of property/value was observed. To compile monstrous fortunes, avaricious men had to devise other means of acquisition than individual effort.

Even by the 1770s, however, the North American mainland colonies were no longer simple agricultural outposts; they had developed a few highly commercial areas (the larger cities), and some of the farming regions had switched from self-sufficiency to commercial agriculture (of course, the staple-growing regions in the South had always been commercially oriented). Fitting the labor theory of property/value to a yeoman agrarian society and deriving therefrom an equality of condition required no majestic flashes of synaptic capacity. Commercial societies and their relation to the labor theory of property/value, however, presented more problems. According to republican purists, commerce fostered a love of gain, ostentatious living, and a desire for luxuries; it denied the virtuous life of frugality, industry, and competence that was earned in agriculture by the sweat of the brows. Commerce thus corrupted the virtuous characteristics of the people and led to the demise of republics.[34] John Adams wrote in 1808 that "commerce, luxury, and avarice" had been the vices that had destroyed all republics in the past.[35]

33. On the Jefferson-Adams discussion of a natural aristocracy, see Merrill D. Peterson, *Adams and Jefferson: A Revolutionary Dialogue* (Oxford, 1978), 39, 43, 47, 54; J. G. A. Pocock, "The Classical Theory of Deference," *American Historical Review,* LXXXI (1976), 522–23; Joseph J. Ellis, *Passionate Sage: The Character and Legacy of John Adams* (New York, 1993), 128–33.

34. For example, Mercy Warren, *History of the Rise, Progress and Termination of the American Revolution. Interspersed with Biographical, Political and Moral Observations* (1805; rpr. New York, 1970), I, 4–5; George Clinton, "Letters of Cato," in Cecelia M. Kenyon, ed., *The Antifederalists* (Indianapolis, 1966), 308–309; J. G. A. Pocock, "Virtue and Commerce in the Eighteenth Century," *Journal of Interdisciplinary History,* III (1972), 129–32; Ralph Lerner, "Commerce and Character: The Anglo-American as New-Model Man," *William and Mary Quarterly,* XXXVI (1984), 13; Pocock, *Machiavellian Moment,* 533–38.

35. John Adams to William Heath, May 11, 1807, and John Adams to Benjamin Rush, September 27, 1808, in Adams, ed., *Works of John Adams,* IX, 595, 602–603; Richard Jackson to Ben Franklin, June 17, 1755, in Labaree and Willcox, eds., *Papers of Franklin,* VI, 81. For details on the relationship between republicanism and commerce, see Banning, *Jeffersonian Persua-*

Yet many political leaders did not necessarily believe that commerce con-
flicted with a republican form of government. Baron de Montesquieu, they
noted, had sanctioned commercial republics under certain conditions. Eminent revolutionaries believed that commerce either fostered republicanism or
at least was inconsequential in affecting wealth distribution. Charles Pinckney at the South Carolina Ratification Convention in 1788 doubted that merchants had any effect on social structure, arguing instead that a nobility and
feudal land laws had far more deleterious results on the distribution of
wealth. Noah Webster wrote that "commerce has been favorable to mankind" precisely because it evoked a new power to contest the older and potentially more dangerous power of an entrenched landed elite.[36]

Many Americans were able to accept commerce despite the advice of republicanism's revered philosophers by combining the labor theory of prop-
erty/value with the doctrine of noncoercion. The labor theory of property/
value indicated justice whenever the laborer could claim the fruits of his labor. In commerce that condition could be sustained when exchanges were
uncoerced by an outside authority, that is, either by government or by private
monopoly. The fruits of labor would be preserved when bargains were struck
without the presence of coercion.

This emphasis on coercion as the enemy of the labor theory of property/
value appeared starkly in the leadership's analysis of maldistribution of
wealth in the past. Previous civilizations, including republics, had been
agrarian; so how did the magnificently rich arise? The answer was coercion
either by military conquest or taxation. Governing authorities stole the fruits

sion, 65–68, 76–77; Appleby, *Capitalism and a New Social Order,* 9; McCoy, *Elusive Republic,*
58, 62, 69–73, 76–104; Thomas L. Pangle, *The Spirit of Modern Republicanism: The Moral Vision of the American Founders and the Philosophy of Locke* (Chicago, 1988), 64, 66, 67–70, 92.

36. Speech of Charles Pinckney, in Elliot, ed., *Elliot's Debates,* IV, 320–22; Noah Webster,
Jr., *A Collection of Essays and Fugitiv* [sic] *Writings on Moral, Historical, Political and Literary
Subjects* (Boston, 1790), 327; Benjamin Franklin, *A Modest Inquiry into the Nature and Necessity of a Paper-Currency* (1729), in Labaree and Willcox, eds., *Papers of Franklin,* I, 147; Benjamin Franklin to Benjamin Vaughan, July 26, 1784, in John Bigelow, ed., *The Life of Benjamin
Franklin, Written by Himself* (3rd ed.; Philadelphia, 1893), III, 274–78; Van Doren, *Benjamin
Franklin,* 711–12. See McCoy, *Elusive Republic,* 96–104; Wood, *Radicalism of the American Revolution,* 325–27, 337–38; Cathy Matson and Peter Onuf, "Toward a Republican Empire: Interest and Ideology in Revolutionary America," *American Quarterly,* XXXVII (1985), 498, 503,
508–19; Pangle, *Spirit of Modern Republicanism,* 67–68; William Letwin, "The Economic Policy of the Constitution," in *Liberty, Property, and the Foundations of the American Constitution,* ed. Ellen Frankel Paul and Howard Dickman (Albany, 1989), 131–33.

of labor of common people by using the coercive powers of the state. When Franklin had been asked about individual fortunes of ancient days, he replied that great riches had been established by three means: "The first is by war, as the Romans did, in plundering their conquered neighbours. This is robbery. The second by commerce, which is generally cheating. The third by agriculture, the only honest way."[37]

Commerce had two tendencies that enabled it to escape the agrarian, egalitarian confines of the labor theory of property/value and so become a danger to egalitarian ideals about wealth distribution. The first was economic growth and its influence on the rewards to mental labor. Republicanism implicitly depended on at least a static economy. Economic growth augured a reward system that could nullify the fruits of labor arising primarily from the sweat of the brow—in particular, it enabled the "natural aristocracy" to become wealthy indeed.[38]

The second tendency would be applicable in the distant future. A commercial economy implied the use of workers who were under the direction of a property owner, such as clerks in a mercantile house or sailors under the governance of a captain. These relations between owners and workers upset the notion of independency in economic undertakings in republicanism and substituted a version of dependency. More individuals worked for others than for themselves. Commerce brought up the possibility of wage labor becoming a standard in society.

37. Franklin quoted in Van Doren, *Benjamin Franklin*, 372. For other examples, see John Warren, *An Oration Delivered July 4th, 1783 at the Request of the Inhabitants of the Town of Boston, in Celebration of the Anniversary of American Independence* (Boston, 1783), 13–15; James Wilson, *An Oration Delivered Before the Providence Association of Mechanics and Manufacturers, at Their Annual Election, April 14, 1794* (Providence, 1794), 10–12; "On the Origin of Nobility," *American Museum*, XI (May, 1792), 218; The Federal Farmer [Richard Henry Lee?], *Observations Leading to a Fair Examination of the System of Government Proposed by the Late Conventions* (1788), in Storing, ed., *Complete Anti-Federalist*, II, 271–73; Fisher Ames, articles in *Palladium*, in Seth Ames, ed., *Works of Fisher Ames: With a Selection from His Speeches and Correspondence* (Boston, 1854), II, 173–76, 22–23, 332–33. Albert O. Hirschman, *The Passions and the Interests: Political Arguments for Capitalism Before Its Triumph* (Princeton, 1977), implies that this idea about how the ancients had accumulated wealth had become widespread; Paul Rahe believes one of the themes of the American revolutionaries was a revulsion at the excessive brutality and imperialism of past republics (*Republics Ancient and Modern*, 733–47, 777–78, and chap. 6 of part III).

38. On how republican characteristics could lead to wealth inequalities in a commercial society, see John Adams to Thomas Jefferson, December 18, 1819, in Adams, ed., *Works of John Adams*, X, 386.

A host of Americans at the time of the Revolution agreed that wage labor was a sign of dependence and of individuals not receiving the fruits of their labor, inherently contradicting the ideal of the labor theory of property/value. Evidently taking this viewpoint from England's experience, some Americans conceived of wage labor as a power relationship between people. To work for another individual meant that the employer controlled the worker's remuneration and thus had the capacity to reward the laborer less than the laborer's efforts merited. For most eighteenth-century Americans, therefore, wages carried a stigma of dependence, and because of dependence, the distribution of wealth worsened because a few absorbed the fruits of others' labors.[39]

At the time of the Revolution, wage labor was not prevalent. The colonial forms of subordinate labor were slavery, indentured servitude, and apprenticeship.[40] Commerce, however, portended a society that would see an escalation of the proportion of individuals who worked for wages. In the 1770s and 1780s, the United States was overwhelmingly a yeoman, agricultural, partially slaveholding society with only a modest group of urban artisans, many of whom were still operating in the artisanal tradition. Yet the question did hang in the air: was it possible to have waged labor in which wages actually reflected the fruits of labor? In the nineteenth century, the upper-income groups would argue yes. Operatives would respond, almost never.[41]

The labor theory of property/value became the standard for evaluating distributive justice, but it was not without its ambiguities and conflicts. In one sense, it was amazing how late-eighteenth-century Americans at virtually all

39. For example, Benjamin Franklin, "The Interest of Great Britain with Regard to Her Colonies" (1760), in Labaree and Willcox, eds., *Papers of Franklin,* IX, 73; Franklin, "Remarks on Agriculture and Manufacturing" (1770s), *ibid.,* XVIII, 274; [Tench Coxe], Citizen of the United States, *Observations on the Agriculture, Manufactures and Commerce of the United States in a Letter to a Member of Congress* (New York, 1789), 78; Thomas Jefferson to John Jay, August 23, 1785, in Boyd *et al.,* eds., *Papers of Jefferson,* VIII, 426; *American Museum,* I (January, 1787), 5–6; Scott, *In Pursuit of Happiness,* 71–74; McCoy, *Elusive Republic,* 14, 21, 37–39, 50–54; John F. Kasson, *Civilizing the Machine: Technology and Republican Values in America, 1776–1900* (New York, 1976), 19–38.

40. See Robert J. Steinfeld, *The Invention of Free Labor: The Employment Relation in English and American Law and Culture, 1350–1870* (Chapel Hill, 1991), 3–14, 126–37.

41. On the question of commerce and the distribution of wealth, see C. B. Macpherson, *"The Rise and Fall of Economic Justice" and Other Papers* (Oxford, 1985), 2–14.

income levels defended their property holdings as the legitimate rewards for their labor. Americans of all types insisted that they labored. Herein lay a few conflicts.

American society was not egalitarian and some individuals possessed impressive amounts of wealth. An elite did exist, and much of its property had come from political favoritism, inheritance, or family connections. This elite had been attacked verbally, sometimes physically, during the Revolution for earning income without labor.[42] Here was an indication of how the labor theory of property/value did not ultimately resolve problems over a commonly agreed-upon standard of distributive justice. And the fault line was socioeconomic status. Different classes and even occupational groups had different ideas of justifiable labor. During Shays' Rebellion in Massachusetts, the insurgents as well as the established authorities appealed to the "fruits of labor," to the labor theory of property/value, to justify their actions. In only one area was there unanimity among Americans: the leisured aristocrat who obtained income without performing any useful activity at all obviously violated the ethical standard in the labor theory of property/value. Use of the labor theory of property/value was going to be a contested affair.[43]

In the long run, the labor theory of property/value would have other shortcomings as well. As an economic theory it had limitations that political economists would explore, especially its failure to account for consumer prefer-

42. On the American upper class, see Wood, *Radicalism of the American Revolution,* 24–77; Richard B. Morris, *The American Revolution Reconsidered* (New York, 1967), 56, 60–69; Main, *Social Structure of Revolutionary America, passim;* John Richard Alden, *The South in the Revolution, 1763–1789* (Baton Rouge, 1957), 26–39. For conflicts between small farmers, mechanics, and elite members of society during the revolutionary era, see, for example, Alfred F. Young, *The Democratic Republicans of New York: The Origins, 1763–1797* (Chapel Hill, 1967), 4–6, 26, 59–63, 92–105; Edward Countryman, *A People in Revolution: The American Revolution and Political Society in New York, 1760–1790* (Baltimore, 1981), 11–23, 46–60, 186–87; James Kirby Martin, *In the Course of Human Events: An Interpretive Exploration of the American Revolution* (Arlington Heights, Ill., 1979), 10–21, 58–59, 84–87. For the urban mechanic's belief in the fruits of labor, private property, and independence, see Eric Foner, *Tom Paine and Revolutionary America* (New York, 1976), 39–42; Schultz, *Republic of Labor,* 4–11, 59–64, 106; Nash, *Urban Crucible,* 161–76, 297–300; Hoerder, *Crowd Action in Revolutionary Massachusetts,* 355–58.

43. See Szatmary, *Shays' Rebellion,* 33–34, 44, 71–74; Young, "Afterword," 319–25; Carl Bridenbaugh, *Myths and Realities: Societies of the Colonial South* (Baton Rouge, 1952), 15; Wood, *Radicalism of the American Revolution,* 277–80. The definitional problems are discussed in Chapter 3.

ences.[44] Moreover, the theory was irredeemably individualist, propertarian, and ethnocentric—a product of English social norms and intellectual trends. Hidden within the labor theory of property/value was a landed imperialism.

But these tendencies would have to wait to grow and become more visible. For all types of Americans at the end of the eighteenth century, the labor theory of property/value explained most satisfactorily the legitimate means of property acquisition in their semicommercial agricultural society. With the standard set, all that remained was to determine the enemies of the labor theory of property/value. The revolutionary leaders thought they had found the enemy: the social system of aristocracy and its monopoly over the coercive powers of government.

44. See chapter 10 below and Emil Kauder, *A History of Marginal Utility Theory* (Princeton, 1965), 56–63.

2

The Enemy of the Republic:
The Political Economy of Aristocracy

Having determined that the standard for evaluating economic justice and a fair distribution of wealth was to allow each laborer to reap the fruits of his labor, the revolutionaries then required an explanation of how a naturally just distribution of wealth could be distorted into one characterized by the few rich and the many poor. Their answer was aristocracy. From the moment trade and taxation controversies with Great Britain appeared, Americans lashed out at the British, and more generally the western European, social system of aristocracy. Existing political theory held that the nature of a government (democracy, republic, aristocracy, monarchy, and so on) depended on the nature of the society. Yet as they probed the ramifications of British policy, American leaders concluded that economic legislation had the potential to transform a society's character. In particular, laws possessing aristocratic tendencies could undermine and subvert republican equality by producing disparities in the distribution of wealth.

For centuries the system of aristocracy had been the primary social characteristic of European civilization. Although governments differed in the strength of the aristocratic component (absolute monarchy versus oligarchy versus inclusion of a commons), the essential social trait of those nations was hierarchy—society divided into defined castes, estates, or classes. Such divisions often implied political differences as well. Usually (but not in the case of Great Britain) the nobility was exempt from paying taxes and military conscription. Moreover, government was usually reserved for family members of the nobility. Either the aristocracy or the sons of the nobility filled government posts, church offices (in some cases), and high-ranking military positions. And then there was simply social status: commoners were to bow down, obey, and defer to the nobility.[1]

European aristocrats by the mid- to late eighteenth century contrasted greatly in status. Some sons and daughters of aristocrats were penurious and, except for a title, had little to distinguish them from the mass of their nation's population. Many had to make careers in trade or the professions; many were absorbed into the government in one incompetent capacity or another. But there were the grand aristocrats as well, those who possessed untold amounts of wealth. In England, some four hundred landlords possessed one-fifth of all the farmland in 1790. On the Continent, the story varied from country to country except in one particularly important instance. Wherever one went in Europe, the chasm between the unpropertied multitudes and the small but magnificently wealthy elite was obvious. And that material distance between the few and the many, between the rich and the poor, was often the distance between the aristocrat and the commoner.[2]

The American revolutionaries conducted a systems analysis of how politics might distort wealth distribution, and their frame of reference was the aristocratic world of western Europe.[3] Behind the analysis were two closely connected observations. First, European nations exhibited socially destructive distributions of wealth. In Europe Americans could see the existence of the few rich and the many poor. Second, the social and political power of Europe was in the hands of the aristocracy. The mating of these two observa-

1. Daniel A. Baugh, Introduction to *Aristocratic Government and Society in Eighteenth-Century England: The Foundations of Stability*, ed. Baugh (New York, 1975), 2–3, 17–21; R. R. Palmer, *The Age of Democratic Revolution: A Political History of Europe and America, 1760–1800* (Princeton, 1959), I, chaps. 2–3; see Shearer Davis Bowman, *Masters and Lords: Mid-19th-Century U.S. Planters and Prussian Junkers* (New York, 1993), 19–22, 116–19.

2. Figures from Richard L. Bushman, "This New Man: Dependence and Independence, 1776," in *Uprooted Americans: Essays to Honor Oscar Handlin*, by Richard L. Bushman et al. (Boston, 1979), 87; see Gary J. Kornblith and John M. Murrin, "Who Shall Rule at Home?: The Making and Unmaking of an American Ruling Class," in *Beyond the American Revolution*, ed. Young, 29–31; Baugh, Introduction to *Aristocratic Government and Society in Eighteenth-Century England*, ed. Baugh, 9–10, 17; Lewis Namier, *England in the Age of the American Revolution* (2nd ed.; London, 1961), 8–10, 15, 22–23; J. H. Plumb, *The Growth of Political Stability in England, 1675–1725* (Middlesex, Eng., 1967), 78; W. A. Speck, *Stability and Strife: England, 1714–1760* (Cambridge, Mass., 1979), 35–36; D. M. Palliser, *The Age of Elizabeth: England Under the Later Tudors, 1547–1603* (London, 1983), 65–69, 74; Wood, *Radicalism of the American Revolution*, 11–27.

3. See Jack P. Greene, *The Intellectual Construction of America: Exceptionalism and Identity from 1492 to 1800* (Chapel Hill, 1993), 107.

tions resulted in the Americans' second major premise concerning wealth distribution. Aristocrats used their social position to obtain political power to draw away the fruits of labor from the laborer and bestow those fruits upon themselves. Behind this transference stood the naked power of the state: without political power—control of the police and military might of a nation—a person's fruits of labor could not be taken. Thus for the American revolutionaries, unnatural wealth inequality was strictly a political phenomenon. Americans generally found the origin of economic inequality not in an economic but in a political system.

What evolved was a detailed analysis of how politics warped a natural wealth distribution. This was indeed a systems analysis, for the Americans argued that by using political power aristocrats systematically appropriated the fruits of others' labors for themselves. The explanation hinged on the validity of the linkage of the social system of Europe and the maldistribution of wealth.[4] That condition was also its weakness, for, though Americans did not admit it in the eighteenth and nineteenth centuries, their whole understanding of wealth distribution was based on an assumption that aristocracy was the system that produced inequality. Events in the twentieth century would destroy that assumption.

But in the eighteenth century, simple observation and small leaps of logic were all that were necessary to convince Americans about the truth of their forebodings concerning aristocracy. Confirmation of their trepidations came from upper-class Americans touring Europe. Benjamin Franklin and Thomas Jefferson were shocked at the wretchedness of European commoners and found the cause in the power of aristocrats to monopolize the land. Connecticut's William Johnson visited London in the 1760s and was unsettled by the contrasts of wealth and poverty: "There is no equality, all is extremes, and a bad Oeconomy [*sic*] discovers itself in everything."[5]

4. Consult Douglass Greybill Adair, "The Intellectual Origins of Jeffersonian Democracy: Republicanism, the Class Struggle, and the Virtuous Farmer" (Ph.D. dissertation, Yale University, 1943), 111. Compare the different styles of analysis between then and now by examining Immanuel Wallerstein, *The Modern World-System II: Mercantilism and the Consolidation of the European World-Economy, 1600–1750* (New York, 1980), who almost discards politics as an important realm of independent activity.

5. Benjamin Franklin to Joshua Babcock, January 13, 1772, in Labaree and Willcox, eds., *Papers of Franklin*, XIX, 7; Conner, *Poor Richard's Politicks*, 33–34, 132–33; William Johnson quoted in Elizabeth P. McCaughey, *From Loyalist to Founding Father: The Political Odyssey of William Samuel Johnson* (New York, 1980), 74; Thomas Jefferson, "Notes of a Tour into the

In many ways, the American Revolution was the firing of the first gun in the century-long war against European aristocracy and hereditary privilege. By the middle of the eighteenth century, aristocracy had lost favor among intellectuals, political theorists, and political economists. Aristocracy supposedly stabilized a society and provided order and justice. Many Europeans increasingly found aristocracy guilty of mindless passion, bloodletting, political incompetence, and luxurious dissipation. The colonists' conclusions were part of the general European reaction demanding a new set of institutions to replace aristocratic ones.[6]

Americans had many reasons for condemning aristocracy, but one especially vibrant strand of thought stood out. Aristocracy violated the precepts of the labor theory of property/value. The standard definition of an aristocrat (or perhaps a member of the gentry) was a person who did not perform manual labor, who lived a life of leisure without working for sustenance. Aristocrats, at least the more well known of them, had fabulous wealth and yet did not labor. Therefore, they could enjoy such a circumstance only if they lived off the labors of others, thereby violating the natural order of things and the natural distribution of wealth. Ezra Stiles wrote in 1760 that it was objectionable to have feudal tenure in lands "so that a few Barons and feudal Lords have engrossed the Labors of Millions. Whereas every man has a natural Right to the Fruit of his Industry."[7]

Southern Parts of France, &c., 1787," in Boyd and Catanzariti, eds., *Papers of Jefferson*, XI, 420; Dumas Malone, *Jefferson and His Time* (Boston, 1948–81), II, 108, 129–30, 155. See also Soltow, *Distribution of Wealth and Income*, 9–12.

6. The reaction against aristocracy among political theorists and political economists has been superbly related by Hirschman, *Passions and the Interests;* and Rahe, *Republics Ancient and Modern*, 391, 510–11. On the American reaction, see Wood, *Radicalism of the American Revolution*, 181, 231–43; Bushman, "Massachusetts Farmers and the Revolution," 124; Ralph Ketcham, *From Colony to Country: The Revolution in American Thought, 1750–1820* (New York, 1974), 65–66.

7. Edmund S. Morgan, *American Slavery, American Freedom: The Ordeal of Colonial Virginia* (New York, 1975), 63; Baugh, Introduction to *Aristocratic Government and Society in Eighteenth-Century England*, ed. Baugh, 10–11; Wood, *Radicalism of the American Revolution*, 36–38; Bowman, *Masters and Lords*, 28–29; Ezra Stiles, Thanksgiving sermon, November 20, 1760, quoted in Morgan, *Gentle Puritan*, 213; Benjamin Franklin to Count de Campmanes, June 5, 1784, in Bigelow, ed., *Life of Benjamin Franklin*, III, 268; Edward Handler, *America and Europe in the Political Thought of John Adams* (Cambridge, Mass., 1964), 85. For the religious grounds of the American attack on aristocracy, see Morgan, *Challenge of the American Revolution,* 91; for the early fear of a landed aristocracy in the colonies, see Bushman, "Massachusetts Farmers and the Revolution," 99–101; for the Marxian view of aristocracy and the demand

Aristocracy was the enemy, but to understand this enemy the colonials had to define aristocracy, the way it came to power, and the types of political activity that abetted its growth so they could avoid the wealth imbalances that naturally accompanied the system. This search produced a heated debate. John Adams and Thomas Jefferson swapped arguments over the merits and hazards of a natural aristocracy of talent and wisdom, and indeed a considerable public commentary arose concerning those with superior mental abilities. George Clinton, governor of New York and opponent to the proposed Constitution, fretted that in any community there were tendencies that led to an aristocracy: "These are superior talents, fortunes and public employments." Antifederalists at times insisted that wealth was the true prerequisite for an aristocracy and that, if nothing else, even wealth honestly earned could act as a seedbed for an aristocracy. A Maryland writer flatly stated that titles were meaningless, that what counted was wealth: "Titles are of very little, or no consequence—The *rich* are *nobility,* and the *poor plebians* in all countries."[8]

But for the revolutionary generation, the key element that composed aristocracy was an elite's access to legal privileges that were denied to the rest of the members of the community. It was through this avenue that aristocrats determined the contours of wealth distribution. This was the reasoning behind Tom Paine's assertion in *Common Sense* (1776) that the improper chasms between rich and poor could be accounted for by understanding the mechanics of aristocratic and monarchical government rather than by using the "harsh . . . names of oppression and avarice." In aristocratic societies, the aristocracy had a monopoly on political power and used state coercion to enact laws that transferred the fruits of labor from the masses to themselves. Aristocratic control of politics, then, was the source of the maldistribution of wealth. An aristocracy was any elite group that monopolized political power

---

among late-eighteenth-century radicals for private property, see E. K. Hunt, "Marx's Theory of Property and Alienation," in *Theories of Property: Aristotle to the Present,* ed. Anthony Parel and Thomas Flanagan (Waterloo, Canada, 1979), 300. Gordon Wood, in *Radicalism of the American Revolution,* 186, 277–81, has interpreted the fruits of labor expostulations to indicate a vision of economic growth; the interpretation offered here stresses the desire to create equity among the citizens.

8. Peterson, *Adams and Jefferson,* 39, 43, 47, 54; Handler, *America and Europe in the Political Thought of John Adams,* 141, 148, 191; Cato [George Clinton?], in Kenyon, ed., *Antifederalists,* 316; [John F. Mercer?], "Essays by a Farmer," in Storing, ed., *Complete Anti-Federalist,* V, 19, 20; also 33, 55.

for its own economic aggrandizement. The agrarian radical John Taylor of Carolina pithily encapsulated the economic difference between aristocratic and republican forms of government in 1818: "Monarchies and aristocracies" were fraudulent governments because they were "founded on the principle of distributing wealth by law," whereas in a republic the principle was to let "wealth [be] distributed by merit and industry."[9]

It was in this analytical framework that Antifederalists and those who thought like them feared the wealthy. The Maryland Antifederalist who warned that the rich were nobility did not argue that the wealthy should be eliminated but that they had to be so constricted that they reaped only "what they have lawfully gained, by their own [industry] or the industry of their ancestors." If the wealthy came into possession of the government, then that class would pass laws to wrest property from the poorer classes to give to themselves and so create the few rich and the multitudinous poor. At this point, the wealthy, when they controlled government, were in truth a secret aristocracy. But eventually their domination of the government would become so complete that they would declare their real intentions by elevating themselves legally to hereditary status and thereby become an open aristocracy. This was the route that many feared had enabled an aristocracy to arise in the first place. George Logan, the radical doctor of postrevolutionary Pennsylvania, summed up this way of looking at aristocracy and its source of power by writing, "It is not the distinctions of titles which constitutes an aristocracy: it is the principle of partial association [*i.e.,* special privileges]."[10]

From the moment the Americans went to war to secure their indepen-

9. Thomas Paine, *Common Sense* (1776), in Philip S. Foner, ed., *The Complete Writings of Thomas Paine* (New York, 1945), I, 9–13, quote on 9; John Taylor, *An Enquiry into the Principles and Tendency of Certain Public Measures* (Philadelphia, 1794), 21; Taylor, *Arator: Being a Series of Agricultural Essays, Practical and Political: In Sixty-Four Numbers,* ed. M. E. Bradford (4th ed.; 1818; rpr. Indianapolis, 1977), 93–94.

10. Jackson Turner Main, *The Antifederalists: Critics of the Constitution, 1781–1788* (New York, 1961), 11, 129–30; Herbert J. Storing, "What the Anti-Federalists Were *For,*" in Storing, ed., *Complete Anti-Federalist,* I, 10, 17–19, 44, 48, 51; [John F. Mercer?], "Essays by a Farmer," *ibid.,* V, 19, 20; also 33, 55; Federal Farmer [Richard Henry Lee], *Letters of the Federal Farmer, ibid.,* II, 266–68; James A. Haw, "Samuel Chase's 'Objections to the Federal Government,'" *Maryland Historical Magazine,* LXXVI (1981), 275; Wood, *Radicalism of the American Revolution,* 241–43; Young, *Democratic Republicans of New York,* 105; Main, *Antifederalists,* 105–106; A Farmer [George Logan], *Five Letters, Addressed to the Yeomanry of the United States, Containing Some Observations on the Dangerous Scheme of Governor Duer and Mr. Secretary Hamil-*

dence, their ideological enemy was aristocracy. Despite arguments over the definition of an aristocracy and aristocratic dangers to republican American society, virtually all were agreed that the existence of a European-style aristocracy produced the few rich and the many poor. Americans also determined that the means by which aristocrats stole the fruits of others' labors was political—it was effected through monopolization of government. Aristocratic manipulation of the economy was "the political economy of aristocracy," and it was composed of certain concrete policies that enriched the few and pauperized the multitudes.

By 1790, the American concept of how a natural distribution of wealth became warped into the skewed one of the opulent few and the wretched many was complete. It depended on the existence of an aristocracy that used its privileges and social position to control the state. Resistance to the aristocratic program was nigh unto impossible because all the coercive power of the state was used to enforce the laws that performed the transference, and little outside of revolution—unless a popularly elected commons had become an effective part of the government—could alter the situation. Aristocratic governments, in short, used the powers of government to perform class robbery.

From this understanding of how an aristocracy worked through seizure of government to distort a natural wealth distribution, Americans established the operative principles of the political economy of aristocracy, that is, how the social system of aristocracy used government to obtain its economic ends. Americans in the eighteenth and nineteenth centuries never used the phrase *the political economy of aristocracy,* but it captures the essence of their analysis. Moreover, American revolutionaries provided a specific program that indicated the operation of the political economy of aristocracy. That program was derived from the political philosophy of republicanism.

Republicanism was a vague and imprecise philosophy inherited from ancient and medieval times that explained the functioning of a republican form of government. The basic goal of a republican polity was to provide and safeguard the freedom and property of citizens living in equality and to avoid actions that would plunge the government into despotism so that the citizens

---

ton, to Establish National Manufactories (Philadelphia, 1792), 12. The methods by which the wealthy became a hereditary aristocracy were outlined by John Adams in 1778 in *Defence of the Constitutions,* in Adams, ed., *Works of John Adams,* IV, 381.

lost their equality and ability to control government. A host of side conditions were attached to the theory of republicanism as it developed over the years: republican states should be small, agrarian, and egalitarian in landed possessions. The citizenry should possess the traits of simplicity and frugality, exhibit virtue (the capacity to sacrifice self-interest for the public weal), avoid luxury and idleness, and resist corruption (self-gratification). The citizens should be economically independent, and the nation as a whole should be wary of any sign of increasing dependency. Republican government should be small and elections frequent. During the seventeenth century, English republican theorists added a fear of commerce and the demoralizing influence of banks and public debts.

The republican heritage had many confusing qualities. Not everyone in the society need be a citizen; ancient and medieval republicanism permitted the existence of slaves, aristocrats, and monarchs. Some republicans rejected commerce, while others, following the lead of Montesquieu, argued that commercial republics under certain circumstances were stronger than agrarian republics. Republicans stressed an independence that easily shaded into individualism. Although republicanism argued for community, it offered no institutions to enable community norms to subdue excessive individualism.[11]

American revolutionaries claimed that a certain pattern appeared in the devolution of republican governments. At first, a republican society existed in simplicity and equality. But demagogues arose who desired wealth and fame; to gain control of the government, they led some of the citizenry into a

---

11. For a summary of republicanism, consult Pocock, *Machiavellian Moment*, 334–504; Robert E. Shalhope, "Toward a Republican Synthesis: The Emergence of an Understanding of Republicanism in American Historiography," *William and Mary Quarterly*, XXIX (1972), 49–80; Adair, "Intellectual Origins of Jeffersonian Democracy," 55–109; Banning, *Jeffersonian Persuasion*, 25–71; Linda K. Kerber, "The Republican Ideology of the Revolutionary Generation," *American Quarterly*, XXXVII (1985), 474–95; Pangle, *Spirit of Modern Republicanism*, 49–94; Wood, *Radicalism of the American Revolution*, 100–109. For an understanding of ancient republicanism, see the first part of Rahe, *Republics Ancient and Modern*. A sort of summary as to where the debate over republicanism now stands can be found in Lance Banning, "The Republican Interpretation: Retrospect and Prospect," in *The Republican Synthesis Revisited: Essays in Honor of George Athan Billias*, ed. Milton M. Klein, Richard D. Brown, and John B. Hinch (Worcester, Mass., 1992), 91–117; Daniel T. Rodgers, "Republicanism: The Career of a Concept," *Journal of American History*, LXXIX (1992), 11–38; and Lance Banning, *The Sacred Fire of Liberty: James Madison and the Founding of the Federal Republic* (Ithaca, N.Y., 1995), 214–15, 428 n. 3.

faction. This process involved the elevation of private interests above those of the common welfare, that is, the people were being corrupted out of their simplicity and taught to yearn for luxuries. Once in power, the demagogue or faction led the nation into war, causing a huge debt. The debt could be repaid only by levying taxes on the common citizenry. Tax money was also used to expand the government to create numerous offices for favorites of the ruling faction—a bureaucracy. Most of the jobs were useless and served only as a means to maintain a party's control over the government. Eventually, the party became strong enough to establish an aristocracy or a monarchy (or strengthen the existing ones) and eliminate citizen participation in governmental affairs. The republican state became an oligarchy or perhaps an absolute monarchy. In any case, the citizenry lost its equality and liberty.[12]

The republican explanation of how a free people fell into tyranny was a political one. The revolutionaries were most concerned with the fate of their society in political terms. Their political analysis, however, contained important economic implications, and not the least of these involved the distribution of wealth. In the constitutional quarrel with Britain between 1763 and 1776, Americans disclosed the policies that exemplified the political economy of aristocracy and how it created the few rich and the many poor. The distributionist perspective operating in the colonial imagination was betrayed by the phrase *the fruits of labor,* indicating that the colonists believed the aristocratic policies of Parliament were transgressing against the labor theory of property/value.

The first policy that aristocrats wielded to take away the fruits of others' labors was taxation. At the heart of the American controversy with Great Britain was the right of Parliament to tax the colonists, first brought to prominence by the passage of the Stamp Act. Colonists fought British taxation with arguments concerning colonial charters, rights of Englishmen, sovereignty (no taxation without representation), and economic consequences.[13] But the

---

12. The process is most fully laid out in Bailyn, *Ideological Origins of the American Revolution,* 35–50, 56–128; Banning, *Jeffersonian Persuasion,* 65–84; Wood, *Creation of the American Republic,* 22–40.

13. Thomas O'Brien Hanley, *Charles Carroll of Carrollton: The Making of a Revolutionary Gentleman* (Washington, D.C., 1970), 217; John M. Coleman, *Thomas McKean: Forgotten Leader of the Revolution* (Rockaway, N.J., 1975), 63; Bailyn, *Ideological Origins of the American Revolution,* 99, 128; Reid, *Concept of Liberty,* 69–89. Reid has argued that the revolutionaries did not advocate property redistribution and that liberty should not be conflated with property, a point that conflicts with the presentation here (*ibid.,* 5, 69–89, 109–19).

colonial protest over parliamentary taxation contained a consistent theme that the powers of government were being used to take the fruits of colonial labor to bestow on the undeserving in England. For example, Benjamin Franklin, when in London, attacked parliamentary taxation in 1770 because it inferred that "three Millions, out of Fifteen of which his Majesty is Sovereign, are declared no longer Masters of the Fruits of their own Industry." Alexander Hamilton warned that Parliament's attempt to tax the colonists without their consent meant that the colonist's "fruits of his daily toil are consumed in oppressive taxes." Elbridge Gerry wrote in 1774 that the "point [of the conflict] is, whether Americans shall enjoy the fruits of their labour, or send them in taxes to Great Britain." When Joseph Warren delivered an oration in honor of the Boston Massacre in 1775, he emphasized that Parliament had no right to American property, and in particular no right to dispose of the "property which the Americans have earned by their labor." [14]

The second policy that aristocratic governments used to redistribute wealth from producers to nonproducers (that is, to leisured aristocrats) was to create a vast government bureaucracy. The bureaucracy, or patronage or civil list, was composed of individuals in the civil service, the military, pensioners, and church appointees. In republican theory, republics degenerated when ministers swelled the bureaucracy so as to reward supporters and to maintain a political faction. The appearance of bureaucracy was a sign of corruption and dependence, for individuals now relied on a minister for their opulent livelihoods, and policies were being formulated by mindless devotion to faction instead of consideration of the general welfare. [15]

Beyond the politics of a patronage machine, Americans quickly ferreted out the economics of the situation. For a ministry to obtain such a set of followers, money had to be found. And the money was found in taxing the industrious members of the community. Here the political economy of aristoc-

14. [Benjamin Franklin], "The Colonist's Advocate: I," in Labaree and Willcox, eds., *Papers of Franklin*, XVII, 7; Samuel Adams, "The Rights of the Colonists, a List of Violations of Rights and a Letter of Correspondence," in Cushing, ed., *Writings of Samuel Adams*, II, 360; Alexander Hamilton, *A Full Vindication of the Measures of Congress, &c* (1774), in Harold C. Syrett and Jacob E. Cooke, eds., *The Papers of Alexander Hamilton* (New York, 1961–87), I, 53; Elbridge Gerry to Samuel Adams, May 12, 1774, in James T. Austin, ed., *The Life of Elbridge Gerry* (1828; rpr. New York, 1970), I, 44; Oration of Joseph Warren, March 6, 1775, in Niles, ed., *Principles and Acts of the Revolution in America*, 25. See Bushman, "Massachusetts Farmers and the Revolution," 119–24.

15. See, for example, Bailyn, *Ideological Origins of the American Revolution*, 49–50; Banning, *Jeffersonian Persuasion*, 47–50, 65–66; Wood, *Creation of the American Republic*, 143, 156.

racy was explicit. The producers of wealth, industrious workers, were taxed at exorbitant rates to sustain government placemen who did not labor—society's nonproducers. This was a malevolent redistribution of wealth.

Angry colonists frequently berated the British bureaucracy for the sin of drawing off the hard-earned fruits of labor from producers to support non-producers in idleness and luxury. Alexander Hamilton in 1774 made the transfer of wealth explicit: "How would you like to pay four shillings a year, out of every pound your farms are worth, to be squandered, (at least a great part of it) upon ministerial tools and court sycophants?" Sam Adams, who strove ceaselessly to excite anti-British sentiments in the Massachusetts populace by instilling in them fears of a bloated British bureaucracy, warned that the sole purpose of British taxation was "to feed and pamper a set of infamous wretches, who swarm like the locusts of Egypt; and some of them expect to revel in wealth and riot on the spoils of our country." Josiah Quincy complained of the "pensioners, stipendiaries, and salary men" feasting on tax revenues; he then added, "By the sweat of our brow, we earn the little we possess."[16]

The third policy that Americans saw as a part of the political economy of aristocracy that skewed the distribution of wealth was government creation of an established church. In this instance an established church combined the worst features of the the sins of excessive taxation and bureaucratic growth. All persons in a nation with an established church had to pay taxes for the support of that church, and the political authorities used the church as another dumping ground for ministerial supporters. Because many Americans were dissenters from the Church of England, they understandably insisted on the rights of conscience in religious matters, and they feared the potential effects of a forcible entry of England's state-supported church into their lives. Yet such trepidations about the right of conscience did not preclude an understanding of the economics of an established church.

The model of an established church was the Church of England. In their assessment of the way the Church of England functioned, American leaders noted with dismay the extent to which the church absorbed tax monies, the "tythe." Richard Henry Lee wrote to William Lee that he did not wish to see

16. Alexander Hamilton, *A Full Vindication* (1774), in Syrett and Cooke, eds., *Papers of Hamilton*, I, 67; Candidus [Samuel Adams], Boston *Gazette*, October 14, 1771, in Cushing, ed., *Writings of Samuel Adams*, II, 253; Josiah Quincy to Rev. John Eagleson, September 15, 1768, in Josiah Quincy, *Memoir of the Life of Josiah Quincy Jun. of Massachusetts* (1825; rpr. New York, 1971), 21, 23.

an American bishop appointed from London because "neither Tythes nor Ecclesiastical courts will do in America." John Adams wrote in 1815 that his fear of an American episcopate during the Revolution was grounded in logical observations: "But if Parliament can erect diocesses and appoint Bishops, they may introduce the whole hierarchy, establish tythes . . . [and] impose penalties extending to life and limb, as well as to liberty and property." Many Americans believed the operation of state-supported churches in Europe had ruined small farmers.[17]

The fourth policy of the political economy of aristocracy that produced the many poor and the few rich was the ability of government to bestow monopoly economic privileges upon either single persons or groups of persons. In the seventeenth and eighteenth centuries, monopolies in England usually took the form of corporate charters, in which the corporate entity was given an exclusive right to trade or manufacture in some specified area. Monopolies in England developed from specific circumstances (not the least being a capacity of the Crown to earn funds without having to obtain the approval of Parliament), but in economic thought the granting of monopoly charters was part of the policy of mercantilism. Mercantilism, according to its advocates, was a system designed to create national wealth. Its ties to an aristocratic framework were tenuous at best. But radical seventeenth-century Protestants and later eighteenth-century Americans saw a discomforting conjunction of the principles of monopoly and aristocracy. The aristocratic political principle was rights and privileges (and supposedly obligations) reserved for the few; the monopoly principle was seen as the economic equivalent of the politics of aristocracy—business endeavors reserved for the benefit of the few.[18]

American colonists were alive to the threat of monopoly during the revolu-

17. Richard Henry Lee to William Lee, June 19, 1771, in Ballagh, ed., *Letters of Richard Henry Lee,* I, 59; John Adams to Dr. J. Morse, December 2, 1815, in Adams, ed., *Works of John Adams,* X, 185; Hamilton, *A Full Vindication,* in Syrett and Cooke, eds., *Papers of Hamilton,* I, 67. See *American Museum,* I (1787), 7; Thomas Jefferson, "Rough Draft of Jefferson's Resolutions for Disestablishing the Church of England" (1776), in Boyd and Catanzariti, eds., *Papers of Jefferson,* I, 530; Roger Sherman Boardman, *Roger Sherman: Signer and Statesman* (1938; rpr. New York, 1971), 103–104; Bushman, "Massachusetts Farmers and the Revolution," 87, 96.

18. On monopoly in republicanism, see *Cato's Letters,* no. 64, February 3, 1721, and no. 68, March 3, 1721, in Jacobson, ed., *English Libertarian Heritage,* 147, 179–82; on mercantilism, see John Kenneth Galbraith, *Economics in Perspective: A Critical History* (Boston, 1987), 31–45; McCoy, *Elusive Republic,* 41–45. The relation between radical Protestantism and antimonopoly is given in G. P. Gooch, *English Democratic Ideas in the 17th Century* (1898; rpr. New York,

tionary years, and in economic affairs the period might be considered the first bout of antimonopoly agitation in American history. One of the dark motivations revolutionaries ascribed to British commercial legislation was Parliament's desire to monopolize the trade of North America. Sam Adams, never one to forgo an Anglophobian remark, wrote in 1779 that he believed England desired "an intended Monopoly of all the Trade and I may add of the richest Lands in America." When Great Britain applied the Navigation Acts to Americans at the end of the war, Virginian Richard Henry Lee wailed in antimonopoly tones: Great Britain had reprehensible policies because its "appetite for Commerce has ever been ravenous, and its wishes always for Monopoly." That Americans found monopoly to be a singular economic devil with deleterious results to common citizens was revealed in numerous outbursts during the war years when Americans accused merchants of "monopolizing" goods (or "engrossing" them) to drive up prices. Thomas Jefferson proposed to James Madison that the newly crafted Constitution needed a bill of rights, and one of the rights should be a prohibition on the central government from establishing monopolies.[19]

The revolutionaries quickly connected the aristocratic tendencies in monopolies to the ethical standards of the labor theory of property/value. When in 1773 Parliament passed the Tea Act, colonists read the legislation as the commencement of a policy to ruin the equality of citizens operating in the American economy by granting favoritism to court sycophants residing in England. John Dickinson asked "whether WE, our WIVES and CHILDREN, together, with the HARD EARNED FRUITS OF OUR LABOUR are not *made over*

1959), 33, 58, 128–29, 171–72. In general, refer to Lacey Baldwin Smith, *This Realm of England, 1399 to 1688* (Lexington, Mass., 1966), 229–35; Charles Howard McIlwain, *The American Revolution: A Constitutional Interpretation* (New York, 1923), 175–76.

19. Samuel Adams to Samuel Cooper, February 21, 1779, in Cushing, ed., *Writings of Samuel Adams*, IV, 127; Richard Henry Lee to James Madison, August 11, 1785, in Hutchinson *et al.*, eds., *Papers of Madison*, VIII, 340; Thomas Pleasants, Jr., to Thomas Jefferson, October 24, 1785, in Boyd *et al.*, eds., *Papers of Jefferson*, VIII, 666–67; Thomas Jefferson to James Madison, December 20, 1787, *ibid.*, XII, 440. See also Henry Laurens to the governor of Connecticut, November 10, 1778, in Edmund C. Burnett, ed., *Letters of Members of Continental Congress* (Washington, D.C., 1921–36), III, 486; A Committee of Congress to the Several States, November 11, 1778, *ibid.*, III, 491; Address to the Inhabitants of the United States, May 26, 1779, in Worthington Chauncey Ford et al., eds., *Journals of the Continental Congress, 1774–1789* (Washington, D.C., 1904–37), XIV, 650; [Sullivan], *Path to Riches*, 54, 59; Jackson Turner Main, *The Sovereign States, 1775–1783* (New York, 1973), 170, 252–53.

to *this* almost *bankrupt Company,* to augment their Stock, and to *repair* their *ruined Fortunes.*"[20]

By the 1780s and 1790s, Americans clearly associated monopoly with aristocratic prerogative. Wrote the Antifederalist "Agrippa," "Exclusive companies are, in trade, pretty much like an aristocracy in government, and produce nearly as bad effects." The somewhat conservative Philadelphia legalist James Wilson flatly stated in 1790, "Monopoly and exclusive privilege are the bane of every thing—of science as well as commerce."[21] Antimonopoly had become republican; monopoly was a trait of an aristocratic society.

The fifth policy Americans found in the political economy of aristocracy that upset a natural distribution of wealth was a fluctuating standard of value, or more simply the issuance of paper money and the machinery that surrounded it. Paper money was added to the list of aristocratic practices in the 1780s; it had developed out of American domestic troubles instead of the quarrel with England over trade regulation and taxation. Some Americans, however, applied to paper money emissions the same principles they used on British legislation. Their analysis of paper money and its problems in the late 1770s and 1780s derived from their understanding of aristocracy, and for that reason I include it among the policies that constituted the political economy of aristocracy.

During the war the young republic suffered an enormous amount of inflation caused by the disruption of normal trade patterns, a sudden demand for goods from the military, and the propensity of the Continental Congress and state governments to issue paper money instead of levying direct taxes. The massive inflation caused severe social disturbances and led many of the leaders and the wealthy to deprecate paper money emissions. When the war ended, however, some economic dislocations remained. National and state debts were large, and the nation seemingly had no way to repay them. A depression settled over much of the economy for a few years, not only as a result of the usual economic readjustment to peacetime conditions but also because the British ap-

20. John Dickinson, *Two Letters on the Tea Tax* (1773), in Ford, ed., *Political Writings of John Dickinson,* 459.

21. Letter of Agrippa, January 25, 1788, in Storing, ed., *Complete Anti-Federalist,* IV, 104–105; James Wilson, *Lectures on Law* (1790–91), in Robert Green McCloskey, ed., *The Works of James Wilson* (Cambridge, Mass., 1967), I, 217; Ronald Schultz, "Small Producer Thought in Early America, Part I: Philadelphia Artisans and Price Control," *Pennsylvania History,* LIV (1987), 116–17, 121, 135.

plied the Navigation Acts (the laws that excluded trade from outside the British Empire) to the United States.

The state governments and the Confederation government labored under a monstrous tax load. In the past, the states had successfully met wartime challenges as well as economic recessions by issuing paper money, retired through taxation or a slow depreciation. In the 1780s, however, the debts were enormous and various groups (an "urgency" faction) tried to repay debts too quickly by enforcing draconian tax measures. Many of the states backed down from this process because it caused intense popular anger; Massachusetts did not and brought down upon itself a rebellion of farmers who were losing their farms because of failure to pay assessments. Other states successfully implemented gradualist debt retirement programs that used paper money.[22]

Evidently the wartime inflationary experience had horrified many creditors about state-issued paper money, and they now saw it as a means of evading debts by reducing the value of money. Debtors recognized the same result and supported paper money laws so as to avoid onerous taxes. In the 1780s, the creditor groups tended to be merchants, large landholders, and those engaged in commercial activity; they frequently abhorred paper money. Small farmers and people enmeshed in a semicommercial, partially self-sufficient community favored paper money as a way to escape ruinous taxes that would destroy their communities; they represented the popular forces.

The paper money battles of the 1780s were confusing, partly because the colonies had a history of favoring paper emissions, partly because class lines were not as firm as one might expect, partly because some states pursued masochistic monetary policies, and partly because both sides of the issue had a claim to the antiaristocratic heritage. The followers of Shays's Rebellion could claim that they sought only to preserve the "fruits of their labor" from confiscation through onerous taxes, whereas the creditors could assert that failure to pay debts owed to them represented fraud and deprived them of the money

22. I have generally followed the conclusions of Edwin J. Perkins, who has forcefully shown that the states did a creditable job in using paper money to liquidate the Revolutionary War debts in the 1780s but that a number of hard-nosed ideologues insisted on immediate payment of debts, plunging some areas of the nation into social crisis (*American Public Finance and Financial Services, 1700–1815* [Columbus, Ohio, 1994], chaps. 5, 7, 8, esp. 138–44). For another statement on class divisions in the paper money episode of the 1780s, see Roger H. Brown, *Redeeming the Republic: Federalists, Taxation, and the Origins of the Constitution* (Baltimore, 1993), 33–36, 41, 148–53.

that had been promised them by their sacrifice of consumption in the past. The paper money forces, or, more explicitly, those who favored the use of government to issue a legal tender to solve hard economic times, lost the argument to those who favored a currency that was immune to governmental tinkering.[23]

The reasoning of the hard money or specie advocates ultimately prevailed in American economic thought and became, somewhat unbelievably given its upper-class origin, the egalitarian pronouncement on monetary affairs. Policies governing currency and the institutions connected with it were enlisted in the political economy of aristocracy because it was recognized that currency had distinct distributive effects. Therefore, manipulation of the currency by an elite had the possibility of redistributing wealth from the masses to the few, denying workers their legitimate fruits of labor.

Hard money analysis of currency blended together the economic circumstances of extensive commerce, the need for a standard of value, and the legitimate rewards of labor. Sizable elements of the economy of the United States in the 1780s engaged in commercial dealings.[24] Commerce involved the exchange of the goods of one person for the goods of another; in more advanced economies, ones that had gone beyond simple barter, the transaction required an intermediary—money—so that exchange could be extended over place and time. That is, money acted to allow the transaction to be goods for money, and then, at a later date at a different place, the money could be traded for other commodities.

It was the transaction process in commerce that elevated the importance of the standard of value for exchange. If the intermediary of money was employed, it became vital, to avoid injustice to one of the transactors, to establish a stable medium of exchange that accurately reflected value. Value meant the amount of labor used in fashioning or producing the article of trade. Benja-

---

23. For the background of the 1780s, see Main, *Antifederalists,* chaps. 1–3; Jackson Turner Main, "The American States in the Revolutionary Era," in *Sovereign States in an Age of Uncertainty,* ed. Ronald Hoffman and Peter J. Albert (Charlottesville, 1981), 9–16; Countryman, *People in Revolution,* 254–57; Edwin J. Perkins, "Conflicting Views on Fiat Currency: Britain and Its North American Colonies in the Eighteenth Century," *Business History,* XXXIII (1991), 8–30, esp. 23–27; Mary M. Schweitzer, "State-Issued Currency and the Ratification of the U.S. Constitution," *Journal of Economic History,* XLIX (1989), 311–22. On the paper money forces, see Szatmary, *Shays' Rebellion,* 1–6, 32–34, 40, 45–47, and *passim;* Ramsay, *History of the American Revolution,* II, 134–35.

24. Main, *Social Structure of Revolutionary America,* 16–18, 28, 30, 34–37, 270–71.

min Franklin made this notion explicit in 1729 in his *Modest Inquiry into the Nature and Necessity of a Paper Money.* Addressing the problem of paper money, Franklin noted the usefulness of money for exchange purposes because in trade "Labour is exchanged for Labour, or one Commodity for another."[25]

Before the Revolution Franklin had been a proponent of paper money and had successfully led the colony of Pennsylvania in the experiment. He knew that the goal of paper money had to be price stability. By 1764, he wavered on the appropriateness of a paper currency but not on his abhorrence of depreciation caused by excessive emissions of state notes: paper money had to retain "as steady and fixt a Value, as human wisdom can contrive."[26] At this point, the redistributive power of currency entered leadership opinion, for if values were not stable and reflective of the labor embedded in production, then someone in the exchange mechanism obtained more than he should and someone obtained less. That condition was a prescription for severe social conflict. It violated the labor theory of property/value.

Anti–legal tender forces in the 1780s focused on the redistributive power of currency, that certain groups were earning unmerited rewards because of the absence of industrious labor. John Adams wrote to James Warren in 1777 about the imperatives surrounding currency: "The medium of trade ought to be as unchangeable as truth, as immutable as morality. The least variation in its value does injustice to multitudes, and in proportion it injures the morals of the people, a point of the last importance in a republican government." Tom Paine argued that only specie, gold and silver bullion, maintained value faithfully and that paper currency did not: "Money, when considered as the fruit of many years' industry, as the reward of labor, sweat and toil, as the widow's dowry and children's portion . . . has something in it sacred that is not to be sported with."[27]

The potential of redistribution from paper money emissions led to the

25. Benjamin Franklin, *A Modest Inquiry into the Nature and Necessity of a Paper Money* (1729), in Labaree and Willcox, eds., *Papers of Franklin,* I, 148, 150.

26. Benjamin Franklin, "Argument for Making the Bills of Credit Bear Interest," copy Franklin sent to Richard Jackson in letters of January 13–14 and June 25, 1764, in Labaree and Willcox, eds., *Papers of Franklin,* XI, 12–15, quote on 13. See also Richard Jackson to Franklin, March 17, 1754, *ibid.,* V, 245–46.

27. John Adams to James Warren, February 12, 1777, in Adams, ed., *Works of John Adams,* IX, 455; Thomas Paine, *Dissertations on Government* (1786), in Foner, ed., *Complete Writings of Paine,* II, quote on 405, see 404–409.

awareness that individuals who controlled governmental power could manipulate laws governing currency to reward themselves. That is, aristocrats monopolizing government could write laws about the currency that effectively enabled them to claim the fruits of others' labor. And so paper money emissions, a fluctuating standard of value, became a part of the political economy of aristocracy, one more policy that aristocrats could use to glom onto riches without engaging in labor.

The opponents of paper money came to accept gold and silver as the only commodities that retained their value and so could best act as the medium of exchange. Paine went so far as to say gold and silver were the currency emissions of nature.[28] After the 1780s, many nonconservatives accepted the reasoning of the paper money antagonists and agreed that currency fluctuations violated the ethics of the labor theory of property/value. Through this route, advocacy of a specie currency became an egalitarian rallying cry instead of a plot among conservatives to preserve their wealth.

The inclusion of the paper money question completed the American revolutionaries' understanding of the political economy of aristocracy. Aristocrats, defined as those possessing privileges others did not, used government and its coercive powers to redistribute the fruits of labor from producers to nonproducers, from workers to aristocrats. The policies by which the transference was accomplished were high taxation, creation of a bureaucracy, the granting of monopoly economic privileges, the establishment of a state church controlled by political leaders, and installation of currency laws that permitted manipulation of the standard of value. For a host of individuals, these were the legislative actions that twisted a just and equitable distribution of wealth into a reprehensible one of the few rich and the many poor.

The third axiom of the American concept of the distribution of wealth was the impact of the land laws of primogeniture and entail, by which aristocrats passed their estates entirely to the firstborn male heir and passed the entire estate without division through generations. Although these laws can be subsumed under the idea of the political economy of aristocracy, the revolutionaries and their successors treated them as a separate category of almost transcendent importance, and that emphasis will be retained in this book.

---

28. Thomas Paine, *Dissertations on Government,* in Foner, ed., *Complete Writings of Paine,* II, 404. But see the qualification of Edwin Perkins that most Americans were practical about the question of paper money (*American Public Finance,* 3–4, 261, 270).

Most historians and demographers have doubted the importance of the laws of entail and primogeniture in fostering inequality, and many have dismissed the revolutionary generation's abolition of such laws as inconsequential efforts and hardly revolutionary in any social sense.[29] The revolutionaries did not. For many, the abolition of the laws of entail and primogeniture was the key step to promote republican equality and to eliminate the possibility of an aristocracy arising in the new republic.

The aristocracy of Europe, but of England most emphatically, derived its strength from a near monopoly of the land. This condition resulted from the operation of the laws of entail and primogeniture over the centuries. On the Continent, the laws of primogeniture and entail were not so prominent, although land monopoly was. Americans observed at times with horror the inequalities that land monopoly produced, and land in many European states was concentrated in the hands of the elite. For example, Jefferson wrote in a famous passage that "the consequences of this enormous inequality" in landholdings produced "so much misery to the bulk of mankind" that private possessions had to be restricted by adequate laws, for "the earth is given as a common stock for man to labour and live in."[30]

It took little thought to connect the laws of entail and primogeniture to

29. For those having a positive view of the abolition of primogeniture and entail by the revolutionaries, although admitting that the efforts failed to produce the results expected, consult Morris, *American Revolution Reconsidered,* 79–81; J. Franklin Jameson, *The American Revolution Considered as a Social Movement* (1926; rpr. Princeton, 1967), 36–39; Robert A. Nisbet, *The Social Impact of the Revolution* (Washington, D.C., 1973), 8–12. For more pessimistic views, see Robert E. Brown and Katherine Brown, *Virginia, 1705–1786: Democracy or Aristocracy?* (East Lansing, Mich., 1964), 91–92, 286–87; Toby L. Ditz, *Property and Kinship: Inheritance in Early Connecticut, 1750–1820* (Princeton, 1986), 24–29, 47–52, 61–67; Carole Shammas, Marylynn Salmon, and Michel Dahlin, *Inheritance in America from Colonial Times to the Present* (New Brunswick, N.J., 1987), 30–35, 56, 65–67. An important exception by an econometrician is Soltow, *Distribution of Wealth and Income,* 144.

30. Jefferson to Madison, October 28, 1785, in Boyd and Catanzariti, eds., *Papers of Jefferson,* VIII, 681–82. For an American assessment of European landholding, see David Ramsay, "Oration" (1778), in Niles, ed., *Principles and Acts of the Revolution in America,* 380; Benjamin Franklin to Joshua Babcock, January 13, 1772, in Labaree and Willcox, eds., *Papers of Franklin,* XIX, 7; John Quincy Adams to John Adams, August 21, 1781, and J. Q. Adams to Abigail Adams, September 10, 1783, in Worthington Chauncey Ford, ed., *Writings of John Quincy Adams* (New York, 1913–17), I, 5, 10, 11–13; and Bushman, "Massachusetts Farmers and the Revolution," 99–112, 119–22. Lee Soltow estimates that only 10 to 30 percent of European adult males possessed land, whereas approximately 50 percent of Americans did (*Distribution of Wealth and Income,* 30, 41, 126, and more generally 110–39, 210–14).

the existence of the few rich and the many poor. Moreover, the cure for the situation was relatively simple: abolish the laws. As was customary in the way Americans analyzed the causes of disturbances in the natural distribution of wealth, they simply reversed the logic they saw operating in aristocracy. If the land laws that preserved estates over generations and gave the inheritance to only one family member produced a horrendous wealth distribution, then laws that promoted the division of estates equally among all possible heirs should result in equality. In other words, by removing the props of aristocracy that produced an unnatural inequality of property, the automatic result should have been, though probably unequal, a naturally equitable distribution. This was the logic employed by the English radical Richard Price, who lectured Americans that the two most important steps they could take to preserve equality were to eliminate titles and to abolish the right of primogeniture because the "tendency of this [law] to produce an improper inequality is very obvious."[31]

The land laws of aristocracy violated the American concept of the distribution of wealth at several key points. First, those laws were examples of legislative privilege to a few and so transgressed against the notion of republican civil equality. Second, those land laws established a monopoly, another departure from republican equality.[32] Third, entail and primogeniture captured the idea of hereditary preference, and the American Revolution as a whole was a war against the aristocratic ideal and the hereditary pillars upon which it stood. And finally, in the eyes of American revolutionaries, the laws of entail and primogeniture opposed the standards of the labor theory of property/value. Property was meant to be earned by individual labor; inheritance was not labor—although the revolutionaries failed to take their own premises to their logical conclusions.

Thomas Jefferson indicated that behind his determination to rid Virginia of the law of primogeniture was the labor theory of property/value. In a debate in the Virginia legislature, Edmund Pendleton wanted to give a double portion of the inheritance to the eldest son: "I observed, that if the eldest son could eat twice as much, or do double work, it might be a natural evidence of his right to a double portion." New England inheritance laws beginning in

31. Richard Price, *Observations on the Importance of the American Revolution, and the Means of Making It a Benefit to the World,* in Peach, ed., *Richard Price,* 209.

32. See analysis of Thomas Paine, *Agrarian Justice* (1796), in Foner, ed., *Complete Writings of Paine,* I, 612–13; Stanley N. Katz, "Republicanism and the Law of Inheritance in the American Revolutionary Era," *Michigan Law Review,* LXXVI (1977), 19.

the early eighteenth century mandated partible inheritance (property divided among all the heirs) because all the estates in the colony had been "brought to improvement by the Industry and labour of the Proprietors, with the Assistance of their Children, the Younger Children generally having been longest" in service to their parents and, therefore, in the matter of inheritances should be "recompence[d for] their Labour."[33]

The revolutionaries were certain that their extirpation of the laws of entail and primogeniture guaranteed that the United States would possess the wide diffusion of property needed for republican government. During the heady days of the initial war effort against Britain, John Adams declared that an equitable distribution of wealth was no problem for the future of republicanism in the United States: "The tendency of the laws of inheritance is perpetually to distribute and to subdivide whatever portion of land acquires any great market value." For Adams and other revolutionaries, primogeniture and entail concentrated land in the hands of certain families and enabled the estate to remain intact for centuries. Partible inheritance destroyed aristocratic concentration and was thus republican and egalitarian. Simple comparison between old England and New England demonstrated, so it seemed, the obvious antiaristocratic tendency of partible inheritance.[34]

Later, when John Adams started having doubts about the efficacy of American inheritance laws, others continued to celebrate the demise of entail and primogeniture. Wrote Roger Sherman, "Besides, while the real estates are divisible among all the children, or other kindred in equal degree, and entails are not admitted, it [abolition of primogeniture] will operate as an agrarian law." Thomas Jefferson in 1813—more than enough time after the Revolution to find other causes for maldistribution of wealth—told Adams that an American aristocracy was an impossibility. He bragged about the ending of entail and primogeniture in Virginia: "These laws [that ended entail and primogeniture], drawn by myself, laid the axe to the foot of pseudo-aristocracy." And Noah Webster, who insisted that republics needed a wide diffusion of

---

33. Thomas Jefferson, *Autobiography*, in Andrew A. Lipscomb, ed., *The Writings of Thomas Jefferson* (Washington, D.C., 1904), I, 64; quote of New Hampshire intestacy law, 1718, taken from Shammas, Salmon, and Dahlin, *Inheritance in America*, 34. See Katz, "Republicanism and the Law of Inheritance," 5, 11–20, 26–29; Katz, "Thomas Jefferson and the Right to Property," 467–88.

34. John Adams, *Defence of the Constitutions of Government of the United States of America*, in Adams, ed., *Works of John Adams*, IV, 359–60. Note remarks of Soltow, *Distribution of Wealth and Income*, 77, 146–49, 210–14.

property, gravely intoned that the necessary equality for a republic was obtained by partible inheritance laws, for those laws "hold out to all men equal motivs [*sic*] to vigilance and industry."[35]

The revolutionaries arrogantly boasted about their abolition of the aristocratic laws of entail and primogeniture. Whenever the subject of the distribution of wealth came up, members of the revolutionary generation fairly quickly mentioned the importance of aristocratic land laws in producing an opulent few and the pauperized many. Their proclamations exhibited little doubt that they expected the abolition of those statutes to guarantee for years to come a diffusion of property that was suitable for republican institutions. Historians have overlooked the amazing celebration of this achievement and the expectation by Americans of equality in property holdings for generations to come.

The fourth and final axiom composing the American concept of the distribution of wealth was the population-to-land ratio. Of all the axioms, this was the odd one, for unlike the others it had no relation to politics. Indeed, it was at this juncture that political economy began evolving into economics.

During the seventeenth and early eighteenth centuries, under the influence of mercantilist thought, publicists believed that increases in population augmented national wealth. In the last quarter of the eighteenth century, individuals, including Americans, began to have doubts. To many it seemed that as population increased, so did the wretchedness of the multitude. In American republican doctrines, the idea of population increase was housed in the theory that societies moved through stages (hunting, shepherding, agriculture, and commerce/fine manufacturing) and that the final stage—a commercial, manufacturing society—was one with grievous wealth extremes. Nations turned to manufacturing only to absorb excessive numbers of citizens who no longer could obtain land to farm—the obvious preferred choice of any rational human being—and manufacturing in and of itself indicated pauperized wage earners.[36]

Two Americans particularly aware of the distortions in wealth distribution that population pressure could generate were James Madison and Thomas

35. Roger Sherman to John Adams, July 20, 1789, in Adams, ed., *Works of John Adams,* VI, 438; Thomas Jefferson to John Adams, October 28, 1813, in Lipscomb, ed., *Writings of Jefferson,* XIII, 399; Webster, *Collection of Essays,* 327.

36. McCoy, *Elusive Republic,* 19, 54–55, 107; Dorfman, *Economic Mind in American Civilization,* I, 182.

Jefferson. Madison was more obsessed with population growth, and his ideas concerning it governed his thoughts for the rest of his life. In 1786 Madison and Jefferson exchanged letters discussing the origin of misery on the planet. Jefferson pointed to the aristocracy and its monopolization of farmlands and government. Madison wondered. No doubt, Madison wrote, "the misery of the lower classes will be found to abate wherever the Government assumes a freer aspect, and the laws favor a subdivision of property." Madison simply said republican cures for aristocratic social diseases produced some beneficial results. Yet there was a limit to what those republican remedies could accomplish: "A certain degree of misery seems inseparable from a high degree of populousness." During the Constitutional Convention, Madison warned that abolition of entail and primogeniture was insufficient to arrest for long the division of society into the few rich and the many poor—the power at work was population growth, and it could not be stopped. Therefore, the Constitution had to be framed with that future condition of extreme inequality of property in mind. This concern over population never eased in Madison's thinking. In the 1830s, he continued to interpret events and long-term processes in light of population pressures.[37]

Jefferson seemed not to have feared population growth. Although he abhorred cities and believed that a society should go through stages, he nonetheless thought he could preserve the agrarian nature of the United States and so restrain the agrarian republic from a plunge into the inequality of the commerce/fine manufacturing abyss. The means was westward expansion. By the Louisiana Purchase in 1803 when he was president, Jefferson hoped to forestall any alteration in agrarian America. So long as there was land, Americans would choose farming over manufacturing and commercial pursuits.[38]

Few others shared Madison's gloom about the distant future. Far from fearing population growth, most Americans wanted to stimulate it to develop

37. James Madison to Jefferson, June 19, 1786, in Boyd and Catanzariti, eds., *Papers of Jefferson*, IX, 659–60; Madison speech at Constitutional Convention, in Madison, *Notes of Debates*, 194; Madison to N. P. Trist, January 26, 1828, in Gaillard Hunt, ed., *The Writings of James Madison* (New York, 1900–1910), IX, 304–305; Madison to [?], [Majority Governments], (1833), *ibid.*, IX, 524–25; McCoy, *Elusive Republic*, 128–31; Banning, *Sacred Fire of Liberty*, 63–65.

38. Thomas Jefferson, *Notes on Virginia* (1782), in Lipscomb, ed., *Writings of Jefferson*, II, 118–21, 228–30; Wills, *Inventing America*, 161–62; Malone, *Jefferson and His Time*, II, 129–30; McCoy, *Elusive Republic*, 190–206; Matthews, *Radical Politics of Jefferson*, 32, 38–40. That slaveholders generally viewed Malthus so positively deserves closer scrutiny.

the nation. The extent of uninhabited land—the Indians were always disregarded as the rightful owners of the land—indicated a glorious future. Most recognized that with so much land, pauperized wages were not a possibility in the United States. Population pressure resulted in low wages, and thus a socially debilitating inequality occurred in overpopulated Europe. The United States enjoyed the opposite situation—too much land and too few people. Benjamin Franklin had early seen the lack of population and urged Europeans to migrate to the United States without fear of disrupting society or menacing wage rates. Others joined him.[39]

When Charles Pinckney addressed the Constitutional Convention, he mentioned reasons why an aristocracy was impossible in the United States and the continued existence of a republican form of government was guaranteed. The moderate equality of property in the United States arose from equal protection under the laws, equal access of citizens to positions of power, no institutions or places reserved only for those of a particular parentage, no nobility, and no laws of entail or primogeniture. All these were factors politicians could control. But from the start of his address, Pinckney pointed to the impact of land: "This equality is likely to continue, because in a new Country, possessing immense tracts of uncultivated lands . . . where industry must be rewarded with competency, there will be few poor, and few dependent."[40] Pinckney's observation was fairly commonplace by 1787. The existence of land and the ratio of population to arable land supported a republican form of government by allowing members of the society to obtain an agrarian competency.

It needs to be underscored just how ill-fitting this argument was with the rest of the discussion on wealth distribution or with republicanism in general. Virtually everything connected with republicanism involved either institutions purposefully created by citizens or values purposefully practiced by them. If the citizenry practiced virtue, patriotism, frugality, and simplicity and avoided luxury, dependency, and corruption, a republic would endure. If legislators proved true to republicanism and did not produce aristocratic land

39. Franklin, "On a Proposed Act to Prevent Emigration," [December (?), 1773], in Labaree and Willcox, eds., *Papers of Franklin*, XX, 524–25; Stiles, *United States Elevated to Glory and Honor*, 8–9; "Essay on Population," from London *Repository*, in *American Museum*, VIII (1790), 260–63; William Barton, *Observations on the Progress of Population, and the Probabilities of the Duration of Human Life, in the United States of America* (Philadelphia, 1791), 1–2; McCoy, *Elusive Republic*, 50–51; Dorfman, *Economic Mind in American Civilization*, I, 182.

40. Charles Pinckney speech, in Madison, *Notes of Debates*, quote on 181, speech 181–87.

laws, did not organize into factious political parties, did not grant special privileges and monopolies, did not build up a bureaucracy, and did not tax maliciously, a republic would survive. All these attitudes and practices were choices made by legislators and citizens. The people determined their fate by force of will and foresight.

The population-to-land ratio had nothing to do with human choice or any republican theory whatsoever. It was simply a condition of social activity, a matter of geography and demography over which no individual or group had any say. What Pinckney said at Philadelphia was in many ways not much more than that the Europeans living in North America simply enjoyed good luck because they possessed land. And American republicanism was the product of nothing more than a sly smile from Dame Fortuna.

The population-to-land ratio did not fit the other doctrines of the American concept of the distribution of wealth because it was a condition unamenable to a legislative cure. Americans, nevertheless, found it more and more congenial to believe in as time passed. American equality, always a subject of celebration, became an artifact of a geographical condition. Equality and republican government hinged not on institutions or on citizen participation or on the preachings of ancient and medieval philosophers but entirely on an accident of geography and demography. But lurking in the effervescence of contemporary rejoicings about the egalitarian features of American life because of the population-to-land ratio was the Madisonian darkness. At least Madison had the courage to face what his idea portended for the distant future. Eventually population would overcome available land, misery would be the fate of the masses, wages would plummet to subsistence, and republicanism would devolve into some form of despotism. For those on the Jeffersonian side of the party system, the population-to-land ratio became something of democratic scripture, while others mounted a serious attack on its validity. But the population-to-land ratio became at the same time the most potent and yet the most dangerous justification of American republicanism.

Explanations for distortions in property distribution other than those given by the political economy of aristocracy appeared during the revolutionary period. These included the actions of deceitful individuals, selfish behavior, and the corrosive effects of commerce. At least among the leadership, these ideas were secondary to the political economy of aristocracy. These other notions could be used to explain individual circumstances and idiosyncratic patterns, perhaps, but revolutionary writers seemed to believe that the politi-

cal economy of aristocracy explained better than any other theory the distributive outcomes of a political system. Moreover, the revolutionary generation
easily ascribed many unwanted results not to errors in an economic system
that promoted selfishness and commercial conniving but to the errors of monopoly and privilege as exhibited in the political economy of aristocracy.

A salient belief that many voiced was that riches were amassed simply because some individuals had cheated others out of their just rewards. By the
1790s, Tom Paine wondered if some of the hoards of the wealthy had not originated in "the effect of paying too little for the labour that produced it." A dis-
gruntled New Yorker wrote in 1765 that it was inequitable for most of the
wealth to be held by a few men, "especially when it is considered that Men frequently owe their Wealth to the impoverishment of their Neighbors." Tench
Coxe, interestingly, given his obsession to create a manufacturing capacity in
the new republic, flatly admitted that rich people obtained their wealth by
taking from others, and he viewed the wage relationship—or so his words
would lead one to believe—as a power relationship that allowed one person
to take advantage of another: "The poor, as they are wholly dependent on the
rich for employment, so the rich have it always in their power to fix the price
of the labour of the poor" and thereby "the profitable parts of the labour of
the poor are accumulated by the rich."[41]

Such complaints about the rich grinding the faces of the poor usually arose
when economic crises afflicted the colonies or young states, such as in the inflationary periods between 1777 and 1780 and then again between 1785 and
1788. Frequently in these situations when popular anger rose against the well-
to-do, wrath was aimed specifically at unfair means of property acquisition,
hence the appearance of such terms of disapprobation as *monopolist* and *en-
grosser*. It is likely, though not very demonstrable, that a strain of sentiment
existed among the middling and lower ranks of society that individuals of
great wealth never obtained their fortunes justly but always became rich
through some means of deceit, dishonesty, or political connection. The idea

---

41. Thomas Paine, *Agrarian Justice*, in Foner, ed., *Complete Writings of Paine*, I, xl; New
York *Gazette*, July 11, 1765, quoted in Gary B. Nash, *Red, White, and Black: The Peoples of Early
America* (2nd ed.; Englewood Cliffs, N.J., 1982), 265–66; Brutus, *To the Free and Loyal Inhabi-
tants of the City and Colony of New-York* (Broadside; New York, 1774); Citizen of the United
States [Tench Coxe], *Observations on the Agriculture, Manufactures and Commerce of the
United States in a Letter to a Member of Congress* (New York, 1789), 78. See also Ketcham, *From
Colony to Country*, 89; Hoerder, *Crowd Action in Revolutionary Massachusetts*, 83, 354, 356–57.

that great wealth was always undeserved was (and is) an undying element in American folklore or folk belief.

Another means by which wealth could be redistributed to the benefit of the few that appeared in the revolutionary era was when a society engaged in excessive and unrestrained commercial enterprise. American suspicions about commercial activity to some extent arose from political theorists. English proponents of republicanism in the late seventeenth and early eighteenth centuries—at the moment when commercial growth began to reshape England's economy—warned that commerce, by making luxuries available, enticed individuals away from industry, frugality, and simplicity. Thus commerce emphasized self-seeking and vanity, thereby destroying virtue.

Nonetheless, many of the complaints against commerce fell under the jurisdiction of the political economy of aristocracy. It becomes questionable whether individuals were complaining against a *system* of commerce or the *existence* of monopoly. The fear of monopoly, which was usually tied to some governmental arrangement, invoked a fear of aristocratic privilege.[42] An example of how monopoly invaded the subject of commerce and thereby renders interpretation less precise is a famous letter of Richard Henry Lee to James Madison. Lee, who has been quoted often by historians, railed, "The Spirit of Commerce through out the world is a spirit of Avarice." Before Lee arrived at this generalization, however, he first lambasted not commerce but England for always pursuing monopoly. He then considered the possibility of giving the Continental Congress power over navigation and recoiled in horror at the thought: that would allow the nonslaveholding states to erect a commercial monopoly over the noncommercial slaveholding states. He did not wish the South to be at the "Mercy of our East and North." It does not appear that Lee's self-interest in how Virginia fared was very far from his analysis of commerce. Lee had almost a self-serving definition of wholesome commerce: it was acceptable whenever planters got the better of the deal. One massive peculiarity about the whole of Lee's arguments further leads to the conclusion that he was mostly antimonopoly and not anticommercial. Lee was an advocate of free trade. Indeed, in the letter in which he penned his belief that commerce was the spirit of avarice, he lamented the difficulty the

---

42. For example, Richard B. Morris, *Government and Labor in Early America* (New York, 1946), 97–99, 102–107, 113, 114–19; Main, *Sovereign States*, 234–37, 252–56; Schultz, "Small Producer Thought in Early America, Part I," 115–47.

Americans were having in procuring unfettered, unregulated, free trade—
and free trade was a celebration of the commercial connection.[43]

Numerous Americans did fear commerce and its apparent celebration of
cupidity for material goods as the motivating economic force in human society. Many also demeaned commerce because of the banking apparatus it
seemed to require, machinery that for many seemed susceptible to chicanery
and deception.[44] But many of the trepidations about commerce could be incorporated into the four axioms of the American concept of the distribution
of wealth. Commerce posed problems, but among elite Americans speaking
and writing about the distribution of wealth, commerce was not designated
as a primary influence for producing improper wealth-holdings. As they entered the nineteenth century, American leaders continued to find power in
the four principles of wealth distribution that they had fleshed out during
the Revolution.

After the Revolution, Americans constantly used the political economy of
aristocracy or some of its derivative elements to explain why pernicious
wealth inequalities existed. They affirmed that unnatural inequalities were
preeminently a political act, not an outcome of a particular economic system. Thus Noah Webster could write in 1793 that the United States had the
most just economy in the world because of its low taxes and easy land laws:
"Here the equalizing genius of the laws distributes property to every citizen"—no tithes, no rack rents, no gratuities, no arbitrary taxes, and no exclusive monopolies. In 1816, Thomas Jefferson wrote John Adams about the
follies of Great Britain. William Pitt and George III had squandered the
"fee simple of the kingdom"; "their sinecures, salaries, pensions, priests, pre-
lates, princes and eternal wars have mortgaged to its full value the last foot of
their soil." In the 1825 annual report of the secretary of the treasury, Richard
Rush bowed to the logical power behind the idea that aristocrats warped
wealth distributions through legislation. The United States, Rush wrote,
prospered because of the people's morality and industry, "of the unrivalled
equality of their laws, which, interdicting exclusive rights and monopolies,

43. Richard Henry Lee to James Madison, August 11, 1785, in Ballagh, ed., *Letters of Richard Henry Lee,* II, quotes 383, see 382–84; Maier, *Old Revolutionaries,* 187.

44. For example, Jefferson to John W. Eppes, November 6, 1813, in Lipscomb, ed., *Writings
of Jefferson,* XIII, 427–30.

invites the most energetic exertions of every individual in the field of competition."[45]

But no one captured the invigorating, even revolutionary, sweep of emotions that followed escape from aristocratic institutions in the manner that Michel Guillaume Jean de Crèvecoeur did. His *Letters from an American Farmer* is largely about how the American Revolution lifted the incubus of aristocracy off a people. Crèvecoeur bound tightly a skewed distribution of wealth to the existence of an aristocracy: "It [American society] is not composed, as in Europe, of great lords who possess everything, and of a herd of people who have nothing. Here are no aristocratical families, no courts, no kings, no bishops, no ecclesiastical dominion, no invisible power giving to a few a very visible one; no great manufacturers employing thousands, no great refinements of luxury. The rich and poor are not so far removed from each other as they are in Europe." In the countryside, he observed a parson "as simple as his flock, a farmer who does not riot on the labor of others. We have no princes for whom we toil, starve, and bleed." Crèvecoeur answered his own famous query, "What then is the American, this new man?" They were a people—the only people—who reaped the fruits of their labors. Americans "receive ample rewards for their labors" because of the equality of laws resulting from representative (that is, republican) government. The American equality of condition came from the republicanism that denied aristocrats and monarchs the ability to seize from the masses the fruits of their honest labor.[46]

Crèvecoeur even added a psychological touch to his presentation. The European arrived in America beaten down by the hierarchies of Europe, by aristocratic institutions and pretensions. Slowly he learned his possibilities. "He begins to feel the effects of a sort of resurrection; hitherto he had not lived, but simply vegetated." Republicanism had elevated him as "a man, because he is treated as such." Aristocratic laws had decreed him an "insignificancy; the laws of this [land] cover him with their mantle." The European immi-

---

45. Noah Webster, Jr., *Effects of Slavery on Morals and Industry* (Hartford, Conn., 1793), 31; Jefferson to John Adams, November 25, 1816, in Lipscomb, ed., *Writings of Jefferson,* XV, 82; Richard Rush, "Annual Report of the Secretary of the Treasury" (1825), in U.S. Congress, *Register of Debates,* 19th Cong., 1st Sess., 27; McCoy, *Elusive Republic,* 168–69; Bushman, "Massachusetts Farmers and the Revolution," 77–124.

46. J. Hector St. John de Crèvecoeur, *Letters from an American Farmer* (1782; rpr. New York, 1912), 39–44, 83–87, 91–92, quotes 43, 39–42.

grant probed, tried, and slowly accumulated a competency. In the process he shed his European characteristics. But Crèvecoeur was precise in what he considered the European characteristics to have been: "This great metamorphosis has a double effect, it extinguishes all his European prejudices, he forgets that mechanism of subordination, that servility of disposition which poverty had taught him."[47]

In Crèvecoeur one reads easily enough the hostility to aristocratic institutions that came to characterize the American Revolution. One also sees in it an understanding of why the masses in Europe were poor. The mechanisms of aristocracy demanded wealth for the noble few, which could be obtained only by taking the fruits of the people's labors, thus dooming the multitude to poverty. Crèvecoeur exemplifies how revolutionary Americans used the idea of the political economy of aristocracy to explain the maldistribution of wealth.

By 1789, the American republican theory of the distribution of wealth was complete. It consisted of the four axioms of the labor theory of property/value, the political economy of aristocracy, the land laws of entail and primogeniture, and the population-to-land ratio. This theory proved remarkably enduring and was the standard by which policy measures were evaluated for nearly another century. There were dissenters to it and revilers of it, but eerily enough this theory persisted and even tightened its grasp over the public imagination as time wore on. It was visible even among those who rejected portions of the theory.

The American republican theory of the distribution of wealth was one of the preeminent legacies the revolutionaries left to succeeding generations. But it was not a legacy without ambiguities and misdirections.

47. *Ibid.*, 59–60, quote on 60.

3

The Legacies and Ambiguities of the Revolution

The American Revolution was a mighty torrent that cut a deep channel forward into time, molding the expectations, ideals, and institutions of the American future. For well over a century the United States developed within the boundaries of that channel. Variations occurred, but they revolved around the main artery that the Revolution had bored. Throughout the nineteenth century, citizens referred approvingly to their revolutionary forebears and continuously reaffirmed their decisions as to the direction and institutional structure of the country.

As a specific event delimited by an exact time chronology, the Revolution failed to reshape American society. Indeed, the colonial past lingered on in political and social deference, local regulation of economic endeavor, patterns of collective activity, judicial rulings based on common law, patron-client or master craftsman–journeyman relations, and daily life shaped by personal encounters.[1] The Revolution nonetheless set in motion currents that augured a different nation based on individualism. It was to take a considerable number of years to work out the implications of the Revolution; that essentially was the task of the nineteenth century.

The revolutionary dialogue about the distribution of wealth touched on subjects that would grow in importance as the years passed. These are the areas in which the revolutionaries bequeathed an obvious legacy to their successors—the promises of the Revolution that were left for other genera-

1. Steven Mintz, *Moralizers and Modernizers: America's Pre–Civil War Reformers* (Baltimore, 1995), xiv, chap. 1; Paul A. Gilje, *Rioting in America* (Bloomington, 1996), chaps. 1–2; William E. Nelson, *Americanization of the Common Law: The Impact of Legal Change on Massachusetts Society, 1760–1830* (Cambridge, Mass., 1975), 1–8, 67–68, and *passim*.

tions to keep. The four axioms that composed the revolutionaries' concept of the distribution of wealth had distinct implications for an understanding of slavery, for social mobility and a meritocracy, for the reception of British political economy, for appropriate policies of governance, and for the ideal of sacrifice of self-interest. This chapter explores how the political individualism of the Revolution started pushing the society out of its eighteenth-century deferential patterns into the obstreperous economic individualism of the nineteenth.

The revolutionary heritage seemed clear in some areas, but it was far less so in others. The discussion of the principles of the distribution of wealth contained much ambiguity that was directly attributable to the analysis being conducted in qualitative, verbal terminology. Certain terms, especially *labor* and *property*, were ill-defined and could be interpreted in radically divergent ways. Distribution of property is a subject that demands calculation and the application of simple mathematics. This analysis was never done. In fact, it was not attempted in the United States any earlier than the 1850s and became important only in the 1890s. Behind the axioms were assumptions about the society and economy that were never made explicit. The lack of exactitude on the subject had its own legacy, a legacy of inactivity that would vex attempts of later generations to handle inequalities that were socially dangerous.

In 1786, Thomas Jefferson condemned slavery in the United States and the "boisterous passions" that characterized the master-slave relationship. He powerfully expressed his belief that slaveholding was iniquitous: "Indeed I tremble for my country when I reflect that God is just; that his justice cannot sleep forever." Luther Martin told the Maryland state legislature in 1788 that slavery should be abolished because "*slavery* is *inconsistent* with the *genius* of *republicanism,* and has a tendency to *destroy* those *principles* on which it is *supported,* as it *lessens the sense* of the *equal rights* of *mankind,* and habituates us to *tyranny* and *oppression.*" A black contributor to the *American Museum* argued that the American Revolution sought to establish equality among citizens, and the existence of slavery rendered Americans guilty of hypocrisy.[2]

2. Thomas Jefferson, *Notes on Virginia* (1782), in Lipscomb, ed., *Writings of Jefferson,* II, 226–27; Luther Martin, "Mr. Martin's Information to the General Assembly of the State of Maryland," in Storing, ed., *Complete Anti-Federalist,* II, 61–62; Othello, "Essay on Negro Slavery," *American Museum,* IV (1788), 415. On the revolutionary heritage, see Leon F. Lit-

The constellation of principles that composed the American republican theory of the distribution of wealth had an obvious relevance for contemporary understanding of the peculiar institution. These principles were immediately employed to analyze the antirepublican nature of slaveholding. Those distribution-based arguments against slavery reverberated through the decades, and it is fair to say that by 1800, even by 1790, the essential republican condemnation of slavery was complete and merely reiterated for the next sixty to seventy years.

American propagandists denounced the "slavery" that Parliament intended for them as evidenced, they thought, by the legislation the British government passed. The slavery the colonial protesters had in mind was a civil slavery of citizens, and it could be theoretically separated from the slavery imposed on Africans by stipulating that Africans were not members of the body politic. Yet colonial complaints against Parliament contained a labor theory of property/value that could not be confined only to white colonists; the analysis lent itself directly to an analysis of African slavery. Indeed, even in their attack on parliamentary legislation, the revolutionaries had defined civil slavery as the condition in which citizens were no longer masters of the fruits of their own labors.[3]

When addressing economic doctrines, antislavery advocates turned explicitly and insistently to the labor theory of property/value. When Noah Webster attacked the institution in print in 1793, he argued that "to labor solely for the benefit of other men, is repugnant to every principle of the human heart," and slaves, as normal human beings, would not work industriously "without a well founded expectation of enjoying the fruits of their labor." When Tom Paine announced that slavery was antirepublican, he

wack, *North of Slavery: The Negro in the Free States, 1790–1860* (Chicago, 1961), 3–18; Arthur Zilversmit, *The First Emancipation: The Abolition of Slavery in the North* (Chicago, 1967), chaps. 3–8.

3. Stephen Hopkins, *The Rights of the Colonies Examined* (1765), in Bailyn, ed., *Pamphlets of the American Revolution*, 516; John Dickinson, *Letters of a Farmer in Pennsylvania, to the Inhabitants of the British Colonies* (1768), in Ford, ed., *Political Writings of John Dickinson*, 357, 401. See Allan Gallay, "The Origins of Slaveholders' Paternalism: George Whitefield, the Bryan Family, and the Great Awakening in the South," *Journal of Southern History*, LIII (1987), 390–91; Donald L. Robinson, *Slavery in the Structure of American Politics, 1765–1820* (New York, 1971), 58, 61; James Brewer Stewart, *Holy Warriors: The Abolitionists and American Slavery* (New York, 1976), 12, 19–23; Louis S. Gerteis, *Morality and Utility in American Antislavery Reform* (Chapel Hill, 1987), 4–5.

demanded that the slaves be freed and allowed "the fruits of their labors at their own disposal, and [thereby] be encouraged to industry." A definition of slavery emerged quickly: slaves did not enjoy the fruits of their labors, and that condition violated revolutionary principles.[4]

Use of the labor theory of property/value in the revolutionaries' analysis of slavery then became inextricably bound together with their understanding of the slave master. The slaveholder became an aristocrat because he usurped the fruits of others' labors. Crèvecoeur caustically mentioned the inhumanity of Charlestown planters who paid no heed to the miseries of their slaves from whose "painful labours all their wealth proceeds." Slaveholders, he concluded, liked a "bewitching and pleasurable . . . [life] without labor." The earliest antislavery advocate, Quaker John Woolman, made it explicit that the sin of slavery (and ultimately the sin of the slaveholder) was stealing a person's fruits of labor so that masters "may live at Ease, and fare sumptuously, and lay up Riches for their Posterity."[5]

Eighteenth-century opponents of slavery found a host of character traits of slave masters that smacked of aristocracy—the natural enemy of republicanism—and threatened to destroy the political edifice. Slave owning was seen as a hereditary institution, thereby mocking the revolutionaries' attempt to limit family ascendance through inherited wealth. Slave masters developed hard hearts and became used to living indolently. The most frequent epithet revolutionaries used to describe slaveholders was "tyrant," as did James Mason in the Constitutional Convention: "Every master of slaves is born a petty tyrant." More hostile to neoclassical republican political theory were the traits found wherever slavery existed: "the love of luxury is universal," and the power behind slavery was *"individual interest."* Indeed, for many oppo-

---

4. Webster, *Effects of Slavery on Morals and Industry,* 22; Thomas Paine in *Pennsylvania Journal and Weekly Advertiser,* March 8, 1775, in Foner, ed., *Complete Writings of Paine,* II, 19– 22. David Cooper, who argued against slavery, quoted Locke on the labor theory of value in *A Mite Cast into the Treasury; or, Observations on Slave-Keeping* (Philadelphia, [1772]), 22–23; [Nathaniel Appleton], *Considerations on Slavery in a Letter to a Friend* (Boston, 1767), 4.

5. Crèvecoeur, *Letters from an American Farmer,* 160–61; John Woolman, *Some Consideration on the Keeping of Negroes: Recommended to the Professors of Christianity of Every Denomination* (Philadelphia, 1754), 16; J. P. Brissot de Warville, *New Travels in the United States of America 1788,* trans. Mara Soceanu Vamos and Durand Echeverria, ed. Echeverria (Cambridge, Mass., 1964), 231; remarks of Gouverneur Morris, in Madison, *Notes of Debates,* 411; Edward Rushton, *Expostulatory Letter to George Washington, of Mount Vernon, on His Consenting to Be a Holder of Slaves* (Lexington, Ky., 1797), 4; James Swan, *A Dissuasion, to Great-Britain and the Colonies, from the Slave Trade to Africa* (Boston, [1772]), 38.

nents of slavery the desire for individual gain so evident in slavery bespoke the absence of virtue; self-interest, the love of personal wealth above all else, was the motivating passion of slaveholders.[6]

Slavery's violation of so many republican principles could only result in a lopsided distribution of wealth. Indeed, by 1800 comments abounded that showed that antislavery elements believed wealth in the South was far more concentrated among a few people than in the egalitarian North. David Ramsay wrote that slavery in the South had "led to the engrossing of land, in the hands of a few." Philadelphia physician Benjamin Rush commented that if southerners emancipated their slaves, their economy would improve through greater individual productivity, "a circumstance this, which by diminishing opulence in a few, would suppress Luxury and Vice, and promote that equal distribution of property, which appears best calculated to promote the welfare of Society." One Connecticut antifederalist argued against ratification of the Constitution because it would mate the inegalitarian, slave-ridden South with the egalitarian North, which had industrious people, "small and nearly equal estates, [and] equality of rights."[7]

6. [Cooper], *A Mite Cast into the Treasury,* 11; Philanthropos [David Rice], *Slavery Inconsistent with Justice and Good Policy* (Lexington, Ky., 1792), 40; E[lihu] H[ubbard] Smith, *A Discourse, Delivered April 11, 1798, at the Request of and Before the New-York Society for Promoting the Manumission of Slaves, and Protecting Such of Them as Have Been or May Be Liberated* (New York, 1798), 18, 24; Mason, quoted in Madison, *Notes of Debates,* 504; Henry Clay, "To the Electors of Fayette County," 1798, in James F. Hopkins *et al.,* ed., *The Papers of Henry Clay* (Lexington, Ky., 1959–), I, 6; Jonathan Edwards, *The Injustice and Impolicy of the Slave Trade; and the Slavery of the Africans; . . . A Sermon* (New Haven, 1791), 12; Webster, *Effects of Slavery on Morals and Industry,* 18, 20–21; Timothy Dwight, *An Oration Spoken Before "The Connecticut Society, for the Promotion of Freedom and the Relief of Persons Unlawfully Holden in Bondage"* (Hartford, Conn., 1794), 4, 14–16; Kenneth Roberts and Anna M. Roberts, trans. and ed., *Moreau de St. Mery's American Journey [1793–1798]* (Garden City, N.Y., 1947), 60; Anthony Benezet, *A Short Account of That Part of Africa Inhabited by the Negroes* (Philadelphia, 1762), 4, 21; Benezet, *Observations on the Inslaving, Importing and Purchasing of Negroes* (Germantown, Pa., 1759), 9–15; Othello, "Essay on Negro Slavery," *American Museum,* IV (1788), 415; Paine, "African Slavery in America," in Foner, ed., *Complete Writings of Paine,* II, 16; Woolman, *Some Consideration on the Keeping of Negroes,* 16, 19–20. See David Brion Davis, *The Slave Power Conspiracy and the Paranoid Style* (Baton Rouge, 1969), 11, 14; Davis, *The Problem of Slavery in the Age of Revolution, 1770–1823* (Ithaca, N.Y., 1975), 250.

7. Ramsay, *History of the American Revolution,* I, 24; A Pennsylvanian [Benjamin Rush], *An Address to the Inhabitants of the British Settlements in America Upon Slave-Keeping* (Philadelphia, 1773), 7; [James Winthrop], "Letters of Agrippa," in Storing, ed., *Complete Anti-Federalist,* IV, 94. See also John Woolman, *Considerations on Keeping Negroes; Recommended to*

Antislavery workers took their analysis beyond the recording of aristo-cratic habits, the powers of slaveholders, and slaveholders' denial to the la-borer of the fruits of labor. By 1800 they were claiming that slavery produced a backward economy because slave labor was inherently inferior to free labor. Abolitionist David Rice argued that "slavery produces idleness; and idleness is the nurse of vice." A nation, according to Rice, grew powerful only through the industriousness of its citizens, and slavery destroyed the desire to work. Northerners frequently pointed out that slave labor was inevitably less pro-ductive than free labor. Noah Webster calculated that it took three slaves to match the output of one northerner and used this lackadaisical effort of slaves as a reason to propose a scheme of emancipation. Oliver Wolcott, informing Congress on ways to implement direct taxes, deprecated slave labor: "It is barely necessary to mention that slaves are generally incapable of performing any other than the most simple operations of agricultural labor." According to David Ramsay, slavery destroyed incentive, ruined the work habits of whites by making labor disreputable, taught slave masters habits of dissipa-tion, and divorced physical effort from mental effort. Slavery had no incen-tives: "Nothing stimulates to industry so much as interest . . . he who has an immediate profit from his labor, will disregard tasks, times and seasons."[8]

Benjamin Rush as well as anyone brought many of the republican themes together that pronounced slavery unrepublican. "Liberty and property form the basis of abundance and good agriculture," wrote Rush; "I never observed is [*sic*] to flourish where those rights of mankind were not firmly established." Under the hands of the free laborer, the earth became paradise, but the soil "seems to shrink into barrenness under the sweat of the slave." What was wrong—the great error—was simple: God had commanded that man be free "that he might cultivate his possession with the sweat of his brow; but still should enjoy his Liberty."[9]

Themes other than the economic follies of the peculiar institution domi-

---

the Professors of Christianity, of Every Denomination, Part Second (Philadelphia, 1762), 32; George Buchanan, *An Oration upon the Moral and Political Evil of Slavery* (Baltimore, 1793), 7–8.

8. [Rice], *Slavery Inconsistent with Justice and Good Policy,* 17–18. Webster, *Effects of Slavery on Morals and Industry,* 6, 7, 22; Oliver Wolcott, "Direct Taxes" (1796), in *Annals of Congress,* 4th Cong., 2nd Sess., Appendix, 2711; Ramsay, *History of the American Revolution,* I, 23–25, quote on 24–25. There was also animosity between "free" laborers and slave laborers; see Edgar J. McManus, *A History of Negro Slavery in New York* (Syracuse, 1966), 182–83.

9. Rush, *Address Upon Slave-Keeping,* 6–7.

nated eighteenth-century antislavery literature. Opponents of slavery recoiled at the naked coercion of the practice and its rejection of voluntary agreement among community members.[10] The bulk of antislavery publications relied on two themes: Christian doctrines, especially the application of the Golden Rule, and the visibly excessive cruelty that slavery produced.[11] Some antislavery writers questioned racist beliefs.[12]

By 1800, the revolutionaries had articulated virtually every argument abolitionists would trumpet for the next sixty-five years. In particular, they had fully outlined the two major northern complaints against slaveholding in the United States. They had enunciated the doctrines of the free labor ideology in connection with slavery. Though the free labor ideology became most shrill when the Republican party burst upon the political stage in the 1850s, it had already become a staple of American life before 1800. The revolutionaries' attack on slavery also brought out another major line of argument: slavery produced an aristocracy that actively sought control of government for its own aggrandizement and for the elimination of its rivals. By the 1840s, the concepts embedded in the political economy of aristocracy had become in connection with the antislavery struggle the "slave power conspiracy," the idea that slaveholders sought to control uncontestedly the federal government, to nationalize slavery, to extirpate civil liberties, to extend the empire of slavery, to eliminate freedom and republicanism, and by political means to direct all wealth to themselves. The slave power conspiracy became one of the

10. E. C., "On Slavery," *Gazette of the United States* (Philadelphia), May 2–6, 1789; Benjamin Franklin, "A Conversation on Slavery," printed in the *Public Advertiser,* January 30, 1770, in Labaree and Willcox, eds., *Papers of Franklin,* XIII, 39–44; A Respectable Member of the Community, *Extract from an Address in the Virginia Gazette, of March 19, 1767* (Philadelphia, 1770), 2.

11. See, for example, Granville Sharp, *An Essay on Slavery, Proving from Scripture Its Inconsistency with Humanity and Religion* (Burlington, N.J., 1773), 20–22; [Anthony Benezet], *Brief Considerations on Slavery, and the Expediency of Its Abolition* (Burlington, 1773), 3–16; Benezet, *Observations on the Inslaving,* 2–15; Woolman, *Some Consideration on the Keeping of Negroes,* 6; [Samuel Hopkins], *A Dialogue Concerning the Slavery of the Africans* (Norwich, Conn., 1776), 4–11; Rush, *Address Upon Slave-Keeping,* 9–18; Mack Thompson, *Moses Brown: Reluctant Reformer* (Chapel Hill, 1962), 99–103; Davis, *Problem of Slavery in the Age of Revolution,* 43, 45–47; Stewart, *Holy Warriors,* 12–13; Zilversmit, *First Emancipation,* 55, 93–94.

12. Smith, *Discourse,* 28; [Rice], *Slavery Inconsistent with Justice and Good Policy,* 18–19; Woolman, *Considerations on Keeping Negroes . . . Part Second,* 29; Amynto [?], *Reflections on the Inconsistency of Man, Particularly Exemplified in the Practice of Slavery in the United States* (New York, 1796), 22; Jean R. Soderlund, *Quakers and Slavery: A Divided Spirit* (Princeton, 1985), 174–75.

Republican party's most potent appeals to the northern electorate.[13] It, as well as the free labor ideology, had distinct roots in the revolutionary period and in the republican theory of the distribution of wealth and constituted one of the most potent legacies of the Revolution.

The American concept of the distribution of wealth as it emerged out of the Revolutionary War contained ideas that produced some unintended consequences. The argument possessed a logic that the leaders failed to pursue to some obvious conclusions. Eighteenth-century American society had characteristics of order, stability, personal relationships, patriarchy, and deference. But the Revolution opened up the possibilities of a society based on free labor, social mobility, achievement, and economic individualism—all of which were implied in the revolutionaries' strictures on wealth distribution. The leaders neither foresaw these developments nor welcomed them when they appeared. But the force of their arguments led directly to social mobility and a free labor ideology.

Not long after the war with Great Britain commenced, orators began proclaiming that every political office in the land was open to every adult white male who demonstrated capability and energy. By diligence, industry, and perseverance a person could acquire wealth and high social standing. David Ramsay delivered a speech in Charleston in 1778 that had an interesting mixture of the old republicanism and the new realities. Ramsay first reminded his audience of the excesses and wasteful indulgences of kingly courts, whereas in a republic there would be "truth, sincerity, frugality, industry, and simplicity of manners." In particular, a republic no longer would tolerate advancement by those "that can best please [their] superiors, by the low arts of fawning and adulation." Instead, preferment in a republic went only to those

---

13. Eric Foner first delineated the elements of the free labor ideology and emphasized its importance in bringing about the Civil War in *Free Soil, Free Labor, Free Men: The Ideology of the Republican Party Before the Civil War* (2nd ed.; New York, 1995), chap. 1; see also Foner, "Politics, Ideology, and the Origins of the American Civil War," in *A Nation Divided: Problems and Issues of the Civil War and Reconstruction,* ed. George M. Fredrickson (Minneapolis, 1975), 15–16, 20; Larry Gara, "Slavery and the Slave Power: A Crucial Distinction," *Civil War History,* XV (1969), 5–18. The most recent use of the slave power thesis is contained in two important works: Michael F. Holt, *The Political Crisis of the 1850s* (New York, 1978), 51, 151–52, 189, 201; and William E. Gienapp, *The Origins of the Republican Party, 1852–1856* (New York, 1987), 357–62.

who possessed "extraordinary merit." Then Ramsay hit the social mobility note, though only in embryonic form: even the poorest of men could rise to power "if possessed of abilities equal to the important station." In a contradictory statement that quickly followed, as Ramsay had just outlined a potential scramble by meritorious individuals for office, he said that while the poor would rise to higher stations, nonetheless in a republic the citizens would discard "the law of the pursuit of wealth" and instead work on "the powers of the soul."[14]

Other speakers picked up the theme of social mobility. William Drayton in 1776 argued for separation, and once a republic was founded in North America then "by virtue and merit, the poorest man may arrive at the highest dignity." During the fight over ratification of the Constitution, "Centinel," Samuel Bryan of Pennsylvania, argued against centralization because under the Articles of Confederation, but possibly not under the Constitution, "the field to fame and riches is open to all, [and] it stimulates universal exertion, and exhibits a lively picture of emulation, industry and happiness." Elias Boudinot presented a discourse to the Society of the Cincinnati in New Jersey in 1783 in which he lauded equal rights but not equal conditions. "The road to honors, riches, usefulness, and fame in this happy country," he pontificated, "is open equally to all," a sentiment echoed in a contribution to the *American Museum* in 1790.[15]

American revolutionaries knowingly or not—and generally it was unknowingly—paved the road for the political celebration of a person's opportunity to climb the socioeconomic ladder. The thrust of the Revolution was antiaristocracy, and in particular opposition to the hierarchy that aristocracy foisted upon a society. Aristocratic rules, however, had given order to a society and made explicit how wealth and political position were to be obtained—by birth. Of course, societies never operated completely by these rules, but the norm was supposed to be that birth determined wealth and social position.

14. David Ramsay, Oration, July 4, 1778, at Charleston, in Niles, ed., *Principles and Acts of the Revolution in America,* 375–76.

15. Speech of William Henry Drayton, Charges to the Grand Jury, May 2, 1776, in William M. Dabney and Marion Dargan, *William Henry Drayton and the American Revolution* (Albuquerque, 1962), 190; Centinel [Samuel Bryan], "Letters of Centinel," in Storing, ed., *Complete Anti-Federalist,* II, 176; speech of Elias Boudinot in J. J. Boudinot, ed., *The Life, Public Services, Addresses, and Letters of Elias Boudinot* (1896; rpr. New York, 1971), II, 362–64, 373–74, quote 373; "The Politician. No. IX," *American Museum,* VII (1790), 82.

American revolutionaries attacked the idea of hereditary preferment; they thus effectively disordered society.[16] Without aristocracy to guide choices, without an operative hierarchy, how would rulers and community leaders be chosen?

For most of the leadership, the answer was initially the natural aristocracy, the position held by John Adams and Thomas Jefferson. For Adams and Jefferson, natural aristocracy meant a capacity for public leadership, magnanimous thinking, and virtuous behavior, backed by extensive education in the classics. It certainly was not indicated by birth or, in Jefferson and Adams' estimation, the ability to amass riches. But the problem with the natural aristocracy was simple: how to discern its presence. Ultimately, the only means to find talented individuals to lead government and society was by a demonstration of ability. And ability was revealed in action and in acquiring more responsibility—that is, climbing the ladder of success.

The revolutionary leadership created a child most in that generation did not want to claim. They had a hierarchy in mind for the country in which they, of course, occupied the upper echelon, and they abhorred the notion of a mad scramble among competitors for status, political office, and wealth. In a sense, the original revolutionary leadership wanted the safety of a hierarchy without its actual structures and procedures. It was an impossible situation. By smashing the structures of aristocracy, the revolutionaries left their society fundamentally disordered with no formal means to determine leadership or social position. Into that vacuum flowed rather naturally the idea of a meritocracy: in an egalitarian society in which no preferences were granted by government, merit and talent were the only means to determine position. And so sprang up the idea of social mobility.[17]

When the promise of social mobility was mated with the labor theory of

16. Gordon Wood has strongly argued this position in *Radicalism of the American Revolution*, 231, 241–43, and chaps. 13–17 generally; see also W. J. Rorabaugh, " 'I Thought I Should Liberate Myself from the Thraldom of Others' ": Apprentices, Masters, and the Revolution," in *Beyond the American Revolution: Explorations in the History of American Radicalism*, ed. Alfred F. Young (De Kalb, Ill., 1993), 188, 195–200. For a differing view, see Robert H. Wiebe, *Self-Rule: A Cultural History of American Democracy* (Chicago, 1995), 18–26.

17. For other interpretations of the early emergence of social mobility notions, see Steven Watts, *The Republic Reborn: War and the Making of Liberal America, 1790–1820* (Baltimore, 1987), 68; Van Doren, *Benjamin Franklin*, 109; Isaac Kramnick, "Republican Revisionism Revisited," *American Historical Review*, LXXXVII (1982), 641, 645; Savelle, *Seeds of Liberty*, 220; James M. Banner, Jr., *To the Hartford Convention: The Federalists and the Origins of Party Politics in Massachusetts, 1789–1815* (New York, 1970), 9–10.

property/value, the offspring was the free labor ideology. The free labor ideology was a celebration of the ability of each person to obtain a competency by the act of labor, to rise in wealth and status by merit and talent; it celebrated the dignity and nobility of labor, embraced the market system of competition, and glorified continuous expansion.[18] For the late-eighteenth-century revolutionaries, the notion of free labor had distinct connotations of independent yeoman farmer labor, whereas nineteenth-century northerners extended the concept to embrace urban dependent labor. Except for the explicit embrace of free market mechanisms and an awareness of economic growth, few differences separated what many of the revolutionaries voiced about labor and its prospects and what the Republicans of the 1850s said. The Revolution, not a mid-nineteenth-century market economy, had given birth to the free labor ideology.

The reason individuals in the late eighteenth century did not capture entirely the enthusiasm of mid-nineteenth-century Americans came from a difference in economic structures. The agrarian, semicommercial quality of the late-eighteenth-century economy limited their capacity to act out the possibilities of an unrestricted economy. What tied the ideas of the Republicans of the 1850s to the revolutionaries of the 1770s and 1780s, however, was the fundamental character of the American Revolution: an antiaristocratic explosion based on the idea that the laborer deserved the fruits of his or her labor.[19]

At the same time republicanism took root in the thinking of the American revolutionaries, Adam Smith was forging a set of ideas that became classical economic theory. Smith and his successors explained how the "invisible

18. Foner, *Free Soil, Free Labor, Free Men,* 11–39.

19. During the Revolution, innumerable individuals commented that prosperity depended on property rights being observed and that no one would labor if governmental power stripped individuals of the fruits of their labor. Such expressions are eerily close to Republican speeches in the 1850s. For example, David Ramsay, *The History of the Revolution of South-Carolina, from a British Province to an Independent State* (Trenton, N.J., 1785), I, 7, 10; Nathaniel Niles, *Two Discourses on Liberty* (1774), in Hyneman and Lutz, eds., *American Political Writing during the Founding Era,* I, 267; Charles Thomson to Benjamin Franklin, September 24, 1765, in Labaree and Willcox, eds., *Papers of Franklin,* XII, 278; Boston *Gazette,* September 16, 1782, quoting letter of Quirinus in *Freeman's Journal;* [Logan], *Letters Addressed to the Yeomanry of the United States,* 27–28; A Citizen of Philadelphia [Pelatiah Webster], *An Essay on Free Trade and Finance, Humbly Offered to the Consideration of the Public* (Philadelphia, 1779), 5; Wood, *Radicalism of the American Revolution,* 341–42.

hand" of self-interest in the marketplace produced general well-being in the economy and augmented national wealth. The republicanism of the Americans distrusted self-interest. Thus the two doctrines supposedly clashed in their fundamental values. Yet free trade economic theory as presented by Smith and the republicanism as espoused by the revolutionaries had similar qualities. The specific area in which they reinforced each other was public policy, for both theories found laissez-faire policies antiaristocratic and, for a while, egalitarian. One of the more salient heritages of the revolutionaries' understanding of the distribution of wealth, therefore, was a swelling appreciation and eventual glorification of the egalitarian promise of the negative state.

The essential message of the political economy of aristocracy was that aristocrats used political power to transfer the fruits of labor from producers to themselves. Those policies which the revolutionaries found most aristocratic in operation were taxation, establishment of a large bureaucracy, government sponsorship of a particular religious body, creation of monopolies, and manipulation of currency. Therefore, the natural distribution of wealth could be maintained by doing the opposite. As republicanism was the opposite of aristocracy, so republican policies should be the opposite of aristocratic policies. The economic agenda for a republic became clear: enact the opposite of aristocratic legislation. Thus a republic required low taxes, no bureaucracy, disestablishment of church and state, equal access to economic undertakings by abolition of monopolies, and no financial manipulations by government authorities. This program was a prescription for laissez-faire economic policy.

The revolutionary generation's outline of economic policy and their determination of the impact politics had on the distribution of wealth bore a striking resemblance to the formulations of Adam Smith. The political controversy between the colonials and Parliament must have affected Smith, for much in the *Wealth of Nations* echoed the substance of colonial complaints. Smith's treatise rested (at least partly) on a labor theory of value. Likewise, the Scottish philosopher divided labor into the categories of productive and unproductive labor, the difference between them being determined by whether an act of labor produced "some particular subject or vendible commodity." Thus unproductive labor included the army, navy, the sovereign, "churchmen, lawyers, physicians, men of letters of all kinds, players, buffoons, musicians, opera-singers, opera dancers, &c." This list was not unlike the one colonials made, especially in the common emphasis on court favorites. Adam Smith also continuously struck out at corporations, monopolies, and laws that showed favoritism—hence his attack on mercantilism and the Navigation Acts. He railed at government expenditures, high taxes, and tariffs; rent, he believed, was income arising from a monopoly privilege. He deprecated the laws of entail and primogeniture.[20]

On the distribution of wealth, Adam Smith developed an argument different from that of the colonials. Smith did not consider or comment extensively on the actual diffusion of property among the population or on the forces explaining the distribution of wealth. Instead, he divided earnings into the three categories of profits, rent, and wages. Over time, this became the classical analysis of distributive shares to the factors of production (capital, land, and labor).[21] This was a real innovation, at least to the Americans, because it focused attention away from the fruits of labor to the income earned by occupation. Wages in particular became elevated in importance as a determinant of society's income (and wealth) distribution.

Smith's distribution could not be read as egalitarian, although he made a distinct plea for high wages.[22] But he also emphasized liberty, in particular the right of each person to seek employment in accordance with his desires. Inequalities, he wrote, arose largely from the denial of the natural liberty of economic choice—and the culprit was almost always corporations or a system of "exclusive privilege."[23]

As William D. Grampp has observed, the views of Adam Smith and the American revolutionaries uncannily paralleled each other.[24] This is the point at which historiographical controversies erupt. Adam Smith is generally considered not as the first political economist but as the first organizer of eco-

20. Adam Smith, *An Inquiry into the Nature and Causes of the Wealth of Nations,* ed. Edwin Cannan (1776; rpr. New York, 1937), 30–33, 64, 314–15, 118–21, 423–29, 49, 60, 145, 433–35, 716; Mark Blaug, *Economic Theory in Retrospect* (3rd ed.; Cambridge, Eng., 1978), 39–40; Donald Winch, *Adam Smith's Politics: An Essay in Historiographic Revision* (Cambridge, Eng., 1978), 58–59, 89–90, 62, 80, 97, 101, 144, 66–67, 137; Jacob Viner, *The Long View and the Short: Studies in Economic Theory and Policy* (Glencoe, Ill., 1958), 227; Duncan Forbes, "Sceptical Whiggism, Commerce, and Liberty," in *Essays on Adam Smith,* ed. Andrew S. Skinner and Thomas Wilson (Oxford, 1975), 187.

21. Smith, *Wealth of Nations,* 64–69, 87–98, 144–47, 248–50; Winch, *Adam Smith's Politics,* 60, 92.

22. "Where wages are high, accordingly, we shall always find the workmen more active, diligent, and expeditious, than where they are low" (Smith, *Wealth of Nations,* 81).

23. *Ibid.,* 118–19. This was the argument used against guilds, *ibid.,* 120–23.

24. William D. Grampp, "Adam Smith and the American Revolutionists," *History of Political Economy,* XI (1979), 179–91.

nomic knowledge who offered a systematic presentation of economic principles that governed the entire realm of economic activity. The principles he
propounded were those of laissez-faire capitalism. Several authors assert that
the philosophy of republicanism so pervasive among Americans was fundamentally opposed to capitalism. Capitalism praised the traits of individualism, self-interest, and accumulation; it also emphasized the private sphere of
life over the public sphere and posited competition over cooperation. Republicanism, according to many historians, glorified virtue. The qualities republicanism prized were cooperation, the public sphere over the private sphere,
moderation, and community.[25] Although attempts have been made to mod-
ify Smith's acceptance of self-interest and the market mechanism, they can at
best be marginally successful, for Adam Smith is capitalism's patron saint.[26]

The strange debate over whether revolutionary America was neoclassical
republican or embryonic capitalist can be resolved to some degree by recon-
sidering the idea of egalitarianism. Many historians have called republicanism an egalitarian politics because, at least for citizens, it called for the suppression of self-seeking and an equality of property ownership. In contrast,
the charge against laissez-faire capitalism was that it was inegalitarian because it sanctioned large economic differences among citizens and individual aggrandizement. What needs to be recognized is that laissez-faire capital-

25. The two who have most advanced the notion of virtue, which seems to be the key concept in this debate, are Pocock, *Machiavellian Moment*, ix, 426–36, 459–61, 531–38; and Wood,
Creation of the American Republic, 53–62, 418. For one arguing strenuously (and in many ways
correctly) that the Founders accepted liberal capitalist values, much of which deals with the
influence or noninfluence of John Locke over the revolutionaries, see Kramnick, *Republicanism and Bourgeois Radicalism*, chap. 1. Paul Rahe has stressed that the notion of virtue in the
modern world was not the same as in the ancient (*Republics Ancient and Modern*, 736–47, and
chap. 6, part III); see as well Diggins, *Lost Soul of American Politics*, chap. 1.

26. A prominent work questioning Smith's embrace of self-interest and the market is
Winch, *Adam Smith's Politics*, 7–8, 43, 81–84, 87–90, 181; see also J. Cropsey, "Adam Smith and
Political Philosophy," in *Essays on Adam Smith*, ed. Andrew S. Skinner and Thomas Wilson
(Oxford, 1975), 132–53. Robert E. Shalhope has offered an interesting fusion of American republicanism and Adam Smithian economics; Robert E. Shalhope, "Republicanism, Liberalism, and Democracy: Political Culture in the Early Republic," in *The Republican Synthesis Revisited: Essays in Honor of George Athan Billias*, ed. Milton M. Klein, Richard D. Brown, and
John B. Hench (Worcester, Mass., 1992), 37–90, esp. 56, 69, 78–80; and Shalhope, "Individualism in the Early Republic," in *American Chameleon: Individualism in Trans-National Context*, ed. Richard O. Curry and Lawrence B. Goodheart (Kent, Ohio, 1991), 77–81. Shalhope's
conclusions coincide with those offered here except that this presentation sees classical republicanism as a much weaker intellectual current.

ism in its earliest stages possessed an egalitarian edge in its comments on existing European society—that is, Adam Smithian economics and American republicanism shared a common analysis.[27] That common analysis was the labor theory of property/value. In a semisubsistence agrarian economy, demanding that each laborer obtain the fruits of his labor was an egalitarian doctrine. That was why it was seized so early by the agrarian radicals of North America and why laissez-faire seemed to promise equal wealth-holdings among the citizenry. With no power inhering in any person or group to extract from citizens the just fruits of their labors, only equality could result.

Thus the cry of "free trade" that Adam Smith justified by his economic logic could be seen by many Americans, radical and otherwise, as a demand for a more egalitarian economic system. A primary example of this tendency to find equality in laissez-faire doctrines was the Pennsylvanian George Logan. In 1792 he pleaded in unmistakable abhorrence about Alexander Hamilton's economic program, *"let us alone."* Logan specifically named Adam Smith as his fount of wisdom and praised Smith's notions of allowing people to determine how best to use whatever talents they were blessed with. Logan then made the explanatory leap. Laissez-faire promoted republican equality. It was aristocratic favoritism that resulted in wealth-holding extremes.[28]

Republicanism, at least the form that derived from the English libertarian writers John Trenchard and Thomas Gordon, had earlier sanctified a move toward laissez-faire on the basis that it promoted equality among citizens. *Cato's Letters* certainly did indicate fears of the unduly rich, the grasping, and the avaricious. But at the same time, and somewhat inconsistently, Cato argued, "Let People alone, and they will take Care of themselves, and do it best." Trenchard and Gordon argued for an equality of property, or at least a

27. Shalhope, "Individualism in the Early Republic," 66–86. The phrase *Adam Smithian economics* has to be employed because before long classical economics posited a wretched distribution of wealth. That was not necessarily the case with Adam Smith. Once Malthus added his population formula (see Chapter 5 below), classical economics radically departed from American views on the distribution of wealth. For a dissenting view on emerging American individualism, see Barry Alan Shain, *The Myth of American Individualism: The Protestant Origins of American Political Thought* (Princeton, 1994), xv–xviii, 9, 30–58, and *passim*.

28. Logan, *Five Letters,* 4, 10, 11–12, 19, 27, quote on 19. See Webster, *Essay on Free Trade and Finance,* 5; Sullivan, *Path to Riches,* 5–6; Thomas Paine, "A Serious Address to the People of Pennsylvania on Their Present Situation of Their Affairs" (1778), in Foner, ed., *Complete Writings of Paine,* II, 293; Stiles, *United States Elevated to Glory and Honor,* 30; Letwin, "Economic Policy of the Constitution," 124–26; Matson and Onuf, "Toward a Republican Empire," 503, 508–10.

wide diffusion. They expected to obtain it by laissez-faire techniques because under laissez-faire each person reaped only the fruits of his own labor and could steal no one else's. Adam Smith absorbed that line of thought. Inequalities, wrote Smith, arose from a lack of liberty, and a lack of liberty usually came from the government handing out "exclusive privileges" in the form of corporate charters. Thus laissez-faire had a potential egalitarian thrust that people of the late eighteenth century could perceive because they had known the inegalitarian effects wrought by the favoritism of aristocratic societies.[29]

Both republicanism and free trade theories additionally seized upon past civilizations' use of force to build massive fortunes for the few by inflicting wretched poverty upon the many. The principle for a new economic system provided by theorists such as Adam Smith was an economy based on voluntary association from which the coercive powers of government were removed altogether. Voluntary association in the form of a competitive market reduced (theoretically) the noxious effects of treachery and deceit of merchants by requiring a great number of suppliers to vie for consumers, enabling the consumer to avoid monopolistic effects. Voluntary association as well destroyed what many considered the greatest cause of inequality: governmental favoritism made omnipotent by the physical violence of state police power.[30] For both liberal capitalist economics and neoclassical republicanism in the late eighteenth century the solution to inequality veered toward an embrace of the negative state.

What bound neorepublicanism and liberal capitalism together, as different as they were on the crucial subject of self-interest, was the common enemy of aristocracy, an aristocracy that continuously violated the precept of the laborer deserving the fruits of his labor. The Americans attacked aristocracy largely from a colonial perspective that emphasized political power. Their political perspective led to an economic critique that emphasized the power of the aristocracy to transfer the legitimate fruits of labor from the populace to themselves. Adam Smith approached the matter of current institutions from

29. *Cato's Letters,* January 20, 1721, no. 62, in Jacobson, ed., *English Libertarian Heritage,* 130; see also for Cato's exposition of the labor theory of value, *ibid.,* 127–28; Smith, *Wealth of Nations,* 118–19; Forbes, "Skeptical Whiggism, Commerce, and Liberty," 184, 196.

30. Hirschman, *Passions and the Interests,* esp. 10–11, 58–59, 101–102, implies this idea of wealth acquisition. On Adam Smith, see Smith, *Wealth of Nations,* 122, 420–23, and his egalitarianism on 15, 735; Rahe, *Republics Ancient and Modern,* 510–12, 747, 778; Kornblith and Murrin, "Who Shall Rule at Home?," 31.

an economic angle and found that the system of privilege and monopoly cheated people out of a just return on their labor and retarded economic growth and the general welfare.[31] But the tie that bound Adam Smith and the colonials together was not republicanism; it was the critique of aristocracy, of the European system of privilege and monopoly. The similarity between the policies of the Americans and Adam Smith is worth underlining: both based their systems on antiaristocracy, one politically with economic implications and the other economically with political implications.

The legacy of the revolutionary generation over the proper means to obtain a just and republican distribution of wealth contained some large obfuscations and indeterminacies. The revolutionary concept of the distribution of wealth and the four axioms that composed it would serve and satisfy the nation for several generations. Components of the revolutionary discourse, however, were disturbing in their long-run implications.

A serious confusion in the revolutionaries' ideas about wealth distribution involved the definition of the word *labor*. Even by the time of the Revolution, a division appeared among Americans over manual and mental labor. Those who argued that a basic inequality could not be avoided constructed their viewpoint on differences of individual talent. Tom Paine said nothing could alter the inequalities created by nature. John Adams wrote that equal rights before the law were possible, "but equal ranks and equal property never can be inferred from it, any more than equal understanding, agility, vigor, or beauty [can]." One pamphleteer engaged in the impost (tariff) controversy of 1786 showed an impatience with the reward some felt due a head of state; some believed that just because a head of state sits all day "and does not labour" he needed no more income than a plowman. People did not acknowledge the utility of "head work." Thomas Jefferson made his bias plain in 1803 when he affirmed his apprehension about urban living, for there the "general

---

31. Ralph Lerner notes that Smith's work was antiaristocratic ("Commerce and Character," 6). Smith said, and his interpreters have agreed, that his dispute was over the policy of mercantilism. But in a broader sense, it was over the aristocratic notions of privilege and monopoly; see Winch, *Adam Smith's Politics,* 148; Viner, *Long View and the Short,* 234, 240; Forbes, "Sceptical Whiggism, Commerce, and Liberty," 186–87, 193, 196; Andrew S. Skinner, "Adam Smith: An Economic Interpretation of History," in *Essays on Adam Smith,* ed. Skinner and Wilson, 160; Glenn R. Morrow, *The Ethical and Economic Theories of Adam Smith* (1923; rpr. New York, 1969), 78–79.

desire of men to live by their heads rather than their hands" led to dissipation and wretchedness.[32]

The difficulty lay in the ambiguity in the word *labor*. The mental versus manual labor controversy that began to arise soon after the Revolution displayed the fuzziness in how the word *labor* was applied. For the revolutionaries, it evidently had a distinctly antileisure, antiaristocratic quality. Eventually, though, fortunes amassed through mental labor, among other factors, would emerge, and those who possessed the fortunes relied on the labor theory of property/value to justify their possessions. In the late eighteenth century, few lived the leisured life of an aristocrat and almost everyone was engaged in the activity of earning a living. Yet labor did not carry the same meaning to all persons, and without some refinement in the terminology, the labor theory of property/value could become (as it in fact did) a justification for extremes in the distribution of wealth as well as a condemnation of those extremes. Few caught this problem as did Noah Webster, who lived to witness the ascension of the Jacksonians to power. In 1837 Noah complained to Daniel Webster about Jacksonian speeches exhorting the public to believe that the "rich are enemies and oppressors of the poor." Argued Noah, "But the rich do *not* live on the labors of the poor; they live on the fruits of their own industry and good management or those of their ancestors."[33] The use of the labor theory of property/value, so long as labor went undefined, did not necessarily mean that an expositor was arguing for an egalitarian distribution of wealth.

Another area of verbal obfuscation involved the word *property*. Historians have been quite active in detailing how broad a definition persons in the eighteenth century gave the term *property*.[34] An important question has to be whether the revolutionary generation meant that property, as material possession, was justified by labor, as the labor theory of property/value held, or

32. Thomas Paine, *Rights of Man* (1791), in Foner, ed., *Complete Writings of Paine*, I, 367; John Adams to Thomas Brand-Hollis, June 11, 1790, in Adams, ed., *Works of John Adams*, IX, 570; A Plain Politician, *Honesty Shewed to Be True Policy; or, A General Impost Considered and Defended* (New York, 1786), 13; Jefferson to David Williams, November 14, 1803, in Lipscomb, ed., *Writings of Jefferson*, X, 431. See Bogin, *Abraham Clark and the Quest for Equality*, 32; Schultz, "Small Producer Thought in Early America, Part I," 116. For a discussion of mental versus manual labor between 1830 and 1860, see Jonathan A. Glickstein, *Concepts of Free Labor in Antebellum America* (New Haven, 1991).

33. Noah Webster to Daniel Webster, 1837, in Harry R. Warfel, ed., *Letters of Noah Webster* (New York, 1953), 493.

34. For example, Forrest McDonald, *Novus Ordo Seclorum: The Intellectual Origins of the Constitution* (Lawrence, Kans., 1985), 10–13, and generally 10–36.

whether the revolutionary stand that property was the basis of all civilization simply meant property in possession, with little concern about the means of acquisition.[35]

So long as the United States was a developmental economy and retained the institutional earmarks of an expanding agrarian nation, possession of property and the labor theory of property/value could complement each other instead of conflicting. The day would come when that developmental phase ended, and then the question would have to be faced. Was property justified because of the labor entailed in acquiring it, or was property sacrosanct because somebody possessed it and too much social conflict would erupt if society questioned the rights of possessors to their possessions? The revolutionaries, for all their talk about the fruits of labor, never defined property legally or institutionally as the reward due to labor. Rather, the legal institutions simply defined property as that which someone possessed. That definition leads one to suspect that the revolutionary elite was far more concerned about the sanctity of property rights than the means of acquisition. When the time arose to question property distribution in the United States, dissenters would find that the legacy of the Revolution—the important one provided by institutional structures instead of the ones in speeches and pamphlets—was not the labor theory of property/value but the absolute sanctity of property regardless of the means of acquisition.

A more telling weakness in the American revolutionary discourse about the distribution of wealth was the lack of numerical definitions. The revolutionaries never went beyond a vague literary description about what a good distribution was. They never numerically defined a good versus a bad distribution of wealth. Modern scholarship has established that the top 10 percent of colonial wealth-holders in 1774 possessed approximately 50 percent of colonial net worth.[36] That lopsided a distribution, which the colonists felt was

35. Many threw hedges around the absolute sanctity of property rights; see Thomas Paine, *Agrarian Justice* (1796), in Foner, ed., *Complete Writings of Paine,* I, 620; Benjamin Franklin to Robert Morris, December 25, 1783, in Bigelow, ed., *Life of Benjamin Franklin,* III, 243; Thomas Jefferson to Isaac McPherson, August 13, 1813, in Lipscomb, ed., *Writings of Jefferson,* XIII, 333–34; Matthews, *Radical Politics of Jefferson,* 20–24; Wills, *Inventing America,* 229–30; Jean Yarbrough, "Jefferson and Property Rights," in *Liberty, Property, and the Foundations of the American Constitution,* ed. Ellen Frankel Paul and Howard Dickman (Albany, 1989), 68–69.

36. From Alice Hanson Jones, *Wealth of a Nation to Be: The American Colonies on the Eve of the Revolution* (New York, 1980), Table 6.1, pp. 162–63. See also Williamson and Lindert, *American Inequality,* 9, 28–30, 36–39; Billy G. Smith, "The Material Lives of Laboring Philadelphians, 1756 to 1800," *William and Mary Quarterly,* XXXVIII (1981), 163–202; Smith, "In-

sufficient to sustain a republic and which seemed inordinately better than the distribution that obtained in Europe, hardly seems worthy of the description of an "equal distribution of wealth." Without some explicit standard by which people could judge whether the distribution of wealth was within the proper limits for a republic, virtually any distortion in wealth-holdings could be rationalized as sufficiently equitable for a republican society. This is what happened in later years. Not until the 1880s and 1890s would quantitative assessments of the actual distribution of American wealth appear in print.

Evidently the revolutionaries desired more a widespread diffusion of property than an equal distribution of it. Studies of the distribution of wealth have almost always been done on a relative basis, revealing what proportion of the population possessed what proportion of wealth. It seems that the revolutionaries were more concerned with an absolute than a relative notion of property distribution. For a republic, widespread ownership of property, even in small lots with a few large accumulations, was permissible. Property ownership, regardless of size, provided independence, not relative amounts of it. Size of property holdings became important only in extremes, when the impoverished class became too great and the wealthy class too small. Certainly the revolutionaries feared the avaricious rich man, but on a general basis it may be argued that they were more concerned about the size of the poverty class. It seems that the American revolutionaries believed the way to detect unhealthy wealth accumulations was by detecting widespread poverty.

Another and perhaps most telling omission of the Founders was their failure to produce an agrarian law. According to their words, a widespread diffusion of property was essential to the maintenance of a republican form of government. If they believed such to be the case, one would have thought that they would have acted to enforce an equitable distribution by designing a law mandating a redistribution from the wealthy to the poor to preserve a republican polity. That action certainly would have demonstrated the existence of virtue among society's social, economic, and political leaders. Moreover, the great republican theorists whom the revolutionaries read had endorsed agrarian laws or redistributions, at least to a

equality in Late Colonial Philadelphia: A Note on Its Nature and Growth," *William and Mary Quarterly,* XLI (1984), 629–45; Soltow, *Distribution of Wealth and Income,* 41–59. A thorough review of the literature on the distribution of wealth in colonial America is offered in McCusker and Menard, *Economy of British America,* chap. 12.

limited extent: Montesquieu, Harrington, Francis Hutcheson, and Catharine Macaulay.[37]

In all fairness, many revolutionaries looked upon the abolition of entail and primogeniture as agrarian laws that stopped the creation of large accumulations of landed property. An argument can be made that, despite the conclusions of many historians, abolition of entail and primogeniture was, outside of the emancipation of the slaves in the North, the most radical act of the Revolution. But the elimination of these feudal laws disturbed no mighty interest in the young republic and required little sacrifice from anyone. Agrarian laws were more forceful, demanding possessors of property to yield some of their wealth for redistribution to poorer citizens. The revolutionary leaders wanted no part of agrarian laws of that character, as was evidenced by their reaction to Shays' Rebellion.[38]

One obtains the impression that Americans, upon discovering that their constitutional struggle with Great Britain was serious and leading them to form a separate republic, knew from their reading of past philosophers that a wholesome distribution of wealth was vital for a republic's health. They then, with a sigh of relief and without any numerical investigation into the matter, determined that the American distribution of wealth as it stood in 1776 was sufficient for a republic. Upon further reflection, they outlined a series of policies to avoid so as not to create monstrous divergences in the distribution of wealth, but they also realized that over time such divergences would inevitably come about. They were thankful that circumstances, the frontier, and simple luck had given them a healthy distribution of wealth. But realizing that they would not have to go through the anguish and struggle of recasting institutions, they were mostly thankful that they did not have to do anything at all.

The enduring legacy the revolutionaries bequeathed their successors in regard to the distribution of wealth was inactivity. Distribution in the United States, regardless of republicanism or any other doctrine, was to be achieved

37. Caroline Robbins, *The Eighteenth-Century Commonwealthman: Studies in the Transmission, Development and Circumstance of English Liberal Thought from the Restoration of Charles II Until the War with the Thirteen Colonies* (Cambridge, Mass., 1959), 15, 125, 191–92; Scott, *In Pursuit of Happiness,* 27; Pocock, *Machiavellian Moment,* 387, 468; Thomas L. Pangle, *Montesquieu's Philosophy of Liberalism: A Commentary on "The Spirit of the Laws"* (Chicago, 1973), 77, 149–50.

38. Szatmary, *Shays' Rebellion,* 70–76.

by nature, by the market, by chance, by talent, or by some other nonhuman agency. The legacy was that distribution was *not* to be the product of an act of political will, of a sense of organic responsibility to the society, of a virtuous devotion to community. In the realm of distribution of wealth, the real legacy was utter laissez-faire.

PART II

BUILDING THE HOUSE OF REPUBLICANISM UPON THE REVOLUTIONARY FOUNDATION 1790–1880

To obtain *labor* without rendering a fair equivalent is also a violation of the rights of property. . . . The great disparity in the conditions of the rich and poor is the natural result of unjust laws. . . . *Unjust distribution originates in wrong legislation.*
—Edward Kellogg, *Labor and Other Capital: The Rights of Each Secured and the Wrongs of Both Eradicated*

It is an observation as curious as it is important, that in countries in which industry is respectable, and where the fruits of labor are secure, property always tends toward an equal distribution. Every man possesses as a means of acquirement, his own labor; and though there be a very considerable difference in the capacity, the industry, the good fortune of individuals, yet this difference has its limits; and diversities of acquisition are still more limited.
—Richard Hildreth, *Despotism in America; or, An Inquiry into the Nature and Results of the Slave-holding System in the United States*

Industry well directed is a great source of national wealth. It is well known that the toil, and labour and almost the exercise of ingenuity in the Southern States are left to the slaves. Their Masters are unwilling to labour and they live upon the labour of their slaves.
—Peter O. Thatcher to Nathan Appleton, March 14, 1832

4

Economic Structure, American Values, and the Republican Theory of Wealth Distribution

The American theory of the distribution of wealth ruled economic thought for one and one-quarter centuries. Its four axioms—the labor theory of property/value, the political economy of aristocracy, the laws of entail and primogeniture, and the population-to-land ratio—sailed through the nineteenth century without revision or deviation. And then at the start of the twentieth century the American theory of wealth distribution utterly disintegrated. In this chapter I explore the institutional and environmental reasons why the theory was so explanatory of the economic experience for people in the nineteenth century and so completely inadequate for those in the twentieth.

Quantitative studies of the distribution of wealth and income have revealed the massive skew in American wealth distribution in the nineteenth and early twentieth centuries. The richest 10 percent of Americans possessed some 50 percent of the nation's wealth at the time of the Revolution; by the Civil War, that element owned 73 percent; by 1912, the height of the Progressive campaign, the richest 10 percent owned 90 percent of the nation's wealth. After about 1940, inequality moderated until 1980 or so—a period in which wealth distribution resembled that during the Revolution—and then began to worsen; as of 1996 the distribution of wealth is apparently as miserable as it was in 1929 (see Table 1).

The widespread verbiage extolling economic equality seems odd given the statistics on American wealth distribution for the eighteenth and nineteenth centuries. Except for a few reformers and the early labor movement from 1830 to the turn of the century, most statements by Americans in the nineteenth century were smugly self-congratulatory. Europe had pauperized masses ruled over by the opulent, aristocratic few, but in America, equality ruled in

TABLE I
THE DISTRIBUTION OF WEALTH OVER SELECTED YEARS, 1774–1962

Year	Percentage of Wealth Held by Richest 1%	Percentage of Wealth Held by Richest 10%	Gini Coefficient of Inequality	Poverty (%)
1774	12.6	49.6	.642	—
1860	29.0	73.0	.832	43.86
1870	27.0	70.0	.833	—
1912	56.4	90.0	.93	34.8
1923	45.7	84.1	.90	—
1962	26.0	61.6	.76	26
1977	—	—	.72	12.3

Year	Percentage of Income Held by Richest 20%	Gini Coefficient
1947	43.0	.376
1959	41.1	.361
1969	40.6	.349
1979	41.7	.365
1984	42.9	.385
1988	44.0	—

Sources: Jeffrey G. Williamson and Peter H. Lindert, *American Inequality: A Microeconomic History* (New York, 1980), Table 3.1, pp. 38–39, Table 3.6, pp. 50–51, Table 5.20, p. 132; Frank Levy, *Dollars and Dreams: The Changing American Income Distribution* (New York, 1987), Table 2.1, p. 14; Kevin Phillips, *The Politics of Rich and Poor: Wealth and the American Electorate in the Reagan Aftermath* (New York, 1990), chart 2, p. 13; Alan S. Blinder, Irving Kristol, and Wilbur J. Cohen, "The Level and Distribution of Economic Well-Being," in *The American Economy in Transition*, ed. Martin Feldstein (Chicago, 1980), Table 6.10, p. 435, Table 6.13, p. 438, and pp. 466–67; poverty statistic in the 1977 wealth panel is a 1975 statistic taken from *The Universal Almanac: 1991* (Kansas City, 1992), 211.

politics *and* in economics. Yet wealth distribution worsened over the decades of the nineteenth century. Why did rhetoric not match the reality of worsening wealth distribution?

The answers as to the power, longevity, and sudden demise of the American theory of the distribution of wealth come from the structures and processes of the American economy. Americans were not "hegemonized" into one way of thinking, were not mesmerized by social superiors, and were not guilty of false consciousness or deluded thinking. Rather, the way the American economy evolved supported the American theory of the distribution of wealth and a host of assorted values involving individualism, thrift, frugality, industriousness, and social mobility. The fit between structures and beliefs was not perfect—if it ever has been or ever will be—but the central tendencies of the ideology and the economic processes were close enough to allow Americans to believe their understanding of how wealth was properly and improperly distributed was accurate and a useful guide for formulating public policy.

Current interpretations of the American economy in the eighteenth and nineteenth centuries tend to push in an opposite direction. Instead of a stability that could reinforce a set of ideals over 125 years, historians—especially social historians—have stressed the impact of seismic economic change and how it ignited social upheavals, redistributed wealth, destroyed lifestyles among the masses, and created new and malignant aristocracies. The most important word connected with studies of the social and political effects of the evolution of the American economy is *transformation*. Americans have certainly endured a remarkable number of transformations. The law was transformed, the market was transformed, politics was transformed, social groups were transformed, the North was transformed (the South was not). Transformations occurred in the 1780s, the 1810s, the 1820s, the 1830s, the 1850s, and probably in any given decade between 1870 and 1900.[1] And after 1900 the pace of transformation increased.

1. This observation is also made by Thomas Bender in connection with historians' treatment of the ideal of community in *Community and Social Change in America* (New Brunswick, N.J., 1978), 45–48, and chapter 3 generally. For examples of the idea of nineteenth-century transformation, consult Morton J. Horwitz, *The Transformation of American Law, 1780–1860* (Cambridge, Mass., 1977); Stuart M. Blumin, *The Emergence of the Middle Class: Social Experience in the American City, 1760–1900* (Cambridge, Eng., 1989), 12–13, 66–68, and *passim;* Richard D. Brown, *Modernization: The Transformation of American Life, 1600–1865* (New York, 1976); Ronald P. Formisano, *The Transformation of Political Culture: Massachusetts*

Within the general framework of transformation, historians have worked with two basic themes. The first is the disintegration of classical republicanism (*i.e.,* denial of self-interest) and its replacement by marketplace liberalism (polity based on individual gratification). This is transformation from the vantage point of ideological change and informed by political theory.[2] The second is the shift from a subsistence economy to a commercial market economy.[3] Within the second is the special topic of the transportation revolution from the 1820s to the 1850s.[4] According to some historians, these massive alterations to the fabric of society upset social classes, destroyed skilled labor, gave birth to a new urban middle class, altered the relation of farmers to the land and of people to their communities, produced reformers and abolitionists, and established a new feudalistic moneyed aristocracy.[5]

Here I apply a more restrictive meaning to the word *transformation,* defining it loosely in a statistical sense, although its application relies on intuition rather than on data. A transformation would entail the abrupt movement of a

---

Parties, 1790s–1840s (New York, 1980); Steven Mintz and Susan Kellogg, *Domestic Revolutions: A Social History of American Family Life* (New York, 1988), 43–52, chap. 5; L. Ray Gunn, *The Decline of Authority: Public Economic Policy and Political Development in New York State, 1800–1860* (Ithaca, N.Y., 1988), 26–27, 47, 55–56.

2. See the discussion concerning the secondary literature about republicanism and liberalism in James L. Huston, "Virtue Besieged," 521–26, and generally, 521–47.

3. For example, Main, *Antifederalists,* 2–4, 8–11, 17–18, 27–34, and *passim;* Thomas P. Slaughter, *The Whiskey Rebellion: Frontier Epilogue to the American Revolution* (New York, 1986), 38–40; Watson, *Liberty and Power,* 19–32; Charles G. Sellers, *The Market Revolution: Jacksonian America, 1815–1846* (New York, 1991); Kulikoff, *Agrarian Origins of American Capitalism,* chaps. 1–2.

4. George Rogers Taylor's book *The Transportation Revolution, 1815–1860* (New York, 1951) is seminal on this theme. See also Alfred D. Chandler, Jr., *The Visible Hand: The Managerial Revolution in American Business* (Cambridge, Mass., 1977), chap. 3; Brown, *Modernization,* 123. "[Historians need] to examine more critically the role of the market in the antebellum economy, its interaction with various aspects of preindustrial culture, and the destructive aspect of that interaction," writes W. J. Rorabaugh, "Who Fought for the North in the Civil War? Concord, Massachusetts, Enlistments," *Journal of American History,* LXXIII (1986), 701.

5. On the power of the market revolution, see Watson, *Liberty and Power,* 28–35; Kohl, *Politics of Individualism,* 228; Major L. Wilson, *The Presidency of Martin Van Buren* (Lawrence, Kans., 1984), 1–4; Gunn, *Decline of Authority,* 9, 13; Sellers, *Market Revolution,* 5–32, 202–68; Steven Hahn, *The Roots of Southern Populism: Yeoman Farmers and the Transformation of the Georgia Upcountry, 1850–1890* (New York, 1983), 52–63, chap. 4. I find myself in general agreement with Walter Licht, *Industrializing America: The Nineteenth Century* (Baltimore, 1995), xvi–xvii.

societal norm (that is, its average or central tendency) one standard deviation or more from its previous position. In the nineteenth century, for example, the central tendency was to laissez-faire. If the attitudes about government intervention in the economy could be measured and plotted, the central tendency of nineteenth-century Americans was laissez-faire; the movement of the central tendency to federal regulation in the twentieth century is assumed to be (without any statistical proof, data, or anything else vaguely resembling a measurement) a movement of the societal norm by at least one standard deviation. Admittedly this is an imprecise means of conjecturing about the existence or nonexistence of transformations (all intuition, no data), but it is the standard being employed.

The interpretation offered here is that the *economic* structures of American life had a rough unitary quality between 1765 and 1880 that sustained ideas about the economy and the distribution of wealth. The structures changed—there were distinct and at times powerful fluctuations—but the structures held and did not undergo transformation. These years should be labeled the "Age of the American Revolution" because every aspect of American life was being changed to adhere to the techniques of life appropriate for a republic.[6] The Revolution created institutions at odds with the somewhat hierarchical order existing at the time of the republic's founding, and it would take time for the institutions of individualism to triumph over the social practices of deference. More precisely, in the years after 1789, Americans were continuously working out the implications of the Revolution until the opening of the twentieth century. In the economy, the central thrust was the creation of a national market economy and its slow but inevitable victory over self-contained agricultural communities. Its chief characteristic, however, was the small unit of production. American economic growth, with a few important exceptions, was primarily a continuous multiplication of production units; the American economy over time was like an amoeba, constantly subdividing and expanding outward but *not* consolidating into fewer and larger units. This constant multiplication of

6. The end dates for the period of the Age of the American Revolution are a little flabby and other ones could be proposed. I assume that around 1765 cultural traits were rising in the colonies at considerable variance with those of England. At their emergence, it is fair, I think, to say that the English colonists had experienced a transformation in which elements of British culture had been lost and replaced by new elements. An end date of 1880 is chosen as being the moment before entry into a world of large-scale enterprise, although 1890 or 1900 could be argued for as well.

production units supported the rhetoric about social mobility, industriousness, and individualism and in turn elicited a continuous adherence to the republican theory of the distribution of wealth.

The primary characteristic of the United States in the Age of the American Revolution was that it was an agrarian republic. In 1770, the nation's labor force engaged overwhelmingly in agricultural pursuits; by 1800, nearly 90 percent of all those employed were in agriculture, and even by 1880 a majority of the employed workforce found a livelihood in agriculture (see Table 2). Although agriculture's share of the national wealth declined between 1850 and 1860, it dwarfed the investment in manufacturing as late as the census year of 1900 (see Table 3).[7]

Moreover, the residential pattern in the nation reflected its agrarian underpinnings. A majority of Americans throughout the nineteenth century lived in rural settings (see Table 4). Certainly the period from 1830 to 1860 witnessed an explosion of urban growth, in percentage terms the greatest urban growth the nation has ever known. But the standard for determining an "urban" area in the nineteenth century was a population of twenty-five hundred or more. A town of twenty-five hundred inhabitants for most purposes is perhaps an indication of a move away from isolated farms but hardly a signal of rampant urbanization. If one chooses a population of twenty thousand as a size at which urban needs forced themselves upon the town's citizens and when urban services begin to appear in important ways, then there were only forty urban areas in the United States in 1860, accounting for 11.81 percent of the population. Nearly 90 percent of the population lived on farms or in villages and towns tightly connected with the rural economy (see Table 5). Even though the South was the most thoroughly agrarian part of the nation, even industrial New England in the mid-1870s, where some 46 percent of its male population was employed in manufacturing, retained a rural quality.[8]

7. See Jeremy Atack and Fred Bateman, *To Their Own Soil: Agriculture in the Antebellum North* (Ames, Iowa, 1987), 3.

8. Alexander Keyssar, *Out of Work: The First Century of Unemployment in Massachusetts* (Cambridge, Eng., 1986), 15–18; Stanley Lebergott, *Manpower in Economic Growth: The American Record Since 1800* (New York, 1964), 102; Richard H. Sewell, *A House Divided: Sectionalism and Civil War, 1848–1865* (Baltimore, 1988), 9; John Niven, *Connecticut for the Union: The Role of the State in the Civil War* (New Haven, 1965), 5–6; Theodore Parker, "The Material Condition of the People of Massachusetts," in Francis Power Cobbe, ed., *The Collected Works of Theodore Parker* (London, 1864–71), VIII, 161–72; Robert J. Cook, *Baptism of Fire: The Republican Party in Iowa, 1838–1878* (Ames, Iowa, 1994), 8.

TABLE 2
WORK CATEGORIES OF EMPLOYED AMERICANS, BY CENSUS YEAR, 1800–1900

Year	Total Employed (000s)	Agriculture (000s)	(%)	Manufacturing and Mining (000s)	(%)	Trade and Transport (000s)	(%)	Construction (000s)	(%)	Teachers (000s)	(%)	Domestics (000s)	(%)
1800	972	870	89.5	12	1.2	40	4.1	0	0	5	.5	40	4.1
1810	2,135	1,950	91.3	37	1.7	60	2.8	0	0	12	.6	70	3.3
1820	2,694	2,470	91.7	30	1.1	50	1.9	0	0	20	.7	110	4.1
1830	3,342	2,965	88.7	117	3.5	70	2.1	0	0	30	.9	160	4.8
1840	5,249	3,570	68.0	628	12.0	452	8.6	290	5.5	45	.9	240	4.6
1850	7,504	4,520	60.2	1,429	19.0	685	9.1	410	5.5	80	1.1	350	4.7
1860	10,132	5,880	58.0	1,871	18.5	1,115	11.0	520	5.1	115	1.1	600	5.9
1870	13,236	6,790	51.3	2,863	21.6	1,605	12.1	780	5.9	170	1.3	1,000	7.6
1880	17,567	8,920	50.8	3,875	22.1	2,471	14.1	900	5.1	230	1.3	1,130	6.4
1890	22,491	9,960	44.2	5,201	23.1	3,830	17.0	1,510	6.7	350	1.6	1,580	7.0
1900	27,822	11,680	42.0	7,057	25.4	5,115	18.4	1,665	6.0	436	1.6	1,800	6.5

Source: Computed from Stanley Lebergott, *Manpower in Economic Growth: The American Record Since 1800* (New York, 1964), Table A-1, p. 510. The total column in Lebergott's Table A-1 represents the eligible labor pool and thus includes the unemployed; the estimate given above is the addition of those employed in the subject categories. The unemployed have been excluded.

TABLE 3

SHARES OF NATIONAL WEALTH AND NATIONAL CAPITAL, 1840–1900

A. Estimates of Wealth and Capital (billions of dollars, current prices)

	1840	1850	1860	1870	1880	1890	1900
Wealth (Gallman)*	—	7.89	16.39	24.21	32.22	54.92	73.12
Capital	3.89	6.27	12.27	17.80	23.79	38.98	52.97
Wealth (North)*	—	7.14	16.16	30.07	43.60	65.00	94.00
*See source note							

B. Value of Types of Property (billions of dollars) and Size Ratios of Establishments

	1840	1850	1860	1870	1880	1890	1900
Farm property	—	3.97	7.98	11.12	12.18	16.05	20.44
Value industry	.22	.53	1.01	2.12	2.79	6.53	9.84
Railroad investment	—	.32	1.15	2.48	5.40	10.02	10.26
Workers per estab.	4.31	7.78	9.36	8.15	10.80	11.97	10.38
Capital per worker ($)	480	560	770	1,030	1,020	1,530	1,850
Capital per estab. ($)	2,076	4,333	7,187	8,401	10,993	18,359	19,201

C. Ratio of Category Wealth to Total Wealth

Farm property	55.6	49.4	37.0	27.9	24.7	21.7
Industrial capital	7.4	6.3	7.1	6.4	10.0	10.5
Railroad investment	4.5	7.1	8.2	12.4	15.4	10.9

D. Ratio of Category Wealth to National Capital

Farm property	63.3	65.0	62.5	51.2	41.2	38.6
Industrial capital	8.5	8.2	11.9	11.7	16.8	18.6
Railroad investment	5.1	9.4	13.9	22.7	25.7	19.4

Sources: Section A: Wealth and income statistics taken from Robert E. Gallman, "The United States Capital Stock in the Nineteenth Century," in *Long-Term Factors in American Economic Growth*, ed. Stanley L. Engerman and Robert E. Gallman (Chicago, 1986), 204; other wealth statistics taken from S. N. D. North, *Abstract of the Twelfth Census of the United States, 1900* (3rd ed.; Washington, D.C., 1904). 300–301.

Section B: Value of farm and industry taken from North, *Abstract of the Twelfth Census*, 300–31; railroad investment taken from U.S. Bureau of the Census, *Historical Statistics of the United States, Colonial Times to 1970, Bicentennial Edition* (Washington, D.C., 1975), 734, 735. Number of firms taken from North, *Abstract of the Twelfth Census*, 300–301; number of workers in industry, *ibid.*; value of industry, number of workers, and number of firms in 1840 computed from *Tenth Census*, II, vii. Capital per worker calculated from section A and North, *Abstract of the Twelfth Census*.

Section C: Computed as ratio of categories in Section B divided by the estimate of wealth provided by the *Twelfth Census* in Section A.

Section D: Computed as the ratio of categories in Section B divided by estimate of wealth provided by Gallman in Section A.

TABLE 4

SHARE OF THE RURAL POPULATION IN TOTAL POPULATION
1800–1900

Year	Percentage
1800	93.9
1810	92.7
1820	92.8
1830	91.3
1840	89.2
1850	84.7
1860	80.2
1870	74.3
1880	71.8
1890	64.7
1900	60.3

Source: Robert E. Gallman, "The Agricultural Sector and Discontinuities," in *Essays in Nineteenth Century Economic History: The Old Northwest*, ed. David C. Klingaman and Richard K. Vedder (Athens, Ohio, 1975), Table 1, p. 37.

Agricultural activity demonstrated considerable variations, the most extreme being southern slavery. Until the 1880s, however, it appears that yeoman farms tended to average 80 to 120 acres, except for the much smaller farms in New England, and farm tenancy, while existing, was usually a minor factor in agricultural life.[9]

Not only was the United States an agrarian nation in the Age of the American Revolution, it was also commercial. The commercial quality of life had

9. Atack and Bateman, *To Their Own Soil,* Table 7.1, p. 111, Table 7.2, p. 112, and pp. 107–11 generally; U.S. Bureau of the Census, *Historical Statistics of the United States, Colonial Times to 1970: Bicentennial Edition* (Washington, D.C., 1975), 457; Frederick A. Bode and Donald E. Ginter, *Farm Tenancy and the Census in Antebellum Georgia* (Athens, Ga., 1986), 116–17, 137, 180–85; Paul W. Gates, "Problems of Agricultural History," in *Farming in the New Nation: Interpreting American Agriculture, 1790–1840,* ed. Darwin P. Kelsey (Washington, D.C., 1972), 44–45; Donald L. Winters, *Farmers Without Farms: Agricultural Tenancy in Nineteenth-Century Iowa* (Westport, Conn., 1978), 4–24, and Table 1.1, p. 14.

Table 5

American Cities with Populations Above 20,000
(1860–1880), in Descending Order by Size

1860		1870		1880	
City	Population	City	Population	City	Population
New York	805,651	New York	942,292	New York	1,206,299
Philadelphia	562,529	Philadelphia	674,022	Philadelphia	847,170
Brooklyn	266,661	Brooklyn	396,099	Brooklyn	655,663
Baltimore	212,418	St. Louis	310,865	Chicago	503,185
Boston	177,812	Chicago	298,907	Boston	362,839
New Orleans	168,675	Baltimore	267,354	St. Louis	350,518
Cincinnati	161,044	Boston	250,527	Baltimore	332,313
Chicago	109,260	Cincinnati	216,239	Cincinnati	255,139
Buffalo	81,129	New Orleans	191,418	San Francisco	233,959
St. Louis	77,860	San Francisco	149,373	New Orleans	216,090
Newark	71,914	Buffalo	117,714	Cleveland	160,146
Louisville	68,033	Wash., D.C.	109,199	Pittsburgh	156,389
Albany	62,367	Newark	105,059	Buffalo	155,134
Providence	50,660	Louisville	100,753	Wash., D.C.	147,293
Pittsburgh	49,217	Cleveland	92,829	Newark	136,508
Rochester	48,204	Pittsburgh	86,076	Louisville	123,798
Detroit	45,619	Jersey City	82,546	Jersey City	120,722
Milwaukee	45,246	Detroit	79,577	Detroit	117,340
Cleveland	43,417	Milwaukee	71,440	Milwaukee	115,587
Charleston	40,578	Albany	69,422	Providence	104,857
Wash., D.C.	40,001	Providence	68,904	Albany	90,758
New Haven	39,267	Rochester	62,386	Rochester	89,396
Richmond	37,910	Allegheny	53,800	Allegheny	78,682
Lowell	36,827	Richmond	51,038	Indianapolis	75,056
Montgomery	35,962	New Haven	50,840	Richmond	63,600
San Francisco	34,776	Charleston	48,956	New Haven	62,882
Mobile	29,258	Indianapolis	48,244	Lowell	59,475

(cont.)

TABLE 5 (cont.)

1860		1870		1880	
City	Population	City	Population	City	Population
Jersey City	29,226	Troy	46,465	Worcester	58, 291
Hartford	29,154	Syracuse	43,051	Troy	56,747
Troy	28,785	Worcester	41,105	Kansas City	55,785
Allegheny City	28,702	Lowell	40,928	Cambridge	52,669
Portland	26,341	Nashville	40,226	Syracuse	51,792
Cambridge	26,060	Cambridge	39,634	Columbus	51,647
Roxbury, Mass.	25,137	Hartford	37,180	Paterson	51,031
Reading	23,161	Scranton	35,092	Toledo	50,137
Memphis	22,623	Reading	33,930	Charleston	49,984
Syracuse	22,271	Paterson	33,579	Fall River	48,961
Salem	20,264	Kansas City	32,960	Minneapolis	46,857
Manchester	20,109	Mobile	32,034	Scranton	45,850
Dayton	20,081	Toledo	31,584	Nashville	43,350
		Portland	31,413	Reading	43,278
		Columbus	31,274	Wilmington	42,478
		Wilmington	30,841	Hartford	42,015
		Dayton	30,473	St. Paul	41,473
		Lawrence	28,921	Camden	40,659
		Utica	28,804	Lawrence	39,151
		Charlestown,		Dayton	38,678
		Mass.	28,323	Lynn, Mass.	38,274
		Savannah	28,235	Atlanta	37,409
		Lynn, Mass.	28,233	Denver	35,629
		Fall River	26,766	Oakland	34,555
		Springfield,		Utica	33,914
		Mass.	26,703	Portland	33,810
		Covington	24,505	Memphis	33,592
		Salem, Mass.	24,117	Springfield,	
		Quincy, Ill.	24,052	Mass.	33,340
		Manchester,		Manchester	32,630
		N.H.	23,536	St. Joseph	32,431

TABLE 5 (cont.)

1860		1870		1880	
City	Population	City	Population	City	Population
		Harrisburg	23,104	Grand Rapids	32,016
		Trenton	22,874	Hoboken	30,999
		Peoria	22,849	Harrisburg	30,762
		Kingston, N.Y.	21,945	Wheeling	30,737
		Evansville	21,830	Savannah	30,709
		Atlanta	21,789	Omaha	30,518
		New Bedford	21,320	Trenton	29,910
		Oswego	20,910	Peoria	29,259
		Elizabeth	20,823	Evansville	29,228
		North Prov.	20,495	Mobile	29,132
		Hoboken	20,297	Elizabeth	28,229
		Lancaster	20,233	Erie	27,737
		Poughkeepsie	20,080	Bridgeport	27,643
		Camden	20,045	Quincy	27,268
		Davenport	20,038	Fort Wayne	26,880
		St. Paul	20,030	New Bedford	26,845
				Terre Haute	26,042
				Lancaster	26,769
				Somerville	24,933
				Wilkes-Barre	23,339
				Des Moines	22,408
				Dubuque	22,254
				Galveston	22,248
				Norfolk	21,966
				Auburn	21,924
				Holyoke	21,915
				Augusta	21,891
				Davenport	21,831
				Chelsea	21,782

(cont.)

TABLE 5 (cont.)

1860		1870		1880	
City	Population	City	Population	City	Population
				Petersburg	21,656
				Sacramento	21,420
				Taunton	21,213
				Oswego	21,116
				Salt Lake City	20,768
				Springfield, Ohio	20,730
				Covington	20,720
				San Antonio	20,556
				Elmira	20,541
				Newport	20,433
				Poughkeepsie	20,207
				Bay City, Mich.	20,093
Total for 1860	3,724,209			(11.8% of U.S. population)	
Total for 1870	6,264,569			(16.4% of U.S. population)	
Total for 1880	9,070,405			(18.1% of U.S. population)	

Sources: Joseph C. G. Kennedy, *Preliminary Report on the Eighth Census, 1860* (Washington, D.C., 1862), 242–44; *Tenth Census,* I, 447–56.

penetrated significant portions of the colonies at the time of the Revolution. The large cities, coastal areas, and navigable river areas all engaged in commercial activities with Europe, Africa, and the West Indies. The southern plantation owners were perhaps more enmeshed in the commercial network than any other group in the colonies.

Large segments of the population were not engulfed in a broad market context. The early American republic was almost divided into small, local trading-agricultural districts in which self-sufficiency ruled. Farmers consumed between 60 and 80 percent of their harvest on the farm and used the bulk of the remainder for local purchases and occasionally to obtain a manufactured item. Perhaps at the time of the adoption of the Constitution, a majority of Americans lived in this self-sufficiency (or, more popularly, subsistence) condition.[10]

The limitations of the self-contained economic district had important ramifications for local society and for general economic growth. The obvious problem was transportation. Self-contained communities were usually self-sufficient out of necessity. They lacked natural means of transporting goods into and out of their areas, which put an obvious ceiling on work, effort, and reward. The farmers and craftsmen of these self-sufficient communities (if craftsmen there were) found no reason to produce beyond certain bounds, for excess production could not be disposed of. Surpluses beyond community and family needs made no sense; they could not be transported anywhere because the cost of transportation made the price of the article prohibitive to potential consumers.

The self-sufficient communities therefore could require more community effort, more neighborliness, and more consensual behavior. Or they could require nothing at all from their members. Time was not the constraint it could be in a commercial society where the "time is money" syndrome appears. In a semicommercial region, maximization of income might be accomplished in a fairly short period of time. Because of transportation dilemmas, any extra production above local needs was wasted effort because it could not be shipped elsewhere. Thus the potential arose for the community to demand that individuals expend surplus time on community projects. New Englanders could demand time from each person to work on roads and bridges, to attend religious services, to attend town meetings; southerners could engage in

10. The colonial and early national subsistence-commercial quality of American life has most persistently been presented by Main, *Social Structure of Revolutionary America*, 8–34 and *passim*. See also Atack and Bateman, *To Their Own Soil*, 201–202; Jeremy Atack and Fred Bateman, "Self-Sufficiency and the Marketable Surplus in the Rural North, 1860," *Agricultural History*, LVIII (1984), 298, 306; Clarence H. Danhof, *Change in Agriculture: The Northern United States, 1820–1870* (Cambridge, Mass., 1969), 8–13; Bettye Hobbs Pruitt, "Self-Sufficiency and the Agricultural Economy of Eighteenth-Century Massachusetts," *William and Mary Quarterly*, XLI (1984), 333–64. Two articles stressing the emergence of markets early in the republic's history are Winifred B. Rothenberg, "The Emergence of Farm Labor Markets and the Transformation of the Rural Economy: Massachusetts, 1750–1855," *Journal of Economic History*, XLVIII (1988), 537–66; and Rothenberg, "The Emergence of a Capital Market in Rural Massachusetts, 1730–1838," *Journal of Economic History*, XLV (1985), 781–808.

preindustrial antics of brawling, cockfighting, and horse racing.[11] Communities could respond in a variety of ways to the condition that community members had no reason to spend all their time on economic endeavors.

Transportation improvements—otherwise known as the transportation "revolution"—lifted the production constraints on the self-sufficient community and forged the communities together in one more or less frictionless market system. This was the central economic achievement of Americans in the nineteenth century—not manufacturing or anything even related to manufacturing. And it took nearly a century to complete. The railroad was the chief means of constructing the national market, and railroad construction peaked in the building of new lines and in its share of national product in the 1880–1890 period, when all tracks in the country adopted the standard gauge of $4'8\,^1/_2''$.[12]

Railroads were not the only means of transportation Americans employed in the nineteenth century, though the iron horse became by far the dominant one. Turnpikes had been built in the first part of the century with negligible results in improving the movement of freight. Canal construction, which between 1825 and 1840 inaugurated the transportation revolution, proved far more vital in stimulating the economy and breaking down self-sufficiency. Between 1815 and 1860 some $200 million, most of it public funds, was invested in canal construction, resulting in the opening of three thousand miles of canals, mainly in the northern states. Canals continued to be important carriers of traffic until the 1880s.[13]

Besides the canals, water transport generally remained a vital aspect of commerce throughout the whole of the nineteenth century. Oceanic travel,

11. See Elliot J. Gorn, " 'Gouge and Bite, Pull Hair and Scratch': The Social Significance of Fighting in the Southern Backcountry," *American Historical Review,* XC (1985), 18–43.

12. Chandler, *Visible Hand,* 130, 147; U.S. Bureau of the Census, *Historical Statistics,* Table Q329, p. 732; Albro Martin, *Railroads Triumphant: The Growth, Rejection and Rebirth of a Vital American Force* (New York, 1992), 25. By common parlance, the construction of the transportation network has been dubbed a revolution. The economic change had important consequences, but it does not compare with a political revolution. Nor can it; any economic endeavor requiring long-term investment will not, almost by definition, have the shortened time horizon of a political revolution.

13. Lance E. Davis et al., *American Economic Growth: An Economist's History of the United States* (New York, 1972), 482–84; Taylor, *Transportation Revolution,* chap. 3, esp. 52–55. A good summary of the canal era is Ronald E. Shaw, *Canals for a Nation: The Canal Era in the United States, 1790–1860* (Lexington, Ky., 1990).

especially the shipment of cotton and foodstuffs, and the coastal trade continued to grow in the antebellum years. More spectacular in some respects was the mighty surge of commercial activity on the Ohio–Mississippi River system and its tributaries after the appearance of the steamboat. The steamboat moved more tonnage in 1849 than did the railroads in the 1850s. Not until the 1880s did the western river traffic decline. Finally, shipping on the Great Lakes swelled as population filled the region and sought cheap means of transporting agricultural produce to the east coast and beyond.[14]

Railroads dominated American commerce in the nineteenth century, and although the victory of the railroad over canals and steamboats took more time than originally expected—older technologies have a greater ability to survive than most scholars accord them—Americans poured their money and labor into the iron rail as the means of conquering time and space.[15] The economic role of the railroad has at times caused confusion for historians, however. Frequently railroads have been characterized as part of the industrial revolution in America, and that linkage has some truth.[16] Unlike older forms of commerce, the railroad relied on the steam engine, metallurgy, and engineers—all primary elements of the industrial revolution. But the railroad's function was strictly commercial. Railroads made returns by commer-

14. Erik F. Haites, James Mak, and Gary M. Walton, *Western River Transportation: The Era of Early Internal Development, 1810–1860* (Baltimore, 1975), 11, 120–23; Taylor, *Transportation Revolution,* chaps. 2, 6; Douglass C. North, *The Economic Growth of the United States, 1790–1860* (New York, 1961), chap. 8; John H. Frederick, *The Development of American Commerce* (New York, 1932), 90–93, 106; John G. Clark, *The Grain Trade in the Old Northwest* (Urbana, 1966), 102–23, 277–80; Emory R. Johnson, T. W. Van Metre, G. G. Huebner, and D. S. Hanchett, *History of Domestic and Foreign Commerce of the United States* (Washington, D.C., 1915), I, 332–47.

15. For those stressing the economic role of the railroad, see Albert Fishlow, *American Railroads and the Transformation of the Ante-Bellum Economy* (Cambridge, Mass., 1965), chaps. 2, 8; Jeffrey G. Williamson, "The Railroads and Midwestern Development, 1870–90: A General Equilibrium History," in *Essays in Nineteenth Century Economic History: The Old Northwest,* ed. David C. Klingaman and Richard K. Vedder (Athens, Ohio, 1975), 269–352. Alfred D. Chandler has stressed the organizational aspects of the railroad and its impact, ultimately, on American business practices in *Visible Hand,* chap. 3. A scholar who questions the impact of the railroad is Robert William Fogel, *Railroads and American Economic Growth: Essays in Econometric History* (Baltimore, 1964).

16. One of the strongest statements about the vital role of the railroad in fostering industrialization is provided by W. W. Rostow, *The Stages of Economic Growth: A Non-Communist Manifesto* (2nd ed.; Cambridge, Eng., 1971), 55.

cial activity: they moved passengers and freight from point A to point B. The railroad was only tangentially involved in industrialization. The power of the enterprise and its major effects were commercial.[17]

Besides agriculture, commerce was the major economic endeavor of Americans in the nineteenth century. The estimates of United States employment by enterprise category in Table 2 show that trade and transportation grew quickly between 1830 and 1900, although not as fast as manufacturing. But the manufacturing totals require some qualitative reservations. Somewhat more revealing of the importance of commercial development to nineteenth-century Americans is the share of railroad investment to either total wealth or to national capital between 1850 and 1890 compared to the ratio of investment in industry to total wealth or to national capital (see Table 3, section D).[18] When it is recalled that railroads were a portion of the category of commerce and that capital invested in steamboats, lake transport, canals, and ocean and coastal shipping, along with the physical accoutrements of piers, docks, warehouses, and the like, are not tabulated, it becomes obvious what a monumental effort Americans put into the construction of commercial arteries and carriers in the nineteenth century. The nineteenth century was the Age of Commerce. The industrial revolution in comparison was minuscule; in the nineteenth century, the industrial revolution was not much more than the johnny-come-lately, the bobtail and ragtag ends of the commercial revolution.

Moreover, the surge of commercial activity brought about increased financial activity. Not only did banks first appear in the United States as the pooled efforts of merchants with excess capital, but the basic role of banks from 1781 (the founding of Robert Morris' Bank of North America) to the wizardry of J. P. Morgan in the 1880s was simply to lubricate the commercial sector of the economy. Finance did not exist to make long-term investments in manufacturing; banking existed to provide credit principally for mer-

17. On the relationship of railroads to industrialization, see Fishlow, *American Railroads,* 116–62.

18. These figures possess a certain flabbiness because they all, except possibly for railroad investment, are based on estimates and probably faulty census reports. But the relative magnitudes of investments in railroads, manufacturing, and agriculture can be considered crudely correct, at least enough to establish an interpretation that does not require massive technical precision. See Fishlow, *American Railroads,* 101–106. Peter Temin also noted that commerce seemed more revolutionary in this period than did industry (*Causal Factors in American Economic Growth in the Nineteenth Century* [Houndmills, Eng., 1975], 16).

chants to move agricultural crops, to facilitate exchanges abroad (hence the various bills of exchange with England), to provide credit for landed expansion—which was agricultural expansion—and for improvements in transportation facilities. Even the New York Stock Exchange, which suddenly was vivified by the trading of railroad stocks in the 1850s, served commercial, not industrial, purposes. The number of banks rose in waves between 1784 and 1860; in 1815 there were 208 state banks, in 1840, 901, and in 1860, 1,562. Banking expansions occurred in the second, third, and fifth decades of the nineteenth century. And they were all tied to agricultural expansions and commercial developments. Commerce required credit, and the banking structure responded to expansions and contractions of commerce. Not until the 1880s did investment banking and industrial securities become an important feature of American finance.[19]

The overall importance of the expansion of commerce was simple enough: it created a national market economy.[20] In doing so, it provided the stimulus to break out of the barriers that confined districts to economic self-sufficiency. Transportation improvements—a phrase that simply means enhancing the exchange power of a marketplace—had two effects on aggregate supply and demand. Quite possibly the nineteenth century abetted economic growth by aggregating consumers and so increased the demand for goods and services (that is, shifted the aggregate demand curve to the right). But its major impact was on aggregate supply. The costs of production in the early republic were the traditional ones of labor, capital, and other normal

19. Taylor, *Transportation Revolution*, 319–25; Paul B. Trescott, *Financing American Enterprise: The Story of Commercial Banking* (New York, 1963), 35–38; Vincent P. Carosso, *Investment Banking in America: A History* (Cambridge, Mass., 1970), ix, 10–50; William J. Shultz and M. R. Caine, *Financial Development of the United States* (New York, 1937), 239–41, 431–38; William N. Parker, *Commerce, Cotton, and Westward Expansion, 1820–1860* (Chicago, 1964), 55–56; Chandler, *Visible Hand*, 91–94; Harold Livesay and Glenn Porter, "The Financial Role of Merchants in the Development of U.S. Manufacturing," *Explorations in Economic History*, IX (1971), 65–67, 79.

20. Parker, *Commerce, Cotton, and Westward Expansion*, 61. This is, of course, the brunt of George Roger Taylor's argument in *The Transportation Revolution*. A limitation on the quality of the national market is offered by Taylor and Irene D. Neu in *The American Railroad Network, 1861–1890* (Cambridge, Mass., 1956), 11–14, 49–53. Winifred Rothenberg has attempted to demonstrate the existence of regional markets in Massachusetts before 1800, but it is dubious whether Massachusetts achieved by 1800 the important feat of reducing transportation costs so that goods could move about the region with small charges (Rothenberg, "Emergence of Farm Labor Markets," 537–66).

items of production—plus the cost of transportation. Consumer demand was based on final price, not the price of an article at its point of production. In areas where land transportation was the only means of conveyance, transportation quickly became the major element of cost. Establishment of steamboats, canals, and railroads turned the giant of transportation costs into a dwarf.[21] The aggregate supply curve simply lurched downward and to the right. For all producers, the commercial expansion presented golden opportunities; a potential equilibrium representing a much greater national product now existed. And producers began to buzz in activity to achieve that new potential equilibrium.

Over the space of nearly sixty years transportation services created a national market and spelled the doom of the isolated, self-sufficient market area.[22] In fact, the commercial expansion brought into being the domestic market so desired by Henry Clay and the advocates of the American System. A distinct trade-off seems to have occurred. As transportation connected the trans-Appalachian West to the seaboard East, American interest in the overseas market, except among New Yorkers and southerners, waned while fascination with the internal market waxed. The trade-off between foreign and domestic commerce was in one instance explicit. Since the seventeenth century, the West Indies had been the pivot of American trade patterns and to some extent the determining factor of American well-being, economic growth, and a successful trade relationship with the rest of the world. But the trans-Appalachian West replaced the West Indies as the nexus of trade.[23]

No sector of the economy required more adaptation than did agriculture, but, somewhat surprisingly, the adaptation occurred with a minimum of friction. The expansion of commerce and American agriculture had an odd symbiotic relationship; they fed off each other and together created the commercial agrarian republic.

The major task of American commerce throughout the nineteenth century was twofold: to move people and agricultural staples. Cotton and foodstuffs dominated the oceanic trade, while foodstuffs and manufactured items constituted the canal and Great Lakes trade. The southern railroad system,

21. Diane Lindstrom, *Economic Development in the Philadelphia Region, 1810–1850* (New York, 1978), 14; Taylor, *Transportation Revolution*, 137–41.

22. See Lindstrom, *Economic Development in the Philadelphia Region*, chaps. 4, 5; Taylor, *Transportation Revolution*, 211–15; Watson, *Liberty and Power*, 17–31; Paul W. Gates, *The Farmer's Age: Agriculture, 1815–1860* (New York, 1960), 416.

23. On the role of the West Indies, see Gary M. Walton and James F. Shepherd, *The Economic Rise of Early America* (Cambridge, Eng., 1979), 79–83.

about one-third of the nation's total mileage in 1860, was designed to move inland cotton to port cities. The Ohio–Mississippi River system transported agricultural produce. The massive extension of eastern railroads to the Great Lakes region was motivated by the desire to capture the abundant cereal crops of that area.

But in breaking down the transportation barriers to a full market economy, the transportation revolution reshuffled agricultural activities in the United States. As the Great Lakes states rose in population, the staples of wheat, corn, and wool poured to the east coast via the new trade arteries. Great Lakes farmers were well-served by the new techniques of transportation, and they earned a respectable if not an outstanding return on their labors.[24] While Great Lakes farmers won, eastern farmers had to undergo severe adjustments. Except for a few localities in New York and Pennsylvania, cereal crop farming was no longer profitable because of western competition made possible by transportation improvements. Eastern farms became smaller and focused on dairying, truck gardens, and orchards.[25] Easterners adjusted to western competition in part by simply giving up; a massive migration of New Englanders, New Yorkers, and Pennsylvanians accounted for much of the population gain in the Great Lakes area. Southern states did not undergo such trauma. Cotton really was king in the antebellum period, and the height of cotton's reign was the 1850s. Moreover, transportation networks were not yet complete in the South, resulting in the preservation of semicommercial areas that did not feel the heat of agricultural competition.[26]

24. Atack and Bateman, *To Their Own Soil,* 95–96, 201–203, 250–61.

25. On the role of western competition and its impact on eastern farmers, see Danhof, *Change in Agriculture,* 14–23; Richard A. Easterlin, "Farm Production and Income in Old and New Areas at Mid-Century," in *Essays on Nineteenth Century Economic History: The Old Northwest,* ed. David C. Klingaman and Richard K. Vedder (Athens, Ohio, 1975), 86–87; Stevenson Whitcomb Fletcher, *Pennsylvania Agriculture and Country Life, 1840–1940* (Harrisburg, Pa., 1955), II, 1, 4–5, 30–33, 41, 98–99, 139–41, 169, 317, 331–32, 364; Philip L. White, *Beekmantown, New York: Forest Frontier to Farm Community* (Austin, 1979), 45, 53–56, 69–79; Harold Fisher Wilson, *The Hill Country of Northern New England: Its Social and Economic History, 1790–1830* (New York, 1936), viii–ix, 29–53; Neil Adams McNall, *An Agricultural History of the Genesee Valley, 1790–1860* (Philadelphia, 1952), 147–54; Hal S. Barron, *Those Who Stayed Behind: Rural Society in Nineteenth-Century New England* (Cambridge, Mass., 1984), 21–23, 26–41.

26. Atack and Bateman, *To Their Own Soil,* 76–77; Fletcher, *Pennsylvania Agriculture and Country Life,* II, 4–5, 365; William N. Parker, "From Northwest to Midwest: Social Bases of a Regional History," in *Essays in Nineteenth Century Economic History: The Old Northwest,* ed. David C. Klingaman and Richard K. Vedder (Athens, Ohio, 1975), 6, 12; White, *Beekmantown, New York,* 70; Wilson, *Hill Country of Northern New England,* 48, 56–64; Hahn, *Roots*

The new commercial agriculture introduced society to a feature that had not been especially present in its semicommercial, self-sufficient condition. Suddenly, winners and losers appeared and, of course, the broad spectrum in between. But in a semicommercial society, winning had distinct limits unless someone resorted to physical force, as was the case with feudalism, or if some suffered from natural catastrophe. Because efficiency in production was not the great denominator of social and material worth, an inefficient individual could likely take fairly good care of him or herself and the family unit in the self-sufficient community. In a commercial situation, however, the efficient could reap far greater rewards—and the inefficient could lose everything.

American farmers experienced some strains in adapting to a market economy. They had to make the best use of the resources at their disposal. The number of available seeds multiplied; the different breeds of pigs and cattle increased; farmers had to pay attention to market reports and plan rationally how much of what crop to plant. To keep abreast of competitors, farmers had to purchase new equipment allowing them to cultivate more acres with less labor. They also faced the indebtedness of farm mortgages to obtain credit to engage in commercial agriculture. They had to depend on purchasing goods for hearth and home instead of making such items themselves. The market economy introduced more rationality and foresight than was required in the semicommercial agricultural locality.[27]

Yet agriculturalists both north and south seemed not to have been rocked by the emergence of the market economy. Adaptation was slow and deliberate, and many historians of eastern agriculture point to the 1870s and 1880s as the periods of greatest stress for farmers.[28] Outside of the Grangers, the

of Southern Populism, 139–52; Robert William Fogel, *Without Consent or Contract: The Rise and Fall of American Slavery* (New York, 1989), 64–72; Lacy K. Ford, "Rednecks and Merchants: Economic Development and Social Tensions in the South Carolina Upcountry, 1865–1900," *Journal of American History,* LXXI (1984), 294–318; Ulrich Bonnell Phillips, *A History of Transportation in the Eastern Cotton Belt to 1860* (New York, 1908), 1–9, 20, 390–95; North, *Economic Growth of the United States,* 66–74, 122–34.

27. The best description of these changes remains Danhof, *Change in Agriculture,* 130–51 and chaps. 7–10. For a description of the terrors of a market economy, see Robert A. Gross, "Culture and Cultivation: Agriculture and Society in Thoreau's Concord," *Journal of American History,* LXIX (1982), 42–61.

28. For reactions of farmers to market conditions, consult Barron, *Those Who Stayed Behind,* chap. 4; Barron, "Listening to the Silent Majority: Change and Continuity in the Nineteenth-Century Rural North," in *Agriculture and National Development: Views on the*

antirenters in New York, and to some extent the Know-Nothings, few political protest movements appeared between 1830 and 1880 to act on the plight of distressed agrarians. American farmers seemingly eased from a semi-commercial economy to a full market economy with a minimum of turbulence.[29]

Avoidance of social unrest and political protest in reaction to the change from an economy filled with self-sufficient units to one characterized by market competition resulted from one condition: the existence of western land. The normal pattern for nations undergoing such an alteration in their economies is that efficiencies in agriculture render some of the rural population redundant. Forced off the land, the dispossessed of the countryside migrate to towns and cities for wretched living conditions and wretched wages, forming a volatile pool of discontentment, sullenly resenting the loss of a lifestyle, the disorientation of urban living, and the squalid conditions of a swollen labor market.[30] This potential phalanx of dispossessed did not appear in the United States in the nineteenth century. The essential reason was west-

Nineteenth Century, ed. Lou Ferleger (Ames, Ia., 1990), 8–16; Christopher Clark, *The Roots of Rural Capitalism: Western Massachusetts, 1780–1860* (Ithaca, N.Y., 1990), 195–204, 224–27, 273–313; Paul S. Taylor and Anne Loftis, "The Legacy of the Nineteenth-Century New England Farmer," *New England Quarterly,* LIV (1981), 244–52; Wilson, *Hill Country of Northern New England,* 87–108; Fletcher, *Pennsylvania Agriculture and Country Life,* II, 3–5, 28, 33, 39; Yasuo Okada, "The Economic World of a Seneca County Farmer, 1830–1880," *New York History,* LXVI (1985), 6–19; Danhof, *Change in Agriculture,* 134, 212, 279; Nancy Grey Osterud, *Bonds of Community: The Lives of Farm Women in Nineteenth-Century New York* (Ithaca, N.Y., 1991), 31–39.

29. See, for example, James L. Huston, "Economic Change and Political Realignment in Antebellum Pennsylvania," *Pennsylvania Magazine of History and Biography,* CXIII (1989), 347–95.

30. The obvious example is England in the eighteenth and nineteenth centuries. See J. L. Hammond and Barbara Hammond, *The Village Labourer, 1760–1832: A Study in the Government of England Before the Reform Bill* (1913; rpr. New York, 1967), chaps. 1–6; Peter Mathias, *The First Industrial Nation: An Economic History of Britain, 1700–1914* (2nd ed.; London, 1983), 53–66; Paul Mantoux, *The Industrial Revolution in the Eighteenth Century: An Outline of the Beginnings of the Modern Factory System in England,* trans. Marjorie Vernon (2nd ed.; New York, 1927), 156–90. The current analytical approach is termed proto-industrialization, but it still relies on the same economic mechanism of agricultural efficiencies displacing customary agricultural workers or peasants. For an application of proto-industrialization to the United States, see James A. Henretta, *The Origins of American Capitalism: Collected Essays* (Boston, 1991), 209–11, and generally 203–55. A literature exists which casts doubt that alterations in agriculture displaced workers who then became prey for industrialists; for example, Phyllis Deane, *The First Industrial Revolution* (2nd ed.; Cambridge, Eng., 1979), 45–46, 146–49. But

ward migration of farmers. When the national market took shape, huge numbers of eastern farmers migrated west. There they recommenced farming, but this time as commercial farmers, not self-sufficient ones. This massive migration spared the East from social tumult. Many eastern farmers would have had to leave the land and go penniless to the cities to beg for work had it not been for the West. Urban America had enough problems without the potential catastrophe of adding from 25 to 50 percent of the region's farmers to city populations. Migration eased the transition and permitted farmers to adapt to a commercial agriculture. Few inflammatory outbursts of agrarian agony, save those of the Grangers, rocked the North between 1830 and 1880.[31]

But such a cry did arise in the trans-Mississippi West and in the South in the 1880s and 1890s—the cry of populism. By the 1870s, commerce finally penetrated the South's isolated, self-sufficient agricultural districts.[32] Western farmers, already commercial farmers, found themselves on the losing end of the competitive stick, facing competition in world markets from

see N. F. R. Crafts, "Income Elasticities of Demand and the Release of Labor by Agriculture During the British Industrial Revolution: A Further Appraisal," in *The Economics of the Industrial Revolution,* ed. Joel Mokyr (Totowa, N.J., 1985), 151–64.

31. On agricultural migration, see Atack and Bateman, *To Their Own Soil,* 76–77; Richard K. Vedder and Lowell E. Gallaway, "Migration and the Old Northwest," in *Essays in Nineteenth Century Economic History: The Old Northwest,* ed. David C. Klingaman and Richard K. Vedder (Athens, Ohio, 1975), 160–69; Thomas Dublin, "Rural-Urban Migrants in Industrial New England: The Case of Lynn, Massachusetts, in the Mid-Nineteenth Century," *Journal of American History,* LXXIII (1986), 623–44; Laurence Glasco, "Migration and Adjustment in the Nineteenth-Century City: Occupation, Property, and Household Structure of Native-Born Whites, Buffalo, New York, 1855," in *Family and Population in Nineteenth-Century America,* ed. Tamara K. Hareven and Maris A. Vinovskis (Princeton, 1978), 154–78; Richard A. Easterlin, George Alter, and Gretchen A. Condran, "Farm Families in Old and New Areas: The Northern States in 1860," *ibid.,* 42; John Modell, "The Peopling of a Working-Class Ward: Reading, Pennsylvania, 1850," *Journal of Social History,* V (1971), 71–95; Donald H. Parkerson, "The Structure of New York Society: Basic Themes in Nineteenth-Century Social History," *New York History,* LXV (1984), 159–87; Kulikoff, *Agrarian Origins of American Capitalism,* 187, 209–15; Kathleen Neils Conzen, "Immigrants in Nineteenth-Century Agricultural History," in *Agriculture and National Development: Views on the Nineteenth Century,* ed. Lou Ferleger (Ames, Ia., 1990), 304–306; Richard H. Steckel, "Household Migration and Rural Settlement in the United States, 1850–1860," *Explorations in Economic History,* XXVI (1989), 191–99, 212.

32. Hahn, *Roots of Southern Populism,* chaps. 4, 7; Wayne K. Durrill, "Producing Poverty: Local Government and Economic Development in a New South County, 1874–1884," *Journal of American History,* LXXI (1985), 764–81.

Australia, Canada, and Russia. And now southerners and westerners had no fecund West to remove to. In the 1890s, farmers could not escape the grindstone of competition by simply moving to better land. The West had closed.

Frederick Jackson Turner had been right in one respect. The West had been a safety valve for social and economic discontent. It operated most conspicuously in the period from 1840 to 1860, when hundreds of thousands of eastern farmers gave up the East to resettle in the Great Lakes area. Turner had been wrong, however, in pointing to the working class as the chief beneficiaries of cheap western lands.[33] Rather, farmers obtained the greatest advantage from the public domain, for it enabled them to escape the potential, and to some extent inevitable, results of commercialization: the efficient would be rewarded, and the inefficient would be ruined. The situation rewarded urban workers only in the sense that western lands prevented masses of displaced agrarians from overwhelming urban labor markets and plunging the wage rate to abysmal depths.

What has claimed the attention and the literary prowess of historians has been the advent of industrialization in the United States between 1820 and 1860—the arrival of machines, factories, a new industrial elite, and an immiserated working class. American industrialization, however, had peculiar qualities. First, the progress of industrialization was hardly breathtaking. In capital invested, people employed, the number of workers per establishment, and percentage share of either national wealth or national capital, manufacturing did not exhibit any drastic shifts until the 1880s or 1890s (see Tables 2 and 3). Moreover, throughout the Age of the American Revolution, most laborers retained a skill component that gave them a claim to "republican independence," and they resided in small shops in small communities. In 1860, much of American industry was primitive, and its totals were inflated by numbers of artisans working in rural communities. Several industries did exhibit the traits that characterized the standard interpretation of the industrial revolution—but particularly in 1860, and as well in 1870 and 1880, they were enormously atypical.[34]

33. For example, Fred A. Shannon, "A Post Mortem on the Labor-Safety-Valve Theory," *Agricultural History*, XIX (1945), 31–38; George Rogers Taylor, ed., *The Turner Thesis Concerning the Role of the Frontier in American History* (rev. ed.; Boston, 1956).

34. This is a standard interpretation of business structure. In his text on small business in the United States, Mansel G. Blackford titled his first chapter "The Traditional Business System: Small Firms Before 1880"; see Blackford, *A History of Small Business in America* (New

Manufacturing in the nineteenth century displayed enormous variations. The textile mills were the most technologically sophisticated, and
important advances were made in integrated iron-making and later in steel
production. Likewise, the toolmakers of the federal armories helped to
advance the use of interchangeable parts. Yet steam engines, the power
source of industrialization, were used primarily on steamboats and railroads, not in factories. As late as 1869, the majority of power for the nation's factories came from waterfalls. Most American shops had a low capi-
talization, indicating a greater reliance on labor and human skill than on
machinery. Indeed, one of the most sophisticated areas of American manufacturing, well into the 1870s, was the manufacture of wooden products
such as clocks. Few companies organized along corporate lines. The corporate form of doing business was relegated principally to banks, large commercial carriers (railroads and canals), eleemosynary organizations, and
textile companies. Proprietorships and partnerships ran America's industrial plant.[35]

One of the most telling features of American manufacturing shops was
the size of workforce per establishment. It appears that expansion of work-

---

York, 1991), chap. 1, and pp. 4–11. The persistence of skill is given in the excellent case study by
John K. Brown, *The Baldwin Locomotive Works, 1831–1915* (Baltimore, 1995), 127–45. See also
Licht, *Industrializing America*, 21–44.

35. Nathan Rosenberg, *Technology and American Economic Growth* (New York, 1972), 90–
101, 27–31, 64–72; David A. Hounshell, *From the American System to Mass Production, 1800–
1932: The Development of Manufacturing Technology in the United States* (Baltimore, 1984),
3–8, 20–21, 107, 122; Peter Temin, *Iron and Steel in Nineteenth-Century America: An Economic
Inquiry* (Cambridge, Mass., 1964), 83–117; David Montgomery, *Beyond Equality: Labor and
the Radical Republicans, 1862–1872* (New York, 1967), 4, 8; Joseph G. Rayback, *A History of
American Labor* (2nd ed.; New York, 1966), 51–52; Parker, *Commerce, Cotton, and Westward
Expansion,* 46–55; James Willard Hurst, *The Legitimacy of the Business Corporation in the Law
of the United States, 1780–1970* (Charlottesville, 1970), 13, 22–25; George Heberton Evans, Jr.,
Business Incorporations in the United States, 1800–1943 (New York, 1948), 10, 21–31; John W.
Cadman, Jr., *The Corporation in New Jersey: Business and Politics, 1791–1875* (Cambridge,
Mass., 1949), 97, 160–74; Edwin Merrick Dodd, *American Business Corporations Until 1860
with Special Reference to Massachusetts* (Cambridge, Mass., 1954), 11, 123; Ronald E. Seavoy, *The
Origins of the American Business Corporation, 1784–1855: Broadening the Concept of Public Ser-
vice During Industrialization* (Westport, Conn., 1982), 212–14, 258–72; Lawrence M. Lipin,
*Producers, Proletarians, and Politicians: Workers and Party Politics in Evansville and New Al-
bany, Indiana, 1850–87* (Urbana, 1994), 10–11, 15–23, 31–33; Brown, *Baldwin Locomotive Works,*
17–22.

force per business unit occurred principally between 1815 and 1830 and then slowly increased for the rest of the century. From the time of the Revolution to 1815, the typical business enterprise consisted of the master, a journeyman, and perhaps one or two apprentices. A large shop was evidently considered to be ten or more people. Commercial expansion enabled the firm size to grow to about ten individuals per shop between 1840 and 1870. In this transition, Americans lost the old master-journeyman relationship and the artisanal mobility that had once been a chief characteristic of the hand trades.[36]

Many Americans recognized that the expansion of commerce had increased the size of the manufacturing firm in the United States. Free trade economist George Tucker, evidently accepting Adam Smith's postulate that an increase in the size of the market resulted in a deeper division of labor and larger companies, argued that large-scale enterprise was inevitable. Others early in the century thought that an overabundance of small firms was wasteful. The compiler of Philadelphia industrial establishments, Edwin T. Freedley, perhaps demonstrated the odd middle ground many political economists and literate Americans were taking. Freedley had no hesitation in proclaiming the larger firm a salutary economic evolution, and he welcomed the effects of managed labor and the further division of labor. He also postulated a limit to size. Some, not all, enterprises would grow into "moderately large establishments" but would not displace smaller ones or deskill the worker. Mid-century Americans saw growth in the size of business units; they did not see giganticism.[37]

36. Philip S. Foner, *Labor and the American Revolution* (Westport, Conn., 1976), 3–5; Sean Wilentz, *Chants Democratic: New York City and the Rise of the American Working Class, 1788–1850* (New York, 1984), 27–33, 112–15, 388; Charles G. Steffen, *The Mechanics of Baltimore: Workers and Politics in the Age of Revolution, 1763–1812* (Urbana, 1984), 30–36; Howard B. Rock, *Artisans of the New Republic: The Tradesmen of New York City in the Age of Jefferson* (New York, 1979), 131–32; Montgomery, *Beyond Equality*, 8–15; David Brody, "Labor and Small-Scale Enterprise During Industrialization," in *Small Business in American Life*, ed. Stuart W. Bruchey (New York, 1980), 264–65; Steven J. Ross, *Workers on the Edge: Work, Leisure, and Politics in Industrializing Cincinnati, 1788–1890* (New York, 1985), 6–8; W. J. Rorabaugh, *The Craft Apprentice: From Franklin to the Machine Age in America* (New York, 1986), chap. 3 and passim.

37. George Tucker, *Political Economy for the People* (1859; rpr. Philadelphia, 1970), 94, 110–17; Joseph Holdich, *Political Economy Simplified: A Lecture, Delivered Before the Young Men's Lyceum of the City of Middleton, Conn.* (Middleton, Conn., 1838), 17–20; Edwin T. Freedley,

Certain enterprises concentrated workers more than others. In the United States at mid-century, textile manufacturing was the most advanced and the largest type of manufacturing enterprise. The average textile plant in 1860 employed about 130 individuals. But the textile industry was almost bimodal. The large textile plants were incorporated ones in Massachusetts and employed workforces ranging from 500 to over 1,000 people. Samuel Slater, in contrast, established his cotton textile plants with a far smaller workforce, anywhere from 60 to 150. Around Philadelphia a handicraft industry in textiles arose that exhibited even smaller firms, used traditional craft means of production, and persisted until the end of the century.[38]

Iron making was another activity in which a considerable number of employees were brought together in one company. By 1849, western Pennsylvania rolling mills averaged an employment of 131 persons, whereas in the eastern part of the state the average was 65. The number of employees per firm increased substantially between 1869 and 1879, from an average of 119 for steelworks and rolling mills in the former year to an average of 220 in the latter year and 332 in 1889.[39]

Nonetheless, there is little indication that production processes, once they had been altered in the 1820s and 1830s, made any new metamorphoses until the 1880s and 1890s. Iron and steel, except for the integrated mill starting in the 1850s, had run on traditional skills used in the eighteenth century. Textiles did not innovate much after 1840. And the rest of the economy

---

Philadelphia and Its Manufactures: A Hand-Book Exhibiting the Development, Variety, and Statistics of the Manufacturing Industry of Philadelphia in 1857 (Philadelphia, 1858), 27–44, quote on 43.

38. The figure for average number of textile employees is from Fogel, *Without Consent or Contract,* 24; see Melvin Thomas Copeland, *The Cotton Manufacturing Industry of the United States* (Cambridge, Mass., 1912), 7, 11; Barbara M. Tucker, *Samuel Slater and the Origins of the American Textile Industry, 1790–1860* (Ithaca, N.Y., 1984), chaps. 3, 4; Robert F. Dalzell, Jr., "The Rise of the Waltham-Lowell System and Some Thoughts on the Political Economy of Modernization in Ante-Bellum Massachusetts," *Perspectives in American History,* IX (1975), 229–30, 233; Philip B. Scranton, *Proprietary Capitalism: The Textile Manufacture at Philadelphia, 1800–1885* (Cambridge, Eng., 1984), chap. 2, and pp. 36–71, 83, 136–42, 180–81, 319–23, 344; Peter J. Coleman, *The Transformation of Rhode Island, 1790–1860* (Providence, 1963), 91, 98, 129; Jonathan Prude, *The Coming of Industrial Order: Town and Factory Life in Rural Massachusetts, 1810–1860* (Cambridge, Mass., 1983), xiv–xvi, 84–87. See "The Manufactures of the United States," *De Bow's Review,* XVI (1854), 188–91.

39. Temin, *Iron and Steel in Nineteenth-Century America,* Tables 5.1 and 7.1, pp. 108, 166.

was small-scale. In 1860, the pork-packing companies averaged only eight hands per establishment, breweries were local undertakings, and flour milling averaged only two workers per mill. From furniture making to coal mining to shoe and boot manufacturing, the nation's economy teemed with small companies with few employees fighting for a share of the national income.[40]

A list of the largest manufacturers in the United States *ca.* 1868 shows how few firms had achieved a size of five hundred or more employees. Large-scale enterprise was dominated by textile and iron-making firms (see Table 6). Although compilations are evidently not available, enough information exists to construct a listing of large firms in England up to 1841 (see Table 7). A comparison of the two tables demonstrates that even by the 1860s the English firms were generally larger than their American counterparts. But perhaps as interesting is that English industrialization was born big whereas American industrialization was born little. Part of the difference between the initial reactions of American workers to industrialization compared to the British

---

40. Dalzell, "Rise of the Waltham-Lowell System," 243–44; Paul F. Paskoff, *Industrial Evolution: Organization, Structure, and Growth of the Pennsylvania Iron Industry, 1750–1860* (Baltimore, 1983), chaps. 5, 6; Temin, *Iron and Steel in Nineteenth-Century America*, 83–98; Margaret Walsh, *The Rise of the Midwestern Meat Packing Industry* (Lexington, Ky., 1982), Table 2, p. 3; John P. Arnold and Frank Penman, *History of the Brewing Industry and Brewing Science in America* (Chicago, 1933), 61–62; Thomas C. Cochran, *The Pabst Brewing Company: The History of an American Business* (New York, 1948), 29; Clifton K. Yearley, Jr., *Enterprise and Anthracite: Economics and Democracy in Schuylkill County, 1820–1875* (Baltimore, 1961), 36–38; Lyman Horace Weeks, *A History of Paper-Manufacturing in the United States, 1690–1916* (New York, 1916), 240–41; Herman Steen, *Flour Milling in America* (Minneapolis, 1963), 36–38; Charles Byron Kuhlmann, *The Development of the Flour-Milling Industry in the United States, with Special Reference to the Industry in Minneapolis* (Boston, 1929), 65; John W. McGrain, "'Good Bye Old Burr': The Roller Mill Revolution in Maryland, 1882," *Maryland Historical Magazine*, LXXVII (1982), 154–71; Alan Dawley, *Class and Community: The Industrial Revolution in Lynn* (Cambridge, Mass., 1976), 28–29; Harold B. Hancock, "Delaware Furnituremaking, 1850–1870: Transition to the Machine Age," *Delaware History*, XVII (1977), 250–94; Brian Greenberg, *Worker and Community: Response to Industrialization in a Nineteenth-Century American City, Albany, New York, 1850–1884* (Albany, 1985), 9–16; Richard B. Stott, *Workers in the Metropolis: Class, Ethnicity, and Youth in Antebellum New York City* (Ithaca, N.Y., 1990), 31, 36–66; Ross, *Workers on the Edge*, 80–82, Tables 9.1 and 9.2, pp. 221–22; Clifford S. Griffin and Sally Griffin, "Small Business and Occupational Mobility in Mid-Nineteenth-Century Poughkeepsie," in *Small Business in American Life*, ed. Stuart W. Bruchey (New York, 1980), 124.

Table 6
American Industrial Enterprises with 500 or More Employees, 1867–1868, in Descending Order by Size

Worcester, Mass. 2 cotton firms employing 6,315; average	3,158
Amoskeag, Manchester, N.H.	3,000
Montour Iron Works, Danville, Pa.	3,000
Pacific Mills, Lawrence, Mass.	3,000
Benjamin Bullock's Sons Factory, Conshohocken, Pa.	3,000
Washington Mills, Lawrence, Mass.	2,300
Merrimack Manufacturing Co., Lowell, Mass.	2,120
Reading Iron Works, Reading, Pa.	2,000
Trenton Iron Co., Trenton, N.J.	2,000
Cambria Iron Works, Johnstown, Pa.	1,948
Massachusetts Cotton Mills, Lowell, Mass.	1,700
Werts, Bradly, and Cary's Hoop Skirt Works, New York City	1,600–2,000
Lawrence Manufacturing Co., Lawrence, Mass.	1,650
Pepperell Textile Mill (ca. 1870), Biddeford, Maine	1,600
Troy Iron and Nail Factory, Troy, N.Y.	1,500
Lowell Manufacturing Co., Lowell, Mass.	1,450
Boott Cotton Mills, Lowell, Mass.	1,310
Hamilton Manufactory Co., Lowell, Mass.	1,275
Norris Locomotive Works, Philadelphia	1,000–1,500
Phoenix Iron Works	1,230
Chicopee, Mass. 2 mills, 2,450 workers; average	1,225
Atlantic Cotton Mills, Lawrence, Mass.	1,200
Clark Thread Co., Newark, N.J.	1,000–1,200
Etna Iron Works, New York City	900–1,500
Delmater Iron Works, New York City	1,000–1,200
Wamsutta Mills, New Bedford, Mass.	1,050
Allair Works, New York City	1,000
Androscoggin Mills, Lewistown, Maine	1,000
Novelty Iron Works, New York City	1,000
Hayward Bartlett and Co. Foundry & Locomotive Works, Baltimore	*ca.* 1,000
Rogers Locomotive and Machine Works, Paterson, N.J.	1,000
Morgan Iron Works, New York City	900
Lowell Machine Shop, Lowell, Mass.	900
Suffolk Manufacturing Co., Lowell, Mass.	900

TABLE 6 (cont.)

Tremont Mills, Lowell, Mass.	872
Philadelphia. 1 cotton mill	850
Middlesex Company, Lowell, Mass.	772
Corning, Winslow & Co., Troy, N.Y.	750
Danforth Locomotive and Machine Shops, Paterson, N.J.	700
Brooklyn. 2 hat manufacturers employing 1,377; average	689
E. Remington & Son's Armory, Rochester, N.Y.	600–700
Washburn Iron Works, Worcester, Mass.	640
Ripka Mills, Manayunk, Pa.	600
Bridgewater Iron Company, Bridgewater, Conn.	600
Baldwin and Co., Philadelphia	600
City Point Works, Boston	500–700
Globe Works, Boston	600
American Screw Co., Providence	600
Howe Sewing Machine Manufacturer, Bridgeport, Conn.	550
Mitchell and Ranmelsberg's Furniture Manufactory, Cincinnati	500–600
Appleton Company, Lowell, Mass.	520
Philadelphia. 1 cotton mill	513
Schenectady Locomotive Works, Schenectady, N.Y.	500
Chickering and Son's Piano-Forte Manufactory, Boston	500
Lamson and Goodnow's Cutlery Works, Holyoke, Mass.	500
Nashua, N.H. 3 companies totaling 1,500; average	500
Waring Manufacturing Co., Yonkers, N.Y.	500

Unknown but probably over 500 employees:

    Thomas Iron Co., Allentown, Pa.

    Lehigh Crane, Allentown, Pa.

    Lackawanna Iron and Coal, Scranton, Pa.

    Freedom Iron Company, Lewistown, Pa.

    Samsondale Iron Works, Haverstraw, N.Y.

Sources: Temin, *Iron and Steel in Nineteenth-Century America,* 109; Freedley, *Philadelphia and Its Manufactures,* 250, 309; Montgomery, *Beyond Equality,* 12–13; J. Leander Bishop, *A History of American Manufactures from 1608 to 1860* (3rd ed.; 1868; rpr. New York, 1967), III, 316, 49–50, 211, 314, 253, 316, 218, 336, 125, 128, 130, 132, 135, 224, 314, 251, 213, 226, 261, 50, 283, 257, 285, 435, 340, 465, 451, 347, 213, 314, 231. Bishop often failed to provide the number of employees for the firms enumerated, and thus the table can make no claims to inclusiveness.

TABLE 7
SELECTED LARGE FIRMS IN ENGLAND, 1750–1841,
IN DESCENDING ORDER BY SIZE

Year	Firm Name	Number of Employees
1830	Cyfarthfn (Wales)	5,000
1830	Dowlais	5,000
1825	Grout, Baylis & Co. (7 different works)	3,900
1779	Carron Ironworks	2,000
1814	Samuel Fereday of Bradly	1,500
1814	Butterly	1,500
1765	John Sherrard, silk-throwster	1,500
1842	British Iron Co.	1,400
1833	John Marshall	1,317
1824	Gospel Oak; mines	1,300
1814	Smith of Chesterfield (several places)	1,200
1833	Leys, Masson & Co.	1,152
1829	Benjamin Gott	1,120
1795	Bradly and Co. New Mills	1,000
1799	Parker, Brookhouse, & Crampton	500–1,000
1725–50	Ambrose Crowley, iron	1,000
1776	Coalbrookdale	1,000
1840	Charles Tennant	1,000
1765	Spragg, Hopkins & White	800
1833	S. Pearson	800
1833	John Heathcote	800
1803	Robert Peel and Partners, 20 mills; average	750
1761	Philip Clowes	720
1841	William Chance	700
?	Shropshire	700
1833	T. A. Mulholland	660
1833	T W Stansfield	610
1833	Clark's Market Harborough	600
1830s	Norfolk, 4 silk factories; each averaging	568
1833	Pim, Nevins & Son	552

TABLE 7 (cont.)

Year	Firm Name	Number of Employees
1833	James Akroyd	550
1833	John Wood	527
1833	Matraneu & Overby	500–550
1755	Birmingham	500
1833	Mill, Cruden & Co.	500
1830s	Manchester. 30 mills employing over 500 workers each	500
1765	John Graham	500
1833	William H. Sheppard	500
1833	William Hardisty	500
1833	J. W. Partridge	500
1833	Wilson & Co.	500
1790	Wedgewood	150–160

Sources: Stanley D. Chapman, *The Early Factory Masters: The Transition to the Factory System in the Midland Textile Industry* (Plymouth, Eng., 1967), 40, 91, 116, 133–34; Sidney Pollard, *The Genesis of Modern Management: A Study of the Industrial Revolution in Great Britain* (Cambridge, Mass., 1965), 12–17, 20–23, 48–55, 62–63, 70–71, 78–83, 90–101.

may have been one of scale; Americans did not have to adjust to a factory the same way the British did.[41]

Size of plant in the nineteenth century probably said much about the extent to which workers had lost craft skills. The process of "deskilling" resulting from mechanization of labor routines was a powerful creator of dis-

41. See Peter Temin, "Product Quality and Vertical Integration in the Early Cotton Textile Industry," *Journal of Economic History,* XLVIII (1988), 891–907; V. A. C. Gatrell, "Labour, Power, and the Size of Firms in Lancashire Cotton in the Second Quarter of the Nineteenth Century," *Economic History Review,* XXX (1977), 96–99; Sidney Pollard, *The Genesis of Modern Management: A Study of the Industrial Revolution in Great Britain* (Cambridge, Mass., 1965), 10. Comparisons between Great Britain and the United States are difficult to make. Based on the census of 1851, Peter Mathias reports (taken from an earlier work by G. N. Clark) that 755 firms had one hundred or more employees, 411 of them were cotton manufacturers; however, Britain was very much a land of small workshops. In 1871, 15 percent of the English

content. American workers seemed for a variety of reasons to have escaped the worst of the initial impact of industrialization on craft skills. First, as re-flected in the capital invested per establishment, American plants did not have the machinery to displace workers' skills. Second, the displacement in the first three-quarters of the century was borne by women. It is a revelation to recognize that the early machines most harshly affected women workers. Female labor was used extensively in the textile industry; the displacement of male labor by machines was avoided. Machines endangered male jobs only later in the century.[42]

The continuing importance of skill in American manufacturing can be gleaned from Tables 8 through 10. It is clear that American manufacturing was based on skilled or semiskilled craftsmen. The categories that indicate workers coping with mindless machine-tending tasks such as factory laborer and operative pale before the number of carpenters, coopers, bricklayers, ma-sons, wheelwrights, and other such occupations.[43]

Finally, the extent of industrialization must be questioned, for all the cen-sus totals include individuals who clearly were not participating in the pro-cess of industrialization. Numerous manufacturers grew to serve the national

---

were engaged in agriculture, 43 percent in industry, 20 percent in transportation and trade, and 22 percent in the professions and public service. For comparison (from Table 2), in 1870, 51.3 percent of Americans were employed in agriculture, 21.6 percent in manufacturing, 12.1 percent in trade and transportation, and 14.8 percent in other categories. See Mathias, *First In-dustrial Nation,* 224, 240, 242–48.

42. Susan Estabrook Kennedy, *If All We Did Was to Weep at Home: A History of White Working-Class Women in America* (Bloomington, 1979), 21–24; Thomas Dublin, *Women at Work: The Transformation of Work and Community in Lowell, Massachusetts, 1826–1860* (New York, 1979), 5–6, 26, 64–69, 193–94; Thomas R. Winpenny, *Industrial Progress and Human Welfare: The Rise of the Factory System in 19th-Century Lancaster* (Washington, D.C., 1982), 54–58; Mary H. Blewett, "Women Shoeworkers and Domestic Ideology: Rural Outwork in Early Nineteenth-Century Essex County," *New England Quarterly,* LX (1987), 403–28; Ray Ginger, "Labor in a Massachusetts Cotton Mill, 1853–60," *Business History Review,* XXVIII (1954), 67–91; Gerda Lerner, "The Lady and the Mill Girl: Changes in the Status of Women in the Age of Jackson, 1800–1840," in *A Heritage of Her Own: Toward a New Social History of Ameri-can Women,* ed. Nancy F. Cott and Elizabeth H. Pleck (New York, 1979), 189–90.

43. But see Susan E. Hirsch, *Roots of the American Working Class: The Industrialization of Crafts in Newark, 1800–1860* (Philadelphia, 1978), chap. 2; Amy Bridges, *A City in the Republic: Antebellum New York and the Origins of Machine Politics* (Cambridge, Eng., 1984), 46–57; Iver Bernstein, *The New York City Draft Riots: Their Significance for American Society and Politics in the Age of the Civil War* (New York, 1990), 77–82. Hirsch presents fairly compelling evidence of the degradation of skill in Newark.

TABLE 8

OCCUPATIONS IN 1850 EMPLOYING 10,000 OR MORE
FREE MALES OVER AGE FIFTEEN

Manufacturing Jobs	No.	Nonmanufacturing Jobs	No.
Laborers	909,786	Farmers	2,363,958
Carpenters	184,671	Clerks	101,325
Cordwainers	130,473	Merchants	100,752
Black and white smiths	99,703	Mariners	70,603
Miners	77,410	Students	42,149
Masons and plasterers	63,392	Physicians	40,564
Tailors	52,069	Boatmen	32,454
Coopers	43,694	Teachers	29,587
Cabinet and chair makers	37,359	Planters	27,055
Weavers	31,872	Clergymen	26,842
Wheelwrights	30,693	Grocers	24,479
Painters and glaziers	28,166	Lawyers	23,939
Millers	27,795	Innkeepers	22,476
Machinists	24,095	Servants	22,243
Saddle and harness makers	22,779	Overseers	18,859
Mechanics, unspecified	16,004	Butchers	17,773
Manufacturers, unspecified	15,091	Traders	14,917
Tanners and cutters	14,988	City, county, and town officers	12,579
Printers	14,740	Engineers	11,626
Ship carpenters	14,585	Peddlers	10,669
Teamsters	14,469	U.S. and state officers	10,268
Bakers	14,256		
Stone and marble cutters	14,075		
Coach makers	14,049		
Cutters	13,879		
Joiners	12,672		
Sawyers	11,974		
Tinsmiths	11,749		
Brickmakers	11,514		
Hemp dressers	11,024		

(cont.)

TABLE 8 (cont.)

Manufacturing Jobs	No.	Nonmanufacturing Jobs	No.
Drivers	10,968		
Factory hands	10,869		
Tobacconists and cigar makers	10,823		
Lumbermen	10,070		
Other	22,159		

Source: James D. B. De Bow, *Statistical View of the United States . . . Being a Compendium of the Seventh Census* (Washington, D.C., 1854), 126–28.

market and sent their products throughout the Union, the obvious examples being boots and shoes, textiles, and iron wares. But the pattern exhibited in the census reports reveals that much of what went under the category of "manufacturing" and the "industrial revolution" was not much more than the attachment of skilled or partially skilled artisans to a local agricultural economy. Obviously, the large manufacturing establishments produced for a national market, but throughout the counties and townships of the United States were individuals only marginally connected to this national market economy, and yet their enumeration swells the manufacturing total and leads to improper conclusions. For example, in the census of 1860, the county of Bedford, Pennsylvania, was obviously agricultural, with only slightly over 5 percent of the population engaged in manufacturing pursuits. The census listed for Bedford County the following numbers of people and establishments engaged in manufacturing (the number of establishments is followed by a slash, then the total number of employees):

agricultural implements	1 / 3	iron castings	2 / 8
blacksmithing	15 / 26	iron stoves	1 / 4
boots and shoes	6 / 11	pig iron	2 / 92
carpentering	1 / 2	leather	14 / 38
carriages	7 / 20	distilled liquors	1 / 2
cigars	1 / 6	sawed lumber	6 / 6

TABLE 9
OCCUPATIONS IN 1860 EMPLOYING 10,000 OR MORE PEOPLE

Manufacturing Jobs	No.	Nonmanufacturing Jobs	No.
Laborers	969,301	Farmers	2,423,895
Carpenters	242,958	Farm laborers	795,679
Shoemakers	164,608	Servants	559,908
Miners	147,750	Clerks	184,485
Blacksmiths	112,357	Merchants	123,378
Tailors and tailoresses	101,868	Teachers	110,469
Seamstresses	90,198	Planters	85,561
Factory hands	87,289	Mariners	67,360
Apprentices	55,326	Physicians	54,543
Painters and varnishers	51,695	Students	49,993
Masons (brick and stone)	48,925	Grocers	40,070
Machinists	43,824	Laundresses	38,633
Coopers	43,624	Overseers	37,883
Millers	37,281	Clergymen	37,529
Weavers	36,178	Railroadmen	36,567
Mantua makers	35,165	Lawyers	33,193
Teamsters	34,824	Innkeepers	25,818
Wheelwrights	32,693	Officers (public)	24,693
Butchers	30,103	Boatmen	23,816
Cabinetmakers	29,223	Housekeepers	22,393
Civil and mechanical		Fishermen	21,905
engineers	27,437	Gardeners and nurserymen	21,323
Milliners	25,722	Peddlers	16,594
Mechanics	23,492	Agents	16,478
Printers	23,106	Dealers	14,063
Carters	21,640	Barkeepers	13,263
Tobacconists	21,413	Boardinghouse keepers	12,148
Stone and marble cutters	19,825	Traders	11,195
Drivers	19,521	Barbers	11,140
Coach makers	19,180	Druggists	11,031

(cont.)

TABLE 9 (cont.)

Manufacturing Jobs	No.	Nonmanufacturing Jobs	No.
Bakers	19,001		
Tinsmiths	17,412		
Molders	17,077		
Lumbermen	15,929		
Sawyers	15,000		
Bricklayers	13,736		
Ship carpenters	13,392		
Plasterers	13,116		
Refectory keepers	13,054		
Saddlers	12,756		
Harness makers	12,728		
Hatters	11,647		
Manufacturers	11,283		
Jewelers	10,175		
Other occupations	62,872		

Source: Eighth Census, I, 656–79.

men's clothing	1 / 3	machinery	1 / 18
hulling clover	1 / 1	pottery ware	1 / 1
bituminous coal	1 / 20	newspaper printing	2 / 6
cooperage	2 / 2	saddlery and harness	3 / 5
cotton coverlets	2 / 2	tin, copper, and sheet iron ware	3 / 5
flour and meal	55 / 71	wagons, carts, and the like	3 / 7
cabinet furniture	3 / 7	wool carding	2 / 6
hats and caps	1 / 2	woolen goods	4 / 20
iron blooms	1 / 10		

The census recorded that the county of Bedford contributed 147 establishments, worth approximately $418,250 in capital, employing 406 males and 3 females, to the national effort in manufacturing.[44] It is doubtful whether

44. *Eighth Census,* III, 496–97; Atack and Bateman, *To Their Own Soil,* 3.

TABLE 10
Occupations in 1870 Employing 20,000 or More People

Manufacturing Jobs	No.	Nonmanufacturing Jobs	No.
Laborers, unspecified	1,031,666	Farmers and planters	2,977,711
Carpenters and joiners	344,596	Agricultural laborers	2,885,996
Boot- and shoemakers	171,127	Servants	975,734
Tailors	161,826	Store clerks	222,534
Miners	152,107	Railroad employees	154,027
Cotton mill workers	111,606	Teachers	126,822
Blacksmiths	111,171	Draymen, hackmen, teamsters	120,756
Milliners, dress and mantua		Traders and dealers	
makers	92,084	(unspecified)	100,406
Masons, brick and stone	89,710	Grocers	74,410
Painters and varnishers	85,123	Physicians	62,383
Woolen mill operatives	58,836	Launderers and laundresses	60,906
Machinists	54,755	Sailors	56,663
Sawmill operatives	47,298	Government officials	44,743
Manufacturers	42,877	Butchers	44,354
Cabinetmakers	42,835	Clergymen	43,874
Carriage and wagon makers	42,464	Lawyers	40,736
Coopers	41,789	Dry goods traders	39,790
Mill and factory workers		Restaurant keepers	35,185
(unspecified)	41,582	Gardeners and nurserymen	31,435
Printers	39,860	Bookkeepers and	
Tinners	39,524	accountants	31,177
Iron foundry workers	34,243	Fishermen and oystermen	27,106
Engineers and firemen	34,233	Hotel and restaurant	
Harness and saddle makers	32,817	employees	26,394
Curriers, tanners, and		Barbers and hairdressers	23,935
leathermen	28,702	Soldiers	22,081
Cigar makers	28,286	Boatmen	21,332
Bakers	27,080		
Brick and tile makers	26,070		

(cont.)

Table 10 (cont.)

Manufacturing Jobs	No.	Nonmanufacturing Jobs	No.
Marble and stone cutters	25,831		
Plasterers	23,577		
Iron and steel workers	22,141		
Wheelwrights	20,942		
Employees of manufacturing companies	20,242		

Source: Ninth Census, I, 674–84.

these numbers reveal anything except that the bulk of these individuals were servicing a local economy.

Small shops and the continued demand for craft skills did not guarantee workers a pleasant existence. Life in antebellum America was increasingly short and brutish. An employer of a small shop might be a saint or a sadist. Craft skills were preserved in many ways, but a constant dilution via outwork was going on. And wages were low, hours were long, and prices for consumer goods were high.[45]

The existence of the small shop as the means of American industrial production is not a matter for idle rumination. That structure of smallness had an effect on the expectations of the population and the social relations governing people's lives. The future was the big business establishment. Table 11 provides the employment figures for the large railroads in 1880. These figures dwarf the statistics for employees of large manufacturing establishments in

45. Fogel, *Without Consent or Contract,* 354–60; Dawley, *Class and Community,* 151–66; Norman Ware, *The Industrial Worker, 1840–1860: The Reaction of American Industrial Society to the Advance of the Industrial Revolution* (1924; rpr. Chicago, 1964), 26–70, 106–24, 130–32; Bruce Laurie, *Artisans into Workers: Labor in Nineteenth Century America* (New York, 1988), 58–61, 64; Christine Stansell, "The Origins of the Sweatshop: Women and Early Industrialization in New York City," in *Working-Class America: Essays on Labor, Community, and American Society,* ed. Michael H. Frisch and Daniel J. Walkowitz (Urbana, 1983), 78–95; Ross, *Workers on the Edge,* 36; Wilentz, *Chants Democratic,* 113–15, 124–29. Bruce Laurie, Theodore Hershberg, and George Alter write that the small shop was becoming less the home of artisanal production and more the site of the metropolitan sweatshop ("Immigrants and Industry: The Philadelphia Experience, 1850–1880," *Journal of Social History,* IX [1975], 219–48).

TABLE 11

EMPLOYMENT BY SELECTED RAILROADS, 1880

Railroad	No. of Employees	No. of Officers and Clerks
Pennsylvania	25,736	661
Baltimore and Ohio	14,330	289
New York, Lake Erie, and Western	13,528	139
New York Central and Hudson River	13,007	157
Chicago, Burlington and Quincy	12,065	522
Philadelphia and Reading	11,226	155
Chicago, Milwaukee, and St. Paul	10,368	456
Lake Shore and Michigan Southern	9,652	151
Chicago and Northwestern	8,405	152
Wabash, St. Louis, and Pacific	7,800	204
Chicago, Rock Island, and Pacific	6,843	87
Central Pacific	6,139	178
Atchison, Topeka, and Santa Fe	5,522	173
Michigan Central	4,909	143
Union Pacific	3,865	94

Source: Tenth Census, IV, 20.

1868 in Table 6. The totals in Table 11 bespeak a different society, different social relations, and different expectations than in the small shop economy.

The severe limitations that applied to American manufacturing in the nineteenth century, however, point up the most obvious fact about how Americans accomplished economic growth: they multiplied the units of enterprise. According to the census figures, there were 105,729 manufacturing firms in 1840; 123,025 in 1850; 140,433 in 1860; 252,148 in 1870; 253,852 in 1880; 355,415 in 1890; and 512,276 in 1900.[46] Over much of the nineteenth century the number of workers per establishment remained fairly stable while the value invested per firm increased substantially (see Table 3). Productivity

46. S. N. D. North, *Abstract of the Twelfth Census of the United States, 1900* (3rd ed.; Washington, D.C., 1904), 300–301. The 1840 figure is from *Tenth Census,* II, vii.

undoubtedly came from infusions of capital, but output grew largely because the number of firms grew. The country expanded horizontally over
the continent; in a sense, the manufacturing economy did the same. Instead
of creating a new organization for work—that is, instead of growing ver-
tically—manufacturing expanded horizontally. Manufacturing establishments simply reproduced themselves in size and abilities and spread out over
more territory. Industrialization in the United States was a continually repet-
itive experience. Innovations in organizational structure awaited the years
1880 to 1900.

In the life span of the commercial agrarian republic, during the Age of the
American Revolution, 1765–1880, agriculture passed from subsistence to
commercial activities without great damage; the existence of western land
absorbed the shock of the change. The major area of activity was building a
national network, which used the capital and labor of the country in unprecedented amounts. During this period there was a steady expansion of industrial output. Some of it came from advanced industries and adoption of a
new technology but most originated in a multiplication of producing units;
the number of enterprises increased, not their size. For the laborer, this meant
that craft skills were preserved. The Age of the American Revolution was the
age of the farmer, the merchant, and the skilled and semiskilled male mechanic. Workers lost a measure of their mobility, their opportunity to create
their own small businesses, but they had not lost the intimacy (or tyranny) of
the small shop and the value placed on their craft skills. The Age of the American Revolution had continuities in its politics, its ideology, and its economic
structure. The years 1765 to 1880 are a unit.

The structural elements of the economy explain the origin and the longevity
of the American theory of the distribution of wealth. The particular way the
economy developed—the continuous multiplication of small units of production—supported and justified various American ideals of mobility, education, nobility of labor, equality of opportunity, equality of condition,
laissez-faire economic policies, and small frugal governments. The widespread and repeated faith in nineteenth-century notions of free labor existed
because a congruence between the ideal and reality existed for a broad spectrum of the American public. Many saw the exceptions to the general rule,
and most understood the limitations of their ideas. Nonetheless, the structure of the economy upheld the general applicability of the ideas that composed the American theory of the distribution of wealth.

From the beginning, the colonies were largely composed of self-sufficient agricultural districts with only a few localities possessing a distinct commercial base. In that economic base were people who understood market calculation, rationality, and rules of trade.[47] The economic story of America from 1765 to 1880 is basically the contraction of those self-sufficient areas and the expansion of the commercial realm until the entire country was engulfed in one nearly frictionless market.

When the walls of the self-sufficient agricultural community began crumbling at the touch of commercial expansion, adjustments took place. First, greater production of agricultural goods was now possible, for a means to transport the surplus now existed. Second, farmers had to choose crops that would bring them the most income. Third, farmers had to decide whether to remain in their present surroundings or to migrate where land might produce more. Fourth, a whole retinue of people had to spring forth to move agricultural products from place to place: merchants, grocers, financiers, clerks, and others. Likewise, the surge in purchasing power of commercial farmers gave manufacturers an expanded market so they could successfully produce, ship, and sell more goods.

Increased economic activity caused by the breakdown of self-sufficient agricultural units into a commercial network had a name: opportunity. Many contemporaries understood precisely what the market expansion was doing to the American economy. William H. Seward witnessed the transformation of western New York as a result of the Erie Canal and then the railroad. His expansive notion of American democracy and equality was based on the commercial, not the industrial, revolution.[48]

Opportunity on such a vast scale turned into a celebration of social mobility. Throughout the period 1825 to 1880, the economy created conditions that enabled individuals to establish their own independent businesses in agricul-

---

47. See Thomas C. Cochran, *Challenges to American Values: Society, Business and Religion* (New York, 1985), 16, 22; Cochran, "The Business Revolution," *American Historical Review,* LXXIX (1974), 1449–66.

48. William H. Seward, "The Physical, Moral, and Intellectual Development of the American People" (1854), in George E. Baker, ed., *The Works of William H. Seward* (2nd ed.; Boston, 1887), IV, 162–70. See also Daniel Webster, "Address Delivered at the Laying of the Corner-stone of the Bunker Hill Monument at Charlestown, Mass., June 17, 1825," in J. W. McIntyre, ed., *The Writing and Speeches of Daniel Webster* (Boston, 1903), I, 239, 247; Webster, speech at Buffalo, 1833, *ibid.,* II, 132; *Bankers' Magazine,* III (1848), 329–30; John S. Jenkins, *James Knox Polk and a History of His Administration* (New Orleans, 1854), 58.

ture, commerce, or manufacturing. The continuous multiplication of small enterprises allowed considerable social mobility in the sense that a person had a reasonable chance to move from dependency (working for another) to independency (owning one's own business). For the bulk of the nineteenth century, except for slavery, railroads, textiles, and some iron companies, increasing returns because of size must have been absent. A large enterprise must have been no more efficient in production of goods or services than a small one. And the principal reason for that condition must have been that machinery had not yet tilted the efficiency factor in favor of the large-scale enterprise.

Determining the extent of self-employment in the nineteenth century is tricky, but we can assume that it was probably fairly widespread. Table 12 provides ratios indicating that individual enterprise was fairly prevalent in the United States. Taking the number of manufacturing firms and the number of

TABLE 12

STATISTICS OF FIRMS AND FARMS
COMPARED WITH NUMBER OF EMPLOYED

| | A. Percent of Change over Decades | | |
Decade	No. of Employed	No. of Farms	No. of Manufacturing Firms and Farms
1850–60	35.0	41.1	39.0
1860–70	30.6	30.1	33.3
1870–80	32.7	50.7	46.4
1880–90	32.7	13.9	15.4
1890–1900	24.7	25.7	27.1

B. Ratio of Firms and Farms to Total Employed

Date	Ratio
1850	.209
1860	.216
1870	.220
1880	.243
1890	.211
1900	.215

TABLE 12 (cont.)

| | C. Ratio of Firms and Farms to Total Employed | | | |
Year	Free Males Age 20+	Free Males Age 30+	All Males Age 20+	All Males Age 30+
1850	.228	.369	.196	.318
1860	.219	.383	.195	.339
1870			.221[a]	.346[b]
1880			.226[a]	.354[b]
1890			.202[a]	.286[b]
1900			.193	.283

[a] Males aged 21 years and older.
[b] Estimate.

Sources: The male labor pool aged thirty and above was estimated by calculating the percentage of the male population aged twenty and above and the male population aged thirty and above in the censuses of 1840, 1850, and 1860. The average was then used to calculate the percentage of males in the age categories for 1870, 1880, and 1890; the census of 1900 provided the necessary information without estimation. The assumption that roughly the same percentage held for the rest of the century is manifestly incorrect because the population started aging after 1870, but the procedure permits crude comparisons. In 1860, the 30+ males were 28.47 percent of the total male population; by 1900, that figure had climbed to 38.35 percent. Population figures taken from U.S. Department of State, *Compendium of the Enumeration of the Inhabitants and Statistics of the United States* [Sixth Census, 1840] (Washington, D.C., 1841), 100–101; *Seventh Census,* xlii–xliv; *Eighth Census,* I, 592–95; *Ninth Census,* I, 606, 619; U.S. Department of Interior, Census Office, *Compendium of the Tenth Census* (2 vols.; Washington, D.C., 1885), I, 2, 560–61; U.S. Department of the Interior, Census Office, *Compendium of the Eleventh Census, 1890* (Washington, D.C., 1892), I, 764, 468; figures for employed taken from Table 10.2. The number of farms was adjusted for tenancy by the figures in Lebergott, *Manpower in Economic Growth,* table A.2, p. 511. The self-owned farming rate in 1880 was .69; in 1890, .67; and in 1900, .64. It was assumed that tenancy was no greater in 1850, 1860, and 1870, and so the .69 figure for 1880 was used for the earlier census years.

farms as an indicator of self-owned enterprises—this, of course, leaves out mercantile and financial firms, which Table 2 and Tables 8–10 show obviously rapid growth—it seems that the decadal increase in the number of firms and farms kept pace with the increase in the number of people employed until the decade 1880–1890 (see Table 12). The ratio of firms and farms to the number of persons employed actually rose from .209 to .243 between 1850 and 1880, then dropped in 1890. If one compares the number of firms and farms to the available male population, one age category being twenty years and older and the other category being thirty years and older, then the ratio for the older males approaches .355. Because information concerning the number of independent merchants, financiers, and other persons involved in mercantile activities could be considered only guesswork (as most of this is anyway), it may be surmised that for most of the nineteenth century, males over age thirty would probably have constituted a considerable number of independent economic actors.

The age criterion is of some importance in trying to ferret out how nineteenth-century Americans viewed their society. The society was heavily weighted toward youth (at the time of the Civil War, the median age was 19.4 years) and life expectancy was short (well under 50 years of age). Americans had no reason to believe youths just entering the labor market would instantly possess their own shops and farms. Youths had to learn a business and accumulate skills and capital before making the jump from dependency to independency. Age thirty seems appropriate for that society to determine how independency was faring in the United States. And throughout most of the century, it seemed to be faring modestly well.[49]

American economic opportunity did not promise paradise, however. Small firms popped into existence and then as suddenly dropped out of sight. Failures were common. In the cities, dependency was a normal condition of everyday life. An average manufacturing shop employed ten workers. Manufacturing had already demonstrated that the days of the artisanal economy— the mobility for apprentices to rise to journeymen and to master craftsmen

---

49. Jonathan R. T. Hughes, *American Economic History* (3rd ed.; Glenview, Ill., 1990), 101; U.S. Bureau of the Census, *Historical Statistics,* Table B 107–115 gives a life expectancy of all males and females at birth at 47.3 years; Fogel has written that life expectancy rates plunged at the middle of the century so it may be assumed it was worse in 1850–60 than in 1900 (*Without Consent or Contract,* 307). Some women probably ran their own businesses, but as the nineteenth century was one of distinct separate spheres for the sexes, and as popular ideologies had a distinctly masculine element, I made the calculations in Table 12 based on males only.

—had ended; independent business status for the bulk of employees was a statistical impossibility. What buoyed up the belief in independency in business over time was the agrarian-commercial qualities of American life. The preponderance of the occupation of farming, the agricultural town and village as the center of community activity, and the numerous small shops of the merchant, grocer, and other appendages of the agrarian economy all pointed to independency as a common condition of economic endeavor.[50]

That the economy grew by replicating business units in agriculture, commerce, and finance while maintaining the small shop generally in manufacturing and confining large-scale enterprise to a few areas had obvious repercussions for the American theory of the distribution of wealth. First, to take advantage of the opportunities offered by the transportation revolution, an individual had to labor strenuously—physically and mentally. Some might have had the fortune to fall into positions as a result of birth or privilege, but the existence of so much opportunity meant that many individuals could obtain independency by arduous effort.[51] For many Americans, laboring to become independent seemed to be the ruling order of the day.

50. On social mobility, see doubts of Montgomery, *Beyond Equality*, 26, 30; Pole, *Pursuit of Equality*, 205; Lebergott, *Manpower in Economic Growth*, 119–26. Stephan Thernstrom indicates that some property mobility did exist but nineteenth-century conservatives exaggerated it (*Poverty and Progress: Social Mobility in a Nineteenth Century City* [Cambridge, Mass., 1964], 1–19, 164–66). General critics of mobility in nineteenth-century America include, among numerous others, Pessen, *Riches, Class, and Power*, 2–4, 84–88; Jocelyn Maynard Ghent and Frederic Cople Jaher, "The Chicago Business Elite, 1830–1930: A Collective Biography," *Business History Review*, L (1976), 327–28. The perils of small business life are given in Griffen and Griffen, "Small Business and Occupational Mobility in Mid-Nineteenth Century Poughkeepsie," 122–41; Laurie, Hershberg, and Alter, "Immigrants and Industry," 219–48. The decline in independency was an urban phenomenon, however, and the United States until 1890 was an agrarian, not an urban, nation. Agricultural studies tend more to stress the independent small farmer until the troubles of the last two decades arose; see James T. Lemon, *The Best Poor Man's Country: A Geographical Study of Early Southeastern Pennsylvania* (Baltimore, 1972), 13 and chap. 8; Atack and Bateman, *To Their Own Soil*, 43–45, 107–11; Danhof, *Change in Agriculture*, 87–94.

51. It is generally conceded that few Americans had the luxury of simply living off an inheritance or interest from investments. Active participation in the economy was required of virtually everybody. See Paul Goodman, "Ethics and Enterprise: The Values of a Boston Elite, 1800–1860," *American Quarterly*, XVIII (1966), 437–51; for a different interpretation, see Dalzell, "Rise of the Waltham-Lowell System," 263–67. Deborah Jean Warner, "William J. Young: From Craft to Industry in a Skilled Trade," *Pennsylvania History*, LII (1985), 62–64; Edward C. Mack, *Peter Cooper: Citizen of New York* (New York, 1949), 164.

Thus the expansion of commerce did not disturb the notion that only the act of labor justified the acquisition and possession of private property so tenaciously adhered to by Americans in the self-sufficient, nonaristocratic, agricultural community. Indeed, commercial expansion initially reinforced the truthfulness of the labor theory of property/value. The bountiful crop of economic opportunities, all largely in the form of potential proprietorships or self-owned farms, could be earned only by physical and mental labor; only by the "sweat of his brow" could the individual obtain independency. The colonists had proclaimed in protest against the Stamp Act in 1765 that property was the fruit of labor. The truisms of the revolutionary generation were as applicable to nineteenth-century Americans as they had been to the Founders. In short, the labor theory of property/value not only retained its explanatory power but became more sacred among the citizenry. Americans worshiped property in the nineteenth century because they saw it as the rightful reward of labor.

The realities of economic life in the mid-nineteenth century can also help to explain the extraordinary tenacity of the labor theory of property/value on the popular mind and the division that was appearing between small freehold farmers and wage-earning industrial workers. In an econometric work on antebellum northern farming, Jeremy Atack and Fred Bateman estimated that 15 percent of the physical labor expended by midwestern settlers to establish and maintain their farms produced an appreciation of the value of their farms. Another way to look at that process of clearing and improving a farm is to recognize that it was a direct transformation of physical labor into property. Given the overwhelming agricultural quality of American life before 1890, the understanding of the translation of labor into property must have been tremendously widespread. The view that labor created property had a tangible reality that individuals in the twentieth century have lost.[52]

But individuals in wage-earning positions in society, especially the permanent ones, started to lose this natural (agrarian) sense of the transformation of labor into property. Instead of personally experiencing the transformation of labor into property possessed by the laborer, the industrial worker received only a wage. Theoretically, the industrial worker could save a small amount from his or her wage and by investment earn property either in the form of interest income or capital gains—all of which was contingent on the exis-

---

52. Atack and Bateman, *To Their Own Soil*, 236–41. See Olivier Fraysse, *Lincoln, Land, and Labor, 1809–60*, trans. Sylvia Neely (Urbana, 1994), 25–26, 41, and the "producer" ideology in Brown, *Baldwin Locomotive Works*, 94–96, 128.

tence of high wages, a dubious proposition by mid-century. Nevertheless, the process of capital or property acquisition was different. The farmer experienced a direct conversion of labor into property, a condition that would exist well into the twentieth century, but the wage earner lost that sensation. This contrast in the manner that property could be obtained partially accounts for the different perspectives small farmers and industrial wage earners have exhibited toward the institution of property and as well has a bearing on why distressed farmers and distressed laborers had such difficulty in coalescing politically and developing a common economic platform.

To achieve independency, to take advantage of the multitude of opportunities that the commercial revolution created, individuals not only had to labor but to cultivate a host of character traits to ensure that their attempt at independency would succeed. Those character traits were the oft-expressed and nearly banal ones of integrity, temperance, industriousness, intelligence, attentiveness, and frugality. In an economy of near equals in which individuals competed against each other (not aggregations of people competing against aggregations of other people), the emphasis on individual character traits makes sense. In an anarchistic type of competitive economy, the only mechanism of control a solitary figure could exert to enable him- or herself to attain success was to exercise control over him- or herself.

All these elements added together—the labor theory of property/value, independency, and industrious character traits—became known as the free labor ideology or the small producer ideology. The ideology had a basis in fact.[53] It was not that mobility was open to everyone or that everyone was assured of success; but the improvement of economic standing over time by individual effort—not the spectacular cases but the more average ones—was sufficiently widespread and publicly acknowledged to sustain the exaggerated social mobility rhetoric that filled public speeches. In March, 1860, Abraham Lincoln addressed a New Haven audience in the middle of the greatest strike in antebellum history, the shoemakers' strike. In his speech, Lincoln offered a classic version of mid-nineteenth-century belief in social mobility:

> What is the true condition of the laborer? I take it that it is best for all to leave each man free to acquire property as fast as he can. Some will get wealthy. I

53. See Gerald David Jaynes, *Branches Without Roots: Genesis of the Black Working Class in the American South, 1862–1882* (New York, 1986), 7–12; Montgomery, *Beyond Equality*, 14–30; Harold D. Woodman, "The Reconstruction of the Cotton Plantation in the New South," in *Essays on the Postbellum Southern Economy*, ed. Thavolia Glymph and John J. Kushma (College Station, Tex., 1985), 102–107.

don't believe in a law to prevent a man from getting rich; it would do more harm than good. So while we do not propose any war upon capital, we do wish to allow the humblest man an equal chance to get rich with everybody else. (Applause.) When one starts poor, as most do in the race of life, free society is such that he knows he can better his condition; he knows that there is no fixed condition of labor, for his whole life. I am not ashamed to confess that twenty five years ago I was a hired laborer, mauling rails, at work on a flat-boat—just what might happen to any poor man's son! (Applause.) I want every man to have the chance—and I believe a black man entitled to it—in which he *can* better his condition—when he may look forward and hope to be a hired laborer this year and the next, work for himself afterward, and finally to hire men to work for him! That is the true system.[54]

Not all Americans welcomed the explosiveness of the commercial revolution, of course. All those economic opportunities brought out avaricious behavior that defied conventional morality and republican standards. The fact that so many people seized the chance to improve their economic condition created a dynamism and a devotion to material welfare that not only shocked foreign visitors but disturbed and angered numerous natives. Throughout the nineteenth century a constant wail arose denouncing the haste to become rich.[55] Proslavery writers recoiled at the chaos of commercial society and feared the "isms" the chaos brought to life.[56] Sidney Fisher, a Philadelphian who was certain of the social necessity of hierarchy and his high place in it, found the grubbing for money upsetting to his aristocratic sense of placidity: "The good, respectable, old-family society for which Philadelphia was once

54. Lincoln speech at New Haven, in Roy P. Basler, Marion Dolores Pratt, and Lloyd A. Dunlop, eds., *The Collected Works of Abraham Lincoln* (New Brunswick, N.J., 1953–55), IV, 24–25. See William E. Forbath, "The Ambiguities of Free Labor: Labor and the Law in the Gilded Age," *Wisconsin Law Review* (1985), 767–79, 783–86. The difficulty with Forbath's analysis is that he argues that Lincoln's viewpoint differed from that of the abolitionists regarding the free labor ideology; it did not.

55. For example, James L. Huston, *The Panic of 1857 and the Coming of the Civil War* (Baton Rouge, 1987), 35–36; Beman Brockway, *Fifty Years in Journalism, Embracing Recollections and Personal Experiences, with an Autobiography* (Watertown, N.Y., 1891), 195; entry of August 18, 1843, in Robert F. Lucid, ed., *The Journal of Richard Henry Dana, Jr.* (Cambridge, Mass., 1968), I, 202; Noah Webster to Daniel Webster, 1837, in Warfel, ed., *Letters of Noah Webster,* 478–88; Robert W. Johannsen, *To the Halls of the Montezumas: The Mexican War in the American Imagination* (New York, 1985), 280–82.

56. For example, H. [George F. Holmes], "Greeley on Reforms," *Southern Literary Messenger,* XVII (May, 1851), 263–64.

so celebrated is fast disappearing, & persons of low origin & vulgar habits, manners & feelings are introduced, because they are rich, who a few years ago were never heard of."[57] Workers, because their prospects for mobility and property acquisition had dimmed, were far less celebratory about the commercial age and complained that commercialization had largely allowed the quick-witted to feast upon the honest and hardworking.[58] Intellectuals as a group reacted negatively; the pursuit of wealth seemed sordid compared to the pursuit of wisdom at Walden Pond.[59] In politics, individuals more accustomed to the slow-paced activity of the self-sufficient agricultural community tended to rally behind the Jeffersonian and Jacksonian parties.[60]

Many literate Americans saw matters differently and argued that commercialism was the natural enemy of aristocracy and that under certain conditions commercialism reinforced the basic precepts of republicanism. Robert Rantoul among others held that aristocracy brought forth the military chieftain who created a military state of high taxes and privileged orders. Commerce was the economic force that eroded that military despotism, and thus commercialism served the ends of republicanism. Unitarian minister Henry W. Bellows worried about the potential victory of materialism over spiritual values, yet commercial nations were an improvement over aristocracies where wealth "is necessarily confined to a few, while here it is open to all." "Commerce," proclaimed Bellows, "is to become the universal pursuit of men. It is to be the first result of freedom, of popular institutions everywhere." As early as 1790, a publicist knew that republicanism implied social mobility and that aristocracy implied caste: "In great commercial states, individuals of every rank are continually rising from obscurity into light, and from small beginnings frequently become rich."[61]

In a society in which economic growth was achieved by multiplication of

57. Entry of January 15, 1837, in Nicholas B. Wainwright, ed., *A Philadelphia Perspective: The Diary of Sidney George Fisher Covering the Years 1834–1871* (Philadelphia, 1967), 18.

58. Implication in Watson, *Liberty and Power*, 30–32; Kohl, *Politics of Individualism*, 22, 35, 54.

59. Irvin G. Wyllie, *The Self-Made Man in America: The Myth of Rags to Riches* (New Brunswick, N.J., 1954), 136–39.

60. For example, Rowland Berthoff, "Independence and Enterprise: Small Business in the American Dream," in *Small Business in American Life*, ed. Stuart W. Bruchey (New York, 1980), 31–34; Kohl, *Politics of Individualism*, 15, 55, 59.

61. Robert Rantoul, "Oration at South Reading," July 4, 1832, in Luther Hamilton, ed., *Memoirs, Speeches and Writings of Robert Rantoul, Jr.* (Boston, 1854), 166–70; see also "The Progress of Society," *North American Review*, LXIII (1846), 344–49, 353–54; Henry W. Bel-

the number of business units, success depended on individual character traits, and property was understood as the appropriate reward for labor, the notion of the fairness of the distribution of wealth had an obvious connection to economic structure. Inequality was inevitable but was thought to be bounded because all effort was individual. The reward of the marketplace was appropriate because the market was a boiling cauldron of hundreds of thousands of equals. Individuals had a fair chance at obtaining a competency so long as the laborer was assured of receiving his or her fruits.

The only disturbing element in the picture of a commercial society populated by thousands of equal producing units was politics. Where all the actors were small proprietors—where equality seemed to be the *natural* rule—no one could take unfair advantage of another and cheat or inveigle away the fruits of someone else's labors. Politics was the one power by which the *natural* equality of the economic actors could be made unequal. By using the coercive power of the state, governmental decrees could favor some over others and create an unjust and skewed distribution of wealth. The obvious means of doing so was political favoritism: exemption from taxation and particular laws of inheritance (entail and primogeniture).

Moreover, government could tip the natural equality operating in the economy of hundreds of thousands of competing business units by legislation. By creating monopolies via corporate charters, government introduced inequality into the economic contest. The corporation had more resources to draw on than did the individual and was as well granted exclusive rights to act in certain areas. And government could unbalance an equitable distribution by use of patronage, taxation, and war-making powers to enlarge the fortunes of the favored few at the expense of the laboring multitude.

When Americans declared that governments could distort the natural distribution of wealth and reward the undeserving and punish the meritorious, they had a factual basis for their claim. The American republican fear of the political economy of aristocracy received justification not only from the power of individual observation but from data that were widely distributed. In comparison with the twentieth century, of course, the power of western European governments in the nineteenth century was puny except during times of war. Nineteenth-century European governments did not tax their

---

lows, "Influence of the Trading Spirit upon the Social and Moral Life of America," *American* [Whig] *Review,* I (1845), 95–98; E. C., "The Politician, Number V," *American Museum,* VII (1790), 16.

citizens as greatly as have twentieth-century governments, welfare programs were nonexistent, and government expenditures minuscule. But it must be kept in mind that the economies of the nineteenth century were not far removed from brutal subsistence. Small amounts of taxation in such an economy could be sufficient to drive large portions of the citizenry from a modest competency to complete economic despair.[62]

The *Encyclopaedia Britannica* in the 1850s published material on the finances of European governments that was reprinted in American periodicals. Those reports were illuminating because they estimated the national debts, the annual income, and the standing armies of the European nations. Table 13 provides the results of those articles (in dollar values) plus roughly comparative data from the United States. The table exhibits some striking differences between republics and aristocracies and most emphatically between the United States and Great Britain. It is no wonder that American republicans quivered in fear of national debts; the cost of winning the Napoleonic Wars had placed a monstrous burden on the British people, and Britain in the mid-1850s had only slightly more people than the United States. In fact, all of Europe's debts—with the exception of the republics—were outrageous when compared with those of the United States. The large nations of Europe—the great powers of Britain, France, Russia, and Austria—also exhibited two startling features: massive armies and large national annual incomes. Not only did European powers have to tax citizens heavily to pay off national debts, but high taxes were also required to maintain an expensive and unproductive military establishment. It is hardly any wonder that nineteenth-century American republicans saw aristocratic governments as the agency of the distortion of the distribution of wealth through taxation and patronage policies.

But the differences did not stop with armies and national debts. The finances of Great Britain also filled the pages of American periodicals. In the year ending April 1, 1845, the British government's annual income was about $207,230,812; 38.9 percent came from impost duties, whereas 46.5 percent

62. For example, the effect of Republican Reconstruction programs in the South, though ultimately very modest, created havoc among the small self-sufficient white farming population and, besides the pervasive racial reasons, provided an economic impetus to overthrow Republican state organizations; see J. Mills Thornton III, "Fiscal Policy and the Failure of Radical Reconstruction in the Lower South," in *Region, Race, and Reconstruction: Essays in Honor of C. Vann Woodward,* ed. J. Morgan Kousser and James M. McPherson (New York, 1982), 349–94.

TABLE 13
COMPARISON OF FINANCES OF EUROPEAN NATIONS
AND THE UNITED STATES

	Debt (millions)	Annual Income (millions)	Soldiers (thousands)	Population (millions)	Per Capita Gov. Debt	Per Capita Gov. Income
Britain and Ireland	3,040	224	129	27.5	110.6	8.14
France	1,100	248	265	36	30.6	6.89
Austria	720	100	500	36	20.0	2.78
Russia	680	140	700	70	9.7	2.00
Prussia	128	60	121	17	7.5	3.53
Spain	480	60	160	13	36.9	4.62
Republics						
Swiss Cantons	0	3	70	2.5	0	1.04
Bremen	12	NA	[500]	[80,000]	150	NA
Lubeck	24	NA	[490]	[50,000]	480	NA
Frankfort	28	NA	[1,300]	[65,000]	431	NA
United States (1853)	59.8	62	21	25.7	2.32	2.41

Sources: "The Debts and Armies of Europe," *Bankers' Magazine,* X (1856), 658; "Population, Finances, etc., of the European States," *Hunt's Merchants' Magazine,* XXVIII (1853), 95; U.S. Bureau of the Census, *Historical Statistics,* 8, 1106, 1118, 1142. The *Bankers' Magazine* article lists the debts and incomes in pounds; the *Hunt's* article lists the same in Prussian dollars. The figures in the table are from *Bankers' Magazine.* The exchange rate between pounds and dollars in 1850 was $3.98 to £1 (Jones, *Wealth of a Nation to Be,* table 1.2, p. 10). I rounded the conversion to $4 to £1.

originated from direct taxation of British citizens. What is astounding is that nearly three-fourths of the income (72.1 percent) went to service the public debt. Out of the over $200 million in revenue, only $53 million was required to run the government. But a further caution is needed. The money to run the government went to pay court officials (the patronage of the aristocracy), the military (more patronage of the aristocracy in the officer corps), and to support the monarchy (see Table 14).

The comparison with the United States government in 1853 is striking.[63] All United States revenue came from the tariff; no income was derived from direct taxes. As internal taxes, or direct taxes, were always regressive, proportionately taxing lower-income groups more than upper-income groups, the republican economy offered Americans an escape from the tax burden England imposed. Direct taxes in England accounted for over 46 percent of the nation's income; the regressive nature of those taxes must have had a major impact on lower-income groups. Moreover, that tax revenue was being leached from the producing classes in unbelievable amounts to pay the national debt. In 1853, only 7.5 percent of the United States' annual income went to service the national debt versus 72 percent of Great Britain's. Such figures explain why John Taylor, Thomas Jefferson, Andrew Jackson, and others were horrified about a national debt. The simple reality was that the mass of the population in England worked under a major tax burden to pay the bondholders of Britain's national debt. The many were being taxed for the benefit of the few.[64] The actual expenses of both the United States and Great Britain for the normal functioning of government were similar, but England's debt situation required it to tax its citizens three to four times as much as the United States government had to tax its citizens.

Throughout the Age of the American Revolution, 1765–1880, the federal government exhibited fairly common statistics. For a century, the federal government relied for its income on the tariff, the major exception being the direct taxes levied during the Civil War and then kept in force afterward. Nevertheless, the tariff was the major source of income for the government until World War I. After World War I, the income tax became

63. The year 1853 was chosen to avoid the effects of the Mexican War and the low incomes of the 1840s; 1853 seemed representative of the United States and reasonably close to 1845.

64. Of course, the people of Britain supposedly received something in return; they had not been absorbed into the Napoleonic Empire. Whether the generations of Englishmen after 1815 thought the price was worthwhile is another question.

TABLE 14

RECEIPTS AND EXPENDITURES OF GREAT BRITAIN AND THE UNITED STATES, MID-NINETEENTH CENTURY

England, Year Ending April 1, 1845	Amount ($)	Percent of Total
Income		
Customs	80,706,924	38.9
Excise	48,899,628	23.6
Stamps	26,859,360	13.0
Taxes	20,417,792	9.9
Post office	2,716,000	1.3
Crown lands	500,000	.2
Miscellaneous	4,269,416	2.1
Total ordinary income	201,240,112	
With adjustments	207,230,812	
Expenditures		
To consolidated fund (public debt)	149,450,152	72.1
To advances	4,014,008	1.9
To ways and means	53,766,652	25.9
Total	207,230,812	

United States, 1853	Amount ($)	Percent of Total
Income		
Customs	58,932,000	95.7
Internal taxes	0	0
Other	988,000	1.6
Public Land Sales	1,667,000	2.7
Total	61,587,000	

TABLE 14 (cont.)

	United States, 1853 Amount ($)	Percent of Total
Expenditures		
Department of Army	9,947,000	20.6
Department of Navy	10,919,000	22.7
Interest on public debt	3,666,000	7.6
Other	23,652,000	49.1
Total	48,184,000	

Sources: "Public Revenues of Great Britain," *Bankers' Magazine,* I (1846), 81; U.S. Bureau of the Census, *Historical Statistics,* 1106, 1114.

the dominant source of income.[65] As well, Americans sought to keep the national debt within bounds by making sure that servicing the debt required only a small fraction of the annual income. The only exceptions were the years following the Revolution and the Civil War (see Table 15). Finally, nineteenth-century Americans heeded revolutionary warnings about the dangers of a bureaucracy.[66] The military and the postal service

65. U.S. Bureau of the Census, *Historical Statistics,* Table Y 352–357, p. 1106, for years 1916–39. See Bennett D. Baack and John Edward Ray, "Special Interests and the Adoption of the Income Tax in the United States," *Journal of Economic History,* XLV (1985), 607–25.

66. It is understandable that European visitors to the United States marveled at the lack of government there. Historians have long stressed the lack of bureaucracy in the United States: Cochran, *Challenges to American Values,* 61–69; Eric Foner, *Reconstruction: America's Unfinished Revolution, 1863–1877* (New York, 1988), 143–48; Morton Keller, "Power and Rights: Two Centuries of American Constitutionalism," *Journal of American History,* LXXIV (1987), 679–81; Donald J. Pisani, "Promotion and Regulation: Constitutionalism and the American Economy," *Journal of American History,* LXXIV (1987), 740–68; Morton Keller, *Affairs of State: Public Life in Late Nineteenth Century America* (Cambridge, Mass., 1977), 239–44; William E. Nelson, *The Roots of American Bureaucracy, 1830–1900* (Cambridge, Mass., 1982), 3–5. Matthew A. Crenson sees more bureaucracy in Jacksonian America than was there (*The Federal Machine: Beginnings of Bureaucracy in Jacksonian America* [Baltimore, 1975]). The research of Theda Skocpol has revealed a welfare agency in the post–Civil War years based on soldiers' pensions, yet the citizenry retained its antibureaucratic animus (*Protecting Soldiers and Mothers: The Political Origins of Social Policy in the United States* [Cambridge, Eng., 1992], 48–50, 87–149).

TABLE 15

INCOME SOURCES AND DEBT PAYMENTS

OF THE UNITED STATES, 1790–1900

Census Year	Income (millions)	% Income from Customs	% Income from Direct Taxes	% Outlay to Service Public Debt
1789–91	4.42	99.5	—	55.02
1800	10.85	83.7	7.5	31.29
1810	9.38	91.5	.1	34.88
1820	17.88	83.9	0	28.07
1830	24.84	88.2	0	12.64
1840	19.48	69.3	0	00.72
1850	43.60	91.0	0	09.56
1860	56.07	94.9	0	05.03
1870	411.26	47.3	45.0	41.74
1880	333.53	55.9	37.2	35.78
1890	403.08	57.0	35.4	11.35
1900	567.00	41.1	52.1	07.71

Source: U.S. Bureau of the Census, *Historical Statistics,* 1106, 1115.

regularly accounted for some 88 percent of federal employees between 1815 and 1880. Only in the years 1880 to 1900 was there a sudden and dramatic rise of federal employment unrelated to postal or military occupations (see Table 16).

The nature of the economy with its preponderance of small producing units reinforced republican preachings concerning the evils of national debts, the patronage power, high taxes, and policies that bestowed economic privileges on the few. The mass of individual producing units in the economy meant that many, if not most, Americans lived close to the edge of economic ruin. A competence was possible, but given the rudimentary nature of American life in the nineteenth century it must have been precarious. Governmental policies could quickly tip the balance from competency and independency to subsistence and loss of property. Maintaining a small government, a

TABLE 16

U.S. GOVERNMENT PERSONNEL, 1816–1901

Date	Total Civilian and Military Employment	% Post Office	% Military	% Other
1816	21,580	15.5	77.6	6.9
1821	17,501	27.2	60.5	12.3
1831	22,664	38.7	49.3	12.0
1841	38,831	36.8	53.5	9.7
1851	46,973	45.5	44.1	10.4
1861	253,784	11.9	85.5	2.6
1871	87,716	41.8	48.2	10.0
1881	137,888	40.9	27.4	31.7
1891	195,310	48.9	19.4	31.7
1901	351,738	38.7	31.9	29.4

Source: Computed from U.S. Bureau of the Census, *Historical Statistics,* 8, 1102–1103, 1142–43.

small national debt, and low taxes made sense for an economy founded on the small shop and the small farm.[67]

American politics also reflected the essential structure of the economy. The great economic dividing line between the parties aligned with Jeffersonian principles and those with Hamiltonian ones was largely a matter of understanding and acting on expansion of commerce. The Jeffersonian parties never repudiated the market; they always accepted commercial society. But their ideas of states' rights reflected the lingering memory of life in the self-sufficient agricultural districts, they always favored agriculture, and above all they feared the speed of the commercial revolution. The new compression of time in commercial society, the quickness with which financial and commer-

67. A different explanation is offered by Gerald N. Grob, "The Political System and Social Policy in the Nineteenth Century: Legacy of the Revolution," *Mid-America,* LVIII (1976), 5–19. Grob argues that Americans, inheriting an antibureaucratic bias from the Revolution, had no model to create the interventionist welfare state. Actually, the Americans did have a model: England. But it was the model to avoid, not emulate.

cial transactions might be completed, evidently bothered and angered them. Those who lacked the mental agility to handle the new speed required for transactions could be robbed, plundered, or cheated out of their just rewards.[68] The Jeffersonian parties and their followers never really attacked the market or property earned as the fruit of labor, but they were highly sensitive to governmental action that might allow some to take advantage of the many by simple mental calculations.

The Hamiltonian parties welcomed the commercial nation. The parties and individuals who adhered to Hamiltonian policies wanted the government to encourage and extend commerce. Some, like Lincoln and Seward, saw commercialization as a democratizing force that upheld social mobility, property, and high wages. Others probably had a superiority complex. They could ride the calculating anarchy of decision making in the time-shortened business life of a commercial society; they did not apprehend being taken advantage of, but rather savored the prospect of benefiting from the new conditions that transportation had wrought. Yet the parties reflecting the Hamiltonian viewpoint did not travel far from essential republican ideas concerning the size of government, national debts, and intervention in the economy. Both parties were dominated by belief in small government and the American theory of the distribution of wealth. The economic dividing line was simply that one constellation of parties welcomed the Age of Commerce and wanted to goad it into greater action while the other party was suspicious and wanted a slower pace of development.[69]

A commercial agrarian republic that grew by multiplication of business units also helps to explain the issues basic to American politics between 1776 and 1896. Land laws and the disposition of the public domain would, of course, be of primary interest to a growing agricultural society. Likewise, a commercial society would demand activity to promote the linkage of markets, that is, internal improvements. The republican heritage demanded a tax

68. Kohl, *Politics of Individualism*, 22, 35–38, 50; Watson, *Liberty and Power*, 193–94, 210; Ashworth, *"Agrarians" and "Aristocrats,"* 17–19, 23–24, 28–39, 94–95.

69. Some authors emphasize too strongly the anticapitalist bias of the Democrats; see Kohl, *Politics of Individualism*, 61; Ashworth, *"Agrarians" and "Aristocrats,"* 113, 131; Watson, *Liberty and Power*, 237–40; Sellers, *Market Revolution*, 333, 346; Bridges, *City in the Republic*, 18–25, 69. Emphasis on the role of government in the economy has been exquisitely laid out by James Willard Hurst, *Law and Social Order in the United States* (Ithaca, N.Y., 1977), 267; and Hurst, *Law and the Conditions of Freedom in the Nineteenth-Century United States* (Madison, 1956), 34–57.

power that was fairly innocuous and controlled: the tariff best suited the conflicting desires of American republicans in regard to taxation. Finally, commerce implied the presence of credit mechanisms to enable goods to be moved and stored; hence the importance of currency and banking issues. Because small businessmen and independent farmers provided the bulk of productive power in the economy, the presence of small producing units also explains what was missing in governmental policy: regulation. The cost of regulating such huge numbers of individuals was probably prohibitive. So long as an essential equality among the producing units existed and most participants could obtain only a competence, not many citizens could offer a cogent justification for government intervention based on equitability. The equitability already existed and was maintained by the smallness of the competitors.

The American republic had enemies from 1765 to 1880, and those enemies all had one feature in common: bigness. Both the First and the Second Banks of the United States had elicited paranoid reactions from the Jeffersonian party groups because they were enormous institutions compared with the rest of the economy. And slavery also had a reputation for bigness. It became a target of vituperation for a variety of reasons, but in a land of small proprietors the might of the institution and the size of the large slaveholders' operations were ominous. John Hume, an Ohio abolitionist who lived to witness the trust-busting activities of Theodore Roosevelt, made a telling observation about how out of place slavery was in small-business America:

> The slave-owners were numerically a lean minority even in the South, but their mastery over their fellow-citizens was absolute. Nor was there any mystery about it. As the owners of four million slaves, on an average worth not far from five hundred dollars each, they formed the greatest industrial combination—what at this time we would call a trust—ever known to this or any other country. Our mighty Steel Corporation would have been a baby beside it. If to-day all our great financial companies were consolidated, the unit would scarcely come up to the dimensions of that one association.

When bigness occurred in the industrial and commercial realm, a new crusade against bigness was launched.[70]

70. See Robert V. Remini, *Andrew Jackson and the Bank War: A Study in the Growth of Presidential Power* (New York, 1967), 39; John F. Hume, *The Abolitionists: Together With Personal Memories of the Struggle for Human Rights, 1830–1864* (New York, 1905), 32; Gerald Gunderson, "The Origin of the American Civil War," *Journal of Economic History*, XXXIV (1974), 916–20, 940.

*

The commercial agrarian republic could not last forever, but when it disappeared, it disappeared suddenly. The commercial agrarian republic was based on widespread individual proprietorship, and eventually simple population growth would have made it impossible for units of production to expand by multiplication. Commercialization was also a process that portended future organizational change. For several decades commerce allowed the small shop to exist and multiply, but a few individuals recognized that commerce had changed the rules of economic life. Opportunities for individual ownership existed, but so did opportunities to create new vertical structures. The few people who understood the new principles ruthlessly applied them and earned the sobriquet of robber barons. Ultimately, the transportation revolution encouraged an increase in the size of the production unit.[71]

The unexpected intrusion of gigantic firms in the midst of a small business economic structure produced massive social trauma and shattered expectations, ideals, and policies. In 1854, Amasa Walker, a Massachusetts political economist and abolitionist, provided in the pages of *Hunt's Merchants' Magazine* the rule of equitability for an economy composed of small shops: an "equitable division" of income—that is, the rewards of labor—depended on "the equality on which they [factors of production] stand. . . . For if one partner should from any cause whatever be so situated that he can dictate terms to the other, those terms may be altogether unequal and unjust." In an economy in which all economic actors were equally small, fairness of income distribution was assured (at least theoretically). But in the "core-periphery" economy in which big business dominated small business, how could equitability be achieved?[72]

For generations, Americans had maintained their equality by achieving an essentially horizontal pattern of growth. Equality was almost implicitly defined as proprietorship or independency, and expansion meant expansion

71. The term comes from Matthew Josephson, *The Robber Barons: The Great American Capitalists, 1861–1901* (1934; rpr. New York, 1962). See Charles S. Ashley, "The Distribution of Wealth," *Popular Science Monthly,* XXIX (October, 1886), 726–27; Keller, *Affairs of State,* 431–35 and chaps. 12, 15.

72. Amasa Walker, "Political Economy—Wages," *Hunt's Merchants' Magazine,* XXXI (1854), 179; see also C. F. Adams, Jr., quoted by Shelton Stromquist, *A Generation of Boomers: The Pattern of Railroad Conflict in Nineteenth-Century America* (Urbana, 1987), 15; Hurst, *Legitimacy of the Business Corporation in the Law,* 42.

outward, not upward. Instead of creating larger units of production, Americans created more units of production. Instead of remaining on one site, Americans expanded horizontally out west—which for the Indians was pure and simple imperialism. Even the cities lacked large buildings. The development of skyscrapers in the 1890s and the erection of the Brooklyn Bridge in 1883 were profound metaphors for the entire society. Growth became vertical. The large corporation, the large organization, became the dominant force in the American economy and was so patently visible because it towered massively over the remaining small and scattered units of production.

Vertical growth meant hierarchy, and Americans were confronted with a condition that, except for slavery, they had escaped for one and one-quarter centuries. Early republicanism with its emphasis on independency and Adam Smithian laissez-faire with its stress on individual competition had both been systems that in one way or another attacked the layered society of aristocracy. Strong antihierarchical notions were embedded in both. The commercial agrarian republic lacked hierarchy. The corporation brought hierarchy into American life.[73]

The concentration of economic power in a few firms brought out the traditional fears of republicanism. Monopoly was abroad in the land, and it would deprive the laborer of the just fruits of his or her labor. Monopoly would drive out the small business, destroy the small farm, possess the government, and snuff out social mobility and independency.[74]

But for American industrial workers, the emergence of large corporations carried other, more devastating menaces. Of all Americans, laborers were the first to face hierarchy. The initial jump in the size of firms from the artisan workshop to the small manufactory created a somewhat permanent laboring class. It also shattered the idea that most workers could obtain independence over time. Now workers had to become accustomed to taking orders from someone higher in the organizational ranking, even if that ranking included no more than a foreman or the proprietor himself. No matter how personal

73. See R. Jeffrey Lustig, *Corporate Liberalism: The Origins of Modern American Political Theory, 1890–1920* (Berkeley, 1982), 46–47, 52; Rayback, *History of American Labor*, 187.

74. The impact of bigness on Americans in the 1880s and 1890s might not have been much different than the impact of bigness in textile manufacturing in England in the 1830s. V. A. C. Gatrell quotes a general opinion in Lancashire that because of machinery, "I believe no working man can [now] rise from his low condition by his own exertions" ("Labour, Power, and the Size of Firms in Lancashire Cotton," 124).

the relations between employer and employee in the small shop might be, an element of hierarchy was inescapable. The casual tyranny that such hierarchy might invoke, its infuriating arrogance, was described by Samuel Gompers. In the 1870s in New York City, Gompers, a cigar maker, asked a foreman why he placed an old man in a dark area of the shop and a new man in a lighted area. The terse response was, "That is my business and I will do just as I please." Hierarchy gave one person power to order others around at pleasure without any act of bargaining or negotiation or mutuality. Gompers responded with a walkout.[75]

The horrid conditions of American manufacturing antagonized industrial workers, but so did the irritating presence of hierarchy. But American industrialization during commercialization did not produce deskilled workers. A sort of equilibrium in industrial relations was maintained between 1830 and 1880 by the presence of craft skill in many areas of industrial work. The industrial worker lost the artisanal shop as a source of independence but did not lose the craft skills upon which another sense of independence was based.[76] The existence of the small shop and the continuance of craft skill were the structural elements that allowed workers to find some truth in the free labor ideology. The experience of hierarchy and the conditions of industrialization also made the worker certain that a continuous violation of the labor theory

75. Samuel Gompers, *Seventy Years of Life and Labor* (New York, 1925), I, 66; Mary H. Blewett, *Men, Women, and Work: Class, Gender, and Protest in the New England Shoe Industry, 1780–1910* (Urbana, 1988), 261.

76. Labor historians have created a disjointed history regarding craft skill and the position of the American worker in society. Labor historians who deal with antebellum time periods tend to stress loss of craft skill, the impact of machinery, and the subjugation of the worker to the control of the capitalist. For example, Dawley, *Class and Community,* 42–50, 90–96; Cynthia J. Shelton, *The Mills of Manayunk: Industrialization and Social Conflict in the Philadelphia Region, 1787–1837* (Baltimore, 1986), chaps. 3, 5; Carl Siracusa, *A Mechanical People: Perceptions of the Industrial Order in Massachusetts, 1815–1880* (Middleton, Conn., 1979), 6–7; Ware, *Industrial Worker,* x–xii, chap. 4. Postbellum studies stress workers' control over job content, inside contracting, and craft skill: Francis G. Couvares, *The Remaking of Pittsburgh: Class and Culture in an Industrializing City, 1877–1919* (Albany, 1984), chap. 2; David Bensman, *The Practice of Solidarity: American Hat Finishers in the Nineteenth Century* (Urbana, 1985), xix–xx, 212–20; David Montgomery, *Workers' Control in America: Studies in the History of Work, Technology, and Labor Struggles* (Cambridge, Eng., 1979), 4–5, 9–11; Roderick N. Ryon, "Baltimore Workers and Industrial Decision-Making, 1890–1917," *Journal of Southern History,* LI (1985), 565–80. A good periodization of labor history is offered by Ross, *Workers on the Edge,* 71–83, 219–39; see also David Grimsted, "Ante-Bellum Labor: Violence, Strike, and Communal Arbitration," *Journal of Social History,* XIX (1985), 5–18.

of property/value was occurring—the fruits of labor were not being awarded to the laborer.[77]

When the large corporation emerged and captured the bulk of manufacturing jobs in the United States, it not only brought business bureaucracy, hierarchy, and impersonalization but was accompanied by the most massive deskilling of workers in American history. Between 1880 and 1920 the unskilled worker was born, a person nearly invisible before 1880. In industry after industry, machines replaced skill: in glassblowing, in mining, in quarrying, in automobile assembling, in iron and steel-making, in printing.[78] The wretched conditions of labor in the Gilded Age, the sudden intrusion of large-scale shops and impersonal management, and the cycles of boom and bust were bad enough, but the loss of skill was the loss of self-identification and was unbearable.[79]

In the social transformation of working for proprietors to working for corporate supervisors, laborers lost the skills they had preserved for at least one-half century. In an economic sense, American workers earned a considerable amount of money from their skills; their knowledge of the skills to produce goods represented a form of human capital. The new technology deskilled the worker and destroyed his investment in human capital; in a real sense the

77. On ideological studies, see Greenberg, *Worker and Community,* chap. 2; Paul G. Faler, *Mechanics and Manufacturers in the Early Industrial Revolution: Lynn, Massachusetts, 1780–1860* (Albany, 1981), 30–35; Blewett, *Men, Women, and Work,* 204, 320–22; Lipin, *Producers, Proletarians, and Politicians,* 187–206.

78. For example, Nathan Rosenberg, *Perspectives on Technology* (Cambridge, Eng., 1976), 117; Hounshell, *From the American System to Mass Production,* chap. 6 and *passim;* Pearce Davis, *The Development of the American Glass Industry* (Cambridge, Mass., 1949), 180–91, 197–99, 205–19, 239–40, 271–74; Augusta Emile Galster, *The Labor Movement in the Shoe Industry with Special Reference to Philadelphia* (New York, 1924), 35; David Brody, *Steelworkers in America: The Nonunion Era* (Cambridge, Mass., 1960), 27–31, 51–58. Note the title of chapter 4 in Mark Wyman's work on mining: "Betrayed by the New Technology," Wyman, *Hard Rock Epic: Western Miners and the Industrial Revolution, 1860–1910* (Berkeley, 1979), 84–117.

79. On conditions of labor, see for the most general treatment Melvyn Dubofsky, *Industrialism and the American Worker, 1865–1920* (Arlington Heights, Ill., 1975), 4–28. For the demise of the foreman's authority over labor relations and production, see Daniel Nelson, *Managers and Workers: Origins of the New Factory System in the United States, 1880–1920* (Madison, 1975). On Taylorism and control of production, see Harry Braverman, *Labor and Monopoly Capital: The Degradation of Work in the Twentieth Century* (New York, 1974), chaps. 1–7; David Montgomery, "Workers' Control of Machine Production in the Nineteenth Century," *Labor History,* XVII (1976), 485–509; Sanford M. Jacoby, *Employing Bureaucracy: Managers, Unions, and the Transformation of Work in American Industry, 1900–1945* (New York, 1985), 3, 14–16.

late-nineteenth-century worker was robbed of his property, his mental property.[80] The usual reaction for a person of small means when robbed of his property is to resort to violence.

Between 1880 and 1900, the nation experienced the great upheaval among workers. The wave of strikes and unrest among American workers was unique among western European states. But the great upheaval in the United States was not so much exceptional as misplaced in time. Labor unrest in the Gilded Age should be compared to early industrialization in England and in Europe, where the impact of machine displacement of skills evoked angry riots among artisans. In the United States, that response to deskilling was delayed because of the novelties of the American founding, the feminine quality of the early advanced textile force, and the small shop quality of American industrialization. Skill in the United States was diluted but was not displaced or eliminated between 1800 and 1880. The preservation of craft skills from the impact of the machine could not be maintained forever, and in the 1880s the barrier burst and large-scale organization proceeded with an unprecedented assault on the skilled worker in mass-production facilities. The great upheaval was the result.[81]

Not only did strikes proliferate, they frequently became violent; and state and federal officials called in troops to quell them. The usual outcome was a death toll sometimes climbing into two digits. Such industrial violence did not exist before 1877, the year of the great railroad strike. Before 1877, strikes had community attributes and a fatality was almost never recorded and certainly not from a state official shooting a striker. Americans had boasted that they lived without a true police force, that the purpose of the army was not to maintain law and order. Such use of the coercive power of the state belonged only to aristocracies. After 1880, in the midst of the reorganization of American life, state coercion became a daily fact of life, and strikes in which some-

---

80. On human capital theory, see Ronald A. Wykstra, Introduction to *Education and the Economics of Human Capital,* ed. Wykstra (New York, 1971), 1–19. For the impact of deskilling in the twentieth century, see Daniel Bell, *Work and Its Discontents: The Cult of Efficiency in America* (Boston, 1956); Robert Blauner, *Alienation and Freedom: The Factory Worker and His Industry* (Chicago, 1964); and Ely Chinoy, *Automobile Workers and the American Dream* (Garden City, N.Y., 1955).

81. For the great upheaval and strike violence, consult Walter Licht, *Working for the Railroad: The Organization of Work in the Nineteenth Century* (Princeton, 1983), 245, 249–53; Licht, *Industrializing America,* 168–91; Gerald Friedman, "Strike Success and Union Ideology: The United States and France, 1880–1914," *Journal of Economic History,* XLVIII (1988), 5, 17–25.

one was *not* injured or killed by state authorities became a rarity. Whatever the form of society that was replacing the commercial agrarian republic, it drew its power from military coercion and not from the republican mid-century boast of voluntarism.[82]

The strength and longevity of the republican theory of the distribution of wealth—the labor theory of property/value, the political economy of aristocracy, the land laws of entail and primogeniture, and the population-to-land ratio—sailed through 125 years of national existence without a change or even slight modification because the ideas matched well an economic structure of numerous proprietors in a commercial agrarian republic. Economic structure and ideas fit not perfectly but close enough to avoid severe dissonance.

Events in the United States between 1765 and 1880 had a unitary quality. In politics it was the period of the working out of the institutions and ideas and implications of the Revolution; in economics, it was sustaining and extending horizontally the commercial agrarian economy, with its mass of proprietorships and skilled and semiskilled work routines. In society, it was finding the social patterns necessary for an atomistic, individualist, voluntary society to replace those of deference and local coercion. Although historians have created smaller divisions for these years (the Federalist Era, the Era of Good Feelings, the Jacksonian Era, the coming of the Civil War, the Civil War and Reconstruction, the Gilded Age), they are mainly variations on the revolutionary theme. Nothing that occurred in the years 1765 to 1880 drastically revised the revolutionary heritage. Even the Civil War inaugurated nothing new; it was fought, by both North and South, explicitly on the principles of 1776 and produced no new institutions (with the exception of

82. For example, [John L. O'Sullivan], "Introduction," *United States Magazine and Democratic Review*, I (October, 1837), in Charles M. Wiltse, ed., *Expansion and Reform, 1815–1850* (New York, 1967), 151; "Civilization: American and European," *American* [Whig] *Review*, III (June, 1846), 622; Richard B. Morris, "Alexander Hamilton After Two Centuries," in *Alexander Hamilton: A Profile*, ed. Jacob E. Cooke (New York, 1967), 30–31; Edward Payson Powell, *Nullification and Secession in the United States: A History of the Six Attempts During the First Century of the Republic* (New York, 1897), 424–25; William H. Seward, address at Ogdensburgh, in Baker, ed., *Works of Seward*, III, 211–12. Historians have overlooked the theme of coercion in U.S. history; see, for example, George E. McNeill, "The Problem of To-Day," in *The Labor Movement: The Problem of To-Day*, ed. McNeill (Boston, 1887), 454; Herbert Spencer, *The Man Versus the State* (1892; rpr. Caldwell, Idaho, 1965), 16–17, 41.

the Freedmen's Bureau) and no new ideas. The Civil War was not a "second" American Revolution as much as a completion of the first American Revolution.[83]

For contemporaries and contemporary historians, the 1880s and 1890s were the turning point in American life.[84] The rise of bigness in American life shook the nation to its core and shredded but did not obliterate entirely the revolutionary heritage—at least not that portion that had been given institutional form. The transformation of the 1880–1920 period affected almost all areas of people's daily lives. Urbanization became the norm, and from a nation of rural communities and towns the country evolved into a land of cities; urban dependence replaced the rural communities' practice and idea of self-sufficiency and independence. The new wave of immigration from central, southern, and eastern Europe changed the demographics of the country. The large-scale business unit dominated the industrial output of the nation; science and technology replaced skill and learning by experience. From a land with no visible hierarchy the nation passed to a land with a very visible hierarchy. Political agendas were reversed. Laissez-faire once was the popular cry of the masses; now interventionism became the order of the day. And politics itself was fundamentally different. The nineteenth century did in fact live up to a model of change by realignment. But the twentieth century was a different system altogether: mass participation dwindled, the party played a

83. The idea that the Civil War profoundly changed the United States was partially a product of southern lamentations about the death of states' rights, which, given the strength of the states' rights doctrine in the twentieth century, seems a little absurd. Charles A. Beard proclaimed the Civil War a turning point in economic history, as have others, but such authors have exaggerated the political change, not the economic change, and the former was nothing more than the adoption of a milquetoast Whig program in the 1860s. I agree with Licht, *Industrializing America,* chap. 4. For historians stressing the Civil War as a point of pivotal change, see William B. Hesseltine, *Lincoln's Plan of Reconstruction* (Tuscaloosa, 1960), 16, 19, 33–37; Jean H. Baker, *Affairs of Party: The Political Culture of Northern Democrats in the Mid-Nineteenth Century* (Ithaca, N.Y., 1983), 13; Charles A. Beard, *Contemporary American History, 1877–1913* (1914; rpr. New York, 1918), 27–28; Leonard P. Curry, *Blueprint for Modern America: Nonmilitary Legislation of the First Civil War Congress* (Nashville, Tenn., 1968), 244–52; Richard Franklin Bensel, *Yankee Leviathan: The Origins of Central State Authority in America, 1859–1877* (Cambridge, Eng., 1990), chap. 1 and *passim.* But see Sewell, *House Divided,* 1–5; Foner, *Reconstruction,* 242; William L. Barney, *Flawed Victory: A New Perspective on the Civil War* (Lanham, Md., 1980), ix–x, 184–86, 193.

84. See chapter 10 below and the general treatments of Keller, *Affairs of State;* Nell Irvin Painter, *Standing at Armageddon: The United States, 1877–1919* (New York, 1987); John A. Garraty, *The New Commonwealth, 1877–1890* (New York, 1968).

less prominent role, political agendas were different, the structure of authority changed.[85]

In *Looking Backward*, Edward Bellamy captured the essence of the transformation that had so disoriented the society and left its ideology, including the American theory of the distribution of wealth, in shambles. Leete, the instructor of Julian West, the 1887 inhabitant of Boston spirited into the year 2000, explained why strikes no longer existed. Strikes had occurred because of the sudden concentration of capital

> in greater masses than had ever been known before. Before this concentration began, while as yet commerce and industry were conducted by innumerable petty concerns with small capital, instead of a small number of great concerns with vast capital, the individual workman was relatively important and independent in his relations to the employer. Moreover, when a little capital or a new idea was enough to start a man in business for himself, workingmen were constantly becoming employers and there was no hard and fast line between the two classes. Labor unions were needless then, and general strikes out of the question. But when the era of small concerns with small capital was succeeded by that of the great aggregations of capital, all this was changed. The individual laborer, who had been relatively important to the small employer, was reduced to insignificance and powerlessness over against the great corporation.[86]

Between 1880 and 1890 the Age of the American Revolution ended, and the commercial agrarian republic passed away. The industrial empire had been born.

---

85. On politics, see Joel Silbey, *The American Political Nation, 1838–1893* (Stanford, 1991), 237–51; Walter Dean Burnham, *Critical Elections and the Mainsprings of American Politics* (New York, 1970), 71–90; Richard L. McCormick, *The Party Period and Public Policy: American Politics from the Age of Jackson to the Progressive Era* (New York, 1986), 217–26, 279–80; John F. Reynolds and Richard L. McCormick, "Outlawing 'Treachery': Split Tickets and Ballot Laws in New York and New Jersey, 1880–1910," *Journal of American History,* LXXII (1986), 835–58; John F. Reynolds, *Testing Democracy: Electoral Behavior and Progressive Reform in New Jersey, 1880–1920* (Chapel Hill, 1988), 2–3, 168–71; Keller, *Affairs of State,* chap. 16; Michael E. McGerr, *The Decline of Popular Politics: The American North, 1865–1928* (New York, 1986), chaps. 7, 8.

86. Edward Bellamy, *Looking Backward* (1888; rpr. New York, 1968), 56–57.

5

Political Economists, 1790–1860

While Americans at the end of the eighteenth century argued over the policies that best promoted an equitable distribution of wealth for an agrarian republic, intellectual developments in Europe altered the ideological boundaries of the debate. Adam Smith's work on national economic progress
stimulated further inquiry into the economic realm. A succession of writers
changed the method of analyzing the topic of wealth and income distribution so that by 1830 distribution meant for political economists the relative
proportions earned by capitalists (profits), laborers (wages), and landholders
(rent). These new categories implied a great deal about a society's wealth or
income distribution and how commercial maturation had altered the nature
of the investigation. European handling of the subject had shifted dramatically away from the concerns of the American revolutionaries.

The followers of Adam Smith left no doubt as to the shape wealth distribution would assume in any advanced, populous society. They concluded that
inequitable wealth distribution was a law of nature and perhaps even of the
Divinity. Because the United States was bound mentally to England and Europe, the discoveries of European political economists—abstruse as they
sometimes were—were quickly acknowledged by a large segment of the literate American public.

British political economy swept over North America and invaded nearly
every political and public debate concerning economic health and governmental policy. The background of British classical economics was vitally important to the public discourses raging in North America. Americans did not
accept all aspects of classical political economy or apply it in all fields; on the
contrary, the doctrines induced immense political battles. But the nature of

the battles can hardly be recognized unless one understands the framework that the English economists had thrust upon the Americans. This was certainly the case for the distribution of wealth because the findings of British political economists directly challenged the formulations of the Founders. British laws of political economy were hostile to republicanism, as many Americans realized.

American political economists, grappling with the formulations of their European counterparts, usually divided into two camps—free traders and protectionists (advocates of high tariffs). In one fashion or another, both sides rejected the wealth distributions the Europeans forecast. Indeed, although Americans in a few cases actually concocted new theories of distribution, the most impressive element in their discussions was their adherence to the revolutionary generation's belief that wealth inequalities arose from governmental practices—taxes, monopolies, bureaucracies, financial manipulations, an established church, aristocratic laws of entail and primogeniture, and control of politics by an aristocracy. Nevertheless, a clear division emerged in the American camp. At the heart of this division was the problem of securing high wages for the laborer to ensure that all workers—now broadly defined to include urban dwellers as well as independent farmers—received the fruits of their labor. Free traders ascribed to the analysis of their British peers but escaped the dire conclusion by rejoicing in the effects of western land. Protectionists rejected the landed imperialism that free trade required for egalitarianism; the protectionists located a just distribution of wealth in the Founders' understanding of aristocratic manipulations but added to it a condition that government must promote a special type of market in which equality in earnings could flourish.

Adam Smith had accepted inequality in his discussion of income distribution among landlords, laborers, and capitalists. Smith, however, had been an optimistic systematizer of England's economic developments. His book argued for increasing wealth through a division of labor, free trade, accumulation of capital stock, and improved machinery. Smith's hopeful view of the economic future soon dissipated in the glare of the three dominant political economists of the early and middle nineteenth century: the Reverend Thomas Malthus, financier David Ricardo, and philosopher John Stuart Mill.[1] By 1848 and probably into the 1870s, these three men succeeded in

1. See the comparison between American and British economists in Hovencamp, *Enterprise and American Law,* 68–77.

transforming political economy into a "dismal science" that foretold of over-bearing wealth for landlords, unending physical deprivation for laborers, and an end to human improvement and economic growth—the arrival of societies at the "stationary state" where economic life becomes eternally stagnant.

The first component to be added to Adam Smith's analysis was the impact of population growth. From Smith's time to the 1790s, the world was becoming more frightening to many English leaders because of the French Revolution and the apparently unbounded enthusiasm of some intellectuals for human improvement through enlightened reason. One person who reacted strongly to such ideas of advancement was Thomas Malthus, who in 1798 wrote his (in)famous pamphlet, *An Essay on the Principle of Population as It Affects the Future Improvement of Society with Remarks on the Speculations of Mr. Godwin, M. Condorcet, and Other Writers.* Malthus' thesis was relatively simple. The mass of mankind lived by wages, and wages were determined solely by the supply of labor. The supply of labor was regulated by population, and population in turn depended on available food supplies. When civilization finally used the last parcel of arable land, the food supply would become restricted. The animal passions of the lower orders led to procreation whenever available food supplies existed, ensuring that population would always press on the means of subsistence. Wages, therefore, always fell to the lowest possible level. Malthus added to his explanation the proposition that a "wage fund," consisting of the year's productions out of which labor could be paid, governed the welfare of the lower class. The fund was stationary; the larger the laboring class, the lower the wage level.[2]

Malthus at first claimed that human intervention could not alter the un-reasoning and unthinking course of population expansion. People simply procreated too much, and as a result some would have to starve. Thus wars,

---

2. Thomas Robert Malthus, *On Population* (1798), ed. Gertrude Himmelfarb (New York, 1960), 8–15, 74–75; Thomas Robert Malthus, *Principles of Political Economy Considered with a View to Their Practical Application* (2nd ed.; 1836; rpr. New York, 1968), 223. Herbert Hoven-camp has called attention to the wage fund as the focus for discussions on the distribution of wealth; however, the wage fund was one of the vehicles for explaining subsistence wages, and subsistence wages rather than the wage fund was the fulcrum on which distributionist dis-course centered (Hovencamp, *Enterprise and American Law,* 193). On Malthus, see H. Scott Gordon, "The Wage-Fund Controversy: The Second Round," *History of Political Economy,* V (1973), 14–15; Lionel Robbins, *The Theory of Economic Policy in English Classical Political Econ-omy* (London, 1952), 75–76; Robert L. Heilbroner, *The Worldly Philosophers: The Lives, Times, and Ideas of the Great Economic Thinkers* (5th ed.; New York, 1961), 60–61, 70–75; Blaug, *Eco-nomic Theory in Retrospect,* 69–79.

famines, plagues, and other disasters were a positive check on overpopulation. Unfortunately, once population was reduced, the lower class ate better and again let their sexual appetites overwhelm them, resulting in a population surge that again superseded the ability of the civilization to provide subsistence, leading to famines and wars. One of the gloomiest of political economists, Malthus wrote in the first edition of his book, "Man cannot live in the midst of plenty," and later added, "It has appeared, that from the inevitable laws of our nature, some human beings must suffer from want."[3]

Malthus' original theory was altered over time as he and David Ricardo disputed everything the other wrote or said. In the second and following editions of his essay on population, Malthus agreed that perhaps the lower orders could be taught to restrain their sexual habits and so possibly improve their lot (preventive checks). He also came to advocate equal rights and equal laws. He remained a spokesperson for landholders, however, and vigorously denied Ricardo's depiction of rent. Malthus never surrendered the notion of a wage fund, and although his later writings may have contained some hope for common people, he basically argued that wages could never rise much above subsistence.[4]

Malthusian economics led to a skewed distribution of wealth, for the overriding implication was that the fate of most people was subsistence wages. A second feature in the reverend's musings was the absence of a labor theory of value. Supply determined wages, the value of labor. Malthus' analysis also presumed that expansion of capital stock could never outpace population growth, so demand for labor was never as important as its supply. At one point Malthus agreed that man had "rights," but one right he did not have was "a right to subsistence when his labour will not fairly purchase it."[5] Here Malthus made two important statements: wages were determined by the market, and the fruits of labor were meaningless except as a market-determined wage. The fruits of labor, in short, did not imply subsistence, let alone comfort or competence.

Malthus explained why Americans possessed high wages and hence a more

3. Malthus, *On Population,* 1st ed., 66, 74.

4. *Ibid.,* 3rd ed., ed. Himmelfarb, 158–60; 7th ed., 338–44, 385–87, 495–500; Malthus, *Principles of Political Economy,* 140–52, 218–23; Heilbroner, *Worldly Philosophers,* 65–68, 79.

5. Malthus, *On Population,* 7th ed., 518; on the question of value in Malthus, see Morton Paglin, *Malthus and Lauderdale: The Anti-Ricardian Tradition* (New York, 1961), 46; Allen Kaufman, *Capitalism, Slavery, and Republican Values: Antebellum Political Economists, 1819–1848* (Austin, 1982), 28.

equitable distribution of wealth. As Madison and Jefferson had hypothesized a decade earlier, the reason was available land. Because of the amount of unoccupied land the United States possessed, population increases could easily be accommodated by settling the surplus people on western lands, thus avoiding the trap of a stationary wage fund. But the rule of population growth and human misery could not be thwarted forever. Malthus forecast that "it may be expected that in the progress of the population of America the labourers will in time be less liberally rewarded." The land could not last forever.[6]

David Ricardo, Malthus' contemporary and intellectual competitor, extended the theory of population into a much broader theory of distribution. A London stockbroker, Ricardo developed many essential ideas about economic activity that made important advances in the discipline. But it was his theory of distribution of income among landlords, laborers, and capitalists that won him fame in the nineteenth century. Ricardo may not have been the best economist of his day, but he probably had the most penetrating mind. Unfortunately, he wrote his penetrating insights in almost impenetrable English, resulting in what amounts to an academic industry trying to decipher exactly what he meant.[7]

Ricardo began his theory of distribution by positing that society fell into the three categories of landlords, laborers, and capitalists. He relied on a strict labor theory of value to determine value in a cost-of-production approach, and he then translated value into equivalents of amounts of wheat. (It was Ricardo's peculiar idea that physical labor alone created value that led critics of market economics to grab onto it and to become known as "Ricardian" socialists.) To determine the reward given labor, that is, wages, Ricardo turned

6. Malthus, *On Population,* quote from 7th ed., 336; see also 1st ed., 49, 7th ed., 392; Malthus, *Principles of Political Economy,* 226, 233.

7. The best description of Ricardian economics is Blaug, *Economic Theory in Retrospect,* 91–140; and Mark Blaug, *Ricardian Economics: A Historical Study* (New Haven, 1958). For examples of some of the controversy surrounding Ricardo, consult George J. Stigler, "The Ricardian Theory of Value and Distribution" and "Ricardo and the 93 Per Cent Labor Theory of Value," both in Stigler, *Essays in the History of Economics* (Chicago, 1965), 156–97, 326–42; Overton H. Taylor, *A History of Economic Thought* (New York, 1960), 173–213; Samuel Hollander, *The Economics of David Ricardo* (Toronto, 1979); H. Barkai, "Ricardo on Factor Prices and Income Distribution in a Growing Economy," *Economica,* XXVI (1959), 240–49; Frank W. Fetter, "The Rise and Decline of Ricardian Economics," *History of Political Economy,* I (1969), 67–84; David Levy, "Ricardo and the Iron Law: A Correction of the Record," *History of Political Economy,* VIII (1976), 235–51.

to Malthusian population strictures. Population pressed wages down to subsistence levels: "The natural price of labour is that price which is necessary to enable the labourers, one with another, to subsist and perpetuate their race, without either increase or diminution." The reward for capitalists depended on the wage rate, and here Ricardo proposed the inverse law between wages and profits that set up the classical notion of conflict of interests, soon to be translated into class conflict: "It has been my endeavour to shew throughout this work, that the rate of profits can never be increased but by a fall in wages." Profits were therefore a residual; they depended on the income remaining once all the costs of production had been met (basically, labor costs).[8]

Ricardo then closed his system by considering the returns to landlords. Employing Malthus' model of population pressure, Ricardo asserted that landlords began to cultivate less fertile lands to meet the increased food requirements of a growing population. Here he enunciated the principle of diminishing marginal returns. At a certain point, the yield (output) obtained from the addition of an extra unit of resource (input) fell. Hence the yield of grain on new soil was less than on the plots originally cultivated, yet the price of all grain was regulated by the yield on the most infertile plots. Prices rose because it became more difficult to raise as much grain. Thus farmers who possessed the best land earned more money than previously for no reason except that prices rose because production had moved to inferior soil. Earning income not from labor but from monopoly of a natural resource has since become known as earning a rent or a quasi-rent.[9]

Then the political economist turned to the implications of his system. Population pressures required resorting to less and less fertile land to feed a swelling population. Foodstuff prices rose, and so landlords earned more income from the operation of rent. Laborers, already at the subsistence level, had to earn more wages to survive. Thus wages rose but not the workers' standard of living—the workers remained at subsistence. Because wages and profits were inversely related, profits had to fall—capitalists earned less.

8. David Ricardo, *On the Principles of Political Economy, and Taxation* (3rd ed., 1821), in Piero Sraffa, ed., *The Works and Correspondence of David Ricardo* (Cambridge, Eng., 1951), I, 49; on labor theory of value, 12; on wages, 93–94; quotes on 93, 132; see also 35 and chap. 6; on cost of production, see David Ricardo, *Notes on Malthus's Principles of Political Economy* [*ca.* 1820], *ibid.,* II, 38, 46.

9. Ricardo, *On the Principles of Political Economy, ibid.,* I, 67; a full explanation of his idea is *ibid.,* chap. 2.

Eventually this process reached its limit at which time no new land could be acquired, population increases had to stop or the Malthusian positive check would occur, landlords reaped immense incomes, laborers stayed at subsistence, and capitalists earned only enough to maintain the industry already established. At some point, then, society reached a steady state because no further improvement was possible—the limits of human achievement had been reached.[10]

Foreign trade provided a temporary means out of the dilemma. England's arable land was fast diminishing, thereby bringing about the upward march of wages that stymied manufacturing profits and expansion. Ricardo argued that this situation was avoidable by resorting to foreign trade and importing foodstuffs: "If, therefore, by the extension of foreign trade, or by improvements in machinery, the food and necessaries of the labourer can be brought to market at a reduced price, profits will rise." Blocking this route were the landlords, who expected to reap large returns from rent and who supported the high taxes on imported foodstuffs, the Corn Laws.[11]

Together Malthus and Ricardo gave birth to the "iron law of wages" and the prediction that laborers faced only a future of misery. It was a grim forecast, deservedly earning the discipline the title of the "dismal science." Any number of scholars have tried to exculpate Ricardo from these charges, but most commentators in the nineteenth century equated Ricardian economics with starvation wages.[12]

Ricardo disclosed his basic Malthusian population perspective when he discussed the American economy. Capital might outpace population in new settlements "where the arts and knowledge of countries far advanced in refinement are introduced," for there "it is probable that capital has a tendency to increase faster than mankind." That condition would not last. True, the United States had high wages. Where would "the high real wages of America . . . finally go? I answer they will go with almost the whole of the rest of the surplus produce to rent." He elaborated: "First, they [wages] will, when they fall, raise profits.—High profits lead to new accumulations—new accumula-

10. *Ibid.,* 120–26. The basics of the Ricardian system can be gleaned from any number of works, but see Blaug, *Ricardian Economics,* 22–33; Heilbroner, *Worldly Philosophers,* 62–64, 75–79; Hollander, *Economics of David Ricardo,* 6–12, 124–25, 398–99.

11. Ricardo, *On the Principles of Political Economy,* in Sraffa, ed., *Works and Correspondence of Ricardo,* I, quote on 132; see 129–33.

12. For a defense of Ricardo's views on labor, see Hollander, *Economics of David Ricardo,* 6–7, 11–12, 268; Blaug, *Ricardian Economics,* 24; Vincent Bladen, *From Adam Smith to Maynard Keynes: The Heritage of Political Economy* (Toronto, 1974), 189–90.

tions to an increased demand for labour, to an increase of people—to the cultivation of poorer land and finally to an increase of rent."[13] And so Ricardo agreed with Malthus about the essentials of the American economy. Extensive land momentarily propped up wages, providing a facade of wealth and income equality, but eventually population pressure would overwhelm that condition, rents would rise, real wages would fall to subsistence, and profits would stagnate. The exceptionalism of the United States would pass, and Americans would eventually confront class conflict and the stationary state.

The economic doctrines of Malthus and Ricardo held sway over political economists during the 1820s, but then a counterattack mounted that lasted from the late 1820s until John Stuart Mill joined the battle over economic principles in the 1840s. Various investigators, including Jean-Baptiste Say, Robert Torrens, J. R. McCulloch, Nassau Senior, and Robert Whately, found innumerable problems with Ricardo's wage theories, rent doctrines, and value definitions and with Malthus' population strictures. These writers implied that there was more equity and optimism in political economy than Malthus and Ricardo had allowed because of the effects of productivity, birth control, education, and human capital generally. The Ricardian wage theory came under particular attack. English economist Nassau Senior found the inverse wage relation to be fraught with error: "The consequence has been that, since the publication of his [Ricardo's] great Work, an opinion has prevailed that high wages and high profits are incompatible, and that whatever is taken from the one is added to the other." This, Senior snorted, was an "absurdity." Moreover, no one except socialists could make sense of the labor theory of value, remarked Senior, "and by this one ambiguity has rendered his great work a long enigma."[14]

13. Quotes from Ricardo, *On the Principles of Political Economy,* in Sraffa, ed., *Works and Correspondence of Ricardo,* I, 98; Ricardo, *Notes on Malthus's Principles of Political Economy, ibid.,* II, 138–39.

14. Mark Blaug, "The Empirical Content of Ricardian Economics," *Journal of Political Economy,* LXIV (1956), 44–45; Blaug, *Ricardian Economics,* 111, 113, 119; Maxine Berg, *The Machinery Question and the Making of Political Economy, 1815–1848* (Cambridge, Eng., 1980), 81–82; D. P. O'Brien, *J. R. McCulloch: A Study in Classical Economics* (New York, 1970), 316–18; Barry Gordon, "Criticism of Ricardian Views on Value and Distribution in the British Periodicals, 1820–1850," *Journal of Political Economy,* I (1969), 370, 380–85; Nassau William Senior, *An Outline of the Science of Political Economy* (1836; rpr. New York, 1939), 143, 228; James Mill, *Elements of Political Economy* (3rd ed.; London, 1844), 74; J. R. McCulloch, *The Principles of Political Economy; with a Sketch of the Rise and Progress of the Science* (Edinburgh, 1825), 366–67; On the labor theory of value, see O'Brien, *J. R. McCulloch,* 126–30; Blaug, *Ricardian Economics,* 52–61; Fetter, "Rise and Decline of Ricardian Economics," 76–80. Fetter argues that

These interesting forays came to naught. John Stuart Mill published his *Principles of Political Economy* in 1848, revised it six times, resuscitated Malthus and Ricardo, and crushed anti-Ricardian ideas in England. Mill reestablished the primacy of population growth, the infertility of inferior soils, and the inverse relationship between profit and wages. He prophesied the end of economic growth and inevitable attainment of the stationary state. Not until the late 1870s and the early 1880s, when marginal utility value theory gained ground, did Ricardian economics once again come under attack.[15]

Mill's economics called for a redistributive scheme like that of Ricardo's, but he injected suitable modifications to allow wage earners to live a modestly comfortable life. Production, Mill wrote, was a science, but distribution "is a matter of human institution solely." The "distribution of wealth, therefore, depends on the laws and customs of society," and political rulers often determined those laws and customs. Although Mill tackled wealth distribution in a manner reminiscent of the eighteenth century, he nonetheless did not hesitate to pronounce population growth the major villain in the question of equitable distribution and social welfare. The new doctrines of socialism and communism troubled him, for their attacks on capitalism—or, in his estimation, on property rights—were based on the injustice of wealth inequality. On behalf of property rights, which he sought to preserve because of their connection with individual liberty, Mill argued that economic systems based on property rights had not yet received a fair trial because the initial wealth distribution had been so awful. That realization may have nudged Mill to adopt the position that society should alter inheritance laws which made inequalities loom so great.[16]

---

the only reason Ricardian value theories ever became important was their acquisition by Marxian socialists (*ibid.,* 80). For rejection of the stationary state, see O'Brien, *J. R. McCulloch,* 294–98; Blaug, *Economic Theory in Retrospect,* 180. On rent, see O'Brien, *J. R. McCulloch,* 298–99; Senior, *Outline of the Science of Political Economy,* 26; Blaug, "Empirical Content of Ricardian Economics," 51.

15. On the resurgence of Ricardian economics because of the arguments of John Stuart Mill, see N. B. de Marchi, "The Success of Mill's *Principles,*" *History of Political Economy,* VI (1974), 122–57; Blaug, *Ricardian Economics,* 117–19, 190; Fetter, "Rise and Decline of Ricardian Economics," 81–82; Gordon, "Criticism of Ricardian Views on Value and Distribution," 385. Fetter argues that Mill reformulated Ricardo into a theory that Ricardo would not have approved ("Rise and Decline of Ricardian Economics," 81).

16. John Stuart Mill, *Principles of Political Economy with Some of Their Applications to Social Philosophy,* ed. J. W. Ashley (1871; rpr. London, 1926), quote on 200; discussion of communism and socialism, 201–33; remarks on private property, 201–204, 208, 218–19, 221; on distribution, 199–202, 242.

Though Mill offered more interesting thoughts on the distribution of wealth than did other political economists of the Manchester school, he was a Ricardian. Despite his desire to see an intelligent, skilled, and happy working class, workers suffered the usual fate of a Malthusian world.[17]

Mill also had occasion to remark on the economy of the United States. On the one hand, Mill found high wages in North America to be the result of the boundless land that enabled capital easily to absorb excessive population growth. But the process could not go on forever; "therefore, if wages do not fall, profits must; and when profits fall, increase of capital is slackened." On the other hand, Mill found a phenomenon he could not interpret. In comparing different nations, he noted that the United States had an unusual comparative advantage in international trade even though daily earnings were so much higher there: "But the productive power of American labour is so great—." That observation might have led to important alterations in his theories, but Mill could not escape the Ricardian framework from which he viewed the world. His observation on productivity remained merely an observation.[18]

Ricardo created a distribution theory that remained dominant in European and English circles until the 1870s and 1880s—and in some ways lasted beyond that time. The distribution of income in the categories of wages, rents, and profits became the standard mode of discussion in political economy for the rest of the century. In the form that Malthus and Ricardo fashioned classical distribution theory, the implication was that wealth was enormously unequally distributed because of the subsistence wage doctrine. The question of an equitable distribution of wealth, such as the American revolutionaries spoke of, was driven out of European economics except to the extent that authors claimed that the distribution theory of Ricardo and Malthus was natural and thereby moral. Equality in wealth distribution, or even equity, had to find a home other than classical economics. It found such a home in radical political philosophies such as socialism. But in the United States, the older idea of an equal or equitable distribution of wealth was not driven out of economic inquiry.

The Americans learned the boundaries of disputes over wealth distribution and its analysis from the European discussion of political economy between 1776 and 1860. First, they had to deal with Ricardian distribution and its inequitable implications. Second, they continued to define value, with in-

17. *Ibid.,* 757–62.
18. *Ibid.,* 350–51, 681–82; on wages, see 688–90, 757–62.

creasing reservations and qualifications, in terms of a labor theory of property/value. Unlike the Europeans, who found the morality inherent in the labor theory of value useful for alternative economic schemes such as socialism, North Americans kept the labor theory of property/value in the mainstream of political economy and did not relegate it to peripheral groups. Third, the key to the debate over an equitable distribution of income, and hence wealth, was the determination of wages. The validity of subsistence wage theory held the key to human happiness.

Fourth, the Americans learned that they had escaped the fate of Europe because of their possession of western land. Indeed, in terms of political economy, the answer to "American exceptionalism" was easy enough to understand and explain. The vast expanse of land gave Americans an economy in which capital was preponderant in relation to population, in which wages were high by European standards, and in which the distribution of wealth was uncommonly good—all of which led to the corollary of an absence of class animosities and working-class unrest. But nineteenth-century European political economists quickly pointed out that American exceptionalism would last only as long as there were boundless tracts of land. When that condition ended, so did American exceptionalism. The laws of political economy did not brook exceptions over time and place.

British ideas in the form of books and articles swiftly flowed over the Atlantic to the United States. It was not long before Americans responded to the theories and conclusions of Malthus, Ricardo, and John Stuart Mill. Various circumstances affected the American response, however. Americans, with a few exceptions, were not as sophisticated as the important European political economists, and it is debatable how many really understood Ricardo and the implications of his rent theory. Furthermore, Americans used political economy in the service of the questions that most befuddled them, and those were not the questions over which Europeans quarreled. For American political economists, the immediate concerns were the proper policy toward international trade, government encouragement of industrialization, the creation of a suitable medium of exchange, the power of the central government, the funding of internal improvements, and the settlement of western lands. The fact that the United States was in a developmental stage colored the attitudes of economists as to what they believed was important and what was not. The comparison with Europe and especially England was obvious: political economy in those lands was not only how to sustain economic growth but how to rationalize the sufferings of the working class. Americans felt little of the latter motivation.

Two camps dominated American economic thinking—free traders and advocates of protectionism. They had much in common because both were securely lodged in the house of capitalism. They adhered to the essential primacy of property rights, a competitive marketplace, the supremacy of individual choice, a division of labor, and capital accumulation. In a formal sense, they divided over the policy of international trade. Free traders wanted no tariff barriers, or at most a tariff for revenue only, whereas protectionists argued for restricting the importation of foreign wares by high tariff duties so as to allow a native manufacturing establishment to take root and spread.

American free traders had a strange relationship with the distribution theories of classical economics. Though attaching many reservations, they tended to accept Malthusian doctrines but had problems with Ricardo. They found ways to argue for an egalitarian distribution of wealth even though the theory they used unavoidably established an immensely skewed distribution. For the free traders, the saving grace was land. The American proponents of the lessons of Smith, Malthus, Ricardo, and Mill could save the egalitarian wealth strictures of the revolutionaries only by glorifying the existence of the American West. American republicanism, in the free trade camp, increasingly became solely dependent on westward expansion.

American free traders in their strange dance with the British economists further altered the revolutionary inheritance. Free trade economics tended to take republicanism out of economic concerns. This result was probably unavoidable and was directly traceable to the theories of Malthus and Ricardo. Revolutionary republicanism posited a tight relationship between government structure, society, and the economy. Republican governments had republican economies, aristocratic governments had aristocratic economies. But in the economics of Malthus and Ricardo, government had no vital role, and in the important processes, government did not matter. According to Malthus and Ricardo (but not necessarily Adam Smith), all economies were powered by the fertility of the soil and the extent to which a society had resorted to marginal land, the nearly invincible sexual lusts of the lower class which propelled population growth to the limits of subsistence, and the desire of capitalists to make a profit. Those three features determined economic relationships and outcomes. Politics was not an essential feature in the Malthusian-Ricardian model. Ultimately what Malthus and Ricardo said was that proper political policies could advance or retard the stationary state, could depress or elevate the condition of the working class, could augment or decrease profits, but could not over time change the final outcome or the fundamental forces at work. Whereas republicanism joined politics and economics, free trade theory divorced them.[19]

Free trade theorists in the United States were amateurs, obtaining no certification or notoriety except by publishing. A few claimed academic chairs, yet individuals from vastly different occupations contributed to economic doctrines. By 1860 a corpus of free trade works had appeared that were considered standard treatments of the subject. Three prominent authors hailed from the South: Jacob N. Cardozo (1786–1873), a South Carolinian who functioned as an editorialist and economics reporter; Thomas Cooper (1759–1840), an English-born radical who had migrated to the United States and eventually became a professor of moral philosophy at the University of South Carolina; and George Tucker (1775–1861), a professor who taught political economy at the University of Virginia. The northern contingent of free trade theorists included Francis Wayland (1796–1865), a Baptist minister who became president of Brown University; John McVickar (1787–1868), a New Yorker who became a professor of moral philosophy; Henry Vethake (1792–1866), a British Guinea–born economist who eventually taught at Columbia, Dickinson College, Washington College, and the University of Pennsylvania; George Opdyke (1805–1880), a Republican politician who became mayor of New York City during the Civil War; and Amasa Walker (1799–1875), an important Boston shoe merchant, abolitionist, and father of the postbellum labor economist Francis Amasa Walker.[20]

Most free traders ascribed to some degree to the labor theory of value, although many qualifications began to appear. Wayland probably most completely relied on the notion that labor created values and thereby justified private property. Others believed that other influences helped create value. Thomas Cooper in 1826, while underlining the importance of labor, also stressed the contributions of capital and raw material. George Tucker emphasized the role of labor in creating value but suggested that value was simply a subjective emotional quality that could not be totally ascribed to labor inputs alone. Jacob Cardozo, writing in response to Ricardian doctrines in 1826, re-

19. Francis Lieber, *Notes on the Fallacies of American Protectionists* (4th ed., 1870; rpr. New York, 1974), 33; see also John McVickar, *Outlines of Political Economy* (New York, 1825), 48.

20. For information on these individuals, consult John Roscoe Turner, *The Ricardian Rent Theory in Early American Economics* (New York, 1921); and Dorfman, *Economic Mind in American Civilization*, II, 516–22, 527–66, 713–71.

jected the labor theory of value and pointed out how other circumstances such as transportation facilities created value.[21] Thus American free traders quibbled over the proper definition of value and saw labor as a chief component of value but not the only component.

Free traders found Malthusian population theory relatively easy to digest, understand, and popularize, although they did not necessarily conclude as did Malthus that humankind was doomed to inevitable misery. Because they grasped Malthus' theory without difficulty, most free traders agreed that an ever-expanding population would press wages down to subsistence. Wayland understood Malthus' logic but could not accept the result, arguing instead that Malthus demonstrated the need for capital to accumulate faster than population to ensure that the masses never fell into penury (thus missing the point of the argument: with a rising population, capital could not accumulate fast enough to employ the population when agriculture moved onto infertile soils).[22]

Thomas Cooper took a more interesting approach. He saw Malthus not as a harbinger of doom but as a messenger of salvation and human happiness. Like Wayland, Cooper considered capital accumulation the means of assuring workers a decent wage. But he also stressed Malthus' proposition that a society that exercised restraint could avoid overpopulation. He then teased out

21. Francis Wayland, *Elements of Political Economy* (4th ed.; Boston, 1856), 15, 17–20; Thomas Cooper, *Lectures on the Elements of Political Economy* (Columbia, S. C., 1826), 31, 63; George Tucker, *The Laws of Wages, Profits and Rent Investigated* (1837; rpr. New York, 1964), 1–7; J[acob] N. Cardozo, *Notes on Political Economy* (Charleston, 1826), 108–11. Although many saw labor as the only way to wealth, free traders had trouble with labor being the sole determinant of value: see John Bascom, *Political Economy: Designed as a Text-Book for Colleges* (1859; rpr. Andover, Mass., 1874), 19–21; John McVickar, *First Lessons in Political Economy; For the Use of Primary and Common Schools* (Boston, 1835), 59; Henry Vethake, *The Principles of Political Economy* (Philadelphia, 1838), 51; Melvin M. Leiman, *Jacob N. Cardozo: Economic Thought in the Antebellum South* (New York, 1966), 27–29.

22. Cardozo, *Notes on Political Economy*, 123–24; Tucker, *Laws of Wages, Profits and Rent Investigated*, 97; Tucker, *Political Economy for the People*, 81–82; on Vethake, see Turner, *Ricardian Rent Theory*, 68–69. See also Samuel P. Newman, *Elements of Political Economy* (Andover, Mass., 1835), 254; George Johnson Cady, "The Early American Reaction to the Theory of Malthus," *Journal of Political Economy*, XXXIX (1931), 609, 611–13, 616–18; Joseph J. Spengler, "Population Doctrines in the United States, I: Anti-Malthusianism," *Journal of Political Economy*, XLI (1933), 436; Spengler, "Population Doctrines in the United States, II: Malthusianism," *Journal of Political Economy*, XLI (1933), 640–42, 648–50; Francis Wayland, *The Elements of Political Economy* (Boston, 1840), 308–23, esp. 312–13. For a different interpretation, based on the wage fund, see Hovencamp, *Enterprise and American Law*, 194–96.

of that discovery a new way to look at saving and accumulation. According to republican principles, accumulation, particularly in the hands of a few people, was not socially healthy. Not so to Cooper, given Malthusian economics: "Frugality therefore, and accumulation, are public virtues." It was virtuous to accumulate money and invest it because that process ensured that capital would be available to employ the entire population.[23]

What Cooper had done to virtue, free trade economics did to the republicanism of the Revolution. The economics of free trade was forcing republicanism to accept market structures and the pursuit of self-interest.[24] Under the impress of the Malthusian population dilemma, free traders saw only two ways to maintain the population: sexual restraint and an increase of capital. Because capital accumulation employed people and avoided massive death by famine, disease, and wars, accumulation became a public service—a virtue.

If American free traders found Malthus' population ideas straightforward and understandable, Ricardo's views of rent gave them fits. Francis Wayland and Amasa Walker ascribed rent to location and fertility, among other things, and frequently talked of rent as equivalent to interest paid on capital. Cooper provided a decent summary of Ricardo, but he did not elaborate what Ricardo's rent theory implied in terms of distributive shares. George Tucker attempted a refutation of Ricardian rent theory in 1837, but it was close to being a disastrous exercise. Tucker simply did not understand the nature of a closed system and Ricardo's premises. The Virginian found no reason to assert that when food prices rose, wages would rise and profits fall. The reason, he suggested, was that Ricardo did not comprehend subsistence wages: Tucker argued that of course wages could go below subsistence—there was no need to feed a wife and children, only oneself. Because wages could always fall further (he rejected the notion of a minimum wage that labor had to be paid), profits could rise when food prices rose.[25]

Cardozo was one of the few American free trade economists who under-

23. Cooper, *Lectures on the Elements of Political Economy,* quote on 12; also discussion 48–49, 232–40.

24. Jean V. Matthews has argued that early free trade economists, like McVickar, stayed within the confines of virtue. It was not possible for free trade economists to espouse virtue because of the individualist, self-seeking nature of the theory; moreover, McVickar's work was largely a reprint of David Ricardo's *Principles,* and no one to my knowledge has ever accused Ricardo of being a monument to classical republican virtue. See Matthews, *Toward a New Society: American Thought and Culture, 1800–1830* (Boston, 1991), 139.

25. Wayland, *Elements of Political Economy* (1856), 339–55; Amasa Walker, "Rent," *Hunt's Merchants' Magazine,* XLII (April, 1860), 302–10; Cooper, *Lectures on the Elements of Political Economy,* 81–84; Tucker, *Laws of Wages, Profits and Rent Investigated,* iv, 32–42, see also 56–57,

stood Ricardo, and his response was quick and incisive. Though Cardozo did consider population growth a potential long-run problem, he saw no great difficulty with increasing soil infertility and rejected the Ricardian scheme that related wages inversely to profits. After quoting extensive portions of Ricardo's *Principles,* Cardozo got to the underlying assumption of the Ricardian scheme: soil could not be improved by the wit of man. This concept Cardozo rejected. Soil was as responsive to science and technology as any other natural element. Because diminishing returns did not need to exist in agriculture, rent did not have to absorb all surpluses, and thus the inverse relation of wages and profits under the condition of rising food prices was no longer valid: "Wages do not encroach on profits nor profits on wages. All that is necessary to the final result is, that science and skill should be able to overcome the difficulty of production on land of a decreasing fertility."[26] Cardozo's emphasis on science in undermining Malthus and Ricardo would be developed by protectionists rather than by free traders.

When free traders turned to the vital question of distribution, their conclusions were messy and unsure. They offered a direct division of national income into proportionate shares to profits, rent, and wages, as did Ricardo, but they were uncertain as to how rents and profits were related to each other—a common practice was to consider rent as another form of profit. If the Ricardian notion of distribution was muddled, however, the Malthusian postulate of subsistence wages was clear and usually precise. Free traders generally accepted the idea that wages would be kept down by population pressure.[27]

Free traders' writings implied that they sanctioned a large imbalance in the distribution of income and wealth. With wage earners receiving so little, it was difficult to argue for an equality of wealth in the sense that the revolutionary generation did. Indeed, the distribution of wealth was not even talked about in the same manner it was in the days of the War for Independence. Only Wayland, who made a distinct plea for inequality based on tal-

---

60–62, 64–76, 104–108. See also Turner, *Ricardian Rent Theory,* 60, 65, 68, 71, 73, 92–105. For Ricardian apostles, see Bascom, *Political Economy,* 155–56; Dorfman, *Economic Mind in American Civilization,* II, 713–16.

26. Cardozo, *Notes on Political Economy,* quote on 41; see also 13–15, 19–26.

27. On subsistence wages, see Cardozo, *Notes on Political Economy,* 123–24 (but also p. 40 when he states that real wages can rise over time); Cooper, *Lectures on the Elements of Political Economy,* 30, 90–94, 98, 233–39; Tucker, *Laws of Wages, Profits and Rent Investigated,* 21–23, 39, 69; Richard Sulley, "Free Trade and Protection: Review of HC Carey," *Hunt's Merchants' Magazine,* XL (May, 1859), 532, 540.

ents, actually talked of the distribution of wealth. Free traders tended rather to contemplate distributive shares and, evidently, to allow readers to infer from their statements whatever they wished concerning the distribution of wealth. Although the free traders implied a highly unequal distribution of wealth, under Malthusian conditions, free traders, like George Opdyke in the 1850s, could argue that nonetheless it was a natural distribution and therefore legitimate.[28]

Free traders did not find republicanism a true shaper of economic relationships, but they did ascribe to parts of the revolutionary analysis of the distribution of wealth. The four axioms of the revolutionary generation appeared in their works. They were especially unified in condemning the economic effects of aristocracy.[29] By using the political economy of aristocracy, they fashioned an explanation for the economic injustices occurring in England.

Jacob Cardozo, who in many ways retained more revolutionary doctrines than other free traders, criticized Ricardian rent theory not only for its lack of faith in science and knowledge but also because he saw that Ricardo had overlooked politics in the origin of rent. Throughout his work, Cardozo returned again and again to the effects of entail and primogeniture. Those laws, he said, were the true reason rent existed. He ended his book with a nearly complete litany of the defects of England that the revolutionaries had propounded: "Without indulging, therefore, in dreams of perfectibility, it is not venturing on visionary speculations of unattainable or impossible improvement to infer, that if the institution of primogeniture were abolished wherever it prevails, with every species of monopoly, supposing the security of person and property complete, and the public burthens moderate, the rate of increase in the production of food might greatly augment."[30]

Either explicitly citing England as an example or relating how governments could deflect distribution from its natural course, the free traders ticked off the items singled out by the revolutionaries of 1776. First was excessive taxation. A swollen government was also a source of economic waste and potentially unfair redistribution. Cooper evoked the revolutionary view of patronage in his discussion of unproductive labor and the definition of aris-

---

28. Wayland, *Elements of Political Economy*, 119–21; George Opdyke, *A Treatise on Political Economy* (New York, 1851), 260.

29. On republicanism, see Cardozo, *Notes on Political Economy*, iii; Opdyke, *Treatise on Political Economy*, iv–v; on fruits of labor, McVickar, *First Lessons in Political Economy*, 49–50; Newman, *Elements of Political Economy*, 19; Tucker, *Political Economy for the People*, 30.

30. Cardozo, *Notes on Political Economy*, 124; see also 25–30, 36.

tocracy: the unproductive class was "those members of society, who do not labour in any manner," and those individuals were most likely "All Sinecure
holders" such as "Kings, Nobles, the Hierarchy, with all their tribe of retain-
ers." Free traders called for equal laws and an end to special privileges and
monopolies, including, needless to say, their denunciation of high tariffs.
And free traders were especially bitter about paper money issued by governments. They warily approached the subject of the value of commercial bank
paper and had little but scorn for a paper legal tender.[31]

Free traders used aristocracy to explain inequities in American wealth distribution. No free trade political economist ever argued for an equal division
of property among a nation's inhabitants, but they all possessed an equitability standard. Aristocracies violated the principle of equal laws for all citizens,
resulting in one group's appropriation of another group's fruits of labor.
George Tucker remarked that people would be "neither industrious nor frugal, if a rapacious government is ready to seize on the fruits of his labor." By
aristocratic follies such as monopolies, court favorites, taxation, and feudal
dues, "mankind . . . [has] been down-trodden and oppressed by their rulers."
As late as 1859, John Bascom was explicit about the economic evils of aristocracy. "An aristocracy, on the other hand," he wrote, "gathers up the rewards
of labor, the enjoyments and luxuries of life, and bestows them not on those
who have produced them, and where falling they are the needful stimulus of
industry, but upon the most unproductive." When considering distribution,
American free traders, rather than drawing out and living with the bitter
fruits of Malthusian-Ricardian logic, opted for the blissful but unexplained
doctrine that when wealth was permitted to flow "unchecked and unim-
peded," then "its diffusion becomes most general and salutary."[32]

But despite their common analysis, American free traders were not as pessimistic as their European counterparts. The reason derived entirely from the
fourth axiom of the revolutionaries' concept of the distribution of wealth.

31. Wayland, *Elements of Political Economy*, 394, 116, 259–71; Tucker, *Laws of Wages, Profits
and Rent Investigated*, 139–40, 118, 206, 210–11; Cardozo, *Notes on Political Economy*, 76–80,
42–46, 24–26, 83, 87–88; Cooper, *Lectures on the Elements of Political Economy*, 213–15, 219–20,
50, 132–42, 157, quote on 34; Opdyke, *Treatise on Political Economy*, 292; Charles H. Carroll,
"On the Nature of Commercial Value," *Hunt's Merchants' Magazine*, XL (March, 1859),
309–13.

32. Tucker, *Political Economy for the People*, 30–31; Bascom, *Political Economy*, 59; Newman, *Elements of Political Economy*, 234. See also "The Applications of Political Economy,"
New Englander, VII (August, 1849), 432–38.

Land was not available in Europe, and the social implications of that condition saturated European economic tracts with morbid foreboding. Land was plentiful in the United States (if Europeans ignored, as they regularly did, the claims of American Indians). Land was the savior of the revolutionary generation's concern about acquiring the proper distribution of wealth for a republic. Western lands would preserve a republican polity in the United States.

Because of the West, Americans could take care of their surplus population for generations, maintain wages, and thus ensure equality of wealth so long as no monopolization of the land occurred. American free traders recognized this condition and sought to keep the United States on the agrarian path of economic development. The southern free traders, for instance, harbored no particular love for industrialism, and Thomas Cooper was bitter in his portrayal of factory establishments in England.[33] American free traders tended to be agrarians who romanticized rural life. Although many motives may have spurred them to support commercial agricultural development in the United States, the choice to do so was logically correct given their theory and the state of American resources: the existence of uninhabited land promised a rough equality of property for the bulk of the people and thereby a continuation of the republican experiment.

Of course, the free trade analysis of land also propounded a definite end to the republican experiment. And in that sense, the free traders were dishonest about the prospects of the nation.

The distribution of wealth and income was a core topic for protectionists. Their treatment of the subject differed considerably from that of the free trade school, and protectionists preserved much of the revolutionary analysis. They confronted the Manchester school of free trade economics on two fronts. One was the use of the doctrines of revolutionary republicanism in explaining the skewed wealth distribution of England and the miseries of the English working class. The second was decidedly more theoretical. Protectionists sought to and, indeed, succeeded in overthrowing the Malthus-Ricardo-Mill apparatus of subsistence wages.

Protectionism in the United States first appeared in the realm of politics, a product of the mercantilist leanings of Alexander Hamilton and the nationalistic motivations of Henry Clay. In the early years of the republic, protec-

33. Cooper, *Lecture on the Elements of Political Economy*, 119–22; David A. Wells, *The Creed of Free Trade* (N.p., n.d., reprinted from *Atlantic Monthly*, August, 1875), 5–8.

tionism lacked a theoretical foundation and instead appealed overtly to "common sense," the realities of international trade and power politics, and practical actions rather than idealistic concerns. Except for Canadian John Rae (1796–1872) and Baltimorean Daniel Raymond (1786–1849) in the 1820s, protectionism was largely advocated by politicians rather than academics or literary figures, and a full theoretical exposition of the high-tariff position would not appear until the 1830s and 1840s.[34]

Protectionists, who were usually found above the Mason-Dixon line, were a varied lot. In one fashion or another all criticized free trade theory. Two early developers of protectionist ideas were Daniel Raymond, a Baltimore lawyer, and John Rae, a British émigré to Canada who was influential in New England for his writings on capital growth. Boston produced two leading protectionists in Edward Everett (1794–1865), a Whig politician and outstanding orator, and Alexander Everett (1790–1847), brother of Edward, who became a publisher and a Democrat. New England also produced Francis Bowen (1811–1890), a conservative protectionist who served a tumultuous professorship at Harvard. Ezra Seaman (1805–1880) practiced law at Ann Arbor, Michigan; on economic matters he seemed more iconoclastic than most.

One of the important propagandizers for the Whigs and the tariff was Calvin Colton (1789–1857), biographer of Henry Clay and collector of his works. Pennsylvania contributed several protectionist theorists. Mathew Carey (1760–1839), an Irish émigré to the United States, was an early advocate of protection. Perhaps Mathew's greatest gift to protectionism was his son, Henry Charles Carey (1793–1879), who became the chief theoretician of protectionism and during the nineteenth century the bitterest foe of Ricardian economics in the United States. Closely connected with Henry Carey was the New Yorker Erasmus Peshine Smith (1814–1882), who worked with Senator William H. Seward and later traveled to Japan and adopted that nation's culture—a fitting conclusion for one who believed that protectionism preserved cultural integrity. Also allied with Henry Carey was Stephen Colwell, an

---

34. Michael Hudson, *Economics and Technology in 19th Century American Thought: The Neglected American Economists* (New York, 1975), 7–8, 11–15; Charles Patrick Neill, *Daniel Raymond: An Early Chapter in the History of Economic Theory in the United States* (Baltimore, 1897), 10–16. The early protectionists Hezekiah Niles and Mathew Carey were more crusaders and pamphleteers than theoreticians; see Richard Gabriel Stone, *Hezekiah Niles as an Economist* (Baltimore, 1933), 58–68, 121–29; Kenneth Wyer Rowe, *Mathew Carey: A Study in American Economic Development* (Baltimore, 1933), 50–55, 58–68.

evangelical ironmaster and divinity student who fretted over the inability of industrial workers to obtain sufficient wages. Protectionists also obtained the able services of Horace Greeley, mercurial reformer, zealous Whig and Republican, presidential nominee in 1872, and owner of the nation's most widely read newspaper in the 1850s, the New York *Tribune*.[35]

Revolutionary republican sentiments ran throughout protectionist antebellum writings. Unlike free traders, protectionists believed governmental structure vitally affected the operations of an economy and its social results. Daniel Raymond declared in the 1820s, "As our country has had the high honour of laying the true foundations of civil government, it must also have the honour of laying the true foundations of political economy." In 1848, Colton proclaimed that a free country, or representative government, meant economically high wages: "The great object of the American revolution was *to vindicate the rights of labor,* which, with the American fathers, comprehended all other valuable rights."[36]

Protectionists frequently resorted to the vocabulary of revolutionary republicanism and postulated on occasion a morality, usually biblical, that overruled any market-derived morality. They investigated the topics of luxury and virtue. The fear of importing foreign luxury goods was for John Rae an important reason for establishing a tariff. Moreover, in consideration of virtue, protectionists launched a crusade against the avarice and self-interest they saw lying behind free trade economics. Seaman warned that avarice was a natural passion, but it became a vice when "it is in excess and leads to covetousness and oppression." Colwell deprecated "the right of doing as every one pleases, which is included in free trade" as an unsound social principle "because it is a right which can inure only to a few; it is in fact the principle of savage rather than of civilized life."[37]

35. Biographical information can be obtained from Hudson, *Economics and Technology in 19th Century American Thought;* Turner, *Ricardian Rent Theory;* Dorfman, *Economic Mind in American Civilization,* II, 771–844, 952–55; Paul Conkin, *Prophets of Prosperity: America's First Political Economists* (Bloomington, 1980); R. Warren James, "The Life and Work of John Rae," *Canadian Journal of Economics and Political Science,* XVII (1951), 141–63; Daniel Walker Howe, *The Political Culture of the American Whigs* (Chicago, 1979), 107–22; Kaufman, *Capitalism, Slavery, and Republican Values,* chap. 3.

36. Henry C. Carey, *The Past, the Present and the Future* (1847; rpr. New York, 1967), 227–32; Daniel Raymond, *The Elements of Political Economy, in Two Parts* (2nd ed. 1823; rpr. New York, 1964), II, 395; Calvin Colton, *The Rights of Labor* (3rd ed.; New York, 1847), 9.

37. Raymond, *Elements of Political Economy,* I, 18, 21–22, chap. 19, esp. 408–10; Ezra C. Seaman, *Essays on the Progress of Nations in Productive Industry, Civilization, Population, and Wealth* (Detroit, 1846), 6, 297, quotes on p. 43; Francis Bowen, *The Principles of Political Econ-*

These protectionists still clearly harbored the notion of the general welfare and the use of politics to achieve it. That meant, of course, rejection of the free traders' favorite nostrum for enhancing economic activity, laissez-faire. Protectionists thought competition and free enterprise best, but they believed free traders had taken the principle too far. In particular, from Daniel Raymond and John Rae in the 1820s to Carey and Bowen in the 1850s, protectionists argued that government had to act to procure the conditions most conducive to national prosperity. Included in this list were prohibiting foreign luxury goods, maintaining full employment, providing education for the masses, and securing high wages for labor. In all these activities, save education, the role of the tariff was easily rationalized as the proper means of governmental intervention.[38] Unlike the free traders, protectionists kept alive the idea of an active government and argued for community over individualism. Protectionism, in short, grew out of the Revolution's communal heritage, whereas free trade economics evolved from its libertarian legacy.

Protectionists wrote about the distribution of wealth in the manner of the American revolutionaries. Daniel Raymond based much of his second volume about political economy on the necessity for a republic to maintain an equitable distribution of wealth: "A great portion of the evils in society arise from a too unequal division of property." Henry Carey denounced the multiplication of paupers and millionaires, "furnishing conclusive proof of decline in civilization and in freedom." By the mid-1850s, Francis Bowen, perhaps frightened by the revolutions of 1848 and the advance of socialist doctrines, warned that political economy must concern itself with more than the accumulation of national wealth: "We may admit that it is so, *if the wealth*

---

omy (Boston, 1856), ix, 123–24, 127; Stephen Colwell, *The Claims of Labor, and Their Precedence to the Claims of Free Trade* (Philadelphia, 1861), 42; Horace Greeley, "Protection of Industry," *Whig Almanac*, 1843, pp. 8–9. On luxury and virtue, see esp. John Rae, *The Sociological Theory of Capital, Being a Complete Reprint of the New Principles of Political Economy, 1834*, ed. Charles Whitney Mixter (New York, 1905), Appendix, 277–81. For the use of the golden rule in economics, see Henry C. Carey, *Principles of Political Economy* (1837–40; rpr. New York, 1965), II, 55.

38. Greeley, "Protection of Industry," 6; Francis Bowen, *American Political Economy* (New York, 1870), 18–21; Willard Phillips, *Propositions Concerning Protection and Free Trade* (Boston, 1850), 11; E. Peshine Smith, *A Manual of Political Economy* (New York, 1853), 257; Horace Greeley, *Essays Designed to Elucidate the Science of Political Economy . . .* (Boston, 1870), 23; Rae, *Sociological Theory of Capital*, 364–67; Raymond, *Elements of Political Economy*, I, 207–10, 219, 220–22, II, 276; Willard Phillips, *A Manual of Political Economy, with Particular Reference to the Institutions, Resources, and Conditions of the United States* (Boston, 1828), 226; Calvin Colton, *Public Economy for the United States* (New York, 1848), 275.

be distributed with some approach to equality among the people. But if the vast majority of the nation is beggared, while enormous fortunes are accumulated by a few,—if pauperism increases at one end of the social scale as rapidly as wealth is heaped up at the other,—then . . . if a remedy be not applied, society will rush into degradation and ruin."[39]

To explain why a nation's distribution of wealth became lopsided, protectionists fastened on the example of England, using almost the same analysis as free traders. The reason for England's maldistribution of wealth was the enactment of the policies of the political economy of aristocracy—primogeniture and entail, high taxes to pamper court favorites, a subsidized state church, bureaucracy, monopoly, and exclusive privileges. Although protectionists added a few new twists to the explanation of poor wealth distribution, on the whole they stayed within the comfortable confines of the political economy of aristocracy. Inequality arose from improper political activity.

By the beginning decades of the nineteenth century and certainly by the century's third and fourth decades, the poverty and misery of England's working class had become common knowledge and something of an international scandal. Equally well-known was the munificence of England's upper class. In contemplating the reasons for this awful wealth distribution, protectionists paid no heed to the Manchester school's explanation—the operation of the natural law of Malthusian population pressure—nor did they find any more attractive the ideas of socialists and labor leaders that the poor were ground down by capitalists. The reason for England's appalling number of poor was the system of aristocracy.[40]

Specific reasons why the political system of aristocracy generated inequalities quickly followed. Among the first objects protectionists attacked were the laws of English inheritance—primogeniture and entail. By the time of the Civil War, Americans still saw primogeniture and entail as the major rea-

39. Raymond, *Elements of Political Economy,* II, 15, also 9–26; Henry C. Carey, *Financial Crises: Their Causes and Effects* (Philadelphia, 1864), in Carey, *Miscellaneous Works of Henry C. Carey* (Philadelphia, 1865), I, 21; see also Carey, *The Harmony of Interests: Agricultural, Manufacturing and Commercial* (1851; rpr. New York, 1967), 63; Bowen, *Principles of Political Economy,* 16–17.

40. Raymond, *Elements of Political Economy,* II, 15, 63. The same sentiment is consistently found in protectionist works: Carey, *Principles of Political Economy,* II, 32; Seaman, *Essays on the Progress of Nations,* vii, 96; Calvin Colton, *The Junius Tracts and the Rights of Labor* (1844, 1847; rpr. New York, 1974), 83–84; Colton, *Rights of Labor,* 7–8; Horace Greeley, "Protection of Industry," 7–8; Smith, *Manual of Political Economy,* 126–28.

sons for England's concentration of wealth in the hands of the few. A second feature protectionists pointed to in England as creating a maldistribution of wealth was the granting of monopolies and privileges to the aristocratic few. Carey remarked that England had one of the most prized classes of all, "the class of small capitalists," but in England, unlike the United States, the small entrepreneur was thwarted from wholesome economic activity by monopolists. A third element skewing wealth distribution was the poor laws and trade unions, which tended to immobilize labor. The fourth component was heavy governmental taxation. Henry Carey, in his free trade phase during the 1830s, even went so far as to proclaim that taxation was the sole reason for the difference between high American wages and low British wages.[41]

The problem of the low wages of British workers, however, demanded more scrutiny. Protectionists denied that industrial activity under a free enterprise system necessitated the degradation of the worker. After all, they intended for the United States to become a manufacturing powerhouse, and they could hardly recommend a system of production that entailed such agony for the masses. Protectionist investigation of the miseries of British labor revealed some interesting attitudes on the part of the investigators, if not convincing explanations of the fate of British workers.

"High wages," intoned Calvin Colton, "and a high value of every species of property, as compared with those of Europe, are identical with freedom." Protectionists were thus arguing, correctly, that the inheritance of the American Revolution was workers' privilege of receiving fully the fruits of their labor. Francis Bowen stressed this point in a discussion of the conditions that led to the United States' rapid development: "1. That the laborer shall be sure of receiving the full amount of his wages, or shall be protected in the ownership of the values which he had produced." Because republicanism meant equal laws for all people with no favoritism shown to any group, the laborer should always receive ample remuneration. Alexander Everett made the difference between republicanism and aristocracy even more emphatic regarding the fruits of labor: "But if the products of labor of the community are distributed among its members upon any other principle than that of giv-

41. Raymond, *Elements of Political Economy*, II, 41–46, 70–71, 73–78; Colton, *Junius Tracts*, 102; Seaman, *Essays on the Progress of Nations*, 96–97; Carey, *Past, Present and Future*, 147, 323–34, 83–86; Henry C. Carey, *The Principles of Social Science* (1858; rpr. Philadelphia, 1867), III, 278; Smith, *Manual of Political Economy*, 127, 120–22, 134–36; Henry C. Carey, *Essay on the Rate of Wages* (1835; rpr. New York, 1965), 145, 62–63, also 9–10, 37; Carey, *Principles of Political Economy*, II, 218–20.

ing to each member the fruits of his own labor, it is evident that the productiveness of labor in general will form no certain criterion of the reward of individual labor, or in other words, of the rate of wages."[42]

Besides inheritance laws, taxes, monopolies, and poor laws, protectionists pointed to other features in Britain's economy that were destroying the well-being of the worker. Bowen detected the operation of a caste system that did not permit social mobility. Many protectionists focused on the size of British manufacturers. English establishments "were gigantic," they were "monster undertakings of large houses wielding an immense capital."[43] The large-scale undertakings of the British—somewhat exaggerated by American economists—resulted in a monopoly of capitalists over the supply of jobs. Thus in England, said Bowen, "the capitalists have the advantage." That advantage was that laborers had nowhere else to go and so the owners took fearful advantage of the British worker's circumscribed economic position.[44] On top of this pernicious condition, the English government used its police power to suppress wages, thereby making "paupers of her millions for the purpose of underselling other manufacturers in all the markets of the world."[45]

The reverse of demonstrating how the political economy of aristocracy crushed the manufacturing laborer was to reveal how a republican economy produced high wages and thus a proper distribution of wealth. Protectionists asserted that in the United States laborers were the equals—sometimes the

---

42. Colton, *Rights of Labor,* 8, 13; Bowen, *Principles of Political Economy,* 76, 52, 203; Alexander H. Everett, *New Ideas on Population: With Remarks on the Theories of Malthus and Godwin* (Boston, 1823), 111–12.

43. Carey, *Harmony of Interests,* 54; Bowen, *Principles of Political Economy,* 200–201, 129; John Aiken, *Labor and Wages, at Home and Abroad: In a Series of Newspaper Articles* (Lowell, Mass., 1849), 6–7. On the caste system in England, see Bowen, *Principles of Political Economy,* 124. Protectionists wanted local development and were suspicious of large international or even national markets; see Tony A. Freyer, *Producers Versus Capitalists: Constitutional Conflict in Antebellum America* (Charlottesville, 1994), 4–5, 7–9; James L. Huston, "A Political Response to Industrialism: The Republican Embrace of Protectionist Labor Doctrines," *Journal of American History,* LXX (1983), 35–57.

44. Bowen, *Principles of Political Economy,* 129; Colton, *Rights of Labor,* 7–8; Colton, *Junius Tracts,* 105; Carey, *Past, Present and Future,* 323–24. Seaman saw an unjust division of the products of labor, but he also believed population pressure was to blame (*Essays on the Progress of Nations,* 307).

45. Stephen Colwell, *The South: A Letter from a Friend in the North. With Special Reference to the Effects of Disunion upon Slavery* (Philadelphia, 1856), 13; Carey, *Harmony of Interests,* 71–72. On government support of the British manufacturing "monopolists," see Colton, *Rights of Labor,* 7–8, 14; Carey, *Past, Present and Future,* 254.

masters—of capitalists, had wages two or three times those of British workers, and had the capacity to save and become capitalists themselves. Of
course, republican institutions aided workers by ensuring that they obtained
the full rewards of their labor. Because the United States had extended the political power to workers, no aristocratic group could control legislation and
legislate workers' earnings into elite pockets. But there were two other interesting arguments as well.[46]

American protectionists tended not to claim that high American wages
were the result of the existence of western lands. Instead they used a productivity argument. Henry Carey best exemplified this approach. He castigated
the free trade nostrum of devoting the resources of an entire nation to the
production of a few goods and relying on division of labor to enhance output:
"Men are crowded into large towns and cities, to labour in great shops, where
the only idea ever acquired is the pointing of a needle and that is acquired at
the cost of health and life." British political economy treated "man as a *mere*
machine." But under protection, workers earned high wages, saved, invested,
and, most important, acquired an education: "To increase the productiveness
of labour, education is necessary. Protection tends to the diffusion of education, and the elevation of the labourer." By the antebellum decade, protectionists had clearly seized upon the notions of human capital and productivity and their influence on wage rates.[47]

A second feature of the protectionist investigation of laboring conditions
in England was a redefinition of independence. Since the Revolution, independence had been considered to be the acquisition of property that could
support a family; most commonly it meant a freehold farmer or an independent, self-employed artisan. By the mid-1840s, protectionists were challeng-
ing the old idea of property ownership as the sole basis for independence with
a new commercial one of economic opportunity. British workers were oppressed, wrote Calvin Colton, because they had only one employer. But
American workers were independent because they had a variety of bidders for
their skills. Said Colton, "It should be observed that labor is never *independent* when it has not *alternatives;* that is, when it is not strong enough in its

46. Colton, *Junius Tracts,* 103–106; Bowen, *Principles of Political Economy,* 129, 199; Colton, *Rights of Labor,* 8; Carey, *Harmony of Interests,* 64.

47. Carey, *Harmony of Interests,* 210, 212–13; see also Bowen, *Principles of Political Economy,* 76, 203; Seaman, *Essays on the Progress of Nations,* 305. On productivity among protectionists, see Hudson, *Economics and Technology in 19th Century American Thought,* 23, 50,
52–53.

own position to accept or reject the wages offered to it in a given case." Henry Carey came to the same conclusion by the late 1850s. "Two men competing for its [a commodity's] purchase, its owner becomes a freeman. The two competing for its sale, become enslaved. The whole question of freedom or slavery for man is, therefore, embraced in that of competition."[48] The protectionists had thus found a way to justify wage laborers as a group possessing economic independence that met the requirements for participation in a republican form of government. Wage labor to eighteenth-century republicans such as Thomas Jefferson was the epitome of dependence. Protectionists had found a way to reconcile commercial, industrial America and its wage earners with the republican dogmas of eighteenth-century agrarian republicanism. The core idea was to generate high wages; high wages became the new equivalent of the old notion of landed independence.

Protectionists had to confront their true enemy when they came to postulating a distribution of wealth that was sufficiently equal to sustain a republic. They had to discredit the British model erected by Malthus, Ricardo, and Mill. Once that monumental obstruction to human happiness was reduced, the path was clear for the optimism of the republican experiment and its hopes for political and economic equality. It was here that protectionists made their greatest contribution to distribution theory, and they did so by developing a forerunner to human capital theory, applied it to productivity and wages, and then disassembled the whole of the Malthus-Ricardo-Mill economic structure.

All protectionists denounced the Malthusian-Ricardian model of economic evolution, but often their complaints lacked a logical counterargument. More often than not, protectionists simply did not like the negative conclusions of Ricardo and Malthus. They saw more clearly, it would seem, that the Malthusian theory of population pressure and the Ricardian theory of rent made republicanism utterly untenable. Moreover, protectionists were not going to rely on the expedient of American free traders of giving thanks for western lands. Western lands were not eternal, and protectionists were uninterested in a theory of society, politics, and economics that posited only a transitory equality. Protectionists as well disliked the abstract, unempirical quality of the Manchester school—its reliance on the deductive

48. Colton, *Rights of Labor,* 7; Carey, *Principles of Social Science,* III, 234, also 235. For comparison, see Joan Wallach Scott, *Gender and the Politics of History* (New York, 1988), 143–45.

method. As E. P. Smith once wrote to Henry Carey, "If social science could have been *thought* by a man with his eyes shut Ricardo would have done wonders."[49]

In their economic doctrines, protectionists moved to the ideas of productivity and intellect to explain how human welfare and wages could increase over time. Most protectionists adhered to some idea of the labor theory of value, although the inevitable disagreements arose, and, good republicans that they were, they insisted that social equity meant that each laborer received the fruits of his labor.[50] But protectionists added one feature that markedly distinguished them from the Manchester school. All protectionists stressed the role of human creativity and invention. They were fascinated by the discoveries of science and how they improved the material life of humankind. By the antebellum decade, protectionists had developed a nearly complete theory of human capital on the macroeconomic level.[51]

John Rae maintained that accumulation of capital stock depended on several variables, but the overriding one was knowledge. Capital stock reached decreasing marginal returns when "*knowledge of their powers and qualities remain stationary.*" Colton's view of labor's contribution to value was qualified by the fact that "a man's power of labor is limited, but his skill is unlimited," and, after all, skill was "the fruit of the labor of mind." Ezra Seaman agreed that Adam Smith was correct in discerning the importance of the division of labor for economic growth, but Smith overemphasized this feature and gave "too little [attention] to invention, to the combination of labor, and to immaterial [intellectual] capital." It was by the route of human capital that protec-

49. E. P. Smith to H. C. Carey, July 17, 1858, in Henry C. Carey Papers, Edward Carey Gardiner Collection, Historical Society of Pennsylvania, Philadelphia. See Rodney J. Morrison, *Henry C. Carey and American Economic Development* (Philadelphia, 1986), 8–9.

50. Raymond, *Elements of Political Economy*, I, 21, 56–64; Carey, *Principles of Political Economy*, I, 18–19; Henry C. Carey, *Manual of Social Science: Being a Condensation of the "Principles of Social Science" by H. C. Carey*, ed. Kate McKean (Philadelphia, 1866), 82–83; Colton, *Junius Tracts*, 98. Seaman disputed the labor theory of value and opted entirely for utility; see Seaman, *Essays on the Progress of Nations*, 204, 314–19; Morrison, *Henry C. Carey and American Economic Development*, 13–17.

51. This is the conclusion of Hudson as well, in *Economics and Technology in 19th Century American Thought*, 11. On human capital, see B. F. Kiker, "The Historical Roots of the Concept of Human Capital," in *Human Capital Formation and Manpower Development*, ed. Ronald A. Wykstra (New York, 1971), 2–12.

tionists ultimately overthrew Malthusian population theory and Ricardian distribution theory—at least among themselves.[52]

Although the protectionists took special pleasure in displaying their horror at and rejection of the Malthusian-Ricardian paradigm, they had trouble in constructing a replacement. By the time of the Civil War, Henry C. Carey had produced a new theory of wages and rent. In effect, he had created a new theory of factor distribution and had overthrown the Malthusian-Ricardian model. Although Carey is now best known for his tariff advocacy and his diatribes against merchants, his protectionist contemporaries understood precisely what he had done: his contribution had been a new theory of distribution.[53]

Carey's dissection of the classical model of income distribution rested on an awareness of the economic roles of knowledge, human capital via education, and productivity. The crucial assumption in the Malthus-Ricardo theory was that soil had a limited capacity for producing foodstuffs which mankind could not alter. This constraint governed the entire economy. Carey lifted the constraint. He initially argued that people first settled and farmed infertile soils rather than the most fertile ones. Thus, as population increased, they would move on to better land and obtain higher yields. This claim reversed the order proposed by Ricardo and supposedly invalidated Ricardo's theory, but it was at best a weak argument and not an accurate one. Carey supplemented his criticism of the Malthusian-Ricardian view of soils by pos-

52. Rae, *Sociological Theory of Capital,* quote 42, 66; Colton, *Junius Tracts,* 98; Seaman, *Essays on the Progress of Nations,* 136. See also Raymond, *Elements of Political Economy,* I, 209; Joseph J. Spengler, "John Rae on Economic Development: A Note," *Quarterly Journal of Economics,* LXXIII (1959), 393–404. Human capital theory really developed in the mid-twentieth century, and the contributions protectionists made to the idea, embedded in their attacks on Ricardo and Malthus, have been noted only by historians.

53. Seaman, *Essays on the Progress of Nations,* 310; Edward Everett, address delivered before the Boston Provident Society, December 22, 1857, in Edward Everett, *Orations and Speeches on Various Occasions* (12th ed.; 1830–68; rpr. Boston, 1895), III, 573; Edward Everett, *A Lecture on the Working Men's Party, ibid.,* I, 303–304; Colton, *Rights of Labor,* 3–4; Rae, *Sociological Theory of Capital,* xlviii, 349, 354–56; Raymond, *Elements of Political Economy,* I, 195–97, II, 20, 67–70; Hudson, *Economics and Technology in 19th Century American Thought,* 152–64; Turner, *Ricardian Rent Theory,* 26, 35, 41–47, 157–59. William Elder, *A Memoir of Henry C. Carey* (Philadelphia, 1880), 16; Kate McKean, Introduction to Carey, *Manual of Social Science,* viii; Smith, *Manual of Political Economy,* 83. See esp. Conkin, *Prophets of Prosperity,* 261–66, 275; more generally, Hovencamp, *Enterprise and American Law,* 184–89; and Freyer, *Producers Versus Capitalists,* 3–5, 7.

iting that soil could be improved by educated farmers armed with scientific knowledge. He created a "manure" theory of soil improvement, but the important link that Carey uncovered was the one that bound the productivity of the soil to scientific knowledge.[54]

His overall depiction of economic development was that people living in close proximity to each other not only developed natural resources but also fostered educational facilities. Knowledge of science grew and thereby enabled humankind to obtain continually increasing returns (productivity) in every area of economic activity. Productivity increases elevated the material well-being of the laborer: "The higher the degree of intellect applied to the work of production, the larger will be the return to labour, and the more rapid will be the accumulation of capital." Ricardo's distribution theory concluded that over time rents rose, wages rose (to maintain subsistence), and profits declined. Carey, from his understanding of human capital, knowledge, and productivity, reversed Ricardo and offered a "true" theory of distribution: "Increased productiveness [is] followed necessarily and certainly by an increase of the labourer's proportion. His wages rise, and the *proportion* of the capitalist falls, yet now the latter accumulates fortune more rapidly than ever, and thus his interest and that of the labourer are in perfect harmony with each other."[55]

Only population pressure remained to hinder Carey's bright vision of increasing rewards to labor. He had little difficulty with the proposition. In a very modern analysis, he simply wrote: "The greater the development of the individual faculties, the more perfect is the physical and mental power of the individual man, and the more absolute is his responsibility to himself, to his family." Population, in short, naturally limited itself when labor received a just and increasing reward for its toils.[56]

Whereas the Malthus-Ricardo-Mill model led to a maldistribution of wealth, a bloated landed aristocracy, subsistence laborers, and stagnant capitalists, Carey's theory posited a future of income equality in which present ill-paid workers gained more from knowledge and technological advance than did capitalists. Carey's was a democratic vision. Moreover, it was a natural

54. Carey, *Harmony of Interests*, 29; Carey, *Past, Present and Future*, 63, 94, 306; Carey, *Principles of Social Science*, I, v, II, 25–28.

55. Carey, *Harmony of Interests*, 209; Carey, *Principles of Social Science*, I, 381, II, 25, Carey, *Past, Present and Future*, 67; see also Carey, *Manual of Social Science*, 392–96.

56. Quote from Carey, *Principles of Social Science*, III, 274; see also *ibid.*, 278; Carey, *Past, Present and Future*, 92–93.

process if politics—particularly the policies of the aristocracy—did not destroy normal economic evolution.

But of course Carey found that normal economic evolution was being violated by English free trade policies. England had suppressed the wages of its workers so as to undersell all other manufacturers in the world. Its free trade policy was therefore designed to erect a worldwide monopoly in which England remained the manufacturing center and the rest of the world supplied it with raw goods. In the "colonies" only rude and unintelligent labor would be used—such as slaves—and the division of labor that occurred stupefied people instead of elevating them. To fasten its system of free trade on the rest of the world, England also fostered the class of merchants to drain earnings from the colonies to the mother country. Free trade produced class divisions and hostilities, an unequal distribution of wealth, rude and elementary production for colonial peoples, and a shriveling of educational advancement. To stop the free trade system of England from destroying natural economic development, Carey advocated the use of prohibitory tariffs: protection was a defense measure "against a system that tends to lessen everywhere the value of labour," and "the road to absolute freedom of trade lies through perfect protection."[57]

The analysis of the distribution of wealth by American political economists between the adoption of the Constitution and the outbreak of the Civil War revealed the fractures that were occurring in understanding the forces that molded a society's distribution of wealth. Economists continued to adhere to three of the axioms of the revolutionary generation and indeed applied them everywhere: the labor theory of property/value, the political economy of aristocracy, and the perniciousness of the laws of primogeniture and entail. At the same time, both free traders and protectionists began the process of adjusting republicanism to a pure market economy. Somewhat amazingly, neither side ever offered a quantitative assessment of the distribution of wealth or income. Although these were economists with something of an empirical bent, they conducted their discussion of the distribution of wealth entirely in literary descriptions.

Yet a major rift was occurring over two particular policies, which mirrored

57. Quotes from Carey, *Harmony of Interests,* 66, 67. This very brief description of Carey's critique of English free trade policy is based on Carey, *Harmony of Interests,* 36–38, 52–54, 61–64; Carey, *Principles of Social Science,* I, 218–19, 234–43, 261, III, 235–40.

the division of political parties. One side found population pressure the ultimate key to distribution schemes and accepted a large portion of the dismal science propagated by Malthus, Ricardo, and Mill. The other side developed new theories and continued to stress that equitable distribution was a political act, not purely a natural one.

These ideas permeated the public. They infused politics. By the middle of the nineteenth century, economic viewpoints had become entangled in virtually every topic imaginable. And much of it was a repetition of the views and values of the revolutionary generation.

6

The Transatlantic Discourse
on the Distribution of Wealth

Between 1790 and 1860 the literate public in Europe and the United States sporadically but not infrequently discussed the distribution of wealth in the North American republic. This analysis did not deviate from that of the political economists, and to a surprising degree the essential ideas of the revolutionary generation were verified and approbated. Indeed, during these years the general consensus of those commenting on the subject was that the Americans had achieved a strangely egalitarian society by emphasizing individual labor and rooting out any tendency toward an aristocratic establishment. Europeans in particular marveled at the two circumstances they believed were unique to the Americans: the crucial importance of the abolition of primogeniture and entail, and the existence of western land.

During the first half of the nineteenth century, many of the implications of the revolutionary generation's understanding about wealth distribution grew from a quiet infancy to an obstreperous maturity. Social mobility and free labor rhetoric deafened the ears as Americans of all persuasions tried to justify whatever rewards they received as the fruits of their labor. Any number of authors were certain that they understood the systematic means by which pauperism became a social phenomenon and how to distinguish voluntary from involuntary poverty. Not quite so noisily but perhaps as important, numerous Americans revealed how the language of republicanism was transmogrifying into the language of market economics. Wages became not merely the fruits of labor but the determination of supply and demand. Moreover, the ramifications of Madison's contemplations about population also became magnified, and the widely acknowledged relationship between land and the distribution of wealth had a direct bearing on the ideas sustaining Manifest Destiny.

Most authors, usually from the upper-income groups, celebrated the equality of the American distribution of wealth and its principles. The general discourse—there were dissenters—rejoiced over the condition of wealth-holding in the republic. Part of the reason for this consensus, it must be underscored, was the nature of the comparison: Americans weighed the justice of their system by comparing themselves with aristocratic Europe, not with a simple absolute standard. This mood of self-congratulation nonetheless had its paradoxes, for the distribution of wealth was not particularly egalitarian during the first half of the nineteenth century and was indeed deteriorating. The way so many writers argued for equality in the face of growing inequality provides an instructive exercise in the art of selective inclusion and exclusion.

Most literate Americans between 1790 and 1860 believed that their nation had a "good," or just, distribution of wealth, although by the latter three decades of the period there arose a growing number of vociferous doubters. John Adams, turning sour in retirement, still found in 1817 that Americans enjoyed a wide diffusion of property, although he suggested to James Madison that there were more unpropertied persons than was commonly recognized. In 1820, Daniel Webster presented to the people of Plymouth a patriotic version of the settling of America. In his address, he emphasized the lack of landlords, nobles, and feudal relics in the New World, which allowed all European newcomers to prosper in accordance with their talents and exertions. The result had been for contemporaries "a great equality of condition." While warning an audience of New Yorkers in 1833 about the dangers of free trade policies, the Whig congressman and novelist John Pendleton Kennedy remarked, "Wealth is . . . [in Europe] distributed rather in lakes than rivers, and these large reservoirs are perpetually attracting to themselves the smaller accumulations." A Jacksonian economist, Theodore Sedgwick, argued that the implementation of republican principles in the United States had created an equal division of property "such as has never been known among mankind." European travelers to the United States affirmed the boasts of its citizens. The perspicacious sojourner Alexis de Tocqueville began his penetrating work on American society by recounting that what shocked him most forcefully about the country was "the general equality of condition among the people," a sentiment shared by numerous other Europeans.[1] Similar expressions were abundant in antebellum America, and individuals who lived to the first decade of the twentieth century wrote about the first half of the nineteenth century in almost utopian terms, exhibiting a sort of distribution-of-wealth nostalgia.[2]

No part of the revolutionary leadership's understanding of equity in wealth-holding received more adulation than did the labor theory of property/value. That individuals deserved the fruits of their labor was endlessly reiterated and was the single most used phrase in the popular economic lexicon. Moreover, Americans celebrated this Lockean conceptual device in a particular way. Early-nineteenth-century writers emphasized the *creation* of property and not simply its ownership, especially ownership that came through inheritance. Francis Bowen made precisely this point in the *North American Review* in 1848. Even as he justified property obtained via inheritance laws, Bowen admitted that acquisition of property through inheritance was inferior in terms of natural rights than acquisition of property through labor: "The property which a man does not inherit, but actually creates by his own industry, seems to be his own by a higher and stronger title than any which society can confer."[3]

It is almost incredible how nineteenth-century Americans unfailingly testified to their belief in the labor theory of property/value. The primary means of self-identification was labor; to be an American citizen, one had to labor.

1. John Adams to James Madison, June 17, 1817, in Adams, ed., *Works of John Adams*, X, 268; Daniel Webster, "First Settlement of New England," in McIntyre, ed., *Writings and Speeches of Webster*, I, 212; John P[endleton] Kennedy, *An Address Delivered Before the American Institute . . . October 17, 1833* (New York, 1833), 13; Theodore Sedgwick, *Public and Private Economy* (New York, 1836), II, 84; Henry Barnard to Henry Watson, October 31, 1841 [typescript], Henry Watson Papers, Duke University Library, Durham, N.C.; Alexis de Tocqueville, *Democracy in America,* ed. Phillips Bradley (1835–40; rpr. New York, 1945), I, 3. See also Sir Charles Lyell, *A Second Visit to the United States of North America* (New York, 1849), I, 57–59; Harriet Martineau, *Society in America* (1837; rpr. New York, 1966), I, 16; A Citizen of the World [James Boardman], *America and the Americans* (1833; rpr. New York, 1974), 11–12.

2. George F. Hoar, *Autobiography of Seventy Years* (New York, 1903), I, 40; Henry Cabot Lodge, *Early Memories* (New York, 1913), 126; Samuel G. French, *Two Wars: An Autobiography of Gen. Samuel G. French* (Nashville, Tenn., 1901), 6. For a historian who disputes the extent of American egalitarianism, see Edward Pessen, *Jacksonian America: Society, Personality, and Politics* (Homewood, Ill., 1969), 46–58.

3. [Francis Bowen], "The Distribution of Property," *North American Review,* LXVII (July, 1848), 119–21, quote on 121; on the American understanding of property, see 110–17.

Anyone who did not labor was either a pariah or an aristocrat. To labor was to participate in American life; to avoid labor was to remove oneself from the American community, from the nation. Talk of labor was so thick in antebellum America that it almost suffocated every form of discourse, especially when done by political partisans. Europeans nearly gagged on the American obsession. Tocqueville noted that in the United States, labor was presented "on every side, as the necessary, natural, and honest condition of human existence." Two Hungarian visitors who ventured into the United States with Louis Kossuth, Francis and Theresa Pulszky, offered a glowing picture of democratic practices: "Yet the wonderful effect of democratic institutions strikes me always afresh. The principle, that *labour is never degrading,* is here carried into life." Michael Chevalier, who feared extirpation of aristocracy but who nonetheless admired the laboring society of North America, closed his book with a statement very similar to the one made by Ezra Stiles in 1783: "This is the first time since the origin of society that the people have fairly enjoyed the fruits of their labor and have shown themselves worthy of the prerogatives of manhood. Glorious result!"[4]

Northerners, as one would expect, had no difficulty in continuously trumpeting the labor theory of property/value.[5] Nathan Appleton, a Massachusetts politician and cotton textile magnate, contributed an amazing piece to the discussion. He wrote an article for *Hunt's Merchants' Magazine* that was seized by the Whigs and used in the 1844 presidential campaign. Appleton praised American social mobility and its work ethic—to be expected from one justifying industrial capitalism and his own fortune—but his framework was instructive. Appleton posed the question of labor in an aristocratic versus republican context, not in a capital versus labor context. He stated forthrightly that labor was the only source of wealth and that the precise form of that assertion was to be found in the writings of John Locke. Appleton insisted that the conflict between capital and labor was created by Europeans and applicable only to them. In the United States the notion of economic conflict made little sense because the United States had none of the aristo-

4. Tocqueville, *Democracy in America,* II, 152; Francis Pulszky and Theresa Pulszky, *White Red Black: Sketches of Society in the United States During the Visit of Their Guest* (1853; rpr. New York, 1968), III, 128; Martineau, *Society in America,* II, 295, 302; Roger Boesche, *The Strange Liberalism of Alexis de Tocqueville* (Ithaca, N.Y., 1987), 174; R. K. Webb, *Harriet Martineau: A Radical Victorian* (New York, 1960), 139, 170; Michael Chevalier, *Society, Manners, and Politics in the United States,* ed. John William Ward (1839; rpr. Garden City, N.Y., 1961), 418.

5. Note the comments of Diggins, *Lost Soul of American Politics,* 117, 143–49.

cratic apparatus (entail, primogeniture, political control) that belittled labor socially and beggared it economically. Americans believed in property by creative labor, not inheritance. "Manual labor has a position with us, which it has never possessed in any period of the world," he wrote. No aristocrats, no great families, ruled the country: "It is true, ours is a working-day world."[6]

Southerners and advocates of slavery did not shy away from the labor theory of property/value, and the literary record is teeming with southerners offering hosannas to it. At the beginning of the nullification crisis, South Carolinian James Hamilton, a leader in the movement, argued that it was unconstitutional for "the labour of one member of the league [to] pay tribute to nourish and reward the labour of another." The labor theory of value was even embedded in one of the fundamental documents of the slaveholding South—John C. Calhoun's *Exposition and Protest* (1828). In complaining about the protective tariff policy, Calhoun wrote that "the fruits of our toil and labour, which on every principle of justice ought to belong to ourselves, are transferred from us to them [northern manufacturers]." The obstreperous South Carolina free trader George McDuffie often invoked the labor theory of property/value. Speaking on the tariff in 1844, McDuffie approvingly referred to Adam Smith and free trade science: "The fundamental principle of this theory is that labor is at once the only source and the true measure of all those values which constitute individual or national wealth." He then thanked "God that it is so; for I have always regarded the sentence by which he doomed fallen man to eat bread by the sweat of his brow, as in fact a mercy." McDuffie next affirmed the Lockean and Smithian ideal of government: "to secure to the people the free use and enjoyment of the products of that labor."[7]

Nineteenth-century Americans went to extreme lengths to justify their behavior in terms of toiling or laboring. Not only did they fill their discourses and orations with phrases about working, the fruits of labor, and the sweat of their brows, but they also placed such expressions in their personal correspon-

6. Nathan Appleton, "Labor—Its Relations in the United States and Europe, Compared," *Hunt's Merchants' Magazine*, XI (September, 1844), 217–23.

7. James Hamilton, *A Speech on the Operation of the Tariff on the Interests of the South, and the Constitutional Means of Redressing Its Evils* (Charleston, 1828), 5; John C. Calhoun, draft of *Exposition and Protest*, in Robert L. Meriwether *et al.*, eds., *The Papers of John C. Calhoun* (Columbia, S. C., 1959–), X, 456; speech of George McDuffie on tariff, *Congressional Globe*, 28th Cong., 1st Sess., Appendix, 141; Richard N. Current, *John C. Calhoun* (New York, 1944), 44.

dence and diaries. Politicians often referred to their campaigns in terms of their labors on the stump, entrepreneurs wrote of their labors in establishing working enterprises, and even speculators wrote about how hard they labored at making a killing in some stock market transaction. One correspondent to Thomas Corwin even had the gall to use the labor theory of property/value to obtain a patronage position: "I have toiled *hard day* and *night* at the loss of much time and money, [and] am now out of employment;" he therefore deserved a position in government.[8]

Some striking mid-nineteenth-century ideological currents had their roots in the primary axiom of the American concept of the distribution of wealth, the labor theory of property/value. Americans increasingly defined a republican citizenry in an economic sense by the words *toil* and *labor.* The difference between an aristocratic and a republican society was that only in the latter did the laborer receive the fruits of his labor. As Crèvecoeur noted in the 1780s, lifting the aristocratic damper on economic activities resulted in a citizenry that was eager, enterprising, and laboring. By the middle of the nineteenth century, the magnification of the labor theory of property/value as the preeminent economic principle of republicanism led many Americans to idealize republican society as enterprising, busy, active, and participatory, in motion, a citizenry that radiated energy. An aristocratic society was characterized by dullness, torpor, sullenness, languidness. As John Pendleton Kennedy said, the United States was a land "of busy men. . . . Unlike the European States, we have no piles of hoarded wealth destined to be transmitted in mass to our posterity."[9] The celebration of the labor theory of property/value in nineteenth-century America led irresistibly to two obvious rhetorical manifestations: the free labor ideology and the creed of social mobility.

In 1853 the Maryland Know-Nothing, soon to be Republican, Henry Winter Davis exhibited the hallmarks of the free labor ideology and its connection to the labor theory of property/value. He declared in an address that "labor is honorable in all. . . . It is a product of our free and equal condition. . . . American Republicanism does not look on labor as a necessity; it imposes it as a duty, and, therefore, it is honorable in all, and idleness is not

8. Joseph K. Hartwell to Thomas Corwin, November 6, 1850, in Thomas Corwin Papers, Library of Congress, Washington, D.C.

9. Kennedy, *Address Delivered Before the American Institute,* 27; see also Crèvecoeur, *Letters from an American Farmer,* 42, 44, 57, 59–60, 83–84, 91–92; [Henry W. Bellows?], "Influence of the Trading Spirit upon the Social and Moral Life of America," *American* [Whig] *Review,* I (January, 1845), 95–96.

honorable in any." Such exclamations were not restricted to the free labor North. Even in the secessionist South the cry of free labor echoed. The editor of the Vicksburg *Daily Whig* in 1860 affirmed, "Let us sedulously cultivate the sentiment, so true in itself, that *labor is honorable and dignified.*"[10]

The celebration of free labor—labor free of aristocratic shackles—began during the Revolution but by the 1850s had become a dominant theme in political rhetoric. And in one sense, it was almost inevitable that a free labor ideology would present itself so noisily. Once Americans defined republicanism economically in terms of the labor theory of property/value and the fruits of labor, it was only a small jump to stressing the noble, egalitarian, democratic features of toiling for one's own bread—especially when it was compared with the aristocratic way of immorally stealing bread from others.

Likewise, idealization of upward mobility was an almost unavoidable outcome of the American embrace of the labor theory of property/value.[11] The natural distribution of wealth was to give each laborer exactly the fruits of his toils; only by toiling was one justified in possessing property. Because no hereditary privilege existed in a republican society and no partial laws disturbed the natural distribution of wealth, any person—regardless of family situation or initial conditions—could rise as far as his talents let him (but not her). And this, of course, was the process of social mobility, of climbing the ladder of success.

Most commentators in the first half of the nineteenth century probably believed a well-structured society and economy (one based on republican principles) permitted every willing worker to obtain a comfortable competence or subsistence. The act of labor ensured a decent, but not ostentatious, livelihood. Social mobility advocates celebrated the possibility of moving beyond the average position. But they were not saying only the very talented could escape poverty. In a republican society, where each obtained the full value of the fruits of labor, anyone who toiled would rise above poverty, but

10. Speech of Henry Winter Davis at Maryland Institute, 1853, in Bernard C. Steiner, *Life of Henry Winter Davis* (Baltimore, 1916), 76; Vicksburg *Daily Whig*, January 18, 1860, in Dwight Lowell Dumond, ed., *Southern Editorials on Secession* (New York, 1931), 15. The basic (and best) book on Republican free labor ideology remains Foner, *Free Soil, Free Labor, Free Men*, chap. 1. On southern free labor ideals, see Huston, *Panic of 1857*, 84–90.

11. See Pole, *Pursuit of Equality*, 4–9, 36–37; Joseph L. Blau, Introduction to Blau, ed., *Social Theories of Jacksonian Democracy: Representative Writings of the Period, 1825–1850* (New York, 1947), xx–xxi; Robert H. Wiebe, *The Opening of American Society: From the Adoption of the Constitution to the Eve of Disunion* (New York, 1984), 131–35, 354–55.

only the very talented could expect very great rewards.[12] Social mobility rhetoric invaded political speech-making, but in antebellum times it was not limited only to the Whigs or Republicans; Democrats employed the mobility ethic as well.[13]

Social mobility was possible only when the fruits of labor were substantial. As the economy became more urban and commercial because of the transportation revolution in the 1830s and 1840s, the question soon became how to ensure that wages were sufficiently high to enable an industrious and ambitious worker the opportunity to save and ultimately to buy his own farm, store, or artisanal manufactory. Social mobility was meaningless if people never earned a wage at the start of economic life sufficient to allow them to escape pauperism. Thus by the 1830s, one of the major political and economic questions of the republic was how to implement the policies most conducive to a high-wage republic. The debate over high wages followed the free trade–protectionist dichotomy in American political economy.[14]

But a more basic problem was becoming manifest. Ultimately, what mech-

12. On the rhetoric of mobility in antebellum America, see Edward K. Spann, *The New Metropolis: New York City, 1840–1857* (New York, 1981), 205–206; Rush Welter, *The Mind of America, 1820–1860* (New York, 1975), 118–21. The most important work is probably still by Irvin G. Wyllie, who intelligently reminds twentieth-century inhabitants that the myth of the self-made man was originally developed for democratic reasons, not to celebrate only the heroic few (*The Self-Made Man in America*, 10–23, 41, 133–37, 152–55). For the working-class belief that republican wages meant a competence, see Blewett, *Men, Women, and Work*, 36–37.

13. On social mobility among the Whigs and Republicans, see Foner, *Free Soil, Free Labor, Free Men*, 30–37; Ashworth, *"Agrarians" and "Aristocrats,"* 66–68; Thomas Brown, *Politics and Statesmanship: Essays on the American Whig Party* (New York, 1985), 39; Kohl, *Politics of Individualism*, 66. For the Democrats, see speech at Reading Town Meeting, June 30, 1845, in Charles Henry Jones, *The Life and Public Services of J. Glancy Jones* (Philadelphia, 1910), I, 116; H. M. Flint, *Life of Stephen A. Douglas* (Philadelphia, 1865), 3; Andrew Johnson to William W. Pepper, July 17, 1854, in Leroy P. Graf, Ralph W. Haskins, and Paul H. Bergeron, eds., *The Papers of Andrew Johnson* (Knoxville, 1967–), II, 238; Francis J. Grund, *Aristocracy in America: From the Sketch-Book of a German Nobleman* (1839; rpr. New York, 1959), 108. Rush Welter also finds a (limited) appeal for social mobility among antebellum Democrats (*Mind of America*, 121, 129, 133).

14. For example, Ashworth, *"Agrarians" and "Aristocrats,"* 68, 97–98, 250–52; Thomas R. Hietala, *Manifest Design: Anxious Aggrandizement in Late Jacksonian America* (Ithaca, N.Y., 1985), 88–101; Watson, *Liberty and Power*, 241–42; Elliott Barkan, "The Emergence of a Whig Persuasion: Conservatism, Democratism, and the New York State Whigs," *New York History*, LII (1971), 380–90; Alfred A. Cave, *An American Conservative in the Age of Jackson: The Political and Social Thought of Calvin Colton* (Fort Worth, Tex., 1969), 58.

anism did middle- and upper-class American public officials depend on to set high wages? The answer was the market. Supply and demand set the price for all commodities, and labor was simply another commodity. By the 1830s calculation of prices by reference to market forces was omnipresent; it probably was widespread in the 1820s. To preserve social mobility via high wages, Americans had to arrange supply and demand in such a fashion as to obtain the desired outcome.[15]

Agreement on the mechanism that determined wages among well-placed Americans has important ramifications for historical understanding of the first half of the nineteenth century, for the answer reveals where ideological consensus broke down in the republican experiment and where conflict arose. It was relatively easy to get most segments of society to agree about the evils of aristocracy, the means by which aristocrats kept themselves in power, the horrors of high taxation, excessive bureaucracy, a bloated military, and an established church. Virtually everyone affirmed that a republican society should possess social mobility and that labor was dignified. All subscribed to the republican notion that the laborer deserved the fruits of his labor.

The specific problem was carrying into effect in a concrete fashion the phrase *fruits of labor.* How in real life did one calculate the fruits? What was the quantitative assessment? How did one know whether the fruits obtained from his or her labor were just?

One may imagine, but not really prove, that for many Americans throughout the eighteenth and nineteenth centuries the fruits of labor were a tangible presence. From an overwhelmingly yeoman agrarian society (excluding slaves), the fruits of labor became the actual harvest in self-sufficient communities. For artisans, the fruits of labor were the handcrafted, finished products they bartered or sold to others. In a neoclassical economic sense, a "wage" manifested itself in these operations, but the connection between work and its fruits probably had a sensory association largely lacking in a commercial society where money intervened between the creation of a product and the reward for its creation. This notion of the just fruits of labor—an agrarian, self-sufficient notion—probably persisted in various degrees among all classes of citizens for all of the nineteenth century.

A clear socioeconomic line was portending, however. The upper and middle classes, and certainly public leaders, finally opted for explaining wages in

---

15. The other method of obtaining high wage rates found by protectionist economists was developed in chapter 5; high wages came from productivity and human capital.

terms of market determination—supply and demand acting together established the wage rate. Moreover, when supply and demand established a wage level, it was, or became, the just wage, the natural wage—the true fruits of labor. Those who possessed little property or who entered life as wage earners found the market-determined wage to be at best parsimonious and oppressive. Somehow the laborer was not receiving the fruits of labor, and it was this perception that then became the backbone for the concept of the moral economy. Thus the argument over how to determine the fruits of labor reveals how republicanism and political economy split along socioeconomic lines.[16]

As they did with the labor theory of value, Americans in the first half of the nineteenth century elaborated on but did not challenge or revise the revolutionary generation's definition of the political economy of aristocracy. Political manipulations, as exhibited in European states, created the few rich and the many poor. In many ways, the European context dominated American thinking on the subject.[17] Certainly, European travelers to the United States did nothing to persuade Americans that their analysis was faulty.

The two basic equations of the political economy of aristocracy—aristocracy equals inequality, republicanism equals equality—found emphatic articulation from the beginning of the government. In 1792, William Branch Giles, Democratic-Republican from Virginia, explicitly used the aristocracy equals inequality theme:

> Under a just and equal Government, every individual is entitled to protection in the enjoyment of the whole product of his labor, except such portion of it as is necessary to enable Government to protect the rest; this is given only in consideration of the protection offered. In every bounty, exclusive right, or monopoly, Government violates the stipulation on her part; for, by such a regulation, the product of one man's labor is transferred to the use and enjoyment of another. The exercise of such a right on the part of the Government can be justified on no other principle, than that the whole product of the labor of every individual is the real property of Government, and may be distributed among the several parts of the community by governmental discretion; such a suppo-

16. The "moral economy" was the invention of E. P. Thompson, "The Moral Economy of the English Crowd in the Eighteenth Century," *Past and Present*, L (1971), 76–136; for examples of its use, see Wilentz, *Chants Democratic*, 102; Steffen, *Mechanics of Baltimore*, 103.

17. Robert Wiebe has written, "Only Europe could define America" (*Opening of American Society*, 18).

sition would directly involve the idea, that every individual in the community is merely a slave and bond[s]man to Government, who, although he may labor, is not to expect protection in the product of his labor. An authority given to any Government to exercise such a principle, would lead to a complete system of tyranny.

Free trade New York congressman Churchill C. Cambreleng explained the poverty of England by reference to the political economy of aristocracy: "In Europe where the labour of the nation is the property of the aristocracy, that is, the *masters of the labourers,* it is proper for royal political economists to speculate on what quantity of productive labour can be drawn out of the *bodies* of men, at the least possible expence, keeping the labourers in perpetual poverty and augmenting the capital of their masters."[18]

During debate over tariff revision in 1832, Kentucky representative John Bell gave an emphatic definition of how aristocracy produced inequality. To have courts and sovereigns, Europe had to have inequalities in property. This was not an appropriate model for the United States. The true system for republicanism was "a perfect equality of rank, rights and privileges" and absolutely no monopolies, the economic disease of aristocratic systems. Americans must discourage "the accumulation of great wealth in the hands of individual citizens." That would be accomplished by having a policy opposite that of European nations. The source of inequality was government, according to Bell; whenever a few obtained disproportionate rewards for their labor, it indicated that the government's "laws and policy are hostile to equality in the rank and influence of its citizens, and consequently to liberty itself."[19]

Jacksonian Democrat and Locofoco ideologue William Leggett described aristocracy more pithily as a political system designed "to concentrate all wealth and privilege in the hands of a few." The editor of the *United States Magazine and Democratic Review,* John L. O'Sullivan, wrote in the first issue that aristocracy amounted to government by the few, and the tendency of a "minority, entrusted with governmental authority is, to surround itself with

18. Speech of Representative William Branch Giles, on cod fisheries, February 3, 1792, *Annals of Congress,* 2nd Cong., 1st Sess., 363–64; One of the People [Churchill C. Cambreleng], *An Examination of the New Tariff Proposed by the Hon. Henry Baldwin, a Representative in Congress* (New York, 1821), 165.

19. Speech of Representative John Bell, June 8, 1832, on the tariff, *Register of Debates,* 22nd Cong., 1st Sess., 3356–57, 3359, 3361; John Bell's 1832 speech is also noted in Joseph Howard Parks, *John Bell of Tennessee* (Baton Rouge, 1950), 52–55.

wealth, splendor, and power, at the expense of the producing mass, creating and perpetuating those artificial social distinctions which violate the natural equality of rights of the human race." O'Sullivan was explicit about how aristocracies created inequalities: "Legislation has been the fruitful parent of nine-tenths of all the evil, moral and physical, by which mankind has been afflicted since the creation of the world, and by which human nature has been self-degraded, fettered, and oppressed."[20]

In a multitude of ways, European commentators on American society demonstrated the correctness of the American understanding of the political economy of aristocracy. Several Englishmen used the occasion of a trip to North America to disparage republican/democratic tendencies and to justify the system of aristocracy. Basil Hall, for example, toured the United States in the 1820s. He criticized the Americans for being crazed about money and offhandedly said spending money was more difficult than making it: "I mean, of course, the art of spending it like a gentleman." Americans had industry and frugality but knew nothing of spending money gracefully because of the lack of an aristocracy, "a permanent money-spending class in the society." Another British sojourner in America, Thomas Hamilton, wrote that the United States was a flawed civilization because it had no aristocracy and allowed universal male suffrage. But "the man who labours with his hands cannot be raised to an equality of knowledge with those who have greater wealth and time to bestow on its acquisition."[21]

European travelers were defining aristocrats as a class of people who obtained wealth without labor, and other visitors pointed out this difference as well. William Cobbett, once a Federalist but after the Napoleonic Wars a re-

20. William Leggett, "Utopia—Sir Thomas More—Jack Cade," New York *Evening Post,* December 18, 1834, in Theodore Sedgwick, Jr., ed., *A Collection of the Political Writings of William Leggett* (New York, 1840), I, 128; John L. O'Sullivan, Introduction, *United States Magazine and Democratic Review,* I (October, 1837), in Wiltse, ed., *Expansion and Reform,* 147, 148, 151. Several historians have implied that American economic thinking was dominated by an awareness of a political economy of aristocracy: Ashworth, *"Agrarians" and "Aristocrats,"* 16–19; Brown, *Politics and Statesmanship,* 97; Kohl, *Politics of Individualism,* 202–203; Robert E. Shalhope, *John Taylor of Caroline: Pastoral Republican* (Columbia, S. C., 1980), 79–81; Frederick B. Tolles, *George Logan of Philadelphia* (New York, 1953), 131.

21. Hall, *Travels in North America,* II, 305, 306; Thomas Hamilton, *Men and Manners in America* (2nd ed., 1843; rpr. New York, 1968), xxx, also pp. 51, 61–62. Frederick Marryat, *A Diary in America: With Remarks on Its Institutions,* ed. Sydney Jackman (1839; rpr. Westport, Conn., 1962), 307. For a retelling of European observation of American democracy, see Wiebe, *Self-Rule,* 41–60, 65.

born radical in British politics, praised the United States for having a government "under which every one enjoys his earnings, *and no more.*" He objected to those few Americans who had the same attitude as English "Borough-mongers and Priests: namely, *to live without labour on the earnings of others.*" The Polish exile Adam Gurowski made his contempt of aristocracy and his praise of laboring Americans plain: the European upper class were "dead-weights and drones, turning the scales on one side, absorbing the results of the labor of the mass of the people, and rendering difficult its free ascension and normal expansion."[22] But Europeans did not believe the Americans had totally freed themselves from aristocracy, pointing immediately to slaveholders.[23]

Moreover, Europeans testified that the different forms of society—republican versus aristocratic—were revealed most emphatically in modes of governance. For many, republican government was almost nonexistent. They noticed that republicanism in America removed many of the governmental structures and institutions they were used to. Michael Chevalier, a traveler in 1839, after talking about the federal government, came to the conclusion that "the supreme authority is null and void; there is no government here in the true sense of the word." Several Europeans were startled because Americans paid low taxes and deduced that wages were high simply because government did not take anything from anybody. Isaac Holmes even asserted in the 1820s that the total revenue collected by federal government would be insufficient to pay the salaries of the tax collectors in England. Several pointed out that enterprise actually was free in the United States, that systems of privileges were absent, and that wealth tended to change hands rapidly.[24]

22. William Cobbett, *A Year's Residence in the United States of America* (1819; rpr. Carbondale, Ill., 1964), 212–13; Adam G. de Gurowski, *America and Europe* (New York, 1857), 193; Chevalier, *Society, Manners and Politics in the United States,* 418. The same idea of the aristocracy living off the labors of others can be found in Martineau, *Society in America,* I, 159, 163; Tocqueville, *Democracy in America,* I, 3–4.

23. On whether the Americans would have to establish an aristocracy, see, for example, Hall, *Travels in North America,* II, 310; Hamilton, *Men and Manners in America,* xx, xxx; Chevalier, *Society, Manners, and Politics in the United States,* 395–97; Marryat, *Diary in America,* 467–68; Martineau, *Society in America,* I, 159; Pulszky and Pulszky, *White Red Black,* 178–79.

24. Chevalier, *Society, Manners, and Politics in the United States,* 42–43, 62–63; Tocqueville, *Democracy in America,* I, 70–87, 215–18. David Montgomery, however, has argued for coercion in American society to make capitalism work (*Citizen Worker: The Experience of Workers in the United States with Democracy and the Free Market During the Nineteenth Century* [New York, 1993], chap. 2). See Cobbett, *Year's Residence in the United States,* 12; Martineau,

American views on the centrality of the political economy of aristocracy in creating inequality were fortified by their enormously dismal view of England and its social woes. Commentators always remarked on the political power of the aristocracy in England (and Europe generally) and how it managed to thrust the burden of government on others and receive rewards for its members. Many were appalled by the extent of pauperism in Europe. Senator Aaron V. Brown, a Tennessee Democrat, said in 1842 that to avoid social calamity Americans must look at the "shame" of England—its "awful mass of individual poverty." It was reported as a shocking statistic that one out of every eight persons in England was on poor relief and thus a pauper (which was the poverty rate for the United States in 1994).[25]

The list of reasons Americans concocted for the maldistribution of wealth in England and Europe was the same one the American revolutionaries compiled and American political economists unearthed. First was the monstrous load of taxation, most of which fell upon the laboring and middle classes.[26] Three subthemes in regard to taxation were clear. First, high taxes were required in Europe to pamper the dependents of aristocrats by employing them in the bureaucracy.[27] Second, Americans commented frequently and acidly about the sums of money taken by taxes to support established churches in

Society in America, I, 29; Isaac Holmes, *An Account of the United States of America, Derived from Actual Observation During a Residence of Four Years in That Republic* (1823; rpr. New York, 1974), 121–22; Francis J. Grund, *The Americans in Their Moral, Social and Political Relations* (1837; rpr. New York, 1968), 22, 252–53.

25. [Francis Bowen], "The Social Condition of England," *North American Review,* LXV (October, 1847), 483. See Cave, *American Conservative in the Age of Jackson,* 6–7, 13–14; Lilian Handlin, *George Bancroft: The Intellectual as Democrat* (New York, 1984), 227–34; Kohl, *Politics of Individualism,* 120; Jean V. Matthews, *Rufus Choate: The Law and Civic Virtue* (Philadelphia, 1980), 73; Speech of Senator Aaron V. Brown of Tennessee, June 18, 1842, on the tariff, *Congressional Globe,* 27th Cong., 2nd Sess., Appendix, 485; Sedgwick, *Public and Private Economy,* I, 82; "The Creation of Values," *American* [Whig] *Review,* IV (December, 1846), 643.

26. Samuel J. Tilden, "Currency, Price, and Wages" (1840), in John Bigelow, ed., *The Writings and Speeches of Samuel J. Tilden* (New York, 1885), I, 152–55; Representative Charles Jared Ingersoll, June 29, 1813, speech on taxes, *Annals of Congress,* 13th Cong., 1st Sess., 359; speech of Representative George Evans, June 11, 1832, *Register of Debates,* 22nd Cong., 1st Sess., 3432; [A. Ritchie], "Mad. de Stael's Considerations on the French Revolution," *North American Review,* VIII (December, 1818), 28.

27. For example, speech of Representative William Drayton (South Carolina), on the tariff, February 6, 1827, *Register of Debates,* 19th Cong., 2nd Sess., 983. A partial confirmation of bureaucratic English excess can be found in W. D. Rubinstein, "The Victorian Middle Classes: Wealth, Occupation, and Geography," *Economic History Review,* XXX (1977), 608.

Europe, but especially the Church of England. Reports in American maga-
zines, culled from the British press, indicated that several British sees took in
well in excess of £100,000 per year—an astounding sum to Americans.[28]
Third, Americans found the expense of the European military establishment
abhorrent. John Quincy Adams wrote in 1801 that the "great problem" that
occupied the minds of European statesmen was "what proportion of the
people's sweat and blood can be squeezed from them to maintain an army
without producing absolute death."[29]

American commentators also discussed other key aspects of European
aristocratic society. Protectionists focused on the lack of social mobility. Bar-
ricades were erected to keep individuals in their appropriate social circle.[30]
Americans did not overlook the misery of Ireland, and they ascribed Irish
troubles, as Benjamin Franklin had done, to absentee landlords.[31] Granting
of privileges and favoritism to a select class was a case of monopoly privilege.[32] In nineteenth-century America, the word *monopoly* conjured up the
dark vision of an aristocratic conspiracy to deprive the people of their justly
earned property.

American travelers to Europe, as opposed to European travelers to the
United States, commented on economic systems and the existence of poverty.
Americans were usually dumbfounded by European conditions and enraged

28. For discussion of established churches, see *Aurora*, February 9, 1807, in Ronald
Schultz, "Small Producer Thought in Early America, Part II: William Duane's 'Politics for
Farmers and Mechanics,'" *Pennsylvania History*, LIV (1987), 219; Sedgwick, *Public and Private
Economy*, I, 33–34; Thomas Aspinwall to Hugh Legaré, October 19, 1832, in Hugh Legaré Pa-
pers, Duke University Library, Durham, N.C.; reports on the annual income of English sees
in "Archbishops and Bishops of England," *Bankers' Magazine*, I (April, 1847), 561.

29. John Quincy Adams to Thomas Boylston Adams, February 14, 1801, in Ford, ed., *Writings of John Quincy Adams*, II, 502. See also William H. Seward, Address at Ogdensburgh, August 15, 1839, in Baker, ed., *Works of Seward*, III, 211–12; "Civilization: American and European," *American* [Whig] *Review*, III (June, 1846), 622.

30. Speech of Senator Samuel Latham Mitchell, November 21, 1808, on the tariff, *Annals
of Congress*, 10th Cong., 2nd Sess., 90; Colton, *Public Economy*, 282–85; John Pendleton Kennedy, *Letter of J. P. Kennedy to His Constituents, Citizens of the Fourth Congressional District in
the State of Maryland, on the Principles and Value of the Protective System* (N.p., n.d., [Balti-
more, 1842?]), 17.

31. For example, William H. Seward, *Autobiography*, in Frederick W. Seward, ed. *Autobiography of William H. Seward, from 1801 to 1834, with a Memoir of His Life and Selections from
His Letters from 1831 to 1846* (New York, 1877), I, 107.

32. For example, speech of Representative William Segar Archer, February 5, 1827, *Register
of Debates*, 19th Cong, 2nd Sess., 946–47.

by aristocratic control of politics and society. Theodore Sedgwick, who visited England in 1837, recorded his shock at seeing the unbelievable wealth of a few while the masses suffered the worst penury he had ever witnessed. He explained the awful British wealth distribution by pointing to the large expense for the British military, the lack of an education system for the common man, obstacles to enterprise and to social mobility, the lack of equal rights, the rage for speculation, the ability of nonproducers to take away the earnings of producers, the patronage of the king and court, and the ridiculous costs of aristocratic and monarchical ceremonies. Abram Hewitt wrote in 1844 that in England he had seen "more beauty and more deformity, more wealth and more poverty than my eyes have rested upon during the whole course of my life." The abolitionist Samuel J. May visited Prague in 1859 and was stunned at how the aristocracy lived: "I came away saying with more emphasis than ever: 'What a pity, what a wrong, that so much wealth and power should be allowed to accumulate, and to be retained by inheritance in the hands of one person.'" Thurlow Weed, New York Whig chieftain and one not known for radical proclivities, wrote from Ireland that "by far the most painful scenes I have witnessed are in the crowds of wretched poor who surround and beleaguer strangers."[33]

Americans of many backgrounds found the European elite insufferable. James Buchanan said the Russian nobility in the 1830s were "fond of extravagance and show and have not the least taste for Republican simplicity and economy." He harbored grudges against England in the 1850s when he was appointed ambassador. There, "Society [was] in a most artificial position," and the aristocracy wielded power undeservedly: "I confess, however, that when in looking over the Peerage, I found that many of the nobles had from 5 to 20 & even thirty livings in their gift, my Republican spirit was vexed at this abuse." The social power of the English aristocracy impressed Richard Henry Dana in 1856, and when he saw the luxury at Versailles he vented his republican preferences for utilitarianism and modesty: "Such wanton luxury, such unrestrained and frantic lavishness of expense, is more than the Almighty in-

---

33. Sedgwick, *Public and Private Economy*, II, 55–56, 63, 74–75, 84–85, 87–88, 122, 131–32, 139, III, 30, 42–53, 102. On Sedgwick in general, see Marvin Meyers, *The Jacksonian Persuasion: Politics and Belief* (New York, 1957), chap. 8. Letter of Abram Hewitt, 1844, quoted in Allan Nevins, *Abram S. Hewitt: With Some Account of Peter Cooper* (New York, 1935), 37; Samuel Joseph May, *Memoir of Samuel Joseph May* (Boston, 1873), 205; Thurlow Weed to [?], June, 1843, and Weed to eldest daughter, August 9, 1843, in Harriet A. Weed, ed., *Autobiography of Thurlow Weed* (Boston, 1884), II, 103, 108.

tended for any race of human beings to enjoy or any other to be taxed for, and the penalty must be paid." The penalty, of course, was the French Revolution.[34]

How through political power the aristocracy managed to amass wealth unto itself and skew the distribution of wealth in its favor was given distinct form by three abolitionists who directly linked aristocracies to specific policies that created the few rich and the many poor. In 1841 Wendell Phillips was in Naples, and he was shocked by the extremes of wealth and poverty. He wrote to William Lloyd Garrison that art and luxuries "are no balance to the misery which bad laws and bad religion alike entail on the bulk of the people." At approximately the same time, James and Lucretia Mott were in London attending an antislavery convention. James Mott later wrote, "Windsor Castle is one of the many monuments of the extravagance and folly of the English nobility and aristocracy, *which oppresses the laborer by taking from him in the shape of impost and taxes, so much of his earnings, as to leave but a scanty subsistence for himself.*" A few years earlier, William Lloyd Garrison wrote of London that "I have seen dukes, marquises, and earls, and royalty itself, in all the hereditary splendor of an ancient monarchy, surrounded with luxury, and pomp, and the people impoverished and oppressed to sustain it all; but here, in New England, one looks for such inequality in vain."[35]

The experience of seeing Europe's social condition sometimes had a strong effect on otherwise staid Americans. John Sherman, a moderate antislavery Republican in the 1850s and conservative financial politician in the postwar years, upon seeing the social degradation of England in 1859, almost declared himself a revolutionary. The British government was "a government of the aristocracy, more exclusive, repelling, and narrow than I conceived of." There was no representation in England. "The idea that all this stock and property belonged to a few, that the great mass of the people merely labored for others,

34. James Buchanan to General Jackson, October 1–13, 1832, in John Bassett Moore, ed., *The Works of James Buchanan: Comprising His Speeches, State Papers, and Private Correspondence* (Philadelphia, 1908–11), II, 239–40; Buchanan to Miss [Harriet] Lane, August 26, 1853, *ibid.,* IX, 38; Buchanan to Rev. Mr. Edward Y. Buchanan, September 8, 1853, *ibid.,* IX, 47–48; Charles Francis Adams, *Richard Henry Dana: A Biography* (rev. ed.; Boston, 1891), II, 34, 118.

35. [Wendell Phillips to William Lloyd Garrison], "Letter from Naples," April 12, 1841, in Wendell Phillips, *Speeches, Lectures, and Letters* (Boston, 1884–91), II, 219, 221; James Brewer Stewart, *Wendell Phillips: Liberty's Hero* (Baton Rouge, 1986), 79; Anna Davis Hallowell, ed., *James and Lucretia Mott: Life and Letters* (Boston, 1884), 195 (emphasis added); Garrison speech quoted in Bernard Mandel, *Labor Free and Slave: Workingmen and the Anti-Slavery Movement in the United States* (New York, 1955), 91.

and that the whole government was conducted and a system of laws passed simply to continue and intensify this state of things, and that the favored class had the possession of all the powers of government, securely hedged about, made me feel a rebel from the beginning." What was the solution to the state of social affairs in England? How could the laboring groups reclaim the fruits of their labor? The answer was that Great Britain required equal representation based on actual population and "a law against entailment, and a law of descent and distribution, which would divide property among children equally."[36] For Sherman, abolition of entail and primogeniture was an act of revolution, a means to pull down a social order.

The political economy of aristocracy defined how Americans generally understood the existence of poverty, for it was more complex than a simple reliance on individual character traits. Certainly some Americans did try to explain the world on the basis of individual moral habits, but they were only part—and not necessarily the larger part—of the dialogue concerning poverty and the distribution of wealth.[37] The larger and more widespread explanation of poverty and imbalances in wealth-holding was not individualistic but a systems analysis.

Americans insisted that the *political* (not the *economic*) system determined the extent of poverty and maldistribution of wealth. The system of privileges, monopoly, restrictive government—that is, aristocracy—immediately doomed the masses to poverty and unnaturally concentrated wealth in the hands of a few. Republicanism, because of its stress on equal rights, its allowance of participation in tax and expenditure decisions through representation, and its rejection of elite attempts to use government to enrich the few at the expense of the many, normally produced a healthy distribution of wealth and eliminated the artificially created mass of poverty. Under republican regimes, all individuals who labored were rewarded with the full fruits of their labors, and though the masses would not grow rich, they would at least have

36. John Sherman to William T. Sherman, June 19, 1859, in Rachel Sherman Thorndike, ed., *The Sherman Letters: Correspondence Between General and Senator Sherman from 1837 to 1891* (New York, 1894), 73–74.

37. For example, see Sedgwick, *Public and Private Economy*, II, 69–70, 87; Robert H. Bremner, *From the Depths: The Discovery of Poverty in the United States* (New York, 1956), 16–19; David J. Rothman, *The Discovery of the Asylum: Social Order and Disorder in the New Republic* (Boston, 1971), 161–65, and more generally 154–79; Charles C. Cole, Jr., *The Social Ideas of the Northern Evangelists, 1826–1860* (New York, 1954), 175, 186–87; Spann, *New Metropolis*, 70–77; Kohl, *Politics of Individualism*, 70, 97.

a healthy competence. Therefore, once a person lived under a republican system, poverty was seen as an individual failure because the system had already been made as favorable as possible (although most people admitted that natural misfortune also sometimes entered the picture). Americans did blame the poor for their own poverty when they lived in a republican system; but they never blamed the European poor for their poverty, for the root of poverty in Europe was the system of aristocracy.

Theodore Sedgwick mentioned two other factors influencing Britain's obviously ill-distributed wealth. Although Sedgwick disparaged Malthus and mocked the British for using Malthusian population doctrines to explain poverty, he did comment that he believed the land may have had too many people. More important, Sedgwick pointed out that inequality naturally came from monopolization of the soil, and under aristocracy that monopolization was most apparent when the laws of primogeniture and entail were most deeply entrenched.[38] Sedgwick was not alone. The revolutionary generation had laid great stress on the importance of abolition of primogeniture and entail and instituting the laws of partible inheritance in their stead so that no intergenerational transfers of concentrated amounts of property occurred. It is perhaps not unreasonable that Americans living in the late eighteenth century should have been so impressed with the wealth-distributing potential of these laws. But Americans in the nineteenth century continued to think that the laws of primogeniture and entail were the primary determinants of wealth distribution. It is startling when one looks over antebellum discussions of the distribution of wealth to realize how signally important the laws of entail and primogeniture were to them.

Advocates of the use of governmental powers to build up the American economy commonly seized upon the American practice of partible inheritance to argue that the distribution of wealth in the country would always be equal because of the absence of the laws of entail and primogeniture. In one of the classic statements of protectionism, Henry Clay argued in March, 1824, that his plan for a high tariff to promote manufactures would not upset a healthy wealth distribution and ruin the republic: "We may safely confide in the laws of distributions, and in the absence of the rule of primogeniture, for the dissipation (perhaps too rapid) of large fortunes." "A republican form

---

38. Sedgwick, *Public and Private Economy*, on Malthus, II, 59; overpopulation, III, 30; see also I, 47, 53–55, 237–38, 242, III, 69.

of government," preached Daniel Webster, "rests not more on political constitutions, than on those laws which regulate the descent and transmission of
property." The glory of the Pilgrim settlers was their avoidance of feudal restrictions; they divided the land equally and later outlawed entail and primogeniture.[39]

Protectionists made continual reference throughout the antebellum years
to the laws of partible inheritance as regulators of the distribution of wealth.
During the nullification battle, Senator Archer Robbins of Rhode Island felt
some government intrusion in the economy would not upset a just distribution of wealth. The people prized the spirit of liberty too greatly for improper
wealth inequalities to appear, and the country had "no mortmain, no perpe-
tuities, [that] prevent alienation and check circulation; where the accumulations of one generation are broken down in the next by distribution." A writer
for the Boston *Journal* in 1853 also relied on partible inheritance to preserve a
just distribution of wealth. "In a community like ours," wrote the author,
"there can result no permanent evils from the successful acquisition of great
wealth. If fortunes could be rendered inalienable, if the law of primogeniture
and entail could devolve upon the son the miserly accumulation of the [fa-
ther], and restrain its dissipation by spendthrift heirs, very few generations
would pass before a moneyed aristocracy would arise which would darken the
heavens, and overshadow the land; but as it is under our wise statutes of distribution, the wealthy son not unfrequently [*sic*] finds himself in the end
where the wealthy [father] found himself in the beginning, at the very bot-
tom of fortune's wheel."[40]

Free trade politicians seemed to scoff publicly at the idea that abolition of
the laws of entail and primogeniture was sufficient to secure a republican distribution of wealth. Yet one does not have to look very far to find numerous
declarations by free traders that the laws of entail and primogeniture were indeed aristocratic laws that purposefully transferred wealth from producers to
nonproducers. John Taylor of Caroline was an early, vociferous, and violent
opponent of using tariffs to encourage American manufacturing. Yet even in
his most famous antitariff publication, *Tyranny Unmasked,* Taylor admitted

39. Speech of Representative Henry Clay, March 31, 1824, *Annals of Congress,* 18th Cong.,
1st Sess., 1993; Webster, "First Settlement of New England," in McIntyre, ed., *Writing and
Speeches of Webster,* quote on 211; on primogeniture and entail, 211–12, 213–14; on need for
equality, 215–16.

40. Quotes from Senator Robbins, tariff speech, March 2, 1832, *Register of Debates,* 22nd
Cong., 1st Sess., 492; Boston *Journal* quoted by Clearfield (Pa.) *Republican,* March 18, 1853.

that the principal means of consolidating wealth in the hands of the aristocracy was the feudal system of land tenure, followed by manufacturing monopoly. John Bell of Tennessee, who forcefully brought up the issue of the distribution of wealth in Congress in the nullification battle, mentioned that, although he attacked protectionism, the first measure a republic should enact was the abolition of the laws of entail and primogeniture. James Buchanan in 1828 also testified that division and "subdivision of estates, under our laws, without any other cause, will of itself, in the course of a few generations cut up the largest estates into small fractions." Senator James Barbour of Virginia said about the laws of entail and primogeniture that "these principles are two of the strongest pillars upon which a monarchy rests, because they concentrate the property of the country, and with it the power and influence of a few."[41]

The extreme laissez-faire Jacksonian Democrats of the 1830s and 1840s did not forget to mention the wealth-distorting power of the laws of primogeniture and entail while they were attacking banks and tariffs. Robert Rantoul believed the idea of landed power in the United States had in the main died: "The abolition of entails, and a statute of distributions, will indeed do much to prevent, or help to break up a landed aristocracy." The New York Locofoco Samuel J. Tilden, while attacking paper money and national banks, disparaged England for keeping property "in large masses in the hands of the few by the law of primogeniture and the system of entails." Both Gideon Welles and Andrew Johnson in the 1840s found aristocracy abroad supported by a landed monopoly.[42]

European wayfarers to the United States reinforced the American ten-

41. John Taylor, *Tyranny Unmasked* (Washington, D.C., 1822), 200; speech of John Bell on the tariff, June 8, 1832, *Register of Debates*, 22nd Cong., 1st Sess., 3359; James Buchanan, "Address on the Establishment of Common Schools," in Moore, ed., *Works of Buchanan*, I, 378; speech of Senator James Barbour, April 27, 1820, *Annals of Congress*, 16th Cong., 1st Sess., 2063.

42. Robert Rantoul, "The Education of a Free People," 1839, in Hamilton, ed., *Memoirs, Speeches and Writings of Rantoul*, 135; Tilden, "Divorce of Bank and State: An Address to the Farmers, Mechanics, and Workingmen of the State of New York," February 26, 1838, in Bigelow, ed., *Writings and Speeches of Tilden*, I, 83; Andrew Johnson, speech on Homestead Bill, clerk's version, July 25, 1850, in Graf, Haskins, and Bergeron, eds., *Papers of Andrew Johnson*, I, 559. John Ashworth believes the use of entail and primogeniture to explain the distribution of wealth was most prominent among conservative Democrats (*"Agrarians" and "Aristocrats,"* 138).

dency to single out the laws of entail and primogeniture as the main determinants of a distorted distribution of wealth. The Europeans seemed obsessed with discovering the effects of the absence of the laws of primogeniture and entail in the United States and willingly generalized that the lack of these laws laid the foundation for American democracy and the general diffusion of property. Francis J. Grund even declared that the absence of primogeniture had "done more towards equalizing conditions than the spirit of exclusiveness will ever be able to overcome." Tocqueville, after setting the tone of his work by exclaiming about the novelty of American material equality, immediately launched into an extended commentary on the impact of the Americans' abolition of entail and primogeniture.[43] Among foreign observers in the antebellum period, the subjects of primogeniture and entail were of crucial importance and received extended analysis and commentary. Europeans entertained no doubt that primogeniture and entail were key elements in explaining a skewed distribution of wealth.

Near the middle of the century, Francis Bowen made some acute observations about the importance of the laws of primogeniture and entail in regard to the distribution of wealth. No one doubted the importance of the laws in establishing and perpetuating an aristocracy. But the United States was no longer the leader in fomenting republican laws of inheritance. Revolutionary France had decreed that all inheritances must be equally divided among the children; republican America's inheritance laws merely covered the disposition of the deceased's property when there was no will (*i.e.,* the person died intestate). A person who made out a will, however, could leave the entire fortune to a first son. As Bowen pointed out, American law on inheritance now occupied the middle ground between aristocratic England and egalitarian France. Moreover, Bowen noticed that if estates, in this case farms, became too small, then a law demanding equal partition among the children and spouse would do a disservice to the public welfare by creating inefficient farms. Yet in the case of England, no one doubted that primogeniture and entail had created a privileged caste and had brought the notion of property

43. Grund, *Americans in Their Moral, Social and Political Relations,* 22; Tocqueville, *Democracy in America,* I, 46–51, 293. See also Hamilton, *Men and Manners in America,* 61–62; Gurowski, *America and Europe,* 118; Charles Lyell, *Second Visit to the United States,* I, 58–59, 83; Holmes, *Account of the United States,* 102; Chevalier, *Society, Manners, and Politics in the United States,* 396–97; Hall, *Travels in North America,* II, 320–31; Pulszky and Pulszky, *White Red Black,* III, 172.

rights into disrepute. The only way to cure England of its social evils, Bowen stated, was to abolish entail and primogeniture: "That such measures would destroy the aristocracy, there can be no doubt; but they would save the people."[44]

No economic doctrine in the nineteenth-century United States penetrated more deeply into economic controversies, and indeed into all kinds of controversies, than Malthusian population theory. It was literally omnipresent. As much as Americans and some European visitors insisted that political institutions affected any society's distribution of wealth, the literate public increasingly came to accept the validity of Malthusian population doctrines. By 1860 the population-to-land ratio had become a major part of the American discussion of the distribution of wealth and had affected policy making in a variety of ways. Free traders and Democrats increasingly came to believe, regardless of their shrill warnings about the effect of aristocrats on economic equality, that the existence of land for population expansion governed the distribution of wealth. This was a prescription for the justification of a policy of landed imperialism.

Throughout the nineteenth century, Americans understood that overpopulation—which was never numerically defined but only presented impressionistically—created widespread poverty. English social problems were often ascribed to excessive populousness.[45] The important element in the population-to-land ratio was its effect on wages, and it was primarily through high wages that American political and public leaders had come to believe that an equitable distribution of wealth in the United States could be maintained. Where land was plentiful in relation to population, wages were high; where land was scarce in relation to population, wages were low. This relationship, visible to most at the time of the Revolution, became widespread knowledge as the nineteenth century wore on. It is almost fair to say that for some the relationship became an obsession.

Protectionists bowed to the importance of the population-to-land ratio and its impact on wages. They offered a variety of arguments to show why

44. [Bowen], "Distribution of Property," 119–56, quote on 152; see esp. 126–34, 137–52.

45. Nevins, *Abram S. Hewitt,* 38; Henry M. Baldwin, "Protection to Manufactures," report of Committee on Manufactures, January 15, 1821, in *Annals of Congress,* 16th Cong., 2nd Sess., Appendix, 1574; Speech of John J. Crittenden at Pittsburgh, June 24, 1848, in Mrs. Chapman Coleman, *The Life of John J. Crittenden* (Philadelphia, 1871), I, 313; Lynn (Mass.) *News,* March 7, 1860.

American wages were high and English wages low, yet when it came to the central core of why Americans could expect high wages, many protectionists in the end relied on the West to sustain an equitable distribution of wealth. Henry Clay in his great tariff speeches of 1820 and 1824 said that the West would sustain high wages so none needed to fear that manufacturing would plant a pauper element in American society. Other proponents of high tariffs uttered the same sentiments. Protectionists bowed to the omnipresence of the doctrine. High wages in the United States at the very least partially originated in the low land-to-population ratio.[46]

Free traders did not hesitate to attribute the wholesome American distribution of wealth and existence of high wages to the population-to-land ratio. The Malthusian population doctrine became an immovable feature of free trade economics. Political and public figures declaring their preference for free trade just as frequently bestowed their approval on Malthus' population doctrines. The reason they could do so, of course, was that the United States had the land that Europe lacked.[47]

From the start of political life under the Constitution, free traders explained high American wage rates as the result of the existence of uninhabited, arable western lands. The leaders of the Democratic-Republicans all testified, even gloried in, the possession of western lands. When the anticonsolidation elements of American politics regrouped in the 1820s under the banner of Jacksonian Democracy, the new party continued to trumpet the view that high wages arose from possession of western lands. Indeed, a visible strain of thought in the free trade argument emphasized that the agrarian nature of American society should be preserved and manufacturing avoided because of the comparative advantage western land gave American agriculture. The Democratic attitude by the time of the Civil War was exemplified by the editor of the Hartford, Connecticut, *Daily Times:* "The skill and enterprize

---

46. Henry Clay, speech on tariff, April 26, 1820, in Hopkins *et al.*, ed., *Papers of Clay*, II, 829; Henry Clay, tariff speech, March 31, 1824, in *Annals of Congress*, 18th Cong., 1st Sess., 1986, 1991, 1994; Friends of Domestic Industry, *Address of the Friends of Domestic Industry, Assembled in Convention, at New-York, October 26, 1831, to the People of the United States* (Baltimore, 1831), 20, 21; Joseph Fitz Randolph, tariff speech, June 20, 1842, *Congressional Globe*, 27th Cong., 2nd Sess., Appendix, 821. For Whig views, see Brown, *Politics and Statesmanship*, 45; Matthews, *Rufus Choate*, 66. Henry Carey was the exception to the belief that western land propped up wages.

47. See Wiebe, *Opening of American Society*, 131–35, 288–90; Watson, *Liberty and Power*, 241–42.

of our people, and above all our advantages over all other nations in rich and super-abundant agricultural productions, will be quite sufficient to pay labor fair [and] remunerative prices."[48]

The history of American land laws exhibits several major tendencies. First, western lands were used for social experimentation and as a fund to finance certain eastern projects such as education and transportation. Second, public policy evolved from high land prices sold in large amounts to low land prices sold in small amounts to the homestead policy of granting settlers 160 acres if over a period of time they improved the land. Between the Northwest Ordinance of 1787 and the Homestead Act of 1862, the disposal of western lands was a heated political controversy.[49]

The republican theory of the distribution of wealth meandered around and through most of the crucial aspects of the political debates over western lands. Proponents of low land prices and small acreage purchases were hoping to preserve an egalitarian and agrarian society. The debates over land policies give eloquent testimony to the power that the Malthusian relation of population to land had over the American imagination. Every time a land law was debated in Congress, representatives denounced monopoly, the economic manifestation of aristocratic evil. A leader in homestead legislation, George Washington Julian of Indiana, explained that land monopoly produced surplus population and deprived people of independence: "It was never designed that men should be wholly dependent upon his fellow for the bread and breath of life. It was never designed that he should be deprived of a

48. James Madison, speech on tariff, April 9, 1789, *Annals of Congress,* 1st Cong., 1st Sess., 117; Thomas Jefferson to David Humphreys, June 23, 1791, in Boyd *et al.,* eds., *Papers of Jefferson,* XX, 565; Thomas Jefferson to Jean Baptiste Say, February 1, 1804, in Lipscomb, ed., *Writings of Jefferson,* XI, 2; Jefferson to Thomas Cooper, September 10, 1814, *ibid.,* XIV, 182; Albert Gallatin to La Fayette, May 12, 1833, in Henry Adams, ed., *The Writings of Albert Gallatin* (1879; rpr. New York, 1960), II, 471; Hartford *Daily Times,* September 8, 1858; "Memorial of Free Trade Convention," *Senate Executive Document* 55, 1832, 22nd Cong., 1st Sess., 10–11; William M. Gouge, *A Short History of Paper Money and Banking in the United States to Which Is Prefixed an Inquiry into the Principles of the System* (1833; rpr. New York, 1968), 44. Note the comments of Major L. Wilson, *Space, Time and Freedom: The Quest for Nationality and the Irrepressible Conflict, 1815–1861* (Westport, Conn., 1974), 95, 109–10.

49. For a history of land laws generally, see the standard accounts in Roy Marvin Robbins, *Our Landed Heritage: The Public Domain, 1776–1936* (1942; rpr. New York, 1950), chaps. 1–6, 10–13; Gates, *Farmer's Age,* chaps. 3, 4; Benjamin Horace Hibbard, *A History of the Public Land Policies* (New York, 1939), chaps. 3–17.

homestead for himself and his family, as a defense against the cold-blooded rapacity of avarice."[50]

The subject of western land and its relation to the republican theory of the distribution of wealth, however, leads to some disconcerting features about the application of specific doctrines. The leaders of the United States acquired western lands through purchase, annexation, or conquest—the Louisiana Purchase of 1803, Florida in 1819, Texas in 1845, the Mexican Cession in 1848, Oregon in 1846, and the Gadsden Purchase of 1854. These lands were not uninhabited, and property rights were not unknown. Native American Indians possessed these lands and had a property right in them that was evidenced by the fact that the federal government made treaties to obtain land. Why did not the labor theory of property/value and the belief in property rights protect American Indians?

The labor theory of property/value contained many cultural prejudices, and in some ways it is fair to say that in the extreme it is not much more than the individualism of the Anglo-Saxon world writ into universal law. The labor theory of property/value implied a culture in which individualism reigned and labor meant certain specific activities. When the labor theory of property/value ran into a culture lacking Anglo-Saxon individualism and based on a different technology—such as the tribal cultures of North American Indians and particularly the Plains tribes—the labor theory of property/value became an argument for dispossession and even extermination.[51]

The use of the labor theory of property/value against the property rights of

50. Mary E. Young, "Congress Looks West: Liberal Ideology and Public Land Policy in the Nineteenth Century," in *The Frontier in American Development: Essays in Honor of Paul Wallace Gates,* ed. David M. Ellis (Ithaca, N.Y., 1969), 80–112; Huston, *Panic of 1857,* 100–103; George W. Julian, speech in House of Representatives, January 29, 1851, in George W. Julian, *Speeches on Political Questions* (1872; rpr. Westport, Conn., 1970), 59. On the land question, see Daniel Feller, *The Public Lands in Jacksonian Politics* (Madison, 1984), esp. 25–29, 75, 113, 116, 196–97, for his discussion of the yeoman ideal.

51. Kauder, *History of Marginal Utility Theory,* 3–9, 32–38, 70–80; T. W. Hutchison, "The 'Marginal Revolution' and the Decline and Fall of English Classical Political Economy," in *The Marginal Revolution in Economics: Interpretation and Evaluation,* ed. R. D. Collison Black, A. W. Coates, and Craufurd D. W. Goodwin (Durham, N.C., 1973), 176–202. On Indian relations and Eurocentric individualism, see Alexander Saxton, *The Rise and Fall of the White Republic: Class Politics and Mass Culture in Nineteenth-Century America* (London, 1990), 6, 28, 54–59; Fraysse, *Lincoln, Land, and Labor,* 5, 14; Greene, *Intellectual Construction of America,* 124.

Indians had begun with the Revolution, if not earlier. Colonists had used the theory to justify their forcible seizure of Indian lands, attaching an appendix that stated that groups who possessed land but did not use it had no property rights at all. Thus wrote James Wilson, "Those nations that live by hunting, and have more land than is necessary even for the purposes of hunting, should transfer it to those who will make a more advantageous use of it." In 1775 Joseph Warren delivered an oration that extolled property rights earned by labor and denounced British taxation as an unjust seizure of the colonists' property. In the same speech he explained why Indians had no right to property—they did not labor in the manner of the Europeans and instead sought to take the colonists' fruits of labor. When Ezra Stiles proclaimed the United States a unique experiment because it sought to give each worker the full fruits of his labor, he justified American absorption of Indian land because the European settlers had improved it and the Indians had not.[52]

Nineteenth-century free traders clung to the same argument. The immigrant scholar Francis Lieber easily disposed of the tribes' title to land. Western Europeans in America were the superior race because "labour has risen to honour, and that industry has at length been closely wedded to science and knowledge." A more emphatic use of the labor theory of property/value to condone seizure of Indian land was provided by Jacksonian Democrat and immigrant Francis J. Grund. Indians never possessed the soil because "they never cultivated it to any extent, nor had they, individually, any distinct title to it arising from actual labor." Because the Indians did not labor in a way recognized by English civilization, they did not possess the land as a property right. The land could be taken away in accordance with natural law or God's law. This imperialism was the Manifest Destiny of the Jacksonian period.[53]

52. James Wilson, "Lectures on Law," in McCloskey, ed., *Works of James Wilson,* I, 158; Warren, *Oration Delivered March Sixth, 1775,* 9; Stiles, *United States Elevated to Glory and Honor,* 8–14. See also Johnson, *American Economic Thought in the Seventeenth Century,* 71, 269; Scott, *In Pursuit of Happiness,* 15–17; Wilcomb E. Washburn, *Red Man's Land/White Man's Law: The Past and Present Status of the American Indian* (2nd ed.; Norman, Okla., 1995), 28–34, 56–68.

53. Francis Lieber, *Essays on Property and Labour as Connected with Natural Law and the Constitution of Society* (New York, 1841), 76; Grund, *Americans in Their Moral, Social and Political Relations,* 225. Economists have been attracted to the issue of Indian property rights, largely from the obtuse angle of government intervention in Indian property rights in the twentieth century; see essays in Terry L. Anderson, ed., *Property Rights and Indian Economies* (Boston, 1992); Terry L. Anderson and Fred S. McChesney, "Raid or Trade: An Economic Model of Indian-White Relations," *Journal of Law and Economics,* XXXVII (1994), 39–74.

One of the most disturbing features connected with the relationship between landed expansion and the republican theory of the distribution of wealth is its implications for the way Americans intended to maintain their egalitarian society. Landed expansion was the policy of the Democratic party in antebellum America, and several authors have noted that James K. Polk and the advocates of Manifest Destiny, among numerous other motives, wanted western lands to preserve an agrarian nation of small yeoman farmers. That is, to avoid the Malthusian population crush, to thwart the development of manufactures, to maintain the wide diffusion of property necessary for a republican form of government, to avoid any changing of institutions so as to acquire a broad diffusion of property, it was necessary for the United States government to war continually on neighboring lands and to subjugate and dispossess the people living there. American equality of property was thus the product of extirpating other people's property rights—those of people distinctly not ethnically western European. Americans obtained their equality of property by enlarging the number of dispossessed non-Europeans. The policy of Manifest Destiny was essentially a phase of "*herrenvolk* democracy," a democracy that includes only those of a certain race or ethnicity and assigns to all others a social and economic status of dependency and inferiority.[54]

Yet citizens of the United States knew that their well-being was to some extent dependent on the supply of western lands, regardless of who lived on them. Foreign visitors reiterated the theme that American prosperity and lack of a poverty class was owing to western lands that drew surplus population from the East. Indeed, some foreign travelers stated explicitly that republican institutions had no influence on the distribution of wealth in the United States—the sole determinant was land. An English visitor, Thomas Hamilton, who came to the United States in the 1820s, was emphatic that the American republican experiment could not last. At the moment the United States had land, but eventually population would rise and overwhelm it; "THEN will come the struggle." Hamilton believed that eventually a manufacturing population would develop and receive only subsistence

54. On the interpretation that Manifest Destiny was bolstered by a desire to maintain an agrarian equality among Americans of European descent, see Hietala, *Manifest Design,* 96–101, 105–17; Paul H. Bergeron, *The Presidency of James K. Polk* (Lawrence, Kans., 1987), 66–68; Ashworth, *"Agrarians" and "Aristocrats,"* 221. On *herrenvolk* democracy, see George M. Fredrickson, *The Black Image in the White Mind: The Debate on Afro-American Character and Destiny, 1817–1914* (New York, 1971), 61.

wages. Because of republican institutions, the masses would pass an agrarian law and redistribute wealth. An aristocracy would then take over the nation, suppress the people to maintain property rights, and finally extinguish republicanism.[55]

Hamilton's exposition of the fate of the United States received fuller form and much more attention in 1860 when American biographer Henry S. Randall revealed a letter from the eminent English historian Thomas Babington Macaulay about Jeffersonian principles. Macaulay was unimpressed. Because Europe had a dense population, it was necessary for power to be concentrated and used to force the rabble to accept their miserable existence. The United States escaped the same fate only because it possessed "a boundless extent of fertile and unoccupied land," thus ensuring high wages. "But the time will come when New England will be as thickly peopled as Old England," Macaulay wrote. "Wages will be as low. . . . Then your institutions will be fairly brought to the test. Distress everywhere makes the laborer mutinous and discontented, and inclines him to listen with eagerness to agitators, who tell him that it is a monstrous iniquity that one man should have a million while another cannot get a full meal."[56]

The question hung in the air: was an equitable distribution of wealth determined by Malthusian doctrine, the population-to-land ratio, or was it instead the product of republican political institutions? Many Americans, even though continuing to worry about Malthus, possessed an abundant faith that inequalities in wealth were caused by aristocratic machinations and that by following the labor theory of property/value, European imbalances could be avoided. On the question of the distribution of wealth in 1860, Americans were optimistic though perhaps troubled.[57] Europeans, however, probably held a different belief. American exceptionalism could be explained in two words: western lands. When the lands ran out, American exceptionalism would die.

Between 1800 and 1860, in numerous political speeches, popular tracts, sermons, books, and pamphlets, literate Americans referred to their distribution

55. Chevalier, *Society, Manners, and Politics in the United States,* 143, 331; Tocqueville, *Democracy in America,* I, 290–96; Marryat, *Diary in America,* 467–68; Hamilton, *Men and Manners in America,* quote on xx, analysis on 162–66.

56. T. B. Macaulay to Henry S. Randall, May 23, 1857, in *Littell's Living Age,* May 19, 1860, p. 430; see Huston, "Political Response to Industrialism," 38.

57. See Huston, *Panic of 1857,* 97–110.

of wealth, and they found it enormously satisfactory. So did Europeans. Except for a few vocal dissenters and Cassandras, the record Americans left concerning their attitude toward the existing distribution of wealth in antebellum times was celebratory. Therein lies a paradox.

On occasion Americans counted the number of unemployed, the number of immigrants, the number of millionaires, the number of factories, the number of working women, the number of orphans, the number of morons, the number of sheep, and the number of anything else that seized their imagination. But they never figured out their distribution of wealth. Antebellum Americans were content with descriptions and impressions rather than with close estimates. The entire discourse on the distribution of wealth in the United States was verbal, not numerical. Some pamphlets detailing the wealth of the upper class circulated, but never was there a description of the division of wealth among all of society's classes.[58] Twentieth-century investigators have not been as content with impressions as had been their forebears.

Historians and econometricians have investigated American nineteenth-century wealth-holding patterns, and generally they all agree that the antebellum United States had severe wealth inequalities.[59] Economists estimate that nearly one-third of Americans in 1860 were poor, that cities—where poverty was most extensive—had poverty rates as high as 50 percent, that the top 10 percent of wealth-holders possessed over 70 percent of the nation's physical wealth. Using the "Gini coefficient of inequality," in which 0.00 represents perfect equality and 1.00 represents perfect inequality, economists have found that wealth distribution in the United States distinctly worsened between the Revolution and the Civil War. In 1774 the Gini coefficient was .694; by 1860 it was .832. Scholars concede that the Great Lakes region was the most egalitarian in the United States, and even there the Gini coefficient was between .58 and .62. More dramatically, the share of wealth possessed by

58. [Moses Y. Beach], *Wealth and Biography of the Wealthy Citizens of New York City* (6th ed.; New York, 1845); A. Forbes and J. W. Greene, *The Rich Men of Massachusetts: Containing a Statement of the Reputed Wealth of About Fifteen Hundred Persons, with Brief Sketches of More Than One Thousand Characters* (Boston, 1851). Some statistics were published about Great Britain in the labor press; see "Distribution of Wealth," *Voice of Industry* (Lowell, Mass.), July 23, 1847.

59. For example, Pessen, *Jacksonian America,* 39–55; Richard B. DuBoff, *Accumulation and Power: An Economic History of the United States* (Armonk, N.Y., 1989), 16–25; Douglas T. Miller, *The Birth of Modern America, 1820–1850* (New York, 1970), 79, 105–107, 118, 123–24, 154; Clark, *Roots of Rural Capitalism,* 155, 160, 227, 263, 274; Peter R. Knights, *The Plain People of Boston, 1830–1860: A Study in City Growth* (New York, 1971), 82–89.

the highest 10 percent of the population had increased from 53.2 percent in 1774 to 73 percent in 1860.[60]

The reason for the inequality has been a bone of contention among academics interested in this particular historical problem. A few have recognized that population pressure created some inequalities, especially in a rural society when further division of farms—as in New England—became uneconomical and a surplus rural population developed. Some historians have tended to blame the creation of a market economy, with its commercial webs of dependence that allowed owners of capital to take advantage of persons less well situated. Many immediately point to industrialization as the cause of inequality, especially the transition from an agrarian to an industrial economy in the first half of the nineteenth century. Although historians have not been very precise in explaining why industrialization produces wealth inequalities, it seems clear that they lean to the idea that a hierarchical institution such as a corporation generates inequalities of power, thus enabling some to take monetary advantage of others. Less well developed but obviously implicit in the discussion is the way manufactures developed historically. From the English example, manufactures used cheap, even pauper, labor, and over time the lords of the loom became established as a new wealthy aristocracy. Many historians believe that the basic reasons for American inequality were industrialization and the capitalist marketplace.[61]

60. See Table 1, Chapter 4, and Soltow, *Men and Wealth in the United States,* 24–25, 35–36, 38–39, 47, 108; David C. Klingaman, "Individual Wealth in Ohio in 1860," in *Essays in Nineteenth Century Economic History: The Old Northwest,* ed. David C. Klingaman and Richard K. Vedder (Athens, Ohio, 1975), 183; Atack and Bateman, *To Their Own Soil,* 88–89, 95–96; Williamson and Lindert, *American Inequality,* 36–37. See Davis et al., *American Economic Growth,* 50–54; Richard H. Steckel, *Poverty and Prosperity: A Longitudinal Study of Wealth Accumulation, 1850–1860,* NBER Working Papers Series on Historical Factors in Long-Run Growth No. 8 (Cambridge, Mass., 1989), i, 3, 6–7, 13. In 1989, in *Distribution of Wealth and Income,* 5, 45–46, 174–75, 190–91, Lee Soltow argued that between 1798 (or 1774) and 1870 wealth inequality remained the same and did not worsen. I have decided to accept earlier findings concerning worsening wealth inequality, if for no other reason than that the sudden shifts in the labor supply caused by immigration argue for a deterioration in wealth equality. Steckel reported a Gini of .771 for 1860, whereas Soltow's 1989 study reports a Gini of .657 (p. 42). Although Carole Shammas has questioned whether the distribution of wealth has really changed over time, I have elected to follow the determination of earlier investigators. See Shammas, "A New Look at Long-Term Trends in Wealth Inequality in the United States," *American Historical Review,* XCVIII (1993), 412–31.

61. On the role of market relationships producing inequality and the pressure of population on farmers, see Clark, *Roots of Rural Capitalism,* 160–90, 246–53, 263, 318, 320–25. On in-

Econometricians differ as to why wealth-holding patterns assume the shape they do. The general position among economists is that age, nativity, length of residence, and education are the main determinants of wealth-holding, both in the present and in the past.[62] Jeffrey G. Williamson and Peter Lindert have offered some novel views of inequality in the nineteenth and twentieth centuries. American inequality was at its worst between 1820 and 1930 for three reasons. First, the labor market experienced greater growth in these years than in any before or after. Second, a huge gap emerged between the pay of skilled and unskilled workers. Third, and most important to Williamson and Lindert, a large differential occurred in the productivity and income acquisition of various sectors of the economy, the starkest being between agriculture and industry. Inequality began to lessen after 1940 or so, when the rates of income growth and productivity for agriculture and industry equalized.[63]

Such studies as exist on the distribution of wealth in foreign countries do not reveal massive differences between the United States and other lands. Existing studies of the nineteenth century reveal that England led in inequality. In ownership of land, the republican United States was more egalitarian than European states but otherwise did not seem by the mid-nineteenth century much different from aristocratic Europe.[64]

Scholarship, in short, disputes nineteenth-century Americans (and Europeans) on almost every conceivable point relating to the outline and causes of

---

dustrialization, see Pessen, *Jacksonian America,* 94, 114–18; DuBoff, *Accumulation and Power,* 5–10; Miller, *Birth of Modern America,* 103–10, 118–24, 154.

62. Soltow, *Men and Wealth in the United States,* 16–17, 124, 148–58, 16–17. An interesting and informative exchange about antebellum wealth distribution and its causes took place in *Social Science History* between the econometrician Robert Gallman and the historian Edward Pessen. Gallman argued the importance of age and that American wealth distribution really was egalitarian; Pessen fired back that egalitarian means equal, which American wealth distribution was not, and that the inequality was rooted in capitalism. See Robert Gallman, "Professor Pessen on the 'Egalitarian Myth,'" *Social Science History,* II (1978), 194–207; Edward Pessen, "On a Recent Cliometric Attempt to Resurrect the Myth of Antebellum Egalitarianism," *Social Science History,* III (1979), 208–27.

63. Williamson and Lindert doubt the importance of government transfers, unions, age, and immigration, although if they emphasize growth of labor supply it is difficult to see how immigration cannot be a factor (*American Inequality,* 41–42, 57, 135–49, 161–62, 204, 249).

64. Soltow, *Men and Wealth in the United States,* 93–94; Lee Soltow, "Wealth Distribution in England and Wales in 1798," *Economic History Review,* XXXIV (1981), 64–67, 70; Soltow, "The Rich and the Destitute in Sweden, 1805–1855: A Test of Tocqueville's Inequality Hypothesis," *Economic History Review,* XLII (1989), 43–63; Williamson and Lindert, *American Inequality,* 33.

wealth distribution. No twentieth-century scholar finds equality in the mid-nineteenth-century United States, and most assert a growing inequality. The republican theory of the distribution of wealth, the idea that wealth was redistributed by aristocrats using government for their own enrichment, has drawn largely a bitter laugh from scholars when it has been recognized at all. One would never know from twentieth-century productions that western lands existed or that there was such a thing as a safety-valve thesis.[65]

American students of wealth distribution have totally ignored the absence of primogeniture and entail. Lee Soltow has argued that partible inheritance increased inequality, although he has recently indicated that the removal of entail and primogeniture did have important effects for wealth distribution in the United States. A British economist, A. B. Atkinson, at least offered one different perspective. Inspecting the top one-tenth of 1 percent of wealthholders in the United States and England in the twentieth century, he found that in 1900, 88 percent of the elite in England obtained their positions through inheritance and in 1960, 69 percent. The United States was the reverse—the wealthiest of Americans were entrepreneurs. Atkinson believes the cause of this difference was the existence of entail and primogeniture in England and partible inheritance in the United States.[66]

How, then, did mid-nineteenth-century Americans *and* Europeans find the American distribution of wealth so equal when scholars have found it so unequal? Some, of course, did find it inegalitarian, but the political and economic leadership crowed about economic equality. The answer lies in part in the imprecise language of nineteenth-century Americans. Citizens of the United States evidently talked about a wide diffusion of property—they cele-

65. Williamson and Lindert, *American Inequality,* 30, 141; Steckel, *Poverty and Prosperity,* i, 10, 13; Soltow, *Distribution of Wealth and Income,* 9, 13–14. Soltow did estimate that inequality in the 1790s would have worsened considerably if there had not been a western frontier (*ibid.,* 160). Historians have attacked the notion that political equality would produce economic equality and have essentially shredded the propositions that supported the republican theory of the distribution of wealth; see Pessen, *Jacksonian America,* 202–89, 293–95; Miller, *Birth of Modern America,* 50, 141, 163–67.

66. Lee Soltow cited in Atack and Bateman, *To Their Own Soil,* 97; see also E. Digby Baltzell, *Puritan Boston and Quaker Philadelphia: Two Protestant Ethics and the Spirit of Class Authority and Leadership* (New York, 1979), 207; Soltow, *Distribution of Wealth and Income,* on entail and primogeniture, 111, 144–47, and other land warrant systems, 89–90, 155–68; A. B. Atkinson, *The Economics of Inequality* (Oxford, 1975), 143–55. Atkinson's book is excellent for a discussion of the factors causing inequality and some of the techniques used in quantitative research.

brated the widespread ownership of property. Its relative amounts may not have impressed Europeans as much as that the mass of American society seemed propertied. The distribution of wealth, after all, is a relative statistic—it divides society into deciles or quintiles and then compares the amounts of wealth held by each category. But a society in which property ownership was widespread could easily have had the same wealth distribution statistics as a poor society in which great numbers had no property at all. In the latter case, an observer would be impressed with the extent of pauperism and draw very negative ideas about the distribution of wealth—which seems to have been the case for England, France, and other European nations. But an observer looking at a nation in which property ownership was widespread, even though the actual distribution between decile groups was inegalitarian, might easily come away impressed with the egalitarian nature of the society and its "good" distribution of wealth. But observers, American and European, were actually recording their impression of widespread ownership of small amounts of property, not its size distribution.

An important second element in how Americans understood their distribution of wealth at mid-century is also apparent. They made exceptions and did not factor into their calculations people whom they considered to be exceptions or insignificant. Three examples are obvious. The first were slaves. The second were Indians, who to this day are never included in calculations of wealth inequality for the United States in the nineteenth century. The third were immigrants, who for ethnic reasons easily became a scapegoat for poverty and inequality. The Irish influx between 1840 and 1860 in particular showed how a technique of excepting ethnic groups enabled native Protestants to argue for income equality; wealth was distributed well among the important people with the right habits—individuals like themselves. Others were different, and the differences meant they had to be considered separately and not as a part of the "nation." Immigrants, slaves, and Indians were exceptions that disfigured the distribution of wealth but could be overlooked. They also accounted for probably 25 to 30 percent of the total population of North America.[67]

67. On immigration and the distribution of wealth, see Soltow, *Men and Wealth in the United States,* 47; Fogel, *Without Consent or Contract,* 354–62; Allan Nevins, *Ordeal of the Union* (New York, 1947), II, 277, 286–88, 329–30; Holt, *Political Crisis of the 1850s,* 159–61; Ray Allen Billington, *The Protestant Crusade, 1800–1860: A Study of the Origins of American Nativism* (1938; rpr. Chicago, 1964), 193–94, 199–200, 322–25; Maldwyn Allen Jones, *American Immigration* (Chicago, 1960), 131–34, 152–53. The question of slavery in the distribution of

Finally, one other factor explains how so many Americans could believe that the distribution of wealth of their country was so much superior to that of European nations. Commentators on the distribution of wealth never made it clear whether they were talking about income or about wealth, and the difference is important. Income is always more evenly distributed than wealth. It appears that American incomes were significantly higher than European incomes, and even individuals who did not possess much property could impress observers with their incomes.[68]

By one means or another, Americans convinced themselves that they possessed a republican distribution of wealth and congratulated themselves on their superiority over Europe in egalitarian economics. They intended to stay that way by acquiring land for excess population. They also wanted to ensure that aristocrats did not ruin the existing property relationships by manipulating government power. And so in the arena of public policy, they applied the republican theory of the distribution of wealth consistently and ferociously.

---

wealth has produced a small debate. Robert Fogel argues that southern wealth was no more poorly distributed than in the North, while others such as Gavin Wright and Roger Ransom argue that it did produce severe skews. See Fogel, *Without Consent or Contract,* 81–84; Gavin Wright, *The Political Economy of the Cotton South: Households, Markets, and Wealth in the Nineteenth Century* (New York, 1978), 24–37; Roger L. Ransom, *Conflict and Compromise: The Political Economy of Slavery, Emancipation, and the American Civil War* (Cambridge, Eng., 1989), 60–66; Lacy K. Ford, Jr., *Origins of Southern Radicalism: The South Carolina Upcountry, 1800–1860* (New York, 1988), 48–50, 258–63.

68. On American income in the antebellum period, see Stott, *Workers in the Metropolis,* 77–78, 134–40, 160, 167–89. On income inequality, consult Alan S. Blinder, Irving Kristol, and Wilbur J. Cohen, "The Level and Distribution of Economic Well-Being," in *The American Economy in Transition,* ed. Martin Feldstein (Chicago, 1980), 419–21. For example, the Gini coefficient of inequality for income distribution in 1967 was .376 for families and .552 for unrelated individuals (*ibid.,* Table 6.13, p. 438) while the Gini coefficient of inequality for wealth-holding was about .70 (*ibid.,* 466–67).

7

Antebellum Political Parties

American attitudes toward the distribution of wealth found their fullest expression in the political arena in the decades preceding the Civil War. Two topics in particular—the tariff and banking—elicited from politicians a discussion on the necessity of an equitable distribution of wealth and the means of obtaining it. Banking and tariff controversies plagued American politics from the founding of the Constitution to the Civil War, and each episode drew out comments concerning the distribution of wealth. These struggles revealed how thoroughly the axioms of the revolutionary theory of the distribution of wealth dominated the minds of nineteenth-century Americans.

The political wrangling over banking and tariff policies also illuminates American expectations on several important social and economic issues. These political wars over national policies revealed how Americans valued stasis and change. They also throw light on the extensive discussion that erupted in the middle decades of the century over industrialization, the factory system, and the economic direction of society. As well, these debates resolve a problem that has irritated and frustrated historians and other scholars for nearly the whole of the twentieth century: how negative government and equal political rights could translate into, as contemporaries so fervently declared, a nearly equal property distribution, or at least a socially equitable one.

Questions about the appropriate policies to be implemented by the national government soon led to the creation of political parties. Largely because of the nature of the presidency, the American system of politics became a competitive contest between two parties for control of the presidency (and the patronage attached thereto) as well as the legislative agenda. Political scientists have labeled the organization of American politics by competitive parties a "party system," and these systems possessed distinctive characteristics in the nineteenth century. Parties were not stable over time, tending to disappear every thirty or so years. Why a two-party system disintegrated and a new one arose is a bone of contention among historians and political scientists. The pattern of party-system dissolution and "realignment" was characterized by the emergence of a new and intractable politico-social issue that the old party system could not manage, the entrance of some new power into the social realm that carried unforeseen political implications, a sudden eruption of short-lived, single-purpose third parties, a surge of young and inexperienced voters to a party, a rearrangement of the coalitions of social groups (religious, wealth-holding, ethnic, familial) that had framed the earlier party system, and the formal construction of at least one new party to replace one of the older ones. After the original alignment of parties in the 1790s, three major realignments occurred in 1832–1840, 1854–1860, and 1892–1896.[1]

Many reservations have to be attached to any generalizations about the political experience of Americans in the nineteenth century, but research over nearly twenty-five years has produced some conclusions about these party systems. Participation in political activity and voting were exceptionally high after 1840 and remained so until 1896. Probably over 80 percent of the eligible electorate voted in most elections. American politics was open to third-party challenges, accomplished simply by dissidents printing their own ballots for voters to cast in elections. Parties tended to attract people on the basis of their religious views and ethnicity rather than their economic status, although this theory may be the most contested conclusion of researchers working in the area of partisan affiliation.[2]

1. On the party system in general and for a discussion of realignment theory, see Burnham, *Critical Elections and the Mainsprings of American Politics;* James L. Sundquist, *Dynamics of the Party System: Alignment and Realignment of Political Parties in the United States* (2nd ed.; Washington, D.C., 1983); Jerome M. Clubb, William H. Flanigan, and Nancy H. Zingale, *Partisan Realignment: Voters, Parties, and Government in American History* (Beverly Hills, 1980); McCormick, *The Party Period and Public Policy.* There is much debate over the duration of the realignment period and when each realignment occurred; the times I have provided are somewhat standard but imprecise, depending on the authority one consults. Joel Silbey (*American Political Nation*) is one of many scholars having doubts about the realignment synthesis.

2. The literature on the history of the two-party system is vast. The works that most informed me about the machinery of nineteenth-century politics are Silbey, *American Political Nation;* McCormick, *The Party Period and Public Policy;* Gienapp, *Origins of the Republican*

On the question of party agendas and economic programs, however, the party systems exhibited some essential continuities. The first is that a core set of economic issues moved from one realignment to another without the slightest alteration. Hamilton's program—banks and currency, tariff duties, internal improvements and government expenditures, and congressional use of western lands—remained basic to all nineteenth-century party systems. In every realignment, new issues appeared that perhaps took precedence over the old economic core, yet banking and currency, tariff, public lands, and internal improvements remained the foundation of public controversy and were essential in defining the ideology and values for all nineteenth-century political parties.

A second continuity in American politics between 1790 and 1896 was a struggle between individualism and community. One of the parties normally reduced economic issues to a matter of individual self-interest. The other party publicly spoke about the general welfare, the welfare of the community, and community obligations.

The third continuity was a controversy over the power of the central government over the economy. One party argued for minimal federal power and the negative state. The other cautiously called for federal intervention to stimulate enterprise (usually) or to rectify some social imperfection (unusually).

The fourth continuity was that one party represented dynamic economic growth and the other either cautioned wariness or denied the need for any change.

On the basis of these continuities in economic programs and agendas, nineteenth-century American politics had two axes, one of Democratic-Republican/Democracy groups and the other of Federalist/National Republican/Whig/Republican groups. The first, or Jeffersonian, axis was characterized by advocacy of negative government, economic self-interest, slow economic growth, and support of a program calling for low tariffs, easy access to western lands, restricted federal funds for internal improvements, and a government retreat from financial regulation. The second, or Hamiltonian,

---

Party; Holt, *Political Crisis of the 1850s;* Dale Baum, *The Civil War Party System: The Case of Massachusetts, 1848–1876* (Chapel Hill, 1984); Paul Kleppner, *The Third Electoral System, 1853–1892: Parties, Voters, and Political Cultures* (Chapel Hill, 1979); Richard J. Jensen, *The Winning of the Midwest: Social and Political Conflict, 1888–1896* (Chicago, 1971). Party histories can be found in William Nisbet Chambers and Walter Dean Burnham, eds., *The American Party Systems: Stages of Political Development* (New York, 1967); and Paul Kleppner et al., *The Evolution of American Electoral Systems* (Westport, Conn., 1981).

axis was the opposite: it emphasized dynamic economic growth, government intervention in the economy, a collective sense of economic duty, and a program affirming the need for high tariffs, federal regulation of the banking system, federal subsidization of internal improvements, and a slow disposition of western lands.[3]

These continuities have an important implication for the American perspective on wealth distribution. So long as the basic issues remained the same, the same economic values were repeated from one party system to another, and the same economic policies were the subjects of debate between each set of two parties, the analysis of the distribution of wealth was likely to remain the same. And this is precisely what happened. The revolutionaries filled the ranks of the first party system of Democratic-Republicans and Federalists, and they brought with them the revolutionary understanding of what generated and distorted a sound distribution of wealth. Quickly the notions of the labor theory of property/value, the political economy of aristocracy, the laws of entail and primogeniture, and the population-to-land ratio were applied to federal policy. Once the basic formulations were made about how to interpret the tariff, western lands, banking, and internal improvements, politicians applied the analysis without fail in party system after party system.

Congressional debaters seldom added to or modified the revolutionary generation's understanding of the distribution of wealth. Rather, as the century wore on, the original views about wealth distribution grew stronger, more refined, and more powerful. The same ideas were endlessly—one is

3. Rather than go through the party histories to demonstrate the existence of these two axes, I simply affirm their existence. Besides the literature cited in notes 1 and 2, the conclusions about the party systems were also formulated from the research offered in Richard Buel, Jr., *Securing the Revolution: Ideology in American Politics, 1789–1815* (Ithaca, N.Y., 1972); John C. Miller, *The Federalist Era, 1789–1801* (New York, 1960); David Hackett Fischer, *The Revolution of American Conservatism: The Federalist Party in the Era of Jeffersonian Democracy* (New York, 1965); Banner, *To the Hartford Convention;* Manning J. Dauer, *The Adams Federalists* (Baltimore, 1953); McCoy, *Elusive Republic;* John R. Nelson, Jr., *Liberty and Property: Political Economy and Policymaking in the New Nation, 1789–1812* (Baltimore, 1987); Appleby, *Capitalism and a New Social Order;* Richard P. McCormick, *The Second American Party System: Party Formation in the Jacksonian Era* (New York, 1966); Lee Benson, *The Concept of Jacksonian Democracy: New York as a Test Case* (Princeton, 1961); Glyndon G. Van Deusen, *The Jacksonian Era, 1828–1848* (New York, 1959); Watson, *Liberty and Power;* Kohl, *Politics of Individualism;* Ashworth, *"Agrarians" and "Aristocrats";* Welter, *Mind of America;* Baker, *Affairs of Party;* Brown, *Politics and Statesmanship;* Howe, *Political Culture of the American Whigs.*

tempted to say mindlessly—repeated for one hundred years. The great repetition had begun.

The subject of currency and banking commenced when the government was established in 1789 and had strong roots in the paper money crises of the 1780s. Throughout the nineteenth century the banking issue was probably the single most important economic policy debate in the United States. It first arose because Alexander Hamilton, the first secretary of the treasury, developed and implemented a program to deal with the nation's pressing difficulties over the national debt and economic growth. Between 1790 and 1792 he advocated and Congress approved a new taxing policy, funding of the old Confederation debt, assumption of state debts, and the establishment of the National Bank; he failed to obtain congressional support for bounties and higher tariffs to goad industrialization, but this setback did not disturb him much, and probably most of the Federalist party disliked the concept anyway.[4]

Hamilton's financial initiatives elicited a quick response from the Jeffersonians, and by 1800 and certainly by 1815 the critique of banking and currency by the Jeffersonian axis was complete. It rested on the labor theory of property/value and the political economy of aristocracy. These ideas were propagated with great force by Jefferson, Madison, Albert Gallatin, John Taylor of Caroline, and George Logan of Pennsylvania, among others. John Taylor had unusual influence among succeeding generations, who referred constantly to his works.[5] With few alterations, the Jeffersonian analysis of the 1790s persevered throughout the nineteenth century.

The foundation of the Jeffersonian critique of currency and finance was the labor theory of property/value. The two agrarian radicals, George Logan and John Taylor, insisted that all wealth came from manual labor.[6] In a society in which individuals exchanged products for money, the operative currency had to reflect accurately the labor that had gone into the production of

4. The Hamiltonian program can be found in numerous places; a standard account is in Miller, *Federalist Era,* chaps. 3, 4, but see the excellent revision in Nelson, *Liberty and Property,* chaps. 3, 4.

5. For biographies of these individuals with insight into their economic thought, see Dorfman, *Economic Mind in American Civilization,* I, 287–99, 301–307, 433–47. On the role of John Taylor in the Jacksonian era, see Ashworth, *"Agrarians" and "Aristocrats,"* 16.

6. [Logan], *Letters Addressed to the Yeomanry of the United States,* 27–28; John Taylor, *Enquiry into the Principles and Tendency of Certain Public Measures,* 21–22, 30.

an item. If the currency fluctuated, some people obtained more from exchange than they deserved and others received less.

From the labor theory of property/value, then, came two primary fears continually voiced by those viewing economic life from the Jeffersonian perspective. The first was a desperate anxiety about being manipulated and defrauded by others. Those on the Jeffersonian axis exhibited a pervasive fear in their writings that individuals who understood finances and financial institutions could manipulate currency and enrich themselves by impoverishing others. John Adams, speaking for the agrarian side of the Federalist party, deprecated banks that issued paper money that could not be immediately redeemed in specie because it "represents nothing, and is therefore a cheat upon somebody." Albert Gallatin, continuing his fight against irresponsible banking into the Jacksonian era, once wrote that a fluctuating standard of value "impair[s] the performance of every contract, make[s] invariably the ignorant and the weak dupes of the shrewd and the wary, and demoralize[s] the whole community."[7]

The second paranoiac fear the labor theory of property/value aroused in the Jeffersonians when considering financial subjects was a belief that the institution of banking offered rewards entirely out of proportion to its contribution to wealth production. Jeffersonians belittled bankers, stockholders, and speculators in financial securities as individuals who obtained wealth without labor. Bankers and speculators were rich because they cheated honest labor out of its due reward. John Taylor constantly complained that the financiers and bondholders prospered because they lived "upon the labour of the other classes."[8]

The initial Jeffersonian dissection of the banking issue directed attention to the dichotomy between physical labor and mental labor. The Jeffersonians' attack on banking contains obvious strains of small-producer thought and agrarianism. For many Americans, the labor theory of property/value meant physical labor, the exertion sanctioned by the biblical injunction to eat bread

7. John Adams to F. A. Vanderkemp, February 16, 1809, in Adams, ed., *Works of John Adams,* IX, 610; Albert Gallatin to Robert Potter, December 3, 1830, in Adams, ed., *Writings of Gallatin,* II, 442.

8. John Taylor, *An Examination of the Late Proceedings in Congress Respecting the Official Conduct of the Secretary of the Treasury* (Richmond, Va., 1793), 7; Taylor, *Tyranny Unmasked,* 41–42; Taylor, *A Definition of Parties: The Political Effects of the Paper System Considered* (Philadelphia, 1794), 6; Thomas Jefferson to Colonel Charles Yancey, January 6, 1816, in Lipscomb, ed., *Writings of Jefferson,* XIV, 381.

by the sweat of one's brow.[9] In a land where the bulk of the population earned their livelihood by handicraft artisanship or farming, a natural jealousy emerged toward those who made their living entirely by mental activity—by wit, cunning, intelligence, or possession of important information. Much of the political controversy over banking exhibited a society struggling to adapt itself to an economy in which rewards to mental labor outstripped those to physical labor.

Besides the idea of finance in general, the Jeffersonians pointedly attacked the institution of banking. Although private banks existed in the United States and merchant houses at times acted as creditors, almost all early banks were creatures of legislative enactments. On the state level, banks were chartered by state legislatures and given specific rules and regulations to follow. They were usually given monopoly privileges and the ability to provide a paper currency. Alexander Hamilton goaded Congress into chartering the National Bank for the United States that incorporated features of both private and public banking.[10] The obvious political connection between legislation and banking instantly invoked the fear of the political economy of aristocracy.

The first element Jeffersonians noted about banks was that they were not "natural" enterprises as were farming, handicraft manufactures, and commerce. Banks were "artificial" creations of legislation. Second, legislatures endowed banks with special privileges. The word *monopoly* came readily to the lips and pens of Jeffersonians considering banking institutions.[11] Third, the bestowing of special or monopoly privileges meant that the receivers of the privileges had become an aristocracy in fact if not in name.[12]

Because the National Bank housed the funds of the government obtained from taxes, and because the funded debt had to be paid back with tax reve-

---

9. Kulikoff, *Agrarian Origins of American Capitalism,* 74, 79, 82.

10. There is a question as to whether Hamilton hoped to use the bank as an engine for his ambitions: see McCoy, *Elusive Republic,* 146–48. On the bank in general, see Hughes, *American Economic History,* 195–96.

11. For Jeffersonians who castigated chartered banks as privileged institutions with monopoly advantages, see [Sullivan], *Path to Riches,* 54, 59; Taylor, *Enquiry into the Principles and Tendency of Certain Public Measures,* 11, 19–20. See Hovencamp, *Enterprise and American Law,* 4, 27–28, 36–37, 56.

12. The best example of a Jeffersonian insisting that banking legislation amounted to the creation of an aristocracy is Taylor, *Enquiry into the Principles and Tendency of Certain Public Measures,* 16–17; Taylor, *An Inquiry into the Principles and Policy of the Government of the United States,* ed. Loren Baritz (1814; rpr. Indianapolis, 1969), 17, 21, 26, 46, 51.

nue, the Jeffersonians cried that they were being taxed to serve the avarice of bondholders. The notion of public funds going to private investors was galling. John Adams wrote to Benjamin Rush that he never approved of the funding system because "it was contrived to enrich particular individuals at the public expense." James Madison in 1791 interpreted the scramble to buy National Bank stock as an example of the few stealing from the many: "The subscriptions are consequently a mere scramble for so much public plunder which will be engrossed by those already loaded with the spoils of indi-[vi]duals."[13]

The second feature of early American banking that shocked Jeffersonians was the provision made by states and by the federal government to allow banks to issue a paper currency, supposedly redeemable in specie on demand. On the subject of paper money, the Jeffersonians outfederalized the Federalists of 1787–1788 in the debate over the ratification of the Constitution. Jefferson's correspondence is filled with an undying animus to paper money, and he faulted Adam Smith for being insufficiently calamitous on the subject.[14] James Monroe complained to Jefferson in 1813, "We are now at the mercy of monied institutions, who have got the circulating medium into their hands." John Taylor argued that paper money, besides the system of funding, was the principal means of transferring "the property of others" to the few. James Madison wrote in 1820 that "a discretion vested in a few hands over the currency of the nation, & of course over the legal value of its property, is liable to powerful objections."[15]

Jeffersonians' fears of manipulation, of cunning brains taking pecuniary advantage of brawny backs, led them to demand a currency and a standard of value that were not subject to manipulation. The choice was specie, gold and silver coins. In retirement Jefferson advised Secretary of the Treasury John Eppes that for reasons of international trade at the least the nation required a

13. John Adams to Benjamin Rush, August 28, 1811, in Adams, ed., *Works of John Adams,* IX, 638; James Madison to Thomas Jefferson, July 10, 1791, in Hutchinson and Rachal, eds., *Papers of Madison,* XIV, 43.

14. For Jefferson on Adam Smith, see Jefferson to John Eppes, November 6, 1813, in Lipscomb, ed., *Writings of Jefferson,* XIII, 413; Jefferson to John Adams, March 21, 1819, *ibid.,* XV, 185. For Jefferson's comments on paper money, Jefferson to John Taylor, November 26, 1798, *ibid.,* X, 64–65; Jefferson to John Adams, January 24, 1814, *ibid.,* XIV, 76–77; Jefferson to Albert Gallatin, October 16, 1815, *ibid.,* 356–58.

15. James Monroe to Thomas Jefferson, October 1, 1813, in Stanislaus Murray Hamilton, ed., *The Writings of James Monroe* (New York, 1898–1903), V, 273; Taylor, *Definition of Parties,* 6; James Madison to C. D. Williams, Feb. [?], 1820, in Hunt, ed., *Writings of Madison,* IX, 27.

stable measure of value. The best choice was specie because of its "universal value." Jefferson found the idea of a reserve ratio insufficient. For each dollar note a bank issued, that bank should possess in its vaults a dollar in specie. To Charles Pinckney he confided that he desired a *"metallic currency,"* and he earlier had hoped at least to drive out small paper denominations ($5, $10, $20 notes) and establish gold and silver coins as the nation's circulation.[16]

Between 1791 and 1815 Jeffersonians testified to the intimate connection between financial establishments and the distribution of wealth. No individual acted more like a Cassandra concerning the impact of credit, paper money, and a funded debt on the distribution of wealth than John Taylor of Caroline. Taylor insisted that Federalist financial policies created a "dangerous inequality of rank" that could subvert the republic. In the middle of the 1790s he warned that "a democratic republic is endangered by an immense disproportion in wealth" and that credit systems were the principal means of erecting aristocracies and producing "tyrants and slaves—an aristocracy enormously rich, and a peasantry wretchedly poor."[17]

In the 1780s James Madison believed that inequalities in wealth were unavoidable, but the Hamiltonian financial program led him to declare that such a natural inequality could be disastrously worsened by federal policies. To retain the general political equality among the citizenry, he argued in favor of "withholding *unnecessary* opportunities" from the talented elite because by giving those governmental favors, legislators increased "the inequality of property, by an immoderate, and especially an unmerited, accumulation of riches."[18]

Jeffersonians thus used the revolutionary heritage to elaborate more fully

16. Jefferson to John Eppes, November 6, 1813, in Lipscomb, ed., *Writings of Jefferson,* XIII, 412; Jefferson to Charles Pinckney, September 30, 1820, *ibid.,* XV, 280; Jefferson to Colonel Charles Yancey, January 6, 1816, *ibid.,* XIV, 383. Edwin Perkins believes that Jefferson and his followers objected not only to the central government's connection with banks but to state government alliances as well; however, the Jeffersonians were pragmatic and accepted commercial banking. The interpretation offered here is the more traditional one of the animus of Jeffersonians to banking in general. See Perkins, *American Public Finance,* 261–65.

17. Taylor, *Examination of the Late Proceedings in Congress,* 12; Taylor, *Enquiry into the Principles and Tendency of Certain Public Measures,* 30.

18. [James Madison], "Parties," for the *National Gazette,* [*ca.* January 23, 1792], in Hutchinson and Rachal, eds., *Papers of James Madison,* XIV, 197; see also "Property," for the *National Gazette,* March 27, [1792], *ibid.,* 267; speech of John Francis Mercer, March 30, 1792, on public debt, *Annals of Congress,* 2nd Cong., 1st Sess., 510; John Adams to Thomas Brand-Hollis, June 11, 1790, in Adams, ed., *Works of John Adams,* IX, 570.

the means by which chartered banks, paper currency, and a funded debt could result in an unfair distribution of wealth. Seldom did they provide a full explanation of the distribution of wealth, however; almost always the concern about the distribution of wealth was limited to one or two sentences or at most a paragraph—the same way the topic was handled by the revolutionary generation itself. The logic behind Jeffersonian assertions about the tie between banking and the distribution of wealth, however, derived from an extensive discussion and use of the labor theory of property/value and the ideas contained in the political economy of aristocracy. The Jeffersonian analysis of banking and currency dominated political debates over finance for the rest of the century, with a few modifications in programs and pragmatism.

The Democrats of the second and third party systems adhered fairly strictly to the labor theory of property/value. Theophilus Fisk, a radical Democrat and supposed orator for workingmen, entitled an oration on banking "Labor the only True Source of Wealth." William Leggett, the New York Locofoco and newspaper editor, emphasized the manual labor component in the labor theory of property/value. Although the publicist and influential Democratic financial writer William M. Gouge doubted that labor constituted an absolute standard of value, he nonetheless used the labor theory of value as a means of detecting inequities in social arrangements.[19]

To understand the nature of banking, Democrats turned to the political economy of aristocracy and wielded it like a club to beat down their opponents. First, banking in the 1830s, both in the states and most emphatically in the Second Bank of the United States, was done under government charter—that is, banks were corporations with special privileges and monopolistic advantages. Legislation allowed financiers to associate among themselves, combine forces, and then erect shields against competition. Individuals had no chance of fair competition against a combination of financiers girded with the strength of the state.[20] Privileges to corporations (ability to emit a paper

---

19. Theophilus Fisk, *An Oration on Banking, Education, &c. Delivered at the Queen-Street Theatre, in the City of Charleston, S. C. July 4th, 1837. Also an Oration on the Freedom of the Press* (Charleston, 1837), title page, 4; William Leggett, "Rich and Poor," December 6, 1834, in Blau, ed., *Social Theories of Jacksonian Democracy,* 69; Gouge, *Short History of Paper Money and Banking,* 8–14, 91; on Gouge, see Joseph Dorfman, Introduction, *ibid.* For the 1850s, see Huston, *Panic of 1857,* 68–69.

20. New Hampshire governor Henry Hubbard, "Gubernatorial Address," 1842, in Michael Brewster Folsom and Steven D. Lubar, eds., *The Philosophy of Manufactures: Early De-*

currency, right to associate, right to longevity beyond a normal life span, and limited liability) gave immediate rise to the charge of monopoly. The most consistent label Democrats put on state-sponsored banking was monopoly, and the Democracy became something of an antimonopoly party, at least in matters involving finance.[21]

As the ideas behind the political economy of aristocracy implied, those who received dispensations, privileges, and monopolies from government were aristocrats. Democrats called bankers and their political friends "aristocrats" throughout the nineteenth century, much to the anger and consternation of the political opposition.[22] As aristocrats in fact if not in title, bankers exhibited two socially unwholesome traits that made them a danger to society and to honest people. First, they did not labor; as Theophilus Fisk said, banks instill the desire "to live without labor and to grow rich without industry." William Leggett also declaimed against the laziness of bankers, for the government provided "favours to bankers and others, who choose to live in idle-

---

bates over Industrialization in the United States (Cambridge, Mass., 1982), 405; William Leggett, "Joint-Stock Partnership Law," *Evening Post,* December 30, 1834, in Sedgwick, ed., *Collection of the Political Writings of William Leggett,* I, 142–44; Carl Brent Swisher, *Roger B. Taney* (New York, 1935), 297; message of Governor Joseph Brown of Georgia in *Federal Union* (Milledgeville), November 9, 1858. See William Gerald Shade, *Banks or No Banks: The Money Issue in Western Politics, 1832–1865* (Detroit, 1972), 222–23; Richard H. Timberlake, Jr., *The Origins of Central Banking in the United States* (Cambridge, Mass., 1978), 39–41.

21. For example, on the monopoly charge, see William Leggett, "Objects of the Evening Post," January 3, 1835, in Blau, ed., *Social Theories of Jacksonian Democracy,* 72; [John C. Calhoun], Address of the Republican Members of Congress, July 6, 1838, in Meriwether *et al.,* eds., *Papers of Calhoun,* XIV, 369; Stephen A. Douglas, "To the Democratic Republicans of Illinois," in Robert W. Johannsen, ed., *The Letters of Stephen A. Douglas* (Urbana, 1961), 44, 49; James Fenimore Cooper, in Blau, ed., *Social Theories of Jacksonian Democracy,* 55; 1840 editorial of Edwin Stanton in George C. Gorham, *Life and Public Services of Edwin M. Stanton* (Boston, 1899), I, 27–28; Andrew Jackson, Farewell Address, March 4, 1837, in *Register of Debates,* 24th Cong., 2nd Sess., 2174; "Prospectus of the *Mississippi Free Trader,"* *Mississippi Free Trader* (Natchez), February 8, 1858.

22. For example, Tilden, "Divorce of Bank and State," in Bigelow, ed., *Writings and Speeches of Tilden,* I, 82; Andrew Jackson, "Paper Read to the Cabinet, September 18, 1833," in John Spencer Bassett, ed., *Correspondence of Andrew Jackson* (Washington, D.C., 1916–33), V, 193; Robert Rantoul, Jr., "Oration at Worcester, July 4, 1837," in Hamilton, ed., *Memoirs, Speeches and Writings of Rantoul,* 582; Leggett, editorial in *Evening Post,* August 26, 1834, in Sedgwick, ed., *Political Writings of Leggett,* I, 56; Fisk, *Oration on Banking,* 2–4; Arthur M. Schlesinger, Jr., *The Age of Jackson* (Boston, 1949), 164; Shade, *Banks or No Banks,* 57, 124–26, 156–57.

ness by their wits rather than earn an honest livelihood by the useful employment of their faculties."[23] The public was harmed because the banking
aristocracy obtained its wealth the way all aristocracies obtained wealth—by
absorbing the fruits of other people's labor.[24]

In his farewell address, Andrew Jackson explained how bankers, armed
with legislative monopoly, obtained wealth without labor through the agency
of paper money. By monopoly legislation, the Bank of the United States controlled the currency of the nation, and by changing the amount of currency,
it had the ability "to regulate the value of property and the fruits of labor in
every quarter of the Union." In the *United States Magazine and Democratic
Review,* one contributor, possibly the editor John L. O'Sullivan, criticized the
credit system of the United States for granting "combinations of irresponsible individuals with the monopoly of an artificial measure of value, by which
arbitrary control over the subsistence of all other classes is conferred upon
them." Hence legislation opened the door to manipulation of the currency so
that a few could steal the rewards of industrious labor. American workers
were being swindled by those who possessed the strange knowledge of
banking.[25]

While some Democrats saw only a Machiavellian manipulation of currency emissions by bankers to enrich themselves, others outlined a less personally pernicious incentive but a more socially disastrous consequence.
According to William Gouge, the desire of bankers to obtain great profits
led them to expand credit by expanding the supply of banknotes (*i.e.,* paper
money). The unnaturally easy credit swayed normally cautious individu-

23. Fisk, *Oration on Banking,* 8; Leggett, "The Inequality of Human Condition," *Plain-
dealer,* December 31, 1836, in Sedgwick, ed., *Political Writings of Leggett,* II, 161–62.

24. For example, Robert Rantoul, "Oration at Worcester," in Hamilton, ed., *Memoirs,
Speeches and Writings of Rantoul,* 582. Some scholars insist that the Democrats had an anticapitalist bias. The Democrats were certainly antiaristocracy, but antiaristocracy is not anticapitalist. An example of one who finds anticapitalism in the Democracy is John Ashworth, *Slavery,
Capitalism, and Politics in the Antebellum Republic,* Vol. I: *Commerce and Compromise, 1820–
1850* (Cambridge, Eng., 1995), 289–97.

25. Andrew Jackson, "Farewell Address," March 4, 1837, in *Register of Debates,* 24th
Cong., 2nd Sess., 2174; [John L. O'Sullivan?], "The Credit System," *United States Magazine
and Democratic Review,* III (1838), 196; for comments on the secretive, swindling character of
financial dealings, see Fisk, *Oration on Banking,* 22, 30; editorial, *Democratic Watchman*
(Bellefonte, Pa.), October 8, 1857; Rantoul, "Oration at Worcester," in Hamilton, ed., *Memoirs, Speeches and Writings of Rantoul,* 575.

als into making silly and unremunerative investments; it led others to lust after extravagance and to abandon industrious positions in the economy for speculative ones. And because so many untenable investments were made, the economy would eventually crash. American free traders thus found the boom-and-bust cycle of the economy to be the result solely of the credit system.[26]

Of course, the Democratic party between 1830 and 1860 was not a party of ideologues, and a considerable variety of opinion was expressed on establishing the proper banking institutions for the nation. A few wanted merely a divorce between the federal government and banking, some wanted state banking only, some believed an independent treasury would both regulate the currency and distance itself from the avarice of bankers, some demanded a wholly specie currency and elimination of all banknotes, some argued merely for the establishment of a specie circulation for small dollar amounts, and some simply exercised political pragmatism.[27] In one fashion or another, the United States by 1830 was a commercial society and banking services were indispensable. The Democracy fitted its policy advocacies to that fact.

But the Democratic party tended to favor laissez-faire, the negative state, and free banking, if not necessarily a specie-based economy. Although on the matter of banking and currency, most Americans were willing to consider various degrees of intervention in the economy, the Democrats' adoption of

26. Gouge, *Short History of Paper Money and Banking,* 23–24, 28–39. See also speech of Benjamin F. Hallett in Boston *Post,* October 24, 1857; William Leggett, "Causes of Financial Distress," New York *Evening Post,* October 24, 1836, in Sedgwick, ed., *Political Writings of Leggett,* II, 105; Leggett, "Stock Gambling," *Evening Post,* March 25, 1835, *ibid.,* I, 248; Richard B. Latner, *The Presidency of Andrew Jackson: White House Politics, 1829–1837* (Athens, Ga., 1979), 187; Shade, *Banks or No Banks,* 76–77, 117.

27. On the divisions within the Democratic party on banking issues, see Shade, *Banks or No Banks,* 118, 130, 146–48, 167, 171–73; John M. McFaul, *The Politics of Jacksonian Finance* (Ithaca, N.Y., 1972), 6, 140–42; James Roger Sharp, *The Jacksonians Versus the Banks: Politics in the States After the Panic of 1837* (New York, 1970), 13–18; Donald B. Cole, *Martin Van Buren and the American Political System* (Princeton, 1984), 273–78, 304–10; James C. Curtis, *The Fox at Bay: Martin Van Buren and the Presidency, 1837–1841* (Lexington, Ky., 1970), 36, 66; Wilson, *Presidency of Martin Van Buren,* 68, 72–74, 79. Recent research has shown the Democratic fear of banking, although not exactly an anticapitalist content: Nicole Etcheson, *The Emerging Midwest: Upland Southerners and the Political Culture of the Old Northwest, 1787–1861* (Bloomington, 1996), 36–42; Robert J. Cook, *Baptism of Fire: The Republican Party in Iowa, 1838–1878* (Ames, Iowa, 1994), 18–29; Daniel Feller, *The Jacksonian Promise: America, 1815–1840* (Baltimore, 1995), xiii–xiv, chap. 9.

the republican theory of the distribution of wealth pushed them ideologically to a divorce between government and banking.[28]

At one point or another in the Democratic dissection of American banking institutions, some comment about the distribution of wealth invariably surfaced, usually to the effect that existing banking laws had skewed the distribution of wealth in favor of those already possessing natural advantages. When Democrats looked at the banking issue in relation to the distribution of wealth, the culprit was always the government. What caused inequality? For William Gouge, unequal "political and commercial institutions *invert* the operation of the natural and just causes of wealth and poverty," a position that John L. O'Sullivan had turned into the guiding light of the Jacksonian Democratic party. John Bigelow observed that "if human regulations did not produce artificial and unjust distributions of property, a state of things could never exist in which property would be endangered." The "avaricious few," that is, the aristocracy, sought governmental control "to concentrate and perpetuate property in themselves." Even Theophilus Fisk, denominated by historians as a radical antibanker, claimed he wanted no "agrarian" redistribution of wealth but was merely opposed to artificial inequalities "created by partial legislation, by monopolies and exclusive privileges—it is the granting of exclusive favors by the legislature to a privileged nobility of growing rich without industry."[29]

And of course the most famous expression of the impact of government regulation on the distribution of wealth came from Andrew Jackson in his veto message of the recharter of the National Bank in 1832:

> It is to be regretted that the rich and powerful too often bend the acts of government to their selfish purposes. Distinctions in society will always exist under every just government. Equality of talents, of education, or of wealth can

28. Several authors believe that the independent treasury was not a retreat from government involvement in the economy but a clever way for the government to regulate state banks without becoming a central bank. For example, see Wilson, *Presidency of Van Buren*, 72–74; McFaul, *Politics of Jacksonian Finance*, 196–209; Curtis, *Fox at Bay*, 147–48; Cole, *Van Buren and the American Political System*, 304–305. William G. Shade has shown, however, a hostility of Great Lakes Democrats to all banks and to free banking (*Banks or No Banks*, 119–20, 129–30, 146–72).

29. Gouge, *Short History of Paper Money and Banking*, 91; John L. O'Sullivan, quoted in Wiltse, ed., *Expansion and Reform*, 151; Tilden, "Divorce of Bank and State," in Bigelow, ed., *Writings of Tilden*, I, 86; Fisk, *Oration on Banking*, 3–4; Hovencamp, *Enterprise and American Law*, 18, 27, 56.

not be produced by human institutions. In the full enjoyment of the gifts of Heaven and the fruits of superior industry, economy, and virtue, every man is equally entitled to protection by laws; but when the laws undertake to add to these natural and just advantages artificial distinctions, to grant titles, gratuities, and exclusive privileges, to make the rich richer and the potent more powerful, the humble members of society—the farmers, mechanics, and laborers—who have neither the time nor the means of securing like favors to themselves, have a right to complain of the injustice of their Government. There are no necessary evils in government. Its evils exist only in its abuses. If it would confine itself to equal protection, and, as Heaven does its rains, shower its favors alike on the high and the low, the rich and the poor, it would be an unqualified blessing.[30]

Jackson encapsulated perhaps as well as any single American between 1776 and 1890 the republican theory of the distribution of wealth. Nature provides amply for all people, and though nature's distribution is not equal, it is just. Only human intervention by government construction of monopolies and special privileges creates the skewed distribution of wealth that had become the hallmark of human and especially European civilization. It was through use of governmental power that aristocrats first warped the natural distribution of wealth, that aristocrats maintained their wealth possessions, and that would-be aristocrats in the United States saw a path to enormous wealth without labor.

The advocates of centralized banking had few weapons to parry the thrust of Jeffersonian lances. From the beginning, proponents of national banking justified a central bank on the grounds of expediency. As Alexander Hamilton remarked in his 1790 "Report on the Bank," banks increased capital, and increased capital "generates employment; which animates and expands labor and industry." Banks evolved in response to commerce, and as commerce expanded, a substitute for specie in commercial transactions was required, and that substitute was bank paper or banknotes. Hamilton preferred to have a central bank that could make the most economic leverage of the federal government's funds and act as a regulator of credit.[31] Over time, the expedient

30. Andrew Jackson, "Veto Message," in James D. Richardson, ed., *A Compilation of the Messages and Papers of the Presidents, 1789–1902* (Washington, D.C., 1904), II, 590.

31. Hamilton, "Report on the Bank," December 13, 1790, final version, in Syrett and Cooke, eds., *Papers of Hamilton,* VII, 317; Broadus Mitchell, *Alexander Hamilton: A Concise Biography* (New York, 1976), 137, 198–202; McCoy, *Elusive Republic,* 148.

reasons for a central bank grew. Out of the distasteful experiences of the War of 1812 came the realization that a nation without a central bank was incapable of adequately defending itself.

When Andrew Jackson and Locofoco Democrats attacked the Second Bank of the United States in particular and chartered banking in general, the forces in favor of banking were left with nothing but expedient reasons to combat the powerful legacy of the Revolution. They had no real moral appeal, as the Jeffersonians did when they used the labor theory of property/value. Whigs stormed, as had their predecessors, that banks were useful, that the assault on banking was an assault on commerce and property rights, that the Jacksonian forces sought a reversion of civilization to a wholly agrarian base. In political terms, they complained that Jackson had twisted the purpose of representative government by elevating the presidency above Congress, thereby ruining the separation of powers in the Constitution and the principle of majority rule. For a public appeal, the advocates of central banking focused on the vital role of finance in economic affairs, the necessity of public watchfulness over those who might debase the currency by paper note inflation, the possibility of avoiding the business cycle, and the importance of credit for generating an economic expansion that raised wages and permitted farmers to extend their operations.[32]

For all their posturing on the bank and currency issue, however, the Whigs were on the horns of a dilemma. Generally, Whigs and Federalists shared an organic view of society, and part of that perspective allowed public institutions to be created that had public regulatory functions—agencies to serve the general welfare and the public interest, not any private one. Jacksonian charges that all public agencies partook of a monopoly character in which only private interests were served stung the Whigs. The Whigs did possess,

32. Richard N. Current, *Daniel Webster and the Rise of National Conservatism* (Boston, 1955), 84; Robert C. Winthrop, "The Sub-Treasury System," in Robert C. Winthrop, *Addresses and Speeches on Various Occasions* (Boston, 1852–86), I, 233–48; New York *Tribune,* September 10, 1857; *Daily National Intelligencer* (Washington, D.C.), October 8, 1857; Charles Francis Adams, "The Theory of Money and Banks," *Hunt's Merchants' Magazine,* I (1839), 110–24; Holt, *Political Crisis of the 1850s,* 23–25, 33–35; Remini, *Andrew Jackson and the Bank War,* 142–47; Kohl, *Politics of Individualism,* 155–56; Howe, *Political Culture of American Whigs,* 139; Arthur Charles Cole, *The Whig Party in the South* (Washington, D.C., 1913), 25–27, 64–65; Brown, *Politics and Statesmanship,* 28–31, 37–41, 172–75; Shade, *Banks or No Banks,* 92–93, 121–22, 130–33; Maurice G. Baxter, *Henry Clay and the American System* (Lexington, Ky., 1995), 89; Baxter, *One and Inseparable: Daniel Webster and the Union* (Cambridge, Mass., 1984), 198–99.

after all, an antimonopoly, antifavoritism tradition.[33] In the aftermath of the recharter episode in 1832, Nicholas Biddle's actions convinced many Whigs that the Bank of the United States did possess an irresponsible monopoly power.[34]

The Whigs capitulated and gave up the vital principle that the public had a right to create agencies to regulate business enterprise whether by charter or independent government agency (such as a canal commission). They abandoned that ideal for two reasons. First, the antimonopoly charge hurt and contained a valid criticism from the revolutionary past. Not long into the 1830s, the New York Whig governor William Henry Seward addressed the state legislature with the message that banking by special charter was wrong "because odious as a monopoly." But, second, just as important, an alternative existed. Free banking, first pioneered in Michigan, was a system that prescribed certain general conditions for banks to obtain a legal right to operate but excluded nobody and gave no special privileges. Moreover, free banking, though unwieldy and subject to abuses, solved the commercial needs of the economy by allowing financial functions to be performed. The conservative Democrat George Mifflin Dallas summed up the attitude most Whigs eventually adopted: "As to the Bank—let that go—we ought to have it, but we can do without it."[35]

33. Shade, *Banks or No Banks,* 132; Herbert Ershkowitz and William G. Shade, "Consensus or Conflict? Political Behavior in the State Legislatures During the Jacksonian Era," *Journal of American History,* LVIII (1971), 592–617, esp. 614–16; Paul Goodman, *Towards a Christian Republic: Antimasonry and the Great Transition in New England, 1826–1836* (New York, 1988), 25–31 and *passim;* John Quincy Adams in *Columbia Sentinel,* July 13, 1791, in Ford, ed., *Writings of John Quincy Adams,* I, 99; Robert J. Rayback, *Millard Fillmore: Biography of a President* (Buffalo, N.Y., 1959), 74. For those believing in "vested" and almost eternal rights, see Stanley I. Kutler, *Privilege and Creative Destruction: The Charles River Bridge Case* (Philadelphia, 1971), 62–67, 96–98, 101. Herbert Hovencamp disputes Kutler's interpretation by insisting that Whigs differentiated between a franchise and a monopoly in the Charles River Bridge case (*Enterprise and American Law,* 112–13).

34. Remini, *Andrew Jackson and the Bank War,* 168; Howe, *Political Culture of American Whigs,* 106, 301–302; Brown, *Politics and Statesmanship,* 175, 218; Current, *Daniel Webster,* 117; Holt, *Political Crisis of the 1850s,* 107–11, 119–20; Bray Hammond, *Banks and Politics in America from the Revolution to the Civil War* (Princeton, 1957), 513–14.

35. Seward, "Annual Message to the Legislature," in Baker, ed., *Works of Seward,* II, 225; Glyndon G. Van Deusen, *William Henry Seward* (New York, 1967), 45; George Mifflin Dallas to Henry Gilpin, July 13, 1832, in George Mifflin Dallas Papers, Historical Society of Pennsylvania, Philadelphia.

Historians have sometimes argued that the Jacksonians wanted a new form of regulatory agency for banking (the original subtreasury scheme under Martin Van Buren failed of passage) and that the Whigs designed and supported free banking systems to foster greater capitalist enterprise.[36] Such a view stretches the impulses of the party to the snapping point. The logic of the Democratic argument ended up in free banking, not regulation; the only valid criticism Democrats had against free banking laws—which were voiced by Leggett and others—were that even the general laws of free banking called for some governmental intervention. The pure Democratic solution to finance was the same as the party's stand on commercial exchanges—free trade and free money. Let anyone engage in banking under any rules he saw fit, and let the market choose the winners and the losers.

Those on the Hamiltonian axis of American politics accepted the free banking system but not joyfully. Individuals choosing political life on the Hamiltonian axis believed in regulation in the public interest. American banking practices until the Federal Reserve Act of 1913, and really until the Banking Acts of 1933 and 1935, were not regulated. The free banking system of the 1840s and 1850s and then the national banking system founded during the Civil War established guidelines and standards for all engaged in state and national banking—but not regulation. On the banking issue, the Democrats routed the Whigs. It was one more example of the libertarian, individualist tradition of the Revolution triumphing over the communal notion of virtue and individual restraint.

Throughout the nineteenth century, political battles over tariff policy produced voluminous comments on the distribution of wealth. As in the case of the banking issue, debate between free traders (actually, those who favored a tariff for revenue only) and protectionists was built around the labor theory of property/value and the lessons learned from the political economy of aristocracy. Unlike the banking issue, in which those on the Hamiltonian economic axis had to capitulate because of the animus of the revolutionary legacy toward aristocracy and special privilege, the individuals who supported high tariffs had a more potent appeal. American protectionists felt no compulsion to wave a flag of surrender on the question of tariffs. Protectionists

36. For example, McFaul, *Politics of Jacksonian Finance*, 196–209; Curtis, *Fox at Bay,* 147–48; Wilson, *Presidency of Van Buren,* 72–74; Van Deusen, *Seward,* 45.

had an appeal based on wealth distribution that carried as much weight as did that of the free traders.[37]

The important debates over the tariff erupted after the War of 1812 when Henry Clay devised his American System to promote economic growth and thereby avoid future military debacles. Political struggles over tariff policy were few before 1815. In 1792 Hamilton issued his "Report on Manufactures" that became for successors a treasure trove of American protectionist thought. Its policy recommendations were not implemented, and Hamilton never pressed the subject further. In fact, it is dubious that Hamilton even deserves to be considered in the protectionist camp, for his basic instinct was commercial-financial rather than industrial. The Federalist party, with the exception of the Pennsylvanians, protected and fostered commercial activity, not industrial undertakings.[38]

The Democratic-Republicans under the leadership of Jefferson and Madison did not challenge the equitability or usefulness of the tariff. On the contrary, Jefferson almost rejoiced over the imposition of duties on foreign goods. In fiscal policy Jefferson sought two goals: low taxation and as small a number of officeholders as possible. His hatred of taxation focused on land taxes, excise taxes, and direct taxation in general but not on the indirect taxes of tariffs. In 1811 he wrote to E. I. Dupont de Nemours: "We are all the more reconciled to the tax on importations because it falls exclusively on the rich, and with the equal partition of intestate estates, constitutes the best agrarian law."[39] Before 1816, Jefferson saw in the tariff only egalitarian possibilities.

Complaints against the tariff surfaced early, of course, but they were con-

---

37. Tariff debates evoked three principal themes: first, the distribution of wages and profits among the sections of the country; second, the distribution of labor and capital among the then-conceived primary sectors in the economy (agriculture, commerce, and manufacturing); third, the distribution of wealth among the inhabitants. It is the third distribution that is the subject of this section.

38. See Nelson, *Liberty and Property,* 45–51; also McCoy, *Elusive Republic,* 148–51; John C. Miller, *Alexander Hamilton: Portrait in Paradox* (New York, 1959), 288–95. A good introduction to the American System but one that does not go deeply into the protectionist rationale is Baxter, *Henry Clay and the American System.*

39. Jefferson to Dupont de Nemours, April 15, 1811, in Lipscomb, ed., *Writings of Jefferson,* XIII, 39. For Jefferson's attitudes to taxes, see also Jefferson to John Dickinson, December 19, 1801, *ibid.,* X, 302–303; message of Jefferson, November 8, 1804, in *Annals of Congress,* 8th Cong., 2nd Sess., 77. See early debates on the tariff, *Annals of Congress,* 4th Cong., 2nd Sess., remarks of Robert Goodloe Harper, 1866–70; remarks of Joseph B. Varnum, 1879–80. A pro-

fined largely to agrarian radicals such as George Logan, John Taylor, and others.[40] With the proposed tariff of 1820 and then the tariffs of 1824 and 1828, however, the attack on tariff policy and indirect taxes in general commenced. That battle lasted the whole of the nineteenth century.

The critique of the distributive consequences of protectionism by those on the Jeffersonian axis rested first and foremost on the labor theory of property/value and evolved into free trade. They defined economic republicanism strictly in terms of individualism and the freedom to choose markets without any governmental interference whatsoever. In 1791, when criticizing Federalist policies, George Logan complained, "Of what advantage is the free disposal of a man's person, if the whole property acquired by his labor, is to be wrested from him by an arbitrary power?" The 1820 Fredericksburg, Virginia, "Remonstrance Against the Increase of Duties" declared emphatically that "to buy as cheap as you can, no matter where, and to sell as dear, is the maxim" applicable to all people in the market. In the tariff debates of 1846, Representative Edward W. Hubard of Virginia explicitly defined republicanism as competitive capitalism. Republics, he argued, were based "upon *equal* rights and privileges," and freedom had to be the foundation of all activities. "The democracy are now vindicating the freedom of labor and enterprise to seek its own employment, and the right of the people to *sell* where they can get the *highest* price, and to purchase wherever they can *buy* on the *best* terms." Shortly before the start of the Civil War, a contributor to the Charleston *Mercury* reiterated the tie between the labor theory of property/value, republicanism, and marketplace competition: "No man can be said to enjoy his full right in his own property, in the proceeds of his industry, unless he is at liberty to exchange it at the highest price he can get, in the best market he can find for the commodities of his choice."[41]

In the debate over the first tariff of the United States, James Madison, apol-

---

tariff element did exist within the Democratic-Republican ranks; see Steven E. Siry, *De Witt Clinton and the American Political Economy: Sectionalism, Politics, and Republican Ideology, 1787–1828* (New York, 1990), 225.

40. Taylor, *Tyranny Unmasked*, 160–64 and *passim;* [Logan], *Five Letters,* 10, 24–28; remarks of Theodorick Bland, April 14, 1789, in *Annals of Congress*, 1st Cong., 1st Sess., 129; Representative James Jackson of South Carolina, May 9, 1789, *ibid.*, 326; Henry Lee to James Madison, January 29, 1792, in Hutchinson and Rachal, eds., *Papers of Madison*, XIV, 204; Lee to Madison, April 4, 1792, *ibid.*, 279.

41. [Logan], *Letters Addressed to the Yeomanry of the United States*, 27; Fredericksburg Convention, "Remonstrance Against Increase of Duties" (1820), *Annals of Congress,* 16th Cong., 1st Sess., Appendix, 2299; speech of Representative E. W. Hubard, June 26, 1846, *Congressional*

ogizing for his support of a measure that obstructed trade, gave a classic explanation of how free choice in occupations and markets produced the most beneficial diffusion of wealth. It was "a truth, that if industry and labor are left to take their own course, they will generally be directed to those objects which are the most productive, and this in a more certain and direct manner than the wisdom of the most enlightened legislature could point out." The less the government interfered in individuals' exchange of surpluses, "the greater are the proportions of benefit to each."[42] Madison thereby pointed out a significant and popular phrase used by free traders to describe an economy void of governmental or private coercion: capital and labor flowed into their "natural channels."

The impact of the tariff, especially when it took the form of high duties to protect certain Americans from foreign competition, was to direct labor and capital into other channels of enterprise—and necessarily into unnatural ones because the activity was coerced by government instead of being chosen freely by individuals. The mechanism for altering resource allocation was price. Using the tariff as a taxing device raised the price of protected articles and enticed people to produce such goods. In sum, protection increased the profitability of certain enterprises by lifting the price of the finished product, and the enhanced price enticed entrepreneurs to redirect capital and labor out of enterprises favored by free choice and into ones favored by government proclamation.[43] Extremists, such as the South Carolina nullifiers, claimed that the use of tariffs to readjust the flows of capital and labor meant that "Congress [has] assume[d] the right to regulate the labor of the country."[44]

At this juncture, the fears of the political economy of aristocracy emerged, for the very fact that government sought to adjust prices to stimulate certain areas of the economy smacked of privileges and favoritism to an elite group.

Globe, 29th Cong., 1st Sess., Appendix, 735; CASSANDRA, "The Political Position of the South," no. 1, Charleston *Mercury,* September 8, 1857.

42. Speech of Representative James Madison, *Annals of Congress,* 1st Cong., 1st Sess., 116–17.

43. One of the best free trade explanations of this price-changing mechanism is by Albert Gallatin, who wrote the "Memorial of the Free Trade Convention," [1831], 22nd Cong., 1st Sess., Sen. Ex. Doc. No. 55, pp. 7–9, 30; see also "Memorial of Sundry Citizens of Charleston, S.C., Against the Tariff," [1820], 16th Cong., 2nd Sess., House Doc. No. 17, p. 3.

44. Bolling Hall to Nathaniel Macon, February 22, 1833, in "Letters on Nullification, [Part II]" *American Historical Review,* VII (1901), 100; see also J. F. H. Claiborne, *Life and Correspondence of John A. Quitman* (New York, 1860), II, 185; J. Fred Rippy, *Joel R. Poinsett: Versatile American* (Durham, N.C., 1935), 83.

Free traders stated explicitly that the tariff "simply transfers it [wealth] from hand to hand, and can enrich one class only by impoverishing others." During a tariff debate in 1841, Representative Robert Barnwell Rhett of South Carolina explained how the tariff illustrated the principles of the political economy of aristocracy. Legislation passed to aid one group was "aristocracy or oligarchy." "One interest allures or purchases another to follow; they multiply—they combine—they seize the government. . . . Soon palaces may arise, from the forced contributions of the many; but around their marble steps will gather wan pauperism." The result of governmental favoritism was a maldistribution of wealth.[45]

The tariff created the few rich and the many poor in two ways. The first was by taxing the people to benefit the few. As C. W. Gooch complained to George Thompson in 1828, "And what right has the *government* in a free country, to take money out of the pockets of one set of laborers and put it into the pockets of any other?"[46] The tariff was a tax on consumers. But the greatest complaint of free traders was the preeminent republican one of monopoly. Monopolies, created by government laws at the behest of aristocrats, transferred wealth via monopoly prices from the many to the few. As the Alabama legislature insisted, the "natural offspring" of the tariff was "monopoly, and its natural tendency is to divide the community into nabobs and paupers; to accumulate overgrown wealth, in the hands of the few; and to extend the poverty, the vices, and the miseries of the many."[47]

45. Report of Committee on Memorial from Boston Merchants, *Annals of Congress,* 18th Cong., 1st Sess., Appendix, 3081; speech of Rhett, December 22, 1841, *Congressional Globe,* 27th Cong., 2nd Sess., Appendix, 40. The topic of protectionism provoked John Bell of Tennessee to delineate carefully the republican (albeit free trade) notion of the distribution of wealth; see *Register of Debates,* 22nd Cong., 1st Sess., June 8, 1832, pp. 3348–78.

46. C. W. Gooch to Col. George Thompson, August 29, 1828, in Gooch Family Papers, University of Virginia Library, Charlottesville; see also speech of Representative Theodorick Bland of Virginia, April 14, 1789, *Annals of Congress,* 1st Cong., 1st Sess., 129; Joseph Emory Davis to William M. Smyth, April 15, 1845, in Haskell M. Monroe, Jr., and James T. McIntosh, eds., *The Papers of Jefferson Davis* (Baton Rouge, 1971–), II, 240; Andrew Jackson, Farewell Address (1837), *Register of Debates,* 24th Cong., 2nd Sess., 2170–71.

47. Remonstrance of the General Assembly of Alabama (1828), Sen. Ex. Doc. No. 86, 20th Cong., 1st Sess., 4. See Hamilton, *Speech on the Operation of the Tariff,* 6; William Leggett, "Direct Taxation," *Evening Post,* April 22, 1834, in Sedgwick, ed., *Collection of the Political Writings of William Leggett,* I, 261–62; Charles Buxton Going, *David Wilmot, Free-Soiler: A Biography of the Great Advocate of the Wilmot Proviso* (New York, 1924), 83; speech of James Mason, March 1, 1855, *Congressional Globe,* 33rd Cong., 2nd Sess., 1057; Taylor, *Tyranny Unmasked,* 37–40.

The Jeffersonian charge of monopoly against tariffs had two components. As soon as the free traders conjured the specter of monopoly, those who owned companies that received protection became monopolists and aristocrats. In the Senate, John Taylor warned of a new "pecuniary aristocracy" arising from the tariff. Democrat Edmund Burke of New Hampshire in a widely reprinted congressional speech admonished that the purpose of protection was to "build up and fortify capital in this country, thus establishing the basest, most sordid, most grovelling of all aristocracies . . . a *moneyed aristocracy.*"[48]

Besides castigating manufacturers as monopolists and aristocrats, free traders insisted that workers obtained no rewards from protection, that only the owners of capital benefited. In his famous treasury report advocating the tariff of 1846, Robert J. Walker took special care to show that protection did nothing materially for factory workers but only added to the piles of wealth of capitalists: "That is its object, and not to augment the wages of labor, which would reduce those profits." In the 1846 congressional tariff battle, Pennsylvania congressman David Wilmot was more explicit about the motives of protected industrialists: "Your lords of the spindle seek by every means in their power to depress American labor." In 1841, Democrat Ira A. Eastman was equally blunt: "A capitalist does not, will not, cannot, sympathize with the employees in his mills."[49] Free traders lined up decade after decade to proclaim that protectionism merely allowed industrial monopolists to squeeze money out of consumers and to drive laborers into subsistence wages.[50]

In pressing the claims of free trade as national policy, the Jeffersonians

48. Speech of Senator John Taylor, May 4, 1824, *Annals of Congress,* 18th Cong., 1st Sess., 683–84, 687; Edmund Burke, *The Protective System Considered in Connection with the Present Tariff, in a Series of Twelve Essays, Originally Published in the Washington Union over the Signature of "Bundelcund"* (Washington, D.C., 1846), 8.

49. Robert J. Walker, Annual Report of the Treasurer (1845), House Ex. Doc. No. 6, 29th Cong., 1st Sess., 7–8; speech of Wilmot, July 1, 1846, *Congressional Globe,* 29th Cong., 1st Sess., Appendix, 768; speech of Ira A. Eastman, December 28–29, 1841, *Congressional Globe,* 27th Cong., 2nd Sess., Appendix, 47.

50. For example, Calhoun, "Exposition and Protest," Calhoun's draft, in Meriwether and Hemphill, eds., *Papers of Calhoun,* X, 480, 482; "The Tariff—Its History and Influence," *United States Magazine and Democratic Review,* XIX (1846), 174; Burke, *Protective System,* 8, 26–27; John O. Bradford to James K. Polk, August 23, 1844, in Herbert Weaver, Wayne Cutler, and Paul H. Bergeron, eds., *Correspondence of James K. Polk* (Nashville, Tenn., 1969–), VII, 464.

consistently upheld the social degradation of England as the natural result of
protection. Numerous ways were available to explain England's lopsided
wealth distribution, but Jeffersonians found it easy to invoke a simple linkage
of cause and effect. England had once been a land of egalitarian yeoman
farmers, but it adopted a prohibitive tariff policy and thus over time became a
land of the few rich and the many poor. Protection caused that result. In 1842,
Edmund Burke used the analogy of England to frighten Americans from
adoption of the protective principle: "It is this system which, more than any
other cause, has introduced the vast disparity of conditions among the people
of England." And James K. Polk celebrated the repeal of the British corn laws
as ending the system that built up "immense fortunes in the hands of the few,
and . . . [reduced] the laboring millions to pauperism and misery."[51] The politics behind such statements were obvious enough, but the argument was
sufficiently logical and consistent to credit antebellum Jeffersonians with a
sincere belief, varying in intensity from individual to individual, that protectionism generated wealth for the few and pauperism for the many.

One other Jeffersonian attitude had a powerful influence on their position
on tariff policy and some bearing on their perspective on the distribution of
wealth. In 1789, in the nation's first tariff debate, James Madison, while arguing for a 5 percent ad valorem tariff, simply stated, "If we compare the
cheapness of our land with that of other nations, we see so decided an advantage in that cheapness, as to have full confidence of being unrivalled." Nature
had decreed the United States to be an agrarian nation; the doctrine of free
trade, in the form of the theory of comparative advantage, conveniently accepted nature's decision. The notion that the United States should be a land
of yeoman farmers predominates in free trade Jeffersonian literature
throughout the nineteenth century. Agrarian radicals thus found free trade a
most comforting economic theory.[52]

From the free trade ranks, there arose a considerable attack on the idea of
manufacturing. Agrarians seemed to believe that only farmers really toiled

---

51. Speech of Edmund Burke, July 8, 1842, *Congressional Globe,* 27th Cong., 2nd Sess., Ap-
pendix, 565; Polk, Annual Message of the President (1846), 29th Cong., 2nd Sess., Sen. Ex.
Doc. No. 1, p. 28. See also Taylor, *Tyranny Unmasked,* 196–98; Remonstrance of the General
Assembly of Alabama (1828), 20th Cong., 1st Sess., Sen. Ex. Doc. No. 86, p. 5.

52. Speech of Madison, April 9, 1789, *Annals of Congress,* 1st Cong., 1st Sess., 117. For the
agrarian radicals, see [Logan], *Five Letters,* 8–9; Taylor, *Tyranny Unmasked,* 4–5, 25–28, 35–40,
50, 138; [Cambreleng], *Examination of the New Tariff,* 10; Tolles, *George Logan,* 105–106,
110–13.

and that manufacturing was an attempt to escape honest manual labor. Aaron V. Brown once grumped, "Men were not satisfied with hard toil, but attempted to get their living by handicraft inventions." Moreover, there was an undefined suspicion, confirmed perhaps by the social experience of England, that manufacturers produced masses of unruly, starving working people who slaved for the benefit of capitalists. The early agrarian attitude toward manufactures was summed up in 1820 by future president John Tyler: "Sir, gentlemen may tell me what they please about their rotten manufactories"—he argued on behalf of the farmer.[53]

Usually American free traders relied on concepts of favoritism and monopoly to convince the public that high tariffs were inimical to a republican distribution of wealth. But in their analysis of manufacturing versus agriculture, one political element in the determination of wealth kept surfacing. Free traders never could break free of the Malthusian shadow over the distribution of wealth and the general welfare. Ultimately it was the population-to-land ratio that decided human happiness.[54] American free traders avoided the essence of their intellectual dilemma. By adhering to the Malthusian paradigm, they had no need to refer to political institutions or economic systems to explain the distribution of wealth. They continued to use ideas from the political economy of aristocracy even though their resort to Malthusian economics undercut their institutional approach. They never resolved this inconsistency.

Individuals who adhered to the Hamiltonian economic axis in the nineteenth century did not surrender in their fight for high tariff duties their regulatory and communitarian ideals to those on the Jeffersonian axis as they had done in the battle over national banking. On financial policy, the Jeffersonians were simply more persuasive and in line with the legacy of the Revo-

53. Speech of Aaron V. Brown, June 18, 1842, *Congressional Globe,* 27th Cong., 2nd Sess., 653; Memorial of the Citizens of Laurens District, South Carolina (1828), 20th Cong., 1st Sess., Sen. Ex. Doc. No. 28, p. 6; speech of Representative T. H. Bayly, June 30, 1846, *Congressional Globe,* 29th Cong., 1st Sess., Appendix, 819; speech of Representative Whitman, April 25, 1820, *Annals of Congress,* 16th Cong., 1st Sess., 2001; Memorial of Sundry Citizens of Charleston, S. C., Against the Tariff (1820), 16th Cong., 2nd Sess., House Ex. Doc. No. 17, pp. 3–6; speech of John Tyler, April 24, 1820, *Annals of Congress,* 16th Cong., 1st Sess., 1961.

54. For example, Memorial of the Committee of the Free Trade Convention (1832), 22nd Cong., 1st Sess., Sen. Ex. Doc. No. 55, pp. 10–11, 30; speech of Representative Nathaniel Macon, June 1, 1809, *Annals of Congress,* 11th Cong., 1st Sess., 186.

lution. But this was not the case with protectionism. Protectionists had a valid claim that high tariffs fostered a distribution of wealth suitable for a republic, and they pressed it forcefully upon the public.

Between 1789 and 1828 various Americans fleshed out the essential elements of the protectionist appeal, if not the theoretical structure of protectionism. Early protectionism was essentially a cry for patriotism, for Americans to buy American-made products. The early high-tariff proponents often based their advocacy on national grandeur and power. Strong, important European nations, like England, manufactured; weak nations farmed. At times, trade restrictionists desired high tariffs to stop European luxuries from entering American life and corrupting the simple ways of the citizenry.[55] By 1828, protectionists had absorbed and propagated the basic ideas that government was vital to establish manufactures, infant industries required protection from overseas manufacturers, merchants were of dubious national worth, machinery and productivity (along with women and children) were the keys to overcome the alleged American labor shortage, high tariffs were needed to foster industries that contributed to the national defense, competition was maintained and monopoly avoided by creating a keen home market competition, and high tariffs were useful in sustaining full employment for artisans and farmers.[56]

As vital as these separate concepts were to later protectionists, tariff arguments between 1789 and 1820 were theoretically barren. The important advo-

55. "An Oration," at Petersburg, Va., July 4, 1787, *American Museum,* II (1787), 421; "An Oration," by Robert Strettel Jones, March 17, 1777, *American Museum,* V (1789), 265–67; Benjamin Rush, "A Speech," March 16, 1775, *American Museum,* V (1789), 581–82; Noah Webster, "The Patriot," no. V, May 16, 1791, in Warfel, ed., *Letters of Noah Webster,* 102; Richard Rush, "Annual Treasury Report" (1827), *Register of Debates,* 20th Cong., 1st Sess., Appendix, 2825; [Coxe], *Observations on the Agriculture, Manufactures and Commerce of the United States,* 5–6; Hamilton, "Report on Manufactures," [final version], in Syrett and Cooke, eds., *Papers of Hamilton,* X, 257–58, 261–63, 287–89, 291.

56. Many of these elements of protectionism were present in Hamilton, "Report on Manufactures," [final version], in Syrett and Cooke, eds., *Papers of Hamilton,* X, on productivity, 239, 244–45, 251; on machinery, 240–41, 251, 272; on the money market, 274–83; necessity of government encouragement, 266–68. On stimulating employment, see Memorial of the Farmers, Manufacturers, Mechanics, and Merchants, of the County of Rensselaer (1824), 18th Cong., 1st Sess., House Ex. Doc. No. 48, pp. 3–4; on infant industry, Edward Everett, "American Manufactures," Address at American Institute, New York City, October 14, 1831, in Everett, *Orations and Speeches,* II, 78; on national defense, see Andrew Jackson to L. H. Coleman, April 26, 1824, in Bassett, ed., *Correspondence of Jackson,* III, 249–50; and Report of Committee on Manufacturing, *Annals of Congress,* 14th Cong., 1st Sess., 963.

cacies lacked a sufficient grasp of European political economy to develop a coherent alternative system. Alexander Hamilton was a practical politician who never devised a complete economics. Tench Coxe, Hamilton's assistant in the Treasury Department before he switched allegiance to the Democratic-Republicans, was a brute compiler of statistics, but he was no theoretician. Mathew Carey, the Catholic Irish immigrant who established an important Philadelphia publishing house, was a political antagonist more adept at venting spleen on his opponents than at concocting economic explanations.[57]

The first expostulation of high-tariff principles made no mention of the distribution of wealth, a topic that became important in protectionist thought with the publication of Daniel Raymond's *Elements of Political Economy* in 1820. Alexander Hamilton's famous "Report on Manufactures" had a number of insightful glances into economic operations—especially productivity and machinery—but had nothing to say on the distribution of wealth. Tench Coxe did on occasion mention wealth distribution, and he foreshadowed the road later protectionists would travel. True, Coxe asserted, he and others favoring manufacturing called upon government to bestow favors on manufactures that in other countries had led to oppression. But, Coxe insisted, those nations were monarchies and aristocracies in which rulers purposefully sought to reduce the population "to poverty and distress" for their own emolument. The United States was a people's government, a republican government. Thus its actions would not have the same effect as those of monarchies and aristocracies.[58]

In the four decades before the Civil War (and the four decades after it), the protectionist argument regarding the distribution of wealth followed a standard format. Protectionists avowed that government had a duty to act on behalf of its citizens and fulfill the promises of the Revolution. Because the United States was republican in form, its government would act in the interest of the general welfare. Protection merely restricted foreigners from engaging in the American market, but no barriers thwarted Americans from entry. The domestic market thereby encouraged competition and eliminated monopoly. Finally, high tariffs benefited artisans and operatives more than the

---

57. On Hamilton, see Jacob E. Cooke, "The Reports of Alexander Hamilton," in Cooke, ed., *Alexander Hamilton: A Profile* (New York, 1967), 68, 78–82; Miller, *Hamilton*, 290; on Tench Coxe, see Jacob E. Cooke, *Tench Coxe and the Early Republic* (Chapel Hill, 1978), 201; on Mathew Carey, Rowe, *Mathew Carey*, 113–14, and 107–21 generally.

58. [Coxe], *Observations on the Agriculture, Manufactures and Commerce of the United States*, 6, 77–79.

wealthy by multiplying employment opportunities and ensuring that no competition would arise based on starvation wages. By maintaining high wages, politicians of the Hamiltonian axis affirmed that the United States would continue to exhibit the equitable distribution of wealth so vital to the health of a republic.

Protectionists always claimed that protectionism was a legacy of the Revolution and was indeed in the broadest sense the purpose of the Revolution. "Protection may be said," wrote Maryland Whig John Pendleton Kennedy, "to be the eldest born of the Constitution." Daniel Webster in 1837 insisted that the Constitution came into effect only because working people wanted a protective system: "It had been the operatives spread along the Atlantic coast whose voices brought the constitution into being." During an 1860 Republican rally, Joseph Hoxie, exercising some hyperbole, told a crowd that "it was not the tax on tea that the people cared for at Boston, it was the principle of protection."[59]

Tariff advocates in the antebellum decades made explicit just what the Revolution and then the Constitution were intended to protect. American institutions, in the words of Charles Hudson, were designed "to secure to the laborer an ample remuneration for his toil. This raises the price of labor—it makes the laborer a *man.*" A republican polity presupposed widespread popular participation in government that would be biased to self-interest if a maldistribution of wealth occurred and the many were paupers. By creating a republic, the revolutionaries devolved onto the national government the responsibility of ensuring a high standard of living, or in Edward Everett's phrasing, "It has been the object of the economical system of the United States to secure to the labor of the country a just and equitable, but not an extravagant, portion of the products."[60]

Political protectionists were adamant that political institutions and forms of government shaped economic systems. For them, the political economy of aristocracy meant simply that aristocratic governments created widespread poverty. But the United States was based on equal rights and no special privi-

---

59. Kennedy, *Letter of J. P. Kennedy to His Constituents,* 9; speech of Webster, February 24, 1837, *Register of Debates,* 24th Cong., 2nd Sess., 958–59; Joseph Hoxie's speech in New York *Tribune,* June 19, 1860, p. 3; John M. Belohlavek, *George Mifflin Dallas: Jacksonian Patrician* (University Park, Pa., 1977), 45.

60. Charles Hudson, "Protection of American Independence," *Whig Almanac,* 1844, p. 25; Edward Everett, "American Manufactures," in Everett, *Orations and Speeches,* II, 79. See also James H. Lanman, "American Manufactures," *Hunt's Merchants' Magazine,* V (1841), 140.

leges; thus the wealth of the wealthiest in a republic should be reduced to human dimensions, and the material well-being of the many should rise well above subsistence. Protectionist authors did not hesitate to find the problem of wealth distribution in other lands to be preeminently a political problem because aristocrats stole the fruits of labor.[61]

The first of the two major points protectionists made in regard to the distribution of wealth was an absolute denial of the free trade charge of monopoly. Protectionists correctly pointed out that Jeffersonians employed a false definition of monopoly. Nathan Appleton remarked, "A monopoly is an exclusive privilege. What exclusive privilege attaches to a business which is open to every individual in the United States[?]" The Pennsylvania Society for the Encouragement of American Manufacturing in 1820 defined a monopolist as "one who, by engrossing or by patent, obtains the sole power or privilege of vending any commodity."[62] A monopolist was not a nation but a single person or firm who had the power to bar others from entering a field of business. The monopolist could then restrict output, raise prices, lower wages, and extort monopoly profits. The tariff bestowed no such power. It restricted competition to citizens of the United States, but it did not eliminate competition.

The question of competition led protectionists to one of their favorite subjects: the home market. By eliminating foreign competition, Americans could step in and fill the void. Initially a high tariff raised prices of consumer goods. But those higher prices attracted entrepreneurs who then entered the field, increased the supply, and lowered the price (this process, incidentally, is exactly the free trade explanation of sectoral growth on an international scale). For political purposes, many protectionists argued that protection, by increasing domestic competition, would eventually lower the price beneath that of foreign competition. That dubious claim has to be weighed against the more accurate point that protection did not permit monopoly profits. As

---

61. For example, H. G. O. Colby, "The Relations of Wealth and Labor," in Horace Greeley, ed., *The American Laborer, Devoted to the Cause of Protection to Home Industry* (1843; rpr. New York, 1974), 233–38; C. C. Haven, "Home League to the People of the United States," *Hunt's Merchants' Magazine,* VIII (1843), 72; Kennedy, *Letter of J. P. Kennedy to His Constituents,* 17.

62. Speech of Nathan Appleton, January 22, 1833, *Register of Debates,* 22nd Cong., 2nd Sess., 1209; Memorial of the Pennsylvania Society for the Encouragement of American Manufactures (1820), 16th Cong., 1st Sess., Sen. Ex. Doc. No. 126, p. 8; speech of Fillmore, June 9, 1842, *Congressional Globe,* 27th Cong., 2nd Sess., Appendix, 906.

Robert Winthrop stated in 1837, "Domestic competition will take care that these [profits] are not too high."[63]

The other major point high-tariff advocates made about the distribution of wealth after explaining their fealty to competition and abhorrence of monopoly was that high tariffs elevated wages. Tariffs enhanced the standard of living of ordinary workers and only marginally enhanced the profitability of capitalists. Protectionists believed an equitable distribution of wealth could be maintained through high wages.

The labor argument did not appear in protectionism's infancy. Early protectionists were concerned with evading the implications of high wages—this was the brunt of Hamilton's "Report on Manufactures." The early proponents of the American System of high tariffs, a national bank, internal improvements, and slow westward migration justified the tariff to create internal markets for farmers and to multiply employment opportunities for manual labor. Some argued that by creating employment, tariffs reduced indolence and the immorality to which it led. During the 1810 debate on Macon's Bill Number 2, one of the statistical compilers for protection, Adam Seybert, even denied that wages of the American and English working classes differed. The argument that the tariff aided the working class and not the employing/capitalist class evidently first made its entry in 1826 in a pamphlet by Caleb Cushing, Massachusetts politician, and in an 1828 congressional speech by the Federalist-turned-Jacksonian Louis McLane. After 1828, the high wage doctrine of protectionism became its outstanding quality and one that those on the Jeffersonian economic axis vehemently attacked, realizing its strength in attracting votes.[64]

63. Robert Winthrop, "Protection to American Industry," in Winthrop, *Addresses and Speeches*, I, 207. For examples of other references to internal competition and antimonopoly sentiments of protectionists, see speech of Representative John Paul Verree, April 27, 1860, *Congressional Globe*, 36th Cong., 1st Sess., 1880; speech of Representative Andrew Stewart, February 26, 1833, *Register of Debates*, 22nd Cong., 2nd Sess., 1799; speech of Representative Almon H. Read, July 9, 1842, *Congressional Globe*, 27th Cong., 2nd Sess., Appendix, 570; speech of Representative Jacob Collamer, June 24, 1846, *Congressional Globe*, 29th Cong., 1st Sess., Appendix, 962.

64. Hamilton, "Report on Manufactures," [final version], in Syrett and Cooke, eds., *Papers of Hamilton*, X, 251–53, 269–74; Baldwin, "Protection to Manufactures," *Annals of Congress*, 16th Cong., 2nd Sess., Appendix, 1573–75; speech of Representative Francis Baylies, January 31, 1823, *Register of Debates*, 17th Cong., 2nd Sess., 789; speech of Senator James Ross, March 31, 1801, *Annals of Congress*, 7th Cong., 1st Sess., 219–20; speech of Representative Adam Seybert, April 18, 1810, *Annals of Congress*, 11th Cong., 2nd Sess., 1894–97; A Friend of

Protectionists fashioned their labor ideals to appeal to republican sensitivities and to the need for a just distribution of wealth. Caleb Cushing seems to have paved the way. His short book commenced by insisting that different political systems created different economic systems. A republican form of government necessitated an equal or equitable distribution of wealth. An equitable distribution of wealth existed only in the presence of high wages, for the masses of humankind lived on wages, "and the higher the wages the more equal will be the distribution of wealth." When wages were high, republican government was safe. The masses would not avail themselves of political power to divide the honest earnings of the wealthy because there was no mass of paupers looking enviously upon the accumulations of others. Hence "the high wages of labor in this country are nearly connected with the permanence of our political institutions and the progress of the general welfare."[65]

The intertwining of the ideas of high wages, an equitable distribution of wealth, and the preservation of political republicanism was an incessant theme in the protectionist appeal from 1828 to 1860 (and really to 1896 and perhaps even to 1932). High wages provided for social mobility, access to education, proper care of families, and accumulations of property. Without high wages, the American experiment in republicanism was doomed.[66]

The interplay of republican institutions, high wages, and the distribution of wealth in the nineteenth-century protectionist mind explains the prevalence of one of the most famous warnings of high-tariff advocates: the fear of pauper labor. Protectionist literature is filled with the omnipresent admonition that free trade would drag American wages down to those of the debased

Domestic Industry [Caleb Cushing], *Summary of the Practical Principles of Political Economy; with Observations on Smith's Wealth of Nations and Say's Political Economy* (Cambridge, Mass., 1826), 42–46; speech of Senator Louis McLane, April 28, 1828, *Annals of Congress,* 16th Cong., 1st Sess., 2095. On the labor argument in protectionism, see George Benjamin Mangold, *The Labor Argument in the American Protective Tariff Discussion* (1906; rpr. New York, 1971); Huston, "Political Response to Industrialism," 35–57.

65. [Cushing], *Summary of the Practical Principles,* 43–44.

66. For example, speech of Representative Andrew Stewart, March 13, 1844, *Congressional Globe,* 28th Cong., 1st Sess., Appendix, 282; speech of Senator Isaac C. Bates, February 21, 1844, *ibid.,* 297–98; speech of Senator Samuel S. Phelps, February 19, 1844, *ibid.,* 294; Memorial of the Association of Mechanics, Farmers, and Other Working Men, of the Towns of Amesbury and Salisbury, in the State of Massachusetts, (1832), 22nd Cong., 1st Sess., House Ex. Doc. No. 258, p. 2; speech of Representative John Davis, June 6, 1832, *Register of Debates,* 22nd Cong., 1st Sess., 3306–3309; Friends of Domestic Industry, *Address of the Friends of Domestic Industry,* 21.

English operative or of the even more depressed Irish tenant. Robert Winthrop cautioned that "if our labor be levelled off to the grade of European
labor, our liberty must be cut down to the standard of European liberty."
Some memorialists of Easton, Pennsylvania, told Congress that it was "pecu-
liarly requisite in our free Government, to protect the free laborers of America
from being brought to the level of the pauper and slave laborers of other
countries."[67]

The pauper labor argument of the protectionists had much more logic,
electoral appeal, and republicanism than many have conceded. Protectionists adhered to the labor theory of property/value and understood the tenets
of the political economy of aristocracy. Wealth (and income) achieved an equitable distribution when laborers received the fruits of their toil. That fair
and natural distribution was mangled when aristocratic powers controlled
governmental policies and enacted aristocratic legislation that transferred the
fruits of labor from the many to the few. Where republican economic principles held sway—that is, where laborers received the full fruits of their labor—
government did not interfere with private enterprise or needlessly regulate
business.

When nations competed, however, more than trade was at stake. Foreign
trade was not competition of different economic elements, it was the competition of different political systems. Republican economies were high wage
economies because laborers obtained their just reward. Aristocratic economies were low wage economies because aristocrats, via legislation, stole the
fruits of labor. When a republican economy traded openly with an aristocratic economy, a built-in and disastrous unfairness manifested itself. Aristocratic nations purposefully created low wages and thus could undersell virtuous republican products. Free trade mechanisms were not natural because the
intervention of aristocratic government had unnaturally tampered with
wages. Thus the unnaturally low-cost aristocratic product would drive the
higher-cost (but naturally priced) republican product out of the market—
unless wages in the republican nation fell to pauper levels. If wages in a republic were reduced, social mobility, widespread distribution of property, an
equitable distribution of wealth, and the political apparatus of popular sover-

67. Robert C. Winthrop, "The Wants of the Government and the Wages of Labor," in
Winthrop, *Addresses and Speeches,* I, 547; Memorial of the Inhabitants of the Borough of Easton, Pennsylvania (1833), 22nd Cong., 2nd Sess., House Ex. Doc. No. 73, p. 2.

eignty would be threatened. Whatever economic benefit free trade with aristocratic lands conferred, to protectionists it could not begin to compare with the social and political cost of the demise of republicanism.

Those on the Hamiltonian political axis had one further argument concerning the distribution of wealth. It had none of the creativity of the pauper labor argument or the synthesis of high wage economics, republicanism, and the concepts of the political economy of aristocracy. But this charge by protectionists against free traders was utterly devastating. American free traders took their economics from English free traders, whose hallmark was the belief that the masses were mired in wretched poverty by natural processes and deserved to be there. Free trade economics justified mass poverty. Such a doctrine hardly squared with republican notions of an equitable distribution of wealth, and the protectionists knew it. In 1831, the Friends of Domestic Industry castigated any attempt to implement the policies of the English free trade school: "It [free trade theory] assumes the fact, that the wages of labour are barely sufficient to support the labourer, but leave him nothing for accumulation."[68] And the protectionists were correct. Like it or not, Malthus and Ricardo had saddled the free trade theory with mass misery, starvation wages, and a lopsided distribution of wealth. Until the doctrine of free trade was rescued from the palsying embrace of Malthus and Ricardo, it was indeed the "dismal science." And free trade theory regarding the distribution of wealth was antirepublican.

Businessmen and their dealings with wage earners and consumers should have been major topics covered by politicians in discussions of the distribution of wealth. They were not. Political debate contained more than a few hostile remarks about the moral standards of capitalists and entrepreneurs and led to a significant debate about corporations. Yet few ever concentrated wholly on business manipulations and how such operations could affect the distribution of wealth. The reason for this lapse in economic analysis concerning businessmen was the emphasis placed on legislative favoritism in the form of special privileges and monopolies. The power of the concepts in the political economy of aristocracy tended to obfuscate the internal workings of the business world in regard to the distribution of wealth.

68. Friends of Domestic Industry, *Address of the Friends of Domestic Industry,* 19; see also Kennedy, *Letter of J. P. Kennedy to His Constituents,* 20; speech of Nathan Appleton, May 30, 1832, *Register of Debates,* 22nd Cong., 1st Sess., 3206.

The question of business organization most frequently appeared in debates over industrialization. Agrarian Jeffersonians consistently denounced the social results of the factory system—lordly capitalists and servile laborers—whereas those on the Hamiltonian political axis usually defended factories as places of alternative employment, advanced machinery, and intelligent and skilled operatives.[69]

The focus of political leaders' concern regarding business structures was the corporation, of which the factory was perhaps the most obvious manifestation. Politicians on the Hamiltonian political axis exhibited few reservations about encouraging corporate development in the United States. They knew that economic growth, including enhanced wages, depended on increasing accumulations of capital. Corporations encouraged the pooling of resources, the use of machinery, the division of labor, and greater output. Henry Clay said that ownership of corporations by stockholding made them more "democratic" than individually owned businesses, and John Quincy Adams, in one of his rare ebullient moods, proclaimed that northerners turned to associated organizations to effect common goals and employed "the truly republican institution of joint stock companies, of which every class of the community may share in the benefit, proportionate to their means and their resources."[70]

69. These early debates are discussed in the Introduction to Gary Kulik, Roger Parks, and Theodore Z. Penn, eds., *The New England Mill Village, 1790–1860* (Cambridge, Mass., 1982); McCoy, *Elusive Republic,* 37–39, 50–51; Kasson, *Civilizing the Machine,* 22–27, 55–69; Jennifer Clark, "The American Image of Technology from the Revolution to 1840," *American Quarterly,* XXXIX (1987), 431–49. For good examples of antimanufacturing attitudes, see Memorial of the Citizens of Laurens District, South Carolina (1828), 20th Cong., 1st Sess., Sen. Ex. Doc. No. 28, p. 6; Memorial of Delegates of United Agricultural Societies of . . . Virginia (1820), 16th Cong., 2nd Sess., House Ex. Doc. No. 22, pp. 5–7. For promanufacturing statements, see speech of Representative Francis Baylies, January 31, 1823, *Annals of Congress,* 17th Cong., 2nd Sess., 788–89; speech of Senator Henry Clay, February 2, 1832, *Congressional Debates,* 22nd Cong., 1st Sess., 277; Philadelphia Society for Promotion of National Industry, *Addresses* (Philadelphia, 1819), 65–72.

70. Speech of Representative Washington Hunt, *Congressional Globe,* 29th Cong., 1st Sess., Appendix, 967; A Pennsylvanian [Mathew Carey], *An Examination of the Report of a Committee of the Citizens of Boston and Its Vicinity, Opposed to a Further Increase of Duties on Importation* (Philadelphia, 1828), 18–19; George S. White, "Memoir of Samuel Slater" (1836), in Kulik, Parks, and Penn, eds., *New England Mill Village,* 349–53; *North American and United States Gazette* (Philadelphia), March 4, 1858; speech of Nathan Appleton, January 22, 1833,

Why the corporation posed no problem to society or to an equitable distribution of wealth in the estimation of the Hamiltonian political contingent was transparent. The corporation was enabled to produce, but it was given none of the coercive powers it had in Europe. John C. Calhoun used this line of reasoning when he argued for the tariff of 1816. Discussing Europe's caste-ridden society, the dismal condition of the English working class, and the stupefying impact of the division of labor, he said that those conditions originated not in manufacturing corporations or factories but in England's "poor laws, and statutes regulating the price of labor, with heavy taxes." The writers of a memorial from Philadelphia explained that corporations operated differently in republics than in aristocracies. "It is true," the memorial read, "in foreign countries, where the Government, the law, and the employer, are all in combination, or rather conspiracy, against the employed, poverty and its concommitant [*sic*], disease, must be very frequent among the people *employed*." But the United States was a republic, and republics gave no such powers to corporations. In short, by avoiding the political connection, by employing the lessons taught by the political economy of aristocracy, corporations were shorn of any true wealth-distorting power.[71]

Some of the politicians of the Jeffersonian political axis recognized that size might be a factor in depressing wages, that corporations might contain internal mechanisms that skewed the distribution of wealth in spite of republican political institutions. Churchill C. Cambreleng noted that in yeoman agriculture, "each appropriates to *himself* a large share of the produce of his labour," but in manufacturing establishments "the larger portion of it would go to enrich his employer." Robert J. Walker explained in 1845 that when manufacturers were small in size, their power to regulate wages was "inconsiderable," but as the size of the firm grew, "there is a corresponding increase of power until the control of such capital over the wages of labor becomes irresistible." Senator John M. Niles in 1837 made an unusual observation:

Register of Debates, 22nd Cong., 2nd Sess., 1209–11; speech of Senator Clay, February 2, 1832, *Register of Debates,* 22nd Cong., 1st Sess., 277; John Quincy Adams, Report from Committee on Manufactures (1832), *Register of Debates,* 22nd Cong., 1st Sess., Appendix, 84.

71. Speech of Representative John C. Calhoun, April 4, 1816, *Annals of Congress,* 14th Cong., 1st Sess., 1335; Memorial of the Artisans and Manufacturers of Philadelphia (1803), in U.S. Congress, *American State Papers: Documents, Legislative and Executive, of the Congress of the United States* (Washington, D.C., 1832–61), Class III, Vol. II, Doc. No. 206, p. 62.

"Whether a monopoly is created by legal enactments or arises from other causes, it is not the less a monopoly."[72] Further exploration of the corporation, however, seldom extended beyond such flat declaratives.

In almost every instance when politicians of the Jeffersonian axis considered corporations, the political connection was the source of their fear about imperfections in the distribution of wealth.[73] Corporations obtained powers from legislation—limited liability, infinite longevity—that amounted to special privileges and in some cases were monopolistic. Special legislative privileges and monopolies distorted wealth distribution. Once the political connection was removed, however, the Jeffersonians had only an unease with the corporation but virtually no analysis or explanation of how an agency of production that possessed no privileges or legislative power could warp the distribution of wealth. As with the Hamiltonians, although producing a different outcome, the concepts of the political economy of aristocracy dominated understanding of the corporation.[74]

At least one strand of thought hostile to corporate enterprise, however, was discernible. Many commentators believed in individual proprietorships and individual responsibility. Managers, not owners, ran corporations, and managers did not have the same sense of individual responsibility that owners did. Management of corporations by nonowners offered the possibility of "sinecures" for incompetent family members or personal friends.[75] The enterprise that began creating popular disturbances was the railroad corporation. By

72. [Cambreleng], *Examination of the New Tariff,* 186; Robert J. Walker, Annual Report of the Treasurer (1845), 29th Cong., 1st Sess., House Ex. Doc. No. 6, pp. 7–8; speech of Senator John M. Niles, February 24, 1837, *Register of Debates,* 24th Cong., 2nd Sess., 945.

73. This is also the conclusion of Hovencamp, *Enterprise and American Law,* 37, 56.

74. For example, editorials of William Leggett in Sedgwick, ed., *Collection of the Political Writings of William Leggett,* I, 91–94, 142, 73, 77–78; Gouge, *Short History of Paper Money and Banking,* 41–44; Hamilton, ed., *Memoirs, Speeches and Writings of Rantoul,* 313–16; Fisk, *Oration on Banking,* 3–4; "The Credit System," *United States Magazine and Democratic Review,* III (1838), 196–98; S. F. Glenn, "Corporations," *De Bow's Review,* I (1846), 508–509; Andrew Jackson, Farewell Address, 1837, *Register of Debates,* 24th Cong., 2nd Sess., 2171; [Cambreleng], *Examination of the New Tariff,* 165–66; James Madison to J. K. Paulding, March 10, 1827, in Hunt, ed., *Writings of Madison,* IX, 281–82. See Welter, *Mind of America,* chap. 4; Walker Lewis, *Without Fear or Favor: A Biography of Chief Justice Roger Brooke Taney* (Boston, 1965), 282–88; Kutler, *Privilege and Creative Destruction,* 4–5, 15–27, 46, and *passim.*

75. On sinecures, Hartford (Conn.) *Daily Times,* September 8, 1858; see also E. B. Bigelow, *Remarks on the Depressed Condition of Manufactures in Massachusetts* (Boston, 1858), 11–12, 16, 25; *Harper's Weekly,* I (1857), 658; Harrisburg *Pennsylvania Telegraph,* September 22, 1860.

1860, some politicians and editors started to investigate the internal workings of the railroad corporation but without weighing all phenomena in the scale of the political economy of aristocracy. Railroads were upsetting people on both the Jeffersonian and Hamiltonian axes of American politics. But in 1860, nothing indicated that, even in the case of the railroad, the grip of the political economy of aristocracy had loosened its hold on the American mind.[76]

By 1860, American politicians, academics, and journalists had reiterated endlessly the idea that political equality led to economic equality. Statements that an equal distribution of wealth resulted from a society based on political equality and an unregulated economy saturated public discourse from the time of the Revolution to the Civil War. William H. Seward in 1853 told a crowd at the American Institute, "While our Constitutions and laws establish political equality, they operate to produce social equality also, by preventing monopolies of land and great accumulation of wealth." The German academic Francis Lieber, a fanatical supporter of property rights, wrote: "The natural and unfailing tendency is towards a constant distribution and diffusion of wealth. It is by legislation, by positive enactments only, that this natural course can be arrested, and that riches can be made to accumulate in a degree so disproportionate to the general standard of wealth, that they become dangerous to liberty and public welfare." After the Civil War, Samuel A. Goddard, an Englishman connected to the abolitionist Samuel J. May by marriage, pontificated, "With equal laws, without monopolies, with no class legislation, property becomes distributed amongst all."[77]

A marvelous example of this leap of faith that political equality produced economic equality and the frustration involved in trying to understand the

76. Rowland Gibson Hazard, *Economics and Politics: A Series of Papers upon Public Questions Written on Various Occasions from 1840 to 1885,* ed. Caroline Hazard (Boston, 1889), 33–34, 37, 44, 72–73, 86–87; Know-Nothing resolution 14 in New York *Tribune,* September 11, 1858; *American Railroad Journal,* XXXI (1858), 152, XXX (1857), 392, 408–409. See David Lowenthal, *George Perkins Marsh: Versatile Vermonter* (New York, 1958), 289–92; Alfred D. Chandler, Jr., *Henry Varnum Poor: Business Editor, Analyst, and Reformer* (Cambridge, Mass., 1956), 155–77; Thomas C. Cochran and William Miller, *The Age of Enterprise: A Social History of Industrial America* (rev. ed.; New York, 1961), 67–71; Hurst, *Legitimacy of the Business Corporation in the Law,* 25–30.

77. William H. Seward, "The True Basis of American Independence," in Baker, ed., *Works of Seward,* IV, 149; Lieber, *Essays on Property and Labour,* 214; Samuel A. Goddard, *The American Rebellion: Letters on the American Rebellion, 1860 to 1865, &c* (London, 1870), 5.

logic underlying such assertions is provided by the abolitionist lawyer and re-former Lysander Spooner. He wrote a pamphlet in 1846 detailing the cause of and cure for poverty in the United States. He commenced by bewailing the horrid distribution of wealth and the rise in the number of paupers. The first economic proposition Spooner offered to cure this condition was that "every man . . . should be allowed to have the fruits, and all the fruits of his own la-bor." That following such a rule would create an equal distribution of wealth, wrote Spooner, "is a proposition too self-evident almost to need illustration." The rest of the pamphlet demonstrated that the only way to enable each per-son to possess all the fruits of his or her own labor, to end poverty, and to cre-ate an equal distribution of wealth was to repeal the usury laws. Freeing credit from legislative trammels would make poverty disappear.[78]

These are the declarations of laissez-faire economics, and they have amused, puzzled, bewildered, annoyed, irritated, and enraged historians for most of the twentieth century. Scholars fail to comprehend how nineteenth-century Americans could have ever honestly believed that equal political rights—the suffrage—could guarantee equality of property. Political equal-ity has had little impact on distribution unless some party openly pursued a redistributive goal. But in nineteenth-century America, political equality was paired with laissez-faire policy. Many twentieth-century academics see an unregulated economy as a recipe for a horrendously skewed distribution of wealth. Some historians have found the attack on banks and tariffs under-standable (in some cases laudable), but the justification for the attacks by the "equal rights" doctrine has been almost an impenetrable enigma.[79] Scholars

78. Lysander Spooner, *Poverty: Its Illegal Causes and Legal Cure* (Boston, 1846), 5–12, quote on 7.

79. For example, see the comments of William Appleman Williams, *The Contours of American History* (New York, 1973), 266–69, 285, 292–96; Charles Maurice Wiltse, *The Jeffer-sonian Tradition in American Democracy* (Chapel Hill, 1935), 221–24, 236–37; Michael H. Frisch, ed., "Notes and Documents: 'Is the World Governed Too Much?'" *Pennsylvania Maga-zine of History and Biography,* CV (1981), 209–10; Edwin C. Rozwenc, Jr., ed., *Ideology and Power in the Age of Jackson* (Garden City, N.Y., 1964), 301; and the discussion in James L. Hus-ton, "The American Revolutionaries, the Political Economy of Aristocracy, and the American Concept of the Distribution of Wealth, 1765–1900," *American Historical Review,* XCVIII (1993), 1102–1103. At least three articles stress the connection between republicanism, the de-centralized state, and the humane side of John Locke: Major L. Wilson, "The 'Country' Ver-sus the 'Court': A Republican Consensus and Party Debate in the Bank War," *Journal of the Early Republic,* XV (1995), 642; Richard J. Ellis, "Radical Lockeanism in American Political Culture," *Western Political Quarterly,* XLV (1992), 827–44; John Gerring, "A Chapter in the

have had trouble grasping the nineteenth-century doctrine of equal rights for three reasons. First, they have not probed the economic thought of the nineteenth century sufficiently, and, second, they have not fully appreciated the early American conception of the distribution of wealth. The third reason is fundamental. In the twentieth century, the pattern of thinking about the relation between economics and politics has been reversed. In the nineteenth century, politics caused economic relationships. In the twentieth century, the normal pattern of investigation asserts that economics causes political relationships. The logic of political economy in the nineteenth century can be understood only if one accepts the contemporary assumption about the flow of causality from politics to economics.

Both the Jeffersonian and Hamiltonian political axes approved of laissez-faire, the Hamiltonians in the domestic sphere (with some reservations) and the Jeffersonians in the domestic and foreign spheres.[80] Behind the original justification of laissez-faire were the concepts of the labor theory of property/value and the political economy of aristocracy. Because the differences in individuals' quality and quantity of labor were not seismic—but were observable—the resultant property distribution would display inequalities, but those inequalities had boundaries. No excuses existed for individual poverty except the unavoidable whim of fate or character flaws (intemperance, gambling, laziness). The labor theory of property/value, in the American imagination, indicated a reward well above subsistence. Diligent labor earned its reward; when laborers received the full fruits of their labor, that reward was sufficient to maintain a family in relative comfort, provide for education, and set aside a surplus for old age. Laborers did not receive the fruits of their labors when aristocrats controlled the government—when the political economy of aristocracy was in operation. Aristocrats used the government to gorge themselves on the fruits of others' labors, thus creating the few rich and the many poor.

How equal political rights then became the means of reestablishing a natural and equitable distribution of wealth becomes clear. By using the vote,

---

History of American Party Ideology: The Nineteenth-Century Democratic Party (1828–1892), *Polity*, XXVI (1994), 747–51. These scholars find egalitarianism in republican ideology; I believe it stems more from the antiaristocratic impulse and an understanding of the political economy of aristocracy.

80. Hamilton was more of an interventionist than most, probably the best example of a true believer in mercantilism in North America. He nonetheless believed in using government to stimulate entrepreneurs, not to direct or control them.

the masses—the laborers, Jackson's humbler members of society—elected representatives who stopped the avaricious from manipulating government so as to transfer the fruits of labor from the people to themselves. The popular vote thwarted the designs of would-be aristocrats as long as the "people" remained vigilant and "virtuous." Republics had this capacity of popular participation and so could check the ambitious. But monarchies, aristocracies, and other forms of elite rule did not. In those governmental systems, nothing stopped the elite from plundering the people. Without equal rights, without the vote, there could be no equal distribution of wealth.

And so it was by this logic that, with some hesitation and reservation, most Americans argued that laissez-faire and equal political rights inexorably led to an equitable and nearly egalitarian distribution of wealth. Twentieth-century historians have been unable to accept this logic. Quite a few mid-nineteenth-century Americans began questioning its veracity as well.

8

Dissenters

The standard American interpretation of the forces that shaped a nation's distribution of wealth constituted the whole of the thinking of both the Jeffersonian and Hamiltonian political axes. Distributions were equitable when the laborer received the just fruits of his or her labor, and the only agency of distortion was government coercion when directed by aristocrats or some other self-interested force. Party divisions reflected disagreement as to what constituted aristocratic intrusions into the individual's claim to the rewards of labor. Politicians proclaimed that equal rights ensured an equitable distribution, and many believed the United States had obtained as just a distribution of wealth as was humanly possible. The general literary public usually did not dispute these claims of egalitarianism.

Vigorous dissenters appeared in the four decades preceding the Civil War to challenge the mainstream political explanation of the equitability of the existing American distribution of wealth and the forces that created it. Individual reformers, spokesmen for the working class, leaders of women's rights, and communitarians had a different perspective on the revolutionary heritage in regard to the distribution of wealth. Yet most of these groups adhered to the basic outlines of the republican theory of the distribution of wealth. Somewhat surprisingly, the most radical of the dissenters—in fact, the people who announced an undeniable rejection of republicanism—were the communitarians, the utopian socialists.

In 1828, the mechanics, artisans, operatives, and journeymen of Philadelphia, New York City, and Boston began to agitate for a revamping of the economic processes and social tendencies in American life, a movement that persisted with varying degrees of intensity and success for the rest of the century. Workers complained of horrendous hours, unsafe conditions, the degradation of craft skills, low wages, an insensitive political system, the loss of community sharing, and permanent pauperization.[1] They also bitterly denounced the American distribution of wealth. The 1828 preamble to the governing document of the Mechanics' Union of Trade Associations affirmed that laborers needed an organization to combat the "evils which result from an unequal and very excessive accumulation of wealth and power in the hands of a few." Nearly twenty years later, some labor spokesman or sympathizer warned, "If the few rob the many, till the many begin to starve, nature will assert her rights, and a new distribution will be made."[2] Unlike most other periodicals, working-class journals began publishing numbers to show how skewed the distribution of wealth had become in the United States.[3]

Antebellum working-class understanding of the distribution of wealth began with the labor theory of property/value, although for the working class the theory may more accurately be called only the labor theory of value. Labor leaders endlessly and continually declared that wealth was the product of labor—male *or* female—and the laborer alone deserved the fruits of his or her toil. "Whereas," said one 1848 workers' meeting at Ohio City, "Labor is the only source of wealth, it follows that working men and working women are the producers and rightful owners of all wealth."[4] Artisans and jour-

1. See Henry Pelling, *American Labor* (Chicago, 1960), 21–47; Laurie, *Artisans into Workers*, chaps. 1–3; Rayback, *History of American Labor*, 47–108; Ware, *Industrial Worker*.

2. Philadelphia *Mechanic's Free Press*, October 25, 1828, quoted in John R. Commons et al., eds., *Documentary History of American Industrial Society* (Cleveland, 1910), V, 84; *Mechanic's Advocate* (Albany), October 7, 1848; "The System of Wages," in *Voice of Industry* (Fitchburg, Mass.), December 10, 1847. See Ware, *Industrial Worker*, xi; William A. Sullivan, *The Industrial Worker in Pennsylvania, 1800–1840* (Harrisburg, Pa., 1955), 162–63.

3. The labor press is the only source I have been able to locate in the pre–Civil War decades that made even a feeble attempt to provide some numbers on the distribution of wealth. These are highly rudimentary, showing how many times one workingman's wage was needed to equal the income of one rich person: *Mechanic's Advocate* (Albany), March 4, 1847; *Voice of Industry* (Fitchburg, Mass.), July 3, 1846; *Voice of Industry* (Lowell, Mass.), July 23, 1847; "British Pauperism," *Young America* (New York), July 12, 1845; see also Theodore Parker, "The Material Condition of the People of Massachusetts," in Cobbe, ed., *Collected Works of Parker*, VIII, 161–72.

4. *Mechanic's Advocate* (Albany), March 18, 1848. Similar quotations could be repeated endlessly. Labor historians have recognized the centrality of the labor theory of value to nineteenth-century working-class thought: Dawley, *Class and Community*, 9–10; Maurice F.

neymen celebrated the Revolution because of its promise of equality by smashing hierarchical feudal institutions and by establishing the standard that laborers deserved the fruits of their labor.[5]

Having established that only the worker creates wealth, spokesmen for the working class then easily filled out the rest of the social analysis. Society was divided into producers and nonproducers. The producers were mechanics, journeymen, and yeoman farmers; the nonproducers—the useless class—were lawyers, doctors, soldiers, merchants, bankers, and the like, and "many of these can be dispensed with."[6] Those who did not labor, who were not producers, and yet were rich were aristocrats. Stephen Simpson, an ally, spokesperson, and agitator of and for Philadelphia's working-class movement in the early 1830s, wrote, "Aristocracy has received the maxim from feudal Europe, and proclaimed it with all the bloated importance of imitative pride, that NATURE HAD DOOMED THE MANY TO LABOUR FOR THE BENEFIT OF THE FEW." The reason for the riches of the aristocracy was simple: the few took the fruits belonging to the many, resulting in a skewed distribution of wealth. "It is a well known fact," said the labor organ the *Voice of Industry*, "that rich men, capitalists and non producers, associate to devise means for securing to themselves the fruits of other men's labor, and that schemes for this purpose are invented and accomplished by combinations." The condition that as the nation

---

Neufeld, "Realms of Thought and Organized Labor in the Age of Jackson," *Labor History,* X (1969), 13; Ira A. Berlin and Herbert G. Gutman, "Natives and Immigrants, Free Men and Slaves: Urban Workingmen in the Antebellum American South," *American Historical Review,* LXXXVIII (1983), 1195; Wilentz, *Chants Democratic,* 157–59; Laurie, *Artisans into Workers,* 66, 68, 94; Edward Pessen, *Most Uncommon Jacksonians: The Radical Leaders of the Early Labor Movement* (Albany, 1967), 28–33; T. J. Jackson Lears, "The Concept of Cultural Hegemony: Problems and Possibilities," *American Historical Review,* XC (1985), 574–76.

5. "Miscellany," for *Ohio State Tribune* in *Voice of Industry* (Fitchburg, Mass.), September 11, 1845; see also William Dealtry, *The Laborer: A Remedy for His Wrongs; or, A Disquisition on the Usages of Society* (Cincinnati, 1869), 162; speech of Robert Townsend, in *National Trades' Union* (New York), January 17, 1835; "Equal Rights," *Mechanic's Free Press* (Philadelphia), December 26, 1829; Faler, *Mechanics and Manufacturers,* 36; Helen L. Sumner, "Citizenship," in John R. Commons et al., *History of Labour in the United States* (New York, 1921), I, 177; Herbert G. Gutman, "Work, Culture, and Society in Industrializing America, 1815–1919," *American Historical Review,* LXXVIII (1973), 568–69.

6. Quote from Dealtry, *The Laborer,* 9. See letter by PHILO in Lynn (Mass.) *Weekly Reporter,* December 5, 1857; A Hand That Thinks, "Non-Producers," *Mechanic's Advocate* (Albany), June 26, 1847; Faler, *Mechanics and Manufacturers,* 31, 34; Rorabaugh, *Craft Apprentice,* 88.

grew wealthier the laborers grew poorer led one person to state, "Distributive justice is not a law of the present social order."[7]

The essential position of those representing the working class was that imbalances in wealth-holding arose from nonproducers obtaining the fruits of labor from producers. The question then arises, What social or economic mechanism did working-class leaders find responsible for the transference of wealth from laborers to would-be aristocrats?

Frequently working-class leaders explained the maldistribution of wealth afflicting the United States by an analysis that came from republican political economy and did not differ greatly from that of the political parties. Laborers, at least in speeches and in print, had no use for feudalism or medieval Europe and entertained absolutely no romantic notion about those centuries of domination and hierarchy. In particular, they denounced the laws of entail and primogeniture but less often than did politicians. And workers were certainly aware of the population-to-land ratio. Thomas Skidmore, one of the earliest New York City working-class radicals, found the origins of wealth inequality in the first partition of land, which was then continued and exacerbated by inheritance laws. The idea that free western land supported high eastern wages had taken root early in the Jacksonian working-class outburst and became the center of labor reform efforts under the leadership of New York City radical George Henry Evans and the National Reform Association in the 1840s.[8]

Boston's labor organizer and union advocate Seth Luther stated in 1834 that

7. Stephen Simpson, *The Working Man's Manual: A New Theory of Political Economy, on the Principle of Production the Source of Wealth* (Philadelphia, 1831), 136; Preamble of a Constitution of Industrial Brotherhood in *Voice of Industry* (Fitchburg, Mass.), November 7, 1845; A Hand That Thinks, "Non-Producers," *Mechanic's Advocate* (Albany), June 26, 1847; *Mechanic's Free Press* (Philadelphia), November 29, 1828, in Commons et al., eds., *Documentary History of American Industrial Society,* V, 70; mass meeting for Lynn strikers at Cooper Institute, in New York *Tribune,* March 28, 1860; John Pickering, *The Working Man's Political Economy, Founded upon the Principle of Immutable Justice, and the Inalienable Rights of Man; Designed for the Promotion of National Reform* (Cincinnati, 1847), 16–24, 43–44; Wilentz, *Chants Democratic,* 159, 164–65; Pessen, *Most Uncommon Jacksonians,* 119; Sumner, "Citizenship," in Commons et al., *History of Labour in the United States,* I, 190, 193.

8. "The System of Compensation—As It Is, and as It Should Be," *Mechanic's Advocate* (Albany), January 29, 1848; speech of Ely Moore, 1833, in Blau, ed., *Social Theories of Jacksonian Democracy,* 290; *Liberator* quoted in *Voice of Industry* (Fitchburg, Mass.), April 3, 1846; Report by J. C. Stanley in *Working Man's Advocate* (New York), October 3, 1829, in Commons et al., eds., *Documentary History of American Industrial Society,* V, 149–52. See *Working Man's Advocate,* 1845–47, for George Henry Evans' views, which are in virtually every issue; Roy Marvin Robbins, "Horace Greeley: Land Reform and Unemployment, 1837–1862," *Agricultural History,* VII (1933), 18–41; Helene Sara Zahler, *Eastern Workingmen and National Land Policy,*

"in England the poor are ground down to the starving point, by unjust laws[,] banking and other wicked monopolies."[9] Laborers quickly pointed to the machinery of government as a cause of their poverty and wealth-holding imbalances. They used, in short, the lessons of the political economy of aristocracy. A bitter and loud howl from labor leaders deafened the rest of American society as the working class denounced monopoly and special privileges. Perhaps only Locofoco Democrats used the term *monopoly* more often than those representing the working class.[10] The objects of the attack were frequently banks and tariffs. Thus working-class political demands and the platform of the equal rights wing of the Democratic party converged.[11]

Yet working-class leaders and (presumably) their followers went beyond the confines of the republican theory of the distribution of wealth. At best, the revolutionary generation's teachings were only a subset of their ideas. Even though American workers found other mechanisms for improper wealth distribution, their concepts about the distribution of wealth—and especially their solutions—remained fuzzy.

Compared to the members of the Jeffersonian political axis (not to mention those on the Hamiltonian axis), working-class leaders called for a drastic narrowing of the legitimate and justifiable boundaries on the distribution of wealth. Few individuals in the nineteenth century—one is tempted to say none—ever called for absolute equality in wealth-holdings.[12] Three concerns seem to have influenced working-class thinking on the distribution of wealth.

1829–1862 (New York, 1941), 14, 19–25, 33–38, and *passim;* Pickering, *Working Man's Political Economy,* 24, 31; Henry Hoagland, "Humanitarianism (1840–1860)," in Commons et al., *History of Labour in the United States,* I, 524–25.

9. Speech of Seth Luther in *National Trades' Union* (New York), August 16, 1834.

10. For example, speech of Ira Hutchinson, 1858, in Thomas Earle and Charles T. Congdon, eds., *Annals of the General Society of Mechanics and Tradesmen of the City of New-York, from 1785 to 1880* (New York, 1882), 325–26; memorial in *Mechanic's Free Press* (Philadelphia), October 25, 1828, in Commons et al., eds., *Documentary History of American Industrial Society,* V, 43–44; *Voice of Industry* (Fitchburg, Mass.), February 12, 1847; Simpson, *Working Man's Manual,* 76–78, 86, 180–84; Pickering, *Working Man's Political Economy,* 71–74, chaps. 15, 16.

11. The close affinity between working-class leaders and Locofoco Democrats based on antimonopoly has been noted by many historians: Pessen, *Most Uncommon Jacksonians,* 27; Schlesinger, *Age of Jackson,* 79, and chap. 11; and Bruce Laurie, *Working People of Philadelphia, 1800–1850* (Philadelphia, 1980), 109–15.

12. For example, Simpson, *Working Man's Manual,* 28, 52; William Sylvis, speech, July 5, 1859, in James C. Sylvis, ed., *The Life, Speeches, Labors and Essays of William H. Sylvis* (Philadelphia, 1872), 30–31; "The Rothschild's Wealth," *Voice of Industry* (Fitchburg, Mass.), July 3, 1846; Seth Luther, *An Address on the Origin and Progress of Avarice and Its Deleterious Effects on Human Happiness . . .* (Boston, 1834), 40.

First, a rough equality of wealth arose because, in Stephen Simpson's words, "the true and just mode of distributing labour is, by giving value for value." When equivalents were exchanged without force or coercion—a laissez-faire criterion—then justice and equality were served. Second, trade favored the few and deprived the many when something—such as government—intervened to offset the natural and uncoerced exchange of equivalents so that one side could take advantage of the other.[13]

The third element in working-class understanding of wealth distribution was its battle with the rest of society over a particular reading of the labor theory of property/value, which involved the amount of reward mental toil deserved. Since the time of the Revolution, and probably much before, the elite elements in American society always affirmed that mental activity was labor, that it was worthy labor, and that it merited great reward—this was in essence the spirit behind the "natural aristocracy" ideas of Jefferson, Adams, and Hamilton. The advent of industrialization and commercialization increased the employments requiring exercise of mental powers, creating heroes out of lawyers, inventors, and others. Many politicians and commentators believed that widespread education would advance wages, and more than a few argued that one of the benefits of republicanism was to demolish the aristocracy's monopoly on knowledge. Workingmen joined the crusade to institute free public schools partially because they thought education promised a better distribution of wealth and as an act of antimonopoly.[14] But mental power was clearly receiving more reward than manual labor. Horace Greeley once argued to San Francisco mechanics that while republicanism recognized "all useful labor as essentially laudable and honorable," nevertheless "simple manual labor can never achieve the highest reward, nor command the greatest regard."[15]

Workers lambasted the division of toil into mental and manual spheres and especially the huge differential in reward between the two types of work. The editor of the *Mechanic's Advocate* asked in 1848, "On what authority is based the existing distinction between the compensation of intellectual and physical

13. Simpson, *Working Man's Manual,* 70–78, 87, quote on 69.

14. For example, *Working Man's Advocate* (New York), November 14, 1829, March 6, 1830; *Mechanic's Free Press* (Philadelphia), October 3, 1829; Philipsburg, Pa., Working Men's meeting, *ibid.,* October 24, 1829.

15. Speech of Greeley at San Francisco, in New York *Tribune,* September 13, 1859, p. 7. A recent contribution on this theme, stressing the inegalitarian nature of American middle-class, free labor thought, is Glickstein, *Concepts of Free Labor in Antebellum America.*

labor?" Stephen Simpson, though admitting that some inequality of wealth was bound to exist, nonetheless asserted that "the difference between the powers of man, is not so great, as to produce a vast disparity in their productions and acquisitions."[16] Working-class leaders thus envisioned a natural wealth distribution as one without either true poverty or true opulence—only gradations around a middling level.

When the laboring community considered the forces distributing the nation's wealth and income, they passed beyond the confines of the republican theory of the distribution of wealth. Ultimately, the employer was responsible for depriving laborers of their just fruits. The first indication that workers faulted the economic reasoning of republicanism was the rejection of the central belief that inequality was solely a political phenomenon that took form in legislative enactments. Laborers poked beyond the political realm into the socioeconomic realm to find the source of inequality.[17]

In 1805, in the preamble to their organization's governing document, New York cordwainers stated that they organized "to guard against the intrigue or artifices that may at any time be used by our employers to reduce our wages." A report by J. McCune Smith in 1851 blamed the "enormous combination of capital" for inevitably "grind[ing] the face of the poor in the cities." In a New York City sympathy meeting for the striking Lynn cordwainers, Charles McCarthy stated, "The bosses had ground them down to the lowest point."[18] The notion of grinding down wages that was widespread among artisans and operatives between 1830 and 1860 indicated that working people believed a specific villain caused a maldistribution of wealth. Employers, owners of plants and equipment—not necessarily or even primarily governments and laws—caused laborers to take less than they deserved.

How the employer stole the fruits of labor from the worker was not clearly explained. The attacks by labor spokesmen on corporations and factories indicate that part of the explanation lay in their bigness—a violation of the small

16. *Mechanic's Advocate* (Albany), June 10, 1848; Simpson, *Working Man's Manual*, 52.

17. "Distribution of Wealth," from the *Budget* [?], in *Mechanic's Advocate* (Albany), March 4, 1847; address of W. F. Young in *Voice of Industry* (Fitchburg, Mass.), June 5, 1845; see Sumner, "Citizenship" in Commons et al., *History of Labour in the United States*, I, 192.

18. Quote of 1805 cordwainers from David J. Saposs, "Colonial and Federal Beginnings," in Commons et al., *History of Labour in the United States*, I, 119–20; New York *Tribune*, March 20, 1851, quoted by Commons, ed., *Documentary History of American Industrial Society*, VII, 97; remarks of McCarthy in New York *Tribune*, March 28, 1860, p. 8; Faler, *Mechanics and Manufacturers*, 170.

shop and its relationship to the craft tradition. Some rough equation was at work: size equaled power, and power equaled ability to suppress wages.[19]

Beyond the fear of bigness, explanations of how employers stole the fruits of labor from employees were seldom precisely detailed and more often left nebulous. Some recognized that under market conditions workers never could be free "while we have no controul over the price of the only commodity we have to dispose of—our labor."[20] Employers had the advantage of inventory, control of machinery and buildings, and the ability to wait for laborers to quit resisting and accept terms the owners laid down. The deciding capability was the time and resources capitalists had on their side, for workers who needed food immediately had no capacity to wait and so had to surrender to capitalist dictation.[21] At times various labor spokesmen approached the idea of "ownership of the means of production" as the source of capitalists' power, but never said so directly and unambiguously.[22]

More commonly, labor activists simply invoked the magical word *monopoly*. All capitalists became monopolists, and monopolists dictated market terms. An example of how working-class leaders used the monopoly theme is a proclamation given by the Labor Reform League of New England in 1846. Manufacturing by the "giant incorporate system" led to monopoly of the industry; and a monopoly could "prescribe such terms for the government of the operatives, as their own selfish and grasping interest suggest. Thus entirely abrogating the right of mutual contract, between the employer and employed, and leaving no other alternative on the part of the operatives, but submission

19. "Our Manufacturing System," *Voice of Industry* (Fitchburg, Mass.), September 4, 1845; comments of John Commerford and John Ferral, in *National Trades' Union* (New York), September 13, 1834, in Commons, ed., *Documentary History of American Industrial Society*, VI, 222–24; "Cause of Surplus Labor," *Voice of Industry* (Lowell, Mass.), August 7, 1847; Simpson, *Working Man's Manual*, 66–67; "The Factory System," *Working Man's Advocate* (New York), March 24, 1832; "Privileges," *ibid.*, January 10, 1835; Progress, "Government and Corporations," *Mechanic's Advocate* (Albany), June 3, 1847; Sullivan, *Industrial Worker in Pennsylvania*, 55–56.

20. *Pennsylvanian*, April 4, 1835, in Commons, ed., *Documentary History of American Industrial Society*, VI, 26; on discovery of property as the source of working-class problems, see "Anti-Monopoly," *Working Man's Advocate* (New York), June 27, 1835; Senex, *ibid.*, July 13, 1833; *New England Artizan*, "The Right to Property," *ibid.*, August 3, 1833.

21. *Voice of Industry* (Fitchburg, Mass.), November 7, 1845.

22. For example, "The Condition of Laborers," in Haverhill *Banner*, cited in *Mechanic's Advocate* (Albany), January 8, 1848; see Christopher L. Tomlins, *Law, Labor, and Ideology in the Early American Republic* (Cambridge, Eng., 1993), 9.

to laws, in the framing of which they had no voice, and the stringency of which increases in a fearful ratio to the growth of the system." Almost all working-class complaints about capitalists stealing the fruits of labor relied on a charge of monopoly.[23]

Convinced that employers, companies, and corporations mysteriously used monopoly powers to enrich themselves at the expense of workers, American laborers created an institutional device to right the injustice: the union. The verbiage surrounding unionization was pragmatic and earthy; the verbal analysis of the power of capital was imprecise and confused; but the behavior of workers was clear and unmistakable. Employers—not simply bankers, professionals, and legislators—stole the fruits of labor from the worker, and the union was established to get those fruits back. Ely Moore urged his working-class audience to join unions because they would enable "the producer to enjoy the full benefit of his productions, and thus diffuse the streams of wealth more generally." The union was the instrument of redistribution. One resolution of a shoe workers' meeting at the end of the Lynn strike of 1860 stated simply the redistributive purpose of unions: "Therefore, that we set our faces firmly in favor of combination, being fully convinced that it is the only effectual way whereby labor can successfully compete with capital." The weapon workers employed was the strike. The early unions of the 1830s disappeared, but, after a bout of utopian reform activity, numerous local unions sprang up in the mid-1840s, and in the 1850s several permanent national unions were established.[24] Workers expected the union to be the agent of redistributive justice, to restore to them their independence, the fruits of labor, and the full promise of republicanism.

It would appear that by 1860 American workers did not deny that capitalists

23. Address of the Labor Reform League of New England in *Voice of Industry* (Lowell, Mass.), October 9, 1846.

24. Ely Moore, Address, in *National Trades' Union* (New York), September 6, 1834; *Haverhill* (Mass.) *Gazette,* March 16, 1860; see also remarks of Robert Bruce, in Philadelphia *Public Ledger,* November 13, 1857; speech of Ely Moore, in Blau, ed., *Social Theories of Jacksonian Democracy,* 292. For nearly a quarter of a century, labor historians have eschewed institutional history in favor of a cultural/ideological approach. That perspective has reawakened and energized the field, making it probably the most creative of the "new" histories in the "new social history." But ignoring institutional approaches, in some cases blatantly denouncing institutional perspectives, has had costs. One of them has been a failure to incorporate the institution of the union into working-class culture. On the drive to unionization, see Ware, *Industrial Worker,* 227–30; Philip Taft, *Organized Labor in American History* (New York, 1964), 34–43; Laurie, *Artisans into Workers,* 50–51, 83–89, 101–103.

or employers were devoid of any productive function. Capitalists and company managers had a right to their fruits of labor just as the workers had a right to theirs. The union and the recourse to strikes were primarily to ensure an equitable distribution of the company's income. This insistence became the "equal rights" doctrine that flourished among labor leaders struggling to establish and spread unions. Thus Isaac J. Neal, president of the Moulder's Union, told a group of workingmen in Pittsburgh that unions were necessary "not to invade the rights of capital, but to protect those of the laborer."[25]

The impulse to form unions among American workers had two specific purposes: to reclaim an equitable distribution of wealth by ensuring that workers obtained the fruits of their labor and to contest subsistence Malthusian wages. Much of the pro-union literature of the antebellum period depicts subsistence wages as unfair and unrepublican. In no place was workers' rejection of political economy stronger than on wage determination. Wages were not to be set by market forces or competition. For many workers, competition meant competition among laborers to drive down wages for the benefit of capitalists. Rather, antebellum working-class literature posited a personal bargain based on "fair and full equivalents" between employers and wage earners. The conditions and remuneration of labor came from agreement between people, not the hidden workings of a strange mechanism called supply and demand.[26]

Beyond the idea of mutuality as a means of obtaining just compensation for labor, there is the important question of what labor leaders meant by "wage slavery." Working-class representatives rejected the idea of relative wages— that is, wages shaped by the changing conditions of supply and demand. Working-class literature advanced an absolute notion of wages, clothed in re-

25. Speech of Neal in Pittsburgh *Dispatch*, May 16, 1860; see also toast of R. C. Smith in Chicago *Tribune*, May 10, 1858. On the equal rights doctrine, see Dawley, *Class and Community*, 2–3, 9; Faler, *Mechanics and Manufacturers*, 186; Greenberg, *Worker and Community*, 26–27, 40; Siracusa, *A Mechanical People*, 163–66; Licht, *Industrializing America*, 46–56.

26. Simpson, *Working Man's Manual*, 66–67; "Capital and Labor," *Voice of Industry* (Fitchburg, Mass.), November 7, 1845; Pickering, *Working Man's Political Economy*, 90–91, 96; "The System of Wages," *Voice of Industry* (Boston), December 10, 1847; A Hand That Thinks for Itself, "Distributive Justice," *Mechanic's Advocate* (Albany), July 10, 1847; "War on Labor," *Voice of Industry*, May 22, 1846; "The Condition of Laborers," Haverhill *Banner*, quoted in *Mechanic's Advocate*, January 8, 1848; National Trades Union Convention, resolutions, 1834, quoted in Commons et al., eds., *Documentary History of American Industrial Society*, VI, 205. See also Wilentz, *Chants Democratic*, 90–93; David A. Zonderman, *Aspirations and Anxieties: New England Workers and the Mechanized Factory System, 1815–1850* (New York, 1992), 287, 293–94.

publicanism but probably independent of political philosophy. Wages should be high enough to afford a comfortable existence for a family, provide for old age, and permit education of children. The most insistent lament of working-class broadsides was that "wages [were] not sufficient to support a moderate family." According to the previously mentioned preamble to the Mechanics' Union of Trade Associations constitution, unions were vital to avert "the desolating evils which must inevitably arise from a depreciation of the intrinsic value of human labour."[27]

The idea of wage slavery filled the air and infiltrated the speeches and writings of working-class leaders, perhaps partly inspired by the crusade against slavery. When the term *wage slavery* appeared, it almost always meant starvation wages. As one person said in a protest meeting in 1857, "The way things are fixed we are mere serfs and slaves. The men that work the most get the poorest wages." Workers were spared the ignominy of an auction block but had to "sell themselves year after year, to toil like slaves for the bare necessities of life." Although workers had the rights of citizens, if they obtained only subsistence wages "what'll those there privileges amount to, if they come to nothing."[28]

Wage slavery is susceptible to at least two different interpretations, each of which spins off a train of consequences. The protests of antebellum workers and their use of the slavery analogy can be understood as a denunciation of the loss of independence. Instead of working for themselves through the honored route from apprentice to journeyman to master of the craft, urban laborers discovered that they remained frozen in a journeyman status and hence were always dependent on someone else—the capitalist—for employment and subsistence. Thus they were always in the position of taking orders and following the directions of another. A hierarchy had been established, and they occupied the lower portion of it. The analogy to slavery inhered in the word *dependence:* wage earning was similar to slavery in that production was divided into task-

27. On mutuality, see Wilentz, *Chants Democratic,* 93–95, 102. Quote from preamble of the Mechanics' Union of Trade Associations governing document in Commons et al., eds., *Documentary History of American Industrial Society,* V, 89; Trenton *True American,* November 9, 1857; William Sylvis, preamble of Iron Moulders' Union constitution, 1859, in Sylvis, ed., *Life, Speeches, Labors and Essays of William H. Sylvis,* 32. The phrase *family wage* is a gendered notion; see Boydston, *Home and Work;* 30, 155–56; Scott, *Gender and the Politics of History,* chap. 7.

28. Speech of Amos Cook, in Trenton *True American,* November 9, 1857; "Abolitionists" from the *Pleasure Boat* [?] in *Voice of Industry* (Lowell, Mass.), February 26, 1847; report of correspondent in New York *Tribune,* February 25, 1860, p. 6.

masters and task doers. And the task doers had lost their independence. This sense of wage slavery fit snugly into revolutionary republicanism's emphasis on citizens possessing economic independence.[29]

Yet the cry against wage slavery was often tied to the obvious comparison between the remuneration of free workers and southern slaves and was based on an anger at subsistence wages. For American workers, the level of wages said much about dependence or independence, about freedom or slavery. Free labor always received a just reward—the fruits of labor—that permitted a full material competence. Healthy wages indicated the value of a citizen in economic life and validated participation in political life. Low wages established dependence because subsistence not only disclosed how little one's productive contributions were valued but also starkly revealed that someone had the power to take from another the fruits of his or her labor. An independent citizen claimed and received a competence; a dependent person submissively accepted a subsistence. The cry of "wage slavery" most often meant little about working for others or the wage bargain or the commodification of labor; it was a denunciation of Malthusian wages.[30] High wages, regardless of the economic system, indicated independence, mastery, and freedom. In this sense, therefore, unions sought to elevate workers' wages (to reclaim their just fruits of labor) and to combat monopoly, and so they were inherently antimonopoly *and* antislavery institutions.

The rest of American society was not ready for working-class explanations and certainly not for working-class behavior in the form of unions and strikes. Denunciations of strikes and unions pervaded newspaper columns and political speeches. Among the multitude of reasons non-working-class leaders provided for fearing unions, one strain merits elaboration. Editors and politicians broadly asserted that equal political rights were sufficient to

29. For example, "The Condition of Laborers," Haverhill *Banner,* in *Mechanic's Advocate* (Albany), January 8, 1848; Frederick Robinson, speech in Blau, ed., *Social Theories of Jacksonian Democracy,* 327–28; "Black Slavery and White Slavery," *Voice of Industry* (Lowell, Mass.), August 14, 1847. For an elaboration of the dependence theme, see Wilentz, *Chants Democratic,* 91–95, 232, 244–45.

30. Norman Ware made this point seventy years ago in *Industrial Worker,* 50. David Roediger interprets working-class oratory in the antebellum decades differently. He maintains that the term *wage slavery* was seldom employed, that wage slavery had a racist connotation, and that workers viewed themselves differently from slaves because of citizenship rather than economic status. See Roediger, *The Wages of Whiteness: Race and the Making of the American Working Class* (London, 1991), 66–72 and *passim.*

enable each person to enjoy the fruits of his or her labor and that no illegitimate transfers of income or wealth from producers to nonproducers could be accomplished without the exercise of political power. The marketplace, journalists and politicians stated, set the wages of labor. The only way wages could be pushed out of a natural position (*i.e.,* out of a competitive marketplace determination) was by monopoly. Yet most non-working-class observers of the American economy did not see monopoly, except in cases of government favoritism. Rather, most saw a plethora of small shops competing with one another. Non-working-class commentators might agree that individual employers were mean, stingy, and cruel, but in a competitive situation, the obvious answer was to "strike out" for a new job with a different employer. As long as production appeared competitive and not monopolistic, upper- and middle-class Americans told workers that republicanism and free labor gave them the right to switch employers. Indeed, from the non-working-class perspective, the monopolists were the workers themselves. The only element of size many commentators saw in various economic pursuits was the union, not the employers. During the Lynn strike of 1860, the largest strike in American history before the Civil War, the cry of monopoly had a dull tone to many when they realized that the city of Lynn had several hundred employers and large-scale operations were not characteristic of the industry.[31]

The reaction of the rest of society to unionization and strikes hinged on the perception of what side possessed monopoly power. Throughout much of the nineteenth century, the economy looked competitive and it appeared that workers sought a form of monopoly control, even though they couched all their actions in the name of equal rights. When the middle classes acknowledged that production had become monopolized and saw business behavior as monopolistic and reprehensible, a shift emerged favoring unions as an appropriate means to curb industrial avarice and reestablish an equitable division of earnings between labor and capital. This is essentially what happened in the 1930s when large-scale corporations lost their legitimacy and came to resemble grasping, arrogant monopolies; middle-class opinion swung to labor unions as a means of halting the power of large corporations.

31. On the Lynn strike, see Faler, *Mechanics and Manufacturers,* 222–33; Dawley, *Class and Community,* 78–89; James L. Huston, "Facing an Angry Labor: The American Public Interprets the Shoemakers' Strike of 1860," *Civil War History,* XXVIII (1982), 197–212.

Much institutional development in the United States has derived from public understanding of the word *monopoly* and who the public believed exercised illegitimate power.

Working-class discussion of the distribution of wealth in the pre–Civil War years had an odd character. On one hand it contained with some fuzziness a radical critique of the market system—opposed to the existing distribution of wealth, competition, political economy, and political parties. On the other hand, the labor movement did not offer a radical solution to those ills—labor unions and antimonopoly caused trouble enough, but they would not destroy basic republican institutions or traditions.[32] An example of one who exhibited this tendency to a radical critique but not a radical solution was George Henry Evans, who scorched capitalism and American economic development with some of the most vitriolic columns in the period. But the availability of inalienable yeoman farms in the West for settlers was no radical reform and in fact was wholly understood and even framed within the Malthusian population-to-land ratio. The working-class critique of the operation of the American economy is deservedly called radical. But the solutions advanced were largely republican.

The four decades after 1815 were exciting, innovative, and anxious times for many Americans. A market economy developed, grew, and thrived, resulting in a multiplication of wealth, a quickening pace of activity—and a number of people upset with the tendencies of the age. Besides many members of the working class and not a few Whigs and Democrats, a group emerged that advocated withdrawal from marketplace operations into communitarian villages. The European socialist ideas of Robert Owen, Frances Wright, Etienne Cabet, Claude-Henri Saint-Simon, Charles Fourier, and German Marxists circulated in the antebellum United States. Many Americans became proponents of utopian, associationist, or socialist schemes, influenced either by secular visions or by a communal rereading of the New Testament of the Bible. John Humphrey Noyes at Oneida, George Ripley at Brook Farm, Adin Ballou at Hopedale, Robert Owen at New Harmony, Bronson Alcott at

32. Ronald Schultz implies that in Philadelphia the artisans began to absorb a socialist perspective in the late 1820s and 1830s; that interpretation probably anticipates developments by sixty years. See Schultz, *Republic of Labor*, 201, 214, and chap. 7. The reader should compare American working-class solutions to those proposed by the English Chartists. For the Chartists, see Richard Ashcraft, "Liberal Political Theory and Working-Class Radicalism in Nineteenth-Century England," *Political Theory*, XXI (1993), 251–52.

Fruitlands, Albert Brisbane, and to some extent Horace Greeley were a few of the individuals involved in the several scores of community experiments in the United States between 1820 and 1860.[33]

Historians have had some difficulty dealing with the communitarians of the antebellum period. Not only has antebellum socialism been ignored, somewhat surprisingly, by recent scholars, but those researchers who have delved into the communal experiments have often questioned the radicalism and motivations of their founders, the means by which the rest of society was to be affected by the experiments, and the organizational structure that was formulated. What appeared to have been radical was not very radical at all.[34] In their understanding and criticism of the distribution of wealth, however, the utopians were indeed the most radical of all Americans. Not only did they reject almost every philosophical argument of classical economics, but they also attacked many of the economic tenets of republicanism, the American proclivity to explain all events in political terms, and the individualism implicit in both the revolutionary heritage and neoclassical republicanism.

Communitarians did not hide their belief that the American distribution of wealth was immoral and getting more so. In his associationist-Fourierist phase, the Whig editor Horace Greeley, probably the most conservative associationist of the lot, nevertheless denounced vehemently the way American wealth was divided, for the wealth "goes into the hands of the Capitalist who owns the machinery, and not into those of the Laborer." The organ of John Humphrey Noyes's community, the Oneida *Circular*, noted the "passion for

---

33. For general treatments of utopian reform activities, see Alice Felt Tyler, *Freedom's Ferment: Phases of American Social History from the Colonial Period to the Outbreak of the Civil War* (1944; rpr. New York, 1962), chaps. 6–9; Whitney R. Cross, *The Burned-Over District: The Social and Intellectual History of Enthusiastic Religion in Western New York, 1800–1850* (New York, 1950), 238–48, 275, 332–38; Edward K. Spann, *Brotherly Tomorrows: Movements for a Cooperative Society in America, 1820–1920* (New York, 1989), chap. 5. Carl J. Guarneri's work will become the standard on utopian socialism in the United States: *The Utopian Alternative: Fourierism in Nineteenth-Century America* (Ithaca, N.Y., 1991).

34. Whitney Cross wrote about Fourier attempts, "But they grasped in no very realistic fashion the broader problems of an entire society and kept the movement an essentially emotional proposition, a fad, and a panacea" (*Burned-Over District*, 275). See also Ware, *Industrial Worker*, 167, 171–78; Henry E. Hoagland, "Humanitarianism (1840–1860)," in Commons et al., *History of Labour in the United States*, I, 498–507. A more favorable assessment is implied by Laurence Veysey in Introduction to *The Perfectionists: Radical Social Thought in the North, 1815–1860*, ed. Veysey (New York, 1973), 1–13. But see Guarneri, *Utopian Alternative*, 3–6.

acquisition" of wealth among Americans, but it was "at the present time so unjustly distributed, and so little enjoyed." A member of the Brook Farm community saw some classes increasing in wealth while others were decreasing, and "the extremes of riches and poverty [are] constantly increasing."[35]

The one axiom of republican wealth distribution that communitarians accepted was the labor theory of property/value. George Ripley wrote that the object of association was to secure to all "the fruits of their industry," and Albert Brisbane made it a point to underline that Fourierist phalanxes sought to dignify labor and to divide "equitably the product of their labor, every individual receiving a share according to the part taken in producing it, and giving to Labor, Skill and Capital, each, a just proportion or dividend." In explaining the evil of America's economic system, the associationist Earl Joslen wrote, "It does not secure to the laborer the proper, legitimate, and just reward of his labor." Robert Owen, founder of the communitarian experiment at New Harmony, Indiana, in 1825–1827, was probably the first reformer who tied anticapitalist critiques to the labor theory of value.[36]

At this point, however, the utopian socialists parted company with the republican theory of the distribution of wealth. Communitarians, especially Greeley, occasionally talked of land reform, and the word *monopoly* was thrown about to describe evil concentrations of power. In describing wealth concentrations over time, Albert Brisbane noted the impact of entail and primogeniture in England, and perhaps a few spoke about special privileges backed by governmental power. These comments, however, were simply asides. They were not the essence of the communitarian critique of the distribution of wealth.[37]

The communitarians followed a pronouncement by Albert Brisbane that is one of the rarest statements in antebellum political literature and is an utter

35. Horace Greeley, "Lectures for the People—No. 2," in *Voice of Industry* (Lowell, Mass.), April 9, 1847; Oneida *Circular,* December 10, 1857; John Thomas Codman, *Brook Farm: Historic and Personal Memoirs* (Boston, 1894), 36; Charles Crowe, *George Ripley: Transcendentalist and Utopian Socialist* (Athens, Ga., 1967), 192; Guarneri, *Utopian Alternative,* 36–44.

36. George Ripley to Ralph Waldo Emerson, November 9, 1840, in Henry W. Sams, ed., *Autobiography of Brook Farm* (Englewood Cliffs, N.J., 1958), 6; Albert Brisbane and Osborne Macdaniel, "What Is Association?" *Phalanx,* quoted *ibid.,* 93; Earl Joslen quoted in *Phalansterian Record,* I (1858), 16; on Robert Owen, see J. F. C. Harrison, *Robert Owen and the Owenites in Britain and America: The Quest for the New Moral World* (London, 1969), 66–72, 76–77.

37. For example, Codman, *Brook Farm,* 101; Marianne (Dwight) Orvis to Anna Qu. T.

repudiation of republican economic perspectives: "The EVILS *which afflict so-ciety are social, not political in their nature,* and a Social Reform only can eradi-cate them." Another interpreter of Fourier, the New York journalist Parke Godwin (who in the 1850s receded from his earlier radicalism) made the same point. Legislation had damaged society, he conceded, but "it is not the law, it is not political principle, that erects barriers . . . —it is our economical ar-rangements." Indeed, in an analysis that would fit in the twentieth century, Godwin related that the American and French Revolutions had overthrown feudal tyranny so as to establish a middle-class tyranny, the tyranny of the competitive market.[38]

The brunt of American republicanism on topics of political economy was simply that politics dictated economics and, more precisely, the distribution of wealth. From the time of the American Revolution to the 1840s—and in popular opinion several decades beyond—most Americans believed that once the political institutions were perfected and then safeguarded, social and economic ills would disappear. Figuratively, Brisbane, Godwin, and the communitarians cleared the air and basically said political institutions were irrelevant—a position not even working-class radicals dared assume. The communitarians argued that there were social and economic forces that acted independently of politics.

The "present system is false," wrote Brisbane, and there was agreement as to where the falsity lay: the system of "hired labor," the "Wages system." Laborers had no right to secure a position and when they did obtain jobs, they had no right to the fruits of their labor. George Ripley called the American economy an example of "Commercial Feudalism," while the Oneida *Circular* said that "the mercenary system of hiring one to help in executing the schemes of an-

---

Parsons, December 22, 1844, in Marianne (Dwight) Orvis, *Letters from Brook Farm, 1844–1847,* ed. Amy L. Reed (1928; rpr. Philadelphia, 1972), 54–55; [Cornelius C. Blatchly], *An Essay on Commonwealths* (New York, 1822), 14; T. D. Seymour Bassett, "The Secular Utopian Social-ists," in *Socialism and American Life,* ed. Donald Drew Egbert and Stow Persons (Princeton, 1952), I, 177.

38. A Fourierist [Albert Brisbane], "On Association and Attractive Industry," *United States Magazine and Democratic Review,* X (1842), 31, 33; Parke Godwin, *A Popular View of the Doctrines of Charles Fourier. With the Addition of Democracy, Constructive and Pacific* (1844; rpr. Philadelphia, 1972), 10. See also [Brisbane], "On Association and Attractive Industry," 167; Albert Shaw, *Icaria: A Chapter in the History of Communism* (1884; rpr. Philadelphia, 1972), 8; Guarneri, *Utopian Alternative,* 109.

other, fills society with a horde of unenthusiastic operatives—a class having no vital and living relations to their proper work." Improper wealth distribution was caused by the ability of capitalists to control money, machinery, and terms of employment. To some extent, communitarians found the source of the power of the capitalist class in the competitive struggle that modern economies established, and the communitarians found competition repugnant. Not only did competition create a social war of human against human, it allowed the immoral vice of avariciousness to flourish. On this point, a gulf widened between communitarian reformers and the main current in the rest of society. For many, laissez-faire was a path to equality. For the communitarians, laissez-faire was "pure selfishness," a means by which the mentally strong could overpower and subjugate and rob the mentally weak.[39]

Communitarians differed in their attitudes to property, but they harbored a sense that private property was held too sacredly in American society.[40]

39. Brisbane in New York *Tribune*, July 12, 1858; *Harbinger*, June 5, 1847, quoted in Commons et al., eds., *Documentary History of American Industrial Society*, VII, 217; Oneida *Circular*, June 24, 1858; George Ripley, "The Working Men's Movement," *Harbinger*, III (June 13, 1846–December 5, 1846), quoted in Sams, ed., *Autobiography of Brook Farm*, 191–92; Review of "Social Destiny of Man; or, Association and Re-organization of Industry," *United States Magazine and Democratic Review*, VIII (November–December, 1840), 433; Adin Ballou, *History of the Hopedale Community, from Its Inception to Its Virtual Submergence in the Hopedale Parish*, ed. William S. Heywood (1897; rpr. Philadelphia, 1972), v, xii, 10–11; Codman, *Brook Farm*, 34–35; "Association," *Mechanic's Advocate* (Albany), February 25, 1847; Horace Greeley, *Hints Toward Reforms, in Lectures, Addresses, and Other Writings* (New York, 1850), 235, 248; Albert Brisbane, *Social Destiny of Man: Or, Association and Reorganization of Industry* (1840; rpr. New York, 1968), III; J. J. S. in Oneida *Circular*, December 10, 1857; Charles Land, "Brook Farm," *Dial*, IV (1844), quoted in Sams, ed., *Autobiography of Brook Farm*, 89; John Sullivan Dwight, "Association in Its Connection with Education," *ibid.*, 105; George Ripley, "Life in Association," *Harbinger*, II (1845), *ibid.*, 159. On laissez-faire, quote in Georgiana Bruce Kirby, *Years of Experience: An Autobiographical Narrative* (1887; rpr. New York, 1971), 107; [New England Social Reform Society], *The Social Reformer and Herald of Progress* (Boston, 1844? 1845?), 6; Godwin, *Popular View of the Doctrines of Fourier*, 11–12; Cornelius C. Blatchly, "Some Causes of Popular Poverty," in [Thomas Branagan], *The Pleasures of Contemplation* (Philadelphia, 1817), 195–97.

40. Attitudes toward private property varied; see speech of John A. Collins in [New England Social Reform Society], *Social Reformer*, 69–73, 78; Harrison, *Robert Owen*, 76; [Blatchly], *Essay on Commonwealths*, 24–25; Spann, *Brotherly Tomorrows*, 11, 33; Godwin, *Popular View of the Doctrines of Fourier*, 50, 69–70; Horace Greeley, *Recollections of a Busy Life* (New York, 1868), 157; Ira L. Mandelker, *Religion, Society, and Utopia in Nineteenth-Century America* (Amherst, Mass., 1984), 37; Mark Holloway, *Heavens on Earth: Utopian Communities in America, 1680–1880* (London, 1951), 123–25.

Among the other aspects of American society that communitarians found obnoxious were social mobility and individualism.[41] Ultimately, the utopian socialists rejected every principle of market economics. And in rejecting individualism and qualifying property rights, the utopians as well broke away from republicanism.

The utopians championed values that were not central to antebellum American civilization. They argued for cooperation and sharing. The *Phalansterian Record* rejected entrepreneurial activity and self-seeking in work: "All our labor should be co-operative; we should work with others, for ourselves and others at the same time." Communitarians advocated socialism and communism. Utopians frankly avowed an egalitarian society and deprecated hierarchy. And they tried to unite manual and mental labor instead of reserving the rewards mainly for mental labor. George Ripley, the Unitarian leader of Brook Farm, wrote Ralph Waldo Emerson that the purpose of his experiment was "to insure a more natural union between intellectual and manual labor than now exists; to combine the thinker and the worker, as far as possible, in the same individual."[42]

As many have pointed out, the radicalism of the communitarians requires considerable qualification, especially from the standpoint of many mid- and late-twentieth-century standards. The utopians continued to harp on individual faults and seemed obsessed with religious moral principles. They repudiated violence and revolution and argued that they posed no threat to those enjoying unnatural amounts of wealth. Often communitarian experiments were established on a joint-stock-company basis, private property was not banned,

41. George Ripley, in *Harbinger,* July 17, 1847, in Commons et al., eds., *Documentary History of American Industrial Society,* VII, 222; Crowe, *George Ripley,* 192, 213–14; *Phalansterian Record,* I (March, 1858), 13–14; "God Owns All Things," Oneida *Circular,* March 18, 1858; Ballou, *History of the Hopedale Community,* 389–90; *Practical Christian* (Milford, Mass.), August 22, 1857.

42. *Phalansterian Record,* I (1858), 7, 14; *Practical Christian* (Milford, Mass.), August 22, 1857; E. H. H., Oneida *Circular,* July 22, 1858; "Genius and Communism," *ibid.,* June 24, 1858; John Humphrey Noyes, *History of American Socialisms* (1870; rpr. New York, 1961), 656–57; Codman, *Autobiography of Brook Farm,* 36–38; George Ripley to Ralph Waldo Emerson, November 9, 1840, in Sams, ed., *Autobiography of Brook Farm,* 6. See also W. G. B. in *Practical Christian* (Milford, Mass.), November 14, 1857; Oneida *Circular,* September 16, 1858, December 1, 1859; Michael Fellman, *The Unbounded Frame: Freedom and Community in Nineteenth Century American Utopianism* (Westport, Conn., 1973), 5; Sterling F. Delano, *The Harbinger and New England Transcendentalism: A Portrait of Associationism in America* (Cranbury, N.J., 1983), 39, 50; Crowe, *George Ripley,* 140, 166–67, 192–93.

and great attention was paid to marital and familial organization. Brisbane touted that the trouble with the modern economy was its inefficiency, wastefulness, and lack of scientific principles. For these and other reasons, the utopian attack on antebellum American society contained moderating elements.[43]

Whatever the shortcomings of the communitarians by any radical standards, in the antebellum period they articulated the most thoroughly radical analysis of political economy and distribution of wealth of any contemporary group. They broke with basic republican and revolutionary traditions. Moreover, unlike virtually any other group, the utopians went beyond articulation; they tried to create and live in alternative environments. Articulation of a critique has always been the easiest part of radicalism; actually developing alternative structures that embody and foster radical objectives had proved a formidable, almost an impossible, task. Their actions and behavior made the communitarians the radicals of their generation.

Utopian reformers were only a small segment of the frenzied reform movement that occurred in the United States between 1830 and 1860. While the utopians castigated the entire American institutional apparatus, other reformers chose a particular area in American life that required either a new mode of thinking or a new set of institutions. These "piecemeal" reformers agitated on such topics as intemperance, slavery, wars, care of the insane, incarceration of criminals, and education. Powered largely by evangelical conviction and confined principally to northern states, the reform movement at times sought to liberate individuals from repressive institutions of the past but at other times seemed to fasten new means of social control.[44]

43. G. W. N. in Oneida *Circular,* December 3, 1857; *Practical Christian* (Milford, Mass.), August 22, December 26, 1857. For an example of how religion became a vital issue, see [New England Social Reform Society], *Social Reformer,* 11–41. The authoritarian, free love aspect of communes has drawn more attention than its economic base; see, for example, Maren Lockwood Carden, *Oneida: Utopian Community to Modern Corporation* (Baltimore, 1969); Fellman, *Unbounded Frame,* chaps. 1, 3.

44. On the reform movement generally, see Tyler, *Freedom's Ferment,* 227–462; Veysey, ed., *Perfectionists;* Clifford S. Griffin, *The Ferment of Reform, 1830–1860* (New York, 1967); Mintz, *Moralists and Modernizers.* On social control, see Clifford S. Griffin, "Religious Benevolence as Social Control, 1815–1860," *Mississippi Valley Historical Review,* XLIV (1957), 423–44; James

Women's rights was a part of the antebellum reform activity, but it had an odd relationship to the discussion of wealth distribution. Women certainly suffered economic disabilities, as the rights' advocates pointed out. Women's earnings belonged to their husbands; women lost inheritances and property to men when they married; women were barred from most occupations because the doctrine of "separate spheres" and the "cult of domesticity" relegated them to familial tasks; and when women did work, they received much less pay than men for the same work.[45] Yet the antebellum women's rights campaign was oddly silent on distribution of wealth issues, unlike politicians, labor leaders, and communitarians. Women's rights activists seemingly aimed more at achieving full and equal participation in American life than obtaining an equitable distribution of its rewards.

The early women's rights movement showed fealty to distributionist themes that reflected the revolutionary heritage. Among the prominent complaints of women in the economic realm was the denial of access to employment. Mary F. Davis at a Utica, New York, convention in 1858 argued for college education for women so that they could be "released from the hopeless, protracted, wasting toil of unhealthy work-shops" and could instead enter "honorable and lucrative avenues of industry, where a just remuneration" permitted "independent character." Indeed, women's rights activists most commonly invoked the labor theory of property/value when discussing women's economic status. Elizabeth Cady Stanton called woman the "great unpaid laborer of the world" who was "not paid according to the value of the work done, but according to sex." During the Seneca Falls convention in 1848, a Mrs. Galloy made a speech that included a complaint that women still make at the close of the twentieth century: women agreed on "woman's right to equal wages for equal work." The legal doctrine that upon marriage the man assumes all the property of the woman and controls her earnings struck

---

L. McElroy, "Social Control and Romantic Reform in Antebellum America: The Case of Rochester, New York," *New York History*, LVIII (1977), 17–46; Ronald G. Walters, *American Reformers, 1815–1860* (New York, 1978), 34–35, 209.

45. Ellen Carol DuBois, Introduction to DuBois, ed., *Elizabeth Cady Stanton, Susan B. Anthony: Correspondence, Writings, Speeches* (New York, 1981), 8–9, 17, 99–100; Barbara J. Berg, *The Remembered Gate: Origins of American Feminism, the Woman and the City, 1800–1860* (New York, 1978), 5–7, chap. 4; Catherine Clinton, *The Other Civil War: American Women in the Nineteenth Century* (New York, 1984), 15, 17–19, 31, 72–73.

Mariana Johnson of Ohio as leveling women to the stature of slaves: "All that she has, becomes legally his, and he can collect and dispose of the profits of her labor without her consent, as he thinks fit."[46]

Nor did nineteenth-century feminists disdain the concepts behind the political economy of aristocracy. Ida Harper, an early biographer of Susan B. Anthony, remarked that in a convention at Syracuse in 1852 Anthony learned the essence of the political economy of aristocracy: "Any class which is compelled to be legislated for by another class always must be at a disadvantage." Caroline Dall, an upper-class Bostonian who called for more female entrepreneurs and better wages for women factory workers, agreed that superior talent deserved more reward than inferior talent, "but he [*sic*] has no right to increase any natural difference in his favor . . . by laws or customs which cripple the inferior." Often the women's rights activists translated the male enemy into an aristocracy—Stanton used the term the *aristocracy of sex*—and frequently talked of man's "monopoly" of women. Nineteenth-century feminists found the revolutionary heritage of antiaristocracy most suitable to their attack on gender biases and on that basis women demanded the suffrage. When representation was lacking, aristocrats used political power to enslave the politically powerless, and only by gaining a measure of political participation could women make sure that rulers observed their natural rights. As Lucy Blackwell's father once told her, "No governed class was ever yet without a grievance. Yet no governing class has ever been able to see that the grievance existed."[47]

46. New York *Tribune,* September 11, 1858, p. 5; Elizabeth Cady Stanton, Susan B. Anthony, and Matilda Joslyn Gage, eds., *History of Woman Suffrage* (2nd ed.; Rochester, N.Y., 1889), I, 28, 79, 105; speech of Stanton at Albany Convention, 1854, *ibid.,* I, 599–601; D[exter] C. Bloomer, ed., *Life and Writings of Amelia Bloomer* (1895; rpr. New York, 1975), 151; Caroline H. Dall, *"Woman's Right to Labor"; or, Low Wages and Hard Work: In Three Lectures, Delivered in Boston, November, 1859* (Boston, 1860), 6–7. See Suzanne Lebsock, *The Free Women of Petersburg: Status and Culture in a Southern Town, 1784–1860* (New York, 1984), 162; Amy Dru Stanley, "Conjugal Bonds and Wage Labor: Rights of Contract in the Age of Emancipation," *Journal of American History,* LXXV (1988), 471–500.

47. Ida Husted Harper, *The Life and Work of Susan B. Anthony, Including Public Addresses, Her Own Letters, and Many from Her Contemporaries During Fifty Years* (Indianapolis, 1898–1908), I, 81; Dall, *"Women's Right to Labor",* quote on 6, see 9, 48, 53–54, 62–63; Lois W. Banner, *Elizabeth Cady Stanton: A Radical for Woman's Rights* (Boston, 1980), 72–73; Memorial of New York City Convention, 1858, in Stanton, Anthony, and Gage, eds., *History of Woman Suffrage,* I, 675; first resolution of 1854 Albany convention, *ibid.,* I, 593; C. J. James, "Injustice of Our

Yet the calls for economic justice that emanated from the women's rights movement seemed to ask more for participation than for a better distribution. Together with the other demands of the group—entrance into the professions, acquisition of the ballot, and procurement of civil liberties—the distributive justice argument within the women's rights crusade, though present, was weak. The infirmity of an argument claiming a need to establish a just wealth distribution becomes obvious when a comparison is made with women workers in the mills, for example, the appeals of Sarah G. Bagley, president of the Lowell Female Reform Association. In their literature working women expressed outrage at minuscule wages, the grasping nature of bosses, the unsafe and noxious quality of work, and the sense that labor had been cheated out of its just reward.[48]

From the perspective of antebellum conceptions of wealth, a considerable distance opened between the analysis offered by those in the women's rights camp and those in the antislavery camp, let alone those in the working-class or the communitarian movements. Antislavery proponents could hardly overlook the economic function of slavery, and the distribution of wealth was tightly woven into northern understanding of the peculiar institution. Although leaders in the women's rights crusade incessantly compared the lot of woman with that of the slave—lack of civil rights and the suffrage, domination by others—the appeals were different. The women's rights leadership pleaded for participatory justice—the right to engage in activities and earn any rewards possible.[49] But much of the antislavery argument was based on distributive justice, the idea that slavery was characterized by a more visible

Labor System," *Revolution,* July 23, 1868, [37]; Otelia Cromwell, *Lucretia Mott* (Cambridge, Mass., 1958), 78; E. C. S., "The Laboring Man a Slave," *Revolution,* May 28, 1868; Alice Stone Blackwell, *Lucy Stone: Pioneer of Woman's Rights* (Boston, 1930), 6.

48. See *Voice of Industry* (Fitchburg, Mass./Lowell, Mass.), October 2, 1846, August 12, 19, 1848, June 12, December 26, 1845; Alice Kessler-Harris, *Out to Work: A History of Wage-Earning Women in the United States* (New York, 1982), 41–43, 61–63; Dublin, *Women at Work,* 91–94, 106, 110; Christine Stansell, *City of Women: Sex and Class in New York, 1789–1860* (Urbana, 1987), 46–52.

49. The discrimination by gender seems to have been more apparent to women's rights advocates than was distributive justice; see Jane Grey Swisshelm, *Half a Century* (3rd ed.; Chicago, 1880), 48; Lucy Stone, "Speech" (1855), in Aileen S. Kraditor, ed., *Up from the Pedestal: Selected Writings in the History of American Feminism* (Chicago, 1968), 71–73; Stanton, "Address Delivered at Seneca Falls" (1848), in DuBois, ed., *Elizabeth Cady Stanton,* 31; Stanton, "Address to the Legislature of New York on Women's Rights" (1854), *ibid.,* 45, 50. See Kraditor,

and forceful act of deprivation. In one case, the chance to exercise capabilities was thwarted; in the other, the rightful return to labor was denied.

A deeper gulf may have in fact separated antislavery and women's rights crusaders. In one sense, the Europeans had created a community in which women were incorporated. European men patriarchally granted women an inferior role, but they were nonetheless a part of the community. The women's rights activists sought a redefinition of their role in the community and possibly threatened the community. Perhaps the white male response, so often viscerally opposed to women's rights, was understandable in these terms. The family became one of the last vestiges of community in the United States, after all other established relationships had broken down. To lose the familial relationship was to lose the last remnant of community in American life and to be finally plunged into the darkness of totally atomized life.[50]

Slaves, however, were never incorporated into the white community as white women were. Slaves, on the basis of race, had always been kept separate from the European community. As a consequence, their appeals would have different forms and emotional underpinnings. White women, already in the society that wielded power, sought a different role in that society. Slaves, and to some extent their allies in the antislavery movement, sought the termination of the white community's war on the black community and hoped for some way to share power in a new community. These conditions may have shaped the different responses to the question of the distribution of wealth. For the women's rights crusade, distributive justice was a minor issue.

A host of reformers sought to reorganize the United States between 1830 and 1860, but the distribution of wealth was seldom a primary topic in their advocacies. Throughout the nation and at certain moments, discussion of the distribution of wealth flared and then quickly faded. Outside of the republican notion of the distribution of wealth, the working-class literature, and utopian reformers, no sustained analysis appeared as to why wealth distribution

---

Introduction to Kraditor, ed., *Up from the Pedestal,* 15–19; Gerda Lerner, *The Grimké Sisters from South Carolina: Pioneers for Woman's Rights and Abolition* (New York, 1967), 173; Banner, *Stanton,* 34, 72–76.

    50. The idea of the family as the last bastion of community in an atomized society has been propounded by Norma Basch, *In the Eyes of the Law: Women, Marriage, and Property in Nineteenth-Century New York* (Ithaca, N.Y., 1982), 140–41.

assumed the shape it did. Most of the reformers were unremarkable in their analyses, including the transcendentalists and educational reformers.

One who did see maldistribution but who could not escape the revolutionary analysis was the Unitarian minister Theodore Parker. Parker held that individual wealth had natural limitations, because "a man's hands will give him sustenance, not affluence." Parker saw the new aristocracy as the source of the problem, especially its materialist and avaricious ways, but he seemed uncertain as to how the aristocracy of gold manufactured its wealth. There were no political causes for New England's poverty, and so Parker found the problem to be a general moral weakness. The poor gave in to temptation, while the rich refused to abide by biblical ideas of human relationships and instead worshiped market relationships. Rejecting the associationist solution, Parker found that the only cure to American social evils was "the application of Christianity to social life."[51]

The exodus of Germans to the United States between 1840 and 1860 brought over not only republican liberals but individuals versed in adolescent European socialism and a few who were acquainted with Karl Marx. An active German press evolved, and it spread socialist ideals. Those concepts blamed the distribution of wealth on the economic system of free markets and on the preponderance of might in the hands of the middle class through its ownership of the means of production, applying class analysis to socioeconomic affairs, disclosing the evils of property and private ownership, establishing the inevitability of starvation wages, and revealing the increasing need for revolution in the name of proletarians. This analysis contained twentieth-century perspectives and broke cleanly with the American revolutionary republican tradition. But as of 1860 (or before 1880) it influenced immigrants but seldom the native-born citizenry. For many years, European socialism was confined to specific immigrant ethnic groups.[52]

51. Theodore Parker, "A Sermon on the Perishing Classes in Boston," in Cobbe, ed., *Collected Works of Parker,* VII, 54, quote on 58; Parker, "A Sermon on Merchants," *ibid.,* 5–7; Parker, "A Sermon on Poverty," *ibid.,* 98–109; Parker, "A Sermon on the Consequences of an Immoral Principle and False Idea of Life," *ibid.,* VI, 195, 198, 201–202. See also Octavius Brooks Frothingham, *Theodore Parker: A Biography* (Boston, 1874), 134–36; Anne C. Rose, *Transcendentalism as a Social Movement, 1830–1850* (New Haven, 1981), 112–13; Henry Steele Commager, *Theodore Parker* (Boston, 1936), 160, 163, 171, 183–84.

52. On immigrant German radicals, consult Karl Obermann, *Joseph Weydemeyer: Pioneer of American Socialism* (New York, 1947), 49–50, 55–65, 92–103; David Herreshoff, *American Disciples of Marx: From the Age of Jackson to the Progressive Era* (Detroit, 1967), 48–70; Carl

Four individuals discussed the distribution of wealth in greater detail than most and have become almost commonplace names in the American annals of protest. Langton Byllesby, Orestes A. Brownson, Josiah Warren, and Thomas Skidmore all developed and propagated distinct theories of the distribution of wealth.

Langton Byllesby (1789–1871), an Easton, Pennsylvania, mechanic and printer, had been influenced by the novel doctrines of Robert Owen. In 1826 Byllesby wrote *Observations on the Sources and Effects of Unequal Wealth,* probably the earliest attempt by an American to devote extensive space to the topic. Byllesby did not break away from the basic trends of republican ideas.[53]

Byllesby argued from a broad labor theory of value and posited that the wealthy grew rich by taking the fruits of others' labors. He found the origins of inequality in military despotism that captured governments and then oppressed the people. The military victors divided up the land and monopolized it. He split the population into producers and nonproducers and showed an enormous distaste for banking and merchandising. Byllesby insisted that the laws of inheritance must be changed; he was especially adamant about maintaining yeoman freeholds and eliminating large estates. At the close of his treatise, Byllesby quoted extensively from Robert Owen and William Thompson. To obtain equality in the distribution of wealth, Byllesby affirmed the labor theory of value, and he demanded that exchange should be "equal quantities of labour for other equal quantities."[54] Nothing in Byllesby's proposals deviated abnormally from the revolutionary heritage except his obvious belief that American republican institutions were producing an inequitable distribution of wealth.

Perhaps the most caustic, insightful, and abnormal explanation of the American distribution of wealth came from the quill of the momentarily

---

Wittke, *Refugees of Revolution: The German Forty-Eighters in America* (Philadelphia, 1952), 163–73; Wittke, *The Utopian Communist: A Biography of Wilhelm Weitling, Nineteenth-Century Reformer* (Baton Rouge, 1950), 27–53, 155–57.

53. Joseph Dorfman, Introduction, to Langton Byllesby, *Observations on the Sources and Effects of Unequal Wealth; with Propositions Towards Removing the Disparity of Profit in Pursuing the Arts of Life, and Establishing Security in Individual Prospects and Resources* (1826; rpr. New York, 1961), 6–23.

54. *Ibid.,* 28, 32–39; on land, 40–42; on bankers and merchants, 42–58; on producers and nonproducers, 59–62; quote on 104; chap. 3 on Owen and Thompson; for Byllesby's proposals, 104–106.

reform-minded Democratic activist Orestes A. Brownson (1803–1876). Hailing from a Yankee evangelical background, Brownson gravitated to New York City working-class politics in 1829 and 1830. He adopted universalism, preached in Boston in the 1830s, and became a confirmed Democrat. Shocked at the social misery following the Panic of 1837, he tried to rally workingmen to Van Buren's camp in the presidential election of 1840. This was the circumstance that led to his writing "The Laboring Classes," a review of Thomas Carlyle's *Chartism,* in the July, 1840, issue of the *Boston Quarterly Review,* followed by another article in October. The articles created a firestorm, and Brownson's essays became a separate issue in Massachusetts politics. Democrats lost in 1840, and Brownson evidently lost faith in the common man. He commenced a reevaluation of his ideas and by 1844 converted to Catholicism, adopted ideas of hierarchy, and eventually sustained the existing order.[55] Brownson's work demonstrates a frustrating aspect of much antebellum writing on the distribution of wealth: he devised a devastatingly radical critique of the forces that created a lopsided distribution of wealth but then offered bland solutions.

Between 1840 and 1844 Brownson believed that everywhere industrialization had occurred a profound inequality of wealth had emerged. In England this inequality did not come from the aristocracy but from the "middling classes." For the working class the "only real enemy is the employer." Workers had been transformed into slaves; they owned no means of production but instead were "solely dependent on their hands." In 1843 he emphasized that competition ensured starvation wages. The problem with the modern economy was a worship of mammon—its "supreme selfishness." "The evil is inherent in the system," proclaimed Brownson. "We say it is inherent in the *system of wages,* of cash payments."[56]

Yet for all of Brownson's radical analysis—the wage system was the problem, employers stole the fruits of labor, capitalists monopolized the means of production—his solutions were thin gruel. Brownson agreed that some inequality of wealth was to be expected, but the grotesque distortions came from politics. He went straight back to the ideas in the political economy of aristocracy. Legislation merely aided the wealthy; chartered privileges to

55. See Americo D. Lapati, *Orestes A. Brownson* (New Haven, 1965), chaps. 2, 3.

56. Orestes A. Brownson, "The Laboring Classes," *Boston Quarterly Review,* III (1840), 362, 364; Brownson, "The Present State of Society," *United States Magazine and Democratic Review* (1843), in Henry F. Brownson, ed., *The Works of Orestes A. Brownson* (1843; rpr. New York, 1966), IV, quotes on 449, 453, and generally 436–56.

banks were to be repealed and a revenue tariff installed. The ultimate determinant of maldistribution of wealth was excessive government: "There has been thus far quite too much government, as well as government of the wrong kind. The first act of government we want is a still further limitation of itself." The only adventuresome proposal Brownson made was that inheritance be eliminated. He argued that upon a person's death, the property that individual had acquired should be given to the state and then disposed of for the general welfare. Even this proposal, which Brownson intimated could not be implemented without a violent class struggle, was not much more than an extrapolation of the revolutionary generation's animus to the inheritance laws of entail and primogeniture.[57]

After Brownson converted to Catholicism, he altered many of his previous Protestant notions—indeed, he traced his own radicalism to the anarchist, antihierarchical, individualist tendencies in Protestantism. Over time, Brownson came to support a more activist government, almost to the point of being labeled a Whig. He also came to believe that political equality was dangerous and had no relationship to social equality except in foolishly stimulating people to achieve it. By the 1850s Brownson called for a return to a craft industry in which the workers owned their own tools. Only in one way did Brownson truly deviate from American norms: he justified social relations in European medieval society. Except for the writings of some extreme proslavery advocates, no period in the world's past drew more scorn and rebuke from every class of Americans than the "Dark Ages." In his support of the positive side of feudalism, Brownson was unique among northerners.[58]

An inconsistency pervades Brownson's approach that tended to be true for most radical egalitarians addressing the distribution of wealth in the antebellum era. When politicians said that politics generated imbalances and solutions had to be found in political operations, they were at least consistent. The source of the evil was found, and the remedy had a direct relationship to

57. Brownson, "The Laboring Classes," 391–94; Brownson, "Our Future Policy," in Brownson, ed., *Works of Brownson*, XV, 126–27; Brownson, "Come-Outerism," *ibid.*, IV, 542–43.

58. O. A. Brownson, "Socialism and the Church," in Brownson, ed., *Works of Brownson*, X, 86; Brownson, "The Convert," *ibid.*, V, 104. On feudalism and Brownson, see O. A. Brownson, "The Present State of Society," *ibid.*, IV, 439–41. On his later economic views, see his "Socialism and the Church," *ibid.*, X, 84–85, 98; "The Convert," *ibid.*, V, 62–64, 114–17; Lapati, *Brownson*, 63–64, 82–89.

the cause. But in Brownson's case, the analysis of the cause of the evil did not at all match the proposed solution. Even in his later period, Brownson said the "mother-evil" of economic life was the separation of labor and capital into antagonistic classes in which capitalists had the ability to exploit workers and depress wages to the subsistence level.[59] If the cause of the inequality was the capitalists' ability to depress workers' wages, then the proposed solutions of negative government, a lower tariff, antimonopoly, the gold standard, and even drastic inheritance laws, seem beside the point. None of the remedies had any tangible effect on the suspected causes of wealth imbalances. The obvious implication for an explanation of wealth imbalances created by the economic power of capital over labor was either some redesign of economic institutions or the intervention of a new power in the wage process. It appears that only communitarians were consistent in this regard.

One of the lesser known but most intriguing figures who investigated the distribution of wealth was Josiah Warren (1798–1874). Warren, evidently related to the Revolutionary War hero Dr. Joseph Warren, had been a member of the New Harmony commune led by Robert Owen and Frances Wright. The commune failed within two years, and Warren wrote that he spent the next sixteen years trying to lay out the basis for a new and more just society. In 1846 he published the result of his musings, *Equitable Commerce.* His solution rejected socialism and communitarianism, however, and instead developed a fierce individualism that was an outburst of pure anarchist thought. Warren pushed the labor theory of property/value to its logical conclusion.

Warren believed that since the coming of industrialization and commercialization, society had experienced constant revolution and class warfare. The preeminent question before humankind was "the proper, legitimate, and just reward of labor." To solve the problem, Warren insisted on individuality, the "sovereignty of self," that each person was a "SUPREME LAW UNTO HIMSELF." Governments failed in their basic function, protection of person and property, and therefore each person must be his or her own government. The source of American economic problems was the determination of value. Because nations refused to adopt the right standard of value, prices, which were supposed to reflect value, fluctuated wildly. This price fluctuation caused competition, as individuals combated each other to take advantage of price

59. O. A. Brownson, "The Convert," in Brownson, ed., *Works of Brownson,* V, quotes on 114, 115, and see 115–17.

changes, and that allowed a few to grab great rewards with a minimum of work—hence the maldistribution of wealth.[60]

To rectify the situation, Warren went to its source. Since labor was the foundation of all value, labor must be made the standard. The cost of any item in Warren's economics was the labor bestowed on the object. Therefore, for the price to encompass the actual value of the object, it must account for labor cost, or the amount of labor time embedded in the good. This was Warren's great principle: "COST, then, is the only rational ground of price." Warren next outlined a society in which laborers traded labor-time notes among themselves for exchange, say four hours of cobbling for four hours of wheat harvesting. Each laborer was assured of his fruits—his property—and no one could steal the fruits of labor from another because all values were based on labor time— not supply and demand as expressed in market prices. This system of complete individuality led to cooperation instead of competition, and because coopera- tion was an absence of coercion no need arose for an agent of coercion, which was government.[61]

Warren slowly put his ideas in practice around Cincinnati, but his program blossomed when the Boston abolitionist, then anarchist and free-love advocate Stephen Pearl Andrews, read *Equitable Commerce.* For Andrews, the revealed truth of cost the limit of price burned away all other economic principles. In 1851, the two established on Long Island an anarchist commune called Mod- ern Times. Modern Times had no government and no rules; economically, it ran on labor-time notes (evidently figured out on a basis of corn value). The colony worked quite well. During the Panic of 1857, when banking notes be- came worthless, some Long Islanders used Warren's labor-time notes—which lost none of their value—to pay taxes. It was not the radicalism of the experi- ment that caused its downfall, however, but the social disapproval emanating from a group of devout free-lovers who moved into the commune, giving it a most scandalous reputation. Andrews and Warren could not protect their col- ony, ironically, because sovereignty-of-self precepts denied them the justifica- tion to expel the free-lovers, and anarchism left the colonists with no means to enforce standards. Modern Times disintegrated during the Civil War as popu-

60. Josiah Warren, *Equitable Commerce: A New Development of Principles for the Harmoni- ous Adjustment and Regulation of the Pecuniary, Intellectual, and Moral Intercourse of Mankind, Proposed as Elements of New Society* (New Harmony, Ind., 1846), 10–13, 15–17, 19–24, 26, 36, and generally 3–10. This tract is mispaginated.

61. *Ibid.,* 7, 12–14, quote on 14, 15, 51–53, 69–70.

lar animosity over the colonists' sexual proclivities was reinforced by a patriotic war fever.[62]

Josiah Warren took the labor theory of property/value to its logical end point—not communitarianism or socialism but anarchy, individualism, and property. The labor theory of property/value had, of course, an important drawing power for economic dissidents because it conceptualized how the distribution of wealth became lopsided, how the few took advantage of the many; it had the promise of being a measuring stick to calculate oppression. But the labor theory of property/value was irredeemably propertarian and individualistic. It stated simply and forcefully that only individuals created values, those values were created only by labor, and only laborers—absolutely no others—deserved possession of those values. Even in the case of oppression, the remedial action was to give the fruits of labor, that is, property, to the individual who deserved it. One cannot possibly read into the labor theory of property/value a program for ending property rights and for establishing communitarian institutions. The Lockean equation that the individual act of labor created and justified property rights is inherent in the doctrine, no matter how badly the generations mangled its distribution through government machinery or inheritance laws.

The most unusual and insightful commentator on the American distribution of wealth was Thomas Skidmore. Skidmore, born in Connecticut and apprenticed as a machinist, gravitated to New York City in the 1820s. He became a leading organizer and spokesman for the Working Man's party of 1829–1830 and fought with Frances Wright, Robert Dale Owen, and George Henry Evans over the appropriate program for the nation's mechanics. Skidmore hoped for an agrarian division of property, whereas Wright and Owen emphasized education and equal rights. The Working Man's party divided over leadership problems—evidently Skidmore had an imperious personality—and Skidmore died in 1832 before he could further develop his ideas.[63]

62. Madeleine B. Stern, *The Pantarch: A Biography of Stephen Pearl Andrews* (Austin, 1968), 73–86; Eunice Minette Schuster, *Native American Anarchism: A Study of Left-Wing American Individualism* (Northampton, Mass., 1932), 98, 100–110; James J. Martin, *Men Against the State: The Expositors of Individualist Anarchism in America, 1827–1908* (De Kalb, Ill., 1953), 13–64, 81–82.

63. On Skidmore, see Pessen, *Most Uncommon Jacksonians*, 58–60, 65, 69, 177; Veysey, ed., *Perfectionists*, 83; Sumner, "Citizenship," in Commons et al., *History of Labour in the United States*, I, 234–45.

In 1829 Skidmore wrote *The Rights of Man to Property,* in which he laid out his analysis of the causes of the maldistribution of wealth and its solution. The tract is not particularly remarkable. Skidmore revealed his preference for an equalization of property, but he cautioned that he most feared property when it was "so enormously unequal, as we see it at present." He found that the few were stealing the fruits of other people's labor. Inequality originated from governmental action, when "mankind having suffered governments, to cheat much the greater part of the posterity, who succeeded them, out of their rights of property, through the instrumentality of wills." He attacked monopolies, business charters, and banking in general.[64]

At the heart of his proposals were inheritance laws. Skidmore denied the necessity or legitimacy of property rights. Over time property had accumulated in a few hands because of inheritance laws. To equalize property, Skidmore argued—and presented an elaborate plan for effecting the goal—that upon death a person's estate should be confiscated by the state and then doled out equally to all males over eighteen years of age.[65]

Skidmore's insistence on equality and the importance of inheritance laws was extreme, perhaps unique, but not out of the mainstream of American thinking on wealth distribution. Ever since the Revolution, Americans had stressed the skewing effects of improper inheritance laws. Skidmore simply pressed further. His radicalism was most evident in his willingness to sanction government intervention and reallocation. But his attack on banks, paper money, and legislation were all in the mainstream of American thought on wealth distribution. Indeed, Skidmore suffered the same defect as did Brownson. After declaring that much inequality was traceable to the ability of capitalists to take advantage of laborers, Skidmore offered a remedy—confiscation of inheritance—that would not remedy the mechanics of inequality, the capitalist-laborer relationship.[66]

---

64. Thomas Skidmore, *The Rights of Man to Property! Being a Proposition to Make It Equal Among the Adults of the Present Generation* (1829; rpr. New York, 1964), quotes on 3–4, 155, generally see 60–61, 160–72, 179–89.

65. *Ibid.,* 137–39, 144, 270–357.

66. Of course, having found the origin of inequality in transmission of property through the generations, Skidmore was consistent in emphasizing a new inheritance procedure that would halt the perpetuation and enlargement of that sin. By that standard, Noah and Daniel Webster were radicals, for they believed improper wealth accumulations came from the same source, but they averred that partible inheritance would rectify the situation.

Skidmore's real radicalism lay in another part of his analysis. He denied the labor theory of property/value. From 1776 to 1900 the labor theory of property/value was the hinge upon which almost all American economic analysis swung. A few doubted its veracity as an explanation of all value, but almost no one denied that it was an important element of value. In the popular realm, the labor theory of property/value reigned supreme.

Skidmore denied the labor theory of property/value and so in his own way became the unique American investigator of the forces that shaped the distribution of wealth. And he saw to the heart of the matter—a community could not be built on a principle of uncompromising individuality and property rights, and the labor theory of property/value was the ultimate pillar of the legitimacy of property rights and individualism. Skidmore began his treatise in an out-of-date eighteenth-century Enlightenment discussion of the state of nature. He declared by page 5 "that no man has any just and true title to his possessions at all." Whereas proponents of the labor theory of property/value always focused on the act of an individual bestowing labor time and labor skill on some natural object, Skidmore perceptively asked who gave any single individual the right or permission to bestow labor upon a natural object belonging to the community. All agreed that in the original state of nature only common ownership, not private property, existed. For an individual to appropriate something from nature to bestow his labor upon, the person had first to ask permission of the community. So community will ruled the question of property, determining its nature, disposition, and distribution. Property rights beyond the community's control did not exist because the community first sanctioned the creation of property. Skidmore was willing to use the labor theory of property/value as a practical standard; yet property rights were justified on functional, not natural, grounds. And when property rights became dysfunctional, society could decree a new order of things.[67]

Of all the American approaches to the distribution of wealth in the nineteenth century, Skidmore's was among the most unusual and most radical. Few others so decisively challenged property rights; only communitarians and abolitionists (in a highly limited way) made such attempts. Save for some communitarians, no other American discussion of the distribution of wealth rests

---

67. *Ibid.*, quote 5, 32–46. Cornelius Blatchly argued in the same vein; see Arthur Eugene Bestor, *Backwoods Utopias: The Sectarian and Owenite Phases of Communitarian Socialism in America, 1663–1829* (Philadelphia, 1950), 98–99.

on the premises devised by Skidmore—an open avowal of community rights. But no one else picked up Skidmore's contribution or trumpeted his doctrines. His theory did not influence the course of the debate on the distribution of wealth.

The question of property rights and the relations between labor and capital developed a sharper edge in the 1840s and 1850s. The words *socialism, communism,* and the *Left* entered the language. European, especially French, revolutions in 1830 and 1848 made the divisions of industrial society clearer and added to the discussion a growing apprehension of class warfare and bloodshed. One journal picked up a report that French communism was rapidly advancing in Paris in its "most hideous and abominable form—perfect community of goods, even perfect community of women." During the Panic of 1857, newspaper editors constantly referred to unemployment meetings as the work of "red republicans" and "Parisian red republicans." American journals discussed socialism with some frequency, and proslavery writers taunted northerners with the inevitability of class conflict, revolution, and the destruction of property rights as a result of the social conflicts produced by free market capitalism.[68]

Many Americans saw an explosion of socialist sentiments in the 1850s, and they did not shy away from comparing republicanism with socialism. Because so many newspaper editors commented on the merits and defects of each, it is hardly surprising that most mainstream Americans found socialism incompatible with republican institutions. And the clash was distinctly narrowed down to two areas: socialism violated the necessity of limited government and the labor theory of property/value.

Antebellum detractors of socialism had disparate complaints against the proposed system. Socialists destroyed the separate spheres between the sexes and so endangered femininity. Also, socialism was a philosophy of infidelity,

---

68. Correspondent of the *Britannia,* "French Communism," *Littell's Living Age,* XXIX (1851), 109; New York *Times,* October 27, 1857; (Easton, Pa.) *Argus,* November 12, 1857; Lancaster (Pa.) *Examiner and Herald,* November 18, 1857; Huston, *Panic of 1857,* 24–28; "Fourier & Socialists," *Dial,* III [1842], 86–96; [J. A. McMaster], "Societary Theories," *American* [Whig] *Review,* VII (1848), 632–46; "Agrarianism," *Atlantic Monthly,* III (1859), 394–402; Fredrika Bremer, "Impressions of England in 1851: From the Letters and Memoranda of Fredrika Bremer," *Harper's Monthly Magazine,* IV (April, 1852), 619–20; [Francis Bowen], "The Life and Opinions of Sismondi," *North American Review,* LXVI (1848), 34–70. On proslavery, see [George F. Holmes?], "Centralization and Socialism," *De Bow's Review,* XX (1856), 692–94.

lacking a religious base. A transcendentalist wrote that the problem with Brisbane and Fourier was that they conceived a human being as "a plastic thing." The abolitionist Gamaliel Bailey stood foursquare for laissez-faire, but he did concede that socialists—he was talking of Robert Owen—had "taught moralists and the world the immense importance of outward circumstances [*i.e.*, environmental causes] upon inward well-being, character and happiness. He went too far." Another mentioned that what the working class most wanted was possession of private property, not its abolition.[69]

Middle-class opinion of socialism by the 1850s was shaped much less by the nation's bout with utopian communitarianism than by the French revolution of 1848 and the national workshops of Louis Blanc. The national workshops appalled upper-income Americans, and they commenced a dialogue disabusing other Americans of the practicality and morality of this new French socialist development.

One of the first reactions of Americans to the idea of government-sponsored relief was that such programs inflated governmental power and thereby threatened liberty. It was potentially a system that led "to a despotism of the most intolerable character." The despotism was that the people were made dependent on the government for employment and sustenance. They thus lost their independence and with their independence their liberty. Herman Kreismann responded to socialist demands at a meeting of unemployed Chicago Germans in 1857:

> He showed that our government was not like the European despotism which they had escaped; that here there is no obligation on the part of the governing power to secure to the laborer food and work, because it leaves him always free to follow what calling or pursuit he may choose; that where government does not interfere by unequal taxation, unjust laws and the establishment of favored classes in times of prosperity, it cannot be expected to act as the nursing mother in times of distress.

Henry J. Raymond declared, interestingly, that the "doctrine that a man has a *right* to be supplied with labor and wages by the Government or anybody, whether his services are needed or not, is a doctrine which took its rise in aris-

69. [J. A. McMaster], "Societary Theories," *American* [Whig] *Review,* VII (1848), 641–45; "Fourier and Socialists," *Dial,* III [1842], 88; *National Era* (Washington, D.C.), quotes from August 27 and October 29, 1857. See also "On the Elevation of the Laboring Portion of the Community. Second Notice," *United States Magazine and Democratic Review,* VIII (1840), 59–61; "Agrarianism," *Atlantic Monthly,* III (1859), 396, 401–403.

tocratic countries in which the working classes are in a position of degradation and dependence." American newspaper editors read socialism as an outgrowth of aristocracy that created dependency and strong governments. And
aristocracy was the natural enemy of republicanism.[70]

The sudden cry of social and economic equality disturbed Americans.
They believed in equality by nature, but nature allowed for differences in talents and capacities, which implied that some inequality had to exist. Socialists tried to suppress a characteristic of the species implanted by nature, and
such an attempt could only lead to disaster. Wrote one contributor to the
United States [Magazine and Democratic] Review in 1854, socialism "suits the
negro.... Liberty exists among freemen, equality only among slaves."
Laissez-faire, no special privileges, and no monopolies were the true paths to
natural equality; the only path to equitable social relations was the republican
theory of the distribution of wealth.[71]

Moreover, American editorialists sensed that European socialism denied
the labor theory of property/value. It stopped individuals from acquiring as
much property as their labor might allow. Even the erratic editor James Gordon Bennett said that in the United States workers must be "self-reliant," that
"individual exertion is the secret of success in everything. God helps only
those who help themselves." Henry Winter Davis of Maryland, a Know-
Nothing and later Republican, discussed socialism in an address in Baltimore. Although Davis sympathized with the desire to right oppression, he
predicted that socialism would make no inroads in the United States because
free republican institutions "have accomplished the practical ends of the socialist." The republican experiment in the United States already guaranteed
laborers the fruits of their labor. A strong, centralized government worked
against this goal and did not aid in achieving it.[72]

70. Hazard, *Economics and Politics,* 36; speech of Kreismann in Chicago *Daily Tribune,*
November 16, 1857; editorial in New York *Times,* November 10, 1857. See also Philadelphia
Evening Bulletin, November 11, 1857; Cincinnati *Daily Gazette,* November 6, 1857; New York
Evening Post, October 23, 1857.

71. "French Republicanism and American Democracy: The Two Philosophies," *United
States [Magazine and Democratic] Review,* XXIV (1854), 275, quote 276. See also New York
Journal of Commerce quoted by Richmond *Enquirer,* November 20, 1857; *North American and
United States Gazette* (Philadelphia), April 13, 1858.

72. New York *Herald,* November 16, 1857; Henry Winter Davis quoted from Steiner, *Life
of Henry Winter Davis,* 74–76, and Gerald S. Henig, *Henry Winter Davis: Antebellum and
Civil War Congressman from Maryland* (New York, 1973), 64; see also speech of Andrew Johnson on agrarianism, April 29, 1852, in Graf and Haskins, eds., *Papers of Andrew Johnson,* II, 43;

The result of the American discussion of socialism in the 1850s was a middle-class affirmation of laissez-faire—often clothed in terms of the forces of supply and demand—and the republican theory of the distribution of wealth. It also showed one other facet. The driving force behind American republicanism was individualism, not community.

Overall, those who dissented about the quality of the American distribution of wealth did not receive a wide hearing. They barely deflected the overwhelming reliance of Americans on their republican theory of the distribution of wealth to explain appropriate policy choices and equitable outcomes. But in one reform movement, the republican theory about the distribution of wealth played a conspicuous, even overwhelming, role. And that was in the antislavery crusade.

New York *Tribune,* November 11, 1857; S. W. C., "Progress *vs.* Isms," *United States Magazine and Democratic Review,* XXVIII (1856), 109, 112; "Radicalism," *ibid.,* III (1838), 106–109; "Carlyle's Chartism," *ibid.,* VIII (1840), 22–23, 27.

9

The Revolutionary Legacy Confronts Slavery

Since the birth of the North American republic in 1776, slavery had been an institution at odds with the thrust of the Revolution. Slavery clashed most strongly with the two principal axioms of the concept of the distribution of wealth, the labor theory of property/value and the political economy of aristocracy. Several revolutionaries knew this and commenced an attack on the institution that in its core elements did not fundamentally change for nearly seventy years. By the time of Andrew Johnson's presidency the distributionist ideas of the revolutionary generation had reached their fullest expression on the topics of bondage and race.

The northern assault on the bastion of slavery took two particular forms regarding the American concept of the distribution of wealth. Abolitionists exhibited one mode, focusing their denunciations on the effect of the institution on the enslaved. They did not ignore other topics, but the central theme of their criticism was the damage slavery inflicted on the slaves. Abolitionists thus evoked the labor theory of property/value with a clarity and precision unmatched by other groups in society. As a consequence, they had to explain how emancipation would create a better distribution of wealth and how free labor would operate for the betterment of African Americans. Abolitionists were generally not impressive economic thinkers—their power always was in the moral, biblical realm—but the nature of the subject forced them to make some economic formulations.

Northern political leaders conducted the other half of the war on slavery based on distributionist arguments. Compared with the abolitionists, their concern for the welfare of the slave was considerably subdued, although the labor theory of property/value played an interesting role in dissipating some of the dense racism of the time. Antislavery politicians found the lessons stemming from the political economy of aristocracy far more useful to their electoral and political purposes. It was among the politicians that the idea of the slave power took shape, and the politicians, especially the Republicans, incessantly harped on the theme that slaveholders were aristocrats and aristocrats were the natural enemies of republics.

The surge in northern animosity to slavery produced a counterargument from the South in the form of the proslavery argument. The apostles of an eternal slavery had a somewhat ambiguous legacy in regard to the distribution of wealth, but at certain key points a distinct repudiation of the revolutionary legacy was developing. This circumstance was in many ways predictable, for in most areas the Revolution had little to condone the peculiar institution but much to condemn it.

Slavery's demise as a result of the Civil War and the attempt to formulate a position for the freed people led to perhaps one of the most central debates over distribution of wealth before the Progressive era in the first two decades of the twentieth century. In one of a few moments in American history, a desire to redistribute property from the rich to the poor (from the former slave master to the former slave) was considered. That it was not attempted revealed the true limitations of the revolutionary legacy. But it also underscored the relation that politics was supposed to play in achieving an equitable distribution of wealth. Many Republicans, while acknowledging that property redistribution probably was legitimate and conducive to better equitability, found that extension of political rights was a fair substitute for redistribution of land.

The collision between the proslavery and antislavery forces produced as well a fascinating discussion of property rights. Slavery involved the tender subject of property rights, and it becomes a measure of how much radicalism the revolutionary heritage invoked, and how potent was the American concept of the distribution of wealth, to witness the broad discussion of what constituted property among the political entities of the time; for the abolitionists, proslavery writers, Republicans, and Democrats contributed to this discussion. It causes a bit of a shock to recognize that the early Republican party demonstrated by its actions—emancipation—how tenuous property rights really were, even in a society that supposedly worshiped property rights above all else.

The antislavery revolutionaries were able to eliminate slavery in the North, where its roots were shallow and its economic power weakest, but then international affairs and the development of a party system deflected attention away from how suitable the institution was for a republic. Agitation over the peculiar institution resumed in a spectacular way when William Lloyd Garrison of Boston established an abolitionist paper, the *Liberator*, and defiantly and vituperatively attacked slavery and slaveholders in the first issue of January 1, 1831. Abolitionism then evolved and mutated as various individuals formed cliques and agitated in different ways the question of ending slavery. Between 1831 and 1850 abolitionism was largely a movement of individuals and small groups because attempts to create an umbrella organization had failed. All tended to agree, however, that slavery was a moral sin, that emancipation should occur immediately, that slaveholders deserved no compensation for the slaves, and that the most grievous problem connected with slavery and American society was race prejudice.[1]

Abolitionists used a variety of pleas to motivate the northern public to accept emancipation. Theirs was largely an evangelical moral crusade, guided by certain biblical passages. Abolitionists stressed the horrors of slavery, the separation of families, the outrageous brutality of the whipping post, and the immorality of selling human beings on an auction block. They warned of the dangers of slavery to national politics and the national economy; they also attacked pride in color and in caste.[2]

Abolitionists did present an economic analysis of free and slave labor. Yet when dealing with abolitionists and their speeches and literature, it is wise to remember that economic arguments were not foremost in their emphasis. Most abolitionist appeals had an argumentative cadence. Economic analysis was a part of the appeal, but only a part. Morality and sensitivity to suffering pervade abolitionist writing. Economic and political appeals developed par-

1. There are several good histories of abolitionism. See Stewart, *Holy Warriors;* Merton L. Dillon, *The Abolitionists: The Growth of a Dissenting Minority* (De Kalb, Ill., 1974); Gerald Sorin, *Abolitionism: A New Perspective* (New York, 1972); Louis Filler, *The Crusade Against Slavery, 1830–1860* (New York, 1960); and Dwight Lowell Dumond, *Antislavery: The Crusade for Freedom in America* (Ann Arbor, 1961).

2. See James L. Huston, "The Experiential Basis of the Northern Antislavery Impulse," *Journal of Southern History,* LVI (1990), 609–40; John R. McKivigan, *The War Against Proslavery Religion: Abolitionism and the Northern Churches, 1830–1865* (Ithaca, N.Y., 1984), 13, 20–21, 45; Jane H. Pease and William H. Pease, *They Who Would Be Free: Blacks' Search for Freedom, 1830–1861* (New York, 1974), 3–16, 33–41.

tially out of frustration at the lack of public response to the core appeal of humanitarianism and the willingness of some abolitionists to try anything to get northerners to see the evil of slavery. Economic thought was central to antislavery among people not necessarily moved by the plight of the slaves, the morality of slavery, or the damage of race prejudice, but it was less central to abolitionism.

When abolitionists stooped to talk of the material world, however, they revealed themselves the true heirs of the revolutionaries' understanding of the forces that shaped the distribution of wealth.[3] The concepts of the labor theory of property/value and the political economy of aristocracy utterly leap out of the pages of abolitionist writings. And some ironies may be perceived. Even though abolitionists tended to come from a New England culture and a political background of Federalism and Whiggery, their economic ideas tended to be even more slanted toward advocacy of laissez-faire than those of the most radical Jacksonian Democrat.[4]

Abolitionists insisted that they were the torchbearers of the American Revolution and the guardians of the hopes of a pure republican future. Indeed, abolitionists considered the American Revolution an incomplete and half-finished task.[5] The abolitionists brought not novelty to American values but an unyielding insistence that the values of the Revolution be carried out.

Like most other Americans in the antebellum decades, abolitionists did not often provide details about their thinking on the distribution of wealth, but in many ways they implied that wealth should be roughly equally distributed, that skewed distributions were the result of political machinations, and

3. Daniel J. McInerney, in *The Fortunate Heirs of Freedom: Abolition and Republican Thought* (Lincoln, 1994), chap. 5, has tried to explain abolitionist concern about political economy in terms of republicanism. By the middle of the nineteenth century, however, all writers had to confront the conceptual apparatus of British classical economists, and McInerney does not explore abolitionist thought on the economists' terrain.

4. For a different assessment, see Ashworth, *Slavery, Capitalism, and Politics,* I, 157.

5. Elizur Wright, Jr., *The Sin of Slavery, and Its Remedy; Containing Some Reflections on the Moral Influence of African Colonization* (New York, 1833), 3; Alvan Stewart, "Letter to Dr. Bailey," in Luther Rawson Marsh, ed., *Writings and Speeches of Alvan Stewart, on Slavery* (New York, 1860), 250; [Salmon P. Chase], Address of the Liberty Party, 1845, in J. W. Schuckers, *The Life and Public Services of Salmon Portland Chase* (New York, 1874), 72–73; Samuel J. May, *Some Recollections of Our Antislavery Conflict* (Boston, 1869), 4. Louis Gerteis has written in contradistinction to the argument above that in the free labor theorems of political economy, the middle class "transformed the republican values of the Revolution;" see Gerteis, *Morality and Utility in American Antislavery Reform,* xvi.

that absolute material equality was an impossibility. They accepted an inequality, but like so many others, they put a boundary on its extent.[6]

Abolitionists usually stressed the importance of the labor theory of property/value. An equitable society arose when each member obtained the value of his or her labor. Elizur Wright said that for whites—he perceived a racial barrier in the labor theory of property/value that few others did—the United States was a land like no other "country on earth, where a man can reap more fruit of his own honest labor, nor where he can enjoy it with less interference on the part of others." Slavery, of course, produced a disastrously skewed distribution of wealth because the slaveholders unjustly stole the fruits of the slaves' labors. Richard Hildreth put the idea in about the most precise form as any other: "It is an observation as curious as it is important, that in countries in which industry is respectable, and where the fruits of labor are secure, property always tends toward an equal distribution. Every man possesses as a means of acquirement, his own labor; and though there be a very considerable difference in the capacity, the industry, the good fortune of individuals, yet this difference has its limits; and diversities of acquisition are still more limited."[7]

Abolitionists exhibited their clearest thinking on the subject of the distribution of wealth, however, when they referred to the experience of ancient Rome. For them, Rome was a story of horror and evil, hardly a society worthy of emulation by republicans. Rome was an excellent example of what institutions to avoid and why. John G. Whittier flatly declared that Rome's problems with the distribution of wealth were attributable solely to the existence of slavery. In 1858, W. O. Blake castigated the historians who had written narratives of Rome without mentioning slavery; Edward Gibbon, while blaming Christianity for the fall of Rome, devoted only two pages to slavery. Blake

6. See, for example, John S. C. Abbott, *The History of the Civil War in America* (Springfield, Mass., 1863–66), I, 21; Cassius M. Clay, "Fourier Association—The Harbinger," in Horace Greeley, ed., *The Writings of Cassius Marcellus Clay, Including Speeches and Addresses* (1848; rpr. New York, 1969), 375.

7. *Liberator,* January 7, 1832, in Truman Nelson, ed., *Documents of Upheaval: Selections from William Lloyd Garrison's "The Liberator," 1831–1865* (New York, 1966), 41; Wright, *Sin of Slavery,* 25; [Richard Hildreth], *Despotism in America; or An Inquiry into the Nature and Results of the Slave-holding System in the United States* (Boston, 1840), quote on 97, distribution of wealth discussion, 96–99, see also 10, 20–21, 86–92. See also Octavius Brooks Frothingham, *Gerrit Smith: A Biography* (New York, 1878), 95; William E. Channing, *Slavery* (4th ed.; Boston, 1836), 100; [James Russell Lowell], "The Election in November," *Atlantic Monthly,* VI (1860), 498.

emphasized that slavery caused the collapse not only of the Roman empire but, more important, the Roman republic. Blake's interesting history stressed how the use of slaves squeezed out mechanics and yeoman farmers, produced a monopoly in ownership of land, embroiled the Romans in countless and needless wars, and finally prodded the slaveholding aristocracy to overthrow the republic and establish a despotism—all for the purpose of preserving the elite's ownership of slaves. Republicanism died so slaveholding might flourish.[8]

In their analysis of the economic functioning of slavery, the abolitionists ascribed wholeheartedly to the revolutionaries' ideas on the political economy of aristocracy. Abolitionists depicted southern slaveholders as aristocrats. For the abolitionists, however, the key fact of the southern aristocrats was that slave masters lived without laboring themselves and literally stole others' fruits of labor. From the very beginning of abolitionism, the idea that the slave was denied the fruits of his labor and that the slaveholder stole those fruits dominated their economic analysis and much of their moralistic charge as well. Before Garrison founded the *Liberator,* he wrote to a Boston newspaper that slavery brutalizes the slave and that masters stole "day by day, month after month, year after year, the fruits of their [slaves'] unmitigated toil, and give, in return, a little meal and a few herrings." William Ellery Channing said the slave master robbed the slave of his "limbs, faculty, strength, and labor, by which all property is won and held fast."[9]

8. W. O. Blake, comp., *The History of Slavery and the Slave Trade, Ancient and Modern . . .* (Columbus, 1858), 46–60; John G. Whittier, "The Abolitionists," in John G. Whittier, *The Works of John Greenleaf Whittier* (Boston, 1892), VII, 69. Contemporaries knew from Gibbon that at the time of Claudius, the Roman Empire had a population of 120 million, of whom one-half were estimated to be slaves (Blake [comp.], *History of Slavery,* 53). An extensive analysis of the fall of the Roman republic because of slaveholding was (unbelievably) provided by the Jacksonian Democrat and historian George Bancroft in 1834; see [Bancroft], "Slavery in Rome," *North American Review,* XXXIX (1834), 415–33.

9. [Hildreth], *Despotism in America,* 16, 24; Henry Ward Beecher, in *Independent,* February 21, 1850, in Henry Ward Beecher, *Patriotic Addresses in America and England, 1850–1865, on Slavery, the Civil War, and the Development of Civil Liberty in the United States,* ed. John R. Howard (New York, 1888), 168–69; Stephen Alexander Hodgman, *The Nation's Sin and Punishment; or, The Hand of God Visible in the Overthrow of Slavery* (New York, 1864), 58; Mrs. [Lydia Maria] Child, *An Appeal in Favor of That Class of Americans Called Africans* (New York, 1836), 22, 112–13; John G. Whittier, "Democracy and Slavery," in Whittier, *Works of Whittier,* VII, 109; and Whittier, "What Is Slavery," *ibid.,* VII, 103; Rev. Philo Tower, *Slavery Unmasked: Being a Truthful Narrative of a Three Years' Residence and Journeying in Eleven Southern States, to Which Is Added the Invasion of Kansas* (1856; rpr. New York, 1969), 18, 19; Abbott, *History of*

The standard argument of abolitionists (and indeed all antislavery proponents) was that slavery degraded labor and ruined the economy of any region
where it was practiced.[10] Abolitionists argued that because slave masters stole
the fruits of labor, no one had an incentive to labor. But when no force stole
the fruits of labor, when there was no aristocracy or aristocratic mechanism
transferring the fruits of labor from a producer to a nonproducer, then the laborer had every motivation to work arduously and intelligently. As Hildreth
said, people worked diligently for the *"expectation of reward,"* but the system
of obtaining labor by *"fear of punishment"* produced slovenly, uncaring labor.
The difference, which at times abolitionists directly pointed out, was productivity. The knowledge that the fruits of labor belonged to oneself generated
more output per hour per worker; the knowledge that the fruits of labor did
not belong to oneself evoked a minimal work response.[11]

Abolitionists thus plunged into one of the hotly contested areas of political economy, the determination of wages. In this realm one sees their distinct

the Civil War, I, 22; William L. Garrison to editor of Boston *Evening Transcript,* November 6,
1830, in Walter M. Merrill and Louis Ruchames, eds., *The Letters of William Lloyd Garrison*
(Cambridge, Mass., 1971–81), I, 112; Channing, *Slavery,* 53–54; William Goodell, *The American Slave Code in Theory and Practice: Its Distinctive Features Shown by Its Statutes, Judicial Decisions, and Illustrative Facts* (1853; rpr. New York, 1968), 33. See also, *The Bible Against Slavery;
or, An Inquiry into the Genius of the Mosaic System, and the Teachings of the Old Testament on the
Subject of Human Rights* (1838; rpr. Detroit, 1970), 21; George B. Cheever, *God Against Slavery:
And the Freedom and Duty of the Pulpit to Rebuke It, as a Sin Against God* (Cincinnati, n.d.),
94–95, 123–24; Alvan Stewart, speech at Utica, 1838, in Marsh, ed., *Writings and Speeches of
Stewart,* 53; Alvan Stewart, Address to the Abolitionists of the State of New York, October
1836, *ibid.,* 89–90; Betty Fladeland, *James Gillespie Birney: Slaveholder to Abolitionist* (New
York, 1955), 211; Hugh C. Bailey, *Hinton Rowan Helper: Abolitionist-Racist* (University, Ala.,
1965), 28–30.

    10. This aspect of the free labor ideology and abolitionist appeal is well known; see, for ex-
ample, David L. Smiley, *Lion of White Hall: The Life of Cassius M. Clay* (Madison, 1962), 22–
23 and *passim;* Lawrence B. Goodheart, *Abolitionist, Actuary, Atheist: Elizur Wright and the Reform Impulse* (Kent, Ohio, 1990), 92–94; Bailey, *Hinton Rowan Helper,* 27; Stanley G. Harrold,
Gamaliel Bailey and Antislavery Union (Kent, Ohio, 1986), 86–98; Ronald G. Walters, *The
Antislavery Appeal: American Abolitionism After 1830* (Baltimore, 1976), 129; Stewart, *Holy
Warriors,* 79–80.

    11. [Hildreth], *Despotism in America,* 112–13; C. M. Clay, "Abbott Lawrence's Letters to
Wm. C. Rives," 1845, in Greeley, ed., *Writings of Clay,* 390; Channing, *Slavery,* 104–105; Levi
Coffin, *Reminiscences of Levi Coffin: The Reputed President of the Underground Railroad* (2nd
ed.; Cincinnati, 1880), 82–83, 267–72; George Fitzhugh and A. Hogeboom, *A Controversy on
Slavery, Between George Fitzhugh, Esq., of Virginia, Author of "Sociology for the South," etc., and
A. Hogeboom, Esq., of New York* (Oneida, N.Y., 1857), 36.

limitations in regard to political economy and recognizes immediately that they operated on notions of biblical justice. The market mechanism, which is the defining concept of classical capitalism, is *not* in evidence in abolitionist writing.[12] Abolitionists, with certain exceptions, understood wages in biblical terms, not as the product of the forces of supply and demand for labor.

Abolitionists believed that wages had to be voluntary, an agreement between parties for services rendered. The great economic sin of slavery was compulsion. There could be no fair wage without consent.[13] For the abolitionists, when wages were voluntarily agreed upon by two parties, the amount of reward was always adequate and equitable (hence the distribution of wealth in a free labor society was always just because coercion was absent).

Abolitionists also found another pernicious effect of slavery. In a republican setting, where the laborer obtained the full fruits of his or her labor, the worker also used intelligence to complete tasks. That was how free labor societies greatly outstripped slave labor societies. Slavery took away mental power and turned men and women into brutes, animals. As James R. Lowell wrote, slavery "crushes all to one dead level of stupid animalism or sullen despair." Richard Hildreth even argued that stealing from the master was the only intelligent act a slave could perform to obtain the fruits of his labors. For the abolitionists, a free labor society brought mental and manual labor together in one person; all laborers improved their productivity, realizing they would keep the reward of their labors, and hence national wealth was bound to leap forward, especially compared to any society hindered by aristocratic impediments.[14] This vision implies that abolitionists were thinking of a society of independent producers.

Subsistence wages, the backbone of the classical economics of Ricardo, Malthus, and John Stuart Mill, had no place in abolitionist political econ-

12. Without attention to content of classical economics, constructing the bond between the abolitionists and capitalism is tenuous. See, for example, the exchange between David Brion Davis, Thomas Haskell, and John Ashworth in Thomas Bender, ed., *The Antislavery Debate: Capitalism and Abolitionism as a Problem in Historical Interpretation* (Berkeley, 1992).

13. Channing, *Slavery,* 54; George B. Cheever, *The Guilt of Slavery and Crime of Slaveholding, Demonstrated from the Hebrew and Greek Scriptures* (Boston, 1860), i, 68, 108–109, 112; A[ngelina] E. Grimké, *Appeal to the Christian Women of the South* (New York, n.d.), 11.

14. James Russell Lowell, "Putting the Cart Before the Horse," in James Russell Lowell, *The Anti-Slavery Papers of James Russell Lowell* (Boston, 1902), II, 138; [Hildreth], *Despotism in America,* 55, also 51–55, 132. Jonathan Glickstein offers a much different argument in which free labor advocates praised only mental labor and demeaned merely manual labor (*Concepts of Free Labor in Antebellum America,* 19, 28, 32–36, and *passim*).

omy. In one sense or another, abolitionists argued for equitable wages obtained by mutual consent without fraud or coercion. The abolitionists' rejection of subsistence wages is most clear in their brief against slavery. Slave wages, what slaves obtained from the master, were true subsistence wages; and subsistence wages were obviously the result of aristocrats stealing the fruits of the workers' labor. The argument for emancipation could logically mean only that blacks when freed would regain the full fruits of their labors and be better remunerated than when slaves. Some abolitionists foresaw odd examples of the results of future emancipation; William Jay and John G. Whittier, for example, predicted less costs to the planter, the end of various entitlements blacks were accustomed to, and initially a difficult time for blacks receiving ample compensation. But the basic theme was that the switch to a free labor system would result in more productivity, smaller labor costs, yet higher wages. Subsistence wages were the product of aristocratic institutions, like slavery; free contract and mutual agreement established equitable compensation.[15]

What for the abolitionists was the "just" reward, how did they conceive how compensation, or wages, was to be determined—what were the social forces in operation? The answer was a form of biblical morality because abolitionists were usually moralists, not political economists. The ethics embedded in the labor theory of property/value were reinforced by biblical passages stating that the laborer was worthy of his hire, that masters should treat their servants justly (also used by proslavery advocates), and that in the sweat of thy brow shalt thou eat thy bread. For the abolitionists a wage was an independent amount that represented the fruits of labor, a bargain between free agents experiencing no coercion who agreed on services and compensation—a market force was irrelevant. The antislavery radicals described wages as reciprocity of benefits, an exchange of equivalents, a "voluntary contract," a bargain, mutuality, "law of mutual necessity and mutual interest," equitability, the receipt of the full fruits of labor, and fair only when guided by scripture.

15. William Jay, "Inquiry into the Character and Tendency of the American Colonization and American Anti-Slavery Societies," in William Jay, *Miscellaneous Writings on Slavery* (1853; rpr. New York, 1968), 195–99; Henry Cowles to Elizur Wright, January 19, 1833, in Elizur Wright Papers, Library of Congress; William Lloyd Garrison in *Genius of Universal Emancipation,* September 2, 1829, in Wendell Phillips Garrison and Francis Jackson Garrison, eds., *William Lloyd Garrison, 1805–1879: The Story of His Life* (New York, 1885–89), I, 143; Wright, *Sin of Slavery,* 40–41; Amos A. Phelps, *Lectures on Slavery and Its Remedy* (Boston, 1834), 87, 225, 227–31; Whittier, "Justice and Expediency," in Whittier, *Works of Whittier,* VII, 34, 45.

William Goodell wrote in 1853 that a wage, to be "legitimate, must be equitable, or equal," and that meant wages must provide more than a "comfortable sustenance as a mere animal."[16] For the abolitionists, wages represented a moral contract between voluntary agents and not necessarily a determination established by the forces of supply and demand. This was a biblical and not a market economics.[17]

In the first six decades of the nineteenth century, both Manchester economics and American abolitionist thought traveled in the same direction: tearing down the structures of authority and hierarchy. But the justification and the motivations behind those espousing classical economics and those adhering to American abolitionism were different. Classical economics, at least in its English and European manifestation, was incapable of arguing for an acceptably near-equal distribution of wealth from a laissez-faire economy (these economists did argue that it was equitable by natural law). Abolitionists did not live under that constraint and believed that a system of freedom in the economic sphere—that is, a free Christian community—promoted a society characterized by equality.

The situation contained confusions, of course. Some abolitionists, such as Amasa Walker and possibly Gamaliel Bailey, William Elder, and Elizur Wright, were political economists, and they did use an explicit supply-demand analysis.[18] And the abolitionists were increasingly perplexed and confounded by the results of northern industrialization. Their somewhat anarchist vision of a free economy was idealistic; unlike the way they deduced

16. Quotes from Cheever, *Guilt of Slavery,* 67; Grimké, *Appeal to the Christian Women of the South,* 11; [Hildreth], *Despotism in America,* 40; Phelps, *Lectures on Slavery,* 230–31; Goodell, *American Slave Code,* 151–52; also, Whittier, "What Is Slavery," in Whittier, *Works of Whittier,* VII, 102; Rev. William G. Brownlow and Rev. A. Pryne, *Ought American Slavery to Be Perpetuated? A Debate Between Rev. W. G. Brownlow and Rev. A. Pryne. Held at Philadelphia, September, 1858* (Philadelphia, 1858), 115–16; *Bible Against Slavery,* 71; Cheever, *God Against Slavery,* 93–95, 123–24.

17. To a limited extent, Louis Gerteis makes the same point by emphasizing the change in the focus of antislavery from morality to utilitarianism (classical economics), in *Morality and Utility in American Antislavery Reform,* ix–xiii, chap. 4; James L. Huston, "Abolitionists and an Errant Economy: The Panic of 1857 and Abolitionist Economic Ideas," *Mid-America,* LXV (1983), 15–27. For a recent restatement of the market-driven abolitionist interpretation, see Ashworth, *Slavery, Capitalism, and Politics,* 148–55.

18. For example, William Jay, "Inquiry into the Character and Tendency of the American Colonization and American Anti-Slavery Societies," in Jay, *Miscellaneous Writings on Slavery,* 198.

the actual sufferings of the system of slavery, they could not or would not acknowledge the defects of the system of free labor. They maintained an idealistic vision of free labor economic relations, and for that they earned the anger and frustration of working-class radicals. Working-class radicals were far more concerned with the practical results of the free labor system than they were with the idealism of its theory. The failure of abolitionists to use their own insights into the operation of economic systems damaged them in the tumults that followed the Panic of 1873.[19]

An amazing irony, however, pervades abolitionist economic thought. Radical Jacksonian Democrats traced their economic beliefs back to John Taylor of Caroline, who in turn took his ideas from the revolutionary generation, Adam Smith, and European writers on republicanism. It is with a start that one recognizes that abolitionists, though generally from a Federalist-Whiggery–New England political culture, were more Jacksonian in economic thought than the Jacksonians. Abolitionists desired direct taxes, elimination of tariffs (some dissonance here), antimonopoly, and an end to special privileges. Abolitionists were attracted to William Leggett for more than the reason that by the end of his life Leggett was willing to attack slavery as a monopoly. As true heirs of the Revolution, abolitionists pushed the tendency of noncoercion and independency in revolutionary thought to its logical conclusion: anarchy. Abolitionists were closest in their economic thinking to individuals like Josiah Warren and Stephen Pearl Andrews.[20]

19. For abolitionist confusion over the actual functioning of the free labor economy, consult James R. Lowell, "Texas," in Lowell, *Anti-Slavery Papers of Lowell,* I, 9–10; Fitzhugh and Hogeboom, *Controversy on Slavery,* 23–27; Thomas Wentworth Higginson, *Contemporaries* (Boston, 1899), 275–78; Harrold, *Gamaliel Bailey and Antislavery Union,* 101–102. On the tense relations between abolitionism and labor, see Eric Foner, "Abolitionism and the Labor Movement in Antebellum America," in *Anti-Slavery, Religion, and Reform: Essays in Memory of Roger Anstey,* ed. Christine Bolt and Seymour Drescher (Folkestone, Eng., 1980), 255–69; Goodheart, *Abolitionist, Actuary, Atheist,* chap. 11; Forbath, "Ambiguities of Free Labor," 768–93; Jonathan A. Glickstein, " 'Poverty Is Not Slavery': Abolitionists and the Competitive Labor Market," in *Antislavery Reconsidered: New Perspectives on the Abolitionists,* ed. Lewis Perry and Michael Fellman (Baton Rouge, 1979), 195–216; Foner, *Free Soil, Free Labor, Free Men,* x–xxxix, esp. xxii–xxiii.

20. On abolitionists and economic issues and attitudes to the Democrats, see Hugh Davis, *Joshua Leavitt, Evangelical Abolitionist* (Baton Rouge, 1990), 170–73, 195–96; John G. Whittier, "William Leggett," in Whittier, *Works of Whittier,* VI, 184–215; William Goodell, *Slavery and Anti-Slavery; A History of the Great Struggle in Both Hemispheres: With a View of the Slavery Question in the United States* (New York, 1852), 319–25; Harrold, *Gamaliel Bailey and Antislavery Union,* 98–101. On the question of anarchism, see Lewis Perry, *Radical Abolitionism: An-*

It hardly needs mentioning that American blacks during the centuries of slavery did not produce a hefty treatise on the distribution of wealth. Slaves were largely denied opportunities of any kind, and free northern blacks had so many problems to deal with that the distribution of wealth was not uppermost in their writings.[21] Yet to the extent that distributionist themes can be found in antebellum black literature, it appears that black abolitionists mirrored the analysis of white abolitionists. Black abolitionists found no reason to doubt the correctness of the republican axioms of the labor theory of property/value and the political economy of aristocracy.

A strain of argument among some black abolitionists indicated that they found the labor theory of property/value highly insightful in explaining the economic oppression of slavery. In fact, for slaves the labor theory of property/value must have had special meaning because no other Americans had the experience of the fruits of labor literally being beaten out of their grasp to enrich others. Frederick Douglass, the most prominent of the antebellum black abolitionists, wrote about his earnings: "He [the master] did not earn it—. . . . The right to take my earnings was the right of the robber. He had the power to compel me to give him the fruits of my labor, and this *power* was his only right in the case." In 1827, Nathaniel Paul stated that slavery violated the biblical injunction that man must "obtain his bread by the sweat of his brow." New York black abolitionist Charles W. Gardner said slavery was wrong because "it withholds from him [the slave] all the proceeds of his labor, except a scanty subsistence."[22]

---

archy and the Government of God in Antislavery Thought (Ithaca, N.Y., 1973), x, 18–26, 298–302; Lawrence J. Friedman, "The Gerrit Smith Circle: Abolitionism in the Burned-Over District," *Civil War History*, XXVI (1980), 18–32. John Ashworth, in *Slavery, Capitalism, and Politics*, 148–88, 289–97, 307–12, finds the abolitionists totally different from Jacksonian radicals. But see Sean Wilentz, "Slavery, Antislavery, and Jacksonian Democracy," in *The Market Revolution in America: Social, Political, and Religious Expressions, 1800–1880*, ed. Melvyn Stokes and Stephen Conway (Charlottesville, 1996), 202–23.

21. Distribution themes were not particularly visible in a sampling of the remembrances of former slaves taken by the Federal Writers' Project in the 1930s. Anger and horror at slavery abounded in these recollections of slavery but not explicit distributionist themes. I investigated the collections in George P. Rawick, ed., *The American Slave: A Composite Autobiography* (Westport, Conn., 1972), Ser. I, Vols. II, VI, XII, XIII, and XVI.

22. Frederick Douglass, *Life and Times of Frederick Douglass* (rev. ed.; 1892; rpr. New York, 1962), 186; N[athaniel] Paul, "The Abolition of Slavery," in Carter G. Woodson, ed., *Negro Orators and Their Orations* (1924; rpr. New York, 1969), 66; speech of Gardner in Peter C. Ripley, ed., *The Black Abolitionist Papers* (Chapel Hill, 1985–92), II, 206.

And black orators well understood the idea of aristocracy as used by the revolutionary generation: aristocrats were those who commanded the fruits of other people's labors. Slavery, said Douglass, was the means "by which men seek to live without labor, to eat bread by the sweat of another man's brow, to get gold without digging it, and to become rich without using one's own faculties and powers to obtain riches." Three black Philadelphians wrote an appeal for northern black congregations to testify against slavery. They implied the aristocratic power involved in slavery: "Hence, the labor of the slave having been wrested from him by injustice, we deny the right of the 'MASTER' to *transfer the product of that labor,* or anyone to purchase it, except from the slave himself."[23]

Free northern blacks may have absorbed the values of the free labor ideology. They urged their compatriots to work industriously, obtain an education, abstain from drinking, cultivate regular habits, and attend church. In effect, they called upon free blacks to seek no aid from government but to rely on their own talents and to make as much use as possible of the social mobility provided in a free labor society. To some extent, the free black leadership's embrace of the free labor ideology may have been a defensive action to obtain a hearing for their cause and to make the best of a bitterly racist society. Yet reasons abound to explain why black leaders and followers found the essentials of the republican theory of the distribution of wealth suitable for analyzing the circumstance and the results of slavery and its moral and economic ignominy. And it is possible that free blacks and slaves (if they heard such arguments) responded favorably to the basic premises of the free labor ideology. Any set of propositions that promised workers the full fruits of their labor probably would have sounded like deliverance to those accustomed to obtaining nothing from their labor.[24]

Because slavery was preeminently a labor system, the distribution theme

23. Frederick Douglass, "Freedom in the West Indies: An Address Delivered in Pough-keepsie, New York," in John W. Blassingame, ed., *The Frederick Douglass Papers* (New Haven, 1979–), Ser. I, Vol. III, p. 219; Henry Bibb, in Gilbert Osofsky, ed., *Puttin' on Ole Massa: The Slave Narratives of Henry Bibb, William Wells Brown, and Solomon Northup* (New York, 1969), 69; Address by William Watkins, Jacob M. Moore, and Jacob C. White, Sr., of Philadelphia, To the Colored Churches in the Free States, in Ripley, ed., *Black Abolitionist Papers,* III, 191.

24. For interpretations and illustrations of free black use of the free labor ideology, see David E. Swift, *Black Prophets of Justice: Activist Clergy Before the Civil War* (Baton Rouge, 1989), 17, 31, 33, 82, 85; George Levesque, "Boston's Black Brahmin: Dr. John S. Rock," *Civil War History,* XXVI (1980), 344–45; Waldo E. Martin, Jr., *The Mind of Frederick Douglass* (Chapel Hill, 1984), x, 56, 66–69, 254–60; Peter C. Ripley, Introduction to Ripley, ed., *Black Abolitionist Pa-*

among black abolitionists was a salient feature in their writings and speeches. But distributionist themes had to vie for recognition among others in black antislavery advocacy and as a result did not dominate. So many injuries resulted from slavery that the basic theme of black abolitionists, and to some extent white abolitionists, was how racial domination produced social, political, and economic evils. Black abolitionist writings were filled with physical suffering, moral degradation, mental deprivation, familial destruction, and material inadequacy. A particularly strong theme was the effects of racism on blacks in both the free North and the slave South.[25] The overwhelming effect of slavery on every aspect of life thus reduced the visibility of the distributionist theme in black abolitionist writing, but so long as slavery was a labor system the sense of distributive injustice could not be ignored.

From the beginning of political life under the Constitution, friction developed between northerners and southerners over federal policy. Some of the heat was to be expected as the normal result of clashing economic interests of different geographical sections, but arguments between northerners and southerners had a special quality because of the existence of slavery. In the halls of Congress and in politics generally, northern politicians stressed the danger that a new aristocracy, the slaveholders, posed to the nation's republican institutions. Northern politicians employed the political economy of aristocracy and called it the slave power.

Northern politicians must have had a frustrating—really, a maddening—time trying to understand their southern counterparts. Before the political explosions over Henry Clay's American System, northerners almost seemed to have been shocked into silence over the immense gulf between southern words and practices. In the 1820s northerners began to express their venom

---

pers, III, 14–20; Loren Schweninger, "From Assertiveness to Individualism: The Difficult Path from Slavery to Freedom," in *American Chameleon: Individualism in Trans-National Context,* ed. Richard O. Curry and Lawrence B. Goodheart (Kent, Ohio, 1991), 121–32.

25. See R. J. M. Blackett, *Beating Against the Barriers: Biographical Essays in Nineteenth-Century Afro-American History* (Baton Rouge, 1986), 3, 43, 90, 101–106; Blackett, *Building an Antislavery Wall: Black Americans in the Atlantic Abolitionist Movement, 1830–1860* (Baton Rouge, 1983), 12–18; Sorin, *Abolitionism,* 99–118; Gary B. Nash, *Forging Freedom: The Formation of Philadelphia's Black Community, 1720–1840* (Cambridge, Mass., 1988), 172–73; Benjamin Quarles, *Black Abolitionists* (New York, 1969), 47–61; Ripley, Introduction to Ripley, ed., *Black Abolitionist Papers,* III, 184–85. For the status of antebellum African Americans generally, consult James Oliver Horton and Lois E. Horton, *In Hope of Liberty: Culture, Community, and Protest Among Northern Free Blacks, 1700–1860* (New York, 1997).

over the slaveholders' unabashed glorification of simple republicanism while practicing outrageously tyrannical aristocracy.

Northerners could only have been dumbfounded at the impertinence of the writings and effusions of prominent southern slaveholders. Southerners talked and wrote about achieving an equitable distribution of wealth. In the *Arator*, John Taylor said a republic should allow "wealth to be distributed by merit and industry" and government should never take away the property "which we sweat for." In 1858 Lucius Quintus Cincinnatus Lamar proclaimed to the citizens of Jackson, Mississippi, "Yet the general distribution of wealth [in the South] was such as to afford each and every man the necessaries of life; and that we were unlike the other portion of the confederacy, where one might see side by side bloated and overgrown wealth and squalid poverty." The old obstructionist Nathaniel Macon declared in 1828 that "everybody should be let alone and allowed to do that which he can do best." Andrew Jackson wrote in horror of the would-be American aristocrats "who wish to make the labourers of the country Hewers of wood, and drawers of water for the grandees of Texas, as the labourers of England are now for the grandees and aristocracy of England, Ireland, and Scotland." Southerners constantly moaned that northern policies were stealing the fruits of southern labor. At the same time, southerners warned of the horrors of industrialization, the aristocratic power of manufacturers, and the degraded conditions of factory workers.[26]

Northerners knew that something was askew. John Taylor owned more than 140 slaves, possessed thousands of acres of land, and had obtained much of this fortune through inheritance. John C. Calhoun owned eighty slaves in 1828, when he wrote the *Exposition and Protest* charging that southerners were being robbed of the fruits of their labor.[27] According to the Revolution's economic definitions, southern slaveholders were guilty of aristocracy: they lived off the labors of others and manipulated government to ensure that their unearned income would continue. Where else in the republic was a greater vio-

26. Taylor, *Arator*, 94, 96; Speech of L. Q. C. Lamar quoted from Edward Mayes, *Lucius Q. C. Lamar: His Life, Times, and Speeches, 1825–1893* (2nd ed.; Nashville, Tenn., 1896), 620; Nathaniel Macon quoted in William E. Dodd, *The Life of Nathaniel Macon* (Raleigh, N.C., 1903), 346; Andrew Jackson to Andrew J. Donelson, December 2, 1844, in Bassett, ed., *Correspondence of Jackson*, VI, 335–36.

27. Loren Baritz, Introduction to Taylor, *Inquiry into the Principles and Policy of the Government of the United States*, xii; Shalhope, *John Taylor of Caroline*, 183–84; John Niven, *John C. Calhoun and the Price of Union: A Biography* (Baton Rouge, 1993), 156.

lation of the ideas of fruits of labor, the danger of aristocracy, and a lopsided distribution of wealth than the slaveholding South?

Northerners understood early and well how slaveholding clashed with the revolutionary doctrines of the distribution of wealth. John Adams called John Taylor up short on the idea of aristocracy. When Taylor tried to pillory Adams' earlier writing on aristocracy, Adams shot back: what did Taylor think he was if not an aristocrat? "These [the great planters] are every one of them aristocrats, and you, who are the first of them, are the most eminent aristocrat of them all." During the Missouri controversy of 1820–1821, John Quincy Adams had several talks with John C. Calhoun over the fate of the Union and slavery and found aristocracy permeating the facade of southern republicanism: "They fancy themselves more generous and noble-hearted than the plain freemen who labor for subsistence." Some twelve years earlier, in 1808, a High Federalist had said the same thing. Josiah Quincy reprimanded George M. Troup of Georgia for labeling New England's maritime interest an aristocracy: "Sir, the men whom I represent not only raise these humble [agricultural] articles, *but* they do it *with the labor of their own hands,—with the sweat of their own brows.*"[28] Living up to the labor theory of property/value was, according to northerners, the dividing line between North and South, and Quincy was reminding Troup that virtually no one in the North lived off the sweat of a slave's brow. It was in truth an odd situation. Northerners talked aristocracy and lived democracy; southerners talked democracy and lived aristocracy.

It did not take long for proponents of an active government to point out the inconsistency of southern slaveholders berating manufacturers as aristocrats and bewailing the distribution of wealth in industrial England. Henry Clay in his famous 1824 speech on protectionism mentioned that it ill-suited southerners to complain about mercantile nabobs; the nabobs on southern estates had more wealth and power than anyone in the American realm of industry or commerce. Representative Luther Severance of Maine blasted the Treasury Report of Robert J. Walker calling for a lower tariff; the "tirade" in the report depicted capital's oppression of labor and came with "bad grace from a southern cotton-planter, whose extensive lands and fixtures not only

28. John Adams to John Taylor, April 15, 1814, in Adams, ed., *Works of John Adams,* VI, 506; John Quincy Adams quoted in Tyler, *Freedom's Ferment,* 473; Josiah Quincy quoted in Edmund Quincy, *Life of Josiah Quincy of Massachusetts* (Boston, 1869), 158; Siry, *De Witt Clinton and the American Political Economy,* 172, 225–32; William M. Wiecek, *The Sources of Antislavery Constitutionalism in America, 1760–1848* (Ithaca, N.Y., 1977), chap. 5.

are capital, but the living human laborers upon his plantation *are capital also.*" The northern proponents of high tariffs had no difficulty perceiving southern slaveholders as aristocrats.[29]

More important, northern representatives, especially those favoring the American System of Henry Clay, witnessed southern animosity to federal programs rising whenever southerners perceived that the benefits to their region were minimal or simply less than those obtained by other regions (usually New England). They soon recognized the existence of a power that congealed against all legislative initiatives for the North and that vigilantly guarded the slaveholder interest of the South. By 1833 the idea of the slave power was born even if it took the abolitionists, and especially James G. Birney, some time to propagate it. During discussion over the Missouri Compromise, northern anger at the political impact of the three-fifths compromise was widespread. John Quincy Adams noted that slavery bound together southern congressional members around one interest. By the 1840s, the single-interest mania of southern congressmen was widely recognized in the North. Wrote one individual, "The slave system is a bond of united political action, which has no corresponding, counterbalancing interest in the [free] states."[30]

The northern political construction of the slave power thesis grew from infancy to near adulthood in the nullification crisis of 1832–1833. South Carolinians, experiencing internal difficulties with their plantation economy, saw the rise of the manufacturing interest in the North as a competitor for the power of the federal government, and the object of the manufacturer's desire was a protective tariff. After a near collision between the federal government and South Carolina in 1832–1833, a compromise tariff was enacted that successively lowered the impost duties for ten years.[31] But in the congressional

29. Speech of Henry Clay, March 31, 1824, *Annals of Congress,* 18th Cong., 1st Sess., 1993; speech of Representative Luther Severance, June 27, 1846, *Congressional Globe,* 29th Cong., 1st Sess., *Appendix,* 705.

30. Entry of March 3, 1820, in Charles Francis Adams, ed., *Memoirs of John Quincy Adams* (Philadelphia, 1874–77), V, 4; Glover Moore, *The Missouri Controversy, 1819–1821* (1953; rpr. Lexington, Ky., 1966), 16–17, 39, 58, 126–27; Robert F. Durden, *The Self-Inflicted Wound: Southern Politics in the Nineteenth Century* (Lexington, Ky., 1985), 18; Davis, *The Slave Power Conspiracy and the Paranoid Style,* 14–18; *New Englander,* II (1844), 595.

31. The best works on the nullification episode are William W. Freehling, *Prelude to Civil War: The Nullification Controversy in South Carolina, 1816–1836* (New York, 1965); and Richard E. Ellis, *The Union at Risk: Jacksonian Democracy, States' Rights, and the Nullification Crisis* (New York, 1987).

sessions of 1832 and the short session of 1832–1833, northerners exploded at the effrontery of slaveholders who talked in horrified republican tones about northern aristocracy, the destitute and dependent northern laboring class, and the imbalanced northern distribution of wealth. In the cauldron of nullification, the idea of the slave power became a finished and tempered weapon.

Nathan Appleton, a Massachusetts representative who symbolized the enormous financial and political power arising from manufacturing, made two moderate but memorable speeches during nullification. They were remarkable for their implications. On May 30, 1832, Appleton intelligently refuted South Carolinian George McDuffie's "forty bale" theory, which attempted to explain northern oppression of the southern economy. Appleton attacked the English political economists whom southerners so commonly and reverently quoted, and he argued that the republican experiment would work only if wages were high, and wages could be high only if the nation adopted protective tariffs. But Appleton also wondered why all the free states were for protection while all the slave states were opposed. "We hear of no products of these States but those produced by slave labor." The problem with the southern economy was slave labor itself. Why did not the South industrialize like the North when tariff rates rose? The answer, Appleton implied, was that the unintelligent labor of the unrewarded slave was incapable of sustaining manufacturing; slavery was a system of brute labor and could be used only in brute labor occupations.[32]

In the heat of the crisis in January, 1833, Appleton was more emphatic on the economic evils of slavery, though still pleading for moderation and Union. Yet the cause of the conflict was now plain to all. "It is apparent that this great difference of opinion grows out of one great circumstance in the condition of the different sections of the country—the existence and nonexistence of slavery." South Carolinian demands to control the legislation of the federal government were in truth over no single specific policy, such as the tariff, but the "fear and apprehension of the South that the General Government may one day interfere with the right of property in slaves. This is the bond which unites the South in a solid phalanx."[33] The South had not a plu-

32. Appleton speech, May 30, 1832, *Register of Debates,* 22nd Cong., 1st Sess., 3189–92; on free and slave labor states, 3204; on wages, 3205; quoted passage, 3205; on the impact of slavery, 3205–3207. Appleton never referred to race in this speech; it was the system of labor that caused the results, not the race of the enslaved.

33. Speech of Nathan Appleton, January 22, 1833, *Register of Debates,* 22nd Cong., 2nd Sess., 1206.

rality of interests but a unity that demanded control of the federal government; and it was united on the omnipotent and all-governing question of property rights. Appleton had explained why the slave power existed, what it sought to protect, and how it intended to achieve its object.

Appleton had been circumspect and deferential in his speeches, arguing that southerners had no reason to worry about the sanctity of property rights in slaves or a presumed conflict in interest with manufacturers. Not so reassuring were the fulminations of former president, now Massachusetts representative, John Quincy Adams. Adams, who blamed southern opposition for limiting his father's and his own presidencies to one term, found a chance to strike back at southern republican pretensions. As chairman of the House Committee on Manufactures, he was in a position to write virulent reports.[34] Though John Quincy Adams was, like his father, uninformed on anything relating to political economy, he was hypersensitive to the locus and use of political power. His committee reports were landmarks in the creation of the northern awareness of the existence, purpose, and remorselessness of the slave power.

In his report of May, 1832, Adams laid out what seemed to him to be the incredible southern argument. The South could not change, and especially could not industrialize, because its society was always to be divided into "masters and slaves." Between the North and the South on tariff duties there were "irreconcilable interests, and the planter of the South cannot and will not submit to the sacrifice of his interest for the benefit of the Northern manufacturer." The southern viewpoint thus presented "two great, transcendent, opposite, and irreconcilable interests, in deadly hostility to each other," indicating that "no bond of Union under one and the same Government . . . can be maintained."[35] (In typical Adams fashion, he used the occasion to lecture on the moral errors of Bernard Mandeville's "Fable of the Bees" and George Berkeley's philosophical treatise on the nonexistence of matter.)

In his bitter 1833 report, Adams compared wealthy southern slaveholders with European aristocrats and lambasted the Jackson administration for caving in to the legislative demands of America's landed aristocracy instead of taking into consideration urban dwellers. Though Adams tried to argue for Union, he had to agree with the southern slaveholder position that in a nation

34. See Leonard L. Richards, *The Life and Times of Congressman John Quincy Adams* (New York, 1986), 7–10, 58–65, 71–76.

35. Report on Manufactures, May 23, 1832, *Register of Debates,* 22nd Cong., 1st Sess., *Appendix,* 89.

one-half free and one-half slave, "deep, if not irreconcilable collisons of interest must abound. . . . The question whether such a community can exist under one common Government, is a subject of profound, philosophical speculation in theory." He deprecated the political power northerners bestowed on southerners through the three-fifths compromise and bemoaned slaveholders' control of the "general policy of the government." He was incensed that South Carolina dictated policy to the rest of the nation and mortified that the North cowardly submitted to the dictation.[36]

Political abolitionists propagandized the idea of the slave power between 1833 and 1848. The Liberty party of James G. Birney warned northerners of the aristocratic machinations of the slave power, and the Free-Soil party of 1848 ran almost exclusively on the platform that slaveholders endangered the liberties of the people and representative government. When the Republican party formed between 1854 and 1856, its members immediately based the organization on hostility to the designs and might of the slave power.[37]

The Republicans of the 1850s used the revolutionary theory of the distribution of wealth, as was usual among American politicians, in an oblique, implicit manner. Behind most of their criticisms of slavery and slaveholders stood the political economy of aristocracy and the labor theory of property/value. They argued that the existence of slavery threatened a healthy distribution of wealth. This is not to say that the Republican party sprang into existence and the Civil War resulted from a desire on the part of Republicans to protect a particular distribution of wealth in the North. The birth of the Republican party, its sense of urgency, and its relationship to the dissolution of the Union are topics that require more attention to behavior and to institutional structures than a study of popular expectations about wealth distribution can provide. But the perspective of wealth distribution does make some of the major fears of northerners in the 1850s more understandable.

By the time the Republican party had solidified and become the major op-

36. Report of Committee on Manufactures, February 28, 1833, *Register of Debates*, 22nd Cong., 2nd Sess., Appendix, 42–43, 53–55.

37. On Birney, see Fladeland, *James Gillespie Birney,* 187–88, 211; Stewart, *Holy Warriors,* 95–100; John Mayfield, *Rehearsal for Republicanism: Free Soil and the Politics of Antislavery* (Port Washington, N.Y., 1980), 14–15, 22; Gara, "Slavery and the Slave Power," 12–17; William E. Gienapp, "The Republican Party and the Slave Power," in *New Perspectives on Race and Slavery in America: Essays in Honor of Kenneth M. Stampp,* ed. Robert H. Abzug and Stephen E. Maizlish (Lexington, Ky., 1986), 52–73; Davis, *The Slave Power Conspiracy and the Paranoid Style,* 17–20.

ponent of the Democratic party in 1857–1858, its members no longer had any doubts about the slaveholders' essential nature: they were aristocrats. In speech after speech and editorial after editorial, Republicans identified aristocracy with slaveholding. Using the revolutionary analysis, they spoke in horrified tones of the slaveholders' control of the government and how political control impoverished the free labor states.[38]

No individual was more responsible for shaping northern perceptions of southern slaveholders than William Henry Seward, governor of New York in the 1840s and United States senator for New York in the late 1840s and throughout the 1850s. Early in his career, Seward appealed to voters to view slaveholders as aristocrats. In 1844 at Syracuse he said, "These master-slaveholders are an aristocracy." In 1853 he warned an audience that slavery had destroyed the Roman republic and had created huge social divisions: "In such a society the rich and great of course grew always richer and greater, and the poor and low always poorer and more debased." Two years later, he argued that the sectional fight between the North and the South was the ancient fight of equality versus aristocracy. When visiting Wisconsin during the campaign of 1860, Seward used the concepts of the labor theory of property/value and the political economy of aristocracy to explain how wealth became unfairly distributed:

> What is . . . [democracy]? It is the opposite of monarchy or of aristocracy. Aristocracy is maintained everywhere, in all lands, by one of two systems, or by both combined. An aristocracy is the government in which the few privileged own the lands, and the many unprivileged work them, or in which the few privileged own the laborers and the laborers work for them. In either case the laborer works on compulsion, and under the constraint of force; and in either case he takes that which may remain after the wants of the owners of land or labor or both are satisfied.[39]

38. See Detroit *Post and Tribune, Zachariah Chandler: An Outline Sketch of His Life and Public Services* (Detroit, 1880), 112; Francis Fessenden, *Life and Public Services of William Pitt Fessenden* (Boston, 1907), I, 53; editorial, New York *Tribune,* March 11, 1858, p. 4; speech of Lyman Trumbull, in Chicago *Press and Tribune,* September 29, 1859; "The Privileged Class," Chicago *Daily Democrat,* September 22, 1860; speech of Henry Waldron, April 25, 1860, *Congressional Globe,* 36th Cong., 1st Sess., 1871.

39. "The Election of 1844," in Baker, ed., *Works of Seward,* III, 250–51; "The Destiny of America," *ibid.,* IV, 134–35; "The Advent of the Republican Party," *ibid.,* IV, 226–27; Rochester speech in New York *Times,* October 25, 1858; speech at Madison, Wisconsin, in New York *Tribune,* September 17, 1860. William Gienapp has emphasized the antiaristocratic quality of the Republican party in his *Origins of the Republican Party,* 191–92, 360–61.

The Republican party was appropriately named; since the Revolution, aristocracy had been the common enemy of all American republicans.

The Republicans of the 1850s also put the labor theory of property/value to use. Their party celebrated free labor and the right of all laborers to the fruits of their labor. As Horace Greeley wrote in the 1857 *Tribune Almanac,* "The doctrine that no human being was ever created for the benefit or advantage of another—that all service between man and man should be free and reciprocal—that the laborer should not toil and sweat to pamper others' pride or minister to others' luxury" was destined to triumph. The issue of the expansion of slavery into the territories was important to the Republicans because it at least partly portended a collision between free and slave labor systems, with the suppressed wage of the slave surely dragging down the wage of free laborers.[40]

The labor theory of property/value also had an important influence on the Republican party's racial attitudes. Many prominent Republicans declared that they were the "white man's party" and wanted to preserve the fields of the West for free white labor. The Republicans, however, applied the labor theory of value to all human beings. John Wentworth, Chicago editor and former Democrat, wrote, "The right to free labor . . . is a natural right, and no man should be deprived of it, except for crime." Blacks had as much right as whites to the fruits of their labor. During his 1858 debates with Stephen A. Douglas, Lincoln showed that he could be beaten into retreat on some specific issues but not on the universality of the labor theory of property/value: "In the right to eat the bread, without the leave of anybody else, which his own hand earns, *he [a black man] is my equal and the equal of Judge Douglas, and the equal of every living man.*" The labor theory of property/value was thus the source of Republican egalitarianism.[41]

In the South a group emerged to refute the obstreperous Republican

40. Horace Greeley, *Tribune Almanac for 1857,* 3; Foner, *Free Soil, Free Labor, Free Men,* 11–36; Foner, "Politics, Ideology, and the Origins of the American Civil War," in *A Nation Divided: Problems and Issues of the Civil War and Reconstruction,* ed. George M. Fredrickson (Minneapolis, 1975), 29–32; Richard H. Abbott, *Cotton and Capital: Boston Businessmen and Antislavery Reform, 1854–1868* (Amherst, Mass., 1991), 14–19, 53–66. On slavery in the territories, see speech of Andrew Curtin in *Raftsman's Journal* (Clearfield, Pa.), October 5, 1859; speech of Hannibal Hamlin, 1856, in Charles Eugene Hamlin, *The Life and Times of Hannibal Hamlin* (Cambridge, Mass., 1899), 300–301; speech of Abraham Lincoln, August 31, 1858, in Basler, Pratt, and Dunlap, eds., *Collected Works of Lincoln,* III, 77–79; David Wilmot to J. S. Bowen et al., April 22, 1857, in Going, *David Wilmot,* 501; Foner, *Free Soil, Free Labor, Free Men,* 44–45, 59–61.

41. See Eugene H. Berwanger, *The Frontier Against Slavery: Western Anti-Negro Prejudice*

claims of free labor. They concocted a defense of slavery that had extreme implications. Proslavery writers openly denounced Thomas Jefferson, natural rights, natural equality, and John Locke. Instead of praising individualism and market economics, they prized hierarchy and paternalism. Above all, they mocked social relations in the northern states and predicted a class war between the few rich and the many laboring poor.[42]

Proslavery writers repudiated many elements of the revolutionary heritage, but their relationship to the republican theory of the distribution of wealth is more nebulous. More than a few proslavery writers indicated a belief in aristocracy, although it may not have been much different from the notion of natural aristocracy propounded by Jefferson, Adams, and Hamilton. Few proslavery writers indicated a willingness to accept anything smacking of hereditary privileges. The inequality proslavery writers mentioned was almost always linked to race. Many proslavery proponents argued that only southern whites knew and understood true social equality because only Africans were slaves.[43]

The proslavery advocates parted with the revolutionary heritage over the

---

and the Slavery Extension Controversy (Urbana, 1971), 125, 127, 132, and 123–37 generally; Chicago *Daily Democrat,* September 3, 1858; Abraham Lincoln at first joint debate at Ottawa, August 21, 1858, in Robert W. Johannsen, ed., *The Lincoln-Douglas Debates of 1858* (New York, 1965), 53; see also Cassius Marcellus Clay, *The Life of Cassius Marcellus Clay: Memoirs, Writings, and Speeches* (Cincinnati, 1886), I, 233. The case for Republicans advocating amelioration of racism is made by Robert R. Dykstra, *Bright Radical Star: Black Freedom and White Supremacy in the Hawkeye State* (Cambridge, Mass., 1993), 157, 164–67, 189.

42. On proslavery thought in general, see Eugene D. Genovese, *The World the Slaveholders Made: Two Essays in Interpretation* (2nd ed.; Middletown, Conn., 1988); William Sumner Jenkins, *Pro-Slavery Thought in the Old South* (Chapel Hill, 1935); Drew Gilpin Faust, *A Sacred Circle: The Dilemma of the Intellectual in the Old South, 1840–1860* (Baltimore, 1977); and Faust, *James Henry Hammond and the Old South: A Design for Mastery* (Baton Rouge, 1982).

43. Edward A. Pollard, *The Lost Cause: A New Southern History of the War of the Confederates . . .* (2nd ed.; New York, 1867), 50–51; Henry Hughes, *Treatise on Sociology,* excerpt in Drew Gilpin Faust, ed., *The Ideology of Slavery: Proslavery Thought in the Antebellum South, 1830–1860* (Baton Rouge, 1981), 244–45; Claiborne, *Life and Correspondence of Quitman,* I, 18; J. M. Garnett, "The South and the Union," *De Bow's Review,* XIX (1855), 39; "Feudalism in the Nineteenth Century," *Southern Literary Messenger,* XV (1849), 465–66, 471; Robert L. Dabney, *A Defence of Virginia, [and Through her, of the South,] in Recent and Pending Contests Against the Sectional Party* (New York, 1867), 297–300. Fitzhugh, as one might expect, argued for aristocracy because it would allow only the best people to rule; *e.g.,* Fitzhugh and Hogeboom, *Controversy on Slavery,* 8–9; Fitzhugh, "Entails and Primogeniture," *De Bow's Review,* XXVII (1859), 172–78. See also D[aniel] R. Hundley, *Social Relations in Our Southern States* (New York, 1860), 69; George S. Sawyer, *Southern Institutes; or, An Inquiry into the Origins and Early Prevalence of Slavery and the Slave Trade* (Philadelphia, 1859), 14, 198–99. Abel P. Upshur, "Do-

labor theory of property/value. During the Revolution and afterward, southern rhetoric was thick with the phrase *the fruits of labor.* That phrase and the meaning behind it are absent in proslavery (not popular) writing after 1830. Instead, many substitutes appeared that did not square with the verbiage and direction of the Revolution. Instead of labor being reinvigorated by the lifting of the onus of aristocracy, William Harper wrote, in fine European fashion, "If any thing can be predicted as universally true of uncultivated man, it is that he will not labor beyond what is absolutely necessary to maintain his existence." Instead of the revolutionary ardor for individual reward for individual labor, proslavery southerners claimed it was natural for one group of men to live off the labors of another group: it was a "law of society that one portion of the community depended upon the labor of another portion, over which it must unavoidably exercise control," said John C. Calhoun. Abel Upshur flatly claimed that "one portion of mankind shall live upon the labor of another portion."[44]

George Fitzhugh was both like and unlike his proslavery comrades in regard to the labor theory of value/property. Fitzhugh, a Virginian who gained notoriety in the 1850s by publishing works arguing that slavery was the only compassionate means of offering a decent material life to manual workers, had no difficulty in declaring that free labor societies violated the labor theory of value/property and thus courted class warfare. The opening line of his 1857 work on the failure of northern society, *Cannibals All!* (the cannibals were the capitalists), stated: "My chief aim has been to show that *Labor makes values, and wit exploitates and accumulates them.*" He averred that the distribution of wealth was worse in free society, that is, the North, because northern capitalists took values created by labor for themselves and gave only subsistence wages to workers. But under slavery, the master was forced to provide decent living standards for the slaves because the slaves were the master's capital and thus protected from the master's avariciousness.[45]

But Fitzhugh implicitly accepted the idea that one class had to live off the

---

mestic Slavery," *Southern Literary Messenger,* V (1839), 678–79; John Witherspoon DuBose, *The Life and Times of William Lowndes Yancey* (1892; rpr. New York, 1942), I, 40–41.

44. Chancellor Harper, "Slavery in Light of Social Ethics," in E. N. Elliott, ed., *Cotton Is King, and Pro-Slavery Arguments: Comprising the Writings of Hammond, Harper, Christy, Stringfellow, Hodge, Bledsoe, and Cartwright, on This Important Subject* (Augusta, Ga., 1860), 551; John C. Calhoun, Remarks on Receiving Abolition Petitions, Senate, February 6, 1837, in Meriwether and Hemphill, eds., *Papers of Calhoun,* XIII, 389; E. N. Elliott, introduction to Elliott, ed., *Cotton Is King,* vii; Abel Upshur quoted by Faust, ed., *Ideology of Slavery,* 13.

45. George Fitzhugh, *Cannibals All! or Slaves Without Masters,* ed. C. Vann Woodward

fruits of another class's labor. He praised feudalism, believed the laws of entail and primogeniture were progressive and democratic, and argued that land monopoly aided the advance of civilization. He accepted, in short, the idea of a hierarchy that determined the distribution of wealth; his main contention was simply that in slavery a better distribution was obtained than in a "free" society. For Fitzhugh, the essence of society was a natural division of humankind into superiors and inferiors, and the superiors deserved political power and the right to distribute the proceeds of labor.[46]

Proslavery writers are perhaps best known for their consistent attack on free labor economics or capitalism. They were relentless in showing how poorly free laborers lived, especially in comparison to slaves. Some, like George Fitzhugh and Edmund Ruffin, ascribed the miseries of the working class—frequently British—to the system of economics that released avarice but imprisoned responsibilities. More often proslavery writers pointed to the impending Malthusian dilemma that plunged workers into economic desperation. In any case, the system of slavery took care and provided materially for workers whereas the free labor system did not. Proslavery literature did not waste time sneering at the ideas of social mobility or property accumulation of free labor advocates. They simply cast aside theory and went for naked circumstance and behavioral reality.[47]

Another feature of proslavery writing that distinguished it from northern writing was its general attitude toward labor. Northerners, at least rhetori-

---

(Cambridge, Mass., 1960), quote on 5, also see 16–18, 25, 31; [George Fitzhugh], "The Character and Causes of the Crisis," *De Bow's Review,* XXIV (1858), 31; see Harvey Wish, *George Fitzhugh: Propagandist of the Old South* (Baton Rouge, 1943), 174–76; Genovese, *World the Slaveholders Made,* 174–80.

46. On the need for hierarchy and the division of society into superiors and inferiors, see George Fitzhugh, "The Conservative Principle: or, Social Evils and Their Remedies," *De Bow's Review,* XXII (1857), 424; Fitzhugh, *Cannibals All!,* 69, 243–48; Fitzhugh and Hogeboom, *Controversy on Slavery,* 8–9. On his embrace of feudalism and land monopoly, see George Fitzhugh, "Reaction and the Administration," *De Bow's Review,* XXV (1858), 546; Fitzhugh, "Character and the Causes of the Crisis," 28, 30–32; George Fitzhugh, "Entails and Primogeniture," *De Bow's Review,* XXVII (1859), 175; George Fitzhugh, "Origins of Civilization—What Is Property?—Which Is the Best Slave Race?" *De Bow's Review,* XXV (1858), 654.

47. See James C. Hite and Ellen J. Hall, "The Reactionary Evolution of Economic Thought in Antebellum Virginia," *Virginia Magazine of History and Biography,* LXXX (1972), 476–88; Joseph J. Spengler, "Population Theory in the Ante-Bellum South," *Journal of Southern History,* II (1936), 360–89; Wilfred Carsel, "The Slaveholders' Indictment of Northern Wage Slavery," *Journal of Southern History,* VI (1940), 504–20.

cally, celebrated the dignity of labor. By the 1850s they were emphasizing the importance of bringing together the mental and physical aspects of labor to promote both economic progress and a virtuous citizenry. Proslavery writers disdained physical labor and instead prized the intelligent labor of the leisure classes. Edmund Ruffin, for example, explicitly defended slavery on the basis of the division of mental, intelligent labor of whites from the manual, unintelligent labor of Africans.[48]

Proslavery advocates, like virtually everyone else between the Revolution and the Civil War, never precisely defined an equitable distribution of wealth. In their analysis of northern and European labor conditions, proslavery writers either feigned or believed that the distribution of wealth in those lands was horrid. They held that natural ability deserved greater reward and that all societies divided into superiors and inferiors—but the implication of such an attitude toward the actual distribution of wealth was nebulous. Precision on the distribution of wealth was not a hallmark of any American in the pre–Civil War years. With proslavery writers, however, another problem connected with the distribution of wealth intrudes. Much of the inequality proslavery thinkers lauded was based on race; they tended to emphasize equality among whites. Nonetheless, it does not seem unwarranted to assert that proslavery writers were more willing intellectually than any other set of Americans to accept large deviations in the distribution of wealth.[49]

The northern Democratic party in the two decades before the Civil War was in an odd, ironical, and ultimately hypocritical position on the slavery issue. Northern Democrats sought a middle course to avoid the extremism and sectionalism of southern Democrats/proslavery advocates and the Republican party/abolitionist contingent. In trying to do so, they covered their ideologi-

---

48. Entry of March 3, 1820, in Adams, ed., *Memoirs of John Quincy Adams,* V, 10. For a different interpretation, see Glickstein, *Concepts of Free Labor in Antebellum America,* 32–38, 147–59. See also Edmund Ruffin, *The Political Economy of Slavery; or, The Institution Considered in Regard to Its Influence on Public Wealth and the General Welfare* (Richmond, [1857?]), 6–7, 9; Betty L. Mitchell, *Edmund Ruffin: A Biography* (Bloomington, 1981), 83; Ulrich Bonnell Phillips, *The Slave Economy of the Old South: Selected Essays in Economic and Social History,* ed. Eugene D. Genovese (Baton Rouge, 1968), 97.

49. H. [George Frederick Holmes], "Greeley on Reforms," *Southern Literary Messenger,* XVII (1851), 263–64, 266–67; Hughes, *Treatise on Sociology,* in Faust, ed., *Ideology of Slavery,* 244–45; Dabney, *Defence of Virginia,* 298–99; Hammond, "Slavery in Light of Political Science," in Elliott, ed., *Cotton Is King,* 637–39; Wish, *George Fitzhugh,* 224–25.

cal nakedness with Hamiltonian clothing and repudiated the Jeffersonian-Jacksonian analysis of economic processes and the revolutionary heritage.

The northern Democracy did not like slavery. Through the 1850s numerous northern Democrats emphatically called it a social and economic evil. A considerable contingent broke away from the party in the Free Soil revolt of 1848 and then joined the Know-Nothing and Republican parties in the political realignment in the mid-1850s. Often the renegade Democrats acted on the belief that the slave power had become too strong and was taking over the nation.[50] The majority of northern Democrats stayed with the Democracy, however, and struggled to contain and neutralize the sectional rift over slavery.

Northern Democrats employed a variety of stratagems to deflate the importance of the slavery issue. On the matter of slavery's extension into the territories, Democrats argued that free labor was naturally superior to slave labor, northerners had the numbers to bring territories into the Union as free states, and the climate favored free labor rather than slave labor. Northern labor practices, not those of the slaveholding states, were destined to prevail. They also stressed the nature of the constitutional compact between the North and the South and that northerners had no right to violate pledges given in 1788–1789.[51]

In their electoral strategy, northern Democrats relied principally on inciting the voters to reject Republicanism and antislavery through unmitigated

50. On northern Democrats and slavery, see Stephen E. Maizlish, *The Triumph of Sectionalism: The Transformation of Ohio Politics, 1844–1856* (Kent, Ohio, 1983), 55–62; John Niven, *Martin Van Buren: The Romantic Age of American Politics* (New York, 1983), 79. Schlesinger, *Age of Jackson,* 478–79, declared that the true Democrats became antislavery Republicans; the Democratic contingent in the Republican party has been analyzed in Foner, *Free Soil, Free Labor, Free Men,* 149–85; Richard H. Sewell, *Ballots for Freedom: Antislavery Politics in the United States, 1837–1860* (New York, 1976), 263–64; and Dale Baum and Dale T. Knobel, "Anatomy of a Realignment: New York Presidential Politics, 1848–1860," *New York History,* LXV (1984), 61–81.

51. See James Buchanan to Mr. [Wm. R.] King, May 13, 1850, in Moore, ed., *Works of Buchanan,* VIII, 383–84; Andrew C. McLaughlin, *Lewis Cass* (Boston, 1919), 143; speech of Caleb Cushing in Boston *Post,* October 28, 1857; Robert W. Johannsen, *Stephen A. Douglas* (New York, 1973), 340, 419, 570–71; James Buchanan to Charles Kessler et al., August 25, 1847, in Moore, ed., *Works of Buchanan,* VII, 386–87; "The Wilmot Proviso," *United States Magazine and Democratic Review,* XXIII (1848), 224–25; Samuel J. Tilden, "The Union,—Its Dangers; And How They Can Be Averted, Letter to Honorable William Kent," in Bigelow, ed., *Writings and Speeches of Tilden,* I, 295, 306–11; John Niven, *Gideon Welles: Lincoln's Secretary of the Navy* (New York, 1973), 223; Ellis, *Union at Risk,* 152–53, 195.

racist appeals to maintain the nation as a white man's country. "The democracy hold that *white men,*" wrote the editor of the New Hampshire *Patriot,* "should rule this country, and they labor to elevate the character, promote the interests and protect the rights of the white man." Democrats believed antislavery was a trick of old-line Federalists to snatch liberty away from white people, that it was an issue manipulated to hide the oppression of workers by capitalists. But their appeal was frequently nothing more than pure and simple racial bigotry. One individual wrote in the Dayton *Ohio Empire,* "Why the Almighty made the African *black* and gave him a physical organization so averse to labor . . . we do not know, any more than we know why he made the hog to live upon offal, or the hyena upon carcasses." Daniel Voorhees of Indiana showed in 1860 the abysmal depths to which the Democratic celebration of white, European superiority could lead when he rejected all notions of equality of races, argued that the Revolution was fought for a racial aristocracy, demanded the conquest of Mexico and New Mexico, and prophesied genocide for the inferior races that stood in the way of Manifest Destiny. White Americans possessed the "direct sanction of God, to exclude and exterminate, and to reduce to subserviency" the Indians and others who stood in the path of Anglo-Saxon territorial aggrandizement.[52]

One argument northern Democrats used to defend southern rights in slaveholding had trenchant implications for the evolution of the party after the days of Jackson. Northern Democrats told northern audiences they could not interefere with southern slavery because that meant interfering with property rights. By the 1850s, the Democratic party, north and south, was maintaining the inviolable nature of property rights.

Southerners in the antebellum decade screamed that Republicans and abolitionists sought to destroy property rights, and perhaps that was the source

52. New Hampshire *Patriot,* quoted in Boston *Post,* February 19, 1858; Dayton *Ohio Empire* quoted in Richmond *Enquirer,* September 4, 1857; Daniel Voorhees, "The American Citizen," in Daniel W. Voorhees, *Speeches of Daniel W. Voorhees of Indiana, Embracing His Most Prominent Forensic, Political, Occasional, and Literary Addresses,* comp. Charles S. Voorhees (Cincinnati, 1875), 35–57, quote on 40; Justin E. Walsh, "Radically and Thoroughly Democratic: Wilbur F. Storey and the Detroit *Free Press,* 1853 to 1861," *Michigan History,* XLVII (1963), 201–202, 207; Baker, *Affairs of Party,* chaps. 5, 6. The debate between Republicans and Democrats has been exquisitely explored by Dykstra, *Bright Radical Star.* For views mitigating northern Democratic racism, see Ashworth, *"Agrarians" and "Aristocrats,"* 221–23; and Stephen E. Maizlish, "The Meaning of Nativism and the Crisis of the Union: The Know-Nothing Movement in the Antebellum North," in *Essays on American Antebellum Politics, 1840–1860,* ed. Maizlish and John J. Kushma (College Station, Tex., 1982), 166–98.

of northern Democrats' justification of southern slavery. In the South Carolina "Declaration of Causes" for secession, the role of property rights was prominent: regarding fugitive slaves, "the right of property in slaves was recognized by giving to free persons distinct political rights." Jefferson Davis hammered away at the theme that northerners had no right to dictate to southerners what constituted property. Richard Lathers, a South Carolinian who moved to New York City, argued before a crowd in 1861 that the South would never return to the Union until it was convinced that northerners would abide by property rights in slaves. Proslavery writers constantly accused the North of "agrarianism," indicating that they specifically feared that in the North property rights were no longer sacrosanct.[53]

Northern Democrats surprisingly toed the mark on the sanctity of property rights in slaves. President James Buchanan gave an address in July, 1860, to support the nominations of John C. Breckinridge and Joseph Lane for president and vice-president. While explaining the rights of the South, Buchanan asked, "When was property ever submitted to the will of the majority?" Northern Democrats had little hestitation in agreeing with southerners that because slaves were property they were not subject to northern meddling.[54]

The challenge to the sanctity of property rights came from the Republican party. Iowa governor James W. Grimes, a Republican, told the Iowa legislature that property "has its duties, as well as its rights." When in Detroit in 1856, William H. Seward explained to an audience that the two pillars of modern civilization, property and liberty, at times came into conflict: "How

53. "Declaration of Causes Which Induced the Secession of South Carolina," in Frank Moore, ed., *The Rebellion Record: A Diary of American Events* (New York, 1861–65), I, 4; Jefferson Davis, *The Rise and Fall of the Confederate Government* (1881; rpr. New York, 1958), I, 52; speech of Jefferson Davis, Senate, February 13 and 14, 1850, in Dunbar Rowland, ed., *Jefferson Davis, Constitutionalist: His Letters, Papers and Speeches* (Jackson, Miss., 1923), I, 279, 283; Speeches at Pine Street Meeting, 1861, pamphlet, in Richard Lathers Papers, LC; A. P. Upshur, "Domestic Slavery," *Southern Literary Messenger,* V (1839), 684; H. [George Frederick Holmes], "Greeley on Reforms," *Southern Literary Messenger,* XVII (1851), 269–76; Thomas Roderick Dew, "Abolition of Negro Slavery," in Faust, ed., *Ideology of Slavery,* 29–30. Thomas Morris, in *Southern Slavery and the Law, 1619–1860* (Chapel Hill, 1996), 1–2, 61–73, 425–31, believes property was the fundamental aspect of southern slavery.

54. Buchanan, speech of July 9, 1860, in Moore, ed., *Works of Buchanan,* X, 460; William Allen Butler, *A Retrospect of Forty Years, 1825–1865,* ed. Harriet Allen Butler (New York, 1911), 56–57; Roy Franklin Nichols, *Franklin Pierce: Young Hickory of the Granite Hills* (2nd ed.; Philadelphia, 1958), 89; Niven, *Gideon Welles,* 226.

to adjust the balance between property and liberty in States, is the great problem of government." And Seward noted, "Property, therefore, has always a bias towards oppression." James Russell Lowell, with more abolitionist emphasis, backed the election of Lincoln in November in the pages of the *Atlantic Monthly* and said property rights needed to be circumscribed: "Human nature is older and more sacred than any claim of property whatever, and . . . it has rights at least as much to be respected as any hypothetical one of our Southern brethren." Republicans accepted the abolitionist dictum that there never could be property rights in man.[55]

The northern battle over slavery involved a breathtaking reversal of party roles and values. The attack by Republicans, abolitionists, and other antislavery advocates was simple and direct; aside from humanitarian impulses and sensitivity to suffering and domination, the basic condemnation of slavery as an institution came directly from the revolutionaries' economic principles—the labor theory of property/value and the power and malfeasance of aristocracy. Whigs, for example, grew weary and angry at having the Democratic charge of aristocracy leveled at them, and one responded: "In America we know of but one class who transmit political power fram [*sic*] father to son, and who are to be regarded and properly a ruling class, viz., the large planters of the South."[56] Slavery violated almost every axiom of correct economic principles established by the Revolution.

The Republicans saw the contradiction, but why did not northern Democrats? Northern Democrats endlessly used the republican theory of the distribution of wealth on economic issues such as the tariff, western land distribution, expenditures of the federal government, and banking and currency. They certainly saw the utility of the republican theory of the distribution of wealth in dissecting the evils of the monster bank. They utterly failed to transfer the same theory to slavery.

At times, northern Democrats—like southerners—produced some of the

55. Grimes's address to the Iowa legislature, 1854, in William Salter, *The Life of James W. Grimes* (New York, 1876), 56–57; Seward, "The Dominant Class in the Republic," in Baker, ed., *Works of Seward,* IV, 254–55; [James Russell Lowell], "Election in November," *Atlantic Monthly,* VI (1860), 497. For no property rights in man, see Charles Sumner, "Our Immediate Antislavery Duties," in Charles Sumner, *The Works of Charles Sumner* (Boston, 1870–75), II, 414; Providence *Evening Press,* January 23, 1860; Charles Francis Adams, *An Oration, Delivered Before the Municipal Authorities of the City of Fall River, July 4, 1860* (Fall River, Mass., 1860), 6.

56. "Socialists, Communists, and Red Republicans," *American* [Whig] *Review,* X (1849), 417.

most paradoxical statements in antebellum political literature. When John L. O'Sullivan founded the *United States Magazine and Democratic Review* in 1837, his first contribution stressed the "voluntary principle" in creating a new and just society. A contributor returned to the theme of voluntarism in 1855. "THE VOLUNTARY PRINCIPLE" was the principle of self-government, and behind it lay the doctrines of laissez-faire and opposition to monopoly, church and state, and central banking. But the article then moved to a condemnation of abolitionists and antislavery fanatics: they violated the voluntary spirit, the laissez-faire dictum, by interfering with slaveholders' right to live off the fruits of their slaves' labor.[57]

Perhaps Democratic racism or political allegiance with the South inhibited northern Democrats from applying to slavery the simple revolutionary distributionist logic that they did to all other economic issues. Whatever the case, by the 1850s the northern Democratic party had stunningly reversed itself from its Jeffersonian and Jacksonian ancestry. In the political contests over the national banks, the parties ranged on the Jeffersonian axis stood for human rights over property rights, principle over expediency, the fruits of labor over inherited wealth, republicanism over aristocracy. It was the Federalists and the Whigs who argued for, and by the 1850s were the guardians of, property rights, expediency, compromise, and natural inequalities. The Republicans, who economically descended from the Hamiltonian axis of American politics, were the ones who now trumpeted human rights over property rights, principle over expediency, the fruits of labor over inherited wealth, and republicanism over aristocracy.

Several Republicans knew that this had happened, and one suspects that they obtained an intense satisfaction from the reversal of the parties in regard to democracy and human rights. For years those on the Hamiltonian axis honestly protested that they were not aristocrats but pragmatists who wished to see the American republican experiment succeed. They had always been pilloried by those on the Jeffersonian axis who never believed that anyone but themselves espoused the true republican faith and cared for the citizenry. Suddenly, through the slavery issue, the roles changed. Now the Democrats argued for caution and wariness; the Hamiltonian descendants suddenly became the torch-bearers of republicanism and democracy.

The most insightful comments about the Republican and Democratic

---

57. S. W. C., "The Voluntary Principle," *United States Review*, XXXVI (1855), 387–88, 390–92.

stands on property rights came from Horace Greeley. In a reflective mood in January, 1860, Greeley opined, "Originally the [Democratic] party exalted the rights of man over the privileges of property; holding that the former were inherent and inalienable; the latter incidental and conventional." Now Democrats taught that "all *property* is created equal." The northern Democracy "has ceased to prate about the dignity of the toiling masses, while the Southern and ruling wing sneers at farmers and mechanics as 'the mud-sills of society' and declares that the only stable and philosophic basis of the social system is that where the capitalist owns labor!" The old Democracy believed in antimonopoly and antiprivilege, as exemplified, Greeley thought, in the Democratic crusade against the Bank of the United States. But slavery was a far greater monopoly and slaveholders a far more privileged group than the Bank of the United States and its directors ever were. The Democrats had failed their Jeffersonian lineage.[58]

The northern Democracy had in fact experienced a massive failure of will. The Civil War witnessed the greatest assault on the doctrine of property rights ever conducted in the United States. The outcome of the conflagration established in reality the principle that property rights came not from nature but from the given consent of a collective group and that the people composing that group could redefine and restrict property rights in the interest of their civilization whenever it seemed fit to do so. It is one of the paradoxes of American history that this massive assault and redefinition of property rights came not from the logical part of the political spectrum, from the Jeffersonian axis, but from the part that treasured property rights, the Hamiltonian axis. At the moment of decision, at the time of the greatest triumph over property rights in the history of the United States, the descendants of Jefferson trembled, collapsed, and disappeared. The ancestors of Hamilton were the ones emotionally strong enough to complete the final task commanded by the American Revolution.

The Civil War and Reconstruction period, 1861 to 1877, saw no diminution in Republican reliance on the republican theory of the distribution of wealth,

---

58. Editorial by Horace Greeley in New York *Tribune,* January 11, 1860, p. 4. A reading of the Democrats that stresses their reactions to social strains rather than to their Jeffersonian heritage is provided by Joel H. Silbey, "'There Are Other Questions Beside That of Slavery Merely': The Democratic Party and Antislavery Politics," in *Crusaders and Compromisers: Essays on the Relationship of the Antislavery Struggle to the Antebellum Party System,* ed. Alan M. Kraut (Westport, Conn., 1983), 144–61.

most forcibly asserted in the free labor ideology. The war destroyed slavery and left in its wake the monumental task of reestablishing the southern economy with some institutional replacement for slavery as the means of labor organization. Republicans attempted to implement a free labor system in the South. At the same time, certain Radical Republicans, those Republicans most committed to creating a racially egalitarian United States, saw that an economic base for the freed people was a prerequisite for making them an independent citizenry. The solution, advanced by Radicals such as George Washington Julian of Indiana and Thaddeus Stevens of Pennsylvania, was to carve up the large plantations into small freeholds for the former slaves. A few attempts at redistribution were made, but, in keeping with the history of such efforts in the United States, general redistribution did not take place. Instead, a trade-off apparently occurred in which black males obtained the suffrage instead of land. The logic behind that trade-off, that is, voting rights instead of land ownership, can be explained in terms of the political economy of aristocracy. Nonetheless, the Reconstruction episode demonstrated that the set of ideas and values that composed the free labor ideology and the republican theory of the distribution of wealth relied on cultural and social agreements. They were not, as Americans had assumed between 1776 and 1877, universal truths.

During the war, the question of what status to grant the former slaves and how to provide for their future grew in importance, and by the end of the war it loomed as the most pressing topic in national life. After a bitter contest with Andrew Johnson, who succeeded the martyred Lincoln, the Republican party took over direction of the Reconstruction program, mandated a free labor society for the South, set up some appropriate institutions, and granted the freed people citizenship and black males the suffrage.[59]

The Republican design for the postbellum South contained some elements of land redistribution. The Second Conscription Act of July, 1862, and the Freedmen's Bureau (Bureau of Refugees, Freedmen and Abandoned Lands) Act of March 3, 1865, implied the possibility of seizing Confederate land and turning it over to the freedmen. Many Radical Republicans sought a general redistribution. Thaddeus Stevens made an impassioned speech declaring it criminal to release blacks from bondage with no means of indepen-

---

59. For a general overview of Reconstruction with an emphasis on the fate of the free labor ideology, see Foner, *Reconstruction,* esp. 28–29, 156–58, 477–79, 524–26, 602–604.

dent support. In a passage famous to Reconstruction historians, Stevens declared in Congress, "If we do not furnish them with homesteads from forfeited rebel property, and hedge them around with protective laws; if we leave them to the legislation of their late masters, we had better left them in bondage." Calls for confiscation found some approval because dispossession was a sanctioned penalty for those who had engaged in rebellion. As well, the vocal supporters of redistribution indicated that granting homesteads to former slaves would ensure the victory of free labor by creating a middling society in which the fruits of labor were secured to landholding agrarians and were beyond the grasp of aristocrats.[60]

Several attempts at land redistribution were conducted. At Davis Bend in Mississippi and on the South Carolina sea islands, Republican leaders created small freeholds and settled black families on them. Andrew Johnson disliked these trials and through his use of the power of pardon and bureaucratic machinery he destroyed the usefulness of the Freedmen's Bureau, demanded and obtained the return of confiscated land to the previous owners, and generally thwarted any potential Republican program of redistribution. However Reconstruction was to proceed, it was going to have to do so without land redistribution.[61]

60. Thaddeus Stevens, *Reconstruction: Speech of Hon. Thaddeus Stevens, of Pennsylvania. Delivered in the House of Representatives of the United States, December 13, 1865* (Washington, D.C., 1865), 6; see Donald K. Pickens, "The Republican Synthesis and Thaddeus Stevens," *Civil War History,* XXXI (1985), 57–73; Herman Belz, *Emancipation and Equal Rights: Politics and Constitutionalism in the Civil War Era* (New York, 1978), 57, 147–48; Claude F. Oubre, *Forty Acres and a Mule: The Freedmen's Bureau and Black Land Ownership* (Baton Rouge, 1978), 181–83; Jaynes, *Branches Without Roots,* 9–12; Foner, *Reconstruction,* 236, 309; Eric Foner, *Politics and Ideology in the Age of the Civil War* (New York, 1980), 131–48; George W. Julian, *Political Recollections, 1840 to 1872* (Chicago, 1884), 219–20, 238–40; Julian, *Speeches on Political Questions,* 222–25; speech of Thaddeus Stevens, May 8, 1866, *Congressional Globe,* 39th Cong., 1st Sess., 2459–60; *Harper's Weekly,* May 18, 1867, p. 303; Wendell Phillips, "Abraham Lincoln Assassinated," in Louis Filler, ed., *Wendell Phillips on Civil Rights and Freedom* (2nd ed.; Washington, D.C., 1982), 189–91; James Brewer Stewart, *William Lloyd Garrison and the Challenge of Emancipation* (Arlington Heights, Ill., 1992), 181–82, 194.

61. Steven Joseph Ross, "Freed Soil, Freed Labor, Freed Men: John Eaton and the Davis Bend Experiment," *Journal of Southern History,* XLIV (1978), 213–32; Louis S. Gerteis, *From Contraband to Freedman: Federal Policy Toward Southern Blacks, 1861–1865* (Westport, Conn., 1973), 139, 169–81; Willie Lee Rose, *Rehearsal for Reconstruction: The Port Royal Experiment* (Indianapolis, 1964), 199–216, 272–73, 296, 349–58; Edward Magdol, *A Right to the Land: Essays on the Freedmen's Community* (Westport, Conn., 1977), 139–73; John Hope Franklin,

Congressional Republicans would not likely have supported a general land redistribution scheme in any event. Most trembled at such an unabashed denial of the inviolability of property rights. Conservatives argued that the example might lead to alterations in the North as well. The New York *Times* in particular was insistent on exhibiting all the drawbacks of land redistribution. Growing northern labor unrest, in the form of the eight-hour day movement, frightened numerous Republicans.[62] That the Republicans in the 1860s should fail to act on land redistribution is not surprising. Since the Revolution, Americans had excelled only in talking about an equitable distribution of wealth; their record was null when it came to physically transferring wealth from one person to another. The whole of the American experience had been a self-congratulation on being given an equitable distribution of wealth and then following policies to ensure that no aristocratic clique managed to distort that distribution. But when cases arose that called for direct intervention in allocating property from one person to another on the basis of justice, republican necessity, or any other reason, American legislators faded and disappeared.

Instead of a government-mandated transfer of land from the former slave masters to the freed people, Congress bestowed upon freed males the suffrage in the Fourteenth and Fifteenth Amendments to the Constitution. Charles Sumner wrote to the Duchess of Argyll that the black was given the suffrage "for his own protection." In the words of historian William Gillette, the congressional Republican attitude was that "the Negro was now a man, a citizen, and a voter. He could take care of himself. There need be no more talk of Washington giving him land or racially integrated schools."[63]

Historians have been unimpressed with this trade-off. From the late-twentieth-century perspective, land would have done the freedpeople far more good than the ballot. While seldom saying that political power was of

---

Reconstruction After the Civil War (Chicago, 1961), 5, 114. Michael Les Benedict blames Johnson for the failure of Republican redistribution schemes in his *The Impeachment and Trial of Andrew Johnson* (New York, 1973), 17–21, 37–50.

62. New York *Times,* June 13, 27, 1867; "The Reconstruction Discussion," *Nation,* May 22, 1866, p. 648; "The Labor Crisis," *Nation,* April 25, 1867, pp. 334–36; "Confiscation," *Nation,* May 9, 1867, pp. 375–76; *Harper's Weekly,* April 21, 1866, p. 242; Foner, *Reconstruction,* 236–37, 309; Abbott, *Cotton and Capital,* 207.

63. Charles Sumner to the Duchess of Argyll, April 3, 1866, in Beverly Wilson Palmer, ed., *The Selected Letters of Charles Sumner* (Boston, 1990), II, 359; William Gillette, *Retreat from Reconstruction, 1869–1879* (Baton Rouge, 1980), 24.

no consequence, most historians have agreed that without some form of economic independence the ballot had few protective or progressive capacities for the freed people.[64]

An explanation for the granting of political rights rather than economic assistance can be found in the revolutionaries' theory of the distribution of wealth. Too many Republicans and too many northern and southern blacks believed in the power of the ballot to dismiss it as an act of evasion of the freedpeople's monumental problems. No doubt land redistribution would have produced healthier results, but from the standpoint of those living in 1868 wholesome outcomes should have resulted from the implementation of the congressional Reconstruction program. The wretched outcome of Reconstruction by 1910—sharecropping and near peonage—was principally the result of the hidden assumptions of the free labor ideology. Republican congressmen did not realize how vital those assumptions were to the functioning of their favored form of economy.

Scholars have exhibited an attitude to voting somewhat similar to that of true nineteenth-century conservatives. The vote was important to various groups because it enabled them to band together and extract favors, rewards, and even livelihoods from government. The potential of using the vote to control government and redistribute property from the rich to the poor had been the haunting fear of conservatives in regard to universal suffrage since the beginning of the nineteenth century.[65] If nineteenth-century conservatives feared the property-redistributing potential of the ballot, twentieth-century radicals have been dismayed that universal suffrage in western Euro-

64. For debate over Reconstruction policy, see Hans L. Trefousse, *The Radical Republicans: Lincoln's Vanguard for Racial Justice* (New York, 1969), 20–33 and *passim;* Gillette, *Retreat from Reconstruction,* 13–14, 17–23; Michael Les Benedict, *A Compromise of Principle: Congressional Republicans and Reconstruction, 1863–1869* (New York, 1974), 107, 325; Benedict, *Impeachment and Trial of Andrew Johnson,* 10–11; Eric Foner, *Nothing But Freedom: Emancipation and Its Legacy* (Baton Rouge, 1983), 40, 46; Foner, *Reconstruction,* 109, 362–65; Franklin, *Reconstruction After the Civil War,* 222–24; Kenneth M. Stampp, *The Era of Reconstruction, 1865–1877* (New York, 1965), 129–31, 213–15.

65. Cole, *Van Buren and the American Political System,* 71–72; John Adams to James Madison, June 17, 1817, in Adams, ed., *Works of John Adams,* X, 267–68; Hamilton, *Men and Manners in America,* 162–64, 166, 172; Thomas R. Dew, "An Address on the Influence of Federative Republican System of Government upon Literature and the Development of Character," *Southern Literary Messenger,* II (1836), 277–78; A. P. Upshur, "Domestic Slavery," *Southern Literary Messenger,* V (1839), 684; Dabney, *Defence of Virginia,* 298–99; Roland N. Stromberg, *Democracy: A Short, Analytical History* (Armonk, N.Y., 1996), 34–49.

pean nations has failed to produce a redistribution of wealth and income. Time has proven both conservative fears and radical hopes about the ballot to be false; universal suffrage may alter many things economically and politically, but it has almost never produced a major redistribution of income and wealth. For that reason, most historians of Reconstruction have found the Republican grant of voting rights to blacks instead of land redistribution mostly a symbolic measure, devoid of economic content.

This modern analysis of Reconstruction misapprehends the nineteenth-century justification of the ballot. The current interpretation of voting assumes an aggressive use of the ballot to obtain positive rewards from the state. Like-minded people coalesce, vote as a unit, and seek government action to reward or favor their group in a particular way. But in nineteenth-century republican America, the purpose of the ballot and universal suffrage was negative, not positive. And the ideas behind the republican theory of the distribution of wealth explain how congressional Republicans during Reconstruction could with some integrity offer the ballot to black males as a means by which they could advance economically and prosper in American society.

The literature of nineteenth-century egalitarians, not conservatives, in regard to the ballot reveals not the aggressive nature of voting but its protective nature. William Leggett, the radical laissez-faire Jacksonian, for example, editorialized on labor unions in 1837. Leggett understood the purpose of unions—to demand and obtain a higher price for labor—and he was upset by the conflicts that might arise when desired prices did not match lower natural (market) prices. Riots and even unions, however, were not the means to secure a decent income; instead, workers should "through the ballot boxes . . . end, at once and forever" systems "of moneyed monopolies, which impoverish the poor to enrich the rich."[66]

The distribution of wealth was tied to the ballot by the fear of aristocracy and the labor theory of property/value. The ballot stopped those aggressively seeking to use government to transfer by legislation the fruits of another person's labor to themselves. The ballot stopped aristocracy from misusing the powers of government and ensured that each person obtained the fruits of his or her labor, resulting in an equitable distribution of wealth. Joseph Fitz Randolph expressed this attitude in Congress in 1842: "In monarchies and aris-

66. William Leggett, "The Way to Cheapen Flour," in Sedgwick, ed., *Collection of the Political Writings of William Leggett*, II, 221, quotes on 225.

tocracies there are classes of the very wealthy and of the very poor; in a Republic both extremes are avoided; there is more uniformity of character and standing, and all classes assimilate more to each other. In our country we have no class like the miserably poor found in Europe; all are free and equal, and, with our extended right of suffrage, if any should be infamous enough to desire such a degradation, it would be impossible to effect it." Free northern blacks, like Charles Ray, believed that the lack of the suffrage made free northern blacks prey to whites because blacks had no political rights: "The body politic sees in us, therefore, no favors to court, and nothing to fear." Wendell Phillips put the protective feature of the ballot foremost when agitating for the vote for women: "I am speaking in a republic which admits the principle that the poor are not to be protected by the rich, but to have the means of protecting themselves" through "the ballot, which protects each class."[67]

During the first few years of Reconstruction, Republicans gave ample testimony to their belief that the ballot was a protective device, not an offensive weapon. Republicans espoused the ballot because they needed to have their party represented in the conquered South, but they also had expectations about how the ballot would operate. George W. Julian of Indiana made the necessity of the ballot obvious by reminding listeners of the potential damage of "popular sovereignty." Without the ballot, the former slave masters would control legislation and make "the condition of the freedmen more intolerable than slavery itself, through local laws and police regulations." Julian made it clear that slavery was primarily a political condition; the aristocrats of Europe owned labor and "[ground down] the toiling millions of the Old World" because labor had no vote: "The real test of freedom is the right to a share in the governing power." William Stewart of Nevada posed the dilemma forcefully in 1866: "But what are you to do with him [the freedman]? He must either exercise his own political rights or somebody must excercise them for him." James M. Ashley, when in San Francisco, called the ballot the poor man's only defense, and James A. Garfield quoted John Stuart Mill: "That the ballot is put into the hands of men, not so much to enable them to govern others as that he may not be misgoverned by others." Garfield con-

67. Speech of Senator Joseph Fitz Randolph, June 20, 1842, *Congressional Globe,* 27th Cong., 2nd Sess., Appendix, 821; Charles Ray quoted in Swift, *Black Prophets of Justice,* 122; Wendell Phillips, "Suffrage for Women," in Phillips, *Speeches, Lectures, and Letters,* II, 113.

cluded that voting was the principal means of self-defense in political society. Indeed, the radicals insisted on land reform *and* suffrage.[68]

Thus the republican theory of the distribution of wealth was the key element in explaining how the suffrage was so vitally connected to an equitable distribution of wealth. The basic proposition of wealth equitability was that each individual receive the full fruits of his or her labor. That condition allowed for inequalities but not injustices; it assumed the full fruits of labor were considerably above the subsistence wage level. By saving some of the fruits of labor, one accumulated property and over time achieved independence and social mobility, the extent of which depended on moral character and intelligence. That process in a nutshell is the free labor ideology of the Republican party in the Civil War and Reconstruction years. And radicals during Reconstruction clearly envisioned an egalitarian, small-owner, agrarian society growing from free labor doctrines.[69] This was also the economics of American revolutionary republicanism that had been operating since 1776—the Republicans were just better expositors of it than anyone else had been.

Twentieth-century scholars have been reticent to understand this point of view because they have learned their redistributionist theory under the intellectual presuppositions of the twentieth century. These researchers hold, almost to a person, that income inequality derives from the economic and not the political sphere. For the socialist Left, inequality in income and wealth arises from differences in the ownership of the means of production. But for

68. Julian, *Political Recollections*, 265; Julian, "Suffrage in the District of Columbia," in Julian, *Speeches on Political Questions*, 292; see also *ibid.*, 276, 336–37; San Francisco speeches of Ashley in Benjamin W. Arnett, *Hon. J. M. Ashley Souvenir: Duplicate Copy of the Souvenir from the Afro-American League of Tennessee to Hon. James M. Ashley of Ohio* (Philadelphia, 1894), 378, 411; speech of William M. Stewart, May 24, 1866, *Congressional Globe*, 39th Cong., 1st Sess., 2799; speech of James A. Garfield, May 8, 1866, *ibid.*, 2462–63; see also speech of Thaddeus Stevens, January 22, 1864, *ibid.*, 38th Cong., 1st Sess., 316; *Harper's Weekly*, May 12, 1866, p. 290, and March 9, 1867, p. 146; "Political Equality," *Nation*, July 20, 1865, pp. 72–73; George S. Boutwell, *Reminiscences of Sixty Years in Public Affairs* (1902; rpr. New York, 1968), II, 39–40, 45; Julian, *Speeches on Political Questions*, 268–71; William D. Kelley, *Speeches, Addresses and Letters on Industrial and Financial Questions* (Philadelphia, 1872), 169; Wendell Phillips, "The Case for Labor," in Filler, ed., *Phillips on Civil Rights and Freedom*, 198–207.

69. Kelley, *Speeches, Addresses, and Letters*, 168–69, 181–83; Phillips, "The Case for Labor," in Filler, ed., *Phillips on Civil Rights and Freedom*, 204–207; Henry Wilson, *Speech of Hon. Henry Wilson, at the Republican Mass Meeting at Bangor, Me., August 27, 1868* (New York, 1868), 9–10; Julian, *Speeches on Political Questions*, 224–25.

nineteenth-century republicanism, inequality—or, more accurately, inequitability—stemmed from ownership of the means of political coercion. That politics created inequality was a nineteenth-century understanding; that economics created inequality has become the twentieth-century understanding.

The vote preserved the noncoercive, non-government-induced redistribution of wealth from the many to the few. By voting, one protected his (but not *her*) fruits of labor from attack by aristocratic predators. Only by capturing the machinery of government could aristocrats deprive laborers of the fruits of their labors; but the democratic vote denied the aristocracy that power. Without the coercive power of the state, no transference could occur. The economy would simply have to run on voluntary principles, ensuring that every person got the full reward of the fruits of his or her labors. Thus, under the operation of the republican theory of the distribution of wealth, control of the suffrage was critical. Aristocratic influences were always a danger, but under a restricted suffrage the danger grew exponentially. True, a degraded and unvirtuous population might vote for a demagogue and redistribute wealth, but the egalitarian impulse within republicanism spoke to the optimism that a voluntary society and a nonaristocratic government would satisfy the moral sensibilities of the great mass of the people.

The protective quality of the vote may have had some relation to the mass participation in politics and the high voter turnout in the nineteenth century. The notion that the vote was a means of protecting hearth and home from the sinister designs of rapacious aggressors fits the masculine emphasis of American republicanism and American society (and perhaps was one reason for the resistance of men to female voting: protecting was a man's role, nurturing was a woman's). To arouse citizens to protect themselves from a nefarious aristocrat may have had a considerable impact on the psychology of voting. Moreover, the idea of voting to protect what was one's own probably had more appeal than the notion of coalescing with others to ask for government largesse—which, in nineteenth-century terms, was an admission of dependence.[70]

The attempt at a transition from slavery to free labor for the southern states

70. Richard L. McCormick has written that nineteenth-century politics on economic matters was a politics of distribution and promotion, whereas twentieth-century politics has been a politics of administration and regulation (*The Party Period and Public Policy,* 197–227, esp. 203–27). Note the comments of Wiebe, *Self-Rule,* 6, 72–73, on the importance of the ballot.

failed, in part because a free labor society was never established. Republicans knew and understood that racism, ideas, and behaviors inherited from slavery days could impede the practice of free labor, but they naively hoped that such obstacles would fall before the imperatives of supply and demand and a noncoercive, nonaristocratic society. For the first time, Americans had to confront the reality that social forces affected the economic and political realms as well as the reverse. Free labor would never operate beneficially for blacks when white attitudes and behaviors worked to maintain white supremacy and a cheap black agricultural labor force. The free labor ideology required economic actors to allow others to engage in activities of their choice without coercion. The postbellum South was not a land free of coercion. It is hard to say that the Republicans' free labor system failed in the South; in a true sense, it was never tried.[71]

Reconstruction was the last significant trial in which politicians invoked the republican theory of the distribution of wealth. It was used in the debates of the 1870s and 1880s, but its power started to wane. In the 1890s the republican theory of the distribution of wealth was overthrown, and by the twentieth century it was virtually unknown. The grim reaper that mowed down the republican theory of the distribution of wealth was the large-scale corporation.

---

71. Gerald Jaynes has argued in *Branches Without Roots,* 301–306, that free labor never operated in the postbellum South because of violence. There were of course many reasons for Reconstruction's failure, but probably the most fruitful line of inquiry is that of William Gillette, who has suggested that the lack of an active, present, and long-term bureaucracy to adjust racial tensions and economic rights doomed the congressional program (*Retreat from Reconstruction,* 363). For the failure of free labor and the debilitating results of racism, see *ibid.,* 366–76; Foner, *Reconstruction,* 156, 377; Franklin, *Reconstruction After the Civil War,* chaps. 9, 11; Stampp, *Era of Reconstruction,* chap. 7; Martin, *Mind of Frederick Douglass,* 254–59; Woodman, "Reconstruction of the Cotton Plantation," 99–115; Paul A. Cimbala, "The 'Talisman Power': Davis Tillson, the Freedmen's Bureau, and Free Labor in Reconstruction Georgia, 1865–1866," *Civil War History,* XXVIII (1982), 153–71.

PART III

THE FOUNDATION CRACKS, 1880–1920

The farther I went with him [Arthur Lapham Perry] in his way through these flowerless fields, the more I thought I saw the answer to the problem of Accumulated Wealth and Accumulated Power that overhung the barony. Easily I bound cause to effect. The root of the evil was the accursed tariff. . . .

The Free Trade movement died of a profound constitutional malady. Like so many other well-meant reforming inspirations, it had attacked symptoms but stopped short of causations. All that the Free Trade champions said against protection and its evils was true; it was indeed an overflowing fountain-head of trouble. But it was only the outgrowth of an underlying condition. So long as the profit system was to be retained, Protection or Free Trade could make little difference to the lives of the masses, and even Henry George purposed to leave the profit system virtually intact. The real source of the world's distress was production for profit and nothing could remedy or seriously affect the disorders arising from that source except the substitution of production for use.

—Charles Edward Russell, *Bare Hands and Stone Walls: Some Recollections of a Side-Line Reformer*

10

The New Aristocratic Enemy, 1880–1920

The republican theory of the distribution of wealth passed through the furnaces of Civil War and Reconstruction unscathed and unaltered. Since the Revolution, the four axioms of the labor theory of property/value, the political economy of aristocracy, the laws of entail and primogeniture, and the population-to-land ratio had guided Americans in assessing economic phenomena and evaluating economic justice. These elements dominated economic discussion until the mid-1880s and even into the 1890s. But by 1900, the republican theory of the distribution of wealth was dead, its axioms dismissed, its prognosis for political action repudiated. In the space of two decades the nation had undergone the most powerful and wrenching transformation in its history, a transformation that altered customs, habits, expectations, values, institutions, and behaviors. Political agendas were redefined, the understanding of the relation between political and economic processes was reversed, the old economics of laissez-faire was laid to rest, and a new economics was born. The ancient enemy of republicanism, aristocracy, became an impotent and forgettable villain. And a different perspective on the distribution of wealth took form. The agent responsible for this mighty transformation was the large-scale business organization, the corporation.

Between 1865 and 1877, the difficulty of reconstructing the South absorbed the attention of national leaders, but traditional issues of the two-party system once more forced their way into the political arena. In the period described as the Gilded Age, roughly 1877 to 1896, the tariff, western lands, banking and currency, and internal improvements reclaimed their primacy on the congressional agenda just as they had in the days of Hamilton and Jefferson and of Jackson and Clay. For national political issues (but not in other areas) the Gilded Age was indeed the Great Repetition. The issues, the parties, and the understanding of economic and social processes were all borrowed from the antebellum decades.[1]

National politics continued to follow the basic dichotomy that had begun in the 1790s. One party on the Jeffersonian axis, the Democrats, advocated laissez-faire, small government policies for the economy. The other party, the Republicans, situated on the Hamiltonian axis, argued for some governmental intervention to promote economic growth. The Republicans and Democrats of the Gilded Age did not challenge this enduring configuration of American politics.

Kenneth M. Stampp once referred to President Andrew Johnson as the "last Jacksonian." The label was not inappropriate, but the thrust of the interpretation masked an essential feature of the Democratic party between 1865 and 1896: throughout the period the party was thoroughly and irredeemably Jacksonian. When the white supremacist redeemers of the South recaptured state governments between 1872 and 1876, they immediately installed the old laissez-faire doctrines of the 1830s with a vengeance. C. Vann Woodward has written that after 1876, "*laissez faire* became almost a test of Southern patriotism." This was no less true of the North, where Democrats continued to press for free trade (or at least reduced tariffs), small governments, and noninterference in the economy. Among the hotly battled issues of the Gilded Age, strangely enough, were the continuing ones that had inspired Hamilton and Jefferson: centralization and states' rights.[2]

1. For political issues in the postwar period, see Keller, *Affairs of State,* 239–80, 319–40, 412–23, and *passim;* and the general historical accounts of the Gilded Age by Garraty, *New Commonwealth,* chaps. 6, 7; and H. Wayne Morgan, *From Hayes to McKinley: National Party Politics, 1877–1896* (Syracuse, 1969), 277–319, 352–56, 497–519. On banking and currency questions, see Roger L. Ransom and Richard Sutch, *One Kind of Freedom: The Economic Consequences of Emancipation* (Cambridge, Eng., 1977), 110–16, 126–31; John A. James, *Money and Capital Markets in Postbellum America* (Princeton, 1978), 27–29, 48, 119–25, 236; Irwin Unger, *The Greenback Era: A Social and Political History of American Finance, 1865–1879* (Princeton, 1964), chaps. 1–4; Chester McArthur Destler, *American Radicalism, 1865–1901: Essays and Documents* (New London, Conn., 1946), chaps. 1–4. The link between antebellum and postbellum money crusades has been noted by many historians, for example, Sharp, *Jacksonians Versus the Banks,* 7–9, 19, 328–29. On western land, see Robbins, *Our Landed Heritage,* 207–208, 217–20, 222–25, 285–98; Fred A. Shannon, *The Farmer's Last Frontier: Agriculture, 1860–1897* (New York, 1945), 51–67.

2. Stampp, *Era of Reconstruction,* title of chap. 3; C. Vann Woodward, *Origins of the New South, 1877–1913* (Baton Rouge, 1951), 65; Michael Perman, *The Road to Redemption: Southern Politics, 1869–1879* (Chapel Hill, 1984), 80, 174, 179, 191, 199, 203. For the Democratic party in the Reconstruction and Gilded Age periods, see R. Hal Williams, " 'Dry Bones and Dead Lan-

The Republican party continued the Hamiltonian tradition of arguing for an active, interventionist government that promoted economic growth. But the Republican economic program was confused because of the mongrel nature of the origins of the party. During the Civil War, the former Whigs and Democrats in the party almost made a tacit agreement that Democratic thinking would shape financial policies while Whig thinking would control tariff rates. The National Banking Act followed basic Jacksonian notions: no central bank would be founded to act as a national regulator, guidelines for sound banking (to the extent contemporaries believed they knew the foundations for sound banking) were elaborated and instituted, and reserve ratios were established. The Republican program failed to imitate the substance of Whiggery: direct federal control through a bank that could tame the excesses of state banks.[3]

Both parties operated within the confines of a belief in states' rights and laissez-faire. The Hamiltonian axis parties—with the possible exception of Hamilton himself—never envisioned a leviathan for a government. The basic question for national and even state economic policy was complete laissez-faire or modest government promotion and at times regulation of the economy. Although numerous older historians have painted the Republicans as the pawns of industrialists, political centralizers, and oppressors of the people, other studies have shown that Republicans and their economic philosophers did not permit much straying from the laissez-faire, states'-rights path. And the reformers who did appear, the "mugwumps," were not novel. They were adherents to long-standing axioms of republican political economy.[4]

---

guage': The Democratic Party," in *The Gilded Age,* ed. H. Wayne Morgan (rev. ed.; Syracuse, 1970), 129–49; Joel H. Silbey, *A Respectable Minority: The Democratic Party in the Civil War Era, 1860–1868* (New York, 1977), 238–39, 241–44; Jerome Mushkat, *Fernando Wood: A Political Biography* (Kent, Ohio, 1990), viii, 184–244.

3. On the Republican party, see H. Wayne Morgan, *William McKinley and His America* (Syracuse, 1963), 55, 58–64, 211–14; Keller, *Affairs of State,* 238, 251–54; Lewis L. Gould, "The Republican Search for a National Majority," in *The Gilded Age,* ed. H. Wayne Morgan (2nd ed.; Syracuse, 1970), 171–87; Leon Burr Richardson, *William E. Chandler: Republican* (New York, 1940), 400–415; Stanley P. Hirshson, *Farewell to the Bloody Shirt: Northern Republicans and the Southern Negro, 1877–1893* (Bloomington, 1962), 123–26. On Republicans and banking, see Hammond, *Banks and Politics in America,* 722–25, 727.

4. For example, Charles A. Beard and Mary Beard, *The Rise of American Civilization* (New York, 1927), II, 108, 294–95, 297; Stampp, *Era of Reconstruction,* 94–95, 187–88. A recent restatement of the centralizing proclivities of the Republican party can be found in Bernstein, *New York City Draft Riots,* 65, 70, 188–92. A restatement of the Beardian charge that the Re-

American students of political economy added virtually nothing to the body of antebellum knowledge. Into the 1880s, standard books on political economy nitpicked over the appropriate verbiage to define concepts (rent, labor, and so on) and were written from a standard literary format: consumption, production, distribution (rent, wages, and profits), and governmental duties. Not a page of these hefty volumes was sullied by the presence of mathematical formulas or degraded by an elementary chart. Political economy in the Gilded Age was literary and enormously given to the delicacy of word selection. The major topic of debate was free trade or protectionism. As was said in the antebellum era, so political economists said in the postbellum years: the distribution of wealth was determined by natural forces and was beneficent.[5]

Workingmen were stirring in these years, but they were slow to challenge the basic ideas behind the republican theory of the distribution of wealth. Rather, the idea of equal rights continued to pervade working-class movements. Leaders often relied on Jacksonian financial ideas, and the major thrust of working-class reform efforts was to shorten hours and establish unions. In the 1870s and 1880s, Eugene V. Debs revealed the grasp the republican theory of political economy had on union leaders and perhaps on workers in general. The great uprising of 1877, the strike by railroad workers against the Baltimore and Ohio Railroad in July that nearly became a general strike, augured future tense relations and a significant and growing social

publicans were the stalking-horse for industrial capitalism is Bensel, *Yankee Leviathan*, chap. 1 and *passim*. For arguments stressing the essential laissez-faire, states'-rights nature of all American political life, see Keller, *Affairs of State*, 181–85; James C. Mohr, Introduction to *Radical Republicans in the North: State Politics During Reconstruction*, ed. Mohr (Baltimore, 1976), xi–xvi; Sidney Fine, *Laissez Faire and the General-Welfare State: A Study of Conflict in American Thought, 1865–1901* (Ann Arbor, 1956), 3–47. For mugwumps, see Geoffrey Blodgett, *The Gentle Reformers: Massachusetts Democrats in the Cleveland Era* (Cambridge, Mass., 1966), 30–39, 71–79, 96; John G. Sproat, *"The Best Men": Liberal Reformers in the Gilded Age* (New York, 1968), 4–8, 143–84.

5. Paul F. Boller, Jr., *American Thought in Transition: The Impact of Evolutionary Naturalism, 1865–1900* (Chicago, 1969), 70–81; Festus P. Summers, *William L. Wilson and Tariff Reform* (New Brunswick, N.J., 1953), 48–51; Fine, *Laissez Faire and the General-Welfare State*, chap. 1. For examples of standard political economy writing in the Gilded Age, see William G. Sumner, *Lectures on the History of Protection in the United States* (New York, 1886); David A. Wells, *Practical Economics* (New York, 1885); Arthur Latham Perry, *Political Economy* (22nd ed.; New York, 1895); Amasa Walker, *The Science of Wealth: A Manual of Political Economy* (Philadelphia, 1872).

problem. Yet workers did not move much beyond republicanism and craft union principles in their expressed understanding of economic phenomena.[6]

Although the subject of primogeniture and entail did not arise as frequently in postbellum politics as it had in antebellum days, there was still a continuing influx of visitors to the United States and an outflow of Americans to Europe. And a persistent theme of American observers of Europe and of European observers of America was that Europe was laden down with aristocrats and the United States was a land without any aristocratic tradition. The landed aristocracy remained for Americans into the 1880s a touchstone for comparison between the United States and Europe.[7]

The basic idea behind the political economy of aristocracy received continual expression and approval. The analysis of maldistribution had not changed. Democrat Daniel Voorhees of Indiana in 1874 said there were and had been only two parties in the world since the dawn of time: "One, [advocates] that the favored, titled, and noble few should govern and live in idle luxury; the other, that the toiling many should control and shape public affairs for their own benefit." In 1885, John G. Whittier predicted that the Republican mission would probably be completed by the election of Grover Cleveland, for that mission was to ensure that "labor shall everywhere have its just reward, and the gains of it are made secure to the earners." James Garfield, in a famous address in 1873, boldly explained why fears of universal

6. Montgomery, *Beyond Equality*, 249–59, 337, 446–47, and *passim;* Pole, *Pursuit of Equality*, 205–208; Foner, *Reconstruction*, 477–79, 525, 583; Nick Salvatore, *Eugene V. Debs: Citizen and Socialist* (Urbana, 1982), 24–25, 43, 60–68; Herbert G. Gutman, *Work, Culture and Society in Industrializing America: Essays in American Working-Class and Social History* (New York, 1977), 255–57, 266, 311, 319; John B. Andrews, "Nationalisation (1860–1877)," in John R. Commons et al., *History of Labour in the United States* (New York, 1921), II, 53, 119–21; Herbert G. Gutman, "Workers' Search for Power," in *The Gilded Age,* ed. H. Wayne Morgan (2nd ed.; Syracuse, 1970), 31–53; Gerald N. Grob, *Workers and Utopia: A Study of Ideological Conflict in the American Labor Movement, 1865–1900* (Evanston, 1961), viii, 187–88; George Gunton, *Wealth and Progress: A Critical Examination of the Wages Question and Its Economic Relation to Social Reform* (1887; rpr. New York, 1894), 1–5, 15; "The Working-Man's View of Capital," *Nation,* February 4, 1869, pp. 85–86.

7. For example, Richard H. Abbott, *Cobbler in Congress: The Life of Henry Wilson, 1812–1875* (Lexington, Ky., 1972), 239; H. Draper Hunt, *Hannibal Hamlin of Maine: Lincoln's First Vice-President* (Syracuse, 1969), 217–18; Elsie Porter Mende, *An American Soldier and Diplomat: Horace Porter* (New York, 1927), 238–51; Howard I. Kushner and Anne Hummel Sherrill, *John Milton Hay: The Union of Poetry and Politics* (Boston, 1977), 46–51; Oliver Otis Howard, *Autobiography of Oliver Otis Howard* (New York, 1908), II, 499, 529, 540; Allan Nevins, ed. and comp., *American Social History as Recorded by British Travellers* (New York, 1923), 441.

suffrage, expressed so forcefully by Thomas Babington Macaulay, were non-sensical. In the United States social mobility and public education diffused property evenly among the people. Moreover, Garfield insisted that readers had to consider Macaulay's aristocratic frame of reference: "It is hardly possible for a man reared in an aristocracy like that of England to eliminate the conviction from his mind [that there should be no mobility], for the British empire is built upon it. . . . [The English theory is that] there must be a permanent class who shall hold in their own hands so much of the wealth, the privilege, and the political power of the kingdom, that they can compel the admiration and obedience of all other classes."[8] The republican theory of the distribution of wealth, with its emphasis on the political economy of aristocracy, survived hale and hearty into the 1880s. The Gilded Age had not yet tarnished the explanatory power of the revolutionary heritage.

And then the world suddenly and irrevocably changed.

In the last two decades of the nineteenth century, the distribution of wealth in the American republic was questioned and challenged as it never had been before. A paucity of written material between 1765 and 1886 yielded to extended treatments on how distorted American wealth-holding had become. Whereas before one had to hunt for expressions about the distribution of wealth in political speeches on mundane problems and seek for short paragraphs in weighty tomes, now the periodical press erupted with articles devoted solely to the question of wealth distribution. Unlike earlier years, when discussion of American wealth distribution was usually a signal for self-congratulation, the articles and speeches appearing in the 1880s and 1890s were lamentations. Many writers knew that the heritage of the Revolution and republicanism itself were swiftly contracting and, indeed, passing into oblivion.

With a start, Americans realized that their (imaginary) pristine republican distribution of wealth had given way to one disastrously tilted in favor of the few. Tocqueville could not suppress his shock at American equality in the

<hr />

8. Daniel W. Voorhees, *Speeches of Daniel W. Voorhees,* 469; John G. Whittier, "The Republican Party," in Whittier, *Works of Whittier,* VII, 240–41; James A. Garfield, "The Future of the Republic: Its Dangers and Its Hopes," in Burke A. Hinsdale, ed., *The Works of James Abram Garfield* (Boston, 1882–83), II, 50–54; see Samuel S. Cox, *Three Decades of Federal Legislation, 1855 to 1885* (Providence, R. I., 1888), 697–98; Wells, *Creed of Free Trade,* 4; R. W. Thompson, *The History of Protective Tariff Laws* (Chicago, 1888), 500. Fears of a warped distribution of wealth are noted in Foner, *Reconstruction,* 477.

1830s, but a later observer, Englishman James Bryce, could not in the late 1880s escape confronting the existence of an American "plutocracy." Bryce wrote that in 1850 "there were no great fortunes in America, few large fortunes, no poverty." By 1888, he found much poverty and many huge fortunes—"and a greater number of gigantic fortunes than in any other country in the world."[9] Several individuals found the distribution of wealth in the United States to be unacceptable. Numerous citizens recalled in the 1880s and 1890s the simpler days of their youth when equality appeared to be the basic principle of the republic.[10]

A striking feature of the period was the emergence of a protest literature based on the maldistribution of wealth. The first major work flowed from the pen of Henry George, whose emphasis on land monopoly spawned anti-monopoly clubs throughout the United States and England. George's 1879 classic, *Progress and Poverty,* revealed a lopsided distribution of wealth in America, but conceptually it drew on early-nineteenth-century political economists. George's enemies were John Stuart Mill, Thomas Malthus, and particularly David Ricardo. The "unearned increment," which George hoped to eliminate by the "single tax," was simply the rent that Ricardo described as income derived from possession of the soil but whose value increased not from labor but from the encroachment of population and cultivation on marginal lands. The structure of *Progress and Poverty* hardly differed from that of the standard works on political economy of the day. But what made George different and gave him and his work such enormous attention was his avowal that inequality was the inescapable fact of contemporary economic life. The public accepted the statement as true.[11]

Other writers exhibited a more modern cast, pointing at the industrial corporation as the agent of wealth distortion. Laurence Gronlund attempted to

9. James Bryce, *The American Commonwealth* (3rd ed.; New York, 1908), II, 661, quotes on 811. Bryce found other problems more pressing, such as party corruption.

10. Harry Thurston Peck, *Twenty Years of the Republic, 1885–1905* (New York, 1932), 724; Basil W. Duke, *Reminiscences of General Basil W. Duke, C.S.A.* (Garden City, N.Y., 1911), 459–60; John H. Reagan of Texas quoted in Robert H. Wiebe, *The Search for Order, 1877–1920* (New York, 1967), 8.

11. Henry George, *Progress and Poverty: An Inquiry into the Cause of Industrial Depressions, and of Increase of Want with Increase of Wealth. The Remedy* (1879; 4th ed.; New York, 1888), viii, ix–x, 3–8, 49–52, 125, 148–54, 184–195. See Painter, *Standing at Armageddon,* 25; Destler, *American Radicalism,* 12; Garraty, *New Commonwealth,* 316–18; John L. Thomas, *Alternative America: Henry George, Edward Bellamy, Henry Demarest Lloyd and the Adversary Tradition* (Cambridge, Mass., 1983), 106–15.

popularize the writings of Karl Marx for the American public by eliminating class warfare from Marx's theory. Ignatius Donnelly, the Minnesota Populist leader, wrote *Caesar's Columns* to describe (and thereby warn of) a society in which a few plutocrats held all power and pressed the workers to poverty and ultimately to revolution. Henry Demarest Lloyd produced a series of articles on the evils of the Standard Oil Corporation, the nation's first large industrial trust, and brought them together under the title *Wealth Against Commonwealth* (published as the second volume in the Bad Wealth Series). Edward Bellamy penned an account of an American mysteriously transported from strike-plagued Boston in 1887 to Boston in the year 2000. Bellamy described late-nineteenth-century American society as a "prodigious coach" upon which the elite regaled themselves in never-ending festivals but "which the masses of humanity were harnessed to and dragged toilsomely along a very hilly and sandy road. The driver was hunger, and permitted no lagging."[12]

Historians chronicled the rise of monstrous fortunes, and the periodical press in article after article exposed the loss of republican simplicity and equality.[13] In an 1897 article in *Arena,* Robert N. Reeves wrote that "there is something radically wrong with our present economical system," and the wrongness was that "great individual wealth is an anti-social interest." For the first time, investigators began to supply percentages. In one of the pioneering works on the distribution of wealth, Charles B. Spahr provided a historical account of American wealth distribution and then calculated that in Gilded Age America the wealthiest 10 percent received as much income as the remaining 90 percent. Spahr found American income distribution better than that of England and Europe but still highly skewed. An earlier and more cynical writer, Thomas G. Shearman, wrote that for decades Americans had boasted "that there is no danger of any such concentration of wealth in a few hands among us as exists in older and more aristocratic nations." But he fig-

12. Ignatius Donnelly discussed in Martin Ridge, *Ignatius Donnelly: The Portrait of a Politician* (Chicago, 1962), 263; Lloyd discussed in Destler, *American Radicalism,* 136–56; Bellamy, *Looking Backward,* 12; see also Garraty, *New Commonwealth,* 314–24; Edward Chase Kirkland, *Industry Comes of Age: Business, Labor and Public Policy, 1860–1897* (New York, 1961), 309–12. There is a good overview of worries about the distribution of wealth in the Gilded Age in Keller, *Affairs of State,* 182–83, 292–93, 373–74.

13. For historians, see Woodrow Wilson, *Division and Reunion, 1829–1889* (1893; rpr. New York, 1901), 299; Powell, *Nullification and Secession,* 418–23; Ellis Paxson Oberholtzer, *A History of the United States Since the Civil War* (New York, 1917), II, 538–48; James Ford Rhodes, *History of the United States from the Compromise of 1850 to the End of the Roosevelt Administration* (New York, 1895–1922), IX, 168.

ured that in England about one-seventieth of the population owned about 66 percent of the wealth; in the United States, one-seventieth owned between 75 and 80 percent of the wealth. Eltweed Pomeroy showed that the top 8 percent in Massachusetts owned 83 percent of the wealth in the period 1859–1861 but by 1879–1881 had increased their share to 90 percent. Pomeroy added, "Can this [concentration of wealth] continue and the Republic live? No; either the propertyless masses will rise in bloody revolution and snatch from the wealthy some part of their ill-gotten gains" or the country would endure the worst "despotism of wealth" the world had ever seen.[14]

The literature's awful portents for republicanism and especially the republican theory of the distribution of wealth were painstakingly laid out. William M. Dickson, arguing from a historical perspective, reminded his audience that the Founders had established a republic based on "general equality of condition" and that in regard to plutocracy the "natural opponent is republican democracy." A republican government should produce an equitable distribution of wealth. By allowing laborers to obtain the fruits of their labor, by avoiding the wealth-transferring policies of aristocratic governments, by abolishing inheritance monopoly laws, and by possessing a frontier, a republic ought to produce a sound distribution of wealth. Yet the writers found that the distribution of wealth in the American republic was worse than in any European aristocracy. More appalling, the distribution of wealth was no better than that of England. As Shearman accurately pointed out, England had for nearly twelve decades been the target of American egalitarian sneers and derision for its mighty aristocratic landlords and its starving and rebellious working class; its Thomas Babington Macaulay, who cavalierly dismissed Jeffersonian democracy and foretold the collapse of the American experiment; and its elite of 3.5 percent of the population controlling 66 percent of

14. Robert N. Reeves, "Has Wealth a Limitation?" *Arena,* XVIII (1897), 160, 163. See also D. DeW. Smyth, "Wealth and Welfare," *Quarterly Journal of Economics,* XVIII (1903), 138–41; [Charles Eliot Norton], "The Poverty of England," *North American Review,* CIX (1869), 122–54; Edward J. Phelps, "Irresponsible Wealth," *North American Review,* CLII (1891), 523–33; Ashley, "Distribution of Wealth," 721–33; Herman E. Taubeneck, "The Concentration of Wealth: Its Cause and Results," Parts I and II, *Arena,* XVIII (1897), 289–301, 452–69; [Cardinal] Gibbons, "Wealth and Its Obligations," *North American Review,* CLII (1891), 385–94; W. M. Dickson, "The Apotheosis of the Plutocrat," *Magazine of American History,* XVIII (1887), 497–509; Charles B. Spahr, *An Essay on the Present Distribution of Wealth in the United States* (New York, 1896), 123, 129; Thomas G. Shearman, "The Owners of the United States," *Forum,* VIII (1889), 262, 269–72; Eltweed Pomeroy, "The Concentration of Wealth," *Arena,* LVIII (1896), 89–91, 95.

the national wealth. "With what scorn we have long pointed to these figures," lamented Shearman. But now republican America had to admit that the wealthiest class in the United States "is vastly richer than the wealthiest class in Great Britain."[15] This was not supposed to be the outcome of republican economics.

The policies derived from the republican theory of the distribution of wealth had simply and utterly failed. The new wealthy class grew up in spite of republican policies. Writers quickly recognized that not all of the features of republican economics were still valid. Republican institutions no longer provided any certainty that laborers would receive the fruits of their labor; competition became the enemy, not the guarantor, of equitability; some individuals owned far more than any single person should ever possess; private property and sanctity of contract had given birth to outrageous fortunes and had not protected the common person. And what of the hope of Republican party leaders in the 1850s that mental and manual labor would be combined productively in one person to create an independent and prosperous citizenry? Edward P. Powell wrote in a historical account of the years between 1830 and 1890, "The laborer now is exactly like his shovel; to be used, and then put aside till needed again."[16] The republican theory of the distribution of wealth had shrunk and curled up inside itself and died.

If in the 1890s the republican theory of the distribution of wealth was withering at the touch, the protest writers left no doubt as to what agency was doing the touching. The corporation destroyed the republican theory of the distribution of wealth. Indeed, between 1880 and 1920, the discussion of the distribution of wealth was in some senses not about the distribution of wealth at all; it was about the rise of big business in the United States.[17]

The movement toward consolidation in the United States came suddenly

15. Dickson, "Apotheosis of the Plutocrat," 497, 501; Shearman, "Owners of the United States," 263, 267. For an interesting comparison see Peter H. Lindert, "Who Owned Victorian England? The Debate Over Landed Wealth and Inequality," *Agricultural History*, LXI (1987), 25–51.

16. Testimony of R. Heber Newton in John A. Garraty, ed., *Labor and Capital in the Gilded Age: Testimony Taken by the Senate Committee upon the Relations Between Labor and Capital—1883* (Boston, 1968), 171–73; Gibbons, "Wealth and Its Obligations," 386, 393; Reeves, "Has Wealth a Limitation?" 162–64; Smyth, "Wealth and Welfare," 140–41; Fredrick L. Paxson, *Recent History of the United States* (Boston, 1921), 73; Destler, *American Radicalism*, 156; Kirkland, *Industry Comes of Age*, 309; Powell, *Nullification and Secession*, 423.

17. This topic is excellently covered by John Tipple, "Big Business and the New Economy," in *The Gilded Age*, ed. H. Wayne Morgan (2nd ed.; Syracuse, 1970), 14–30.

between 1880 and 1900 but seems to have been particularly virulent from 1897 to 1904. Railroads inaugurated the combination movement in an effort to tame wildcat competition and to ensure that revenues at least covered fixed costs. At first they tried pools and then illegal cartels. Eventually combination was effected by financier-dominated reorganization, especially under the auspices of J. P. Morgan. In industry, John D. Rockefeller pioneered the legal device of a trust in creating the Standard Oil Trust Company in 1881 to evade Ohio legal restrictions. By 1889 or so, the holding company, by which a financial company held shares of other companies, had come into existence. And then there was growth through reinvestment, such as was done by Andrew Carnegie and later Henry Ford. By 1904 some 318 trusts existed, and they held 40 percent of the nation's manufacturing assets. In the merger wave of 1897–1904, some 4,227 firms consolidated into 257 companies. Railroads, industry, and banking all seemed swept into a consolidation frenzy that fundamentally altered the business characteristics of American enterprise. By 1904, the United States was home to the largest companies in the world.[18]

Americans living through this transformation of business structure quaked in apprehension. This was no gradual change. It seemed one day that small shops characterized the economy; the next day, huge firms towered over the economy, the government, the small shop—over every aspect of American life. John Sherman, Ohio representative and senator, secretary of the treasury, and namesake of the impotent 1890 Sherman Anti-Trust Act, left a vivid portrait of the transformation in his memoirs:

Instead of small or moderate workshops with a few hands, we now have great establishments with hundreds of employes [*sic*], and all the capital of scores of stockholders under the control of a few men, and often of one man. This may be of benefit by reducing the cost of production, but it also involves two dangers, one the irrepressible conflict of labor with capital, and the other the com-

18. Thomas K. McCraw, "Rethinking the Trust Question," in *Regulation in Perspective: Historical Essays*, ed. McCraw (Boston, 1981), 1–24, 32. See Chandler, *Visible Hand*, 337–39, 363–76; Naomi R. Lamoreaux, *The Great Merger Movement in American Business, 1895–1904* (Cambridge, Eng., 1985), 1–10; Evans, *Business Incorporations in the United States*, 31; Anthony Patrick O'Brien, "Factory Size, Economies of Scale, and the Great Merger Wave of 1898–1902," *Journal of Economic History*, XLVIII (1988), 639–49; Kirkland, *Industry Comes of Age*, 196–210; Morton Keller, "The Pluralist State: American Economic Regulation in Comparative Perspective, 1900–1930," in *Regulation in Perspective: Historical Essays*, ed. Thomas K. McCraw (Boston, 1981), 64–69.

bination of corporations engaged in the same business to advance prices and prevent competition, thus constituting a monopoly commanding business and controlling the market.

Sherman used the word most uttered in connection with the transformation: *monopoly*. Big enterprise changed everything. Its existence led John Bates Clark to declare that the solution to the trust problem would determine the fate of the United States, for the nation was caught between the "devil of private monopoly and the deep sea of state socialism."[19] No room was left for the republicanism of the Revolution, and certainly no one needed the ideas contained in the political economy of aristocracy.

Nobody expected this shattering change in the size of manufacturing operations. Political economists before 1890 did not discuss size of firm in relation to economic endeavor. The only treatment of large-scale companies was, fatefully, in connection with monopoly. The reigning assumption of protectionists and free traders in nineteenth-century America was that small shops were the natural agents of production and that large concerns were usually inefficient, stumbling giants bloated beyond their natural size by the errant policy of government. Arthur Lapham Perry, in the twenty-second edition of his textbook in 1895, failed to discuss scale of business operations. Amasa Walker in his 1872 textbook mentioned largeness in business only to deprecate it. Although scale offered advantages in wages and profits, mistakes by executives could plunge thousands of people into desperation and destroy the independence of the citizenry. Walker predicted that the optimal business size "turns more and more to the smaller establishments, which secure full, interested personal supervision of labor." In 1870, Henry Varnum Poor cautioned against the railroad combinations that were occurring in England, not the United States. Francis Amasa Walker failed to mention large-scale companies

19. John Sherman, *Recollections of Forty Years in the House, Senate and Cabinet: An Autobiography* (Chicago, 1895), I, 191–92; John Bates Clark and John Maurice Clark, *The Control of Trusts* (1901; rev. ed. New York, 1912), 2; Richard E. Welch, Jr., *George Frisbie Hoar and the Half-Breed Republicans* (Cambridge, Mass., 1971), 165. See Tipple, "Big Business and the New Economy," 14, 17–21; Vincent P. DeSantis, *The Shaping of Modern America, 1877–1916* (St. Louis, 1977), 1–2; Olivier Zunz, *Making America Corporate, 1870–1920* (Chicago, 1990), 12–17, 34–39. Historians in the first quarter of the twentieth century recorded the shock of change from small-shop America to corporate domination; see Beard, *Contemporary American History*, 32–36; John D. Hicks, George E. Mowry, and Robert E. Burke, *The American Nation: A History of the United States from 1865 to the Present* (1933; rpr. Boston, 1963), 109, 136; Lester Burrell Shippee, *Recent American History* (New York, 1924), 113–23, 129–33, 280.

in his 1888 text. David A. Wells did remark on the movement toward industrial combination in 1889, feared excesses and financial manipulations, and
worried that large firms could destroy small companies and crush American
independence. Yet Wells, combative free trader that he was, elaborated more
on the protective tariff than any other subject. Economists, as well as most
other people, did not anticipate the suddenness with which consolidation
would come.[20]

The tie between panic over the suddenly acknowledged warping of the
American distribution of wealth and the equally sudden emergence of large-
scale industrial and commercial firms was made explicit by Andrew Carnegie, the Scottish immigrant poor boy who became one of the nation's richest
industrial barons. In a famous 1889 *North American Review* article entitled
"The Gospel of Wealth," Carnegie laid out the basic changes in the American economy, the alterations in the distribution of wealth, and the inevitability of both. "The problem of our age," he wrote as his first sentence, "is the
proper administration of wealth, that the ties of brotherhood may still bind
together the rich and poor in harmonious relationship." Wealth was good for
the nation and so was industrial combination into large-scale enterprise, for
it was large-scale enterprise that made fantastic new piles of wealth possible.
In older times, articles were made at home or in small shops. "There was, substantially, social equality, and even political equality, for those engaged in industrial pursuits had then little or no voice in the state." In other words, the
republican distribution of wealth and the social and political equality that
stemmed therefrom depended on an economic structure based on small production units.

But those small production units were inefficient, resulting in high prices.
Under the corporation, production was more efficient, prices lower, and output more abundant. Yet the social cost of the new large-scale enterprise was
the acceptance of "rigid castes . . . human society loses homogeneity." The
cost was the loss of republican equality. The advantages were huge increases
in wealth and material welfare, including higher wages. To obtain the new
wealth, the American public must accept "great inequality of environment;
the concentration of business, industrial and commercial, in the hands of a

20. Walker, *Science of Wealth*, 62–63, 79; Perry, *Political Economy;* Henry V. Poor, *Manual
of the Railroads of the United States for 1869–70* (New York, 1869), xxx–xxxi; Francis A. Walker,
Political Economy (New York, 1888); David A. Wells, *Recent Economic Changes and Their Effect
on the Production and Distribution of Wealth and the Well-Being of Society* (1889; rpr. New York,
1899), 73–76, 92–98.

few." After these introductory words, Carnegie then launched into his plan for the stewardship of wealth—the holders of wealth dispensed it for the benefit of society in accordance with their superior wisdom.[21]

The *Independent,* one of the nation's leading periodicals, devoted a 1902 issue to the distribution of wealth and invited a host of authors to contribute. They did mention the distribution of wealth, but the main focus was on industrial combination and the dominance of the large-scale enterprise in the American economy. Most simply followed a standard formula: combination meant power and advantage, which produced enormous fortunes for those at the top of the new corporate pyramid. Carroll D. Wright, the famous data enumerator, doubted the distribution of wealth was that skewed. Charles R. Flint argued for the benefits of size and the difference between the modern corporation and the inefficient businesses of olden days. Russell Sage said intelligence dominated in the corporate mode of business, and James J. Hill sneered at the public outcry against great wealth-holders. William Graham Sumner justified corporations as the products of natural evolution.[22]

Those apprehensive about wealth distribution in the 1902 *Independent* issue revealed that their discontent arose from the industrial consolidation movement. John R. Commons, the labor historian and economist, argued that large-scale firms distorted wealth distribution. J. Harry Selz, a vice-president of a large Chicago shoe manufacturer, fretted about "the effect which centralization will have on the rewards of labor. . . . I am convinced that extreme centralization is at the cost of individuality—that element of character which has made the representative American the force he is." John De Witt Warner worried that two generations ago farmers and laborers were raised to be citizens—could such conditions continue under a plutocracy? Taking a historical view, Ernest Howard Crosby wrote, "In the absence of a centralized social hierarchy the individual was able to claim a high social standing upon his own merits with some hope of success." That independency had disappeared in the face of competition with monster corporations that had unlimited resources to crush the individual who dared to challenge

21. Andrew Carnegie, "The Gospel of Wealth," in Carnegie, *The Gospel of Wealth and Other Timely Essays* (Garden City, N.Y., 1933), 1–4; see also Carnegie, "Popular Illusions About Trusts," *ibid.,* 80, 86–87, 90; Joseph Frazier Wall, *Andrew Carnegie* (New York, 1970), 809–13.

22. *Independent,* May 1, 1902, articles by Carroll D. Wright, "Concentration of Wealth: A Discussion," 1023; Charles R. Flint, "General Survey of the Problem," 1025–27; Russell Sage, "Wealth—A Decree of Justice," 1027–28; James J. Hill, "Consolidation of Wealth Makes Prosperity," 1029–30; William G. Sumner, "Its Justification," 1036–39.

their supremacy. Both William Jennings Bryan and Henry Demarest Lloyd felt that individualism had lost, monopoly had won, and the republic had passed through an evolution that had permanently damaged the revolutionary heritage. Smallness and individuality had passed from American life, and with them went nearly all the precepts of republicanism.[23]

In the last fifteen years of the nineteenth century, the axioms of the revolutionary republican theory of the distribution of wealth unraveled at a breathtaking pace. It was not that all the components died out completely, for they lingered on throughout the twentieth century. No longer, however, did the republican theory of the distribution of wealth dominate political and economic discourse.

The population-to-land ratio had a curious history and demise. Mainstream economic doctrines concerning population pressure certainly did not disappear, but in economic theory they became couched in terms of the capital per capita or per unit of labor. More important for the discussion, however, was a signal fact in American history: the census of 1890 showed that the American frontier had closed, and no longer did the nation have an unexploited region in which to slough off excess population and from which to extract new resources. Frederick Jackson Turner elaborated on the vanishing frontier in 1893 in his seminal work, *The Influence of the Frontier in American History.* Turner's production was in many ways a lament and a portent of evil things to come, for the prediction of Thomas Babington Macaulay haunted the American republican experiment: "Your fate I believe to be certain, though it is deferred by a physical cause. As long as you have a boundless extent of fertile and unoccupied land, your laboring population will be far more at ease than the laboring population of the Old World." Population would soon overwhelm Americans, however, for the frontier could not last forever. Then wages would drop to subsistence levels and the masses would be miserable: "Then your institutions will be fairly brought to the test."[24]

23. *Independent,* May 1, 1902, J. Harry Selz, "Two Sides to the Problem," 1031; John R. Commons, "Its Dangers," 1040–43; John De Witt Warner, "Its Dangers," 1045–47; Ernest Howard Crosby, "The Dangers of an Aristocracy," 1055–58; William J. Bryan, "A Menace to Government and Civilization," 1068–69; Henry Demarest Lloyd, "The Socialistic Re'gime, [*sic*]," 1069–72.

24. Richard Hofstadter, *The Progressive Historians: Turner, Beard, Parrington* (New York, 1968), 53–61; Huston, "Political Response to Industrialism," 38; David M. Wrobel, *The End of American Exceptionalism: Frontier Anxiety from the Old West to the New Deal* (Lawrence, Kans., 1993), chaps. 1–3.

The test seemed to come in the 1890s. One violent strike after another rocked industry. Western and southern farmers enlisted in the Populist party to pass "agrarian" laws. A Socialist party sprang up in the East. A devastating depression in the middle of the decade seemed to foretell enduring misery for the masses. The American experiment in self-government did indeed seem endangered.

Concern in the United States over the population question disappeared in the early twentieth century—never completely, of course, but it was reduced in importance and largely dropped from public discourse. Partly this dismissal of the population-to-land ratio was a function of the change from an agricultural-commercial to an industrial-commercial nation. It was the agrarian republic that riveted attention to issues of land disposition.

Moreover, many soon came to recognize that the nation properly stressed the role of a frontier in promoting economic growth and individual welfare but that land was not the appropriate frontier to applaud and base policy on. In the first two decades of the twentieth century, massive changes occurred in corporations and American universities. The research laboratory was founded and produced inventions that spawned new industries. And the universities moved from concentration on liberal arts to the sciences and particularly to engineering. In short, technology became the frontier, and technological frontiers only expanded, never closed.[25]

For twelve decades Americans had believed that the laws of entail and primogeniture were major props that supported a skewed, aristocratic distribution of wealth. Suddenly, in the last twenty years of the nineteenth century, many Americans rejected the importance of entail and primogeniture and relegated those laws to the status of minor economic phenomena that only antiquarians would be interested in. The statements of Gilded Age writers that the laws of primogeniture and entail were inconsequential in halting the compilation of outrageous fortunes were not social-scientific observations— they were bitter lamentations.

In 1888 former secretary of the treasury Hugh McCulloch published his memoirs, which included a visit to England in 1870. Like so many observers before him, he noted that "the land in Great Britain is owned and controlled by comparatively few of its citizens, and the large estates are entailed." Unlike

25. See Clark and Clark, *Control of Trusts,* 8–12; Leonard S. Reich, *The Making of American Industrial Research: Science and Business at GE and Bell, 1876–1926* (Cambridge, Eng., 1985), 62–96; George Wise, *Willis R. Whitney, General Electric, and the Origins of U.S. Industrial Research* (New York, 1985), 135, 156–58, 169–80.

earlier American travelers, McCulloch basically said such concentration made no difference. Laborers seemed to have good wages, rents were lower in London than in New York City, and clothing and food were cheaper. In fact, from his observations, McCulloch said aristocratic England, the peculiar home of entail and primogeniture, had a better wealth distribution than the United States, and England did not have as many great fortunes as "have been acquired in the United States"—the republican United States. So much for the power of entail and primogeniture to warp a distribution of wealth.[26]

Others thought the failure of the Jeffersonian abolition of entail and primogeniture to secure a republican distribution of wealth was nothing short of cataclysmic. In 1880 General James B. Weaver, Greenback party supporter and future presidential nominee of the Populist party in 1892, warned that the Founders had abolished primogeniture and entail "so that the wealth of the country should diffuse itself among the people according to natural and beneficent laws. They did not contemplate the creation of these corporations that are as real entities as are individuals." In a speech exploring the rise of socialism in the United States, Henry Demarest Lloyd explained how Jefferson had laid the foundation for republican equality by leading the fight to abolish the laws of entail and primogeniture in Virginia. But it was insufficient for modern times. "We have nearly finished democratizing kings," exhorted Lloyd, "and we are now about to democratize the millionaire." William M. Dickson knew that the founders of the republic sought to avoid a plutocracy, and their means of doing so had been to abolish the laws of entail and primogeniture. Dickson lamented, "This has proved a delusion." It was a delusion because the modern corporation, "the telegraph, and the railroad have infinitely multiplied the powers of man."[27]

The fortunes produced by the new corporate economy forced a drastic reevaluation of the potency of the laws of entail and primogeniture in affecting the distribution of wealth. Huge sums were being made in a lifetime that dwarfed any fortune acquired over generations by aristocrats. In 1900, Andrew Carnegie sold his steelworks to J. P. Morgan, who then formed the United States Steel Corporation; the price tag was $480 million, of which

26. Hugh McCulloch, *Men and Measures of Half a Century: Sketches and Comments* (New York, 1888), quotes on 436 and 444; also see 436–37, 441, 443–46.

27. Speech of James B. Weaver quoted in Fred Emory Haynes, *James Baird Weaver* (Iowa City, 1919), 148; speech of Henry Demarest Lloyd, "Revolution: The Evolution of Socialism," in Destler, *American Radicalism,* 214; Dickson, "Apotheosis of the Plutocrat," 497, quote on 505.

Carnegie took one-half. According to Lee Soltow, the value of Carnegie's wealth in 1900 was equal to one-half of 1 percent of the nation's gross national product, thus Carnegie possessed the greatest fortune ever amassed by a single American.[28] Aristocrats in their prime had political might and probably excessive personal control over the lives of thousands; but they had no fortune to compare with that of Andrew Carnegie. The corporation and modern technology were accumulating wealth that those in the aristocratic ages never dreamed of.

One group, however, still used the abolition of entail and primogeniture as a means to argue that American wealth distribution was healthy and proper. The new plutocracy tried to reassure the public that all that was needed to ensure an equitable distribution of wealth was the abolition of entail and primogeniture. Such proclamations emanating from Andrew Carnegie and Jay Gould satisfied almost nobody.[29] Entail and primogeniture were dismissed as important elements in the distribution of wealth. In the twentieth century, even by historians, those laws are usually mentioned only in derision.

It is startling to realize that the foundation of the republican theory of the distribution of wealth was cast aside as well. For at least twelve decades, and probably much longer, Americans believed the test of economic equitability, of a republican distribution of wealth, was ensuring that laborers received the full and just fruits of their labor. For the whole of the existence of the republic until 1900, the economic content of republicanism could almost be reduced to one phrase: laborers deserved the fruits of their labor. That notion still resides in small business America, among laborers, in the unions, and among the disadvantaged. It is, however, no longer a dominant sentiment and has been virtually removed from the public forum. The demise of the labor theory of property/value in the twentieth century has been one of the most monumental changes in popular and intellectual thought in American history. It has, curiously, been one of the most ignored.

Americans had always been attracted to the labor theory of property/

---

28. Harold C. Livesay, *Andrew Carnegie and the Rise of Big Business* (Boston, 1975), 187–88; Soltow, *Men and Wealth in the United States,* 113.

29. Carnegie, "Gospel of Wealth," in Carnegie, *Gospel of Wealth and Other Timely Essays,* 7–8; Carnegie, "The Advantages of Poverty," *Nineteenth Century* (1891), *ibid.,* 50–55; testimony of Jay Gould, 1883, in Senate Hearings, in Garraty, ed., *Labor and Capital in the Gilded Age,* 132. A close look at Carnegie's ideas might promote the interpretation, strange as it may seem, that Carnegie deserves the title of the "Last Jacksonian."

value, although their use of it had been imprecise. Americans permitted a wide definition of labor and so covered many activities that labor spokesmen would have rejected. For European socialists, the labor theory of value meant only the amount of physical labor invested in the production of some good. Americans had generally allowed mental activity (inventiveness, jurisprudence, preaching, engineering, supervision) to be counted as labor activity. English economists understood that socialists had grabbed onto the Ricardian definition of value and used it against capitalists and capitalist economic theory. British economists had for some time retreated from the labor theory of value. That had not been the case in the United States, at least not until the 1880s. Between the 1760s and 1880s, the public air was impenetrably dense with professions of allegiance to the labor theory of property/value. James Bryce observed that Americans had "ground-ideas" upon which the government was based, "as, for instance, his right to the enjoyment of what he has earned, and to the free expression of his opinions, are primordial and sacred."[30]

The labor theory of property/value had always been popular among the American public and politicians, but a major source of support had been students of political economy. Political economy changed in the last two decades of the nineteenth century, and much of the change was concentrated in the question of value. In place of the labor theory of value came marginal utility theory, which by 1900, except for socialist thought, had swept the labor theory of value out of political economy. Marginal utility theory was vital in two areas: it reshaped economists' overall understanding of the distribution of wealth, and it gave birth to a new theory of wages (marginal productivity theory).

The labor theory of value was never a satisfactory means of explaining the value of objects. Rather, it was primarily an expression of the cultural value of individualism that had arisen in English society and had migrated to North America. It is perhaps one of the clearest examples extant of how a cultural norm became reified as an objective, scientific, universal truth. Other Euro-

---

30. Kauder, *History of Marginal Utility Theory,* 57–63; C. B. MacPherson, *"The Rise and Fall of Economic Justice" and Other Papers* (Oxford, 1985), 11–12; Donald Winch, "Marginalism and the Boundaries of Economic Science," in *The Marginal Revolution in Economics: Interpretation and Evaluation,* ed. R. D. Collison Black, A. W. Coates, and Craufurd D. W. Goodwin (Durham, N. C., 1973), 60–72; Ronald L. Meek, "Marginalism and Marxism," *ibid.,* 233–45; Viner, *Long View and the Short,* 209; Bryce, *American Commonwealth,* II, 588.

pean economists, especially in France, Germany, and Austria, never found the labor theory of value to be persuasive and indeed found the Anglo-American allegiance to it rather bizarre. Except for Stanley Jevons, the founders of marginal utility theory (Karl Menger, Leon Walras, Herman Heinrich Gossen, and John Bates Clark) were not British citizens, and its emergence signaled the end of British suzerainty over the theoretical structures of political economy.[31]

There were profound differences between the labor theory of value and marginal utility theory. The labor theory of value was an absolutist doctrine. Values were created by labor, and by estimating the amount of labor in objects one obtained the real differences in values between them. This approach had insuperable problems. It contained no reference to the consumer, and it excluded skill and mental effort. The value of a product thus was absolute, objective, and calculable; the approach was that of a Newtonian seeking an absolute upon which to pin an entire theory, and for nineteenth-century Anglo-American economists, the labor theory of value was the absolute upon which the rest of the theory pivoted. Marginal utility theory more properly stressed the relativistic nature of value. Value was bestowed by consumers, who placed a value on a product in accord with their preferences or tastes, or, as the name implies, their utilities. The values individuals assigned goods could fluctuate wildly, but with a large population statistical regularities in values appeared.[32]

The implications of marginal utility theory were immediately clear. Wealth was not accumulated by those who physically labored hardest but by those individuals or firms who best satisfied consumers' utility cravings. Those who accumulated wealth, in whatever amounts, obtained it because they had successfully met the desires of consumers. So long as the rules of a market economy were obeyed, the distribution of wealth—whatever its shape—was justified because the market rewarded those who best supplied goods that consumers wanted. John Bates Clark wrote that distribution was controlled by a "natural law" that gave "to every agent of production the amount of wealth which that agent creates." A market economy, according to

31. Kauder, *History of Marginal Utility Theory,* chaps. 4–8; Hutchison, "'Marginal Revolution,'" 176–202.

32. For two economists' explanation of marginal utility theory, plus some useful background historical information, see J. P. Gould and C. E. Ferguson, *Microeconomic Theory* (5th ed.; Homewood, Ill., 1980), chap. 13.

marginal utility theory, was inherently and eternally just—so long as rules were obeyed.[33]

From marginal utility theory came marginal productivity theory to explain wages. The Malthusian-Ricardian-Millian subsistence theory finally was overcome by advocates of free trade and laissez-faire. According to John Bates Clark, the law of wages was that the wage was "the market value of its product." As the doctrine matured, it proposed that the wage a firm bestowed upon its employees was determined by the amount of product the hiring of an additional worker would produce; that amount of product times the price of the product was the appropriate wage because the wage earner was rewarded with a wage that equaled his or her contribution to the welfare of society. Once again, however, the implication was that when the rules of the market economy were obeyed, it always produced socially just wages.[34]

In Europe and America a howl arose from socialist theorists over the development of marginal utility theory that continues to this day. John Bates Clark made it explicit that he developed his theories to justify the arrangements of a market economy, and many historians of economic thought have charged, using Clark in particular, that marginal utility theory was a way for economists to avoid questions over class relationships. Few scholars doubt that Bates was reacting to the socialist charge of economic injustice and that he intended to undercut socialist claims by his theory of wage determination. But much of marginalist theory was not developed in the United States but in Europe; marginalism was destined to appear regardless of American social and economic tensions.[35]

33. John Bates Clark, *The Distribution of Wealth: A Theory of Wages, Interest and Profits* (1899; rpr. New York, 1956), v, 3. For a different account, based on the wage fund instead of the labor theory of property/value, consult Hovencamp, *Enterprise and American Law*, 194–96, 222–25.

34. John B[ates] Clark, *The Philosophy of Wealth: Economic Principles Newly Formulated* (Boston, 1886), 21, connection between wage theory and utility theory, 22–25, chap. 5, dismissal of Malthus, 99. Clark, *Distribution of Wealth*, 3–4, 27; Richard T. Ely, *Outlines of Economics*, rev. ed. with Thomas S. Adams, Max O. Lorenz, and Allyn A. Young (New York, 1912), 321; Gould and Ferguson, *Microeconomic Theory*, 352, 370–72.

35. Clark, *Philosophy of Wealth*, 21; see the reviews of Clark's work by T. N. Carver, "Clark's Distribution of Wealth," *Quarterly Journal of Economics*, XV (1901), 578–602, and Richard T. Ely, Review of John Bates Clark, *Science*, December 10, 1886, pp. 551–52. On the American embrace of marginalism, see Craufurd D. W. Goodwin, "Marginalism Moves to the New World," in *Marginal Revolution in Economics*, ed. Black, Coats, and Goodwin, 287–303. The

The field of economics rapidly assumed its present shape after 1900. The term *political economy* died. Between 1776 and 1900, economics had principally been a literary endeavor littered with massive debates over definitions. Mathematical economics had been frequently called for but rarely performed. By 1900, the economics journals began to include articles with a distinct mathematical cast. Moreover, many present-day graphical representations emerged: supply and demand curves started to be used. The present form of the microeconomics textbook was generally in place by 1920.[36]

And the new economics of marginal utility theory and marginal productivity theory had no place for concern over the distribution of wealth, at least not as the original American revolutionaries had conceived of it. Protectionism as an academic field was obliterated and the professionalization of economics eliminated the amateur political economists who had been the backbone of protectionism in the nineteenth century. With the passing of protectionism, no element in economics save the socialists fought to keep alive the old apprehensions over the distribution of wealth. For neoclassical microeconomics, distribution theory was simply determination of wages and profits (rents have pretty much been discarded except as a separate topic in monopoly called "quasi-rents"). In a thorough neoclassical treatment of distribution in 1971, Martin Bronfenbrenner queried in the first line of his first chapter, "Is distribution a sufficiently important problem for serious study, and if so, why?" (One can only imagine the seizure suffered by John Adams' ghost at that pronouncement.) Distribution of income and wealth disappeared from economics texts in the twentieth century, a casualty of the development of marginal utility theory. The response by economists to any question concerning the distribution of wealth or income became a secular rephrasing of scripture: the market giveth and the market taketh away.[37]

The demise of the labor theory of value also revealed a cognizance of the

---

socialist response to marginalism and to Bates in particular can be found in Kauder, *History of Marginal Utility Theory*, 59–63; Winch, "Marginalism and the Boundaries of Economic Science," 60; Meek, "Marginalism and Marxism," 233–38; Viner, *Long View and the Short*, 209.

36. For example, F. Y. Edgeworth, "The Theory of Distribution," *Quarterly Journal of Economics*, XVIII (1904), 159–219; Thomas Nixon Carver, *The Distribution of Wealth* (1904; rpr. New York, 1924), chaps. 1–3. See Kauder, *History of Marginal Utility Theory*, 143–45; Winch, "Marginalism and the Boundaries of Economic Science," 64; George J. Stigler, *Production and Distribution Theories* (New York, 1941), 1–4; Hovencamp, *Enterprise and American Law*, 270–71.

37. Bronfenbrenner, *Income Distribution Theory*, 1; see also vii–ix, 4–6, 12–17.

passing of another feature of American life: individualism. American individualism and the labor theory of property/value had been tightly bound together. Property was sacred because an individual labored to obtain it; meritocracy and mobility existed because the institutions permitted individuals on the basis of their own merits—not political favoritism—to rise to fame and fortune; the individual habits of thrift, honesty, integrity, skill, intelligence, inventiveness, frugality, and industry were prized because they helped individuals to advance; the operation of an open, competitive market produced fair results because individuals competed impersonally with each other and the market rewarded individual effort.[38]

The corporation had no respect for individualism. Corporations operated on teamwork and the suppression of individual idiosyncrasies. The corporation rewrote so many of the traditional rules of American behavior that it could be called in a very fundamental sense antirepublican and un-American. Contemporaries at the beginning of the nineteenth century knew that the corporation challenged American individualism. Wrote John Bates Clark, "What is new in social production is the relation of man to man. Interdependence has supplanted independence."[39]

American individualism and the corporation clashed because the corporation created a hierarchy. And it was the differences connected with hierarchy that explained Americans' almost manic response to the appearance of the corporate economy. The individualism that had taken root in the United

38. See Thurlow Weed to Charles Emory Smith, June 7, 1877, in Harriet A. Weed, ed., *Autobiography of Thurlow Weed* (Boston, 1884), II, 525; Richard T. Ely, *Monopolies and Trusts* (1900; rpr. New York, 1910), 220; Paxson, *Recent History of the United States,* 73; Edwin T. Freedley, *A Practical Treatise on Business: Or How to Get, Save, Spend, Give, Lend, and Bequeath Money, with an Inquiry into the Chances of Success and Causes of Failure in Business* (1852; rpr. Philadelphia, 1866), 43–44 and *passim;* Hurst, *Legitimacy of the Business Corporation in the Law,* 42; Harold C. Livesay, "Lilliputians in Brobdingnag: Small Business in Late-Nineteenth-Century America," in *Small Business in American Life,* ed. Stuart W. Bruchey (New York, 1980), 340–41; Berthoff, "Independence and Enterprise," 29–34; Schlesinger, *Age of Jackson,* 315–17; Lustig, *Corporate Liberalism,* 4, 7.

39. James H. Soltow, "Origins of Small Business and the Relationships Between Large and Small Firms: Metal Fabricating and Machinery Making in New England, 1890–1957," in *Small Business in American Life,* ed. Stuart W. Bruchey (New York, 1980), 193; Chandler, *Visible Hand,* 411–14, 416–18, 450–54; Scott R. Bowman, *The Modern Corporation and American Political Thought: Law, Power, and Ideology* (University Park, Pa., 1996), x, 3, 9; Clark, *Distribution of Wealth,* 12; Paxson, *Recent History of the United States,* 152; Bryce, *American Commonwealth,* II, 591. The title of Clark's piece in the 1902 *Independent* issue devoted to the distribution of wealth was "A Modified Individualism," *Independent,* May 1, 1902, pp. 1066–68.

States produced winners and losers, but generally it did not create a set of persons who guided the lives of others. Individualism was in a structural sense egalitarian: no one stood above anyone else dictating the terms of life or work. Even in the small shop economy of the United States in the nineteenth century that used hired labor, the presence of thousands of small units of production allowed many to believe there was no centralized control of individuals' lives. But in the large-scale corporation the reality was undeniable: corporations created hierarchies, which trampled over numerous elements of the revolutionary heritage.[40]

Individualism had governed the American ideals of mobility and wealth acquisition. It was by individual character traits that one acquired property by labor; individual labor was rewarded by the market. In the corporation, individual character traits no longer meant simply labor, thrift, integrity, frugality, and the like; rather, mobility and income increments depended on evaluation by a supervisor, not by the market. Suddenly a host of traits arose that were basically unrelated to the market: clothes selection, family ties, college training, verbal self-presentation, ability to get along with co-workers or to fit in with the group. Mobility within the corporation was far different from individual productivity in the marketplace. The character traits desired by corporate authorities had far more in common with the "old corruption" of eighteenth-century English politics than with American republicanism— it was who you knew and to whom you were connected, not necessarily meritorious performance, that resulted in political preference. The corporation altered the American ideal of mobility and how it could be obtained.[41]

The corporation also changed the effects of economic power through the establishment of a hierarchy. In an economy of thousands of small produc-

---

40. S. J. Prais, *The Evolution of Giant Firms in Britain: A Study of the Growth of Concentration in Manufacturing Industry in Britain, 1909–70* (Cambridge, Eng., 1976), 139–40; Livesay, *Andrew Carnegie and the Rise of Big Business,* 32; Carnegie, "An Employer's View of the Labor Question," quoted in Carnegie, *Gospel of Wealth and Other Timely Essays,* 98, 104–105; Ernest Howard Crosby, "The Dangers of an Aristocracy," *Independent,* May 1, 1902, p. 1055; Alfred D. Chandler, Jr., "The Emergence of Managerial Capitalism," *Business History Review,* LVIII (1984), 473–75; Alfred D. Chandler, Jr., and Herman Daems, Introduction to *Managerial Hierarchies: Comparative Perspectives on the Rise of the Modern Industrial Enterprise,* ed. Chandler and Daems (Cambridge, Mass., 1980), 2–5; Alfred Marshall, *Principles of Economics* (8th ed., 1920; rpr. London, 1962), 254–55, 503–505; Wiebe, *Self-Rule,* 113–16.

41. Paxson, *Recent History of the United States,* 151–52; Cochran, *Challenges to American Values,* 64, 68; Livesay, *Andrew Carnegie and the Rise of Big Business,* 112; David Halberstam, *The Reckoning* (New York, 1986), 11–12.

tion units, ownership behaviors and styles probably differed. Conditions may have been poor, but workers did have the potential of choosing proprietors with acceptable character traits and disciplining small tyrants by high turnover rates. An employer of bad temperament was limited in how much damage he could inflict on others in a small producer economy. But in a corporation in which power congealed into a hierarchical structure and individualism became redefined as the right of those in the hierarchy to order other people's lives and to expect their decrees to be obeyed, social disasters of immense magnitude could result. When Henry Ford was a small automobile entrepreneur in Detroit in the early twentieth century, he did not have many labor complaints and his eccentricities were looked upon as simply that. In the giant Ford corporation of the 1920s, however, those eccentricities led to a reign of terror, the blatant destruction of civil liberties, the mistreatment of thousands of people, and the near collapse of the company.[42]

In no area did contemporaries see greater abuse of power than in relations between corporate managers and industrial workers. This problem was foreshadowed by the railroad experience. Large companies did not like individualism in their employees. Henry Varnum Poor, chronicler of much of the nation's nineteenth-century railroad activity, wrote an editorial in 1858 on strikes from the perspective of the railroad, even by then a large corporation: "The fault of *strikes,* therefore, may be said always to rest with the chief managers of a road. The degree of discipline necessary to the highest efficiency always consists with the strongest devotion of the subordinate. There is nothing, in the end, that men like so well, as to be made to do their duty. To do it, always begets self-respect, which is contentment. The more perfect the discipline the greater the results achieved."[43] So much for the republican legacy of the Revolution.

And the corporation mangled the old notion of the appropriate distribu-

---

42. Prude, *Coming of Industrial Order,* 144–49, 227–34; Halberstam, *Reckoning,* 93–107; Keith Sward, *The Legend of Henry Ford* (New York, 1948), 327–42. See also J. Harry Selz, "Two Sides to the Problem," *Independent,* May 1, 1902, pp. 1031–32; Cochran, *Challenges to American Values,* 67–72. Microeconomists dispute the influence of hierarchy: Armen Alchian and Harold Demsetz, "Production, Information Costs, and Economic Organization," *American Economic Review,* LXII (1972), 777–95; Gary J. Miller, *Managerial Dilemmas: The Political Economy of Hierarchy* (Cambridge, Eng., 1992), 1–8, 11–12, and *passim.*

43. Editorial, *American Railroad Journal,* January 23, 1858, p. 56. See also Ely, *Outlines of Economics,* 77; Gutman, *Work, Culture and Society in Industrializing America,* 318–19; Brody, "Labor and Small-Scale Enterprise During Industrialization," 263–77.

tion of wealth by personalizing reward. The manager, not the market, set rewards. The cry quickly arose that corporate managers withheld the fruits of labor from employees. The notion was widespread that corporate hierarchies could set the distribution of wealth as they saw fit.[44]

Corporate reorganization of American life also redefined another aspect of nineteenth-century expectations about economic undertakings. For decades Americans had celebrated the unleashing of individual productivity by allowing workers to use both mind and body. Aristocratic economics reduced laborers to mindless brutes, slavery being the most prominent example. Many public figures had hoped that over time Americans would incorporate more intellectual acuity in their manual labor—that manual and mental labor would be combined, not separated. Time was not charitable to this expectation.

Under the new corporate regime, mental labor was decisively and radically separated from manual labor. Suddenly, new mental skills received lavish attention and remuneration: besides the old standard mental professions of law, medicine, education, religion, and politics came the new ones of management and engineering. The new corporate economy prized those who could manage others and who possessed scientific and mathematical talent. Among the justifications of the new large-scale corporation was the stress on mental ability. One contributor to the *North American Review* in 1893 stated that the greatest hoards of wealth in the world "are produced by the exercise not of the universal faculty of labor, but of those mental and moral faculties by which labor is directed and stimulated, and which are exercised and possessed by comparatively few persons." A cynical view was provided by former Civil War general, railroad director, and political Democrat Isaac Wistar: "It remains a well-nigh universal fact that the successful men are not those who labor, but those who by intelligent combination and organization, control the labor of the masses. A cobbler who cobbles, is still a cobbler." In England, the great economist Alfred Marshall noted that the modern corporation required more mental abilities than did small businesses.[45]

44. J. A. Dacus, *Annals of the Great Strikes in the United States* (Chicago, 1877), 18–20; Ashley, "Distribution of Wealth," 722–23; Gibbons, "Wealth and Its Obligations," 386; see justification of wealth distribution by corporations in J. Laurence Laughlin, "Large Fortunes," *Atlantic Monthly*, XCVI (1905), 42; testimony of John W. Britton in Garraty, ed., *Labor and Capital in the Gilded Age*, 125; testimony of Joseph Medill, *ibid.*, 128; testimony of Henry George, *ibid.*, 41.

45. W. H. Mallock, "The Productivity of the Individual," *North American Review*, CLVII (1893), 580; Isaac Jones Wistar, *Autobiography of Isaac Jones Wistar, 1827–1905* (Philadelphia, 1937), 468; Marshall, *Principles of Economics*, 503–505. See also Charles R. Flint, "General Sur-

At the same time, manual labor became for the first time unskilled labor. The evolution of the production process—the rise of the assembly line and mass production, the increasing use of machines to replace skilled labor in the factories—created workers who needed no skills but only hands. A management philosophy even grew up to handle the new unskilled workers and to reduce further their job knowledge and creativity, Frederick W. Taylor's scientific management. Not only did the late nineteenth century witness a sudden awareness of and emphasis on purely mental labor, it also saw a dramatic deskilling of the industrial workforce. Decades of hope for the elevation of the dignity of labor by combining mental and manual labor were mercilessly throttled as the economy lurched into production processes and business forms that resulted in probably the greatest chasm between mental and physical labor in American history.[46]

The emergence of the corporation as the dominant feature in American economic life also damaged one other set of expectations and values. The fruits of labor, the most recurrent American economic notion in the nineteenth century, had always been attached to property. The fruits of labor were property. Americans had consistently argued that a person's right to property found legitimacy in the act of labor. Many persons had argued for a static sense of property rights, of course: property accumulated in certain hands, civilization rested on property rights, the divinity demanded establishment of property rights, and others.[47]

When the corporation emerged, its property rights could not be held inviolate by the same fruits of labor argument for individuals. In corporations, property congealed into a large mass and lawyers and jurists acceded to the old English standard: possessors of property might do what they wished with it. Noticeably absent in the twentieth century has been the justification of property rights because individuals created the property by the act of labor.

vey of the Problem," *Independent*, May 1, 1902, p. 1027; Peck, *Twenty Years of the Republic*, 726; R. C. Floud, "The Adolescence of American Engineering Competition, 1860–1900," *Economic History Review*, XXVII (1974), 58.

46. Montgomery, *Workers' Control in America*, 4, 9–11; Braverman, *Labor and Monopoly Capital*, 85–121, esp. 113, 119, 120, 126, 129–36; Selig Perlman, "Upheaval and Reorganisation (Since 1876)," in John R. Commons *et al.*, *History of Labour in the United States* (New York, 1921), II, 358–59; Brody, *Steelworkers in America*, 31–34, 50–51, 58; Terrence V. Powderly, *Thirty Years of Labor, 1859 to 1889* (Columbus, Ohio, 1890), 23–30. Daniel Nelson qualifies the extent to which scientific management was implemented and its impact on wage earners in *Managers and Workers*, 68–78.

47. See, for example, Schlatter, *Private Property*, 13–15, 25–26, 52, 72–75, 92–94, 98, 101–104, 107.

Rather, the justification for property rights in the twentieth century has been almost exactly the same as the English justification of huge landed estates in the eighteenth century: property rights were expedient; however property was acquired, it would be wrong to deprive any person of property without due process of law; ownership was nine-tenths of possession; the status quo is easier to live with than any wrenching plan of redistribution. The labor theory of property/value justified property rights because individuals created property through their labor. That doctrine is virtually dead.[48]

And so one and one-quarter centuries of discourse filled with the phrase *fruits of labor* came to naught in the first decade of the twentieth century. The strongest pillar of the republican theory of the distribution of wealth had been bulldozed over and buried by the modern corporation. It was the ideological equivalent of the steam engine triumphing over human muscle.

The last element of the republican theory of the distribution of wealth was utterly repudiated and in fact was dramatically reversed. Since the 1760s, Americans believed economic inequality stemmed from aristocratic groups controlling government and implementing legislation backed by the military coercion that transferred the fruits of the labor of the masses to themselves. The solution to inequality was to stop aristocrats from manipulating political power in their favor; the means of doing so was to implement laissez-faire.

In the space of a decade, most Americans reversed that entire analysis. Inequality arose from the economic sphere and only political action—governmental intervention in the economy—could cure it and enable a republic to survive. Behind this reversal of policies and analysis was a startling realization. Aristocracy had been the ancient enemy of American republicanism, but by the end of the nineteenth century aristocracy looked old, enfeebled, and irrelevant. A new consolidator of power had vigorously emerged and had become the enemy of an equitable distribution of wealth, and for many that enemy was the large-scale corporation. When the enemy of republicanism changed, the entire analysis of power changed as well, and the new economic conditions demanded alterations in tactics, understanding, and public policies.

Following the Civil War, laissez-faire doctrines became entangled with the evolutionary theories of Charles Darwin to produce a vicious attitude toward social evolution that historians refer to as Social Darwinism. Social Darwin-

---

48. See interpretation of Hurst, *Law and the Conditions of Freedom*, 28. After the New Deal, property rights no longer held the validity they once had, and, according to legal scholars, that doctrine is diminished, if not extinct. See Ely, *Guardian of Every Other Right*, chaps. 7, 8.

ists, as exemplified by William Graham Sumner, argued that evolution ruled social life, that society was a struggle for survival, and that the best results occurred when the fittest emerged victorious and the weak died out. Social Darwinists hated an interventionist government because they saw government as a means by which the weak attacked the strong and so injured the best possible evolution of the species. Although important differences separated laissez-faire economics and Social Darwinism, the two possessed a great number of overlapping areas: competition in the marketplace, economic rewards to the winners, noninterference by government. It was no surprise that Social Darwinists tended to be the most vocal and obstreperous laissez-faire advocates in the Gilded Age.[49]

But laissez-faire and Social Darwinism came to an impasse on the subject of monopoly. The laissez-faire tradition condemned monopoly under all circumstances. Since the time of Adam Smith, through the years of Jefferson, Jackson, Lincoln, Rutherford B. Hayes, and Cleveland and to the present moment, the economic analysis of monopoly has not altered one iota: monopolists raise prices, lower output, pay less wages, produce decrepit goods, stagnate technologically, and redistribute wealth in their favor.[50]

The difference between Social Darwinists and laissez-faire advocates came over the origins of the trusts and whether the trusts (or simply large corporations) were monopolies. Social Darwinists looked at the consolidation movement as a natural evolution of the economy and so they sanctified it. Laissez-faire economists had far more trouble.

Part of the dilemma facing free traders was the long-hallowed interpretation of monopoly. Richard T. Ely, a progressive economist, undertook a historical study of monopolies and pointed out the obvious origins of monopoly in the Anglo-American universe. Said Lord Coke, "A monopoly is an institution or allowance by the king, by his grant, commission, or otherwise." From the time of the Revolution to the beginning of the twentieth century, Ameri-

---

49. On Social Darwinism and laissez-faire thought, see Richard Hofstadter, *Social Darwinism in American Thought* (rev. ed.; Boston, 1955), 52–60 and *passim;* Maurice R. Davie, *William Graham Sumner* (New York, 1963), 15–29. For distribution in the thought of Herbert Spencer, see Spencer, *Man Versus the State,* 69–70. On laissez-faire, see Fine, *Laissez Faire and the General-Welfare State,* 32–91; Sproat, *"Best Men,"* 4–8, 143–48.

50. The treatment of monopoly either graphically or mathematically in modern texts only confirms the verbal expressions of Adam Smith and other laissez-faire economists of the eighteenth and nineteenth centuries. The real additions to the study of monopoly have been natural monopolies (as in urban utilities, which may exhibit increasing returns to scale), monopolistic competition (William Chamberlain and Joan Robinson), and the impact of research and technology on market expansion for a large, semimonopolistic company.

can and English political economists understood monopoly to arise *only* from "exclusive privileges expressly granted by the legislative branch of government."[51]

From the beginning, laissez-faire advocates in the United States, and protectionists as well, had equated corporations with bigness and inefficiency. The obvious example was the East India Company, originally a joint-stock corporation created by Parliament to run India. The East India Company, filled with patronage places and directed by noneconomic concerns, could not efficiently produce products (tea) and market them. To survive, the company required special privileges from the government, a grant of monopoly power in the American colonies and infusions of cash from the public treasury. On its own, the company would have fallen from its own ineptitude; only government favoritism kept it afloat. Here was the great example of the political economy of aristocracy. Individuals were reaping money and advantages not from their own talents or efforts but from the capability of the state to coerce other people to pay taxes (tribute) to the company and to eliminate competition for its product.[52]

The equating of bigness with monopoly and then monopoly with corporations continued throughout the nineteenth century. Expediency, of course, played a role. Certain tasks required organization beyond the normal size of enterprise (canals, turnpikes, railroads, some charitable agencies) and so corporate charters were issued. Nonetheless, Americans operated on a usually unspoken but deeply held conviction that the *natural* size of business enterprise was small, that bigness was inherently inefficient and incapable of competing with flexible and closely supervised small businesses, and that the only way business could attain great scale in operation was by political favoritism. The political economy of aristocracy taught by experience as much as by theory that monopolies and large-scale firms derived their size and might from the political realm.[53]

51. Ely, *Outlines of Economics,* 190; Ely, *Monopolies and Trusts,* 14, 23–29, quote on 29. See Hurst, *Law and Social Order in the United States,* 239–41, 248–49; Hurst, *Legitimacy of the Business Corporation in the Law,* 1–8; Hovencamp, *Enterprise and American Law,* 13, 125.

52. See the excellent discussion of the East India Company in Hurst, *Law and the Conditions of Freedom,* 15–16; Pollard, *Genesis of Modern Management,* 12–18; and Chandler and Daems, Introduction to *Managerial Hierarchies,* ed. Chandler and Daems, 1.

53. Zunz, *Making America Corporate,* 34. This explanation is extrapolated from discussion of antebellum and postbellum economists on monopolies and is to some degree speculation. Until the 1890s, economists did not investigate the matter of the size of the business firm. There evidently was no need to because most firms had a standard size and only ones with political connections became noticeably large.

Monopolies warped the distribution of wealth in favor of the few.[54] Therefore, laissez-faire economists had to make basic decisions about the character
of the American economy before propounding a course of action. The questions facing laissez-faire theorists were, first, how to explain the rise of the
American combination or trust movement, and, second, whether the trust
movement represented economic efficiency or monopoly power. Monopoly
was the question of the day.

Corporate enterprises did not lack for supporters. One group of economists accepted the new corporate order of business life and did not detect the
presence of monopoly. In fact, the premier reason for justifying the corporation was sheer expediency: corporations produced more goods more efficiently than had the old economy of numerous small firms. Eventually, wages
would rise and a higher standard of living would be achieved, although supporters of the new corporate economy agreed that distribution of income and
wealth would probably be more unequal. Proponents of the new economy
also argued that competition still existed, that the movement from small
units of production to large ones was a natural evolution, and that the cause
of the merger movement was technological, not entrepreneurial. In a preg-
nant analysis, Charles R. Flint wrote that the new system of bigness was
different from that of former centuries. Old big businesses were monopolies,
"held by the favored few," and were political. The modern corporation was
economic, not political: "This is the difference between monopoly and cooperation, between governmental favoritism and natural law." Large-scale
enterprise came not from political machinations but from reverberations in
the growth of the economy. From this set of defenders came the American
conservatives of the twentieth century: the rise of large-scale enterprises had
not altered the principles of political economy or the functioning of the marketplace at all.[55]

But one group of Gilded Age laissez-faire advocates never accepted the

54. For example, "The Rich Richer—the Poor Poorer," *Nation,* April 15, 1869, 291; Ely,
Monopolies and Trusts, v; Ely, *Outlines of Economics,* 208–209; Tipple, "Big Business and the
New Economy," 18.

55. Laughlin, "Large Fortunes," 41–46; Ashley, "Distribution of Wealth," 724, 726, 728–
33; William G. Sumner, "Its Justification," *Independent,* May 1, 1902, pp. 1036–39; Russell
Sage, "Wealth—A Decree of Justice," *ibid.,* 1027; Andrew Carnegie, "The Bugaboo of
Trusts," in Ray Ginger, ed., *The Nationalizing of American Life, 1877–1900* (New York, 1965),
78–83; Fine, *Laissez Faire and the General-Welfare State,* 100–110; Tipple, "Big Business and the
New Economy," 21–23, 28; Charles R. Flint, "General Survey of the Problem," *Independent,*
LIV (May 1, 1902), 1026–27. See comments, for example, of Milton Friedman, with the assis-
tance of Rose D. Friedman, *Capitalism and Freedom* (Chicago, 1962), 121–23, 128–33.

idea that the new political economy of large-scale corporations could be justified by the older laissez-faire economic preachings. The new economy was
emphatically dominated by monopoly. The conviction that monopolists ran
the economy gave birth to twentieth-century liberalism, the belief in the interventionist government, and in a real sense to the birth of American socialism. It was not by chance that socialism became a force in American life only
after the emergence of the large-scale corporation. American socialism, so
strong in the first two decades of the twentieth century, was part of a broader
antimonopoly movement in reaction to the combination movement.[56]

The trust frenzy immediately raised the historic fears of Americans concerning monopoly. Critics of the new big business feared that concentrations
of economic power would be used to crush the small entrepreneur—to destroy the structure of enterprise that had characterized the republic since the
Revolution. The experience of railroads and the antics of such disreputable
entrepreneurs as Jay Gould, Jim Fiske, and Daniel Drew alarmed many about
the bizarre financial arrangements that seemed to follow in the wake of corporate gigantism. Grave concern was expressed that concentration of financial power would permit the new corporations to control legislatures and destroy the essence of republican government, the balanced decisions of the
disinterested citizen.[57]

And the corporation threatened a distribution of wealth suitable for a republic. Richard T. Ely pointed out several times that it had been understood
since the days of Aristotle that republics needed to avoid extremes of wealth

56. Note the emphasis on consolidation in the socialist tract of Alexander Schlesinger, *The
Labor Amendment: Our Next Great Job* (New York, 1910). On the antimonopoly spirit and the
law, consult Bowman, *Modern Corporation and American Political Thought*, 3–6, 61–89.

57. See Robert S. Holzman, *Adapt or Perish: The Life of General Roger A. Pryor, C.S.A.*
(Hamden, Conn., 1976), 128; Robert F. Horowitz, *The Great Impeacher: A Political Biography
of James M. Ashley* (New York, 1979), 167–68; Frank Preston Stearns, *The Life and Public Ser-
vices of George Luther Stearns* (1907; rpr. New York, 1969), 35; John H. Reagan, *Memoirs: With
Special Reference to Secession and the Civil War,* ed. Walter Flavius McCaleb (New York, 1906),
243–52; Richardson, *William E. Chandler,* 596–97, 648; Tipple, "Big Business and the New
Economy," 29–30; Hovencamp, *Enterprise and American Law,* 353–55; Hurst, *Law and the
Conditions of Freedom,* 74–76; Wiebe, *Search for Order,* 45–46, 53; Lawrence M. Friedman,
"Law and Small Business in the United States: One Hundred Years of Struggle and Accommo-
dation," in *Small Business in American Life,* ed. Stuart W. Bruchey (New York, 1980), 308, 310;
Paxson, *Recent History of the United States,* 73; Spahr, *Essay on the Present Distribution of
Wealth,* 40–42; Oberholtzer, *History of the United States,* II, 539–46; Peck, *Twenty Years of the
Republic,* 732; Kirkland, *Industry Comes of Age,* 214–17; Allan Nevins, *John D. Rockefeller: The
Heroic Age of American Enterprise* (New York, 1940), I, 345–46.

and that in a republic it was an ill social condition to have a few employers and a mass of employees. The trust question brought the distribution of wealth question embedded in republicanism to the fore. John R. Commons emphasized the "prime importance of monopoly privileges in the distribution of wealth."[58]

The antimonopolists of the laissez-faire tradition made it explicit why trusts, that is, monopolies, threatened the distribution of wealth: they charged higher prices than in a competitive situation and deprived consumers of the fruits of their labor. John Bates Clark developed a fairly modern treatment of monopoly pricing. A basic unfairness to the wage earner crept into the economic system when monopolization occurred. As Clark mentioned several times, the essence of the just wage under laissez-faire conditions was a "free" bargain between employer and employee, and it was competition that guaranteed economic justice and monopoly that undermined it: "distribution by a bargaining process without true competition is something by which no society could have developed," and "[wages are adjusted] by bargains freely made between individual men." Free bargaining was the assumption girding Clark's marginal productivity theory.[59] Under the economic conditions of consolidation, how could the bargaining process be considered free? How could it even be considered bargaining?

The antimonopolists made no bones about it: the trust movement was monopolistic and was seriously distorting the distribution of wealth. Ely wrote that monopolists obtained "unearned wealth" and created a "privileged class" in society. Edward J. Phelps said in 1891, "Great combinations of capital are organized to enhance unreasonably the price of various necessaries of life, and to extinguish that fair competition in their production which is the safeguard against monopoly and extortion." The Progressive economist Thomas N. Carver called the modern trust movement "the method of terrorism" and said that trusts should be "in the same category with those of the thief, the counterfeiter, and the confidence man."[60]

The antimonopolists knew that combination had to be curbed, tamed, or

58. Ely, *Monopolies and Trusts*, 220, 239; John R. Commons, *The Distribution of Wealth* (New York, 1905), 252; Peck, *Twenty Years of the Republic*, 724.

59. Clark and Clark, *Control of Trusts*, 40, 42–44; Ely, *Monopolies and Trusts*, chap. 3; Clark, *Philosophy of Wealth*, 69; Clark, *Distribution of Wealth*, v. For a comparison, see Amasa Walker, "Political Economy—Wages," *Hunt's Merchants' Magazine*, XXXI (1854), 179.

60. Ely, *Monopolies and Trusts*, 225; Phelps, "Irresponsible Wealth," 530; Carver, *Distribution of Wealth*, 266–67. See also John R. Commons, "Its Dangers," *Independent* (May 1, 1902), pp. 1042–43.

eradicated. Hence the question of the source of bigness became all-important. Monopoly in ages past came from politics, and more than a few in the 1890s and early twentieth century continued to blame the protective tariff and other legislation as the culprit. But most recognized that the lurch in the scale of enterprise was not a product of government laws, as the political economy of aristocracy taught, but was indeed an evolution of the economy. The economy itself became the source of inequality. Without knowing it, Richard T. Ely sealed the doom of the republican theory of distribution with one sentence when he wrote, "At the present time, however, monopolies proceed from the nature of industrial society."[61]

The heart of the republican theory of the distribution of wealth was that natural and equitable distribution succumbed to political manipulations by aristocrats who arranged policy in favor of their class and against the producers of society. Eliminate the laws of favoritism—special privileges—and the distribution of wealth would be equitable. The large-scale corporation obliterated that analysis. The economy, not merely the government, was capable of producing severe inequalities in income and wealth on its own.

Thus commenced a massive historical shift for Americans. Laissez-faire had not been an end unto itself but a means to obtain an equitable distribution of wealth. The evolution of the economy proved that monopoly arose out of new conditions, and laissez-faire policies might permit the monopolists to grow even stronger. And so the antimonopolists became interventionists; the new economists of the late nineteenth century shrugged off 120 years of republican economic analysis and forged a new path—government intervention in the economy.[62] What before had been the source of inequality had now become the fountain of equitability.

Ely had called for public ownership of industry in the 1880s and early 1890s, but by the beginning of the twentieth century he advocated a government regulation that restored competition to the economic realm. In light of

61. For example, Oscar W. Underwood, *Drifting Sands of Party Politics* (New York, 1931), 213–14; William G. McAdoo, *Crowded Years: The Reminiscences of William G. McAdoo* (Boston, 1931), 197; Taubeneck, "Concentration of Wealth, Part I," 299–300; Ely, *Outlines of Economics,* 191; see also Ely, *Monopolies and Trusts,* 29; Destler, *American Radicalism,* 156; Shippee, *Recent American History,* 120, 125.

62. For the "new economists" see Boller, *American Thought in Transition,* 84–90; Richard T. Ely, *Ground Under Our Feet: An Autobiography* (New York, 1938), 132–38; Daniel M. Fox, *The Discovery of Abundance: Simon N. Patten and the Transformation of Social Theory* (Ithaca, N.Y., 1967), 34–45; Fine, *Laissez Faire and the General-Welfare State,* chaps. 6, 7.

the emergence of the corporation, property rights had to be reevaluated, wrote Ely. Whereas before property rights had been sacrosanct because property represented the fruits of individual labor, now the corporation had beclouded the role of property rights—the ethical component was lost. Thus, wrote Ely, property rights were "not an absolute right." John R. Commons agreed; because labor was now organized and associative it was impossible "to determine how much any individual contributes to the social product" and so property rights could no longer be considered inviolable. John Bates Clark was more circumspect, admitting that large-scale organization provided benefits, yet he advocated "regulating competition" instead of abolishing trusts or encouraging socialism.[63]

Distress evinced by intellectuals and economists over the turn in the structure of American business barely preceded outrage in the political arena, although it took politics perhaps a decade to catch up with intellectual and economic currents. The emergence of bigness in firm size had upset Congress sufficiently to goad it to pass two mild regulatory acts, the Interstate Commerce Commission Act (1887) and the Sherman Anti-Trust Act (1890). In the years 1886 to 1896, troubles in the republic exploded. Labor violence crescendoed to the point that the period was called the "Great Upheaval," and farmers in the West and South, facing hard times, revolted from the two-party system and created the last important third-party movement in American history, the People's party, or, more commonly, the Populist party.[64]

The Populists ended the hegemony of the political economy of aristocracy and of the notion that all inequality flowed from aristocratic control of government. Many contradictory trends were apparent within Populist thought. They faced economic hardships and were prone to blame their woes on eastern conspiracies in political, industrial, and financial circles. Many forerunners of Populists, members of the Alliance movement, had demonstrated a preference for cooperatives and a nonaggressive small producer economy. Populists quoted Jefferson at length, talked endlessly of the fruits of labor,

---

63. Quote in Ely, *Outlines of Economics*, 344; Ely, *Ground Under Our Feet*, 251–54; Ely, *Monopolies and Trusts*, 263–71; Richard T. Ely, *Property and Contract in Their Relations to the Distribution of Wealth* (New York, 1922), I, 16–17, 57–66, 80; Commons, *Distribution of Wealth*, 14, 108–11; Clark and Clark, *Control of Trusts*, vi, 20–22, 52.

64. On labor violence, see Rayback, *History of American Labor*, 155–68, 194–226; Licht, *Working for the Railroad*, 245, 249–52; Perlman, "Upheaval and Reorganisation," 356–94. The classic work on the Populist party is John D. Hicks, *The Populist Revolt: A History of the Farmers' Alliance and the People's Party* (Minneapolis, 1931).

and in many ways seemed a typical protest party of the nineteenth century. Not a few scholars have depicted the Populists as embodying the desperate cry of vanishing agrarians against the inevitable urban-industrial future.[65]

Populists were not important or memorable because their organization attracted bizarre personalities, aired unusual ideas, contained dark and menacing tendencies, or revealed a statistically intriguing socioeconomic profile. If any party in American history deserves to be remembered for its platform, save possibly the Republican party of 1856 and 1860, it is the Populist party. In the 1892 Omaha platform, despite their praise of agrarianism and Jefferson, the Populists made a clean break with the revolutionary heritage. Besides the obvious issue of the gold standard (free silver), the Populists called for an income tax, the enactment of a scheme by which government would guarantee the price of important agricultural staples (the subtreasury plan), and nationalization of the telegraph and railroad industries. Even at the close of the twentieth century, this platform has a breathtaking quality, unmatched by any major party in American history in its call for government intervention in the economy, with the exception of the Socialist and Bull Moose parties of 1912.[66]

In the nineteenth century the Populist program must have come to the rest of society as an electrifying jolt. The parties, even until 1896, talked strictly of the traditional issues of American politics: the tariff, currency and banking, public land, and internal improvements. The Populist platform presented a different agenda altogether. And what made the Populists so different from anticorporate forerunners such as the Grange, the Greenback Labor, and the Socialist Labor parties was that the Populists tapped a huge audience. In 1892 they tallied one million votes. By 1896, the question was whether the Populists had the strength to supplant the Democratic party, a possibility that was foreclosed by the nomination of William Jennings Bryan on a free silver

---

65. See Paul W. Glad, *The Trumpet Soundeth: William Jennings Bryan and His Democracy* (Lincoln, 1960), 9–10, 36–38, 52; Hicks, *Populist Revolt*, 55, 59–63, 78–83; Lawrence Goodwyn, *The Populist Moment: A Short History of the Agrarian Revolt in America* (New York, 1978), xi–xxi; Sheldon Hackney, *Populism to Progressivism in Alabama* (Princeton, 1969), 54–55, 72, 78, 81–87; Paola E. Coletta, *William Jennings Bryan: Political Evangelist, 1860–1908* (Lincoln, 1964), 43, 396, 412; Norman Pollack, *The Populist Response to Industrial America* (Cambridge, Mass., 1962), 13–24. On Populist economic thought, see Norman Pollack, *The Humane Economy: Populism, Capitalism, and Democracy* (New Brunswick, N.J., 1990), 13–14.

66. Taken from Kirk H. Porter and Donald Bruce Johnson, comps., *National Party Platforms, 1840–1968* (4th ed.; Urbana, 1970), 89–91. See Pollack, *Humane Economy*, 86, 174.

ticket and fusion of the Democratic and Populist forces. A groundswell of support rose up to embrace the Populist advocacy of the interventionist state. And the groundswell was populated mostly by those who had marched to the Jeffersonian laissez-faire drumbeat, the small farmers.[67]

American politics was forever different after the Populist experience. The Socialist party suddenly became important and growing in the early twentieth century. It broke away from being largely the expression of ethnic immigrants and attracted people of varied backgrounds. Eugene V. Debs, the imprisoned leader of the American Railway Union in the 1894 Pullman strike, became a charismatic spokesman for the cause. In 1912 he attracted 897,000 votes, nearly 6 percent of all those cast.[68]

No doubt existed as to the reason for the appearance of socialism in American life. It was not capitalism per se, it was capitalism conducted by large-scale corporations. While socialists preserved some of the language of the republican theory of the distribution of wealth, in particular, the labor theory of value, in other ways they moved beyond those concepts. They proclaimed class conflict, not a belief in the equal rights doctrine of the mid-nineteenth century. Socialists wanted no part of laissez-faire. Said Debs in 1900, "The working class must get rid of the whole brood of masters and exploiters, and put themselves in possession and control of the means of production, that they may have steady employment without consulting a capitalist employer, large or small, and that they may get the wealth their labor produces, all of it." Socialists talked in a language different from that of the American republican tradition.[69]

The political battles of the early twentieth century pitted progressives against conservatives, that is, those who understood the fundamentals of American life had changed and politics had to change as well versus those

67. See Hicks, *Populist Revolt,* for details on the election of 1896. Destler understood the tensions within the Populist party well and stressed perceptively the interventionist nature of the Populist platform (*American Radicalism,* 18–20). For comparison of the Populist platform with other platforms, see Porter and Johnson, comps., *National Party Platforms,* 37–100.

68. Salvatore, *Eugene V. Debs,* 148, 177; David A. Shannon, *The Socialist Party of America: A History* (New York, 1955), 2–8; T. N. Carver, "How Wealth Ought to Be Distributed," *Atlantic Monthly,* XCVII (1906), 727–31. See Simon Nelson Patten, *Essays in Economic Theory,* ed. Rexford Guy Tugwell (New York, 1924), 219–22.

69. Salvatore, *Eugene V. Debs,* xii; Eugene V. Debs, "Outlook for Socialism in the United States," in Debs, *Writings and Speeches of Eugene V. Debs* (New York, 1948), 38. See Friedrich Engels on trusts in Engels, *Socialism: Scientific and Utopian,* in Arthur P. Mendel, ed., *Essential Works of Marxism* (New York, 1961), 75–82.

who saw no reason why life could not or should not go on as before. Although the Progressive mentality has proven difficult to elucidate, an essential feature of it was a recognition that the old American individualism had died and a new collective entity, the corporation, had replaced it. Democrat William Gibbs McAdoo captured the change as well as anyone. The American Revolution "was a triumph of individualism," its cry was laissez-faire and equal political rights. But the old formula failed in the face of the corporation. The Founders "had not anticipated the rise of Big Business." Theodore Roosevelt recognized that the Jeffersonian call for maximum liberty produced "a perfect freedom for the strong to wrong the weak." Robert Marion LaFollette, perhaps the most ideologically charged Progressive, said Progressives had reconsidered policy because they "have seen this vast revolution in economic conditions."[70]

Huge political contests marked the Progressive era of 1900 to 1920, and fierce battles loomed over the question of the political system's response to the existence of the large corporation. Some wanted to pulverize the trusts, others to go down the road of nationalization, others to let corporations evolve of their own accord, and others to establish some regulation over the marketplace. The answer became regulation of the marketplace and was most blatantly seen in what the Progressives had done to the federal government. In twenty years, the nation acquired a rudimentary bureaucracy that it had never known before (the Pure Food and Drug Act, the Hepburn and Mann-Elkins Acts, the Federal Reserve Act, the Clayton Anti-Trust Act, the Adam-

---

70. McAdoo, *Crowded Years,* 60–61; Theodore Roosevelt, *Theodore Roosevelt: An Autobiography* (New York, 1929), 423; Roosevelt, *Progressive Principles: Selections from Addresses Made During the Presidential Campaign of 1912,* ed. Elmer H. Youngman (New York, 1913), 10–12; John Morton Blum, *The Republican Roosevelt* (New York, 1962), 107–17; Robert M. LaFollette, *LaFollette's Autobiography: A Personal Narrative of Political Experiences* (2nd ed.; Madison, 1918), 104, 763–68; Woodward, *Origins of the New South,* 371–73, 380; Edward N. Doan, *The LaFollettes and the Wisconsin Idea* (New York, 1947), 288. On the fight over the trust question generally, see Martin J. Sklar, *The Corporate Reconstruction of American Capitalism, 1890–1916: The Market, the Law, and Politics* (Cambridge, Eng., 1988), 3, 355–420, and *passim;* James Weinstein, *The Corporate Ideal in the Liberal State, 1900–1918* (Boston, 1968), ix–xv; Arthur S. Link, *Woodrow Wilson and the Progressive Era, 1910–1917* (New York, 1954), 19–22. For the change in the party focus on distribution of resources to administration of interests, see McCormick, *The Party Period and Public Policy,* 24–25, 269–88. For an attack on the idea that a Progressive movement existed at all, see Peter G. Filene, "An Obituary for 'The Progressive Movement,'" in *Twentieth-Century America: Recent Interpretations,* ed. Barton J. Bernstein and Allen J. Matusow (2nd ed.; New York, 1972), 35–51.

son Act, the Fair Trade Commission). The bureaucracy was empowered to alter the practices of actors in the marketplace. The federal government acquired a new means of income. The federal income tax, established by the passage of the Sixteenth Amendment, had the potential of directly redistributing wealth. A new politics had been sanctified by both parties and had been implemented.

But the change in governmental operations wrought by the Progressives had no relationship to the heritage of the American Revolution and was in fact a virtual repudiation of the republican legacy of the distribution of wealth. The republican theory of the distribution of wealth warned against large government, expansive taxing power, and the capability of a central government to come under the sway of aristocrats who plundered the masses for their own benefit. The Progressive era, under the weight of a new corporate economy, had to repeal the economic doctrines that had guided the nation for nearly 130 years.

The Progressive period in one sense had an unusual exhilaration to it, for those individuals knew they navigated in unchartered waters and that the directions of the past had little relevance for them. They had the opportunity to create a new solution, a new synthesis, a new direction that comes to societies very rarely and only once every four or five generations. But the Progressives also knew that they were leaving behind the American revolutionary tradition. In the 1880s and 1890s a part of the American heritage died. Some of the Progressives' memoirs almost seem apologetic for once believing that the tariff, western lands, national banks, paper money, and internal improvements were ever treated as important issues.[71] The important question was regulation of the economy.

Historians have at times not treated this transformation of American politics kindly. A persistent question that haunts the Gilded Age has been the lethargy of politicians in responding to the novel conditions created by the rise of large-scale enterprise. Part of the reason for the hesitation was the continuing power of the revolutionary experience, of the ideas of the political economy of aristocracy that had guided political discussion of economic issues for so many years. It took time to overcome such a precious but now archaic inheritance. For some historians, however, the real problem was dis-

71. For example, Oswald Garrison Villard, *Fighting Years: Memoirs of a Liberal Editor* (New York, 1939), 121–22; Charles E. Russell, *Bare Hands and Stone Walls: Some Recollections of a Side-Line Reformer* (New York, 1933), 44–45; Brand Whitlock, *Forty Years of It* (New York, 1925), 88–90.

carding an unusable past. Wrote historian Chester Destler about the rise of protest in the 1890s: "Both writers [James Bryce and Henry Demarest Lloyd] lifted national thought above the pettiness of contemporary squabbles over tariffs, pensions, free silver, and the tag ends of Reconstruction and focused attention on basic political and economic issues that were never again obscured."[72] Somehow one feels that the political economy of aristocracy deserved a more understanding epithet.

But the idea of the political economy of aristocracy was dead. And so were the other axioms of the republican theory of the distribution of wealth: the labor theory of property/value, the importance of the laws of entail and primogeniture, and the vital role of the population-to-land ratio. They were all gone, dead, and nearly forgotten doctrines.

The republican theory of the distribution of wealth belonged to the agrarian republic, and the agrarian republic was no more.

72. Destler, *American Radicalism,* 135. This was a typical Progressive attitude.

Afterword

About a century has passed since the revolutionaries' ideas about maintaining an equitable distribution of wealth disappeared from discussions of public policy. This temporal distance, because it has enabled other ideas concerning wealth distribution to obtain expression, allows the legacy of the revolutionaries to be put into a broader perspective. By the end of the twentieth century, the limitations of the four axioms that eighteenth- and nineteenth-century American leaders so fervently upheld become more obvious and, in fact, somewhat ironical. The inadequacies of the revolutionaries' understanding of wealth distribution extended beyond the fate of the four axioms; the Founders failed to grapple with the reality that all societies require some redistribution of wealth and income to survive, to be able to claim for themselves the substance, the meaning, behind the word *civilization.* The words of political combat of the nineteenth century endure—*monopoly, privileged, democrat,* and especially *aristocrat*—but now they are fading, diaphanous apparitions, having lost the full-bodied vigor they once radiated when they fully embodied the hopes of constructing a just society.

The twentieth-century discussion of the distribution of income and wealth has been quite different from that of the nineteenth century. In the twentieth century, the topic has been subsumed under other headings, particularly that of poverty. Moreover, wealth distribution has generated considerably different approaches from political groupings in the twentieth century. In this broad discourse the revolutionary heritage had embarrassingly little to say. Most of the formulations of the American concept of wealth distribution have had a weak existence in the twentieth century, and certainly its formulations have not been guides for anyone.

Concerns over wealth distribution in the twentieth century have erupted several times. The first two decades of the century witnessed the Progressive crusade and a socialist outburst, both of which carried distributionist themes in their attack on the newly erected large-scale business structure. During the New Deal years, the distribution of wealth and income as a topic of public debate again surfaced because many New Deal programs had redistributionist potential, and numerous popular movements ran on avowedly redistributionist programs, probably the most notable being Huey Long's "Share the Wealth" campaign. The subject slumbered in the 1940s and 1950s as most turned their attention to the question of economic growth and the problem of securing a full employment economy. Then in the middle of the 1960s, the civil rights movement and the birth of the New Left breathed new life and fire into the question of the equitable distribution of wealth and income. Structural changes in the American economy, the loss of industrial capacity, and the fall in the real wage rate raised the questions of the distribution of wealth and income again in the 1980s.[1]

Three distinct viewpoints about distribution emerged in the twentieth century. One was New Deal–Progressive. It basically argued that free markets were fair, but the emergence of the corporation fouled up the necessary equality between employer and employee and tilted the balance grotesquely toward the employer and stockholders. The second was Marxist-leftist. It insisted that the capitalist system was designed to suppress wage rates and to throw all the earnings of society to the few property holders. The third was academic economics, which at times divided between favoring government intervention and nonintervention in the economy. At least among conservatives—which for precision's sake can be labeled monetarists, supply-siders, and microeconomists in general—the matter of distribution was not a sub-

---

1. I am not aware of a good general historical treatment of the understanding of the distribution of wealth in the twentieth century. Several excellent works exist, however, which imply or provide information on the topic: McClelland, *American Search for Economic Justice;* Lars Osberg, *Economic Inequality in the United States* (Armonk, N.Y., 1984); Jennifer L. Hochschild, *What's Fair? American Beliefs About Distributive Justice* (Cambridge, Mass., 1981); James T. Patterson, *America's Struggle Against Poverty, 1900–1985* (2nd ed., Cambridge, Mass., 1986); Williamson and Lindert, *American Inequality;* DuBoff, *Accumulation and Power.* For empirical studies of the twentieth century, see Frank Levy, *Dollars and Dreams: The Changing American Income Distribution* (New York, 1987); Kevin Phillips, *The Politics of Rich and Poor: Wealth and the American Electorate in the Reagan Aftermath* (New York, 1990); Nan L. Maxwell, *Income Inequality in the United States, 1947–1985* (New York, 1990); Sheldon Danziger and Peter Gottschalk, eds., *Uneven Tides: Rising Inequality in America* (New York, 1993).

ject fit for academic inquiry. Among conservative economists, the rule was the divinelike quality of the market: the market giveth and the market taketh away.[2]

In the twentieth-century debate over the American distribution of wealth, the formulations of the Founders have had little consequence. The Malthusian horror, overpopulation—or, alternatively, the Madisonian killer of republics—was abandoned by the second or third decade of the century as recognition grew that technology and science could alter crop yields. Toward the close of the century, the fear of population expansion rose again but this time in the guise of ecology and the disappearing animal kingdom. Distribution of wealth and income was implied in the analysis but not especially drawn out. The land laws of the aristocracy have barely drawn academic interest, let alone been a part of a twentieth-century public debate. Only the mechanism of inheritance ties current considerations about wealth distribution to the old concern about the effects of entail and primogeniture.

The political economy of aristocracy and the labor theory of property/value have had some influence on distributionist views in the twentieth century, but not in a way nineteenth-century partisans would have recognized. For in the twentieth century, the political economy of aristocracy has been taken over by conservatives or those seeking minimal government. The market, in their estimation, always distributes fairly and efficiently when left to itself. When government acts, it produces a distortion that favors some over others. In a sense, modern conservatism uses the same appeal that existed in the nineteenth century about how government elevates some over others; it is an argument against aristocracy in its own way. The problem with twentieth-century use of the political economy of aristocracy is that the actors are playing the wrong parts and the objective of nonintervention has changed. Laissez-faire advocates in the nineteenth century called for reduced government because they sensed that such a policy would produce equality. They held that in the economic structure where an individual's accomplishments

2. I am not going to explore these positions in any detail. For elaboration of the views contained in the three positions given in the narrative, consult Bronfenbrenner, *Income Distribution Theory;* Lester C. Thurow, *Generating Inequality: Mechanisms of Distribution in the U.S. Economy* (New York, 1975); Donald J. Harris, *Capital Accumulation and Income Distribution* (Stanford, 1978); Assar Lindbeck, *The Political Economy of the New Left: An Outsider's View* (2nd ed.; New York, 1977); Alan S. Blinder, *Toward an Economic Theory of Income Distribution* (Cambridge, Mass., 1974); Friedman, *Capitalism and Freedom;* Arthur M. Okun, *Equality and Efficiency: The Big Tradeoff* (Washington, D.C., 1975).

were wholly confined to what could be performed singly, the end result would be a rough equality of fortune. They also saw laissez-faire as a defense of the poor against the strong.

The twentieth-century advocates of laissez-faire rejoice in inequality, not equality. They demand government inactivity so it does not hamper the talented in accumulating all that they might. And very much unlike those of the nineteenth century, twentieth-century conservatives find the redistribution achieved by government not to be the feared one of the middle to the wealthy (producers to aristocrats) but of the wealthy to the poor. In twentieth-century conservative parlance, the feared aristocracy is the poverty class.

The labor theory of property/value has had a different fate in the twentieth century. "Fruits of labor" and "sweat of our brows" are phrases that have almost disappeared from academic and political parlance. In the academic world, the labor theory of value has been relegated to a struggle between leftists and capitalist economists over the definition of value. For years, the political Left has claimed suzerainty over the labor theory of value and has explained exploitation by stating that labor creates all value, and then capitalists take away the bulk of that value for their own use and enjoyment. Microeconomists have denied the validity of the labor theory of value and have offered some notion of value originating from market evaluation, either marginal utility theory or a similar verbal formulation.[3] As a diffuse notion that effort deserves reward, one may say that the labor theory of value in its fruits-of-labor guise lives on. But in another sense, the term has died out. Instead of acquiring the fruits of labor, one obtains what the market will yield. The connecting bond between effort and reward is considerably different in the twentieth century than it was in the nineteenth.

Human beings do not provide answers for dilemmas that span eternity, and it should not be held against the Founders that they failed to provide an eternal solution to the questions surrounding an equitable distribution of wealth. The explanations they did offer lasted for nearly one and one-quarter centuries, and that longevity was remarkable considering the economic evolutions

3. See Harris, *Capital Accumulation and Income Distribution,* 10–14; Arthur P. Mendel, "The Formation and Appeal of Scientific Socialism," in *Essential Works of Marxism,* ed. Mendel, 6–7; Schlatter, *Private Property,* 273–75; Bronfenbrenner, *Income Distribution Theory,* 185–86 and chap. 6; McClelland, *American Search for Economic Justice,* chap. 3 and pp. 83–85; Colin D. Campbell, ed., *Income Redistribution* (Washington, D.C., 1977); Friedman, *Capitalism and Freedom,* 162–71; Stigler, *Production and Distribution Theories.*

through which their formulations passed. Nonetheless, a hollowness permeates the revolutionary generation's treatment of the distribution of wealth.

On the one hand, the revolutionaries bequeathed to future generations an awareness of and an attention to the distribution of wealth as a measure of societal justice. They found popular government to be far more equitable than aristocracy and monarchy, and from their own musings as well as from the teachings of republican theorists they realized that popular government required fundamental justice in its economic arrangements. The form of that economic justice was displayed in the distribution of wealth. A healthy society for a republic was one in which labor was well rewarded and the disparities between rich and poor were dampened.

On the other hand, a large shadow hangs over the Founders' accomplishments in regard to the distribution of wealth. Their awareness of its importance was mated with an unwillingness to take any positive actions to maintain a healthy wealth distribution. They devised concepts that traced the origin and growth of inequality in European societies, but they evaded the ultimate issue. They ignored the use of political power to establish equitability in wealth distribution and instead relied on "natural" forces to determine poverty and wealth.[4] Behind this timidity was a fear of redistributing property and of legislating agrarian laws. Yet if popular government was so important and vital, it would seem that a political mechanism would have been furnished to allow some amount of redistribution if chance and events had ever enabled a maldistribution to become a threat to republican government. In this sense, the Founders constructed a haunted house. They created a foundation and built a structure for a republican society. They issued warnings about the need for a good distribution of wealth but did not embody those warnings in the structure. And so the warnings served as ghosts to haunt the house, but they had no material existence to affect the distribution of wealth and the ultimate configuration the house took.

4. The theme that the Founders in general and Madison in particular framed the Constitution to remove property rights from popular manipulation is advocated by several scholars. Although more could be said for the constitutional achievement and the Founders' beliefs about property rights, the essential argument is correct: the Constitution was designed to protect property rights and to deny popular majorities, except in extreme situations, the ability to tamper with them. Perhaps the finest exposition of this position is Jennifer Nedelsky, *Private Property and the Limits of American Constitutionalism: The Madisonian Framework and Its Legacy* (Chicago, 1990). For a brief critique of Nedelsky, see Banning, *Sacred Fire of Liberty*, 182–83, 416 n. 70.

Redistribution of wealth and income in American history has not been the most well received topic by the public. Evidently many fear that redistribution means taking from the worthy to give to the unworthy. Another explanation for its lack of popularity may be that, no matter how justifiable the need, somehow the political system will botch the application and turn a magnanimous decision into an evil result. Yet the greatest recalcitrance simply stems from those with the most property, and the source of their distaste is obvious: having obtained property, they cannot countenance the loss of any of it for any reason. The history of American thinking on the justification of holding property is instructive in this instance. All the justifications for private property are after-the-fact apologizing. The real reason is almost wholly psychological; once people obtain property for any reason, they are almost maniacal about keeping possession of it because property dictates the quality of material life and expands a person's field of endeavor.

As the United States prepares to enter the twenty-first century, the failure of its society to enact a just measure of income redistribution—the current method is too little and too incompetent—presents some disturbing comparisons between what the Founders had hoped for the new republic and what the condition of that polity has become. Throughout most of the nineteenth century, Americans prided themselves on the difference between their republican, egalitarian society and the class-ridden aristocratic societies of Europe. To find rampant crime, utter hopelessness, a permanent poverty class, and magnificent fortunes residing next to indescribable hovels, Americans went to Europe. Europeans needed armies to force their populations to obey the law; republican America obtained law-abiding citizens from the reality of republican equality and through voluntary consent, not military coercion. In Europe class was arrayed against class; in the United States the poor and the rich were not so socially distant. In Europe, politics was for the few; in America, it was the jewel possessed by all and elicited widespread participation.

Now, at the close of the twentieth century, Europeans come to the United States to witness the social distance between rich and poor, to observe homelessness and unendurable poverty, to see a political system of republicanism that elicits either apathy or outright hostility from the majority of its citizens, to research rampant crime and the world's largest population of prison inmates, to record the antics and frivolities of the inordinately wealthy. The relationship between Europe and the United States has reversed. In the eighteenth and nineteenth centuries, Americans visited Europe to witness social chasms and unremitting poverty and crime. Now Europeans come to the United States to observe the same conditions that once shocked Americans in European countries. Europe in the late twentieth century is characterized by high participation in politics, low crime, and an acceptable distribution of wealth and income. For Europeans, America has become the land of aristocratic distresses, while Europe is now the land of republican vistas.[5] By looking at the history of the American concept of the distribution of wealth for nearly two and one-half centuries, one comes to the eerie, disquieting conclusion that the late-twentieth-century United States exhibits the traits that the revolutionaries found loathsome in the eighteenth century. The United States has become at the end of the twentieth century the aristocratic disgrace of western European civilization.

5. See the review of Donald Sassoon, *One Hundred Years of Socialism,* in the *Economist,* July 6, 1996, pp. 74–75.

APPENDIX A
Marginal Productivity Theory, Production Functions, and the Distribution of Wealth

In this appendix I argue that it is necessary to reformulate economic doctrines regarding distribution in order to take into account cooperation among productive agents. I also argue—but cannot prove—that distribution of reward among productive agents is indeterminate and is made determinate only by the intervention of an individual situated in a hierarchy and possessing the power to dictate where rewards should go. This discussion focuses on distribution within the firm. It does not tackle the larger question of appropriate distribution to ensure social stability and equitability. For the purposes of this exposition, the object of inquiry is limited to the large-scale corporation.

I suggest that the size of the firm does make a difference in the distribution of income because when groups make a product, an interaction effect appears that is not captured in a traditional economic analysis of distribution. Non-American corporations seem to understand this interaction effect. American corporate officials refuse to acknowledge it, especially when it comes to rewards. The unique feature of American companies when compared to other corporate structures in the industrial world is that American companies are an unholy and generally destructive combination of individualism and cooperation. Other nations have evidently learned that corporations require a cooperative ethic; Americans either have not learned this lesson or, more likely, *refuse* to learn it.[1]

1. This is largely the theme of William Lazonick, who sees the nineteenth century dominated by a market method of distribution of resources (not distribution of income) and the twentieth century as having witnessed the rise of a "collective" means of resource allocation via large institutional structures (*Business Organization and the Myth of the Market Economy*

The cooperation of many individuals with different talents allows a firm to produce a good that earns revenue. The firm earns the revenue; but it is the managers who determine how that revenue is divided up among the cooperating parts. Market forces determine how well the firm does in the marketplace, but not necessarily how well the individuals within the firm do. The market merely establishes boundaries; top management decides where within a boundary an individual is placed. Likewise, compensation is a managerial, not a market, determination. Given this situation and the self-interest of individualism, managers of course maintain that the higher one resides in a hierarchy, the more compensation one deserves. In eighteenth-century terms, American corporations have no virtue (no willingness of individuals to sacrifice for the greater good of the public) but certainly have an abundance of community-destroying self-interest.

This discussion has a bearing on microeconomic analysis of the firm. Business historians, students of industrial organization, and others have complained that microeconomic theory cannot distinguish between a proprietorship and General Motors—and the differences must have some important bearing on economic performance and on such matters as the distribution of income. Microeconomic theory has relentlessly posited individualism as the key to performance of the firm. In a series of lectures given in 1975, Arthur Okun discussed his problems with the ethical quality of market-determined solutions and noted that the idea that an individual reaps in economic values exactly what he contributes to society contained more theoretical bravado than realistic precision. "In view of those dependencies on other people," Okun wrote, "the concept of *my* contribution to output becomes hazy. Production comes out of a complex, interdependent system and may not be neatly attributable to individual contributors."[2]

Marginal productivity theory is not adequate to explain distribution. Outside of the important question of whether assumptions are met (markets are competitive, knowledge of markets is perfect, labor is as liquid as money in its economic applications, and so on), a lingering suspicion arises that marginal productivity theory simply justifies anything that occurs. When incomes are monstrous, they are always the result of some contribution to the economy and therefore legitimate. When incomes

[Cambridge, Eng., 1991], 7–16, 27–31, 37, 64–65). See *Business Week,* January 27, 1992, p. 32; "Japan: All in the Family," *Newsweek,* June 10, 1991, pp. 38–39; "Japan Takes a Good, Hard Look at Itself," *Business Week,* February 17, 1992, pp. 3–35; James Fallows, "Containing Japan," *Atlantic,* CCLXIII (May, 1989), 40–54; Andrea Gabor, *The Man Who Discovered Quality: How W. Edwards Deming Brought the Quality Revolution to America—The Stories of Ford, Xerox, and GM* (New York, 1990), chap. 2; "Japanese Business Methods," *Economist,* April 4, 1992, pp. 19–22. For W. Edwards Deming's assessment of American management practices, see Gabor, *Man Who Discovered Quality,* 58–59, and chap. 9; Deming's opinion in *Forbes,* May 27, 1991, pp. 208–12.

2. Okun, *Equality and Efficiency,* 46.

are virtually Malthusian, they reflect the minuscule contribution of those individuals to society, and so they are legitimate. Most people (I assume) would agree that some individuals, and indeed some occupations, obtain far more remuneration than their contributions merit, while others obtain far less.

A central question about marginal productivity theory is the specification of the key element in the presentation of the theory, the production function. The production function relates mathematically—and, presumably, precisely—the form of the mixture of inputs (usually capital and labor, but it can be extended to research and development, merchandising, different levels of skill, and others) that result in an output. Most presentations concerning the production function use a standard Cobb-Douglas function that yields constant returns to scale. (The standard description is $Y = K^\alpha L^{\alpha-1}$, where alpha is $0 < \alpha < 1$, Y is output, K is capital input, and L is labor input.) The problem with marginal productivity theory is at least partially the adequacy of the production function.[3]

Marginal productivity theory posits that the factors of production obtain the income that they contribute. That condition is usually determined when one more unit of labor (or capital) is added to production; and the price of the product times extra amount of production resulting from the (marginal) infusion of another unit of labor (or capital) then sets the appropriate award for labor (or capital).

Mathematically, the theory operates as follows. For a one-variable case, assume the production function is $Y = f(L)$, that is, all output is a function of labor inputs. Then the production function is placed into a profit function to maximize the situation so that everything operates at an optimal level. The basic profit function is $\pi =$ price of product (p) times the amount of production [$f(L)$] minus total costs (TC). Total costs in this case are entirely labor costs, or the wage rate (w) times the units of labor (L). Thus the profit function can be written as $\pi = pf(L) - wL$. To maximize profits, the profit function is differentiated (with respect to L obviously) and then set to 0. The result is $\delta\pi = pf'(L) - w$. Setting $d\pi$ equal to 0 and solving for w, the expression obtained is $w = pf'(L)$. The wage is equal to the price of the product times the marginal output of an additional unit of labor (by geometric construction, the first derivative of an input function is defined by economists to be the path of marginal contribution of that input). The idea that a person receives a wage (or a profit rate) equivalent to the contribution to production has a nice and straightforward mathematical presentation.

The two-variable input case (*i.e.,* capital and labor are inputs that are allowed to vary) is slightly more complicated but generally ends in the same place as the one-variable example. The production function is taken to be Cobb-Douglas, $Y = K^\alpha L^{1-\alpha}$. The price of the product is given by p. The profit function now becomes

---

3. See Nicholas Kaldor, "Alternative Theories of Distribution," *Review of Economic Studies*, XXIII (1955–56), 89–91; Thurow, *Generating Inequality*, 53–55, 70–72.

π = price of product times amount of production − *TC*, where *TC* (total costs) now equals *wL* (the cost of labor inputs) plus *rK* (the rate of interest times the units of capital, the interest being the cost of borrowing money). The profit function thus looks like:

(1) $\quad \pi = p\ (Y = K^{\alpha}L^{1-\alpha}) - wL - rK$

Taking the profit function and differentiating it with respect to *L*, the expression is obtained:

(2) $\quad \partial\pi/\partial L = p\ (1 - \alpha)\ (K^{\alpha})\ (L^{1-\alpha-1}) - w$

Simplifying this expression,

(3) $\quad \partial\pi/\partial L = p\ (1 - \alpha)K^{\alpha}L^{-\alpha}$

Or (4) $\quad \partial\pi/\partial L = p\ (1 - \alpha)\ (K/L)^{\alpha}$

To maximize, set $\partial\pi/\partial L$ equal to 0 and solve for *w*:

(5) $\quad w = p(1-\alpha)\ (K/L)^{\alpha}$

Once again, it is found that the wage depends on the price of the product times the marginal contribution of labor—in this case, represented by the capital-to-labor ratio; the $(1-\alpha)\ (K/L)^{\alpha}$ portion of equation (5) is the derivative of the production function and thus represents a marginal contribution times the price of the product.

But the theoretical results depend specifically on the production function put into the equation. As Arthur Okun noted, in production dependencies or interdependencies operate that are not captured by the Cobb-Douglas production function (or the CES production function). Large companies seek to establish an intermeshing of people and machines, that is, a coordination of activity. These circumstances argue that the production function, especially for large companies where coordination is more imperative than in small firms and virtually nonexistent in a proprietorship/artisanal shop, should possess an interaction term. The existence of that term would destroy the simplicity of marginal productivity theory because then an extra product arises from the coordination of capital and labor (the interaction term). In short, a production function should be created (and tested) that accomplishes exactly what Arthur Okun implied: the various dependencies of people on each other and on machinery.

What follows is an attempt at such a theoretical production function. This is not an exercise in scientific thinking or reasoning; in fact, there is no science to this exposition because there is no testing. It is only an attempt to create an alternative to existing theory.

For the sake of theory, imagine a production function that displays an interaction term; output *Y* is still a function of *K* (capital) and *L* (labor) (*i.e.*, $Y = f(K, L)$), but say the functional form of the equation now becomes

(6) $\quad Y = K^{\alpha}L^{1-\alpha} + e^{\gamma KL}$

The term $e^{\gamma KL}$ is chosen for specific reasons. First, it is the interaction term. Second, the use of the exponential function is for the expository and illustrative purpose of showing that an extra product comes out of coordination and cooperation; labor and capital must cooperate for additional production to occur. In addition, the exponential function was chosen because when differentiated the basic form remains the same—that is, differentiation does not split capital and labor into separate expressions. This rationalization may be considered whimsy on the part of the author, but the form of the interaction term was designed to reinforce the idea that for extra production to occur as a result of cooperation, the aspect of cooperation cannot be divided into separate spheres of labor and capital but rather must be seen as a single term.

The interaction term also has another feature, the use of gamma (γ) in $e^{\gamma KL}$. Gamma represents a measure of management success in fostering and sustaining cooperation. A large value of γ would mean that management has taken the appropriate steps to ensure harmony within the firm, continued skill development, obtained cooperation among the different departments—and rewards everyone with the understanding that because a company is a joint effort among the participants, no single individual or group of individuals should claim the lion's share of the revenues. Rather, because the work is a joint effort, the reward must be jointly shared. A low number for γ indicates that management has failed at its most basic task: arranging for cooperation among the firm's resources to enhance output. This type of production function with an interaction term has the possibility of explaining variation in production output among companies, whereas traditional production functions (without interaction terms) usually have to *assume* that all companies possess equal managerial ability, technology, and knowledge.

The profit-maximizing equation using the production function with the interaction term then becomes

(7) $\quad \pi = p\,(K^{\alpha}L^{1-\alpha} + e^{\gamma KL}) - wL - rK$

Differentiating π with respect to L, one obtains

(8) $\quad \partial\pi/\partial L = p(1-\alpha)K^{\alpha}L^{-\alpha} + p\gamma K[e^{\gamma KL}] - w$

Simplifying and setting $\partial\pi/\partial L$ equal to 0 to maximize the partial derivative:

(9) $\quad 0 = p(1-\alpha)K^{\alpha}L^{-\alpha} + p\gamma K[e^{\gamma KL}] - w$

Thus, solving for w:

(10) $\quad w = p(1-\alpha)K^{\alpha}L^{-\alpha} + p\gamma K[e^{\gamma KL}]$

This final expression indicates that the wage for an individual in a company in which cooperation is important—that is, large-scale firms—is more than marginal productivity theory determines. The marginal product of labor times the price of the product remains as a key to the determination of wages (the $p(1-\alpha)K^{\alpha}L^{-\alpha}$ term in equation 10 above), but it is no longer the only determinant of wages. Rather, the interaction term ($p\gamma K[e^{\gamma KL}]$) represents the extra output that arises from harmonious cooperation and shows that cooperation should enhance wages.

The first term in equation 10, the marginal productivity term, is set by the marketplace—in a sense, it is market-determined. But the interaction term of wages—the second term in equation 10 that reveals how much production has increased through cooperation—is determined not by the market but by the firm itself. Theoretically the market exerts pressure for the firm to perform up to the standards of others, but any market will have a range of performers, from very good to lackluster, and it is not at all clear that lackluster performers will exit the marketplace in the short term.

One may therefore state that a company may have to pay labor the value of its marginal product, under the influence of the market, but the market has nothing to say about the disposition of the value of production from cooperation, the interaction term. Market forces do not dispose of that value. Rather, the hierarchical nature of the corporation centralizes the decision about the disposition of the value created by cooperative effort and places it in the hands of management. In America, because cooperation has been so little valued and "heroic" management skills so overstated and overvalued, the values created by cooperation have flowed to management officers in the forms of bonuses and "perks" and to stockholders. In short, distribution of the value produced by cooperation is not shared among all the firm's employees but is appropriated by management for its own and for the property holders' aggrandizement. In Japan, the tendency of management has been to recognize the importance of cooperative effort and to distribute the rewards so that each employee obtains something from the values created by cooperative effort.

Economists have always tended to blame workers for irrational behavior in large plants regarding wages and working conditions. As usual in economics, the fault is always with laborers who are "shirkers" and rent-seekers.[4] The working conditions may be set aside for the moment, but the introduction of an interaction effect in the production function explains—*rationally*—why factory workers become upset over wages. It is well known that large-scale production facilities pay higher wages than small-scale companies or proprietorships. Thus when workers in these large corporations demand higher wages, the tendency among laissez-faire economists has been to stress the politics of the situation: workers form unions to coerce politically—not by economic performance—higher wages out of management.

Any person familiar with large companies knows, however, that management never shares its basic financial information or its cost or remuneration figures with workers. Perfect information does not exist for workers—that assumption is stressed as being important only when laissez-faire economists discuss entrepreneurs and upper-income groups; somehow it always seems better for lower-income groups to live in ignorance of wages, costs, and profits. The lack of knowledge breeds a hostile and suspicious attitude on the part of factory workers. And frequently (I assume) workers feel that the company generates huge amounts of cash that is never shared. In short, workers have intuitively believed that a certain amount of production

---

4. See analysis of shirking in Miller, *Managerial Dilemmas,* 4–7, 11–12, 31–36.

comes from cooperative effort and they have never obtained a share of the values created by this effort. Thus even though by marginal productivity theory the wages of workers in large-scale industry may be large, a continuous discontent manifests itself because there is a sense that in proportion to what the company earns, the wage is too little. Equation 10 provides an analytical base for that suspicion.

Distribution thus is not and cannot be exact in economic theory. There is no specifically correct way to divide the rewards of cooperative effort (the value of the interaction term in equation 10). Division of the value of cooperative effort can be accomplished only through collective bargaining (hence the *rational* explanation for the existence of unions in large-scale industrial undertakings) or by simple statesmanship by managers who understand that a good firm must fairly distribute the values created by cooperative effort. In other words, statesmanship in one form or another, not market forces, ultimately determines the distribution of income within a company and thereby has some impact on the larger distribution of income within the entire society.

APPENDIX B
In Defense of Redistribution: A Personal View

A study such as this one evokes a legitimate inquiry as to the author's position on the subject of distribution and the reasons for that position. This appendix is my response. It will be short and sketchy. An easier way to avoid a personal statement is simply to refer readers to the large and ongoing discussion about distribution principles among philosophers, economists, and political scientists, a discourse that has been active for the past two decades. Much of this literature was inspired by the publication of *A Theory of Justice*, by John Rawls, in 1971. A just distribution of resources was the prominent but not the only theme of the work. Rawls argued for redistribution because initial endowments had no moral base. After that, the explosion occurred, with major contributions by Richard J. Arneson, Ronald Dworkin, Amartya K. Sen, Arthur Okun, Alan Blinder, Lester Thurow, G. A. Cohen, and John Roemer. Free market theorists responded: Robert Nozick, Richard Posner, Irving Kristol, David Gautier, and a host of economists fearing powerful government. Their essential argument was that a free market operates without coercion and with voluntary consent; under those conditions, it is impossible for a rational person not to receive the full value of the contributions he makes to society. Any attempt to alter rewards will introduce inefficiency in resource allocation and fail to maximize satisfaction of preferences.[1]

1. John Rawls, *A Theory of Justice* (Cambridge, Mass., 1971); Ronald Dworkin, "What Is Equality? Part 1; Equality of Welfare," *Philosophy and Public Affairs,* X (1981), 185–246; Ronald Dworkin, "What Is Equality? Part 2: Equality of Resources," *Philosophy and Public Affairs,* X (1981), 283–345; Richard J. Arneson, "Liberalism, Distributive Subjectivism, and Equal Opportunity for Welfare," *Philosophy and Public Affairs,* XIX (1990), 158–94; Okun, *Equality and Efficiency;* Blinder, *Toward an Economic Theory of Income Distribution;* Thurow, *Generating Inequality;* John E. Roemer, "A Pragmatic Theory of Responsibility for the Egalitarian Plan-

This is an exceedingly rich literature which I do not presume to have mastered. Undoubtedly, any number of ideas I possess have been introduced or shaped, knowingly and unknowingly, by reading this material. Because some of my views vary slightly from the literature I have perused, however, I will present them briefly. First, the goal of human existence is a civilized life—one within the confines of a civil society. Civil society is made possible by acceptance of rules; that acceptance deserves a material reward regardless of economic contribution. Second, maximum economic efficiency is not the goal of civilization, although it is of economists who have managed to propagandize their theory so much that they have displaced other notions of the meaning of life. What is to be maximized is civilized life, and that maximization may, and in fact does, entail a sacrifice of economic efficiency. Third, reward systems in free markets are not based on economic principles; they are based on gamesmanship principles. This explains why income and wealth distributions have such bizarre skews and do not follow one of the most obvious economic principles: the law of diminishing returns. Minute increments in business talent may result in absurdly exponential returns. And it is the existence of those exponential returns to marginal increases in talent that justifies a redistribution of income to other, less favored members of society to ensure maximization of a civilized life, while still permitting a generous reward for talent that maintains the incentive to excel and ensures further economic growth.

Civilization

Many, if not most, discussions of distribution of income and wealth begin with an investigation of the nature of the human animal. This is a reasonable procedure, and one supposes eventually the topic must be attended to. Nonetheless, it may be more

---

ner," *Philosophy and Public Affairs,* XXII (1993), 146–66; Amartya Sen, *Inequality Reexamined* (Cambridge, Mass., 1992). See comments in Samuel Scheffler, "Responsibility, Reactive Attitudes, and Liberalism in Philosophy and Politics," *Philosophy and Public Affairs,* XXI (1992), 299–323; Ian Shapiro, "Resources, Capacities, and Ownership," *Political Theory,* XIX (1991), 47–72; Robert Nozick, *Anarchy, State and Utopia* (New York, 1974); Irving Kristol, "Thoughts on Equality and Egalitarianism," in *Income Redistribution,* ed. Colin D. Campbell (Washington, D.C., 1977), 35–42; David Gauthier, *Morals by Agreement* (Oxford, 1986); Richard A. Posner, *The Economics of Justice* (Cambridge, Mass., 1981), 101–102; Richard A. Epstein, *Takings: Private Property and the Power of Eminent Domain* (Cambridge, Mass., 1985); George J. Stigler, *"The Economist as Preacher" and Other Essays* (Chicago, 1982), chaps. 2, 3. Most of the literature on property rights and political economy is in this vein; *e.g.,* James M. Buchanan and Gordon Tullock, *The Calculus of Consent: Logical Foundations of Constitutional Democracy* (Ann Arbor, 1962); and Terry L. Anderson and Peter J. Hill, *The Birth of a Transfer Society* (Lanham, Md., 1989), 1–6. For a shortened version of this debate, see McClelland, *American Search for Economic Justice,* chaps. 4, 5.

worthwhile to commence with the objective of human creatures: to live among others according to a set of rules (politics, law, culture) that proves satisfactory to all, or at least to the overwhelming majority. This goal is commonly called civilization, or life in a civil polity.[2] This definition says nothing about technological advance, religion, cultural values, progress, or any other attribute; rather, it is simply a statement that civilization consists of people living harmoniously with each other under a given set of rules that elicit approbation.

It may be assumed (or flatly declared) that the civilization most desired is one with the following characteristics: citizens minimize interpersonal conflict; the governing body does not have to resort to extensive coercion to obtain obedience to the laws; the members have a sufficient opportunity to discover their talents and apply them; and the members have some access to political power and the laws that shape their lives. (Henry C. Carey would call this the mating of individualism and association, the two halves of human life that are inseparably intertwined although they are treated as logically incompatible impulses.) It is not necessary to assume an absolutely egalitarian society where all members are equal in all ways, to argue for uniformity in ideals and values among the citizenry, or to imagine that conflict would evaporate and all violence would be banned. Putting aside the subject of human nature, it can just be imported from other sources, or intuition, or observation, or the properties of the normal curve, and taken as truth that any population will have its deviants, and violence and other ills will beset any civilization formed in the present or in the future. Perfection is not possible. The objective, however, should be to construct the political, economic, and social institutions of a civilization such that the institutions minimize disobedience, disaffection, and nonparticipation. The objective should be to maximize a civil life—acceptance of the personal responsibility to obey the commonly agreed-upon rules of the society—and to observe as well the rules that explain how rules themselves are to be changed.

This formulation of civilization has costs. To obtain the highest degree of civil society possible—the greatest amount of harmony and individual satisfaction—the citizenry must experience a reward. It is true that equal treatment before the law, equal access to political power, and equal recognition of group affiliation (i.e., no discrimination among racial and religious groups or other social divisions) will elicit appreciation and provide various mental rewards—a satisfaction from feeling uncoerced and being permitted to conduct life without undue interference. But these rewards, which may be substantial, will be insufficient to maximize the potential of civilization. Members of a society will not obey its rules without a material reward.

2. Kenneth E. Boulding, "Social Justice in Social Dynamics," in *Social Justice,* ed. Richard B. Brandt (Englewood Cliffs, N.J., 1962), 83–84; Stephen Skowronek, "Order and Change," *Polity,* XXVIII (1995), 92–94.

Or, to put it in its logical obverse, members of society will not accept the rules of a society if obedience is tantamount to punishment—deprivation of material welfare.

The great flaw of a laissez-faire society is that its proponents expect civilized behavior without reward. Indeed, most advocates of laissez-faire society state explicitly that rewards are connected *only* with economic activity and governed by some mechanical device for distribution, such as marginal productivity theory.[3] The central idea behind laissez-faire is that giving people an equal opportunity over time (an attempt to vitiate the problem of initial endowment) is all that can legitimately be asked of institutions. Thus laissez-faire advocates expect the promise of opportunity to be sufficient reward to stimulate individuals to abide by laws and accept institutions. Opportunity is not a material reward, it is only a chance. And if for great numbers of people, or a sizable proportion, it is found that opportunity is meaningless, what is the incentive to obey the rules of society? There is none. Losers in the game will not act "civilized" because there is no reward for doing so.

That leads laissez-faire theorists into the anomaly of advocating state power. It also invokes the shameful cry of "immorality." What is the definition of "morality" in laissez-faire economics? It is ultimately accepting the decrees of the market regarding rewards. If one loses in the marketplace, one accepts the loss and does not violate the rules of the marketplace (institutions of private property and the like, established by law). If one is a member of a society and finds that he or she by the market economy deserves either death (as being totally worthless to the market economy) or starvation wages (as being wholly marginal to the market economy), then the individual is nonetheless expected to obey society's rules and support its functioning. This, quite frankly, is rubbish even on the laissez-faire economist's home turf: self-interest. If the reward is insufficient, self-interest dictates another path of behavior to obtain gratification. Moreover, Darwinism determines the obvious behavioral result. Organisms will struggle to survive. And if some cannot survive by following the rules of the game, they will break the rules in order to survive.

To state it another way: laissez-faire proponents are the greatest welfare cheats the world has ever witnessed. If we define welfare cheats as people who want rewards for nothing, then laissez-faire proponents are guilty as charged. They want a society that operates frictionlessly with people obeying faithfully the rules of society ("morality") without paying for it. They want to maximize civility without paying the price; they want something (civility) for nothing. This is the worst-case scenario of welfare addiction.

Restricting material rewards entirely to the economic realm will never optimize

3. Note the criticism of Douglass C. North, an economic historian, about the neoclassical distrust of the state, in *Structure and Change in Economic History* (New York, 1981), 4–17, esp. 11.

the potentialities of a civil society. To obtain a civil society, a material reward for civil behavior must be present. Somehow, rewards have to be given out, by redistribution from the talented to the less talented, so that all members have the sense of belonging to a "just" society and have an interest in its perpetuation.

Efficiency and Maximization

Behind much of the advocacy of laissez-faire principles is the idea that free market institutions maximize economic growth. These principles do so by essentially two routes: (1) they enable consumer demand to be satisfied as completely as possible according to the existing technology and cultural norms; (2) they permit individuals with the best talents to satisfy consumers to obtain the resources to achieve the task and lay the foundation for further consumer satisfaction.[4] That is, free markets satisfy individual preferences better than any other systems (this is how preference theory and indifference curve analysis have come to dominate the discussion) and guide investment and labor to those areas where consumer preferences are strongest in the aggregate (this is the efficiency argument—the most appropriate allocation of resources to achieve consumer preference).

In a formal sense, the objective is to maximize economic growth, assuming that economic growth automatically enhances a society's welfare. The formulation runs something as follows:

(1) $Y_1 = f(K, L, H, T, P)$

where Y_1 is the rate of economic growth, K is capital stock, L is labor, H is human capital, T is technology, and P is population; frequently all the variables are created in terms of rates of change. The formulation can, of course, be considerably complicated.[5] Among macroeconomists, the goal is to find the specification of the function that maximizes the growth rate.

Regardless of value judgments about whether economic growth in fact makes life better for human beings, it is vital to note that over time equation 1 has become the objective of human life. For economists, this makes sense because it sets a standard for comparative purposes, a means to judge economic performance. Others have trouble with its presumed primary importance. Economic growth by efficient allocation of resources and satisfaction of consumer preferences is continuously paraded as the great desideratum of any society. This represents nothing less than intellectual imperialism. For what has happened is that the other disciplines have been told that

4. For a quick reference, Anderson and Hill, *Birth of a Transfer Society,* 1–6.

5. See, for example, Hywel G. Jones, *An Introduction to Modern Theories of Economic Growth* (New York, 1976).

their objectives are secondary and lesser than that of maximization of economic growth.

The laissez-faire economic formulation has any number of objectionable features, but I will single out only two. First, "economic efficiency" is not a moral argument.[6] Moreover, the implication of maximization of efficiency needs to be drawn out. In this case, economics is capable of a little deconstruction—spelling out the meaning of the opposite. It is taken as a "good" rule that resources should be in the hands of the efficient, the people who use resources best. The opposition here is that resources should not be in the hands of the inefficient. The fate of the efficient is known: they earn rewards. And what is the fate of the inefficient? What do they earn? In the economics of the firm, the answer is that inefficient firms exit from the market. That is, they die. Given a normal distribution of talents or abilities in a population, we can safely conclude that some segment will be totally economically inefficient. Efficiency is achieved by giving nothing to the inefficient; therefore, laissez-faire rules are a sentence of death to a proportion of the population and probably economic misery to another proportion. Killing off the least favored members of the civilization does not maximize the social welfare or achieve the goals of a civilization. It is, however, efficient. This is why efficiency and morality are at odds with each other.[7]

Further, the method of exiting for the inefficient is not only morally odious but insidious for the goals of civilization. Because the laissez-faire society demands non-coercion and no interference with the rights of each person to her or his own body, faculties, and preferences, the inefficient cannot be executed; they are left to starve, commit suicide, or find other means to quit the world by their own action. And the rest of society is supposed to stand idly by and let this process run its course, cheering the triumph of efficiency. This process will sap any civilization of the values worth living for. How any rational person can expect civil society to emerge out of this circumstance is beyond me. And it should not be forgotten that laissez-faire has had its champions of exactly this process: Herbert Spencer and William Graham Sumner. They both argued for death by starvation for the inefficient because it would strengthen the species.

And both Sumner and Spencer argued against charity because it prolonged the life of the inefficient and wasted resources. At least they were consistent. In more recent times, laissez-faire advocates, realizing that there really is a calamity in regard to the inefficient, have attempted to escape the inevitable consequence of their philoso-

6. Richard Posner, however, has developed one, based on the notion that for laissez-faire markets to work, a moral standard is implied (*Economics of Justice*, 66–70).

7. Fine, *Laissez Faire and the General-Welfare State*, 82–84; Spencer, *Man Versus the State*, 23–28; Samuel Freeman, "Reason and Agreement in Social Contract Views," *Philosophy and Public Affairs*, XIX (1990), 134; Serge-Christophe Kolm, "Altruism and Efficiency," *Ethics*, XCIV (1983), 19–24.

phy by calling in "charity" to rescue them. The charity argument is entirely bogus. First, the economic principle of self-interest hardly leads to the behavior of expecting those well-off to help those losing out. The theory is inconsistent in the extreme. Second, the argument is entirely exogenous to the theory. Charity is invoked to avoid the obvious consequences of the economic theory. But where in the economics literature are the two evidences that it has been taken seriously: an estimate of the number of inefficient in a society who would be doomed to the grave by the market system and an estimate of a charity function—the amount of money one could expect the economy to produce for charitable giving? Then, where is a comparison showing that laissez-faire would produce enough charitable giving to cover the needs of the inefficient? These calculations do not exist, and they are not incorporated in any serious economic model (that I know of). Rather, the real argument runs like this: there will be sufficient charity for those who really need it, but others simply will not work and deserve the consequences. And that is merely rephrasing once again the logical inference of the model: to achieve efficiency, the inefficient must be liquidated.

Moreover, we come again to the welfare addiction of laissez-faire apostles. Does anybody rationally expect a worthwhile society to arise on the basis of charity? Does anyone believe that people will give assent to the rules of a society because there is a chance that their misery will be diminished by charity? The charity argument is a monumental waste of time and is counterproductive to a healthy society.

A second and equally fundamental objection to the economists' love affair with economic growth is that it is the wrong function to be maximized for the society. What is desired is civilized life, a healthy civilization; economic growth is only a part of the formulation. In particular, consider the wholly unspecified and ambiguous function:

(2) $CIV = f(P,S,E,PY)$

where *CIV* stands for some measure of civilized behavior, *P* for political activity, *S* for sociological patterns, *E* for economic growth, and *PY* for psychological health. *CIV* could be a combined measure of crime: the extent to which the rules of a society are broken and the amount of force required to stop society from falling apart. The political activity variable might be based on such items as rates of political participation and some scale that indicates access to political power. Sociological indices might be assigned on the basis of group interaction and involvement that the population engages in, and individual psychology might be figured by suicide rates, divorce rates, and perhaps mental health statistics. Economics might be measured by maximum economic growth.

The form of the function, however, probably would not be additive or simply multiplicative. Rather, the maximum economic growth rate of a society would produce enough dissonances in the other areas that the values for civilized life would not be optimized. (To make this read correctly, the function being talked about would seek a minimum of disobedience to the rules of society, and therefore *CIV* would be minimized. To avoid that confusion, it would be understood that minimizing *CIV* is equivalent to maximizing the values that civilization is intended to produce.) One may hypothesize that to obtain the best results in *P, PY,* and *S,* the rate of economic growth would have to diminish and some inefficiency be introduced into the system so that other important values—association, community well-being, essential feelings of fairness and equality—would fully flower. That is, among *P, PY,* and *S,* there is probably a curved relationship with *E,* and eventually the relationship exhibits a negative slope.

The difference between functions 1 and 2 explains a host of writing on political economy. Economists simply assume that what is worthwhile is maximization of economic growth by efficient allocation of resources, allowing government some activity when market failures are encountered. But politicians and other members of society are not interested only in efficiency. They are seeking, at least in the abstract, to obtain the rules by which society holds together as peacefully as possible—in their own way, they are trying to create maximum civility. This does not discount stupidity, venality, greed, and poor judgment in the framing of the laws, for governments, like business firms, run the gamut from the stupid to the wise. But the essential function of politics (or society or psychology) has never been to maximize growth; the function has been to achieve civility. Many economists do not understand this, and therefore they invent strange theories (rent-seeking) to explain political activity.[8]

The formulation of equation 2 is more in line with the objective of creating civilized life. Moreover, it restores to the other fields of endeavor the integrity that they have sacrificed to economics. Economic growth and economic efficiency are useful tools for economists to use to see how the economy performs and the impact of various sociopolitical decisions; but they are not and should not be the objectives of a society.

Gamesmanship and the Distribution of Income and Wealth

All economic behavior is legitimized or tolerated by a set of rules. Supposedly governments compose those rules. But even in the absence of governmental authority, rules dominate economic behavior. In the case of no authority at all, the rule becomes physical violence and survival of the fittest. This does not produce a desirable economy, but it is nonetheless an economic system that follows a rule. Because it is

8. For example, see George J. Stigler, "Law or Economics?" *Journal of Law and Economics,* XXXV (1992), 455–68; Jack Hirshleifer, "The Dark Side of the Force," *Economic Inquiry,* XXXII (1994), 1–9; Gary D. Libecap, *Contracting for Property Rights* (Cambridge, Eng., 1989), 3–21 and *passim;* Keith T. Poole and Howard Rosenthal, "The Enduring Nineteenth-Century Battle for Economic Regulation: The Interstate Commerce Act Revisited," *Journal of Law and Economics,* XXXVI (1993), 837–60.

obvious that wealth can be generated by a better set of rules than physical violence, governments or the operating authorities try to devise them. Over time, at least among economists, the rules that have produced the most wealth permit individual property rights and deny the use of coercion.[9]

By creating rules, societies create winners and losers, and this is unavoidable. Any sizable population will have a distribution of talents, and within each area or category of talent there will be an additional distribution. There will be those with much of a particular talent and those with little of it. Any set of rules will elevate some talents above others and ensure that some segments of society will obtain more reward for no other reason than that the rules favor them rather than others. It is not a matter of effort, training, or discipline; it is a political act that some talents will be considered more valuable than others. In the case of the United States, the rules depreciate physical strength in most instances and instead reward either mathematical and engineering talent (intellectual capability), organizational talent (management), or confrontational verbal talent (lawyers).

This situation sets up a dichotomy that runs through American history and indeed that of most societies. People who have less-valued talents are upset that theirs are not as appreciated as those of people who have been favored by the rules of the game. The most obvious manifestation is the manual labor/mental labor dichotomy. In the late-nineteenth-century United States, it was the basic complaint of the Populists that farmers worked yet obtained no reward while lawyers and financiers merely talked and scribbled yet hoarded all the wealth. This dichotomy also is the bulk of the Marxist complaint against capitalist societies and is the heart of the labor theory of value. If one listens closely, one hears echoes of it all the time: those who labor physically do not receive a commensurate reward for their labor. This circumstance partially explains the rise of special interest groups lobbying political entities because it is widely understood that by changing the rules of the game, the reward system is also changed—that is, one obtains redistribution by definition of what constitutes legitimate economic activity.

More than this, rewards for marginal additions of talent are wholly indefensible on economic principles. Suppose there is such a thing as a "business talent" that has been legitimized by the rules of the game—probably a talent that combines characteristics of calculation, risk-taking, mathematical capability, and organizational ability. Next, assume that within the population there is a distribution of the talent

9. See, for example, Mancur Olson, "Dictatorship, Democracy, and Development," *American Political Science Review,* LXXXVII (1993), 567–76; Douglass C. North and Barry R. Weingast, "Constitutions and Commitment: The Evolution of Institutions Governing Public Choice in Seventeenth-Century England," *Journal of Economic History,* XLIX (1989), 803–32; and Douglass C. North, *Institutions, Institutional Change and Economic Performance* (Cambridge, Eng., 1990), 3–9.

and that it represents a continuum from nearly no business talent to enormous amounts of it. The reward for a marginal increment in talent at the upper end of the talent spectrum disobeys all the normal principles of economics; instead of exhibiting diminishing marginal returns, one obtains exponentially exploding upward marginal returns.

Consider the graphs given below, panels A through C. These are the typical graphs of economics for rate of returns, total revenue, and total product.[10] They exist in almost every standard economics text in the United States. Panels A, B, and C exhibit the principle of diminishing marginal returns. When holding all other factors constant, the return one obtains begins to diminish as an extra input is added. In the case of total revenue and total product (panels B and C), the return eventually becomes negative. The reverse side is that costs begin to dominate as one pushes production beyond certain points; the cost curves begin to rise dramatically.[11]

Now consider panels D and E. They indicate income distribution. Panel D is a Lorenz curve, taken from Alice Hansen Jones, showing the amount of wealth possessed by decile or quintile groups in the society.[12] Panel E is imaginary. It is based on the idea that if one took all the income earners in the United States and lined them up from lowest to highest annual income, this is how the curve would look, with the income level being indicated on the ordinate (Y) axis. The graph drawn is my guess as to the graph's approximate shape (again, this is intuitive, not based on data; such a graph could be constructed more or less, but given the scales on both the X and Y axes, its presentation in normal page format is dubious).

In either case, consider the implications for marginal returns. If we consider the persons lined up on the X axis to be a measure of business talent, from weakest to strongest, what does the graph reveal? That a hypothetical one-unit addition of business talent at the upper end of the spectrum earns exponentially exploding rewards. It is not linear; it is not proportionate; it is exponential.

This explains the popular animus against huge bonuses for executives and fortunes made from the stock market. Most people (I assume) have little complaint about an increase in earnings based on talent but do have a complaint about the excessive amount of the reward. A person with only a few percentage points more talent (however figured) should earn a few percentage points more money. Instead, he or she may earn hundreds of times more.

Panel E is explained not by economic principles but by gamesmanship. That

10. These graphs are styled after those in Gould and Ferguson, *Microeconomic Theory,* 54, 105, 136.

11. *Ibid.*, 187.

12. Jones, *Wealth of a Nation to Be,* 166, of wealth-holders in 1774, total physical wealth. For an example of a Lorenz curve for income, see Blinder, Kristol, and Cohen, "Level and Distribution of Economic Well-Being," 453.

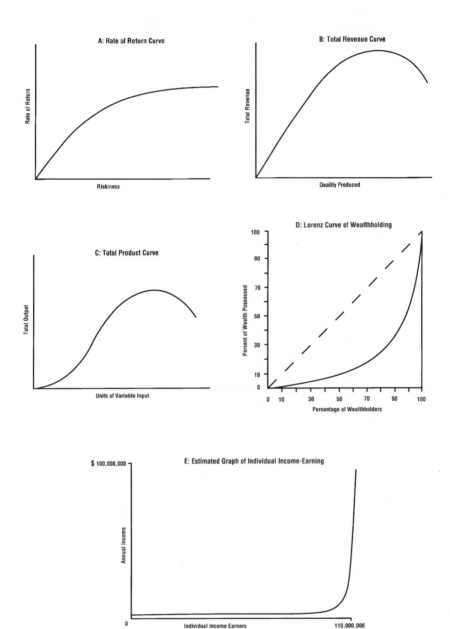

Graph of Wealth/Income Distribution
Compared to Graphs with Diminishing Marginal Returns

shape of reward comes from the winner in the contest. There can be only one champion. If one tried to figure out the reward system for an athletic contest with some one hundred competitors, the recognition or reward system would appear something like panel E. Consider an Olympic champion in either the hundred-meter dash or hundred-meter freestyle swimming. The champion may win by one-tenth of a second or less. What is the difference in talent? From any large perspective—miles per hour—there is no difference. But what is the difference in reward? The Olympic champion may go on to amazingly lucrative endorsements or positions. And for the person who comes in second, there may be some payoffs, but in comparison to the winner he gets nearly nothing. The difference in reward between being first and being second is not proportional; it is exponential. That is what panel E relates.

For athletics, this reward system may be justifiable. It is less so for a society that seeks to maximize civility. Games are sporting events that should not endanger life or entertainments engaged in for leisure reasons. Life deserves more respect; and civilization certainly should not be built on the expectation that the rewards of civil participation are regulated by gamesmanship. Why should citizens permit minor differences in ability to lead to such enormous rewards, especially when the talent itself depends on legal definitions? Change the legal definitions and another person with different talents could achieve the same result.

But the situation—rewards structured by gamesmanship rather than economic principles—justifies and permits redistribution of income. First, economic growth does not hinge on exponential rewarding of economic actors. If one slid backward along the curve in panel E one or two marginal units, there would be virtually no change in overall economic performance, but the change in income earning for the individual would be dramatic. The next best substitute, in other words, for the person with the best talent is perfectly compatible with an advancing economy. For an example, Microsoft Corporation has conquered, momentarily, the software world. In the process, enormous fortunes have been produced for the major stockholders and directors. But if Microsoft never existed, the macroeconomic effect would not be much different. The next best substitutes were very good indeed, and the computer industry was going to fly regardless of the existence of Microsoft. Microsoft earned its rewards because of gamesmanship, not by being vastly superior to its competitors.

Second, given the exponential nature of the income curve at the upper end, it is within the realm of feasibility to tax away a heavy proportion of earnings (say 40 to 60 percent) and not really dampen incentive and use of talents. And individuals so taxed would hardly be pauperized. A person earning one million dollars and taxed at a 60 percent rate would not be happy; but after taxes the person would possess $400,000 and has hardly been impoverished. Moreover, such a person is not likely to quit the "game" when even at a high taxation rate the after-tax income is so substantial. It is true that the wealthy will whine and cry about it; they are trained to do so, and certainly American wealth-holders are especially likely to do so. But in general economic terms, assuming that tax money is spent in a way that elicits civility, the talented will continue to apply their talents and help drive the economic machine. Economic growth will not be injured so long as talent is permitted a substantial reward.[13]

Thus redistributing some of the income earned by the wealthy to those not advantaged by nature or by legal definitions should provide the funds needed to maximize the values of civilization. (One has to assume that for this to work, population growth does not distort the feasibility of redistribution by a continuous increase in the number of impoverished individuals.) How to achieve that redistribution for its maximum effect is another problem that can be solved only by statesmanship. The point of this appendix has been merely to justify the principle of redistribution, not to offer a practical program of redistribution.

I will offer one final observation. The question of redistribution is largely an academic one engaged in by intellectuals of various stripes. In practice, the decision has already been taken worldwide: redistribution is a fact of life, and the only matter worth considering is how to do it so that the values of civilization will be maximized. In my opinion, the twentieth century has destroyed the extreme ends of the political spectrum. Socialists hate the market, and neoclassical economists hate the government. Both have lost. From 1880 to 1950, the world rejected laissez-faire, and, in western Europe, the rout of laissez-faire was complete by 1940. The historical experience—not theory but experience—has been that one cannot take those principles and produce a worthwhile civilization from them. The political entities realized that laissez-faire created too much violence, misery, and hatred for societies to endure. In their own fashion, they all opted for some arrangement that decreased economic growth by establishing economic inefficiencies so that the values of civilization would not be crushed. Between 1965 and 1995, the socialist/Marxist experiment blew apart. One could not take those antimarket ideas and construct a livable society with them, one in which the values of civilization flourished. And at the end of it, the recognition has been that there would be no return to the command economy; as a matter of experience, it could not be made to work. Some type of free market and some type of redistributive government are the fate of the countries of the world for the next sixty to seventy years. The only question that remains is the best way to meld the two together to arrive at a full and satisfying civility. Quite frankly, the Marxist left and the laissez-faire right are irrelevant to the modern world.

13. Only in one sense are the American wealthy understandable: if they are to be taxed heavily, then the government should produce the civility that is the purpose of governmental activity. If the taxes are high and no civility results, the government is failing its function and support starts to be withdrawn.

Bibliography

Primary Sources

Manuscripts

Appleton Family Papers. Massachusetts Historical Society, Boston.

Corwin, Thomas. Papers. Library of Congress.

Dallas, George Mifflin. Papers. Historical Society of Pennsylvania, Philadelphia.

Fish, Hamilton. Papers. Library of Congress.

Gardiner, Edward Carey. Collection. Historical Society of Pennsylvania, Philadelphia.

Garnett, James Mercer, and John Randolph of Roanoke. Letters. University of Virginia Library, Charlottesville.

Gooch Family Papers. University of Virginia Library, Charlottesville.

Lathers, Richard. Papers. Library of Congress.

Legaré, Hugh. Papers. Special Collections Department, Duke University Library, Durham, N. C.

Watson, Henry, Jr. Papers. Duke University Library, Durham, N. C.

Wright, Elizur. Papers. Library of Congress.

Newspapers

Connecticut
    Hartford *Daily Times,* 1858.
Georgia
    Federal Union (Milledgeville), 1858.
Illinois
    Chicago *Daily Democrat,* 1858.

Chicago *Daily Times,* 1857, 1858.
Chicago *Daily Tribune,* 1858.
Daily Illinois State Journal (Springfield), 1857.
Daily Illinois State Register (Springfield), 1858.
Massachusetts
Boston *Gazette,* 1785.
Boston *Post,* 1857, 1858.
Christian (Milford), 1857.
Lynn *News,* 1860.
Lynn *Weekly Reporter,* 1857.
Voice of Industry (Fitchburg/Lowell), 1847.
Mississippi
Mississippi Free Trader (Natchez), 1858.
New Jersey
Trenton *True American,* 1857.
New York
Mechanic's Advocate (Albany), 1847, 1848.
National Trades' Union (New York), 1834, 1835.
New York *Evening Post,* 1857.
New York *Herald,* 1857.
New York *Times,* 1857, 1859.
New York *Tribune,* 1858, 1860.
Oneida *Circular,* 1857, 1858.
Working Man's Advocate (New York), 1845–47.
Young America (New York), 1845.
Ohio
Cincinnati *Daily Gazette,* 1857.
Pennsylvania
Clearfield *Republican,* 1853.
Democratic Watchman (Bellefonte), 1857.
Easton *Argus,* 1857.
Gazette of the United States (Philadelphia), 1789.
Lancaster *Examiner and Herald,* 1857.
Mechanic's Free Press (Philadelphia), 1828, 1829.
North American and United States Gazette (Philadelphia), 1858.
Pennsylvania Telegraph (Harrisburg), 1860.
Philadelphia *Evening Bulletin,* 1858.
Philadelphia *Public Ledger,* 1857.
Pittsburgh *Dispatch,* 1860.
Raftsman's Journal (Clearfield), 1859.
South Carolina
Charleston *Mercury,* 1857.

Virginia
> Richmond *Enquirer,* 1857.
Washington, D.C.
> *Daily National Intelligencer,* 1857.
> *National Era,* 1857.
Wisconsin
> Milwaukee *Daily Free Democrat,* 1858.

Government Publications

De Bow, James D. B. *Statistical View of the United States . . . Being a Compendium of the Seventh Census.* Washington, D.C., 1854.

Kennedy, Joseph C. G. *Preliminary Report on the Eighth Census, 1860.* Washington, D.C., 1862.

North, S. N. D. *Abstract of the Twelfth Census of the United States, 1900.* 3rd ed. Washington, D.C., 1904.

United States. Bureau of the Census. *Historical Statistics of the United States, Colonial Times to 1970: Bicentennial Edition.* Washington, D.C., 1975.

———. *Statistical Abstract of the United States, 1991.* 111th ed. Washington, D.C., 1992.

United States. Congress. *American State Papers: Documents, Legislative and Executive, of the Congress of the United States.* 38 vols. Washington, D.C., 1832–61.

———. *Annals of Congress.*

———. *Congressional Globe.*

———. *Register of Debates.*

United States. Department of State. *Compendium of the Enumeration of the Inhabitants and Statistics of the United States [Sixth Census, 1840].* Washington, D.C., 1841.

United States. Interior Department. Census Office. *The Seventh Census of the United States, 1850.* Washington, D.C., 1853.

———. *The Eighth Census of the United States, 1860.* Washington, D.C., 1865.

———. *Ninth Census of the United States, 1870.* Washington, D.C., 1872.

———. *Tenth Census of the United States, 1880.* Washington, D.C., 1883.

———. *Compendium of the Eleventh Census, 1890.* Washington, D.C., 1892.

United States. President. *Economic Report of the President, 1992.* Washington, D.C., 1992.

Periodicals up to 1865

American Agriculturist.
American Museum.
American Railroad Journal.
American [Whig] *Review.*

Atlantic Monthly.
Bankers' Magazine.
Boston Quarterly Review.
De Bow's Review.
Dial.
Harper's Monthly Magazine.
Harper's Weekly.
Hunt's Merchants' Magazine.
Littell's Living Age.
National Magazine.
New Englander.
North American Review.
Phalansterian Record.
Russell's Magazine.
Southern Literary Messenger.
Tribune Almanac for 1857.
United States Magazine and Democratic Review.
Whig Almanac, 1843, 1844.

Articles After 1865

Ashley, Charles S. "The Distribution of Wealth." *Popular Science Monthly,* XXIX (1886), 721–33.

Carver, T. N. "Clark's Distribution of Wealth." *Quarterly Journal of Economics,* XV (1901), 578–602.

———. "How Wealth Ought to Be Distributed." *Atlantic Monthly,* XCVII (1906), 727–38.

Dickson, W. M. "The Apotheosis of the Plutocrat." *Magazine of American History,* XVIII (1887), 497–509.

Edgeworth, F. Y. "The Theory of Distribution." *Quarterly Journal of Economics,* XVIII (1904), 159–219.

Gibbons, [Cardinal]. "Wealth and Its Obligations." *North American Review,* CLII (1891), 385–94.

Laughlin, J. Laurence. "Large Fortunes." *Atlantic Monthly,* XCVI (1905), 40–46.

Mallock, W. H. "The Productivity of the Individual." *North American Review,* CLVII (1893), 580–90.

[Norton, Charles Eliot.] "The Poverty of England." *North American Review,* CIX (1869), 122–54.

Phelps, Edward J. "Irresponsible Wealth." *North American Review,* CLII (1891), 523–33.

Pomeroy, Eltweed. "The Concentration of Wealth." *Arena,* LXXXV (1896), 82–96.

Reeves, Robert N. "Has Wealth a Limitation?" *Arena,* XVIII (1897), 160–67.

Shearman, Thomas G. "The Owners of the United States." *Forum,* VIII (1889), 262–73.

Smyth, D. DeW. "Wealth and Welfare." *Quarterly Journal of Economics,* XVIII (1903), 138–42.

Taubeneck, Herman E. "The Concentration of Wealth, Its Cause and Results." Parts I and II. *Arena,* XVIII (1897), 289–301, 452–69.

Wells, David A. "The Production and Distribution of Wealth." *Journal of Social Science,* VIII (1875?), 1–22.

Wright, Carroll D., ed. "Concentration of Wealth: A Discussion." *Independent,* May 1, 1902, pp. 1021–72.

Miscellaneous Periodicals

Business Week, 1992.
Economist, 1991, 1992, 1996.
Revolution.
Universal Almanac: 1991.

Published Letters, Speeches, Diaries, and Writings

Adams, John. *The Works of John Adams, Second President of the United States.* Edited by Charles Francis Adams. 10 vols.; Boston, 1856.

Adams, John Quincy. *Memoirs of John Quincy Adams.* Edited by Charles Francis Adams. 12 vols.; Philadelphia, 1874–77.

———. *Writings of John Quincy Adams.* Edited by Worthington Chauncey Ford. 7 vols.; New York, 1913–17.

Adams, Randolph G., ed. *Selected Political Essays of James Wilson.* New York, 1930.

Adams, Samuel. *The Writings of Samuel Adams.* Edited by Harry Alonzo Cushing. 4 vols.; 1904; rpr. New York, 1968.

Ames, Fisher. *Works of Fisher Ames. With a Selection from His Speeches and Correspondence.* Edited by Seth Ames. 2 vols.; Boston, 1854.

Austin, James T., ed. *The Life of Elbridge Gerry.* 2 vols.; 1828; rpr. New York, 1970.

Bailyn, Bernard, ed. *Pamphlets of the American Revolution, 1750–1776.* Cambridge, Mass., 1965.

Blau, Joseph L., ed. *Social Theories of Jacksonian Democracy: Representative Writings of the Period, 1825–1850.* New York, 1947.

Bloomer, Amelia. *Life and Writings of Amelia Bloomer.* Edited by D[exter] C. Bloomer. 1895; rpr. New York, 1975.

Boudinot, Elias. *The Life, Public Services, Addresses, and Letters of Elias Boudinot.* Edited by J. J. Boudinot. 2 vols.; 1896; rpr. New York, 1971.

Brownson, Orestes A. *The Works of Orestes A. Brownson.* Edited by Henry F. Brownson. 20 vols.; rpr. New York, 1966.

Buchanan, James. *The Works of James Buchanan: Comprising His Speeches, State Papers, and Private Correspondence.* Edited by John Bassett Moore. 12 vols.; Philadelphia, 1908–11.

Burnett, Edmund C., ed. *Letters of Members of Continental Congress.* 8 vols.; Washington, D.C., 1921–36.

Calhoun, John C. *The Papers of John C. Calhoun.* Edited by Robert L. Meriwether *et al.* 23 vols. to date; Columbia, S.C., 1959–.

Clay, Cassius M. *The Writings of Cassius Marcellus Clay, Including Speeches and Addresses.* Edited by Horace Greeley. 1848; rpr. New York, 1969.

Clay, Henry. *The Papers of Henry Clay.* Edited by James F. Hopkins *et al.* 11 vols. to date; Lexington, Ky., 1959–.

Commons, John R., *et al.,* eds. *Documentary History of American Industrial Society.* 10 vols.; Cleveland, 1910.

Dana, Richard Henry, Jr. *The Journal of Richard Henry Dana, Jr.* Edited by Robert F. Lucid. 3 vols.; Cambridge, Mass., 1968.

Davis, Jefferson. *The Papers of Jefferson Davis.* Edited by Haskell M. Monroe, Jr., James T. McIntosh, Lynda Crist, *et al.* 9 vols. to date; Baton Rouge, La., 1971–.

Debs, Eugene V. *Writings and Speeches of Eugene V. Debs.* New York, 1948.

Dickinson, John. *The Political Writings of John Dickinson, 1764–1774.* Edited by Paul Leicester Ford. 1895; rpr. New York, 1970.

Douglas, Stephen A. *The Letters of Stephen A. Douglas.* Edited by Robert W. Johannsen. Urbana, Ill., 1961.

Douglass, Frederick. *The Frederick Douglass Papers.* Edited by John W. Blassingame. 5 vols. to date; New Haven, Conn., 1979–.

DuBois, Ellen Carol, ed. *Elizabeth Cady Stanton, Susan B. Anthony: Correspondence, Writings, Speeches.* New York, 1981.

Dumond, Dwight Lowell, ed. *Southern Editorials on Secession.* New York, 1931.

Earle, Thomas, and Charles T. Congdon, eds. *Annals of the General Society of Mechanics and Tradesmen of the City of New-York, from 1785 to 1880.* New York, 1882.

Elliot, Jonathan, ed. *Elliot's Debates [on the Ratification of the Constitution].* 5 vols.; 1836; rpr. Philadelphia, 1937.

Everett, Edward. *Orations and Speeches on Various Occasions.* 12th ed. 4 vols.; Boston, 1895.

Farrand, Max, ed. *The Records of the Federal Convention of 1787.* 3 vols.; New Haven, Conn., 1911.

Faust, Drew Gilpin, ed. *The Ideology of Slavery: Proslavery Thought in the Antebellum South, 1830–1860.* Baton Rouge, La., 1981.

Filler, Louis, ed. *Wendell Phillips on Civil Rights and Freedom.* 2nd ed.; Washington, D.C., 1982.

Folsom, Michael Brewster, and Steven D. Lubar, eds. *The Philosophy of Manufactures: Early Debates over Industrialization in the United States.* Cambridge, Mass., 1982.

Ford, Worthington Chauncey, *et al.,* eds. *Journals of the Continental Congress, 1774–1789.* 34 vols.; Washington, D.C., 1904–37.

Franklin, Benjamin. *The Life of Benjamin Franklin. Written By Himself.* Edited by John Bigelow. 3rd ed. 3 vols.; Philadelphia, 1893.

———. *The Papers of Benjamin Franklin.* Edited by Leonard W. Labaree and William B. Willcox. 28 vols.; New Haven, Conn., 1959–90.

Frisch, Michael H. "Notes and Documents: 'Is the World Governed Too Much?'" *Pennsylvania Magazine of History and Biography,* CV (1981), 203–13.

Gallatin, Albert. *The Writings of Albert Gallatin.* Edited by Henry Adams. 3 vols.; 1879; rpr. New York, 1960.

Garfield, James. *The Works of James Abram Garfield.* Edited by Burke A. Hinsdale. 2 vols.; Boston, 1882–83.

Garraty, John A., ed. *Labor and Capital in the Gilded Age: Testimony Taken by the Senate Committee upon the Relations Between Labor and Capital—1883.* Boston, 1968.

Garrison, Wendell Phillips; and Francis Jackson Garrison, eds. *William Lloyd Garrison, 1805–1879: The Story of His Life.* 4 vols.; New York, 1885–89.

Garrison, William Lloyd. *The Letters of William Lloyd Garrison.* Edited by Walter M. Merrill and Louis Ruchames. 6 vols.; Cambridge, Mass., 1971–81.

Ginger, Ray, ed. *The Nationalizing of American Life, 1877–1900.* New York, 1965.

Hallowell, Anna Davis, ed. *James and Lucretia Mott: Life and Letters.* Boston, 1884.

Hamilton, Alexander. *The Papers of Alexander Hamilton.* Edited by Harold C. Syrett and Jacob E. Cooke. 27 vols.; New York, 1961–87.

Hume, David. *David Hume: Writings on Economics.* Edited by Eugene Rotwein. Madison, Wisc., 1955.

Hyneman, Charles S., and Donald S. Lutz, eds. *American Political Writing During the Founding Era, 1760–1805.* 2 vols.; Indianapolis, 1983.

Jackson, Andrew. *Correspondence of Andrew Jackson.* Edited by John Spencer Bassett. 6 vols.; Washington, D.C., 1916–33.

Jacobson, David L., ed. *The English Libertarian Heritage: From the Writings of John Trenchard and Thomas Gordon in "The Independent Whig" and "Cato's Letters."* Indianapolis, 1965.

Jefferson, Thomas. *The Papers of Thomas Jefferson.* Edited by Julian P. Boyd *et al.* 27 vols. to date; Princeton, 1950–.

———. *Thomas Jefferson: Writings.* Edited by Merrill D. Petersen. New York, 1984.

———. *The Writings of Thomas Jefferson.* Edited by Andrew A. Lipscomb. 20 vols.; Washington, D.C., 1904.

Johannsen, Robert W., ed. *The Lincoln-Douglas Debates of 1858.* New York, 1965.

Johnson, Andrew. *The Papers of Andrew Johnson*. Edited by Leroy P. Graf, Ralph W. Haskins, and Paul H. Bergeron. 13 vols. to date; Knoxville, Tenn., 1967–.

Kenyon, Cecelia M., ed. *The Antifederalists*. Indianapolis, 1966.

Kraditor, Aileen S., ed. *Up from the Pedestal: Selected Writings in the History of American Feminism*. Chicago, 1968.

Kulik, Gary, Roger Parks, and Theodore Z. Penn, eds. *The New England Mill Village, 1790–1860*. Cambridge, Mass., 1982.

Lee, Richard Henry. *The Letters of Richard Henry Lee*. Edited by James Curtis Ballagh. 2 vols.; New York, 1911, 1914.

Leggett, William. *A Collection of the Political Writings of William Leggett*. Edited by Theodore Sedgwick. 2 vols.; New York, 1840.

"Letters on the Nullification Movement in South Carolina, 1830–1834." *American Historical Review*, VI (1901), 736–65, and VII (1901), 92–119.

Lincoln, Abraham. *The Collected Works of Abraham Lincoln*. Edited by Roy P. Basler, Marion Dolores Pratt, and Lloyd A. Dunlap. 9 vols.; New Brunswick, N.J., 1953–55.

Madison, James. *The Papers of James Madison*. Edited by William T. Hutchinson *et al.* 17 vols. to date; Chicago, 1962–.

———. *The Writings of James Madison*. Edited by Gaillard Hunt. 9 vols.; New York, 1900–10.

Marsh, Luther Rawson, ed. *Writings and Speeches of Alvan Stewart, on Slavery*. New York, 1860.

Mendel, Arthur P., ed. *Essential Works of Marxism*. New York, 1961.

Monroe, James. *The Writings of James Monroe*. Edited by Stanislaus Murray Hamilton. 7 vols.; New York, 1898–1903.

Moore, Frank, ed. *The Rebellion Record: A Diary of American Events*. 11 vols.; New York, 1861–65.

Nelson, Truman, ed. *Documents of Upheaval: Selections from William Lloyd Garrison's "The Liberator," 1831–1865*. New York, 1966.

Niles, Hezekiah, ed. *Principles and Acts of the Revolution in America*. Revised by Samuel V. Niles. 1822; rpr. New York, 1876.

Osofsky, Gilbert, ed. *Puttin' On Ole Massa: The Slave Narratives of Henry Bibb, William Wells Brown, and Solomon Northup*. New York, 1969.

Paine, Thomas. *The Complete Writings of Thomas Paine*. Edited by Philip S. Foner. 2 vols.; New York, 1945.

Parker, Theodore. *The Collected Works of Theodore Parker*. Edited by Francis Power Cobbe. 14 vols.; London, 1864–71.

Peach, Bernard, ed. *Richard Price and the Ethical Foundations of the American Revolution*. Durham, N.C., 1970.

Pease, William H., and Jane H. Pease, eds. *The Antislavery Argument*. Indianapolis, 1965.

Phillips, Wendell. *Speeches, Lectures, and Letters.* 2 vols.; Boston, 1884–91.

Polk, James. *Correspondence of James K. Polk.* Edited by Herbert Weaver, Wayne Cutler, and Paul H. Bergeron. 9 vols. to date; Nashville, Tenn., 1969–.

Porter, Kirk H., and Donald Bruce Johnson, comps. *National Party Platforms, 1840–1968.* 4th ed. Urbana, Ill., 1970.

Rantoul, Robert, Jr. *Memoirs, Speeches, and Writings of Robert Rantoul, Jr.* Edited by Luther Hamilton. Boston, 1854.

Rawick, George P., ed. *The American Slave: A Composite Autobiography.* 19 vols.; Westport, Conn., 1972.

Ricardo, David. *The Works and Correspondence of David Ricardo.* Edited by Piero Sraffa. 9 vols.; Cambridge, Eng., 1951.

Richardson, James D., ed. *A Compilation of the Messages and Papers of the Presidents, 1789–1902.* 9 vols.; Washington, D.C., 1904.

Ripley, Peter C., ed. *The Black Abolitionist Papers.* 5 vols.; Chapel Hill, N.C., 1985–92.

Roberts, Kenneth, and Anna M. Roberts, trans. and eds. *Moreau de St. Mery's American Journey [1793–1798].* Garden City, N.Y., 1947.

Rowland, Dunbar, ed. *Jefferson Davis, Constitutionalist: His Letters, Papers and Speeches.* 10 vols.; Jackson, Miss., 1923.

Sams, Henry W., ed. *Autobiography of Brook Farm.* Englewood Cliffs, N.J., 1958.

Schultz, Ronald. "Small Producer Thought in Early America, Part I: Philadelphia Artisans and Price Control." *Pennsylvania History,* LIV (1987), 115–47.

———. "Small Producer Thought in Early America, Part II: William Duane's 'Politics for Farmers and Mechanics.'" *Pennsylvania History,* LIV (1987), 197–229.

Seward, Frederick W., ed. *Autobiography of William H. Seward, from 1801 to 1834, with a Memoir of His Life and Selections from His Letters from 1831 to 1846.* 3 vols.; New York, 1877.

Seward, William H. *The Works of William H. Seward.* Edited by George E. Baker. 2nd ed. 5 vols.; Boston, 1887.

Stanton, Elizabeth Cady, Susan B. Anthony, and Matilda Joslyn Gage, eds. *History of Woman Suffrage.* 2nd ed. 3 vols.; Rochester, N.Y., 1889.

Storing, Herbert J., ed. *The Complete Anti-Federalist.* 7 vols.; Chicago, 1981.

Sumner, Charles. *The Selected Letters of Charles Sumner.* Edited by Beverly Wilson Palmer. 2 vols.; Boston, 1990.

Sylvis, James C., ed. *The Life, Speeches, Labors and Essays of William H. Sylvis.* Philadelphia, 1872.

Thorndike, Rachel Sherman, ed. *The Sherman Letters: Correspondence Between General and Senator Sherman from 1837 to 1891.* New York, 1894.

Tilden, Samuel J. *The Writings and Speeches of Samuel J. Tilden.* Edited by John Bigelow. 2 vols.; New York, 1885.

Veysey, Laurence, ed. *The Perfectionists: Radical Social Thought in the North, 1815–1860.* New York, 1973.

Wainwright, Nicholas B., ed. *A Philadelphia Perspective: The Diary of Sidney George Fisher Covering the Years 1834–1871.* Philadelphia, 1967.

Webster, Daniel. *The Writing and Speeches of Daniel Webster.* Edited by J. W. McIntyre. 18 vols.; Boston, 1903.

Webster, Noah. *Letters of Noah Webster.* Edited by Harry R. Warfel. New York, 1953.

Weed, Thurlow. *Autobiography of Thurlow Weed.* Edited by Harriet A. Weed. 2 vols.; Boston, 1884.

Whittier, John G. *The Works of John Greenleaf Whittier.* 7 vols.; Boston, 1892.

Willard, Margaret Wheeler, ed. *Letters on the American Revolution, 1774–1776.* 1925; rpr. Port Washington, N.Y., 1968.

Wilson, James. *The Works of James Wilson.* Edited by Robert Green McCloskey. 2 vols.; Cambridge, Mass., 1967.

Wiltse, Charles M., ed. *Expansion and Reform, 1815–1850.* New York, 1967.

Winthrop, Robert C. *Addresses and Speeches on Various Occasions.* 4 vols.; Boston, 1852–86.

Woodson, Carter G., ed. *Negro Orators and Their Orations.* 1924; rpr. New York, 1969.

Books and Pamphlets

Abbott, John S. C. *The History of the Civil War in America.* 2 vols. Springfield, Mass., 1863–66.

Adams, Charles Francis. *An Oration, Delivered Before the Municipal Authorities of the City of Fall River, July 4, 1860.* Fall River, Mass., 1860.

Aiken, John. *Labor and Wages. At Home and Abroad: In a Series of Newspaper Articles.* Lowell, Mass., 1849.

Amynto [?]. *Reflections on the Inconsistency of Man, Particularly Exemplified in the Practice of Slavery in the United States.* New York, 1796.

[Appleton, Nathaniel.] *Considerations on Slavery in a Letter to a Friend.* Boston, 1767.

Ballou, Adin. *History of the Hopedale Community, from Its Inception to Its Virtual Submergence in the Hopedale Parish.* Edited by William S. Heywood. 1897; rpr. Philadelphia, 1972.

Barton, William. *Observations on the Progress of Population, and the Probabilities of Duration of Human Life, in the United States of America.* Philadelphia, 1791.

Bascom, John. *Political Economy: Designed as a Text-Book for Colleges.* 1859; rpr. Andover, Mass., 1874.

[Beach, Moses Y.] *Wealth and Biography of the Wealthy Citizens of New York City.* 6th ed. New York, 1845.

Beecher, Henry Ward. *Patriotic Addresses in America and England, 1850–1865, on Slavery, the Civil War, and the Development of Civil Liberty in the United States.* Edited by John R. Howard. New York, 1888.

Bellamy, Edward. *Looking Backward.* 1888; rpr. New York, 1968.

Benezet, Anthony. *Observations on the Inslaving, Importing and Purchasing of Negroes.* Germantown, Pa., 1759.

———. *A Short Account of That Part of Africa Inhabited by the Negroes.* Philadelphia, 1762.

The Bible Against Slavery; or, An Inquiry into the Genius of the Mosaic System, and the Teachings of the Old Testament on the Subject of Human Rights. 1838; rpr. Detroit, 1970.

Bigelow, E. B. *Remarks of the Depressed Condition of Manufactures in Massachusetts.* Boston, 1858.

Bishop, J. Leander. *A History of American Manufactures from 1608 to 1860.* 3rd ed. 3 vols. 1868; rpr. New York, 1967.

Blake, W. O., comp. *The History of Slavery and the Slave Trade, Ancient and Modern. The Forms of Slavery That Prevailed in Ancient Nations, Particularly in Greece and Rome. The African Slave Trade and the Political History of Slavery in the United States.* Columbus, Ohio, 1858.

[Blatchly, Cornelius C.] *An Essay on Commonwealths.* New York, 1822.

———. "Some Causes of Popular Poverty." In [Thomas Branagan], *The Pleasures of Contemplation.* Philadelphia, 1817.

[Boardman, James.] A Citizen of the World. *America and the Americans.* 1833; rpr. New York, 1974.

Boutwell, George S. *Reminiscences of Sixty Years in Public Affairs.* 2 vols. 1902; rpr. New York, 1968.

Bowen, Francis. *American Political Economy.* New York, 1870.

———. *The Principles of Political Economy.* Boston, 1856.

Brisbane, Albert. *Social Destiny of Man; or, Association and Reorganization of Industry.* 1840; rpr. New York, 1968.

Brockway, Beman. *Fifty Years in Journalism, Embracing Recollections and Personal Experiences with an Autobiography.* Watertown, N.Y., 1891.

Brownlow, Rev. William G., and Rev. A. Pryne. *Ought American Slavery to Be Perpetuated? A Debate Between Rev. W. G. Brownlow and Rev. A. Pryne. Held at Philadelphia, September, 1858.* Philadelphia, 1858.

Brutus. *To the Free and Loyal Inhabitants of the City and Colony of New-York.* Broadside. [New York, 1774].

Bryce, James. *The American Commonwealth.* 3rd ed. 2 vols. New York, 1908.

Buchanan, George. *An Oration upon the Moral and Political Evil of Slavery.* Baltimore, 1793.

Burke, Edmund. *The Protective System Considered in Connection with the Present Tariff, in a Series of Twelve Essays, Originally Published in the Washington Union over the Signature of "Bundelcund."* Washington, D.C., 1846.

Butler, William Allen. *A Retrospect of Forty Years, 1825–1865.* Edited by by Harriet Allen Butler. New York, 1911.

Byllesby, Langton. *Observations on the Sources and Effects of Unequal Wealth; with Propositions Towards Removing the Disparity of Profit in Pursuing the Arts of Life, and Establishing Security in Individual Prospects and Resources.* 1826; rpr. New York, 1961.

[Cambreleng, Churchill C.] One of the People. *An Examination of the New Tariff Proposed by the Hon. Henry Baldwin, a Representative in Congress.* New York, 1821.

Cardozo, J. N. *Notes on Political Economy.* Charleston, 1826.

Carey, Henry C. *Essay on the Rate of Wages.* 1835; rpr. New York, 1965.

――――. *Financial Crises: Their Causes and Effects.* Philadelphia, 1864. Also in Henry C. Carey, *Miscellaneous Works of Henry C. Carey* (Philadelphia, 1865), I.

――――. *The Harmony of Interests: Agricultural, Manufacturing and Commercial.* 1851; rpr. New York, 1967.

――――. *Manual of Social Science: Being a Condensation of the "Principles of Social Science" by H. C. Carey.* Edited by Kate McKean. Philadelphia, 1866.

――――. *Miscellaneous Works of Henry C. Carey.* 2 vols. Philadelphia, 1865.

――――. *The Past, the Present and the Future.* 1847; rpr. New York, 1967.

――――. *Principles of Political Economy.* 3 vols. 1837–40; rpr. New York, 1965.

――――. *Principles of Social Science.* 3 vols. 1858; rpr. Philadelphia, 1867.

[Carey, Mathew.] A Pennsylvanian. *An Examination of the Report of a Committee of the Citizens of Boston and Its Vicinity, Opposed to a Further Increase of Duties on Importation.* Philadelphia, 1828.

Carnegie, Andrew. *The Gospel of Wealth and Other Timely Essays.* Garden City, N.Y., 1933.

Carver, Thomas Nixon. *The Distribution of Wealth.* 1904; rpr. New York, 1924.

Channing, William E. *Slavery.* 4th ed. Boston, 1836.

Chastellux, Marquis de. *Travels in North America in the Years 1780, 1781, and 1782.* Rev. translation by Howard C. Rice, Jr. 2 vols. Chapel Hill, 1963.

Cheever, George B. *God Against Slavery: And the Freedom and Duty of the Pulpit to Rebuke It, as a Sin Against God.* Cincinnati, n.d.

――――. *The Guilt of Slavery and the Crime of Slaveholding, Demonstrated from the Hebrew and Greek Scriptures.* Boston, 1860.

Chevalier, Michael. *Society, Manners, and Politics in the United States.* 1839. Edited by John William Ward. Garden City, N.Y., 1961.

Child, Mrs. [Lydia Maria]. *An Appeal in Favor of That Class of Americans Called Africans.* New York, 1836.

Chipman, Nathaniel. *Sketches of the Principles of Government.* Rutland, Vt., 1793.

Claiborne, J. F. H. *Life and Correspondence of John A. Quitman.* 2 vols. New York, 1860.

Clark, John Bates. *The Distribution of Wealth: A Theory of Wages, Interest and Profits.* 1899; rpr. New York, 1956.

—————. *The Philosophy of Wealth: Economic Principles Newly Formulated.* Boston, 1886.

Clark, John Bates, and John Maurice Clark. *The Control of Trusts.* 1901. Rev. ed. New York, 1912.

Clay, Cassius Marcellus. *The Life of Cassius Marcellus Clay: Memoirs, Writings, and Speeches.* 2 vols. Cincinnati, 1886.

Cobbett, William. *A Year's Residence in the United States of America.* 1819; rpr. Carbondale, Ill., 1964.

Codman, John Thomas. *Brook Farm: Historic and Personal Memoirs.* Boston, 1894.

Coffin, Levi. *Reminiscences of Levi Coffin: The Reputed President of the Underground Railroad.* 2nd ed. Cincinnati, 1880.

Colton, Calvin. *The Junius Tracts and the Rights of Labor.* 1844, 1847; rpr. New York, 1974.

—————. *Public Economy for the United States.* New York, 1848.

—————. *The Rights of Labor.* 3rd ed. New York, 1847.

Colwell, Stephen. *The Claims of Labor, and Their Precedence to the Claims of Free Trade.* Philadelphia, 1861.

—————. *The South: A Letter from a Friend in the North. With Special Reference to the Effects of Disunion upon Slavery.* Philadelphia, 1856.

Commons, John R. *The Distribution of Wealth.* New York, 1905.

[Cooper, David]. *A Mite Cast into the Treasury; or, Observations on Slave-Keeping.* Philadelphia, [1772].

Cooper, Thomas. *Lectures on the Elements of Political Economy.* Columbia, S.C., 1826.

Cox, Samuel S. *Three Decades of Federal Legislation, 1855 to 1885.* Providence, R.I., 1888.

[Coxe, Tench.] A Citizen of the United States. *Observations on the Agriculture, Manufactures and Commerce of the United States in a Letter to a Member of Congress.* New York, 1789.

Crèvecoeur, J. Hector St. John de. *Letters from an American Farmer.* 1782; rpr. New York, 1912.

[Cushing, Caleb.] A Friend of Domestic Industry. *Summary of the Practical Principles of Political Economy; with Observations on Smith's Wealth of Nations and Say's Political Economy.* Cambridge, Mass., 1826.

Dabney, Robert L. *A Defence of Virginia, [and Through Her, of the South,] in Recent and Pending Contests Against the Sectional Party.* New York, 1867.

Dacus, J. A. *Annals of the Great Strikes in the United States.* Chicago, 1877.

Dall, Caroline H. *"Woman's Right to Labor"; or, Low Wages and Hard Work: In Three Lectures, Delivered in Boston, November, 1859.* Boston, 1860.

Davis, Jefferson. *The Rise and Fall of the Confederate Government.* 2 vols. 1881; rpr. New York, 1958.

Dealtry, William. *The Laborer: A Remedy for His Wrongs; or, A Disquisition on the Usages of Society.* Cincinnati, 1869.

Detroit *Post and Tribune. Zachariah Chandler: An Outline Sketch of His Life and Public Services.* Detroit, 1880.

Douglass, Frederick. *Life and Times of Frederick Douglass.* Rev. ed. 1892; rpr. New York, 1962.

Duke, Basil W. *Reminiscences of General Basil W. Duke, C. S. A.* Garden City, N.Y., 1911.

Dwight, Timothy. *An Oration Spoken Before "The Connecticut Society, for the Promotion of Freedom and the Relief of Persons Unlawfully Holden in Bondage."* Hartford, Conn., 1794.

Edwards, Jonathan. *The Injustice and Impolicy of the Slave Trade; and of the Slavery of the Africans; . . . A Sermon.* New Haven, 1791.

Elliott, E. N., ed. *Cotton Is King, and Pro-Slavery Arguments: Comprising the Writings of Hammond, Harper, Christy, Stringfellow, Hodge, Bledsoe, and Cartwright, on This Important Subject.* Augusta, Ga., 1860.

Ely, Richard T. *Ground Under Our Feet: An Autobiography.* New York, 1938.

———. *Monopolies and Trusts.* 1900; rpr. New York, 1910.

———. *Outlines of Economics.* Rev. ed. with Thomas S. Adams, Max O. Lorenz, and Allyn A. Young. New York, 1912.

———. *Property and Contract in Their Relations to the Distribution of Wealth.* 2 vols. New York, 1922.

Everett, Alexander H. *New Ideas on Population: With Remarks on the Theories of Malthus and Godwin.* Boston, 1823.

Fisk, Theophilus. *An Oration on Banking, Education, &c. Delivered at the Queen-Street Theatre, in the City of Charleston, S. C., July 4th, 1837. Also an Oration on the Freedom of the Press.* Charleston, 1837.

Fitzhugh, George. *Cannibals All! or, Slaves Without Masters.* Edited by C. Vann Woodward. Cambridge, Mass., 1960.

Fitzhugh, George, and A. Hogeboom. *A Controversy on Slavery, Between George Fitzhugh, Esq., of Virginia, Author of "Sociology for the South," etc., and A. Hogeboom, Esq., of New York.* Oneida, N.Y., 1857.

Flint, H. M. *Life of Stephen A. Douglas.* Philadelphia, 1865.

Forbes, A., and J. W. Greene. *The Rich Men of Massachusetts: Containing a Statement of the Reputed Wealth of About Fifteen Hundred Persons, with Brief Sketches of More Than One Thousand Characters.* Boston, 1851.

Freedley, Edwin T. *Philadelphia and Its Manufactures: A Hand-Book Exhibiting the Development, Variety, and Statistics of the Manufacturing Industry of Philadelphia in 1857.* Philadelphia, 1858.

———. *A Practical Treatise on Business; or, How to Get, Save, Spend, Give, Lend, and Bequeath Money: With an Inquiry into the Chances of Success and Causes of Failure in Business.* 1852; rpr. Philadelphia, 1866.

French, Samuel G. *Two Wars: An Autobiography of Gen. Samuel G. French.* Nashville, Tenn., 1901.

Friends of Domestic Industry. *Address of the Friends of Domestic Industry, Assembled in Convention, at New-York, October 26, 1831, to the People of the United States.* Baltimore, 1831.

George, Henry. *Progress and Poverty: An Inquiry into the Cause of Industrial Depressions, and of Increase of Want with Increase of Wealth. The Remedy.* 4th ed. New York, 1888.

Goddard, Samuel A. *The American Rebellion: Letters on the American Rebellion, 1860 to 1865, &c.* London, 1870.

Godwin, Parke. *A Popular View of the Doctrines of Charles Fourier. With the Addition of Democracy, Constructive and Pacific.* 1844; rpr. Philadelphia, 1972.

Gompers, Samuel. *Seventy Years of Life and Labor.* 2 vols. New York, 1925.

Goodell, William. *The American Slave Code in Theory and Practice: Its Distinctive Features Shown by Its Statutes, Judicial Decisions, and Illustrative Facts.* 1853; rpr. New York, 1968.

————. *Slavery and Anti-Slavery: A History of the Great Struggle in Both Hemispheres, with a View of the Slavery Question in the United States.* New York, 1852.

Gouge, William M. *A Short History of Paper Money and Banking in the United States to Which Is Prefixed an Inquiry into the Principles of the System.* 1833; rpr. New York, 1968.

Greeley, Horace. *Essays Designed to Elucidate the Science of Political Economy, While Serving to Explain and Defend the Policy of Protection to Home Industry as a System of National Cooperation for the Elevation of Labor.* Boston, 1870.

————. *Hints Toward Reforms, in Lectures, Addresses, and Other Writings.* New York, 1850.

————. *Recollections of a Busy Life.* New York, 1868.

————, ed. *The American Laborer, Devoted to the Cause of Protection to Home Industry.* 1843; rpr. New York, 1974.

Grimké, A[ngelina] E. *Appeal to the Christian Women of the South.* New York, n.d.

Grund, Francis J. *The Americans in Their Moral, Social and Political Relations.* 1837; rpr. New York, 1968.

————. *Aristocracy in America: From the Sketch-Book of a German Nobleman.* 1839; rpr. New York, 1959.

Gunton, George. *Wealth and Progress: A Critical Examination of the Wages Question and Its Economic Relation to Social Reform.* 1887; rpr. New York, 1894.

Gurowski, Adam G. de. *America and Europe.* New York, 1857.

Hamilton, James. *A Speech on the Operation of the Tariff on the Interests of the South, and the Constitutional Means of Redressing Its Evils.* Charleston, 1828.

Hamilton, Thomas. *Men and Manners in America.* 2nd ed. 1843; rpr. New York, 1968.

Hazard, Rowland Gibson. *Economics and Politics: A Series of Papers upon Public Ques-

tions Written on Various Occasions from 1840 to 1885. Edited by Caroline Hazard. Boston, 1889.

Higginson, Thomas Wentworth. *Contemporaries.* Boston, 1899.

[Hildreth, Richard.] Author of "Archy Moore." *Despotism in America; or, An Inquiry into the Nature and Results of the Slave-Holding System in the United States.* Boston, 1840.

Hoar, George F. *Autobiography of Seventy Years.* 2 vols. New York, 1903.

Hodgman, Stephen Alexander. *The Nation's Sin and Punishment; or, The Hand of God Visible in the Overthrow of Slavery.* New York, 1864.

Holdich, Joseph. *Political Economy Simplified: A Lecture, Delivered Before the Young Men's Lyceum of the City of Middletown, Conn.* Middletown, Conn., 1838.

Holmes, Isaac. *An Account of the United States of America, Derived from Actual Observation During a Residence of Four Years in That Republic.* 1823; rpr. New York, 1974.

[Hopkins, Samuel.] *A Dialogue Concerning the Slavery of the Africans.* Norwich, Conn., 1776.

Howard, Oliver Otis. *Autobiography of Oliver Otis Howard.* 2 vols. New York, 1908.

Hume, John F. *The Abolitionists: Together with Personal Memoirs of the Struggle for Human Rights, 1830–1864.* New York, 1905.

Hundley, D[aniel] R. *Social Relations in Our Southern States.* New York, 1860.

Jay, William. *Miscellaneous Writings on Slavery.* 1853; rpr. New York, 1968.

Jenkins, John S. *James Knox Polk and a History of His Administration.* New Orleans, 1854.

Julian, George W. *Political Recollections, 1840 to 1872.* Chicago, 1884.

————. *Speeches on Political Questions.* 1872; rpr. Westport, Conn., 1970.

Kelley, William D. *Speeches, Addresses and Letters on Industrial and Financial Questions.* Philadelphia, 1872.

Kellogg, Edward. *Labor and Other Capital: The Rights of Each Secured and the Wrongs of Both Eradicated. . . .* New York, 1849.

Kennedy, John P[endleton]. *An Address Delivered Before the American Institute . . . October 17, 1833.* New York, 1833.

————. *Letter of J. P. Kennedy to His Constituents, Citizens of the Fourth Congressional District in the State of Maryland, on the Principles and Value of the Protective System.* N.p., n.d. [Baltimore, 1842?].

King, Willford Isbell. *The Wealth and Income of the People of the United States.* 1915; rpr. New York, 1922.

Kirby, Georgiana Bruce. *Years of Experience: An Autobiographical Narrative.* 1887; rpr. New York, 1971.

La Follette, Robert M. *La Follette's Autobiography: A Personal Narrative of Political Experiences.* 2nd ed. Madison, 1918.

Lieber, Francis. *Essays on Property and Labour as Connected with Natural Law and the Constitution of Society.* New York, 1841.

————. *Notes on Fallacies of American Protectionists.* 4th ed. 1870; rpr. New York, 1974.

Locke, John. *Two Treatises of Government.* 1690. Edited by Peter Laslett. Cambridge, Eng., 1988.

Lodge, Henry Cabot. *Early Memories.* New York, 1913.

[Logan, George]. A Farmer. *Five Letters, Addressed to the Yeomanry of the United States, Containing Some Observations on the Dangerous Scheme of Governor Duer and Mr. Secretary Hamilton, to Establish National Manufactories.* Philadelphia, 1792.

[————]. An American Farmer. *Letters Addressed to the Yeomanry of the United States, Containing Some Observations on Funding and Bank Systems.* Philadelphia, 1791.

Lowell, James Russell. *The Anti-Slavery Papers of James Russell Lowell.* 2 vols. Boston, 1902.

Luther, Seth. *An Address on the Origin and Progress of Avarice, and Its Deleterious Effects on Human Happiness. . . .* Boston, 1834.

Lyell, Sir Charles. *A Second Visit to the United States of North America.* 2 vols. New York, 1849.

McAdoo, William G. *Crowded Years: The Reminiscences of William G. McAdoo.* Boston, 1931.

McCulloch, Hugh. *Men and Measures of Half a Century: Sketches and Comments.* New York, 1888.

McCulloch, J. R. *The Principles of Political Economy; With a Sketch of the Rise and Progress of the Science.* Edinburgh, 1825.

McNeill, George E., ed. *The Labor Movement: The Problem of Today.* Boston, 1887.

McVickar, John. *First Lessons in Political Economy; For the Use of Primary and Common Schools.* Boston, 1835.

————. *Outlines of Political Economy.* New York, 1825.

Madison, James. *Notes of Debates in the Federal Convention of 1787 Reported by James Madison.* Athens, Ohio, 1966.

Malthus, Thomas Robert. *On Population.* 1798. Edited by Gertrude Himmelfarb. New York, 1960.

————. *Principles of Political Economy Considered with a View to Their Practical Application.* 2nd ed. 1836; rpr. New York, 1968.

Marryat, Frederick. *A Diary in America: With Remarks on Its Institutions.* 1839. Edited by Sydney Jackman. Westport, Conn., 1962.

Marshall, Alfred. *Principles of Economics.* 8th ed. 1920; rpr. London, 1962.

Martineau, Harriet. *Society in America.* 3 vols. 1837; rpr. New York, 1966.

May, Samuel Joseph. *Memoir of Samuel Joseph May.* Boston, 1873.

————. *Some Recollections of Our Antislavery Conflict.* Boston, 1869.

Mill, James. *Elements of Political Economy.* 3rd ed. London, 1844.

Mill, John Stuart. *Principles of Political Economy with Some of Their Applications to Social Philosophy.* 1871. Edited by W. J. Ashley. London, 1926.

[New England Social Reform Society.] *The Social Reformer and Herald of Progress.* Boston, [1844? 1845?].

Newman, Samuel P. *Elements of Political Economy.* Andover, Mass., 1835.

Noyes, John Humphrey. *History of American Socialisms.* 1870; rpr. New York, 1961.

Opdyke, George. *A Treatise on Political Economy.* New York, 1851.

Orvis, Marianne [Dwight]. *Letters from Brook Farm, 1844–1847.* Edited by Amy L. Reed. 1928; rpr. Philadelphia, 1972.

Patten, Simon Nelson. *Essays in Economic Theory.* Edited by Rexford Guy Tugwell. New York, 1924.

Peck, Harry Thurston. *Twenty Years of the Republic, 1885–1905.* New York, 1932.

Perry, Arthur Latham. *Political Economy.* 22nd ed. New York, 1895.

Phelps, Amos A. *Lectures on Slavery and Its Remedy.* Boston, 1834.

Philadelphia Society for the Promotion of National Industry. *Addresses.* Philadelphia, 1819.

Phillips, Willard. *A Manual of Political Economy, with Particular Reference to the Institutions, Resources, and Conditions of the United States.* Boston, 1828.

———. *Propositions Concerning Protection and Free Trade.* Boston, 1850.

Pickering, John. *The Working Man's Political Economy, Founded upon the Principle of Immutable Justice, and the Inalienable Rights of Man; Designed for the Promotion of National Reform.* Cincinnati, 1847.

A Plain Politician. *Honesty Shewed to Be True Policy; or, A General Impost Considered and Defended.* New York, 1786.

Pollard, Edward A. *The Lost Cause: A New Southern History of the War of the Confederates. . . .* 2nd ed. New York, 1867.

Poor, Henry V. *Manual of the Railroads of the United States for 1869–70.* New York, 1869.

Potter, A[lonzo]. *Political Economy: Its Objects, Uses, and Principles, Considered with Reference to the Condition of the American People.* New York, 1841.

Powderly, Terrence V. *Thirty Years of Labor, 1859 to 1889.* Columbus, Ohio, 1890.

Powell, Edward Payson. *Nullification and Secession in the United States: A History of the Six Attempts During the First Century of the Republic.* New York, 1897.

Pulszky, Francis, and Theresa Pulszky. *White Red Black: Sketches of Society in the United States During the Visit of Their Guest.* 3 vols. 1853; rpr. New York, 1968.

Quincy, Edmund. *Life of Josiah Quincy of Massachusetts.* Boston, 1869.

Quincy, Josiah. *Memoir of the Life of Josiah Quincy Jun. of Massachusetts.* 1825; rpr. New York, 1971.

Rae, John. *The Sociological Theory of Capital, Being a Complete Reprint of the New Principles of Political Economy, 1834.* Edited by Charles Whitney Mixter. New York, 1905.

Ramsay, David. *The History of the American Revolution.* 2 vols. Philadelphia, 1789.

———. *The History of the Revolution of South-Carolina, from a British Province to an Independent State.* 2 vols. Trenton, N.J., 1785.

Raymond, Daniel. *The Elements of Political Economy, in Two Parts.* 2nd ed. 2 vols. 1823; rpr. New York, 1964.

Reagan, John H. *Memoirs: With Special Reference to Secession and the Civil War.* Edited by Walter Flavius McCaleb. New York, 1906.

A Respectable Member of the Community. *Extract from an Address in the Virginia Gazette, of March 19, 1767.* Philadelphia, 1770.

[Rice, David.] Philanthropos. *Slavery Inconsistent with Justice and Good Policy.* Lexington, Ky., 1792.

Roosevelt, Theodore. *Progressive Principles: Selections from Addresses Made During the Presidential Campaign of 1912.* Edited by Elmer H. Youngman. New York, 1913.

———. *Theodore Roosevelt: An Autobiography.* New York, 1929.

Ruffin, Edmund. *The Political Economy of Slavery; or, The Institution Considered In Regard to Its Influence on Public Wealth and the General Welfare.* Richmond, Va., [1857?].

[Rush, Benjamin.] A Pennsylvanian. *An Address to the Inhabitants of the British Settlements in America upon Slave-Keeping.* Philadelphia, 1773.

Rushton, Edward. *Expostulatory Letter to George Washington, of Mount Vernon, on His Consenting to Be a Holder of Slaves.* Lexington, Ky., 1797.

Russell, Charles Edward. *Bare Hands and Stone Walls: Some Recollections of a Side-Line Reformer.* New York, 1933.

Sawyer, George S. *Southern Institutes; or, An Inquiry into the Origins and Early Prevalence of Slavery and the Slave Trade.* Philadelphia, 1859.

Schlesinger, Alexander. *The Labor Amendment: Our Next Great Job.* New York, 1910.

Seaman, Ezra C. *Essays on the Progress of Nations, in Productive Industry, Civilization, Population, and Wealth.* Detroit, 1846.

Sedgwick, Theodore. *Public and Private Economy.* 3 vols. New York, 1836.

Senior, Nassau William. *An Outline of the Science of Political Economy.* 1836; rpr. New York, 1939.

Sharp, Granville. *An Essay on Slavery, Proving from Scripture Its Inconsistency with Humanity and Religion.* Burlington, N.J., 1773.

Sherman, John. *Recollections of Forty Years in the House, Senate and Cabinet: An Autobiography.* 2 vols. Chicago, 1895.

Simpson, Stephen. *The Working Man's Manual: A New Theory of Political Economy, on the Principle of Production the Source of Wealth.* Philadelphia, 1831.

Skidmore, Thomas. *The Rights of Man to Property! Being a Proposition to Make It Equal Among the Adults of the Present Generation.* 1829; rpr. New York, [1964].

Smith, Adam. *An Inquiry into the Nature and Causes of the Wealth of Nations.* 1776. Edited by Edwin Cannan. New York, 1937.

Smith, E. Peshine. *A Manual of Political Economy.* New York, 1853.

Smith, E[lihu] H[ubbard]. *A Discourse, Delivered April 11, 1798, at the Request of and Before the New-York Society for Promoting the Manumission of Slaves, and Protecting Such of Them as Have Been or May Be Liberated.* New York, 1798.

Spahr, Charles B. *An Essay on the Present Distribution of Wealth in the United States.* New York, 1896.

Spencer, Herbert. *The Man Versus the State.* 1892; rpr. Caldwell, Idaho, 1965.

Spooner, Lysander. *Poverty: Its Illegal Causes and Legal Cure.* Boston, 1846.

Stevens, Thaddeus. *Reconstruction: Speech of Hon. Thaddeus Stevens of Pennsylvania. Delivered in the House of Representatives of the United States, December 13, 1865.* Washington, D.C., 1865.

Stiles, Ezra. *The United States Elevated to Glory and Honor. A Sermon, Preached Before His Excellency Jonathan Trumbull, Esq L. L. D. . . . at the Anniversary Election May 8th, 1783.* New Haven, 1783.

[Sullivan, James.] A Citizen of Massachusetts. *The Path to Riches. An Inquiry into the Origin and Use of Money; and into the Principles of Stocks and Banks.* Boston, 1792.

Sumner, William G. *Lectures on the History of Protection in the United States.* New York, 1886.

Swan, James. *A Dissuasion, to Great-Britain and the Colonies, from the Slave Trade to Africa.* Boston, [1772].

Swisshelm, Jane Grey. *Half a Century.* 3rd ed. Chicago, 1880.

Taylor, John. *Arator: Being a Series of Agricultural Essays, Practical and Political: In Sixty-Four Numbers.* Edited by M. E. Bradford. 4th ed. 1818; rpr. Indianapolis, 1977.

————. *A Definition of Parties: The Political Effects of the Paper System Considered.* Philadelphia, 1794.

————. *An Enquiry into the Principles and Tendency of Certain Public Measures.* Philadelphia, 1794.

————. *An Examination of the Late Proceedings in Congress Respecting the Official Conduct of the Secretary of the Treasury.* Richmond, Va., 1793.

————. *An Inquiry into the Principles and Policy of the Government of the United States.* 1814. Edited by Loren Baritz. Indianapolis, 1969.

————. *Tyranny Unmasked.* Washington, D.C., 1822.

Thompson, R. W. *The History of Protective Tariff Laws.* Chicago, 1888.

Tocqueville, Alexis de. *Democracy in America.* 1835–40. Edited by Phillips Bradley. 2 vols. New York, 1945.

Tower, Rev. Philo. *Slavery Unmasked: Being a Truthful Narrative of a Three Years' Residence and Journeying in Eleven Southern States, to which Is Added the Invasion of Kansas.* 1856; rpr. New York, 1969.

Trumbull, Benjamin. *Discourse, Delivered at the Anniversary Meeting of the Freemen of the Town of New-Haven, April 12, 1773.* New Haven, 1773.

Tucker, George. *The Laws of Wages, Profits and Rent Investigated.* 1837; rpr. New York, 1964.

———. *Political Economy for the People.* 1859; rpr. New York, 1970.

Underwood, Oscar W. *Drifting Sands of Party Politics.* New York, 1931.

Vethake, Henry. *The Principles of Political Economy.* Philadelphia, 1838.

Villard, Henry. *Memoirs of Henry Villard: Journalist and Financier, 1835–1900.* 2 vols. Boston, 1904.

Villard, Oswald Garrison. *Fighting Years: Memoirs of a Liberal Editor.* New York, 1939.

Voorhees, Daniel W. *Speeches of Daniel W. Voorhees of Indiana, Embracing His Most Prominent Forensic, Political, Occasional, and Literary Addresses.* Compiled by Charles S. Voorhees. Cincinnati, 1875.

Wainwright, Jonathan M. *Inequality of Individual Wealth the Ordinance of Providence and Essential to Civilization. A Sermon Preached Before His Excellency John Davis, Governor, . . . on the Annual Election, January 7, 1835.* Boston, 1835.

Walker, Amasa. *The Science of Wealth: A Manual of Political Economy.* Philadelphia, 1872.

Walker, Francis A. *Political Economy.* New York, 1888.

Warren, Dr. Joseph. *An Oration Delivered March 5th, 1772, at the Request of the Inhabitants of the Town of Boston; To Commemorate the Bloody Tragedy of the Fifth of March, 1770.* Boston, 1772.

———. *An Oration Delivered March Sixth, 1775, at the Request of the Inhabitants of the Town of Boston, to Commemorate the Bloody Tragedy of the Fifth of March, 1770.* Boston, 1775.

Warren, John. *An Oration Delivered July 4, 1783, at the Request of the Inhabitants of the Town of Boston, in Celebration of the Anniversary of American Independence.* Boston, 1783.

Warren, Josiah. *Equitable Commerce: A New Development of Principles for the Harmonious Adjustment and Regulation of the Pecuniary, Intellectual, and Moral Intercourse of Mankind, Proposed as Elements of New Society.* New Harmony, Ind., 1846.

Warren, Mrs. Mercy. *History of the Rise, Progress and Termination of the American Revolution. Interspersed with Biographical, Political and Moral Observations.* 3 vols. 1805; rpr. New York, 1970.

Warville, J. P. Brissot de. *New Travels in the United States of America, 1788.* Translated by Mara Soceanu Vamos and Durand Echeverria. Edited by Durand Echeverria. Cambridge, Mass., 1964.

Wayland, Francis. *Elements of Political Economy.* 4th ed. Boston, 1856.

Webster, Noah, Jr. *A Collection of Essays and Fugitiv* [sic] *Writings on Moral, Historical, Political and Literary Subjects.* Boston, 1790.

———. *Effects of Slavery on Morals and Industry.* Hartford, Conn., 1793.

————. *An Examination into the Leading Principles of the Federal Constitution, Proposed by the Late Convention Held at Philadelphia.* Philadelphia, 1787.

[Webster, Pelatiah.] A Citizen of Philadelphia. *An Essay on Free Trade and Finance, Humbly Offered to the Consideration of the Public.* Philadelphia, 1779.

Wells, David A. *The Creed of Free Trade.* N.p., n.d. Rpr. from *Atlantic Monthly,* August, 1875.

————. *Practical Economics.* New York, 1885.

————. *Recent Economic Changes and Their Effect on the Production and Distribution of Wealth and the Well-Being of Society.* 1889; rpr. New York, 1899.

Whitlock, Brand. *Forty Years of It.* New York, 1925.

Wilson, Henry. *Speech of Hon. Henry Wilson, at the Republican Mass Meeting at Bangor, Me., August 27, 1868.* New York, 1868.

Wilson, James. *An Oration Delivered Before the Providence Association of Mechanics and Manufacturers, at Their Annual Election, April 14, 1794.* Providence, 1794.

Wilson, Woodrow. *Division and Reunion, 1829–1889.* 1893; rpr. New York, 1901.

Wistar, Isaac Jones. *Autobiography of Isaac Jones Wistar, 1827–1905.* Philadelphia, 1937.

Woolman, John. *Considerations on Keeping Negroes; Recommended to the Professors of Christianity, of Every Denomination. Part Second.* Philadelphia, 1762.

————. *Some Consideration on the Keeping of Negroes. Recommended to the Professors of Christianity of Every Denomination.* Philadelphia, 1754.

Wright, Elizur, Jr. *The Sin of Slavery, and Its Remedy; Containing Some Reflections on the Moral Influence of African Colonization.* New York, 1833.

Secondary Sources

Abbott, Richard H. *Cobbler in Congress: The Life of Henry Wilson, 1812–1875.* Lexington, Ky., 1972.

————. *Cotton and Capital: Boston Businessmen and Antislavery Reform, 1854–1868.* Amherst, Mass., 1991.

Abzug, Robert H., and Stephen E. Maizlish, eds. *New Perspectives on Race and Slavery in America: Essays in Honor of Kenneth M. Stampp.* Lexington, Ky., 1986.

Adair, Douglass Greybill. "The Intellectual Origins of Jeffersonian Democracy: Republicanism, the Class Struggle, and the Virtuous Farmer." Ph.D. dissertation, Yale University, 1943.

Adams, Charles Francis. *Richard Henry Dana: A Biography.* 2 vols. Rev. ed.; Boston, 1891.

Adams, Willi Paul. *The First American Constitutions: Republican Ideology and the Making of the State Constitutions in the Revolutionary Era.* Translated by Rita Kimble and Robert Kimble. 1973, rpr. Chapel Hill, 1980.

Alchien, Armen, and Harold Demsetz. "Production, Information Costs, and Economic Organization." *American Economic Review,* LXII (1972), 777–95.

Alden, John Richard. *The South in the Revolution, 1763–1789.* Baton Rouge, 1957.

Anderson, Terry L., ed. *Property Rights and Indian Economies.* Boston, 1992.

Anderson, Terry L., and Fred S. McChesney. "Raid or Trade: An Economic Model of Indian-White Relations." *Journal of Law and Economics,* XXXVII (1994), 39–74.

Andrews, John B. "Nationalisation (1860–1877)." In John R. Commons et al., *History of Labour in the United States.* New York, 1921.

Appleby, Joyce O. *Capitalism and a New Social Order: The Republican Vision of the 1790s.* New York, 1984.

Arnett, Benjamin W. *Hon. J. M. Ashley Souvenir: Duplicate Copy of the Souvenir from the Afro-American League of Tennessee to Hon. James M. Ashley of Ohio.* Philadelphia, 1894.

Arnold, John P., and Frank Penman. *History of the Brewing Industry and Brewing Science in America.* Chicago, 1933.

Ashcraft, Richard. "Liberal Political Theory and Working-Class Radicalism in Nineteenth-Century England." *Political Theory,* XXI (1993), 249–72.

Ashworth, John. *"Agrarians" and "Aristocrats": Party Political Ideology in the United States, 1837–1846.* Cambridge, Eng., 1983.

———. *Slavery, Capitalism, and Politics in the Antebellum Republic.* Vol. I: *Commerce and Compromise, 1820–1850.* Cambridge, Eng., 1995.

Atack, Jeremy, and Fred Bateman. "Self-Sufficiency and the Marketable Surplus in the Rural North, 1860." *Agricultural History,* LVIII (1984), 296–313.

———. *To Their Own Soil: Agriculture in the Antebellum North.* Ames, Ia., 1987.

Atkinson, A. B. *The Economics of Inequality.* Oxford, 1975.

Baack, Bennett D., and John Edward Ray. "Special Interests and the Adoption of the Income Tax in the United States." *Journal of Economic History,* XLV (1985), 607–25.

Bailey, Hugh C. *Hinton Rowan Helper: Abolitionist-Racist.* University, Ala., 1965.

Bailyn, Bernard. *The Ideological Origins of the American Revolution.* Cambridge, Mass., 1967.

Baker, Jean H. *Affairs of Party: The Political Culture of Northern Democrats in the Mid-Nineteenth Century.* Ithaca, N.Y., 1983.

Baltzell, E. Digby. *Puritan Boston and Quaker Philadelphia: Two Protestant Ethics and the Spirit of Class Authority and Leadership.* New York, 1979.

Banner, James M., Jr. *To the Hartford Convention: The Federalists and the Origins of Party Politics in Massachusetts, 1789–1815.* New York, 1970.

Banner, Lois W. *Elizabeth Cady Stanton: A Radical for Woman's Rights.* Boston, 1980.

Banning, Lance. *The Jeffersonian Persuasion: Evolution of a Party Ideology.* Ithaca, N.Y., 1978.

————. "The Republican Interpretation: Retrospect and Prospect." In *The Republican Synthesis Revisited: Essays in Honor of George Athan Billias,* edited by Milton M. Klein, Richard D. Brown, and John B. Hench. Worcester, Mass, 1992.

————. *The Sacred Fire of Liberty: James Madison and the Founding of the Federal Republic.* Ithaca, N.Y., 1995.

Barkai, H. "Ricardo on Factor Prices and Income Distribution in a Growing Economy." *Economica,* XXVI (1959), 240–50.

Barkan, Elliott. "The Emergence of a Whig Persuasion: Conservatism, Democratism, and the New York State Whigs." *New York History,* LII (1971), 367–95.

Barney, William L. *Flawed Victory: A New Perspective on the Civil War.* Lanham, Md., 1980.

Barron, Hal S. "Listening to the Silent Majority: Change and Continuity in the Nineteenth-Century Rural North." In *Agriculture and National Development: Views on the Nineteenth Century,* edited by Lou Ferleger. Ames, Ia., 1990.

————. *Those Who Stayed Behind: Rural Society in Nineteenth-Century New England.* Cambridge, Eng., 1984.

Basch, Norma. *In the Eyes of the Law: Women, Marriage, and Property in Nineteenth-Century New York.* Ithaca, N.Y., 1982.

Bassett, T. D. Seymour. "The Secular Utopian Socialists." In *Socialism and American Life,* edited by Donald Drew Egbert and Stow Persons. Princeton, 1952.

Baugh, Daniel A., ed. *Aristocratic Government and Society in Eighteenth-Century England: The Foundations of Stability.* New York, 1975.

Baum, Dale. *The Civil War Party System: The Case of Massachusetts, 1848–1876.* Chapel Hill, 1984.

Baum, Dale, and Dale T. Knobel. "Anatomy of a Realignment: New York Presidential Politics, 1848–1860." *New York History,* LXV (1984), 61–81.

Baxter, Maurice G. *Henry Clay and the American System.* Lexington, Ky., 1995.

————. *One and Inseparable: Daniel Webster and the Union.* Cambridge, Mass., 1984.

Beard, Charles A. *Contemporary American History, 1877–1913.* New York, 1918.

Beard, Charles A., and Mary Beard. *The Rise of American Civilization.* 2 vols. New York, 1927.

Bell, Daniel. *Work and Its Discontents: The Cult of Efficiency in America.* Boston, 1956.

Belohlavek, John M. *George Mifflin Dallas: Jacksonian Patrician.* University Park, Pa., 1977.

Belz, Herman. *Emancipation and Equal Rights: Politics and Constitutionalism in the Civil War Era.* New York, 1978.

Bender, Thomas. *Community and Social Change in America.* New Brunswick, N.J., 1978.

————, ed. *The Antislavery Debate: Capitalism and Abolitionism as a Problem in Historical Interpretation.* Berkeley, 1992.

Benedict, Michael Les. *A Compromise of Principle: Congressional Republicans and Reconstruction, 1863–1869.* New York, 1974.

————. *The Impeachment and Trial of Andrew Johnson.* New York, 1973.

Bensel, Richard Franklin. *Yankee Leviathan: The Origins of Central State Authority in America, 1859–1877.* Cambridge, Eng., 1990.

Bensman, David. *The Practice of Solidarity: American Hat Finishers in the Nineteenth Century.* Urbana, 1985.

Benson, Lee. *The Concept of Jacksonian Democracy: New York as a Test Case.* Princeton, 1961.

Berg, Barbara J. *The Remembered Gate: Origins of American Feminism, the Woman and the City, 1800–1860.* New York, 1978.

Berg, Maxine. *The Machinery Question and the Making of Political Economy, 1815–1848.* Cambridge, Eng., 1980.

Bergeron, Paul H. *The Presidency of James K. Polk.* Lawrence, Kans., 1987.

Berlin, Ira A., and Herbert G. Gutman. "Natives and Immigrants, Free Men and Slaves: Urban Workingmen in the Antebellum South." *American Historical Review,* LXXXVIII (1983), 1175–1200.

Bernstein, Barton J., and Allen J. Matusow, eds. *Twentieth-Century America: Recent Interpretations.* 2nd ed. New York, 1972.

Bernstein, Iver. *The New York City Draft Riots: Their Significance for American Society and Politics in the Age of the Civil War.* New York, 1990.

Berthoff, Rowland. "Independence and Enterprise: Small Business in the American Dream." In *Small Business in American Life,* edited by Stuart W. Bruchey. New York, 1980.

Berwanger, Eugene H. *The Frontier Against Slavery: Western Anti-Negro Prejudice and the Slavery Extension Controversy.* Urbana, 1971.

Bestor, Arthur Eugene. *Backwoods Utopias: The Sectarian and Owenite Phases of Communitarian Socialism in America, 1663–1829.* Philadelphia, 1950.

Billington, Ray Allen. *The Protestant Crusade, 1800–1860: A Study of the Origins of American Nativism.* 1938; rpr. Chicago, 1964.

Black, R. D. Collison, A. W. Coates, and Craufurd D. W. Goodwin, eds. *The Marginal Revolution in Economics: Interpretation and Evaluation.* Durham, N.C., 1973.

Blackett, R. J. M. *Beating Against the Barriers: Biographical Essays in Nineteenth-Century Afro-American History.* Baton Rouge, 1986.

————. *Building an Antislavery Wall: Black Americans in the Atlantic Abolitionist Movement, 1830–1860.* Baton Rouge, 1983.

Blackford, Mansel G. *A History of Small Business in America.* New York, 1991.

Blackwell, Alice Stone. *Lucy Stone: Pioneer of Woman's Rights.* Boston, 1930.

Bladen, Vincent. *From Adam Smith to Maynard Keynes: The Heritage of Political Economy.* Toronto, 1974.

Blaug, Mark. *Economic Theory in Retrospect.* 3rd ed. Cambridge, Eng., 1978.

———. "The Empirical Content of Ricardian Economics." *Journal of Political Economy,* LXIV (1956), 41–58.

———. *Ricardian Economics: A Historical Study.* New Haven, 1958.

Blauner, Robert. *Alienation and Freedom: The Factory Worker and His Industry.* Chicago, 1964.

Blewett, Mary H. *Men, Women, and Work: Class, Gender, and Protest in the New England Shoe Industry, 1780–1910.* Urbana, 1988.

———. "Women Shoeworkers and Domestic Ideology: Rural Outwork in Early Nineteenth-Century Essex County." *New England Quarterly,* LX (1987), 403–28.

Blinder, Alan S. *Toward an Economic Theory of Income Distribution.* Cambridge, Mass., 1974.

Blinder, Alan S., Irving Kristol, and Wilbur J. Cohen. "The Level and Distribution of Economic Well-Being." In *The American Economy in Transition,* edited by Martin Feldstein. Chicago, 1980.

Blodgett, Geoffrey. *The Gentle Reformers: Massachusetts Democrats in the Cleveland Era.* Cambridge, Mass., 1966.

Blum, John Morton. *The Republican Roosevelt.* New York, 1962.

Blumin, Stuart M. *The Emergence of the Middle Class: Social Experience in the American City, 1760–1900.* Cambridge, Eng., 1989.

Boardman, Roger Sherman. *Roger Sherman: Signer and Statesman.* 1938; rpr. New York, 1971.

Bode, Frederick A., and Donald E. Ginter. *Farm Tenancy and the Census in Antebellum Georgia.* Athens, Ga., 1986.

Boesche, Roger. *The Strange Liberalism of Alexis de Tocqueville.* Ithaca, N.Y., 1987.

Bogin, Ruth. *Abraham Clark and the Quest for Equality in the Revolutionary Era, 1774–1794.* East Brunswick, N.J., 1982.

Boller, Paul F., Jr. *American Thought in Transition: The Impact of Evolutionary Naturalism, 1865–1900.* Chicago, 1969.

Bolt, Christine, and Seymour Drescher, eds. *Anti-Slavery, Religion, and Reform: Essays in Memory of Roger Anstey.* Folkestone, Eng., 1980.

Bowman, Scott R. *The Modern Corporation and American Political Thought: Law, Power, and Ideology.* University Park, Pa., 1996.

Bowman, Shearer Davis. *Masters and Lords: Mid-19th-Century U.S. Planters and Prussian Junkers.* New York, 1993.

Boydston, Jeanne. *Home and Work: Housework, Wages, and the Ideology of Labor in the Early Republic.* New York, 1990.

Braverman, Harry. *Labor and Monopoly Capital: The Degradation of Work in the Twentieth Century.* New York, 1974.

Bremner, Robert H. *From the Depths: The Discovery of Poverty in the United States.* New York, 1956.

Bridenbaugh, Carl. *Myths and Realities: Societies of the Colonial South.* Baton Rouge, 1952.

Bridges, Amy. *A City in the Republic: Antebellum New York and the Origins of Machine Politics.* Cambridge, Eng., 1984.

Brinton, Crane. *English Political Thought in the 19th Century.* 1933; rpr. New York, 1962.

Brody, David. "Labor and Small-Scale Enterprise During Industrialization." In *Small Business in American Life,* edited by Stuart W. Bruchey. New York, 1980.

————. *Steelworkers in America: The Nonunion Era.* Cambridge, Mass., 1960.

Bronfenbrenner, Martin. *Income Distribution Theory.* Chicago, 1971.

Brown, John K. *The Baldwin Locomotive Works, 1831–1915.* Baltimore, 1995.

Brown, Richard D. *Modernization: The Transformation of American Life, 1600–1865.* New York, 1976.

Brown, Robert E., and Katherine Brown. *Virginia, 1705–1786: Democracy or Aristocracy?* East Lansing, Mich., 1964.

Brown, Roger H. *Redeeming the Republic: Federalists, Taxation, and the Origins of the Constitution.* Baltimore, 1993.

Brown, Thomas. *Politics and Statesmanship: Essays on the American Whig Party.* New York, 1985.

Bruchey, Stuart W., ed. *Small Business in American Life.* New York, 1980.

Buel, Richard, Jr. *Securing the Revolution: Ideology in American Politics, 1789–1815.* Ithaca, N.Y., 1972.

Burnham, Walter Dean. *Critical Elections and the Mainsprings of American Politics.* New York, 1970.

Bushman, Richard L. "Massachusetts Farmers and the Revolution." In *Society, Freedom, and Conscience: The American Revolution in Virginia, Massachusetts, and New York,* edited by Richard M. Jellison. New York, 1976.

Bushman, Richard L., *et al. Uprooted Americans: Essays to Honor Oscar Handlin.* Boston, 1979.

Cadman, John W., Jr. *The Corporation in New Jersey: Business and Politics, 1791–1875.* Cambridge, Mass., 1949.

Cady, George Johnson. "The Early American Reaction to the Theory of Malthus." *Journal of Political Economy,* XXXIX (1931), 601–32.

Campbell, Colin D., ed. *Income Redistribution.* Washington, D.C., 1977.

Carden, Maren Lockwood. *Oneida: Utopian Community to Modern Corporation.* Baltimore, 1969.

Carosso, Vincent P. *Investment Banking in America: A History.* Cambridge, Mass., 1970.

Carsel, Wilfred. "The Slaveholders' Indictment of Northern Wage Slavery." *Journal of Southern History,* VI (1940), 504–20.

Cave, Alfred A. *An American Conservative in the Age of Jackson: The Political and Social Thought of Calvin Colton.* Fort Worth, Tex., 1969.

Chambers, William Nisbet, and Walter Dean Burnham, eds. *The American Party Systems: Stages of Political Development.* New York, 1967.

Chandler, Alfred D., Jr. "The Emergence of Managerial Capitalism." *Business History Review,* LVIII (1984), 473–503.

———. *Henry Varnum Poor: Business Editor, Analyst, and Reformer.* Cambridge, Mass., 1956.

———. *The Visible Hand: The Managerial Revolution in American Business.* Cambridge, Mass., 1977.

Chandler, Alfred D., Jr., and Herman Daems, eds. *Managerial Hierarchies: Comparative Perspectives on the Rise of the Modern Industrial Enterprise.* Cambridge, Mass., 1980.

Chapman, Stanley D. *The Early Factory Masters: The Transition to the Factory System in the Midland Textile Industry.* Plymouth, Eng., 1967.

Chinard, Gilbert. *Thomas Jefferson: The Apostle of Americanism.* Boston, 1939.

Chinoy, Ely. *Automobile Workers and the American Dream.* Garden City, N.Y., 1955.

Cimbala, Paul A. "The 'Talisman Power': Davis Tillson, the Freedmen's Bureau, and Free Labor in Reconstruction Georgia, 1865–1866." *Civil War History,* XXVIII (1982), 153–71.

Clark, Christopher. *The Roots of Rural Capitalism: Western Massachusetts, 1780–1860.* Ithaca, N.Y., 1990.

Clark, Jennifer. "The American Image of Technology from the Revolution to 1840." *American Quarterly,* XXXIX (1987), 431–49.

Clark, John G. *The Grain Trade in the Old Northwest.* Urbana, 1966.

Clinton, Catherine. *The Other Civil War: American Women in the Nineteenth Century.* New York, 1984.

Clubb, Jerome M., William H. Flanigan, and Nancy H. Zingale. *Partisan Realignment: Voters, Parties, and Government in American History.* Beverly Hills, 1980.

Cochran, Thomas C. "The Business Revolution." *American Historical Review,* LXXIX (1974), 1449–66.

———. *Challenges to American Values: Society, Business and Religion.* New York, 1985.

———. *The Pabst Brewing Company: The History of an American Business.* New York, 1948.

Cochran, Thomas C., and William Miller. *The Age of Enterprise: A Social History of Industrial America.* Rev. ed. New York, 1961.

Cole, Arthur Charles. *The Whig Party in the South.* Washington, D.C., 1913.

Cole, Charles C., Jr. *The Social Ideas of the Northern Evangelists, 1826–1860.* New York, 1954.

Cole, Donald B. *Martin Van Buren and the American Political System.* Princeton, 1984.

Coleman, Mrs. Chapman. *The Life of John J. Crittenden.* 2 vols. Philadelphia, 1871.

Coleman, John M. *Thomas McKean: Forgotten Leader of the Revolution.* Rockaway, N.J., 1975.

Coleman, Peter J. *The Transformation of Rhode Island, 1790–1860.* Providence, 1963.

Coletta, Paolo E. *William Jennings Bryan: Political Evangelist, 1860–1908.* Lincoln, 1964.

Commager, Henry Steele. *Theodore Parker.* Boston, 1936.

Commons, John R., et al. *History of Labour in the United States.* 4 vols. New York, 1921.

Conkin, Paul K. *Prophets of Prosperity: America's First Political Economists.* Bloomington, 1980.

Conner, Paul W. *Poor Richard's Politicks: Benjamin Franklin and His New American Order.* New York, 1965.

Conzen, Kathleen Neils. "Immigrants in Nineteenth-Century Agricultural History." In *Agriculture and National Development: Views on the Nineteenth Century,* edited by Lou Ferleger. Ames, Ia., 1990.

Cook, Robert J. *Baptism of Fire: The Republican Party in Iowa, 1838–1878.* Ames, Iowa, 1994.

Cooke, Jacob Ernest. *Tench Coxe and the Early Republic.* Chapel Hill, 1978.

———. "The Reports of Alexander Hamilton." In *Alexander Hamilton: A Profile,* edited by Jacob E. Cooke. New York, 1967.

———, ed. *Alexander Hamilton: A Profile.* New York, 1967.

Copeland, Melvin Thomas. *The Cotton Manufacturing Industry of the United States.* Cambridge, Mass., 1912.

Cott, Nancy F., and Elizabeth H. Pleck, eds. *A Heritage of Her Own: Toward a New Social History of American Women.* New York, 1979.

Countryman, Edward. *A People in Revolution: The American Revolution and Political Society in New York, 1760–1790.* Baltimore, 1981.

Couvares, Francis G. *The Remaking of Pittsburgh: Class and Culture in an Industrializing City, 1877–1919.* Albany, 1984.

Crafts, N. F. R. "Income Elasticities of Demand and the Release of Labor by Agriculture During the British Industrial Revolution: A Further Appraisal." In *The Economics of the Industrial Revolution,* edited by Joel Mokyr. Totowa, N.J., 1985.

Crenson, Matthew A. *The Federal Machine: Beginnings of Bureaucracy in Jacksonian America.* Baltimore, 1975.

Cromwell, Otelia. *Lucretia Mott.* Cambridge, Mass., 1958.

Cropsey, J. "Adam Smith and Political Philosophy." In *Essays on Adam Smith,* edited by Andrew S. Skinner and Thomas Wilson. Oxford, 1975.

Cross, Whitney R. *The Burned-Over District: The Social and Intellectual History of Enthusiastic Religion in Western New York, 1800–1850.* New York, 1950.

Crowe, Charles. *George Ripley: Transcendentalist and Utopian Socialist.* Athens, Ga., 1967.

Crowley, J. E. *This Sheba, Self: The Conceptualization of Economic Life in Eighteenth-Century America.* Baltimore, 1974.

Current, Richard N. *Daniel Webster and the Rise of National Conservatism.* Boston, 1955.

———. *John C. Calhoun.* New York, 1944.

Curry, Leonard P. *Blueprint for Modern America: Nonmilitary Legislation of the First Civil War Congress.* Nashville, Tenn., 1968.

Curry, Richard O., and Lawrence B. Goodheart, eds. *American Chameleon: Individualism in Trans-National Context.* Kent, Ohio, 1991.

Curtis, James C. *The Fox at Bay: Martin Van Buren and the Presidency, 1837–1841.* Lexington, Ky., 1970.

Dabney, William M., and Marion Dargan. *William Henry Drayton and the American Revolution.* Albuquerque, 1962.

Dalzell, Robert F., Jr. "The Rise of the Waltham-Lowell System and Some Thoughts on the Political Economy of Modernization in Ante-Bellum Massachusetts." *Perspectives in American History,* IX (1975), 227–68.

Danhof, Clarence H. *Change in Agriculture: The Northern United States, 1820–1870.* Cambridge, Mass., 1969.

Danziger, Sheldon, and Peter Gottschalk, eds. *Uneven Tides: Rising Inequality in America.* New York, 1993.

Dauer, Manning J. *The Adams Federalists.* Baltimore, 1953.

Davie, Maurice R. *William Graham Sumner.* New York, 1963.

Davis, David Brion. *The Problem of Slavery in the Age of Revolution, 1770–1823.* Ithaca, N.Y., 1975.

———. *The Slave Power Conspiracy and the Paranoid Style.* Baton Rouge, 1969.

Davis, Hugh. *Joshua Leavitt: Evangelical Abolitionist.* Baton Rouge, 1990.

Davis, Lance E., et al. *American Economic Growth: An Economist's History of the United States.* New York, 1972.

Davis, Pearce. *The Development of the American Glass Industry.* Cambridge, Mass., 1949.

Dawley, Alan. *Class and Community: The Industrial Revolution in Lynn.* Cambridge, Mass., 1976.

Deane, Phyllis. *The First Industrial Revolution.* 2nd ed. Cambridge, Eng., 1979.

Delano, Sterling F. *The Harbinger and New England Transcendentalism: A Portrait of Associationism in America.* Cranbury, N.J., 1983.

De Marchi, N. B. "The Success of Mill's *Principles.*" *History of Political Economy,* VI (1974), 119–57.

DeSantis, Vincent P. *The Shaping of Modern America, 1877–1916.* St. Louis, 1977.

Destler, Chester McArthur. *American Radicalism, 1865–1901: Essays and Documents.* New London, Conn., 1946.

Diggins, John Patrick. *The Lost Soul of American Politics: Virtue, Self-Interest, and the Foundations of Liberalism.* New York, 1984.

Dillon, Merton L. *The Abolitionists: The Growth of a Dissenting Minority.* De Kalb, Ill., 1974.

Ditz, Toby L. *Property and Kinship: Inheritance in Early Connecticut, 1750–1820.* Princeton, 1986.

Doan, Edward N. *The LaFollettes and the Wisconsin Idea.* New York, 1947.

Dodd, Edwin Merrick. *American Business Corporations Until 1860 with Special Reference to Massachusetts.* Cambridge, Mass., 1954.

Dodd, William E. *The Life of Nathaniel Macon.* Raleigh, N.C., 1903.

Dorfman, Joseph. *The Economic Mind in American Civilization.* 5 vols. 1946; rpr. New York, 1966.

Dublin, Thomas. "Rural-Urban Migrants in Industrial New England: The Case of Lynn, Massachusetts, in the Mid-Nineteenth Century." *Journal of American History,* LXXIII (1986), 623–44.

————. *Women at Work: The Transformation of Work and Community in Lowell, Massachusetts, 1826–1860.* New York, 1979.

DuBoff, Richard B. *Accumulation and Power: An Economic History of the United States.* Armonk, N.Y., 1989.

Dubofsky, Melvyn. *Industrialism and the American Worker, 1865–1920.* Arlington Heights, Ill., 1975.

DuBose, John Witherspoon. *The Life and Times of William Lowndes Yancey.* 2 vols. 1892; rpr. New York, 1942.

Dumond, Dwight Lowell. *Antislavery: The Crusade for Freedom in America.* Ann Arbor, 1961.

Durden, Robert F. *The Self-Inflicted Wound: Southern Politics in the Nineteenth Century.* Lexington, Ky., 1985.

Durrill, Wayne K. "Producing Poverty: Local Government and Economic Development in a New South County, 1874–1884." *Journal of American History,* LXXI (1985), 764–81.

Dykstra, Robert R. *Bright Radical Star: Black Freedom and White Supremacy on the Hawkeye Frontier.* Cambridge, Mass., 1993.

Easterlin, Richard A. "Farm Production and Income in Old and New Areas at Mid-Century." In *Essays in Nineteenth Century Economic History: The Old Northwest,* edited by David C. Klingaman and Richard K. Vedder. Athens, Ohio, 1975.

Easterlin, Richard A., George Alter, and Gretchen A. Condran. "Farm Families in

Old and New Areas: The Northern States in 1860." In *Family and Population in Nineteenth-Century America,* edited by Tamara K. Hareven and Maris A. Vinovskis. Princeton, 1978.

Eaton, Clement. *Jefferson Davis.* New York, 1977.

Egbert, Donald Drew, and Stow Persons, eds. *Socialism and American Life.* 2 vols. Princeton, 1952.

Elder, William. *A Memoir of Henry C. Carey.* Philadelphia, 1880.

Ellis, David M., ed. *The Frontier in American Development: Essays in Honor of Paul Wallace Gates.* Ithaca, N.Y., 1969.

Ellis, Joseph J. *Passionate Sage: The Character and Legacy of John Adams.* New York, 1993.

Ellis, Richard E. *The Union at Risk: Jacksonian Democracy, States' Rights, and the Nullification Crisis.* New York, 1987.

Ellis, Richard J. "Radical Lockeanism in American Political Culture." *Western Political Quarterly,* XLV (1992), 825–49.

Elster, Jon. *Making Sense of Marx.* Cambridge, Eng., 1985.

Ely, James W., Jr. *The Guardian of Every Other Right: A Constitutional History of Property Rights.* New York, 1992.

Engerman, Stanley L., and Robert E. Gallman, eds. *Long-Term Factors in American Economic Growth.* Chicago, 1986.

Ershkowitz, Herbert, and William G. Shade. "Consensus or Conflict? Political Behavior in the State Legislatures During the Jacksonian Era." *Journal of American History,* LVIII (1971), 591–621.

Etcheson, Nicole. *The Emerging Midwest: Upland Southerners and the Political Culture of the Old Northwest, 1787–1861.* Bloomington, 1996.

Evans, George Heberton, Jr. *Business Incorporations in the United States, 1800–1943.* New York, 1948.

Faler, Paul G. *Mechanics and Manufacturers in the Early Industrial Revolution: Lynn, Massachusetts, 1780–1860.* Albany, 1981.

Faust, Drew Gilpin. *James Henry Hammond and the Old South: A Design for Mastery.* Baton Rouge, 1982.

———. *A Sacred Circle: The Dilemma of the Intellectual in the Old South, 1840–1860.* Baltimore, 1977.

Feldstein, Martin, ed. *The American Economy in Transition.* Chicago, 1980.

Feller, Daniel. *The Public Lands in Jacksonian Politics.* Madison, 1984.

———. *The Jacksonian Promise: America, 1815–1840.* Baltimore, 1995.

Fellman, Michael. *The Unbounded Frame: Freedom and Community in Nineteenth Century American Utopianism.* Westport, Conn., 1973.

Ferguson, E. James. *The Power of the Purse: A History of American Public Finance, 1776–1790.* Chapel Hill, 1961.

Ferleger, Lou, ed. *Agriculture and National Development: Views on the Nineteenth Century.* Ames, Iowa, 1990.

Fessenden, Francis. *Life and Public Services of William Pitt Fessenden.* 2 vols. Boston, 1907.

Fetter, Frank W. "The Rise and Decline of Ricardian Economics." *History of Political Economy,* I (1969), 67–84.

Filene, Peter G. "An Obituary for 'The Progressive Movement.'" In *Twentieth-Century America: Recent Interpretations,* edited by Barton J. Bernstein and Allen J. Matusow. 2nd ed. New York, 1972.

Filler, Louis. *The Crusade Against Slavery, 1830–1860.* New York, 1960.

Fine, Sidney. *Laissez Faire and the General-Welfare State: A Study of Conflict in American Thought, 1865–1901.* Ann Arbor, 1956.

Fischer, David Hackett. *The Revolution of American Conservatism: The Federalist Party in the Era of Jeffersonian Democracy.* New York, 1965.

Fishlow, Albert. *American Railroads and the Transformation of the Ante-Bellum Economy.* Cambridge, Mass., 1965.

Fladeland, Betty. *James Gillespie Birney: Slaveholder to Abolitionist.* New York, 1955.

Fletcher, Stevenson Whitcomb. *Pennsylvania Agriculture and Country Life, 1840–1940.* 2 vols. Harrisburg, Pa., 1955.

Floud, R. C. "The Adolescence of American Engineering Competition, 1860–1900." *Economic History Review,* XXVII (1974), 57–71.

Fogel, Robert William. *Railroads and American Economic Growth: Essays in Econometric History.* Baltimore, 1964.

———. *Without Consent or Contract: The Rise and Fall of American Slavery.* New York, 1989.

Foner, Eric. "Abolitionism and the Labor Movement in Antebellum America." In *Anti-Slavery, Religion, and Reform: Essays in Memory of Roger Anstey,* edited by Christine Bolt and Seymour Drescher. Folkestone, Eng., 1980.

———. *Free Soil, Free Labor, Free Men: The Ideology of the Republican Party Before the Civil War.* 2nd ed. New York, 1995.

———. "The Idea of Free Labor in Nineteenth-Century America." Introduction to *Free Soil, Free Labor, Free Men: The Ideology of the Republican Party Before the Civil War.* 2nd ed. New York, 1995.

———. *Nothing But Freedom: Emancipation and Its Legacy.* Baton Rouge, 1983.

———. *Politics and Ideology in the Age of the Civil War.* New York, 1980.

———. "Politics, Ideology, and the Origins of the American Civil War." In *A Nation Divided: Problems and Issues of the Civil War and Reconstruction,* edited by George M. Fredrickson. Minneapolis, 1975.

———. *Reconstruction: America's Unfinished Revolution, 1863–1877.* New York, 1988.

———. *Tom Paine and Revolutionary America.* New York, 1976.

Foner, Philip S. *Labor and the American Revolution.* Westport, Conn., 1976.

Forbath, William E. "The Ambiguities of Free Labor: Labor and the Law in the Gilded Age." *Wisconsin Law Review* (1985), 767–817.

Forbes, Duncan. "Sceptical Whiggism, Commerce, and Liberty." In *Essays on Adam Smith,* edited by Andrew S. Skinner and Thomas Wilson. Oxford, 1975.

Ford, Lacy K. *Origins of Southern Radicalism: The South Carolina Upcountry, 1800–1860.* New York, 1988.

———. "Rednecks and Merchants: Economic Development and Social Tensions in the South Carolina Upcountry, 1865–1900." *Journal of American History,* LXXI (1984), 294–318.

Formisano, Ronald P. *The Transformation of Political Culture: Massachusetts Parties, 1790s–1840s.* New York, 1980.

Fox, Daniel M. *The Discovery of Abundance: Simon N. Patten and the Transformation of Social Theory.* Ithaca, N.Y., 1967.

Franklin, John Hope. *Reconstruction After the Civil War.* Chicago, 1961.

Fraysssé, Olivier. *Lincoln, Land, and Labor, 1809–60.* Translated by Sylvia Neely. Urbana, 1994.

Frederick, John H. *The Development of American Commerce.* New York, 1932.

Fredrickson, George M. *The Black Image in the White Mind: The Debate on Afro-American Character and Destiny, 1817–1914.* New York, 1971.

———, ed. *A Nation Divided: Problems and Issues of the Civil War and Reconstruction.* Minneapolis, 1975.

Freehling, William W. *Prelude to Civil War: The Nullification Controversy in South Carolina, 1816–1836.* New York, 1965.

Freyer, Tony A. *Producers Versus Capitalists: Constitutional Conflict in Antebellum America.* Charlottesville, 1994.

Friedman, Gerald. "Strike Success and Union Ideology: The United States and France, 1880–1914." *Journal of Economic History,* XLVIII (1988), 1–25.

Friedman, Lawrence J. "The Gerrit Smith Circle: Abolitionism in the Burned-Over District." *Civil War History,* XXVI (1980), 18–38.

Friedman, Lawrence M. "Law and Small Business in the United States: One Hundred Years of Struggle and Accommodation." In *Small Business in American Life,* edited by Stuart W. Bruchey. New York, 1980.

Friedman, Milton. With the assistance of Rose D. Friedman. *Capitalism and Freedom.* Chicago, 1962.

Frisch, Michael H., and Daniel J. Walkowitz, eds. *Working-Class America: Essays in Labor, Community, and American Society.* Urbana, 1983.

Frothingham, Octavius Brooks. *Gerrit Smith: A Biography.* New York, 1878.

———. *Theodore Parker: A Biography.* Boston, 1874.

Frothingham, Richard. *Life and Times of Joseph Warren.* 1865; rpr. New York, 1971.

Gabor, Andrea. *The Man Who Discovered Quality: How W. Edwards Deming Brought the Quality Revolution to America—The Stories of Ford, Xerox, and GM.* New York, 1990.

Galbraith, John Kenneth. *Economics in Perspective: A Critical History.* Boston, 1987.

Gallay, Alan. "The Origins of Slaveholders' Paternalism: George Whitefield, the Bryan Family, and the Great Awakening in the South." *Journal of Southern History,* LIII (1987), 369–94.

Gallman, Robert E. "The Agricultural Sector and Discontinuities." In *Essays in Nineteenth Century Economic History: The Old Northwest,* edited by David C. Klingaman and Richard K. Vedder. Athens, Ohio.

———. "Professor Pessen on the 'Egalitarian Myth.'" *Social Science History,* II (1978), 194–207.

———. "The United States Capital Stock in the Nineteenth Century." In *Long-Term Factors in American Economic Growth,* edited by Stanley L. Engerman and Robert E. Gallman. Chicago, 1986.

Galster, Augusta Emile. *The Labor Movement in the Shoe Industry with Special Reference to Philadelphia.* New York, 1924.

Gara, Larry. "Slavery and the Slave Power: A Crucial Distinction." *Civil War History,* XV (1969), 5–18.

Garraty, John A. *The New Commonwealth, 1877–1890.* New York, 1968.

Gates, Paul W. *The Farmer's Age: Agriculture, 1815–1860.* New York, 1960.

———. "Problems of Agricultural History." In *Farming in the New Nation: Interpreting American Agriculture, 1790–1840,* edited by Darwin P. Kelsey. Washington, D.C., 1972.

Gatrell, V. A. C. "Labour, Power, and the Size of Firms in Lancashire Cotton in the Second Quarter of the Nineteenth Century." *Economic History Review,* XXX (1977), 95–139.

Genovese, Eugene D. *The World the Slaveholders Made: Two Essays in Interpretation.* 2nd ed. Middletown, Conn., 1988.

Gerring, John. "A Chapter in the History of American Party Ideology: The Nineteenth-Century Democratic Party (1828–1892)." *Polity,* XXVI (1994), 729–68.

Gerteis, Louis S. *From Contraband to Freedman: Federal Policy Toward Southern Blacks, 1861–1865.* Westport, Conn., 1973.

———. *Morality and Utility in American Antislavery Reform.* Chapel Hill, 1987.

Ghent, Jocelyn Maynard, and Frederic Cople Jaher. "The Chicago Business Elite, 1830–1930: A Collective Biography." *Business History Review,* L (1976), 288–328.

Gienapp, William E. *The Origins of the Republican Party, 1852–1856.* New York, 1987.

———. "The Republican Party and the Slave Power." In *New Perspectives on Race and Slavery in America: Essays in Honor of Kenneth M. Stampp,* edited by Robert H. Abzug and Stephen E. Maizlish. Lexington, Ky., 1986.

Gilje, Paul A. *Rioting in America.* Bloomington, 1996.

Gillette, William. *Retreat from Reconstruction, 1869–1879.* Baton Rouge, 1980.

Ginger, Ray. "Labor in a Massachusetts Cotton Mill, 1853–60." *Business History Review,* XXVIII (1954), 67–91.

Glad, Paul W. *The Trumpet Soundeth: William Jennings Bryan and His Democracy.* Lincoln, 1960.

Glasco, Laurence. "Migration and Adjustment in the Nineteenth-Century City: Occupation, Property, and Household Structure of Native-Born Whites, Buffalo, New York, 1855." In *Family and Population in Nineteenth-Century America,* edited by Tamara Hareven and Maris A. Vinovskis. Princeton, 1978.

Glickstein, Jonathan A. *Concepts of Free Labor in Antebellum America.* New Haven, 1991.

———. " 'Poverty Is Not Slavery': Abolitionists and the Competitive Labor Market." In *Antislavery Reconsidered: New Perspectives on the Abolitionists,* edited by Lewis Perry and Michael Fellman. Baton Rouge, 1979.

Glymph, Thavolia, and John J. Kushma, eds. *Essays on the Postbellum Southern Economy.* College Station, Tex., 1985.

Going, Charles Buxton. *David Wilmot, Free-Soiler: A Biography of the Great Advocate of the Wilmot Proviso.* New York, 1924.

Gooch, G. P. *English Democratic Ideas in the 17th Century.* 1898; rpr. New York, 1959.

Goodheart, Lawrence B. *Abolitionist, Actuary, Atheist: Elizur Wright and the Reform Impulse.* Kent, Ohio, 1990.

Goodman, Paul. "Ethics and Enterprise: The Values of a Boston Elite, 1800–1860." *American Quarterly,* XVIII (1966), 437–51.

———. *Towards a Christian Republic: Antimasonry and the Great Transition in New England, 1826–1836.* New York, 1988.

Goodwin, Craufurd D. W. "Marginalism Moves to the New World." In *The Marginal Revolution in Economics: Interpretation and Evaluation,* edited by R. D. Collison Black, A. W. Coats, and Craufurd D. W. Goodwin. Durham, N.C., 1973.

Goodwyn, Lawrence. *The Populist Moment: A Short History of the Agrarian Revolt in America.* New York, 1978.

Gordon, Barry. "Criticism of Ricardian Views on Value and Distribution in the British Periodicals, 1820–1850." *Journal of Political Economy,* I (1969), 370–87.

Gordon, H. Scott. "The Wage-Fund Controversy: The Second Round." *History of Political Economy,* V (1973), 14–35.

Gorham, George C. *Life and Public Services of Edwin M. Stanton.* 2 vols. Boston, 1899.

Gorn, Elliott J. " 'Gouge and Bite, Pull Hair and Scratch': The Social Significance of Fighting in the Southern Backcountry." *American Historical Review,* XC (1985), 18–43.

Gould, J. P., and C. E. Ferguson. *Microeconomic Theory.* 5th ed. Homewood, Ill., 1980.

Gould, Lewis L. "The Republican Search for a National Majority." In *The Gilded Age,* edited by H. Wayne Morgan. 2nd ed. Syracuse, 1970.

Grampp, William D. "Adam Smith and the American Revolutionists." *History of Political Economy,* XI (1979), 179–91.

———. "A Re-Examination of Jeffersonian Economics." *Southern Economic Journal,* XII (1946), 263–82.

Greenberg, Brian. *Worker and Community: Response to Industrialization in a Nineteenth-Century American City, Albany, New York, 1850–1884.* Albany, 1985.

Greene, Jack P. *The Intellectual Construction of America: Exceptionalism and Identity from 1492 to 1800.* Chapel Hill, 1993.

———. "Society, Ideology, and Politics: An Analysis of the Political Culture of Mid-Eighteenth-Century Virginia." In *Society, Freedom, and Conscience: The American Revolution in Virginia, Massachusetts, and New York,* edited by Richard M. Jellison. New York, 1976.

Griffin, Clifford S. *The Ferment of Reform, 1830–1860.* New York, 1967.

———. "Religious Benevolence as Social Control, 1815–1860." *Mississippi Valley Historical Review,* XLIV (1957), 423–44.

Griffin, Clifford S., and Sally Griffin. "Small Business and Occupational Mobility in Mid-Nineteenth-Century Poughkeepsie." In *Small Business in American Life,* edited by Stuart W. Bruchey. New York, 1980.

Grimsted, David. "Ante-Bellum Labor: Violence, Strike, and Communal Arbitration." *Journal of Social History,* XIX (1985), 5–28.

Grob, Gerald N. "The Political System and Social Policy in the Nineteenth Century: Legacy of the Revolution." *Mid-America,* LVIII (1976), 5–19.

———. *Workers and Utopia: A Study of Ideological Conflict in the American Labor Movement, 1865–1900.* Evanston, 1961.

Gross, Robert A. "Culture and Cultivation: Agriculture and Society in Thoreau's Concord." *Journal of American History,* LXIX (1982), 42–61.

Guarneri, Carl J. *The Utopian Alternative: Fourierism in Nineteenth-Century America.* Ithaca, N.Y., 1991.

Gunderson, Gerald. "The Origins of the American Civil War." *Journal of Economic History,* XXXIV (1974), 915–50.

Gunn, L. Ray. *The Decline of Authority: Public Economic Policy and Political Development in New York State, 1800–1860.* Ithaca, N.Y., 1988.

Gutman, Herbert G. *Work, Culture and Society in Industrializing America: Essays in American Working-Class and Social History.* New York, 1977.

———. "Work, Culture and Society in Industrializing America, 1815–1919." *American Historical Review,* LXXVIII (1973), 531–88.

———. "Workers' Search for Power." In *The Gilded Age,* edited by H. Wayne Morgan. 2nd ed. Syracuse, 1970.

Hackney, Sheldon. *Populism to Progressivism in Alabama.* Princeton, 1969.

Hahn, Steven. *The Roots of Southern Populism: Yeoman Farmers and the Transformation of the Georgia Upcountry, 1850–1890.* New York, 1983.

Haites, Erik F., James Mak, and Gary M. Walton. *Western River Transportation: The Era of Early Internal Development, 1810–1860.* Baltimore, 1975.

Halberstam, David. *The Reckoning.* New York, 1986.

Hamlin, Charles Eugene. *The Life and Times of Hannibal Hamlin.* Cambridge, Mass., 1899.

Hammond, Bray. *Banks and Politics in America from the Revolution to the Civil War.* Princeton, 1957.

Hammond, J. L., and Barbara Hammond. *The Village Labourer, 1760–1832: A Study in the Government of England Before the Reform Bill.* 1913; rpr. New York, 1967.

Hancock, Harold B. "Delaware Furnituremaking, 1850–1870: Transition to the Machine Age." *Delaware History,* XVII (1977), 250–94.

Handler, Edward. *America and Europe in the Political Thought of John Adams.* Cambridge, Mass., 1964.

Handlin, Lilian. *George Bancroft: The Intellectual as Democrat.* New York, 1984.

Hanley, Thomas O'Brien. *Charles Carroll of Carrollton: The Making of a Revolutionary Gentleman.* Washington, D.C., 1970.

Hareven, Tamara K., and Maris A. Vinovskis, eds. *Family and Population in Nineteenth-Century America.* Princeton, 1978.

Harper, Ida Husted. *The Life and Work of Susan B. Anthony, Including Public Addresses, Her Own Letters, and Many from Her Contemporaries During Fifty Years.* 3 vols. Indianapolis, 1898–1908.

Harris, Donald J. *Capital Accumulation and Income Distribution.* Stanford, 1978.

Harrison, J. F. C. *Robert Owen and the Owenites in Britain and America: The Quest for the New Moral World.* London, 1969.

Harrold, Stanley G. *Gamaliel Bailey and Antislavery Union.* Kent, Ohio, 1986.

Haw, James A. "Samuel Chase's 'Objections to the Federal Government.'" *Maryland Historical Magazine,* LXXVI (1981), 272–85.

Haynes, Fred Emory. *James Baird Weaver.* Iowa City, 1919.

Heilbroner, Robert L. *The Worldly Philosophers: The Lives, Times, and Ideas of the Great Economic Thinkers.* 5th ed. New York, 1961.

Henig, Gerald S. *Henry Winter Davis: Antebellum and Civil War Congressman from Maryland.* New York, 1973.

Henretta, James A. *The Origins of American Capitalism: Collected Essays.* Boston, 1991.

Herreshoff, David. *American Disciples of Marx: From the Age of Jackson to the Progressive Era.* Detroit, 1967.

Hesseltine, William B. *Lincoln's Plan of Reconstruction.* Tuscaloosa, 1960.

Hibbard, Benjamin Horace. *A History of the Public Land Policies.* New York, 1939.

Hicks, John D. *The Populist Revolt: A History of the Farmers' Alliance and the People's Party.* Minneapolis, 1931.

Hicks, John D., George E. Mowry, and Robert E. Burke. *The American Nation: A History of the United States from 1865 to the Present.* 1933; rpr. Boston, 1963.

Hietala, Thomas R. *Manifest Design: Anxious Aggrandizement in Late Jacksonian America.* Ithaca, N.Y., 1985.

Hirsch, Susan E. *Roots of the American Working Class: The Industrialization of Crafts in Newark, 1800–1860.* Philadelphia, 1978.

Hirschman, Albert O. *The Passions and the Interests: Political Arguments for Capitalism Before Its Triumph.* Princeton, 1977.

Hirshson, Stanley P. *Farewell to the Bloody Shirt: Northern Republicans and the Southern Negro, 1877–1893.* Bloomington, 1962.

Hite, James C., and Ellen J. Hall. "The Reactionary Evolution of Economic Thought in Antebellum Virginia." *Virginia Magazine of History and Biography,* LXXX (1972), 476–88.

Hoagland, Henry. "Humanitarianism (1840–1860)." In John R. Commons et al., *History of Labour in the United States.* New York, 1921.

Hochschild, Jennifer L. *What's Fair? American Beliefs About Distributive Justice.* Cambridge, Mass., 1981.

Hoerder, Dirk. *Crowd Action in Revolutionary Massachusetts, 1765–1780.* New York, 1977.

Hofstadter, Richard. *The Progressive Historians: Turner, Beard, Parrington.* New York, 1968.

———. *Social Darwinism in American Thought.* Rev. ed. Boston, 1955.

Hollander, Samuel. *The Economics of Adam Smith.* Toronto, 1973.

———. *The Economics of David Ricardo.* Toronto, 1979.

Holloway, Mark. *Heavens on Earth: Utopian Communities in America, 1680–1880.* London, 1951.

Holt, Michael F. *The Political Crisis of the 1850s.* New York, 1978.

Holzman, Robert S. *Adapt or Perish: The Life of General Roger A. Pryor, C. S. A.* Hamden, Conn., 1976.

Horowitz, Robert F. *The Great Impeacher: A Political Biography of James M. Ashley.* New York, 1979.

Horton, James Oliver, and Lois E. Horton. *In Hope of Liberty: Culture, Community, and Protest Among Northern Free Blacks, 1700–1860.* New York, 1997.

Horwitz, Morton J. *The Transformation of American Law, 1780–1860.* Cambridge, Mass., 1977.

Hoselitz, Bert F., et al. *Theories of Economic Growth.* Glencoe, Ill., 1960.

Hounshell, David A. *From the American System to Mass Production, 1800–1932: The Development of Manufacturing Technology in the United States.* Baltimore, 1984.

Hovencamp, Herbert. *Enterprise and American Law, 1836–1937.* Cambridge, Mass., 1991.

Howe, Daniel Walker. *The Political Culture of the American Whigs.* Chicago, 1979.

Howe, John R., Jr. *The Changing Political Thought of John Adams.* Princeton, 1966.

Hudson, Michael. *Economics and Technology in 19th Century American Thought: The Neglected American Economists.* New York, 1975.

Hughes, Jonathan R. T. *American Economic History.* 3rd ed. Glenview, Ill., 1990.

Hunt, E. K. "Marx's Theory of Property and Alienation." In *Theories of Property: Aristotle to the Present,* edited by Anthony Parel and Thomas Flanagan. Waterloo, Canada, 1979.

Hunt, H. Draper. *Hannibal Hamlin of Maine: Lincoln's First Vice-President.* Syracuse, 1969.

Hurst, James Willard. *Law and Social Order in the United States.* Ithaca, N.Y., 1977.

———. *Law and the Conditions of Freedom in the Nineteenth-Century United States.* Madison, 1956.

———. *The Legitimacy of the Business Corporation in the Law of the United States, 1780–1970.* Charlottesville, 1970.

Huston, James L. "Abolitionists and an Errant Economy: The Panic of 1857 and Abolitionist Economic Ideas." *Mid-America,* LXV (1983), 15–27.

———. "The American Revolutionaries, the Political Economy of Aristocracy, and the American Concept of the Distribution of Wealth, 1765–1900." *American Historical Review,* XCVIII (1993), 1079–1105.

———. "Economic Change and Political Realignment in Antebellum Pennsylvania." *Pennsylvania Magazine of History and Biography,* CXIII (1989), 347–95.

———. "The Experiential Basis of the Northern Antislavery Impulse." *Journal of Southern History,* LVI (1990), 609–40.

———. "Facing an Angry Labor: The American Public Interprets the Shoemakers' Strike of 1860." *Civil War History,* XXVIII (1982), 197–212.

———. *The Panic of 1857 and the Coming of the Civil War.* Baton Rouge, 1987.

———. "A Political Response to Industrialism: The Republican Embrace of Protectionist Labor Doctrines." *Journal of American History,* LXX (1983), 35–57.

———. "Virtue Besieged: Virtue, Equality, and the General Welfare in the Tariff Debates of the 1820s." *Journal of the Early Republic,* XIV (1994), 523–47.

Hutchison, T. W. "The 'Marginal Revolution' and the Decline and Fall of English Classical Political Economy." In *The Marginal Revolution in Economics: Interpretation and Evaluation,* edited by R. D. Collison Black, A. W. Coates, and Craufurd D. W. Goodwin. Durham, N.C., 1973.

Jacoby, Sanford M. *Employing Bureaucracy: Managers, Unions, and the Transformation of Work in American Industry, 1900–1945.* New York, 1985.

James, John A. *Money and Capital Markets in Postbellum America.* Princeton, 1978.

James, R. Warren. "The Life and Work of John Rae." *Canadian Journal of Economics and Political Science,* XVII (1951), 141–63.

Jameson, J. Franklin. *The American Revolution Considered as a Social Movement.* 1926; rpr. Princeton, 1967.

Jaynes, Gerald David. *Branches Without Roots: Genesis of the Black Working Class in the American South, 1862–1882.* New York, 1986.

Jellison, Richard M., ed. *Society, Freedom, and Conscience: The American Revolution in Virginia, Massachusetts, and New York.* New York, 1976.

Jenkins, William Sumner. *Pro-Slavery Thought in the Old South.* Chapel Hill, 1935.

Jensen, Merrill. *The Founding of a Nation: A History of the American Revolution, 1763– 1776.* New York, 1968.

Jensen, Richard J. *The Winning of the Midwest: Social and Political Conflict, 1888– 1896.* Chicago, 1971.

Johannsen, Robert W. *Stephen A. Douglas.* New York, 1973.

———. *To the Halls of the Montezumas: The Mexican War in the American Imagination.* New York, 1985.

Johnson, E. A. J. *American Economic Thought in the Seventeenth Century.* 1932; rpr. New York, 1961.

———. *Predecessors of Adam Smith: The Growth of British Economic Thought.* New York, 1937.

Johnson, Emory R., T. W. Van Metre, G. G. Huebner, and D. S. Hanchett. *History of Domestic and Foreign Commerce of the United States.* 2 vols. Washington, D.C., 1915.

Jones, Alice Hanson. *Wealth of a Nation to Be: The American Colonies on the Eve of the Revolution.* New York, 1980.

Jones, Charles Henry. *The Life and Public Services of J. Glancy Jones.* 2 vols. Philadelphia, 1910.

Jones, Maldwyn Allen. *American Immigration.* Chicago, 1960.

Josephson, Matthew. *The Robber Barons: The Great American Capitalists, 1861–1901.* 1934; rpr. New York, 1962.

Kaldor, Nicholas. "Alternative Theories of Distribution." *Review of Economic Studies,* XXIII (1955–56), 83–100.

Kasson, John F. *Civilizing the Machine: Technology and Republican Values in America, 1776–1900.* New York, 1976.

Katz, Stanley N. "Republicanism and the Law of Inheritance in the American Revolutionary Era." *Michigan Law Review,* LXXVI (1977), 1–29.

———. "Thomas Jefferson and the Right to Property in Revolutionary America." *Journal of Law and Economics,* XIX (1976), 467–88.

Kauder, Emil. *A History of Marginal Utility Theory.* Princeton, 1965.

Kaufman, Allen. *Capitalism, Slavery, and Republican Values: Antebellum Political Economists, 1819–1848*. Austin, 1982.

Keller, Morton. *Affairs of State: Public Life in Late Nineteenth Century America*. Cambridge, Mass., 1977.

———. "The Pluralist State: American Economic Regulation in Comparative Perspective, 1900–1930." In *Regulation in Perspective: Historical Essays,* edited by Thomas K. McCraw. Boston, 1981.

———. "Power and Rights: Two Centuries of American Constitutionalism." *Journal of American History,* LXXIV (1987), 675–94.

Kelsey, Darwin P., ed. *Farming in the New Nation: Interpreting American Agriculture, 1790–1840*. Washington, D.C., 1972.

Kennedy, Susan Estabrook. *If All We Did Was to Weep at Home: A History of White Working-Class Women in America*. Bloomington, 1979.

Kerber, Linda K. "The Republican Ideology of the Revolutionary Generation." *American Quarterly,* XXXVII (1985), 474–95.

Kessler-Harris, Alice. *Out to Work: A History of Wage-Earning Women in the United States*. New York, 1982.

Ketcham, Ralph. *From Colony to Country: The Revolution in American Thought, 1750–1820*. New York, 1974.

Keyssar, Alexander. *Out of Work: The First Century of Unemployment in Massachusetts*. Cambridge, Eng., 1986.

Kiker, B. F. "The Historical Roots of the Concept of Human Capital." In *Human Capital Formation and Manpower Development,* edited by Ronald A. Wykstra. New York, 1971.

Kirkland, Edward Chase. *Industry Comes of Age: Business, Labor and Public Policy, 1860–1897*. New York, 1961.

Klein, Milton M., Richard D. Brown, and John B. Hench, eds. *The Republican Synthesis Revisited: Essays in Honor of George Athan Billias*. Worcester, Mass., 1992.

Kleppner, Paul. *The Third Electoral System, 1853–1892: Parties, Voters, and Political Cultures*. Chapel Hill, 1979.

Kleppner, Paul, et al. *The Evolution of American Electoral Systems*. Westport, Conn., 1981.

Klingaman, David C. "Individual Wealth in Ohio in 1860." In *Essays in Nineteenth Century Economic History: The Old Northwest,* edited by David C. Klingaman and Richard K. Vedder. Athens, Ohio, 1975.

Klingaman, David C., and Richard K. Vedder, eds. *Essays in Nineteenth Century Economic History: The Old Northwest*. Athens, Ohio, 1975.

Kloppenberg, James T. "The Virtues of Liberalism: Christianity, Republicanism, and Ethics in Early American Political Discourse." *Journal of American History,* LXXIV (1987), 9–33.

Knights, Peter R. *The Plain People of Boston, 1830–1860: A Study in City Growth.* New York, 1971.

Kohl, Lawrence Frederick. *The Politics of Individualism: Parties and the American Character in the Jacksonian Era.* New York, 1989.

Konzen, Kathleen Neils. "Immigrants in Nineteenth-Century Agricultural History." In *Agriculture and National Development: Views on the Nineteeth Century,* edited by Lou Ferleger. Ames, Iowa, 1990.

Kornblith, Gary J., and John M. Murrin. "Who Shall Rule at Home?: The Making and Unmaking of an American Ruling Class." In *Beyond the American Revolution: Explorations in the History of American Radicalism,* edited by Alfred F. Young. De Kalb, Ill., 1993.

Kousser, J. Morgan, and James M. McPherson, eds. *Region, Race, and Reconstruction: Essays in Honor of C. Vann Woodward.* New York, 1982.

Kramnick, Isaac. "Republican Revisionism Revisited." *American Historical Review,* LXXXVII (1982), 629–64.

———. *Republicanism and Bourgeois Radicalism: Political Ideology in Late Eighteenth-Century England and America.* Ithaca, N.Y., 1990.

Kraut, Alan M., ed. *Crusaders and Compromisers: Essays on the Relationship of the Antislavery Struggle to the Antebellum Party System.* Westport, Conn., 1983.

Kuhlmann, Charles Byron. *The Development of the Flour-Milling Industry in the United States, with Special Reference to the Industry in Minneapolis.* Boston, 1929.

Kulikoff, Allan. *The Agrarian Origins of American Capitalism.* Charlottesville, 1992.

Kushner, Howard I., and Anne Hummel Sherrill. *John Milton Hay: The Union of Poetry and Politics.* Boston, 1977.

Kutler, Stanley I. *Privilege and Creative Destruction: The Charles River Bridge Case.* Philadelphia, 1971.

Lamoreaux, Naomi R. *The Great Merger Movement in American Business, 1895–1904.* Cambridge, Eng., 1985.

Lapati, Americo D. *Orestes A. Brownson.* New Haven, 1965.

Latner, Richard B. *The Presidency of Andrew Jackson: White House Politics, 1829–1837.* Athens, Ga., 1979.

Laurie, Bruce. *Artisans into Workers: Labor in Nineteenth Century America.* New York, 1988.

———. *Working People of Philadelphia, 1800–1850.* Philadelphia, 1980.

Laurie, Bruce, Theodore Hershberg, and George Alter. "Immigrants and Industry: The Philadelphia Experience, 1850–1880." *Journal of Social History,* IX (1975), 219–48.

Lazonick, William. *Business Organization and the Myth of the Market Economy.* Cambridge, Eng., 1991.

Lears, T. J. Jackson. "The Concept of Cultural Hegemony: Problems and Possibilities." *American Historical Review,* XC (1985), 567–93.

Lebergott, Stanley. *Manpower in Economic Growth: The American Record Since 1800.* New York, 1964.

Lebsock, Suzanne. *The Free Women of Petersburg: Status and Culture in a Southern Town, 1784–1860.* New York, 1984.

Leiman, Melvin M. *Jacob N. Cardozo: Economic Thought in the Antebellum South.* New York, 1966.

Lemon, James T. *The Best Poor Man's Country: A Geographical Study of Early Southeastern Pennsylvania.* Baltimore, 1972.

Lerner, Gerda. *The Grimké Sisters from South Carolina: Pioneers for Woman's Rights and Abolition.* New York, 1967.

———. "The Lady and the Mill Girl: Changes in the Status of Women in the Age of Jackson, 1800–1840." In *A Heritage of Her Own: Toward a New Social History of American Women,* edited by Nancy F. Cott and Elizabeth H. Pleck. New York, 1979.

Lerner, Ralph. "Commerce and Character: The Anglo-American as New-Model Man." *William and Mary Quarterly,* XXXVI (1984), 3–26.

Letwin, William. "The Economic Policy of the Constitution." In *Liberty, Property, and the Foundations of the American Constitution,* edited by Ellen Frankel Paul and Howard Dickman. Albany, 1989.

Levesque, George. "Boston's Black Brahmin: Dr. John S. Rock." *Civil War History,* XXVI (1980), 326–46.

Levy, David. "Ricardo and the Iron Law: A Correction of the Record." *History of Political Economy,* VIII (1976), 235–51.

Levy, Frank. *Dollars and Dreams: The Changing American Income Distribution.* New York, 1987.

Lewis, Walker. *Without Fear or Favor: A Biography of Chief Justice Roger Brooke Taney.* Boston, 1965.

Licht, Walter. *Industrializing America: The Nineteenth Century.* Baltimore, 1995.

———. *Working for the Railroad: The Organization of Work in the Nineteenth Century.* Princeton, 1983.

Lindbeck, Assar. *The Political Economy of the New Left: An Outsider's View.* 2nd ed. New York, 1977.

Lindert, Peter H. "Who Owned Victorian England? The Debate over Landed Wealth and Inequality." *Agricultural History,* LXI (1987), 25–51.

Lindstrom, Diane. *Economic Development in the Philadelphia Region, 1810–1950.* Philadelphia, 1978.

Link, Arthur S. *Woodrow Wilson and the Progressive Era, 1910–1917.* New York, 1954.

Lipin, Lawrence M. *Producers, Proletarians, and Politicians: Workers and Party Politics in Evansville and New Albany, Indiana, 1850–87.* Urbana, 1994.

Litwack, Leon F. *North of Slavery: The Negro in the Free States, 1790–1860.* Chicago, 1961.

Livesay, Harold C. *Andrew Carnegie and the Rise of Big Business.* Boston, 1975.

———. "Lilliputians in Brobdingnag: Small Business in Late-Nineteenth-Century America." In *Small Business in American Life,* edited by Stuart W. Bruchey. New York, 1980.

Livesay, Harold C., and Glenn Porter. "The Financial Role of Merchants in the Development of U.S. Manufacturing." *Explorations in Economic History,* IX (1971), 63–87.

Lowenthal, David. *George Perkins Marsh: Versatile Vermonter.* New York, 1958.

Lustig, R. Jeffrey. *Corporate Liberalism: The Origins of Modern American Political Theory, 1890–1920.* Berkeley, 1982.

McCaughey, Elizabeth P. *From Loyalist to Founding Father: The Political Odyssey of William Samuel Johnson.* New York, 1980.

McClelland, Peter D. *The American Search for Economic Justice.* Cambridge, Eng., 1990.

McCormick, Richard L. *The Party Period and Public Policy: American Politics from the Age of Jackson to the Progressive Era.* New York, 1986.

McCormick, Richard P. *The Second American Party System: Party Formation in the Jacksonian Era.* New York, 1966.

McCoy, Drew R. *The Elusive Republic: Political Economy in Jeffersonian America.* Chapel Hill, 1980.

McCraw, Thomas K. "Rethinking the Trust Question." In *Regulation in Perspective: Historical Essays,* edited by Thomas K. McCraw. Boston, 1981.

———, ed. *Regulation in Perspective: Historical Essays.* Boston, 1981.

McCusker, John J., and Russell R. Menard. *The Economy of British America, 1607–1789: Needs and Opportunities for Study.* Chapel Hill, 1985.

McDonald, Forrest. *Novus Ordo Seclorum: The Intellectual Origins of the Constitution.* Lawrence, Kans., 1985.

McElroy, James L. "Social Control and Romantic Reform in Antebellum America: The Case of Rochester, New York." *New York History,* LVIII (1977), 17–46.

McFaul, John M. *The Politics of Jacksonian Finance.* Ithaca, N.Y., 1972.

McGerr, Michael E. *The Decline of Popular Politics: The American North, 1865–1928.* New York, 1986.

McGrain, John W. " 'Good Bye Old Burr': The Roller Mill Revolution in Maryland, 1882." *Maryland Historical Magazine,* LXXVII (1982), 154–71.

McIlwain, Charles Howard. *The American Revolution: A Constitutional Interpretation.* New York, 1923.

McInerney, Daniel J. *The Fortunate Heirs of Freedom: Abolition and Republican Thought.* Lincoln, 1994.

Mack, Edward C. *Peter Cooper: Citizen of New York.* New York, 1949.

McKivigan, John R. *The War Against Proslavery Religion: Abolitionism and the Northern Churches, 1830–1865.* Ithaca, N.Y., 1984.

McLaughlin, Andrew C. *Lewis Cass.* Boston, 1919.

McManus, Edgar J. *A History of Negro Slavery in New York.* Syracuse, 1966.

McNall, Neil Adams. *An Agricultural History of the Genesee Valley, 1790–1860.* Philadelphia, 1952.

Macpherson, C. B. *"The Rise and Fall of Economic Justice" and Other Papers.* Oxford, 1985.

Magdol, Edward. *A Right to the Land: Essays on the Freedmen's Community.* Westport, Conn., 1977.

Maier, Pauline. *The Old Revolutionaries: Political Lives in the Age of Samuel Adams.* New York, 1980.

Main, Jackson Turner. *The Antifederalists: Critics of the Constitution, 1781–1788.* New York, 1961.

———. *The Social Structure of Revolutionary America.* Princeton, 1965.

———. *The Sovereign States, 1775–1783.* New York, 1973.

Maizlish, Stephen E. "The Meaning of Nativism and the Crisis of the Union: The Know-Nothing Movement in the Antebellum North." In *Essays on American Antebellum Politics, 1840–1860,* edited by Stephen E. Maizlish and John J. Kushma. College Station, Tex., 1982.

———. *The Triumph of Sectionalism: The Transformation of Ohio Politics, 1844–1856.* Kent, Ohio, 1983.

Maizlish, Stephen E., and John J. Kushma, eds. *Essays on American Antebellum Politics, 1840–1860.* College Station, Tex., 1982.

Malone, Dumas. *Jefferson and His Time.* 6 vols. Boston, 1948–81.

Mandel, Bernard. *Labor Free and Slave: Workingmen and the Anti-Slavery Movement in the United States.* New York, 1955.

Mandelker, Ira L. *Religion, Society, and Utopia in Nineteenth-Century America.* Amherst, Mass., 1984.

Mangold, George Benjamin. *The Labor Argument in the American Protective Tariff Discussion.* 1906; rpr. New York, 1971.

Mantoux, Paul. *The Industrial Revolution in the Eighteenth Century: An Outline of the Beginnings of the Modern Factory System in England.* Translated by Marjorie Vernon. 2nd ed. New York, 1927.

Martin, Albro. *Railroads Triumphant: The Growth, Rejection and Rebirth of a Vital American Force.* New York, 1992.

Martin, James J. *Men Against the State: The Expositors of Individualist Anarchism in America, 1827–1908.* De Kalb, Ill., 1953.

Martin, James Kirby. *In the Course of Human Events: An Interpretive Exploration of the American Revolution.* Arlington Heights, Ill., 1979.

Martin, Waldo E., Jr. *The Mind of Frederick Douglass.* Chapel Hill, 1984.

Mathias, Peter. *The First Industrial Nation: An Economic History of Britain, 1700–1914.* 2nd ed. London, 1983.

Matson, Cathy, and Peter Onuf. "Toward a Republican Empire: Interest and Ideology in Revolutionary America." *American Quarterly,* XXXVII (1985), 496–531.

Matthews, Jean V. *Rufus Choate: The Law and Civic Virtue.* Philadelphia, 1980.

———. *Toward a New Society: American Thought and Culture, 1800–1830.* Boston, 1991.

Matthews, Richard K. *The Radical Politics of Thomas Jefferson: A Revisionist View.* Lawrence, Kans., 1984.

Maxwell, Nan L. *Income Inequality in the United States, 1947–1985.* New York, 1990.

Mayes, Edward. *Lucius Q. C. Lamar: His Life, Times, and Speeches, 1825–1893.* 2nd ed. Nashville, Tenn., 1896.

Mayfield, John. *Rehearsal for Republicanism: Free Soil and the Politics of Antislavery.* Port Washington, N.Y., 1980.

Meek, Ronald L. "Marginalism and Marxism." In *The Marginal Revolution in Economics: Interpretation and Evaluation,* edited by R. D. Collison Black, A. W. Coates, and Craufurd D. W. Goodwin. Durham, N.C., 1973.

———. *Studies in the Labour Theory of Value.* New York, 1956.

Mende, Elsie Porter. *An American Soldier and Diplomat: Horace Porter.* New York, 1927.

Meyers, Marvin. *The Jacksonian Persuasion: Politics and Belief.* New York, 1957.

Middlekauff, Robert. *The Glorious Cause: The American Revolution, 1763–1789.* New York, 1982.

Miller, Douglas T. *The Birth of Modern America, 1820–1850.* New York, 1970.

Miller, Gary J. *Managerial Dilemmas: The Political Economy of Hierarchy.* Cambridge, Eng., 1992.

Miller, Helen Hill. *George Mason: Gentleman Revolutionary.* Chapel Hill, 1975.

Miller, John C. *Alexander Hamilton: Portrait in Paradox.* New York, 1959.

———. *The Federalist Era, 1789–1801.* New York, 1960.

———. "Hamilton: Democracy and Monarchy." In *Alexander Hamilton: A Profile,* edited by Jacob E. Cooke. New York, 1967.

———. *Origins of the American Revolution.* Boston, 1943.

Mintz, Steven. *Moralists and Modernizers: America's Pre–Civil War Reformers.* Baltimore, 1995.

Mintz, Steven, and Susan Kellogg. *Domestic Revolutions: A Social History of American Family Life.* New York, 1988.

Mitchell, Betty L. *Edmund Ruffin: A Biography.* Bloomington, 1981.

Mitchell, Broadus. *Alexander Hamilton: A Concise Biography.* New York, 1976.

Modell, John. "The Peopling of a Working-Class Ward: Reading, Pennsylvania, 1850." *Journal of Social History,* V (1971), 71–95.

Mohr, James C., ed. *Radical Republicans in the North: State Politics During Reconstruction.* Baltimore, 1976.

Mokyr, Joel, ed. *The Economics of the Industrial Revolution.* Totowa, N.J., 1985.

Montgomery, David. *Beyond Equality: Labor and the Radical Republicans, 1862–1872.* New York, 1967.

———. *Citizen Worker: The Experience of Workers in the United States with Democracy and the Free Market During the Nineteenth Century.* New York, 1993.

———. *Workers' Control in America: Studies in the History of Work, Technology, and Labor Struggles.* Cambridge, Eng., 1979.

———. "Workers' Control of Machine Production in the Nineteenth Century." *Labor History,* XVII (1976), 485–509.

Moore, Glover. *The Missouri Controversy, 1819–1821.* 1953; rpr. Lexington, Ky., 1966.

Morais, Herbert M. "The Sons of Liberty in New York." In *The Era of the American Revolution. Studies Inscribed to Evarts Boutell Greene,* edited by Richard B. Morris. New York, 1939.

Morgan, Edmund S. *American Slavery, American Freedom: The Ordeal of Colonial Virginia.* New York, 1975.

———. *The Challenge of the American Revolution.* New York, 1976.

———. *The Gentle Puritan: A Life of Ezra Stiles, 1727–1795.* New Haven, 1962.

Morgan, H. Wayne. *From Hayes to McKinley: National Party Politics, 1877–1896.* Syracuse, 1969.

———. *William McKinley and His America.* Syracuse, 1963.

———, ed. *The Gilded Age.* 2nd ed. Syracuse, 1970.

Morison, Samuel Eliot. *The Life and Letters of Harrison Gray Otis, Federalist, 1765–1848.* 2 vols. Boston, 1913.

Morris, Richard B. "Alexander Hamilton After Two Centuries." In *Alexander Hamilton: A Profile,* edited by Jacob E. Cooke. New York, 1967.

———. *The American Revolution Reconsidered.* New York, 1967.

———. *Government and Labor in Early America.* New York, 1946.

———. *The Era of the American Revolution: Studies Inscribed to Evarts Boutell Greene.* New York, 1939.

———, ed. *The American Revolution, 1763–1783: A Bicentennial Collection.* Columbia, S.C., 1970.

Morris, Thomas D. *Southern Slavery and the Law, 1619–1860.* Chapel Hill, 1996.

Morrison, Rodney J. *Henry C. Carey and American Economic Development.* Philadelphia, 1986.

Morrow, Glenn R. *The Ethical and Economic Theories of Adam Smith.* 1923; rpr. New York, 1969.

Mushkat, Jerome. *Fernando Wood: A Political Biography.* Kent, Ohio, 1990.

Namier, Lewis. *England in the Age of the American Revolution.* 2nd ed. London, 1961.

Nash, Gary B. *Forging Freedom: The Formation of Philadelphia's Black Community, 1720–1840.* Cambridge, Mass., 1988.

———. *Red, White, and Black: The Peoples of Early America.* 2nd ed. Englewood Cliffs, N.J., 1982.

———. *The Urban Crucible: Social Change, Political Consciousness, and the Origins of the American Revolution.* Cambridge, Mass., 1979.

Nedelsky, Jennifer. *Private Property and the Limits of American Constitutionalism: The Madisonian Framework and Its Legacy.* Chicago, 1990.

Neill, Charles Patrick. *Daniel Raymond: An Early Chapter in the History of Economic Theory in the United States.* Baltimore, 1897.

Nelson, Daniel. *Managers and Workers: Origins of the New Factory System in the United States, 1880–1920.* Madison, 1975.

Nelson, John R., Jr. *Liberty and Property: Political Economy and Policymaking in the New Nation, 1789–1812.* Baltimore, 1987.

Nelson, William E. *Americanization of the Common Law: The Impact of Legal Change in Massachusetts Society, 1760–1830.* Cambridge, Mass., 1975.

———. *The Roots of American Bureaucracy, 1830–1900.* Cambridge, Mass., 1982.

Neufeld, Maurice F. "Realms of Thought and Organized Labor in the Age of Jackson." *Labor History,* X (1969), 5–43.

Nevins, Allan. *Abram S. Hewitt: With Some Account of Peter Cooper.* New York, 1935.

———. *John D. Rockefeller: The Heroic Age of American Enterprise.* 2 vols. New York, 1940.

———. *Ordeal of the Union.* 2 vols. New York, 1947.

———, ed. and comp. *American Social History as Recorded by British Travellers.* New York, 1923.

Nichols, Roy Franklin. *Franklin Pierce: Young Hickory of the Granite Hills.* 2nd ed. Philadelphia, 1958.

Nisbet, Robert A. *The Social Impact of the Revolution.* Washington, D.C., 1973.

Niven, John. *Connecticut for the Union: The Role of the State in the Civil War.* New Haven, 1965.

———. *Gideon Welles: Lincoln's Secretary of the Navy.* New York, 1973.

———. *John C. Calhoun and the Price of Union: A Biography.* Baton Rouge, 1993.

———. *Martin Van Buren: The Romantic Age of American Politics.* New York, 1983.

North, Douglass C. *The Economic Growth of the United States, 1790–1860.* New York, 1961.

Nye, Russel Blaine. *Society and Culture in America, 1830–1860.* New York, 1974.

Oakes, James. *Slavery and Freedom: An Interpretation of the Old South.* New York, 1990.

Oberholtzer, Ellis Paxson. *A History of the United States Since the Civil War.* 5 vols. New York, 1917.

Obermann, Karl. *Joseph Weydemeyer: Pioneer of American Socialism.* New York, 1947.

O'Brien, Anthony Patrick. "Factory Size, Economies of Scale, and the Great Merger Wave of 1898–1902." *Journal of Economic History,* XLVIII (1988), 639–49.

O'Brien, D. P. *J. R. McCulloch: A Study in Classical Economics.* New York, 1970.

Okada, Yasuo. "The Economic World of a Seneca County Farmer, 1830–1880." *New York History,* LXVI (1985), 5–28.

Okun, Arthur M. *Equality and Efficiency: The Big Tradeoff.* Washington, D.C., 1975.

Osberg, Lars. *Economic Inequality in the United States.* Armonk, N.Y., 1984.

Osterud, Nancy Grey. *Bonds of Community: The Lives of Farm Women in Nineteenth-Century New York.* Ithaca, N.Y., 1991.

Oubre, Claude F. *Forty Acres and a Mule: The Freedmen's Bureau and Black Land Ownership.* Baton Rouge, 1978.

Paglin, Morton. *Malthus and Lauderdale: The Anti-Ricardian Tradition.* New York, 1961.

Painter, Nell Irvin. *Standing at Armageddon: The United States, 1877–1919.* New York, 1987.

Palliser, D. M. *The Age of Elizabeth: England Under the Later Tudors, 1547–1603.* London, 1983.

Palmer, R. R. *The Age of Democratic Revolution: A Political History of Europe and America, 1760–1800.* 2 vols. Princeton, 1959.

Pangle, Thomas L. *Montesquieu's Philosophy of Liberalism: A Commentary on "The Spirit of the Laws."* Chicago, 1973.

————. *The Spirit of Modern Republicanism: The Moral Vision of the American Founders and the Philosophy of Locke.* Chicago, 1988.

Parel, Anthony, and Thomas Flanagan, eds. *Theories of Property: Aristotle to the Present.* Waterloo, Canada, 1979.

Parker, William N. *Commerce, Cotton, and Westward Expansion, 1820–1860.* Chicago, 1964.

————. "From Northwest to Midwest: Social Bases of a Regional History." In *Essays in Nineteenth Century Economic History: The Old Northwest,* edited by David C. Klingaman and Richard K. Vedder. Athens, Ohio, 1975.

Parkerson, Donald H. "The Structure of New York Society: Basic Themes in Nineteenth-Century Social History." *New York History,* LXV (1984), 159–87.

Parks, Joseph Howard. *John Bell of Tennessee.* Baton Rouge, 1950.

Paskoff, Paul F. *Industrial Evolution: Organization, Structure, and Growth of the Pennsylvania Iron Industry, 1750–1860.* Baltimore, 1983.

Patterson, James T. *America's Struggle Against Poverty, 1900–1985.* 2nd ed. Cambridge, Mass., 1986.

Paul, Ellen Frankel, and Howard Dickman, eds. *Liberty, Property, and the Foundations of the American Constitution.* Albany, 1989.

Paxson, Frederic L. *Recent History of the United States.* Boston, 1921.

Pease, Jane H., and William H. Pease. *They Who Would Be Free: Blacks' Search for Freedom, 1830–1861.* New York, 1974.

Pelling, Henry. *American Labor.* Chicago, 1960.

Perkins, Edwin J. *American Public Finance and Financial Services, 1700–1815.* Columbus, 1994.

————. "Conflicting Views on Fiat Currency: Britain and Its North American Colonies in the Eighteenth Century." *Business History,* XXXIII (1991), 8–30.

Perlman, Selig. "Upheaval and Reorganisation (Since 1876)." In John R. Commons *et al., History of Labour in the United States.* New York, 1921.

Perman, Michael. *The Road to Redemption: Southern Politics, 1869–1879.* Chapel Hill, 1984.

Perry, Lewis. *Radical Abolitionism: Anarchy and the Government of God in Antislavery Thought.* Ithaca, N.Y., 1973.

Perry, Lewis, and Michael Fellman, eds. *Antislavery Reconsidered: New Perspectives on the Abolitionists.* Baton Rouge, 1979.

Pessen, Edward. *Jacksonian America: Society, Personality, and Politics.* Homewood, Ill., 1969.

————. *Most Uncommon Jacksonians: The Radical Leaders of the Early Labor Movement.* Albany, 1967.

————. "On a Recent Cliometric Attempt to Resurrect the Myth of Antebellum Egalitarianism." *Social Science History,* III (1979), 208–27.

————. *Riches, Class, and Power Before the Civil War.* Lexington, Mass., 1973.

Peterson, Merrill D. *Adams and Jefferson: A Revolutionary Dialogue.* Oxford, 1978.

Phillips, Kevin. *The Politics of Rich and Poor: Wealth and the American Electorate in the Reagan Aftermath.* New York, 1990.

Phillips, Ulrich Bonnell. *A History of Transportation in the Eastern Cotton Belt to 1860.* New York, 1908.

————. *The Slave Economy of the Old South: Selected Essays in Economic and Social History.* Edited by Eugene D. Genovese. Baton Rouge, 1968.

Pickens, Donald K. "The Republican Synthesis and Thaddeus Stevens." *Civil War History,* XXXI (1985), 57–73.

Pisani, Donald J. "Promotion and Regulation: Constitutionalism and the American Economy." *Journal of American History,* LXXIV (1987), 740–68.

Plumb, J. H. *The Growth of Political Stability in England, 1675–1725.* Middlesex, Eng., 1967.

Pocock, J. G. A. "The Classical Theory of Deference." *American Historical Review,* LXXXI (1976), 516–23.

————. *The Machiavellian Moment: Florentine Political Thought and the Atlantic Republican Tradition.* Princeton, 1975.

————. "Virtue and Commerce in the Eighteenth Century." *Journal of Interdisciplinary History,* III (1972), 119–34.

Pole, J. R. *The Pursuit of Equality in American History.* Berkeley, 1978.

Pollack, Norman. *The Humane Economy: Populism, Capitalism, and Democracy.* New Brunswick, N.J., 1990.

———. *The Populist Response to Industrial America.* Cambridge, Mass., 1962.

Pollard, Sidney. *The Genesis of Modern Management: A Study of the Industrial Revolution in Great Britain.* Cambridge, Mass., 1965.

Prais, S. J. *The Evolution of Giant Firms in Britain: A Study of the Growth of Concentration in Manufacturing Industry in Britain, 1909–70.* Cambridge, Eng., 1976.

Prude, Jonathan. *The Coming of Industrial Order: Town and Factory Life in Rural Massachusetts, 1810–1860.* Cambridge, Mass., 1983.

Pruitt, Bettye Hobbs. "Self-Sufficiency and the Agricultural Economy of Eighteenth-Century Massachusetts." *William and Mary Quarterly,* XLI (1984), 333–64.

Quarles, Benjamin. *Black Abolitionists.* New York, 1969.

Rahe, Paul A. *Republics Ancient and Modern: Classical Republicanism and the American Revolution.* Chapel Hill, 1992.

Ransom, Roger L. *Conflict and Compromise: The Political Economy of Slavery, Emancipation, and the American Civil War.* Cambridge, Eng., 1989.

Ransom, Roger L., and Richard Sutch. *One Kind of Freedom: The Economic Consequences of Emancipation.* Cambridge, Eng., 1977.

Rayback, Joseph G. *A History of American Labor.* 2nd ed. New York, 1966.

Rayback, Robert J. *Millard Fillmore: Biography of a President.* Buffalo, 1959.

Reich, Leonard S. *The Making of American Industrial Research: Science and Business at GE and Bell, 1876–1926.* Cambridge, Eng., 1985.

Reid, John Phillip. *The Concept of Liberty in the Age of the American Revolution.* Chicago, 1988.

Remini, Robert V. *Andrew Jackson and the Bank War: A Study in the Growth of Presidential Power.* New York, 1967.

———. *The Legacy of Andrew Jackson: Essays on Democracy, Indian Removal, and Slavery.* Baton Rouge, 1988.

Reynolds, John F. *Testing Democracy: Electoral Behavior and Progressive Reform in New Jersey, 1880–1920.* Chapel Hill, 1988.

Reynolds, John F., and Richard L. McCormick. "Outlawing 'Treachery': Split Tickets and Ballot Laws in New York and New Jersey, 1880–1910," *Journal of American History,* LXXII (1986), 835–58.

Rhodes, James Ford. *History of the United States from the Compromise of 1850 to the End of the Roosevelt Administration.* 9 vols. Rev. ed. New York, 1895–1922.

Richards, Leonard L. *The Life and Times of Congressman John Quincy Adams.* New York, 1986.

Richardson, Leon Burr. *William E. Chandler: Republican.* New York, 1940.

Ridge, Martin. *Ignatius Donnelly: The Portrait of a Politician.* Chicago, 1962.

Rippy, J. Fred. *Joel Poinsett: Versatile American.* Durham, N.C., 1935.

Robbins, Caroline. *The Eighteenth-Century Commonwealthman: Studies in the Transmission, Development and Circumstance of English Liberal Thought from the Restoration of Charles II Until the War with the Thirteen Colonies.* Cambridge, Mass., 1959.

Robbins, Lionel. *The Theory of Economic Policy in English Classical Political Economy.* London, 1952.

Robbins, Roy Marvin. "Horace Greeley: Land Reform and Unemployment, 1837–1862." *Agricultural History,* VII (1933), 18–41.

———. *Our Landed Heritage: The Public Domain, 1776–1936.* 1942; rpr. New York, 1950.

Robinson, Donald L. *Slavery in the Structure of American Politics, 1765–1820.* New York, 1971.

Robinson, Joan. *An Essay on Marxian Economics.* 2nd ed. London, 1969.

Rock, Howard B. *Artisans of the New Republic: The Tradesmen of New York City in the Age of Jefferson.* New York, 1979.

Rodgers, Daniel T. "Republicanism: The Career of a Concept." *Journal of American History,* LXXIX (1992), 11–38.

Roediger, David R. *The Wages of Whiteness: Race and the Making of the American Working Class.* London, 1991.

Roemer, John E. *Analytical Foundations of Marxian Economic Theory.* Cambridge, Eng., 1981.

Rorabaugh, W. J. *The Craft Apprentice: From Franklin to the Machine Age in America.* New York, 1986.

———. " 'I Thought I Should Liberate Myself from the Thraldom of Others': Apprentices, Masters, and the Revolution." In *Beyond the American Revolution: Explorations in the History of American Radicalism,* edited by Alfred F. Young. De Kalb, Ill., 1993.

———. "Who Fought for the North in the Civil War? Concord, Massachusetts, Enlistments." *Journal of American History,* LXXII (1986), 695–701.

Rose, Anne C. *Transcendentalism as a Social Movement, 1830–1850.* New Haven, 1981.

Rose, Willie Lee. *Rehearsal for Reconstruction: The Port Royal Experiment.* Indianapolis, 1964.

Rosenberg, Nathan. *Perspectives on Technology.* Cambridge, Eng., 1976.

———. *Technology and American Economic Growth.* New York, 1972.

Ross, Steven Joseph. "Freed Soil, Freed Labor, Freed Men: John Eaton and the Davis Bend Experiment." *Journal of Southern History,* XLIV (1978), 213–32.

———. *Workers on the Edge: Work, Leisure, and Politics in Industrializing Cincinnati, 1788–1890.* New York, 1985.

Rostow, W. W. *The Stages of Economic Growth: A Non-Communist Manifesto.* 2nd ed. Cambridge, Eng., 1971.

Rothenberg, Winifred B. "The Emergence of a Capital Market in Rural Massachusetts, 1730–1838." *Journal of Economic History,* XLV (1985), 781–808.

———. "The Emergence of Farm Labor Markets and the Transformation of the Rural Economy: Massachusetts, 1750–1855." *Journal of Economic History,* XLVIII (1988), 537–66.

Rothman, David J. *The Discovery of the Asylum: Social Order and Disorder in the New Republic.* Boston, 1971.

Rowe, Kenneth Wyer. *Mathew Carey: A Study in American Economic Development.* Baltimore, 1933.

Rozwenc, Edwin C., Jr., ed. *Ideology and Power in the Age of Jackson.* Garden City, N.Y., 1964.

Rubinstein, W. D. "The Victorian Middle Classes: Wealth, Occupation, and Geography." *Economic History Review,* XXX (1977), 602–23.

Ryan, Alan. *Property and Political Theory.* Oxford, 1984.

Ryon, Roderick N. "Baltimore Workers and Industrial Decision-Making, 1890–1917." *Journal of Southern History,* LI (1985), 565–80.

Salter, William. *The Life of James W. Grimes.* New York, 1876.

Salvatore, Nick. *Eugene V. Debs: Citizen and Socialist.* Urbana, 1982.

Saposs, David J. "Colonial and Federal Beginnings (to 1827)." In John R. Commons et al., *History of Labour in the United States.* New York, 1921.

Savelle, Max. *Seeds of Liberty: The Genesis of the American Mind.* New York, 1948.

Saxton, Alexander. *The Rise and Fall of the White Republic: Class Politics and Mass Culture in Nineteenth-Century America.* London, 1990.

Schlatter, Richard. *Private Property: The History of an Idea.* New Brunswick, N.J., 1951.

Schlesinger, Arthur M., Jr. *The Age of Jackson.* Boston, 1949.

Schuckers, J. W. *The Life and Public Services of Salmon Portland Chase.* New York, 1874.

Schultz, Ronald. *The Republic of Labor: Philadelphia Artisans and the Politics of Class, 1720–1830.* New York, 1993.

Schuster, Eunice Minette. *Native American Anarchism: A Study of Left-Wing American Individualism.* Northampton, Mass., 1932.

Schweitzer, Mary M. "State-Issued Currency and the Ratification of the U.S. Constitution." *Journal of Economic History,* XLIX (1989), 311–22.

Schweninger, Loren. "From Assertiveness to Individualism: The Difficult Path from Slavery to Freedom." In *American Chameleon: Individualism in Trans-National Context,* edited by Richard O. Curry and Lawrence B. Goodheart. Kent, Ohio, 1991.

Scott, Joan Wallach. *Gender and the Politics of History.* New York, 1988.

Scott, William B. *In Pursuit of Happiness: American Conceptions of Property from the Seventeenth to the Twentieth Century.* Bloomington, 1977.

Scranton, Philip B. *Proprietary Capitalism: The Textile Manufacture at Philadelphia, 1800–1885.* Cambridge, Eng., 1983.

Seavoy, Ronald E. *The Origins of the American Business Corporation, 1784–1855: Broadening the Concept of Public Service During Industrialization.* Westport, Conn., 1982.

Sellers, Charles G. *The Market Revolution: Jacksonian America, 1815–1846.* New York, 1991.

Sen, J. R. *The Economics of Sir James Steuart.* Cambridge, Mass., 1957.

Sewell, Richard H. *Ballots for Freedom: Antislavery Politics in the United States, 1837–1860.* New York, 1976.

———. *A House Divided: Sectionalism and Civil War, 1848–1865.* Baltimore, 1988.

Shade, William Gerald. *Banks or No Banks: The Money Issue in Western Politics, 1832–1865.* Detroit, 1972.

Shain, Barry Alan. *The Myth of American Individualism: The Protestant Origins of American Political Thought.* Princeton, 1994.

Shalhope, Robert E. "Individualism in the Early Republic." In *American Chameleon: Individualism in Trans-National Context,* edited by Richard O. Curry and Lawrence B. Goodheart. Kent, Ohio, 1991.

———. *John Taylor of Caroline: Pastoral Republican.* Columbia, S.C., 1980.

———. "Republicanism and Early American Historiography." *William and Mary Quarterly,* XXXIX (1982), 334–56.

———. "Republicanism, Liberalism, and Democracy: Political Culture in the Early Republic." In *The Republican Synthesis Revisited: Essays in Honor of George Athan Billias,* edited by Milton M. Klein, Richard D. Brown, and John B. Hench. Worcester, Mass., 1992.

———. "Toward a Republican Synthesis: The Emergence of an Understanding of Republicanism in American Historiography." *William and Mary Quarterly,* XXIX (1972), 49–80.

Shammas, Carole. "A New Look at Long-Term Trends in Wealth Inequality in the United States." *American Historical Review,* XCVIII (1993), 412–31.

Shammas, Carole, Marylynn Salmon, and Michel Dahlin. *Inheritance in America from Colonial Times to the Present.* New Brunswick, N.J., 1987.

Shannon, David A. *The Socialist Party of America: A History.* New York, 1955.

Shannon, Fred A. *The Farmer's Last Frontier: Agriculture, 1860–1897.* New York, 1945.

———. "A Post Mortem on the Labor-Safety-Valve Theory." *Agricultural History,* XIX (1945), 31–38.

Shapiro, Ian. "Resources, Capacities, and Ownership." *Political Theory,* XIX (1991), 47–72.

Sharp, James Roger. *The Jacksonians Versus the Banks: Politics in the States After the Panic of 1837.* New York, 1970.

Shaw, Albert. *Icaria: A Chapter in the History of Communism.* 1884; rpr. Philadelphia, 1972.

Shaw, Ronald E. *Canals for a Nation: The Canal Era in the United States, 1790–1860.* Lexington, Ky., 1990.

Shelton, Cynthia J. *The Mills of Manayunk: Industrialization and Social Conflict in the Philadelphia Region, 1787–1837.* Baltimore, 1986.

Shippee, Lester Burrell. *Recent American History.* New York, 1924.

Shultz, William J., and M. R. Caine. *Financial Development of the United States.* New York, 1937.

Silbey, Joel H. *The American Political Nation, 1838–1893.* Stanford, 1991.

―――. *A Respectable Minority: The Democratic Party in the Civil War Era, 1860–1868.* New York, 1977.

―――. " 'There Are Other Questions Beside That of Slavery Merely': The Democratic Party and Antislavery Politics." In *Crusaders and Compromisers: Essays on the Relationship of the Antislavery Struggle to the Antebellum Party System,* edited by Alan M. Kraut. Westport, Conn., 1983.

Siracusa, Carl. *A Mechanical People: Perceptions of the Industrial Order in Massachusetts, 1815–1880.* Middletown, Conn., 1979.

Siry, Steven E. *De Witt Clinton and the American Political Economy: Sectionalism, Politics, and Republican Ideology, 1787–1828.* New York, 1990.

Skinner, Andrew S. "Adam Smith: An Economic Interpretation of History." In *Essays on Adam Smith,* edited by Andrew S. Skinner and Thomas Wilson. Oxford, 1975.

Skinner, Andrew S., and Thomas Wilson, eds. *Essays on Adam Smith.* Oxford, 1975.

Sklar, Martin J. *The Corporate Reconstruction of American Capitalism, 1890–1916: The Market, the Law, and Politics.* Cambridge, Eng., 1988.

Skocpol, Theda. *Protecting Soldiers and Mothers: The Political Origins of Social Policy in the United States.* Cambridge, Eng., 1992.

Slaughter, Thomas P. *The Whiskey Rebellion: Frontier Epilogue to the American Revolution.* New York, 1986.

Smiley, David L. *Lion of White Hall: The Life of Cassius M. Clay.* Madison, 1962.

Smith, Billy G. "Inequality in Late Colonial Philadelphia: A Note on Its Nature and Growth." *William and Mary Quarterly,* XLI (1984), 629–45.

―――. "The Material Lives of Laboring Philadelphians, 1756 to 1800." *William and Mary Quarterly,* XXXVIII (1981), 163–202.

Smith, Lacey Baldwin. *This Realm of England, 1399 to 1688.* Lexington, Mass., 1966.

Soderlund, Jean R. *Quakers and Slavery: A Divided Spirit.* Princeton, 1985.

Soltow, James H. "Origins of Small Business and the Relationships Between Large and Small Firms: Metal Fabricating and Machinery Making in New England, 1890–1957." In *Small Business in American Life,* edited by Stuart W. Bruchey. New York, 1980.

Soltow, Lee. *Distribution of Wealth and Income in the United States in 1798.* Pittsburgh, 1989.

———. *Men and Wealth in the United States, 1850–1870.* New Haven, 1975.

———. "The Rich and the Destitute in Sweden, 1805–1855: A Test of Tocqueville's Inequality Hypothesis." *Economic History Review,* XLII (1989), 43–63.

———. "Wealth Distribution in England and Wales in 1798." *Economic History Review,* XXXIV (1981), 60–70.

Sorin, Gerald. *Abolitionism: A New Perspective.* New York, 1972.

Spann, Edward K. *Brotherly Tomorrows: Movements for a Cooperative Society in America, 1820–1920.* New York, 1989.

———. *The New Metropolis: New York City, 1840–1857.* New York, 1981.

Speck, W. A. *Stability and Strife: England, 1714–1760.* Cambridge, Mass., 1979.

Spengler, Joseph J. "John Rae on Economic Development: A Note." *Quarterly Journal of Economics,* LXXIII (1959), 393–406.

———. "Mercantilist and Physiocratic Growth Theory." In Bert F. Hoselitz et al., *Theories of Economic Growth.* Glencoe, Ill., 1960.

———. "Population Doctrines in the United States: I. Anti-Malthusianism." *Journal of Political Economy,* XLI (1933), 433–67.

———. "Population Doctrines in the United States: II. Malthusianism." *Journal of Political Economy,* XLI (1933), 639–72.

———. "Population Theory in the Ante-Bellum South." *Journal of Southern History,* II (1936), 360–89.

Sproat, John G. *"The Best Men": Liberal Reformers in the Gilded Age.* New York, 1968.

Stampp, Kenneth M. *The Era of Reconstruction, 1865–1877.* New York, 1965.

Stanley, Amy Dru. "Conjugal Bonds and Wage Labor: Rights of Contract in the Age of Emancipation." *Journal of American History,* LXXV (1988), 471–500.

Stansell, Christine. *City of Women: Sex and Class in New York, 1789–1860.* Urbana, 1987.

———. "The Origins of the Sweatshop: Women and Early Industrialization in New York City." In *Working-Class America: Essays in Labor, Community, and American Society,* edited by Michael F. Frisch and Daniel J. Walkowitz. Urbana, 1983.

Stearns, Frank Preston. *The Life and Public Services of George Luther Stearns.* 1907; rpr. New York, 1969.

Steckel, Richard H. "Household Migration and Rural Settlement in the United States, 1850–1860." *Explorations in Economic History,* XXVI (1989), 190–218.

———. *Poverty and Prosperity: A Longitudinal Study of Wealth Accumulation, 1850–1860.* NBER Working Paper Series on Historical Factors in Long-Run Growth, Working Paper No. 8. Cambridge, Mass., 1989.

Steen, Herman. *Flour Milling in America.* Minneapolis, 1963.

Steffen, Charles G. *The Mechanics of Baltimore: Workers and Politics in the Age of Revolution, 1763–1812.* Urbana, 1984.

Steiner, Bernard C. *Life of Henry Winter Davis.* Baltimore, 1916.

Steinfeld, Robert J. *The Invention of Free Labor: The Employment Relation in English and American Law and Culture, 1350–1870.* Chapel Hill, 1991.

Stern, Madeleine B. *The Pantarch: A Biography of Stephen Pearl Andrews.* Austin, 1968.

Stewart, James Brewer. *Holy Warriors: The Abolitionists and American Slavery.* New York, 1976.

———. *Wendell Phillips: Liberty's Hero.* Baton Rouge, 1986.

———. *William Lloyd Garrison and the Challenge of Emancipation.* Arlington Heights, Ill., 1992.

Stewart, John B. *The Moral and Political Philosophy of David Hume.* New York, 1963.

Stigler, George J. *Essays in the History of Economics.* Chicago, 1965.

———. *Production and Distribution Theories.* New York, 1941.

Stokes, Melvyn, and Stephen Conway, eds. *The Market Revolution in America: Social, Political, and Religious Expressions, 1800–1880.* Charlottesville, 1996.

Stone, Richard Gabriel. *Hezekiah Niles as an Economist.* Baltimore, 1933.

Storing, Herbert J. "What the Anti-Federalists Were *For.*" In *The Complete Anti-Federalist,* edited by Herbert J. Storing. Chicago, 1981.

Stott, Richard B. *Workers in the Metropolis: Class, Ethnicity, and Youth in Antebellum New York City.* Ithaca, N.Y., 1990.

Stromberg, Roland N. *Democracy: A Short, Analytical History.* Armonk, N.Y., 1996.

Stromquist, Shelton. *A Generation of Boomers: The Pattern of Railroad Labor Conflict in Nineteenth-Century America.* Urbana, 1987.

Sullivan, William A. *The Industrial Worker in Pennsylvania, 1800–1840.* Harrisburg, Pa., 1955.

Summers, Festus P. *William L. Wilson and Tariff Reform.* New Brunswick, N.J., 1953.

Sumner, Helen L. "Citizenship (1827–1833)." In John R. Commons et al., *History of Labour in the United States.* New York, 1921.

Sundquist, James L. *Dynamics of the Party System: Alignment and Realignment of Political Parties in the United States.* 2nd ed. Washington, D.C., 1983.

Sward, Keith. *The Legend of Henry Ford.* New York, 1948.

Swift, David E. *Black Prophets of Justice: Activist Clergy Before the Civil War.* Baton Rouge, 1989.

Swisher, Carl Brent. *Roger B. Taney.* New York, 1935.

Szatmary, David P. *Shays' Rebellion: The Making of an Agrarian Insurrection.* Amherst, Mass., 1980.

Taft, Philip. *Organized Labor in American History.* New York, 1964.

Taylor, George Rogers. *The Transportation Revolution, 1815–1860.* New York, 1951.

———, ed. *The Turner Thesis Concerning the Role of the Frontier in American History.* Rev. ed. Boston, 1956.

Taylor, George Rogers, and Irene D. Neu. *The American Railroad Network, 1861–1890.* Cambridge, Mass., 1956.

Taylor, Overton H. *A History of Economic Thought.* New York, 1960.

Taylor, Paul S., and Anne Loftis. "The Legacy of the Nineteenth-Century New England Farmer." *New England Quarterly,* LIV (1981), 243–54.

Temin, Peter. *Causal Factors in American Economic Growth in the Nineteenth Century.* Houndmills, Eng., 1975.

———. *Iron and Steel in Nineteenth-Century America: An Economic Inquiry.* Cambridge, Mass., 1964.

———. "Product Quality and Vertical Integration in the Early Cotton Textile Industry." *Journal of Economic History,* XLVIII (1988), 891–907.

Thernstrom, Stephan. *Poverty and Progress: Social Mobility in a Nineteenth Century City.* Cambridge, Mass., 1964.

Thomas, John L. *Alternative America: Henry George, Edward Bellamy, Henry Demarest Lloyd and the Adversary Tradition.* Cambridge, Mass., 1983.

Thompson, E. P. "The Moral Economy of the English Crowd in the Eighteenth Century." *Past and Present,* L (1971), 76–136.

Thompson, Mack. *Moses Brown: Reluctant Reformer.* Chapel Hill, 1962.

Thornton, J. Mills, III. "Fiscal Policy and the Failure of Radical Reconstruction in the Lower South." In *Region, Race, and Reconstruction: Essays in Honor of C. Vann Woodward,* edited by J. Morgan Kousser and James M. McPherson. New York, 1982.

Thurow, Lester C. *Generating Inequality: Mechanisms of Distribution in the U.S. Economy.* New York, 1975.

Timberlake, Richard H., Jr. *The Origins of Central Banking in the United States.* Cambridge, Mass., 1978.

Tipple, John. "Big Business and the New Economy." In *The Gilded Age,* edited by H. Wayne Morgan. 2nd ed. Syracuse, 1970.

Tobin, James. "On Limiting the Domain of Inequality." *Journal of Law and Economics,* XIII (1970), 263–77.

Tolles, Frederick B. *George Logan of Philadelphia.* New York, 1953.

Tomlins, Christopher L. *Law, Labor, and Ideology in the Early American Republic.* Cambridge, Eng., 1993.

Trefousse, Hans L. *The Radical Republicans: Lincoln's Vanguard for Racial Justice.* New York, 1969.

Trescott, Paul B. *Financing American Enterprise: The Story of Commercial Banking.* New York, 1963.

Tucker, Barbara M. *Samuel Slater and the Origins of the American Textile Industry, 1790–1860.* Ithaca, N.Y., 1984.

Turner, John Roscoe. *The Ricardian Rent Theory in Early American Economics.* New York, 1921.

Tyler, Alice Felt. *Freedom's Ferment: Phases of American Social History from the Colonial Period to the Outbreak of the Civil War.* 1944; paperback ed. New York, 1962.

Unger, Irwin. *The Greenback Era: A Social and Political History of American Finance, 1865–1879.* Princeton, 1964.

Van Deusen, Glyndon G. *Horace Greeley: Nineteenth Century Crusader.* New York, 1953.

———. *The Jacksonian Era, 1828–1848.* New York, 1959.

———. *William Henry Seward.* New York, 1967.

Van Doren, Carl. *Benjamin Franklin.* New York, 1938.

Vedder, Richard K., and Lowell E. Gallaway. "Migration and the Old Northwest." In *Essays in Nineteenth Century Economic History: The Old Northwest,* edited by David C. Klingaman and Richard K. Vedder. Athens, Ohio, 1975.

Viner, Jacob. *The Long View and the Short: Studies in Economic Theory and Policy.* Glencoe, Ill., 1958.

Wall, Joseph Frazier. *Andrew Carnegie.* New York, 1970.

Wallerstein, Immanuel. *The Modern World-System II: Mercantilism and the Consolidation of the European World-Economy, 1600–1750.* New York, 1980.

Walsh, Justin E. "Radically and Thoroughly Democratic: Wilbur F. Storey and the Detroit *Free Press,* 1853 to 1861." *Michigan History,* XLVII (1963), 193–225.

Walsh, Margaret. *The Rise of the Midwestern Meat Packing Industry.* Lexington, Ky., 1982.

Walters, Ronald G. *American Reformers, 1815–1860.* New York, 1978.

———. *The Antislavery Appeal: American Abolitionism After 1830.* Baltimore, 1976.

Walton, Gary M., and James F. Shepherd. *The Economic Rise of Early America.* Cambridge, Eng., 1979.

Ware, Caroline F. *The Early New England Cotton Manufacture: A Study in Industrial Beginnings.* Boston, 1931.

Ware, Norman. *The Industrial Worker, 1840–1860: The Reaction of American Industrial Society to the Advance of the Industrial Revolution.* 1924; rpr. Chicago, 1964.

Warner, Deborah Jean. "William J. Young: From Craft to Industry in a Skilled Trade." *Pennsylvania History,* LII (1985), 53–68.

Washburn, Wilcomb E. *Red Man's Land/White Man's Law: The Past and Present Status of the American Indian.* 2nd ed. Norman, 1995.

Watson, Harry L. *Liberty and Power: The Politics of Jacksonian America.* New York, 1990.

Watts, Steven. *The Republic Reborn: War and the Making of Liberal America, 1790–1820.* Baltimore, 1987.

Webb, R. K. *Harriet Martineau: A Radical Victorian.* New York, 1960.

Weeks, Lyman Horace. *A History of Paper-Manufacturing in the United States, 1890–1916.* New York, 1916.

Weinstein, James. *The Corporate Ideal in the Liberal State, 1900–1918.* Boston, 1968.

Welch, Richard E., Jr. *George Frisbie Hoar and the Half-Breed Republicans.* Cambridge, Mass., 1971.

Welter, Rush. *The Mind of America, 1820–1860.* New York, 1975.

Weslager, C. A. *The Stamp Act Congress.* Newark, Del., 1976.

White, Morton. *The Philosophy of the American Revolution.* New York, 1978.

White, Philip L. *Beekmantown, New York: Forest Frontier to Farm Community.* Austin, 1979.

Wiebe, Robert H. *The Opening of American Society: From the Adoption of the Constitution to the Eve of Disunion.* New York, 1984.

———. *The Search for Order, 1877–1920.* New York, 1967.

———. *Self-Rule: A Cultural History of American Democracy.* Chicago, 1995.

Wiecek, William M. *The Sources of Antislavery Constitutionalism in America, 1760–1848.* Ithaca, N.Y., 1977.

Wilentz, Sean. *Chants Democratic: New York City and the Rise of the American Working Class, 1788–1850.* New York, 1984.

———. "Slavery, Antislavery and Jacksonian Democracy." In *The Market Revolution: Social, Political, and Religious Expressions, 1800–1850,* edited by Melvyn Stokes and Stephen Conway, Charlottesville, 1996.

Williams, R. Hal. " 'Dry Bones and Dead Language': The Democratic Party." In *The Gilded Age,* edited by H. Wayne Morgan. 2nd ed. Syracuse, 1970.

Williams, William Appleman. *The Contours of American History.* New York, 1973.

Williamson, Jeffrey G. "The Railroads and Midwestern Development, 1870–90: A General Equilibrium History." In *Essays in Nineteenth Century Economic History: The Old Northwest,* edited by David C. Klingaman and Richard K. Vedder. Athens, Ohio, 1975.

Williamson, Jeffrey G., and Peter H. Lindert. *American Inequality: A Macroeconomic History.* New York, 1980.

Wills, Garry. *Inventing America: Jefferson's Declaration of Independence.* Garden City, N.Y., 1978.

Wilson, Harold Fisher. *The Hill Country of Northern New England: Its Social and Economic History, 1790–1830.* New York, 1936.

Wilson, Major L. "The 'Country' Versus the 'Court': A Republican Consensus and Party Debate in the Bank War." *Journal of the Early Republic,* XV (1995), 619–47.

———. *The Presidency of Martin Van Buren.* Lawrence, Kans., 1984.

———. *Space, Time and Freedom: The Quest for Nationality and the Irrepressible Conflict, 1815–1861.* Westport, Conn., 1974.

Wiltse, Charles M. *The Jeffersonian Tradition in American Democracy.* Chapel Hill, 1935.

Winch, Donald. *Adam Smith's Politics: An Essay in Historiographic Revision.* Cambridge, Eng., 1978.

———. "Marginalism and the Boundaries of Economic Science." In *The Marginal Revolution in Economics: Interpretation and Evaluation,* edited by R. D. Collison Black, A. W. Coates, and Craufurd D. W. Goodwin. Durham, N.C., 1973.

Winpenny, Thomas R. *Industrial Progress and Human Welfare: The Rise of the Factory System in 19th-Century Lancaster.* Washington, D.C., 1982.

Winters, Donald L. *Farmers Without Farms: Agricultural Tenancy in Nineteenth-Century Iowa.* Westport, Conn., 1978.

Wise, George. *Willis R. Whitney, General Electric, and the Origins of U.S. Industrial Research.* New York, 1985.

Wish, Harvey. *George Fitzhugh: Propagandist of the Old South.* Baton Rouge, 1943.

Wittke, Carl. *Refugees of Revolution: The German Forty-Eighters in America.* Philadelphia, 1952.

—————. *The Utopian Communist: A Biography of Wilhelm Weitling, Nineteenth-Century Reformer.* Baton Rouge, 1950.

Wood, Gordon S. *The Creation of the American Republic, 1776–1787.* Chapel Hill, 1969.

—————. *The Radicalism of the American Revolution: How a Revolution Transformed a Monarchical Society into a Democratic One Unlike Any That Had Ever Existed.* New York, 1992.

Woodman, Harold D. "The Reconstruction of the Cotton Plantation in the New South." In *Essays on the Postbellum Southern Economy,* edited by Thavolia Glymph and John J. Kushma. College Station, Tex., 1985.

Woodward, C. Vann. *Origins of the New South, 1877–1913.* Baton Rouge, 1951.

Wright, Gavin. *The Political Economy of the Cotton South: Households, Markets, and Wealth in the Nineteenth Century.* New York, 1978.

Wrobel, David M. *The End of American Exceptionalism: Frontier Anxiety from the Old West to the New Deal.* Lawrence, Kans., 1993.

Wykstra, Ronald A., ed. *Education and the Economics of Human Capital.* New York, 1971.

—————. *Human Capital Formation and Manpower Development.* New York, 1971.

Wyllie, Irvin G. *The Self-Made Man in America: The Myth of Rags to Riches.* New Brunswick, N.J., 1954.

Wyman, Mark. *Hard Rock Epic: Western Miners and the Industrial Revolution, 1860–1910.* Berkeley, 1979.

Yarbrough, Jean. "Jefferson and Property Rights." In *Liberty, Property, and the Foundations of the American Constitution,* edited by Ellen Frankel Paul and Howard Dickman. Albany, 1989.

Yearley, Clifton K., Jr. *Enterprise and Anthracite: Economics and Democracy in Schuylkill County, 1820–1875.* Baltimore, 1961.

Young, Alfred F. "Afterword: How Radical Was the American Revolution?" In *Beyond the American Revolution: Explorations in the History of American Radicalism,* edited by Alfred F. Young. De Kalb, Ill., 1993.

—————. *The Democratic Republicans of New York: The Origins, 1763–1797.* Chapel Hill, 1967.

————, ed. *Beyond the American Revolution: Explorations in the History of American Radicalism.* De Kalb, Ill., 1993.

Young, Mary E. "Congress Looks West: Liberal Ideology and Public Land Policy in the Nineteenth Century." In *The Frontier in American Development: Essays in Honor of Paul Wallace Gates,* edited by David M. Ellis. Ithaca, N.Y., 1969.

Zahler, Helene Sara. *Eastern Workingmen and National Land Policy, 1829–1862.* New York, 1941.

Zilversmit, Arthur. *The First Emancipation: The Abolition of Slavery in the North.* Chicago, 1967.

Zonderman, David A. *Aspirations and Anxieties: New England Workers and the Mechanized Factory System, 1815–1850.* New York, 1992.

Zunz, Olivier. *Making America Corporate, 1870–1920.* Chicago, 1990.

Index